LEGACY OF DEVOTION

Father Edward J. Flanagan of Boys Town

Legacy of Devotion
Published by Boys Town Press
13603 Flanagan Blvd., Boys Town, NE 68010
Copyright © 2019, Father Flanagan's Boys' Home
ISBN 978-1-944882-41-9 (Also available in Hardcover: ISBN 978-1-944882-40-2)

Boys Town Press is the publishing division of Boys Town, a national organization serving children and families.

Publisher's Cataloging-in-Publication Data

Names: Stevens, Clifford J., author.

Title: Legacy of devotion : Father Edward J. Flanagan of Boys Town / Father Clifford J. Stevens.

Description: Boys Town, NE : Boys Town Press, [2019]

Identifier: ISBN: 978-1-944882-41-9

Subjects: LCSH: Flanagan, Edward Joseph, 1886-1948. | Father Flanagan's Boys' Home. | Social workers--United States--Biography. | Problem children--Institutional care--United States-- History. | BISAC: BIOGRAPHY & AUTOBIOGRAPHY / Historical. | BIOGRAPHY & AUTOBIOGRAPHY / Religious.

Classification: LCC: HV876.F4 S74 2019 | DDC: 362.74/50924--dc23

10 9 8 7 6 5 4 3 2 1

LEGACY OF DEVOTION

Father Edward J. Flanagan of Boys Town

FATHER CLIFFORD J. STEVENS

Boys Town, Nebraska

CONTENTS

FOREWORD

THE WORK HAS CONTINUED...

By Father Steven E. Boes,
President and Executive Director of Boys Town

Father Edward Joseph Flanagan will always be known as a social reformer, a humanitarian, a revolutionary thinker, and the priest who, against all odds, founded Boys Town, a small haven for homeless youngsters that, over a century of service, has grown into a world-famous leader in child and family care.

But an even greater attribute of Father Flanagan and the virtuous life he led was the genuine compassion and affection he felt for each child he met. His enduring legacy will be that of a kind, caring mentor and advocate who totally immersed himself in his life's mission of ensuring that every child was safe, valued, and loved, and had an opportunity to reach his or her full potential. That, and his unwavering belief that he could bring out the goodness in any youngster by providing a caring family and a trusting home that encouraged that child to be good and to do good.

In his book, *Legacy of Devotion*, Father Clifford Stevens opens a window into Father Flanagan's life that displays all the strengths, complexities, and frailties of a unique man who was driven to make the world a better place for children while preparing them as tomorrow's citizens and leaders.

The ministry he envisioned was revolutionary in its emphasis on treating children as individuals to be loved and cherished. In America at the turn of the century, children were generally not protected from physical and emotional abuse. Child labor was very common, and tens of thousands of kids were homeless, both in the big cities and rural areas.

As a guardian of the weak and defenseless, Father Flanagan would shatter these failures in child care by creating Boys Town, a place of learning, hope, and refuge that has become the model for giving kids second chances. He wrote: "...Rehabilitation rather than retribution is the goal, re-education rather than condemnation... through research and education, can we hope to prevent as well as to cure maladies of personality which for some end in tragedy and for millions of others in frustration and discouragement in life...."

Decades ahead of his time in his understanding of the social and psychological needs of children, Father Flanagan paved the way for a new era of child and family care that continues today in the work of Boys Town and other organizations that have adopted his positive, life-changing approach to helping those in need.

Father Flanagan's extraordinary life was a model of enlightenment, dogged determination, and tireless work. Today, his spirit lives on at Boys Town, and we carry on his dream, inspired by this faithful man of God.

1

LAD OF LEABEG

Leabeg

County Roscommon is the sheep country of Ireland, but in the history of Ireland, it is more than that. It is the site of the ancient Cruachan,[1] where fierce battles were fought in the pre-Christian days of Ireland; the site of the "Tain Bo Cuailgne,"[2] the epic poem of the ancient Gaels who inhabited the island at the time; and of the warrior, Cu Chulainn, the epic hero of the Irish before St. Patrick arrived. It was in this historic land, on the western border of County Roscommon, that Edward Joseph Flanagan was born on July 13, 1886,[3] just across the Suck River from the Galway village of Ballymoe, on a piece of land owned by an English landlord for whom John Flanagan, the child's father, managed the estate.[4]

John Flanagan managed the farm with the help of his many sons and daughters, eleven in all. Among them were Patrick, who early in the life of the future Father Flanagan went off to the seminary; Nellie, who was a second mother to the younger members of the family; and Eddie, the eighth child. Their mother, Nora, was the dominant influence in young Eddie's life and he always consulted her before making any major decision.

On the Sunday after his birth, Edward Joseph Flanagan was baptized in St. Croan's Church[5] in nearby Ballymoe by the local priest, Father William Crofton.

The family farm was on the Leabeg townland of County Roscommon. The Flanagan home had walls white limestone, with a rough exterior, and a thatched roof. In the house there were two fireplaces where Eddie, as he grew older, would curl up with a book or just sit thinking, occupied with his own thoughts.

Eddie was small and frail when he was born, and the attending midwife had warned the family, "He will not last till morning." At one point, the baby turned blue and purple, shaken by a convulsion, and it seemed the end had come.

Suddenly, as the other family members watched, the grandfather, Patrick, took the convulsing baby in his arms, unbuttoned his own shirt, and placed the tiny body inside, rocking him and holding him against his warm chest. Then he spent the night, the baby clasped in his arms, walking up and down in front of the fireplace. By morning, the child was calm, and the family looked upon Eddie's survival as a miracle.[6]

From that moment on, the whole family felt there was something special about Eddie, especially his mother and older sister Nellie. He seemed to have been rescued from certain death and they would always remember the shaking little body and the child struggling for life. They believed that Eddie had been set apart by God Himself. This was a conviction Nellie would carry with her to the grave. Later, when that destiny was made clear to her, she would be at her brother's side until the day he died.

Because of Eddie's frailty, his father watched over him with special care, and took his son with him, even before Eddie started school, as he looked after the sheep and cattle. During Eddie's childhood, he was outdoors most of the time. When he started school at nearby Drimatemple at age five, Eddie tended the sheep and cattle with his father or his brother James, before and after school. He was also expected, like the older sons, to work the turf banks to get fuel for the family home.

The family had faced tragedy before Eddie was born. His brother, Pat, at age three, had been paralyzed from toxic poisoning after a carelessly adminis-tered vaccination. He had been almost bedridden for seven years when the family decided to take desperate measures. They took Pat on a long trip to the shrine of Our Lady of Knock in County Mayo, where they prayed for a cure. He walked out of the shrine unassisted.[7] When Eddie was born, Pat became some-thing of a protector and mentor for his younger brother. Pat left for Summerhill College when Eddie was six years old. Eddie was determined to follow his brother on the way to the priesthood.

The Leabeg farm was an enclave of fertile land, surrounded by heather, moss, and peat. Being a rather large estate, John Flanagan had a hired man, John King, who had been with the family for many years and who was something of a cranky uncle to the children. He loved to tell stories of banshees, leprechauns, ghosts, and little people, and the children would gather around to listen. When Eddie was older, John King would teach him to fish in the Suck River and they could often be seen along its banks, gathering their catch of perch for the family's evening meal.

The family home was set halfway down a meadow that sloped to the River Suck, a short distance away. It was forty feet long and sixteen feet wide, with a small bedroom at each end of the house. The main room was a combination kitchen and living room, where family activities took place. Set against an outer wall were two "settle beds" that were turned down for sleeping or used for sitting when neighbors filled the house. There were two fireplaces – one for heating the house and one for cooking.

The exterior of the house was carefully landscaped with flowerbeds of fuchsias, rhododendrons, daffodils, roses, and violets set along stone walkways and walls, with stone steps built casually along the walls for easy access to the gardens. Open fields beyond the gardens led down to the river, where fish were plentiful.

The closest home was one mile away and the Flanagan home was known as a "rambling house," where neighbors would gather for dancing and song, for neighborhood get-togethers, for "American Wake" celebrations when friends or relatives would leave for America or Australia, and for just plain talk about happenings in Dublin. Occasionally, there was a ceili, a special kind of celebration that drew neighbors from miles around.

When Eddie was born, there were seven other children in the house – two older brothers, Pat and James, and five older sisters, Mary Jane, Nellie, Kate, Susan, and Delia. Before Eddie was ten years old, three other children were born: Nora, Teresa, and Michael.[8] By that time, however, Mary Jane, Nellie, Pat, and Kate had left home.

There is a certain genius that is awakened in childhood, and this awakening is dependent upon the atmosphere and events of childhood itself. Within the intimacy of the family, great dreams are born, and we can see in the lives of a Katharine Hepburn and a Louisa May Alcott the powerful effect of family life and family associations on the future adult. Mozart was a musical prodigy at six and Aloysius Gonzaga was a spiritual prodigy at seven. In both cases, their future was chosen and determined by the atmosphere and events of their childhood.[9]

In this, Edward Joseph Flanagan was extremely fortunate, for he was born into an ancient Irish family, a family of loving intimacy and affective warmth,[10] at a time when the Irish consciousness of its cultural heritage and history was beginning to emerge in families and in villages, in schools, in politics and literature, in art and in music, in drama and the theater, and in those neighborhood and family gatherings called ceilis.[11]

In Eddie Flanagan's case, this awakening was extraordinary, most probably because of his proximity to historical sites such as Cruachan, which was the setting for the classic epic of early Irish history, and for the rich and luminous religious heritage that had shaped Irish families for over 1,400 years.[12]

A Rich Family History

The Flanagans of Roscommon[13] were descended from Cathal, the second son of Muireadhach Muilleathan, King of Connacht, who died in 701 A.D. Cathal's descendants in the direct line became royal chiefs of Clann Cathail and the hereditary stewards of the Kings of Connacht.[14] The head of the clan was one of the twelve great Lords of Cruachan, the ancestral headquarters of the Kings of Connacht at Rathcroghan in County Roscommon, less than ten miles from Ballymoe.[15] The name "Flanagan" apparently was the nickname of a red-headed or ruddy-faced chief, since the word "flann" in Gaelic means red or ruddy. The Flanagans were of royal blood with their own Coat-of-Arms and family crest, emblazoned with the motto: *Audaces Fortuna Juvat* (*Fortune Favors the Bold*).[16]

The Flanagan family was blood relatives of the Kings of Connacht, the Royal House of O'Conor, which distinguished itself in Irish history from the second century when the dynasty was founded by the mythic Conn of the Hundred Battles. He ruled half of Ireland, and after his death, his kingdom was divided into the two kingdoms of Ulster and Connacht, the rivalry between the two made famous by the "Tain Bo Cuailgne," the epic poem of ancient Ireland. Both the name "Connacht" and the name "O'Conor" are variants of the name "Conn," the founder of the dynasty.

The greatest of the Kings of Connacht was the warrior-king Turlough O'Conor, who ruled Connacht from 1106 to 1156. During his long reign, he tried to establish himself as the Ardri, the King of All Ireland, and recruited a large army and navy to war against rival kings. He built fortress-castles all through his domains, from Galway Bay to what are now Longford and Meath, and constructed bridges over the Shannon River for the easy access of his troops through his territory.

On his death in 1156, his son, Rory O'Conor, continued his father's warlike policies and fought with the kings of Ulster and Leinster for the High Kingship. He defeated the King of Ulster, but the King of Leinster appealed to Henry II, King of England, who invaded Ireland and began the Anglo-Norman occupation of the country.

After the defeat of Rory O'Conor, the clans of the Royal House of O'Conor were reduced in status under Norman rule. The clan itself was and remained Catholic after its fall from power and the descendants of the chiefs of Clann Cathail, including the ancestors of John Flanagan and his father Patrick, continued to reside in what had been the Kingdom of Connacht, adjacent to or in the vicinity of the ancient capital at Rathcroghan or in the vicinity of the Clann's headquarters in County Roscommon.

The religious life of the Flanagan family was centered in St. Croan's Church in nearby Ballymoe, about two miles away, across the Suck River in Galway. St. Croan's was a "half-parish." The mother-church and parish was St. Bride's Church in Ballintubber. The pastor resided in Ballintubber and the curate, or assistant priest, in Ballymoe. The priest at the time of Eddie Flanagan's birth and baptism was Father William Crofton, but he was replaced by Father James Fetherstone when Eddie was three years old. Father Fetherstone would remain at Ballymoe for ten years, when he would be replaced by Father Peter Hughes, who would tutor young Eddie in Latin, Greek, and French in preparation for beginning his studies for the priesthood. Father Fetherstone, the priest of Eddie's childhood and his fondest memories, is buried on the grounds of St. Croan's Church.

The history of the Catholic Church in Ballymoe and vicinity begins with St. Patrick, who came to the Ballymoe barony[17] after spending considerable time at Cruachan, the ancient capital of the Kingdom of Connacht. He spent seven years in the area, founding churches and leaving behind priests and bishops to stabilize the faith in the territories he visited. There is no evidence of his stopping at Ballymoe, the village, but he did found churches at Castlerea, ten miles north of Ballymoe, at Oran, southeast of Ballymoe, and at Roscommon, to the south. From earliest times, the village owed its importance to its location beside a strategic ford of the Suck River,[18] in the northeast corner of County Galway. The church in Ballymoe is named after a holy virgin, St. Croan, who was abbess of a monastery in ancient times and whose memory gave the name "Kilcroan" to an original church in the area.

Ballymoe was a rural village with four pubs, a hotel, a courthouse, a police station, a post office, a Protestant Church and a Catholic Church, and homes for about 30 families. The schools were outside the village, across the Suck River, and were reached by crossing a bridge over the river. The village was not a busy commercial center, and most shopping was done in nearby Castlerea or Roscommon, reached by horse and wagon or horse and sidecar, or for the more prosperous, by train from a small railroad station just outside of town.

As a child, Eddie Flanagan would not have been in the village of Ballymoe very often except for Sunday Mass. His local school was not in the village. Rural people were very self-sufficient and most of their food and needs were produced on the land or in the locality. Shopping tended to be concentrated around big occasions or on Sunday while coming from Mass. Big occasions would include seasonal farm operations where help was needed, the arrival of important visitors, and Christmas, or "Stations," where neighbors and priests were invited to a home for the celebration of Mass. The Catholic Church that Eddie attended was an old cruciform structure on the site of the present church. It had mostly plain forms for seating, with some better seats toward the altar, whose owners had special rights to seating and whose rights were respected. Ninety-nine percent of the population of the area was of the Roman Catholic persuasion, and of that number, ninety-five percent of those physically able to attend Mass did so.[19]

The Flanagans were a devout, religious family and attended church in nearby Ballymoe, across the river in Galway. The Rosary was their family prayer, and often when they went looking for young Eddie, he could be found praying his Rosary in some isolated spot. Sometimes he and his father would pray the Rosary in the rain as they searched together for lost sheep.[20]

Leabeg was one of the thirty townlands in that half-parish, the townland being the smallest unit "on which civil and church affairs were organized."[21] John Flanagan's official designation was a "herd," which is the manager of a tract of land for an absentee landlord. In this case, the owners were with the Campbell distillery of Scotland.[22] They lived in London and came once or twice a year to monitor the care of the Leabeg farm and to oversee the sale of their sheep and cattle. Part of the income of the sale was given as salary to the manager.[23]

This was a time of political unrest in Ireland over land reform, since most rural families were merely tenants on their land and had to pay rent to their landlords. Rent could be increased at any time, plunging the tenants into extreme poverty and financial distress. Since the lands were often incapable of producing the income necessary for the rent, the tenants were often evicted from their lands.[24] Herds like John Flanagan were assured of a steady and stable income, and he had his own plot of land to grow potatoes, vegetables, and oats. He could also graze a few of his own cattle or sheep on the farm, which gave him a steady supply of cash.

The herd was a respected professional, his experience and skills essential to the success and profitability of the estate.[25] He looked after the care, feeding, and health of the stock, the proper fencing of the property, and even the buying and selling of the animals. John Flanagan's father, Patrick, had been a herd before him and competent herds were in demand, often moving from smaller estates to larger ones. It is most likely that James, the second Flanagan son, was being trained to follow in his father's footsteps, as the father had followed his father. Part of the herder's expertise included veterinarian skills, since his care of the animals demanded ensuring their health and well-being.

The Flanagan family was, in some sense, a privileged family because of the security of the father's position and the stability of their income. They were undoubtedly generous to their neighbors and friends and those less fortunate than themselves, since their religion mandated this, and they could provide for the education of their children.

Eddie and his father were very close. When they were out on the fields tending the sheep and cattle or sitting in the light of the fireplace at night, John would tell his son adventure stories,[26] perhaps of Fergus mac Roigh and the Red Branch Knights of ancient Ireland or of the warrior Cu Chulainn and his fierce battle with his rival, Ferdia, that took place ninety or a hundred miles from their home, or of the saints, scholars, and patriots he read about in his books, and of the Irish people's struggle for independence going on all around them.[27]

Like every Irish boy, Eddie knew that Ireland had been pirated for over a thousand years, first by the Vikings, then by the Anglo-Normans, and finally, by the English. In 1553, invaders destroyed Clonmacnoise, Ireland's center of art, culture, and learning, carting off or burning its precious books and art treasures and leveling dozens of buildings. Leabeg is not far from the scattered ruins of Clonmacnoise, on the banks of the Shannon River, less than thirty-five miles away.[28]

From being the most learned people in Europe, Ireland had been reduced over the centuries to poverty, hunger, and destitution. It's rulers had been imprisoned, murdered, or exiled, and its land and treasures of art, scholarship, and religion had been pillaged. For all of these centuries, its people endured political occupation under a cruel and oppressive rule that aimed to stamp out every vestige of their unique and glorious heritage. In spite of this, the idea of a free Ireland never died, and its heroes were saints, priests, artists, scholars, soldier-patriots, musicians, poets, slain leaders, teachers, and families, many of whom left Ireland in despair over the oppressive living conditions to seek a better future.[29]

There were stirrings of these things in the Flanagan home: rumors of the doings of the Fenian Brotherhood, and rebel songs sung around the fire by strangers or neighbors who happened to pass by. Some songs were tragic and sad like "Boolavogue," and some were rousing songs of rebellion.[30]

When Eddie was six years old, in 1892, the Flanagan siblings began to move on. Mary Jane, the eldest at twenty, married Matt Naughton of Castlerea, and Kate, who was sixteen, left home to work toward a teacher's certificate. Brother Pat, fourteen, left to begin his first studies for the priesthood at Summerhill College in Sligo. All three would return home in December of that year for the funeral of their grandfather.[31]

By 1893, there had been two deaths in the family: the old grandfather, Patrick, the beloved patriarch of the family, and Honora, a daughter born in 1888, who died a year and a half later. Meanwhile, another child, Teresa, had been born in 1891. Five-year-old Eddie started school in Drimatemple the year Teresa was born, walking the two miles there each day with his two brothers and two sisters. The road to the school was well traveled and bordered by overhanging beech and elm trees on both sides, their tops entwined to form an arch; locals called it a "dark road."

When neighbors would get together, or the men of the families would meet in the pubs, there was always talk of those who emigrated, either to England, Canada, Australia, or the United States. Most had left for the United States, since the opportunities there were the greatest. Even the young men studying for the priesthood were advised to start making plans to join some diocese overseas, since there was already a surplus of priests in Ireland.

Nellie was the first Flanagan child to travel over the ocean water by ship to the United States. In 1894, her mother's brother, Michael Larkin, who had emigrated to New York several years before and was a successful building contractor, returned with his wife to Ireland for a visit and it was decided that Nellie would return with them to the United States. She would come back to Ireland six years later with glowing accounts of opportunities across the ocean, and when Nellie left for the States again, her sister Susan, age eighteen, would go with her.

A Life-Shaping Childhood

Before Eddie was eight years old, four members of the family were no longer at home. In 1894, a younger brother, Michael, was born. Now there were only seven around the supper table and Eddie felt even more alone tending the animals, keeping the cattle out of the bogs and the sheep out of the briers. But by this time he had discovered the world of books. This was company enough for him in the long hours alone. Eddie came to have a love for solitude, and his later memories of his homeland of Ireland would be mostly of spending time outdoors.

It was common knowledge in the family that when Eddie finished his primary school, he would follow his brother to Summerhill College in Sligo to begin studies for the priesthood. From his first days in school, a program of tutoring was set up for him. When he started school, he was tutored in the evening by the schoolmaster, who eventually drank too much and lost his position. After that, Eddie was tutored by his brother Pat when Pat came home each summer from Summerhill College. With his brother's tutoring, Eddie was able to skip three grades in the Drimatemple school. In 1899, when Eddie was thirteen, he was tutored by the local priest, Father Hughes, who started him in Latin, Greek, and French, all on the same day. Over the next two years, the boy could often be found studying under a tree. On days when the sun was shining, he would carry books with him and could be seen walking or sitting somewhere, absorbed in a book. At night, light would last until eleven o'clock, so he was able to read well into the late hours.

Until he was twelve years old, Eddie accompanied his father on long walks through the fields, tending the sheep and cattle and learning to recognize sick animals and how to care for them. Sometimes, he would accompany his uncle, Johnny King, on his rounds and the two became fast friends, King in his tight-fitting breeches and broken-stemmed pipes, regaling the boy with his stories of banshees and leprechauns and the boy running barefoot through the fields, shinnying up a tree or two or chasing the sheep dog that always accompanied him.[32]

By the time he turned twelve, Eddie had become an experienced shepherd and asked if he could tend the sheep and cattle alone. His wish was granted and he traveled over the vast fields of Leabeg, a dog at his side, a book in his hands, his eye alert for any sign of danger to the animals in his care. "I never lost one," he would say in later years.[33]

In that part of Ireland, there were no fences and pastures were divided by digging ditches and piling the dirt to one side. On the piled-up earth were planted thick hedges of hawthorn, designed to keep the sheep in. Eddie's task was to keep the sheep in the open and away from the hedges. If they became entangled in the briery bushes, they could strangle themselves trying to get out or bleed to death from the sharp thorns.[34]

One afternoon, he heard the bleating of a young ram that had become ensnared in the briars. This could be disastrous for the family economy, for not only might the sheep be lost but also its wool. So young Eddie, knowing the value of one sheep, began to extract each thorny brier from the animal's thick wool, his hands soon bleeding as he removed them one by one. It was a heroic deed for one so young, something his father never forgot.[35]

As Eddie grew toward his teens, books were his constant companions: Dickens, Sir Walter Scott, Macauley, or the work of some other literary master that a sister or brother had placed in his hands.[36] He was considered the bookworm of the family and the amount of knowledge he gathered from this casual reading under corn stocks and on the peat moss was considerable.[37] It was from these days that he acquired a passion for books by master novelists, historians, poets, and experts in any field of learning who opened doors and windows for his young mind.

That passion for books was encouraged by the return of his sister Kate to Ballymoe when he was ten years old. As a teenage girl, she had been one of the monitors for the girls' classroom at the Drimatemple school. The school was divided into two sections, one for boys and one for girls, each with its teacher and a teenage monitor. The monitors were paid assistants to the teachers and were in training to become teachers themselves.[38] Kate returned home to teach in a nearby National School and eventually married the head of the school, Owen Staunton. She remained a teacher there for the rest of her life, dearly beloved by several generations of students. She also taught and tutored her younger brother Eddie, supplying him with books and encouraging his widening interests as he grew older.[39]

The most profound influence on his future work was the family intimacy Eddie experienced. He remembered the chimney corner in the kitchen where he would sit and think as a boy, a teakettle hung above the fire and tea always ready. As an adult, he would recall the mist in the dooryard before nightfall came to Leabeg, and himself in a corner by the fireplace, his grandfather's blackthorn shillalah hanging on the wall. Hung on the nails of the plaster wall were hats and coats in various sizes, new pegs being added as each new Flanagan child came along. Suspended from the ceiling was an oil lamp of crinkled blue crystal, a family treasure, perhaps a wedding gift to his father and mother.[40]

John Flanagan usually began his day at five a.m. The first order was to count the sheep and cattle,[41] rescue any animals that had strayed away, and supervise the morning chores. The girls would help their mother get breakfast as other children studied or practiced their music lessons. Each child was expected to be proficient in a musical instrument since music was an important part of family life. In mid-summer, some of the children would be sent out to harvest mushrooms. After breakfast, it was time for school and the Flanagan children would make their way over a well-worn path to the school, a mile or so away, accompanied by their mother. The Drimatemple school was one of the National Schools[42] established by the government[43] for the education of Irish children, Catholic and Protestant. At Drimatemple, the teachers were Catholic[44] and taught primary school[45] classes approved by the state[46] and a religious curriculum approved by the Catholic Church, under the supervision of the local Catholic priest. Children were given instruction in their religion and prepared for the reception of the sacraments, with careful attention paid to their church attendance.[47]

The religious memory of the Irish people goes very deep. The religion of Edward Joseph Flanagan and his family was more than the round of daily devotions and parish rituals. It was part of the culture, the landscape, the local history, almost the air they breathed. Holy sites and sacred ruins were all around them, some within walking distance, and they were so numerous that it is almost too tedious to list them.[48] Most of them were monasteries and churches,[49] vibrant centers of a people's cultural and religious life, educational centers where literary and artistic works were created and diffused, masterpieces of architectural design, which, even in ruins, reflected something of their original artistry and grandeur. Centuries before, they had housed communities of men and women, intent on God, and yet reaching out in service to people of every walk and station.

In spite of wars and persecution, political oppression and tribal strife, these centers lasted for centuries.[50] Clonmacnoise,[51] less than thirty-five miles from Eddie Flanagan's home, was finally destroyed in the 16th century. It had lasted for over a thousand years, founded by the luminous St. Ciaran in 545. The ruins on the banks of the Shannon are but a small remnant of 120 buildings that housed a huge monastic community of artists, artisans, poets, craftsmen, writers, cosmographers,[52] linguists, classical scholars, illuminators, musicians, mathematicians, herbalists, and historians, to say nothing of the practical arts of architecture, engineering, masonry, agriculture, and economics.

These literary geniuses left their mark upon the poetry[53] and literature[54] of ancient Ireland, and on the many texts being carefully collected, translated, codified, and preserved by the Irish Texts Society. Their craftsmen and artisans have left their mark on the high stone crosses that dot the land, and on the chalices,[55] metalwork, and jewelry discovered in bogs or other secret places.[56] Their poets have created epics[57] and invocations[58] and lyric poetry[59] unparalleled in European history. Their illuminators have left behind the *Book of Kells*, the *Book of Durrow*, the *Lindisfarne Gospels*,[60] and thousands of others that were destroyed when the Vikings ravaged the monasteries or the Normans and English pillaged in their rape of the country.

It is a sad history of religion driven underground and kept alive by generation after generation of schoolmasters, bards, sennachie, priests, nuns, and every manner of patriot and tribal chieftain. Many were slaughtered where they slept or were driven from the country, imprisoned, garroted, drawn and quartered, or harried from county to county, sometimes living in caves and hovels, their hands clutching precious manuscripts, sacred vessels, their harps, and collections of poetry.

For the Irish, these are not the dead relics of the past but rather living monuments of a future that never was, the flowering of a cultural explosion that died aborning, the blossoming of a civilization that could have transformed Europe.[61] When the Vikings destroyed their centers of culture and learning, an army of Irish saints and scholars took with them many elements of the Catholic faith in order to re-evangelize Europe.

There is in Ireland, especially since the days of the Catholic Emancipation of 1829, something called the "generational imperative." It's something felt by every Irishman conscious of Ireland's battered and tragic history "to assure the future by preserving the past." This imperative has been at work in Ireland's homes and schools, in its literature and drama, in religion and the arts, and most notably in its struggle for independence and political autonomy. It is the golden thread of Irish education and family life, the family life that Eddie Flanagan so cherished and treasured, which became the foundation and cornerstone of an educational and cultural community that he would someday plant on the plains of Nebraska U.S.A.

Before and after school, young Eddie would accompany his father tending the sheep and cattle, assisting his brother Jamie in the care and feeding of the animals, and tilling the family vegetable garden where produce was grown for the family table.

Years later, Father Edward Flanagan would describe his chores: "Three times a day I would travel over the immense lands of Leabeg, dangerous bogs to the north and south... mostly without shoes... saying my Rosary as I went along, and other times, as I grew older, reading one of Dickens' novels."[62] One day, during his first year in school, while romping in his bare feet through the grassy pasture, he stubbed his foot on a hidden rock and suffered a sprained ankle. His screams brought Johnny King to his side, who lifted the crying boy and carried him into the Leabeg home. He was in bed for several days, crying from the pain. His sprained ankle would bother Eddie for the rest of his life. In later years, at Summerhill College, it prevented him from joining the track team, but he was able to excel in handball, which would be Eddie's favorite sport for the rest of his life.[63]

Eddie did more than read Dickens' novels on the 300 acres of Leabeg. In the summer, there were blocks of turf to be cut, moved, and stored close to Leabeg house. This would be the chore of the boys of the family and the father. With brother Pat away to the seminary when Eddie was six, it was Eddie and his brother Jamie who would tackle this task, with their father supervising. It was a complicated project. Cutting the peat into movable blocks and storing them against one wall of the stone house was an exhaustive and tiring operation. The peat had to be stored just right so that a wall of peat was a protection against the cold and wind of winter.[64]

The cutting of peat was usually done in the summer and the blocks were stored where they were cut, or close by, until the time for "wintering in" came. Since the land was not their own, there was an agreement with the landowner, who lived in London, on how payment for the turf would be made. That cost could be offset by selling some of the family's peat surplus to neighbors, who would come and haul it from the bogs in horse-drawn carts.

The main event of the day was supper in the candlelit dining room, around a huge mahogany table, with plenty for all: father, mother, grandfather, and, over the years, eleven children gathered for the evening meal. There was always music and singing, accompanied by piano, melodeon, concertina, violin, or flute. Before evening prayer, everyone would sing and the girls would play their musical instruments.

In later years, Eddie developed a beautiful baritone voice, and he was known to use it at family celebrations. It was here that he acquired his love of music, which was further developed when he attended Summerhill College. There he made his first acquaintance with the young John McCormack, who was also a student at the college. McCormack, who later became a world-renowned Irish tenor, had his first performances at the college, which Eddie remembered in later years.

As he grew older, classes and reading were not Eddie's only occupations. There were rides sometimes to Roscommon, or Castlerea, ten miles away, for shopping or for just looking at a larger world. It was also fun wandering over Leabeg, with a dog at his heels, and sometimes with a neighborhood boy. When he was twelve, he and a school chum, Jimmie Coan, went fishing on the Suck, far away from home. On one of their jaunts, his friend took out a couple of old clay pipes, lit one up, and offered it to the young Flanagan. Eddie said later that he took a couple of puffs and found himself getting a bit woozy. Another time, his friend led Eddie into something even more daring.

Close by Ballymoe was the estate of Sir Nicholas O'Conor, an important public figure and former Ambassador to Turkey. On his estate was an apple orchard, and the boys once crept into the orchard, hoping to steal apples. Before they could get their hands on the fruit, they were chased by the owner's care-taker, a former policeman, who was guarding the property. Jimmie Coan got away, but Eddie was caught, and, crying with shame, was turned over to his older brother James, who reported the incident to their father. Eddie got a good licking for his escapade, but his biggest punishment was facing his mother when she returned from Galway.

The family was sometimes worried about the quietest of their children, and John taught Eddie more than stories of saints and national heroes. He taught him, as Father Flanagan would later describe it, "the great sciences of life."[65] Somewhere during those long hours of tending sheep and cattle, John Flanagan explained that every boy is like a stallion and that someday he may be challenged to fight, perhaps against the oppressors of their country, like many of the national heroes, but perhaps just to prove that he was not a coward.

The challenge came when Eddie was crossing the fields to school one day and an older boy challenged him to a fight. "Come around tonight and I'll beat you up," the boy told him. Eddie knew the boy would meet him as he crossed the field on his way home, so he went another way to avoid a fight. But the other boy caught up with him and Eddie stood his ground, trouncing the bully at his own game. Later, when the bully himself was threatened by other bullies, Eddie became his protector. "Fight if you must," his father told him, "but never become a bully yourself." It was advice Eddie would remember for the rest of his life… especially when the bully was a judge, a state official, or a law enforcement officer.

The influence of his family on Eddie Flanagan was profound, deeply woven into the very fabric of his thinking. It was a large family, seven girls and four boys, each member a marked and distinct personality, each one shaped by the tenderness and tensions of family living. Through all his later years, Father

Flanagan was strongly bound by ties to his family, and Boys Town, from the very beginning, was a family project. What is important is that the warmth and tenderness of the Flanagan temperament, which became the style of the man, the wit and childlike wonder that endeared him to many, and the resilient toughness and bear-like brusqueness known so well to state officials and juvenile authorities, were products of Flanagan family living.

There is a certain originality of mind that comes from this kind of family life, because Irish family life at the time of Eddie's boyhood was under the heel of an oppressor – even the farm they lived on was not their own. The Irish are by nature poets and deep thinkers, with a gift for metaphor and mystery, and the unusual turning of a phrase. They look at the world obliquely because they think long and hard at what they do and because of the conditions under which they live. There is an Irish lore that has never died, a lore preserved in the hedge schools that were so much a part of 19th-century Ireland, and in the homes and hearths where their outlawed religion and their love of freedom was kept alive by song and story and the neighborhood ceilis that preserved traditions as ancient as Ireland itself.

One wonders about other things that were so much a part of Ireland at the turn of the 20th century: the oral traditions of Great Blasket Island that were coming to light at this time, with the magic names of Peig Sayers, Tomas O Criomhthan, and Gobnaiat Ni Chinneide on everyone's lips.[66] Was he familiar with the itinerant storytellers, the Seanachai,[67] who were common in Ireland and were welcome in every home but outlawed by the English gentry since they kept alive the rich literary, historical, and religious traditions of the Irish people? Eddie Flanagan, by the time he entered Summerhill College in Sligo at the age of fifteen, would have been deeply imbued with the traditions of his people and could look back over fifteen centuries to the heroes and icons who inhabited those centuries.

What is often overlooked is that classical education was flourishing in Ireland when it was dying on the continent. Classical education was taught by Irish scholars like Marianus Scotus,[68] Virgilius of Salzburg,[69] John Scotus Erigena,[70] St. Columbanus,[71] and a host of others[72] who brought it back to the continent after the Barbarian Invasions had devastated Roman Europe. That tradition had never died in Ireland. It was carried on, not only in the seminaries and locally run Irish schools, but in the homes and hedge schools and parish rectories where scholars of the stature of Patrick Augustine Sheehan of Doneraile instructed private students in languages and the classics. It was his brother Pat who introduced Eddie to Letters, enabling him to skip three grades in the educational ladder. But it was the parish priest, Father Hughes, who tutored him in Latin, Greek, and French.

When his young mind began to open to the wider world of learning at Summerhill College, Eddie was ready for the vast world of Catholic and continental scholarship so aptly described in Newman's "Idea of a University," and for the tough meat of philosophical reasoning he would later find at

Emmitsburg, Dunwoodie, Rome, and Innsbruck. Education, even in the secondary schools of Ireland, was based on the Trivium and Quadrivium of classical education, even though that may not have been the designation given them in the school curriculum.[73]

As Eddie reached his teenage years, the Celtic Revival[74] of William Butler Yeats and a host of Irish poets, novelists, and historians was in full swing, and he could not help but be aware of this blossoming of literary genius[75] going on all around him. He was known to be a thoughtful young man, occupied with his own thoughts, with a peculiar fascination for books. Eddie had a quick mind and was still in primary school when he took up the study of Latin, Greek, and French and immersed himself in Scott, Dickens, and Macauley. There was a strange logic to this intellectual grooming.

"I was a little shepherd boy," he wrote later, looking back on those days, "a delicate member of my family and good for nothing else." But Eddie knew what he was good for and he found it in the saints and heroes his father had told him about on their long walks tending the sheep and cattle. Perhaps the only one who had guessed Eddie's logic was his mother, Nora, who heard it from the lips of the priest in Ballymoe one Sunday after Mass when she emerged from the church with six-year-old Eddie at her side.

"And which one of your brood is this thoughtful lad?" Father Fetherstone asked her.

"He's Eddie," she told him.

Placing his hands on the boy's head, almost like a blessing, the priest said, "Someday Eddie will be a priest."[76]

Eddie and his mother looked at each other, but not a word was spoken about it ever again. Yet the mother always looked upon the old priest's words as a prophecy for her son, as she watched Eddie poring over his books and asking for new ones from his sister Kate and brother Pat, when was home from school. Eddie's decision to become a priest came out of a decision to join a long list of local heroes whose names and achievements stretched back to figures like Patrick, Columcille,[77] and Laurence O'Toole,[78] and more recently Oliver Plunkett,[79] Patrick O'Healy,[80] and Father John Murphy of Wexford.[81]

This was just a few years after the encyclicals of Pope Leo XIII had startled the late nineteenth century with their call for social and economic justice in the aftermath of an industrial and technological revolution. This call to action may not have filtered down to the then-fourteen-year-old Eddie, but it was part of the world he was entering when he insisted that he follow his brother Pat on the road to the priesthood. For Eddie's mother, his decision was a fulfillment of Father Fetherstone's "prophecy." For Eddie Flanagan, it was the fulfillment of his heart's desire.

"It was that desire that took hold of me," he wrote in later years, "And I never had any other desire at any time in my life."

A Virtuous Calling

The dreamy little boy who tended his father's cattle and sheep, whose job it was to keep the cattle out of the bogs and the sheep out of the briers, who loved to run and play with the other boys of the village, who went fishing with school chums on the Suck River, and who walked to school with his older brothers and sisters, had decided very early, perhaps at the age of six, that he wanted to be a priest.

What that meant to Eddie we can only judge from the stories he heard about the priests, scholars, and saints of the golden age of Irish history, from the books he read, and from the priests who were part of the Celtic Revival going on all around him.[82]

The image of the parish priest of Ireland in the 19th century was not just that of the parish administrator and celebrant of the sacred rituals and sacraments of the Catholic Church. He was the intellectual and cultural leader, as well as the spiritual guide and religious mentor, usually trained in the classics, with a wide variety of intellectual, pastoral, and pedagogical skills. Some priests were patriots and martyrs, who opposed in their own persons the injustices of the political occupation of their country. Most, however, were living icons and embodiments of Irish culture and history, with a knowledge of that culture and history they passed on in ways that are only coming to light in our time.

At one time, there was a price on their heads: five pounds for turning in a priest and ten pounds for turning in a bishop, and their heroism from Elizabethan times through Cromwell and the Penal Laws was legendary.

For many of them who left Ireland for missionary work or for service in dioceses of England, Australia, Canada, or the United States, there was keen surprise and disappointment that they were confined to the sacristy and sanctuary, where the use of their personal skills was severely limited and where they were expected to confine themselves to doctrinal matters and the inner affairs of their parish and diocese.

Edward Joseph Flanagan, with a naiveté born of long hours of solitude on the fields of Leabeg, and from stories told to him by his father, fashioned an image of the priest that was epic in nature, immersed in the concrete historical situation in which he had to live, looking to create a future rather than merely inhabit it. It is clear from everything Eddie said or did that he never had any other concept of what it means to be priest. This epic sense remained with him until the day he died. Later, as Father Flanagan, he was not surprised that he had to associate with presidents and five-star generals and Hollywood movie stars to accomplish his task. It is also clear that he walked among them as an equal.

From his earliest days as a shepherd boy on the banks of the Suck River, Eddie became aware of the traditions of his own people, and from the songs and stories around the hearthfires and the colorful itinerant storytellers, the Seanachai, he caught glimpses of a glorious past of which he was the recipient and heir.

The liturgy Eddie experienced from the tenderest age was a masterpiece of pedagogy itself, with its feast days and liturgical seasons, its daily and Sunday readings from the Latin Vulgate, translated by sermons and homilies from week to week and from year to year.[83] This panorama of sound and ritual is a feast for the eye, for the ear, and for the mind, weaving a pattern of living unmistakable in its meaning. It was a timely commentary on every aspect of human life – from childhood to old age, from adolescence to mature adulthood, from courtship to marriage, from town hall to marketplace, and from the peasant in his hut to the king on his throne – if one listened, pondered, and was attentive to more than the sound of the words. Its aim was not mere instruction; its aim was to transform human consciousness to an awareness of the Living God and His sovereignty over us.

Edward Joseph Flanagan was Catholic to the core. The Catholic Faith was the lifeblood of his whole existence, but not in the sense of being narrowly Catholic, concerned only about Catholics and Catholic issues. His faith had become theology, a reasoned understanding and insight into the personal and social implications of what he believed. In his growing up, in his journey to the priesthood, Eddie had to face again and again contradictions and setbacks that forced him to work out those implications in the most trying and difficult of circumstances. This mature and luminous faith determined his purposes, his style, his methods, and his manner, and his faith reached out to every human being in distress or in need of any kind. Kindness to every human being he met was his way of life and Eddie made himself the living embodiment of every item of his belief. He did not judge others; he served them with the best that was in him, and in a sense, washed their feet because Eddie saw in them a living image of the God he served.

It is hard to express, much less fathom, the powerful bond with the Living God that the Mass, the Eucharist, builds in the priest who immerses himself in what the ancients called the Sacramentum Tremendum. That tradition of priesthood was the backbone of Irish Catholic life from time immemorial. This can be seen in the rock altars in the side of hills all over Ireland, where the Irish people for centuries risked their lives and the lives of their priests to take part in the stunning ritual of the Mass. Near the Leabeg estate, across the Suck River, close to where Eddie Flanagan spent hours tending cattle and sheep and reading his books, there is such an altar, and he could be found there, praying his Rosary or absorbed in prayer. For centuries before, the Mass Rock had been the place of worship for the Irish where Mass was celebrated in secret. Eddie's growing awareness of a Presence greater than himself, bound up in the Mystery of the Mass, is not unusual among Catholic young men, especially those who later became priests. It nourishes a fascination with God that is the heart of priesthood and a consequent deepening of an interiority out of which such a person begins to live and act.

That young Eddie Flanagan became something of an enigma even to his own family is evident from their remarks and observations over the years, and as time went on, it was the Living Presence of his God in the wonder of the Eucharist that drew him like a powerful magnet.[84] At one time, and several times after his ordination to the priesthood, Eddie mistook this overpowering thrust of his whole inner being as a call to become a Trappist monk. At times, Eddie actually expressed a regret that he had not taken this step.[85]

Eddie had grasped very early the real meaning of the priestly vocation and priestly holiness, and he pursued both with an energy and relentlessness that almost burned him out before his journey had scarcely begun. It was not a conventional view and he did not find it in manuals of piety or ascetical treatises. He got it from a companionship with his Maker that was developed in the long hours of tending his father's sheep, with a book in his hand and a Rosary in his pocket. Eddie had acquired something in those long stretches of aloneness that no seminary could have taught him: that priestly holiness means living under the very gaze of God. His ancient forebearers of Early Ireland called it "the hovering of God,"[86] and it fostered several generations of "saints and scholars" who transformed the world they lived in. Somehow, a young boy with his books and his beads on the peat bogs and flowering heather of Ireland captured a like vision and left behind a legacy as notable as theirs.

Boys who become priests are often minor mystics in their own right. There is some secret part of them that lies hidden from even those who know them well and there is a secret self they never reveal to anyone. Somewhere, they get a tiny glimpse of God and they dwell in a solitary aloneness that seems to envelope them.

There is a certain kind of religious expression that is uniquely Irish and it can be glimpsed in the relics of the Irish age of gold, relics that fill the museums and heritage centers of Ireland. That age was created by contemplative geniuses who left their mark on the great Celtic stone crosses, on their stunning illuminated manuscripts, on their Ardagh Chalices, and in their native literature that rings with a powerful religious passion.

It has been preserved in the songs and prayers of the Scottish Highlands and the Hebrides, where people still pray and sing invocations taught by the Irish monks from Iona or Derry 1,500 years ago. These were collected by an Irishman named Carmichael into a huge collection called "The Carmina Gadelica"[87] fifty years before Eddie Flanagan was born. They express the kind of religious devotion and passion for God that is part of the Irish personality and partially explain the kind of man and priest Eddie would become as Father Flanagan.

When Eddie was a young boy, the Celtic Revival was at its height, and although the literary explosion of this revival was its most prominent feature, there was a religious awakening that was an integral part of it. It can be seen in the work of Robin Flower, Eleanor Hull, George Sigerson, and Kuno Meyer, whose explorations into Irish history began to tap the written religious masterpieces of their Irish ancestors. From their pens came vivid translations of poetry[88] and tales bearing witness to the luminous sanctity of men and women bearing the names of Patrick, Columcille, Brigid, Brendan, Ita, Kieran, Sedulius, Ethna, Columbanus, and Fanchea.

The statement of St. Columcille is typical: "The fire of God's love stays in my heart as a jewel set in gold in a chalice of silver." And every Irish child was familiar with the "Lorica of Saint Patrick," also called "The Deer's Cry," with its lilting lines:

> *I arise today,*
> *through the strength of heaven,*
> *light of sun,*
> *radiance of moon,*
> *splendor of fire,*
> *speed of lightning,*
>
> *swiftness of wind,*
> *depths of sea,*
> *firmness of earth,*
> *strength of rocks...*

and its stirring invocation to Christ, ringing like a drumbeat through the poem:

> *Christ be with me,*
> *Christ before me,*
> *Christ behind me,*
> *Christ beneath me,*
> *Christ above me.*

It is unlikely that Eddie Flanagan was unfamiliar with these poetic and religious masterpieces and it is possible he may have known them in their original Gaelic, from which this treasure of religious devotion was drawn. The conviction behind them was straight out of the Psalms and the Wisdom books of the Bible, translated into the Homeric speech and poetic phraseology of ancient Gaelic. They were part of the repertoire of the itinerant Seanachai and of the hedge school masters who preserved this literary heritage for generations.

When Eddie began to follow in the footsteps of his brother Pat to Summerhill College in Sligo, he was fifteen years old. Leaving home and the security of family life would make him far more dependent upon his own judgment and initiative. He finished primary school at Drimatemple in the spring of 1901 and planned to enter Summerhill College in the fall. There was money set aside for his college education,[89] and perhaps also money provided by friends and relatives. Having two priests in the family was a great honor and other families were happy to share in this honor.

James, Delia, Teresa, and Michael were still at home, so there were two sons to look after the sheep and cattle. Nellie and Susan were in New York, Mary Jane was married, and Kate close by. We do know that Eddie went with his family to

Castlerea to buy a new suit of Donegal Tweed for his train ride to Sligo and Summerhill College.[90] His frail health was a constant worry to the family, something that would plague him for the rest of his life. But the tutoring, the wide reading, and Eddie's intense study had prepared him well. He would breeze through the five years of secondary school in three years and graduate with honors at the top of his class.

Pat was home for that summer, talking about his own plans with the family. At the end of three years, he would make the momentous decision that would set the course for the rest of his life.

Patrick Flanagan had left home in 1892, when Eddie Flanagan was six years old, to begin his studies at Summerhill College in Sligo. When Pat was home in the summer to help on the farm, he would tutor Eddie in the basics of Letters and in the learning skills his younger brother would need to enter Summerhill College.

Pat graduated from Summerhill College in 1896 and prepared to move on to All Hallows missionary college. Eddie was ten years old, and Pat began tutoring him in the primary school subjects in the Drimatemple school. During their whole lifetime, the brothers were close. Later, during his summers home from All Hallows, Pat must have spoken to his brother about the purpose and history of that institution, expecting that Eddie would take his seminary training there.

In the summer of 1901, Eddie, who just turned fifteen, was making plans to leave home for the first time. When Eddie began his studies at Summerhill College later that year, Pat was beginning his second year of theological studies at All Hallows. For the next three years, they would be together every summer, sharing ideas and hopes for the priesthood, discussing their studies and their scholastic progress, and reading letters from their sisters, Nellie and Susan, who were living with relatives in New York. As a matter of fact, the sisters had returned from America in 1900 with glowing reports of life in the United States.

How Eddie's studies at Summerhill College were financed is only a guess. One version says John Flanagan sold a sheep to pay for Eddie's studies, but it is doubtful that a sheep would bring in enough money to pay for three years of study. It is possible that the local bishop footed the bill in anticipation of Eddie being ordained for the diocese of Elphin.[91] Also, Kate was home in Ballymoe, employed as a teacher in one of the local schools, and it is known that Eddie and Kate were close. She had tutored Eddie in his last four years at Drimatemple and must have watched her little brother excel in his classes. It is also not improbable that both Nellie and Susan could send money from America, where they were gainfully employed.

The sale of the sheep could very well have financed Eddie's new suit and travel to Sligo, with perhaps a little in his pocket for spending money. It is mentioned that he frequented the sweet shop in Sligo, so he must have had a few pennies in his pocket for such adolescent pleasures.

Exodus and Goodbyes

Eddie Flanagan was born when the Great Famine[92] was still a terrifying scar in the minds and memories of the people of Ireland. The statistics of this national tragedy are grim and shocking, even 160 years after the event. Agriculture was the mainstay of the Irish economy, with three million people depending on the potato crop as their basic food supply. When that crop failed in 1845, one million people died of starvation and one and a half million left the country.[93] The economy of the country was shattered by the poverty and destitution of those left behind.

John and Nora Flanagan had somehow survived the national tragedy, but the memory of it was still a stark reality in their minds. Even for a competent manager like John Flanagan, employment was unstable and there was always the fear that bad times would come again. But the bonds that held the Irish communities together in love, friendship, and goodwill were deeper and more enduring than the politics and economics that hovered over their heads. The Irish people had cultivated an underground culture for centuries and their unique religious and national heritage was held together by customs, social events, popular movements, and cultural icons that eventually, after the Easter Rising of 1916, gave them independence from an oppressive and powerful neighbor and planted the seeds of a national identity that had been outlawed for centuries.

The poverty and desperation of the days of the Great Famine, and the cruel discrimination of the Penal Laws, still hung over Ireland like a dark cloud, for no one knew when new restrictions on Irish freedom might be handed down from the English Parliament. It was also true that violence could break out anytime and that segments of the Irish community were organizing active resistance to English laws and government. The Young Ireland[94] movement, begun in 1842, was organized as a protest to English rule and very quickly developed into the Fenian Brotherhood, led by Irish-Americans and aimed at overthrowing English rule. The first outcome of this freedom movement was the execution of three Fenians in Manchester, England, in 1867. The three became known as the "Manchester Martyrs,"[95] and their deaths spread political discontent all over Ireland.

This political discontent broke into violence in 1882 with the brutal murders in Dublin of Lord Cavendish, the Chief Secretary of Ireland, and his undersecretary. Trying to stem the discontent and violence, Prime Minister William Gladstone of Great Britain in 1893 proposed his second Home Rule Bill for Ireland, the second in his four terms as Prime Minister. The first, in 1886, was defeated in the House of Commons, and the second was defeated in the House of Lords. Already, the seeds were being planted for the Easter Rising of 1916, which saw Ireland at war with England and her brilliant leaders decimated by mass executions. Eddie Flanagan was only seven years old when the second Home Rule Bill was defeated, which saw Gladstone's retirement from public life.

In 1893, in the wake of that defeat, the Gaelic League was founded by Douglas Hyde[96] to revive the Irish language and to explore and recover the rich traditions of Irish culture that had gone underground for almost a thousand years. This was the beginning of the Celtic Revival under the leadership of William Butler Yeats, Maude Gonne, Lady Augusta Gregory, and a host of poets, novelists, historians, and artists.[97]

This political and economic instability was part of the world Eddie Flanagan would enter when he took the train from Ballymoe to Sligo in 1901 to begin his studies for the priesthood at Summerhill College. The Celtic Revival was in its springtime and the literary renaissance that followed was accompanied by a religious revival. This recovery of Ireland's past began to reveal an astonishing period in Western civilization that had laid hidden for over a thousand years, a cultural explosion comparable to that of classical Greece.[98] This mind-boggling discovery of the roots of Irish culture revitalized the Catholic consciousness of Ireland. There began to emerge from the dust of history the achievements of several generations of artists, poets, scholars, and saints, and a body of writings, poetry, artwork, illumination, and music that created, as the Irish people began to study their historic past, new institutions of learning, new research centers, and new publications like the *Irish Texts Society* and the many issues of the *Studia Hibernica*. Moreover, this new sense of Irish identity began to blossom in education, in literature, in theater, and in the arts, fueling the passion for freedom and political autonomy that had been smoldering for centuries.

Irish families kept in close touch with those who had emigrated.[99] Since the parting often was forever, there began the custom of the "American Wake,"[100] held when someone left for Canada, Australia, or the United States. This was a gathering of family members, friends, and neighbors for a tearful farewell to those who were leaving for a new life far away from home. It was a time for singing, of sad farewells, and for the sharing of memories, together with gifts for the journey and the promise of prayers.

Such events usually meant that adult children were leaving parents for the first time in their life and it might be the last time they would see each other. Communication from distant shores was unreliable at that time, mail service between countries was uncertain, and the final destination of the one leaving often was not known.

An American Wake began at night in the house of the emigrant and continued until the early hours. The young emigrant would have previously visited friends and neighbors, letting them know of the impending departure. All who were close were expected to attend.[101]

There was always some kind of eulogy for the one departing and a kind word or two on the sorrow of those left behind.[102] At the same time, it was a festive occasion, with good food and drinks all around, and settle beds spread generously for seating the gathered company. There was singing and dancing and rousing good cheer, with "jubes, reels, quadrilles, hornpipes, and Irish step dancing" to lighten the sadness of the departure. Next morning, family and friends would accompany the person who was leaving to the train station or portside for a final farewell.

When Nellie Flanagan left with her relatives, the Larkins of New York, in 1894, it is unlikely there was an American Wake. She was going with relatives, eager for her services as a homemaker and her destination was not in doubt. It was almost certain she would return someday and would have the means to do so. (Nellie did return in 1900 when Eddie was about to begin his last year at Drimatemple school. She convinced the family that her sister Susan,[103] who was eighteen, should return with her.[104])

In four years, brother Pat would graduate from All Hallows College in Dublin and be ordained to the priesthood for service in the United States. There were Irish communities all across America, and bishops from the dioceses where the Irish had settled came to All Hallows every year to recruit the newly ordained priests for service in their diocese.[105] The family reasoned, why not let Eddie go with Father Pat when he headed to the United States? Eddie would be leaving for the States after he was ordained anyway, so why not have him take his studies for the priesthood in the country he would eventually move to?

This was the seed of Nellie's plan to bring her parents and the five younger Flanagans to the United States. She would be back in four years to take the next step in carrying it out: begging that Eddie be allowed to accompany her back to America. First Susan, then Eddie, and then perhaps the whole Flanagan clan.

Sligo

"I will arise and go now, and go to Inisfree," wrote William Butler Yeats in 1893, eight years before Eddie Flanagan set foot in Sligo. Inisfree is an island in Lough Gill, just outside of Sligo City, on the border of Leitrim. In Sligo, the young student Eddie would be surrounded by some of the most historic and beautiful landscape in all of Ireland. Sligo is a port city, open to the Atlantic Ocean, with ships coming and going all the time.[106]

Summerhill College was a preparatory school for the Diocese of Elphin,[107] where boys received a classical education fitting them for entrance to the philosophical department of a theological seminary. Eddie's brother Patrick went on to All Hallows in Dublin, but there were other choices: Maynooth in Kildare or St. Kieran's in Kilkenny. The college was, as it is now, conducted under the auspices of the bishop of the diocese, by a competent staff of secular priests and laymen as professors and tutors.

Young Eddie, in a new suit of Donegal Tweeds, took the train from Ballymoe and traveled north to Sligo City, a distance of forty miles. This was the first time he had been away from home for any length of time, but Eddie was following in the footsteps of his brother Pat, who had traveled the same road before him.

Sligo City was a bustling business center, packed with history, and Sligo Harbor was a port from which emigrants left Ireland for Scotland, Canada,

Australia, or the United States; during the famine, they had departed by the tens of thousands. In 1588, ships of the Spanish Armada were wrecked off the coast of Sligo. Many crew members were given refuge by Irish chieftains, but on orders of the English Governor of the Province, both Spanish seamen and their Irish hosts were shot and hanged. One of the chieftains, Brian O'Ruairc, Prince of Leitrim, was arrested, sent to London, and executed on the orders of Queen Elizabeth.

It was at Ballymote Castle, not far from the city, that Red Hugh O'Donnell gathered his army for his final engagement with the English at the Battle of Kinsale in 1601, which drove him in to exile in Spain, and to his tragic death. There was history on every corner and Eddie Flanagan would drink it in during his walks through the city. Sligo was the history of Ireland in miniature, with names like Queen Maeve, Patrick, Columcille, O'Conor, de Burgh, MacDonagh, Fitzwilliam, Fitzgerald, O'Hara, O'Rourke, O'Down, Bingham, O'Gara, Davitt, and Yeats all part of the fabric of its history. The stories that Eddie's father told him by the fireside and in the fields of Leabeg would be brought to life here with a graphic realism and a powerful understanding of the human drama involved in that history. Eddie had to work out for himself what his role in the drama would be.

In 1901, Eddie would meet full force the history of the Irish fight for freedom[108] in Sligo, which had been a hotbed of rebellion against English occupation. Dark mementos were everywhere. In 1867, a warship manned by Irishmen who had fought in the American Civil War sailed into Sligo Harbor, hoping to take the city as a beachhead for further rebellion. It was met by a British gunboat and, after a short skirmish, the Irishmen's ship returned to the United States.

In 1879, an Irish patriot, Michael Davitt, was arrested in Sligo by British authorities and imprisoned in Sligo jail. His trial, a mockery of justice, made headlines all over the world. The English government was forced to bring about a gradual land reform. The Great Famine of 1845 saw 60,000 people leave the port of Sligo for foreign lands, leaving behind over a million dead from starvation and disease. A bronze memorial commemorates the tragedy in the Famine Graveyard at St. John's Hospital in Sligo.

This would be young Eddie's introduction to a larger world, a world quite different from the quiet pastoral life at Leabeg. Other mementos told their own story. "Mass" rocks like the one in Ballymoe dotted the countryside of Sligo, reminders of the days of the Penal Laws when Irishmen could not own land or, closer in time, after the Great Famine, when 15,000 Irish families were evicted from their lands by English landlords and forced to become fugitives in the surrounding hillsides. Eddie would be reminded that Irish priests, risking their own lives, ministered to their people in their agony and danger.[109]

This was a healthy dose of history for this fifteen-year-old student and would solidify his determination to become a priest with no idea of what might lie ahead of him. The Irish Easter Rising, which saw hundreds of his fellow citizens in rebellion and their leaders executed by the British authorities, was only fifteen years away and it was not impossible that he might be caught in this wave of rebellion himself. What Eddie's thoughts were, we do not know. Sligo was the door, not only to a new world and a new experience, but to any number of possibilities for his future priestly work.

His brother Pat's future was already decided. All Hallows Seminary in Dublin was founded specifically to prepare priests for missions in English-speaking countries to serve the "Irish of the Dispersion." Most newly ordained priests from All Hallows were destined for the United States, where most of the Irish emigrants had gone. When Eddie entered Summerhill College, Pat was already halfway through his studies for the priesthood and Eddie could look forward to joining his brother as a candidate for the missions, or to entering St. Patrick's Seminary at Maynooth or St. Kieran's Seminary in Kilkenny for service in Ireland.

It is possible that Eddie had already talked to Pat about his future and caught something of the spirit of the founder of All Hallows, Father John Hand.[110] Father Hand visualized a corps of apostolic-minded priests, trained in languages, the sciences, literature, theology, sacred eloquence, the arts and music, and a host of other skills, prepared to carry their faith and vision of priesthood to the far corners of the world.[111] He recognized that Irish families were the natural seedbeds for the kind of priest he was looking for, since religion was the heart of the Irish home and Irish homes were the best training grounds – he called them "petit seminaires" – for highly motivated and dedicated priests. That was certainly an ideal that would have appealed to Eddie Flanagan, since in later years he talked about his Irish home life in exactly the same terms.

It was not only the landscape of Sligo – its natural beauty and historic surroundings – that came into view as the train from Ballymoe brought the shepherd boy from Leabeg to the threshold of a new world and a new experience. Eddie was already well-versed in Greek, Latin, and French, and undoubtedly in the literature of those languages as well. He would now have a formal introduction to sources of knowledge, in literature and history, in music and the arts, in men and movements, in politics and polemics, which, in the quiet of Leabeg and Ballymoe, had been only a faint echo.

The undercurrent of Irish history and culture, which was linked to a desire for political freedom, was alive in Sligo as it raged in the larger cities and in the journals and national institutions. Out of Sligo would come one of the prime movers of the struggle for Irish independence and one of the founders of Sinn Fein, Father Michael O'Flanagan,[112] who, in the years young Eddie attended Summerhill College, was on the teaching staff of the college.

Sligo was also one of the ports from which the Irish by the thousands were leaving Ireland for a new life in Scotland, America, Canada, and Australia, with news filtering back from ships returning and from letters to relatives. There was much talk of the personal freedom in these countries and of the unique opportunities overseas. It is well-known that young Eddie, during his years at Sligo, carried on intense conversations with a steamship ticket agent named J.G. McDermott,[113] who regaled the lad with stories of the Irish boys he had sent to America and the astonishing things they had accomplished in their new country. One of these successful young men, known to everyone in Sligo, was W. Bourke Cochran, a graduate of Summerhill College thirty years before. Cochran emigrated to the United States at the age of seventeen and became a lawyer and a well-known orator. He was elected to Congress in 1887.[114]

But what hit Eddie as soon as he stepped off the train in Sligo City was an intense homesickness and loneliness, a fifteen-year-old boy away from home for the first time, on his own in a strange city, knowing no one, with no familiar face to talk to. As he walked up Thomas Street toward the massive, stark, gray limestone structure that was Summerhill College, he was surrounded by fog from off the Atlantic and assaulted by a cacophony of sounds from wagons hacks and jarveys that rattled the cobblestone streets and the cries of hucksters with their two-wheeled donkey carts loaded with fresh fish off the ocean, hawking their wares.

Summerhill College was set on a hill on the edge of Sligo, on an elevation overlooking the Cathedral, in a Romanesque style that mirrored the Cathedral itself. It commanded a view of the entire city, with Sligo Harbor and Rosses Point on the left and the Benbulben mountain range straight ahead. Away in the distance was Lough Gill and the isle of Inisfree, both made famous by William Butler Yeats, who spent his boyhood in Sligo.

The college grounds covered nine acres, with four terraces, tennis courts, a football field, a cricket crease, and a track course. In the main building were laboratories for chemistry and physics, a burrow of classrooms and living quarters, a recreation area and dressing rooms, administrative offices, and a chapel. To a young lad from rustic Ballymoe, this was quite overwhelming. The president of the college was Father Martin Kielty, who headed the school under the authority of the Bishop of Elphin.[115]

The curriculum[116] was classical education at its best, a mastery of Greek and Latin classics, English, German, French, Italian, Celtic, mathematics, physics, chemistry, music, mechanical drawing, history, and geography. There also were religion classes and religious devotions and daily attendance at Mass. The three levels of scholastic achievement – Junior, Middle, and Senior – were to be covered in five years. Because of his tutoring at home and his extensive reading, Eddie would cover the three levels in three years, graduating at the head of his class.

Eddie would indicate in later years that it was a lonely time, but his application to study was complete. The ankle he had sprained as a five-year-old prevented him from engaging in major sports like tennis, football, track, and cricket, but he did excel in handball and did a lot of walking in his spare time.[117]

There were, however, two experiences that unsettled Eddie and gave him much to ponder: the lockstep discipline of the school, which was common even in institutions of higher learning at the time, and the urban poverty he found as he walked through the city. He remarked on both of these in later years, seeing no necessity for the first in the education of boys and drawing lessons for his future work from the second. Even at this young age, Eddie was building a mountain of compassion for the suffering of others and already forming keen judgments about policies and institutions that would guide him in his own work.

The lockstep discipline he found especially cruel, since a boy could be expelled and his future compromised by a juvenile infraction as simple as smoking.[118] He carried away from his secondary school days an intense dislike for institutions of any kind and for the grind and impersonal discipline that the young were subjected to in such institutions. He would always remember the lost and lonely Eddie Flanagan, the new boy at school, and the sense of helplessness and lack of comfort that went with it.

The stark poverty that Eddie saw around him as he walked the streets – huge families crowded into makeshift hovels, with small faces staring at him through open doors or windows – was something he would remember for the rest of his life.[119] An even more shocking sight was the small gangs of boy ruffians fighting in the streets, clothes ragged and torn, grubby little hands sometimes outstretched, asking for a "copper or two." It was a grim commentary on the novels of Charles Dickens that had first opened his mind to urban poverty.[120]

But all was not grim and dreary at Summerhill College. Besides being an avid handball player,[121] excelling in this sport,[122] Eddie's baritone voice became part of the choral group of the college. In his freshman year, a senior named John McCormack was delighting the college and Sligo with his golden voice, not only at church services like Benediction but also at social events and even during a concert in the Town Hall of Sligo. This same John McCormack would later delight the world with his Irish tenor voice. Eddie's and John's paths would cross in later years when McCormack appeared in the concert halls of the United States.[123]

Summers, Eddie was home again, with an outstanding scholastic record. Each summer found him taller than the year before, and not only helping his father and brother James tend the cattle and sheep and cut the winter's supply of peat, but also spending afternoons fishing with Johnny King on the banks of the Suck River. Brother Pat was also home summers, closer to ordination to the priesthood and undoubtedly sharing his experiences at All Hallows and expectations for his future as a priest in the United States. Eddie's expectations were to follow Pat to All Hallows and then to the "Irish of the Dispersion," wherever he might be assigned.

It was during Eddie's years at Summerhill that the novels[124] of Canon Patrick Augustine Sheehan[125] were the talk of the seminaries and in the hands of every priest in Ireland. They were unprecedented in the Irish literature of the time and had made Canon Sheehan a household name in Ireland and in the United States.[126] His novels were about priests, about the education of the clergy, about social questions, and about priestly life. These novels faced and discussed some of the critical questions, in the minds of the Irish clergy, in the wake of the Celtic Literary Revival of William Butler Yeats and his literary colleagues, and in the wake of the political ferment generated by the rise and fall of Charles Stewart Parnell.[127]

The novels spoke to the religious consciousness of the Irish people, to the sense of nationalism that was stirring the country after Home Rule had been denied, and to land reform upon which the economic stability of the country depended. These questions were undoubtedly discussed by the Flanagan brothers when they came together each summer, and perhaps also with other members of the family, like their sister Kate, who was a teacher in one of the local National Schools and kept abreast of national issues.

What the novels, especially *My New Curate*, communicated to these two young Irish men aspiring to the priesthood was the vision of a priest whose only limitations were his own efforts, and who dug deep into the Catholic and priestly tradition for new models of priesthood. This image was not lost upon the teen-aged Eddie, who would take that image and give it a startling new direction.

In Leabeg, when he tended the sheep and cattle and dug into the writings of Dickens, Scott, and Macauley, prayer had become almost a second language to Eddie as he fingered his Rosary and opened his mind to the gaze of God. There were bouts of devotion when he had served Mass at Ballymoe for Father Fetherstone or rang the bells and swung the thurible of incense for the stunning ritual of Benediction. Eddie had been caught up in these moments of adoration and there was more of this at Summerhill, where feast days and Sundays were not only more festive, with more voices and more communal participation, but also held a deeper and fuller experience of the sacred Mysteries which had become the glowing center of his existence. In search of solitude, Eddie would sometimes go down to Rosses Point, where deep-sea fishing smacks tied up and captains smoked their long pipes and reviled the English.[128] There was the Holy Well at Tobernalt, "a haven of peace and tranquility (where) cradled in a wooded grove, clear spring waters flow from a cleft in the rocks… and murmur quietly on their way to join Lough Gill."[129] Four miles from the shore of the island Inishmurray, there was an order of monks, who in their solitude and beehive huts, had beeg singing praises to God for a thousand years or more. Around him was a history that spoke to him and beckoned to something deeper than the here and now.

That "something deeper" would be with Eddie until the end of his days, when he seriously considered entering a Trappist monastery. Those "bare ruined choirs" held a fascination for him, where monks lived in solitude intent on God alone. Eddie would always have an attraction for high mountains and monastic solitudes which nourished in him that irritating "impracticality" that made him the despair of some of his contemporaries. His contemplative gifts became the tools for a rich priesthood and were the seeds of the daring projects and bold experiments that led to Boys Town. To his family and his confreres in the priesthood, Eddie seemed to dwell in a place apart, with an inner tranquility and strength of purpose that was beyond them.

We do not know if, during his three years at Summerhill, he was taught by Father Michael O'Flanagan, who was on the staff at the time as a teacher at the college, from which he had graduated six years before. We do know from Eddie's letters to Father O'Flanagan that they knew each other when Eddie was a student there. The tone of their letters indicate more than a passing acquaintance. When Eddie began his tenure at Summerhill College, Father O'Flanagan was a newly ordained priest, fresh from the seminary. It would be at least a dozen years before Father O'Flanagan would become a strong advocate and supporter for land reform and Home Rule for his Irish parishioners, becoming one of the founding leaders of Sinn Fein.

On January 31, 1904,[130] Father Patrick Flanagan was ordained to the priesthood at All Hallows College in Dublin, and immediately returned to Ballymoe for his first Mass. This was also the occasion for another family celebration. Kate Flanagan, now a teacher in one of the local National Schools, had been engaged to Owen Staunton, principal of the school where she taught. They agreed to postpone their wedding until Father Pat could officiate at the service.[131] The wedding took place at Father Pat's first Mass in Ballymoe, with family, friends, and neighbors joining in this double celebration. Undoubtedly, Eddie was also there for this important event for the Flanagan family. He was in his final year at Summerhill and would be home for good at the end of the scholastic year in the spring. After this double celebration, Father Patrick Flanagan would leave for the United States and the Diocese of Omaha, Nebraska.[132]

On returning to Summerhill College, Eddie had to write a Letter of Intention[133] to the head of the school, indicating the subjects of the examination he would be taking at the end of the school year. In order to pass and graduate, he was required to pass in at least two of the subjects he had taken for the three years of his attendance at the school – Greek, Latin, English, math, and one modern language – or to pass in one of these subjects and two other subjects. He took his final exam during June or July of that year, which gave him time for extra study or tutoring by Father Hughes, if this was needed. Eddie not only passed the examination, but passed with honors.

As the summer wore on, news was received that Nellie would be returning from the United States[134] for a visit home. The whole family knew the reason for her visit: to follow through on her proposal four years earlier that Eddie, upon his graduation from Summerhill College, be allowed to accompany her back to the United States to begin his studies for the priesthood there. She most probably had written to Eddie himself about this, since he was known to carry on long conversations in Sligo with a ticket agent named McDermott[135] about the young men he had sent to the United States and the letters he had received back of their success there. Perhaps for the first time, a family council was held. Mary Jane and Kate were close by, happily married now. Father Pat was in the United States, a priest of the Diocese of Omaha in Nebraska. Susan, a nurse, was in New York, taking care of her uncle, Michael Larkin, who had health problems.

Around the great mahogany table sat father and mother, five sisters, and three brothers. The youngest of the children were Teresa, thirteen, and Michael, nine. James, the oldest at twenty-four, was the only son working on the land with his father.

Nellie was persuasive, helped perhaps by a letter from Father Pat, who was eager to have his brother take his studies for the priesthood in the United States.[136] Eddie could study for the Archdiocese of New York, at the diocesan seminary in Yonkers, not far from where the Larkin family lived. Their uncle, Michael Larkin, was a friend of Archbishop Farley and would be happy to pay the expenses for Eddie's further education.[137]

The family was moving forward. Mary Jane, Kate, and Pat had left home in 1892, Nellie had left in 1894, and Susan departed in 1900. It was inevitable that the children should go their own way and stake out a future for themselves. Only James, Delia, Teresa, and Michael remained at home. Eddie would be leaving for All Hallows, if he followed in Pat's footsteps, but then would go to some faraway diocese in the United States. Perhaps their parents, John and Nora, saw the handwriting on the wall. Ireland was changing and the fortunes of the Flanagan family could change with it. The decision was made that Eddie would go to New York with Nellie for whatever the future would hold for him.

In 1903, the Irish Land Act, also known as the Wyndham Land Act,[138] was passed in the British Parliament. It provided for the purchase of land owned by English landlords by their Irish tenants or any Irishman interested in owning land. John Flanagan was growing old and the position of "herd," the basis of his livelihood, was fast disappearing. This new act would hasten it. We do know that within two years, John, Nora, and their four children still at home would emigrate to the United States. Leabeg and the family home would be bought by G.W. Blake Kelly,[139] who would farm it out to William Hanley.

Besides the future of Eddie Flanagan, the future of the Flanagan family may well have been a topic of serious discussion around the great mahogany table.

The remnants of Eddie Flanagan's birthplace and childhood home in Leabeg, County Roscommon, Ireland.

The village of Ballymoe, County Galway, as it looked around 1904, the year Eddie left for America.

The primary school Eddie attended in Drimatemple, County Roscommon.

2

The Immigrant

New York and a New Start

Nellie and eighteen-year-old Eddie Flanagan sailed out of Queenstown in County Cork on the *S.S. Celtic*[140] in late August of 1904, arriving in New York on August 27. They reached Queenstown by train from Ballymoe. Their city of departure was named for Queen Victoria after her visit there in 1849. After the founding of the Irish Free State in 1922, Queenstown, located on the south shore of the Great Island in Cork Harbour, would revert back to its original name of Cobh.

Eddie was leaving an Ireland swirling with violence and discontent, weary of the over-lordship of a British government whose policies for Ireland had left her people impoverished, uncertain of their future, weary of centuries-long conflict, and increasingly demanding a voice in running their own affairs.

In 1886, the year Eddie was born, thousands of tenant farmers were evicted from their lands and their homes.[141] There was violence and killings in the north, and the failure of English Prime Minister William Gladstone's Home Rule Bills brought about the dissolution of Parliament. July 31 of that year saw the election of Lord Randolph Churchill, an avowed foe of Home Rule for the Irish,[142] as leader of the House of Commons. In Chicago, a convention of Irish Americans, deploring the failure of Home Rule, laid the groundwork for a rebirth of the Irish Republican Brotherhood two decades later in 1906.

Eddie also was leaving an Ireland heavy with conflict, ecclesiastical and civil, with the Catholic Church, in the person of its bishops, taking an increasingly larger role in the affairs of the country.[143] Charles Stewart Parnell, in the dozen years preceding Eddie's birth, had brought about an alliance between the Irish Parliamentary Party and the Catholic bishops of the country called the Clerical-National Alliance, whose power was felt in the halls of Parliament and whose influence had brought about a number of important land reforms.

It is doubtful that these things were on Eddie's mind the day he stepped off the *S.S. Celtic* onto Ellis Island, where a whole new world and a whole new life awaited him. He had in his pocket a letter from his mother Nora to her relatives in New York City,[144] and he was welcomed at the port by his brother Patrick, who had traveled from his parish assignment in Omaha, Nebraska.

Father Pat Flanagan had come east not only to meet Eddie and Nellie, but also to help his brother make plans for his priestly studies in the United States. We do not know how long the older brother remained in New York, advising Eddie on the steps he could take to continue his studies for the priesthood, making sure his canonical documents were in order for examination by church authorities, and impressing on him the importance of learning about his new country, its people, and its customs so he could serve them as a priest.

There was undoubtedly another family council with Nellie, Pat, Susan, and perhaps the four Larkin brothers[145] and their sister Jane,[146] to ensure that Eddie would meet the right people who could help him with his plans for the future and introduce him to those church authorities who would be responsible for his future studies. Father Pat would be the advisor and confidante to his brother, first in person and then from Nebraska, keeping in touch with Eddie every step of the way on his journey to the priesthood. (Later, when Eddie's health required him to go far away from the family to the University of Innsbruck in the Tyrolean Alps, it was Pat who paid for his travel and tuition.)

The Larkin brothers had moved to the United States in the waves of immigration that followed the Great Famine of 1845. Michael Larkin and his brothers, Thomas and Patrick, were successful contractors in the city and were well known to the Archbishop of New York. The religious center of these Irish immigrants was St. Ann's Church on East 12th Street. Soon after his arrival, Eddie introduced himself to the pastor of that church, Father Thomas Myhan.

In 1904, St. Ann's Church was the vital center of Catholic life in the East Village of New York City. The East Village was a center of arts and culture, the home of writers, artists, and musicians, and the gateway to life in America for many immigrants. It was from here that Irish immigrants sent letters to their relatives in Ireland, boasting of the freedom and opportunities in the New World.

Four brothers and a sister of Nora Flanagan had settled in the East Village, and into their homes were welcomed brothers, sisters, aunts, uncles, and cousins who were willing to make the trip across the waters to begin a new life for themselves. Nellie and Susan Flanagan had preceded Eddie because they were needed in one of the households as a cook, housekeeper, or nurse to an aged or ailing relative. These family bonds were as strong among the Irish in America as they were in Ireland, and it was the spaciousness of the houses they lived in that made relatives welcome, as well as the Irish traditions of ceili and craq, family and neighborhood get-togethers that were carried on in their new surroundings.

There was a long history of priests in the Larkin clan, going back centuries, and young Eddie was welcomed as an honored member of this extended family.

The financial base of Irish community life was the Emigrants Industrial Savings Bank on Chambers Street in New York City, which came about in the wake of the failure of the Irish rebellion of 1798. The leader of the rebellion was Father John Murphy of Wexford, and the rebellion was a futile attempt for civil and religious liberty, immortalized in the song "Boulavogue."

Irish immigrants in the early nineteenth century, many of them professional men, doctors, teachers, men of letters, poets, and priests who had been driven to exile in the United States, realized that Irish liberty was probably a lost cause. So they took measures to stabilize their presence in their new country and look to the social, spiritual, and economic welfare of the growing Irish population.

Fifty-four years before Eddie Flanagan's arrival in New York, they pooled their financial resources and founded a bank to protect the savings of Irish immigrants and help them on their way to social and economic security. In 1841, with something resembling pre-vision, Archbishop John Hughes encouraged some of the Irish businessmen to organize the Irish Emigrant Society. The Society would help immigrants send some of their earnings to Ireland to support relatives there and enable them to buy homes and provide for the education of their children. On April 10, 1850, the Emigrants Industrial Savings Bank was incorporated.

When Eddie disembarked at Ellis Island in 1904, a president of the bank was his cousin, Thomas Maurice Mulry.[147] Mulry was the titular head of the Irish community in New York. As an outstanding businessman, he was the head of the construction firm of Thos. Mulry & Son, which was founded by his father who had emigrated from Ireland with four brothers in 1851. The firm had become part of the business landscape of New York and had a hand in the construction of Tammany Hall, the Academy of Music, the Long Island Railroad, and other public buildings. Moreover, Mulry had helped the Larkin brothers, Michael, Thomas, and Patrick, begin a construction company of their own and helped to stabilize, in many ways, the lives and fortunes of the Irish immigrants who were flooding the city.

Mulry[148] was also president of the St. Vincent de Paul Society and was deeply involved in the care of orphans and the poor as head of the Catholic Charities of the archdiocese. His four brothers were Jesuit priests and an aunt and a daughter were Sisters of Charity. Two of his sons were also Jesuit priests, and he had been a major player in the founding of St. Joseph's Seminary in the Dunwoodie section of Yonkers eight years earlier. Mulry was the right hand of Archbishop John Murphy Farley in all that concerned the Church in the Archdiocese of New York and was a keen advisor and participant in the affairs of the Archdiocese.[149]

Archbishop Farley was out of town when Eddie met his famous cousin, so Thomas Mulry introduced him to the archbishop's secretary, Father James Lewis.

The Archdiocese of New York was finishing a decade of vast expansion in response to the influx of millions of immigrants to the city, a growing population that required new parishes, new archdiocesan organizations, and new priests to fill the parishes. In 1896, St. Joseph's Seminary in Yonkers was founded[150] and quickly gained a reputation for intellectual excellence and strong spiritual formation. As soon as he arrived, Eddie had his eye on this prestigious institution.

Eddie looked a little older than his years (he was only eighteen). It is possible that Father Lewis considered him to be a little older, since he advised him to apply directly to the rector of St. Joseph's Seminary (also called Dunwoodie Seminary), not realizing he did not have a college degree. (He was lacking at least two years of college credits.) But on the advice of Father Lewis and Thomas Mulry, Eddie wrote a letter[151] to the rector of St. Joseph's Seminary, Father James Driscoll. This was his first step toward priestly ordination.

> *Reverend Dr. Driscoll:*
>
> *Archbishop Farley's secretary, Fr. Lewis, has directed me to write to you, and ask you what are my prospects of getting into Dunwoodie Seminary. Coming from an Irish Seminary, Summerhill, Sligo, with a fairly good education, I have undoubtedly a strong and ardent desire to become a priest, and, if possible, as a student of your college.*
>
> *Mr. Thomas Mulry, President of St. Vincent de Paul Society, who is a cousin of mine, has introduced me to the aforesaid Fr. Lewis. Both have promised all the assistance they can possibly give to me, and would be awfully thankful to you if you could make me a member of that famous ecclesiastical body, of whom you are the ruler. I, too, if I become a member, promise with the grace of Him, Who is Ruler of all, not to throw any cloud, or darken in any way the bright and shining prospects of that body, but to all its fame, piety and renown.*
>
> *I have all the required letters of recommendation from my parish priest, and President of the College I have been in. I have also my certificate of birth and baptism.*
>
> *As regards a money matter, my uncles are very willing to do whatever is needed.*
>
> *I have a brother who was ordained last February, and is now fulfilling his religious duties at St. Agnes Church, South Omaha. It was his ardent desire to give me an American education and make me accustomed to the habits and ways of a country which I intended to come to when I would be a priest, if ever God would be pleased to make one of me.*
>
> *I would now be very thankful to you, as also would Fr. Lewis and Mr. Thomas Mulry, if you would write as soon as you can, and tell me what my prospects of getting in are, and what I am to do.*
>
> *Yours respectfully,*
> *Edward J. Flanagan*

During his first month, after settling in with his mother's relatives, with Nellie no doubt pressuring her uncles and cousins, and on the advice of his older brother, Eddie took strong steps to begin his priestly studies as soon as possible. It was late September when he started to make arrangements for his entrance into the seminary, with the first semester already underway. Dunwoodie Seminary was a well-known and familiar landmark and the center of intellectual life of the Archdiocese. Archbishop Farley was born in County Armagh[152] and had himself come as an immigrant to the city. He was deeply concerned about the growing Irish immigration that deluged the city after the Great Famine of 1845, and was certainly interested in any young man aspiring to the priesthood. After Eddie's letter to the rector of Dunwoodie Seminary, a meeting between Eddie and the Archbishop was arranged by the applicant's cousin and the Archbishop's secretary.

Archbishop Farley met with young Eddie at the Archbishop's residence on Madison Avenue. Any request for admission to the seminary would have to go through his office, and Archbishop Farley was deeply interested in the intellectual formation of the seminarians of his archdiocese.

In his meeting with the Archbishop, perhaps with an uncle or a cousin accompanying him, Eddie presented letters and documents from the president of Summerhill College and from his parish priest, together with his scholastic record.[153] He was barely eighteen at the time; this alone would have barred his entrance to Dunwoodie, where students were usually received after four years of college.

What he lacked was a formal college education and the spiritual formation a seminary would provide. The Archdiocese already had its own "minor" seminary: Cathedral College[154] in New York City, opened in 1903 and part of the Chancery Office complex of the Archdiocese. Although it was called a "college," it was really a high school preparatory school for day students only. Not all the students were destined for entrance to a seminary.

Archbishop Farley apparently determined that day student status was not suitable for Eddie. Besides, his scholastic record surpassed the courses offered at Cathedral College. Instead, the Archbishop chose Mount St. Mary's Seminary and College in Emmitsburg, Maryland, one of the first centers for priestly training in the United States. It was the spiritual home of several Archbishops of New York and had a reputation for intellectual excellence as well as solid spiritual formation. Within a few days, Eddie was on his way to Emmitsburg, his canonical documents with him. Expenses for his seminary training would be paid by his uncle, Thomas Larkin.[155]

Eighteen-year-old Eddie was eminently prepared for the rigorous study and discipline of Mount St. Mary's. His was an outstanding scholastic record and his intense three years at Summerhill College had given him a mastery of several languages, including Greek, Latin, Italian, French, and German.

With documents in hand, Eddie would have taken a ferry boat from New York City, across the Hudson River to Jersey City, and boarded the Central Railroad of New Jersey, which would have connected with the Baltimore and

Ohio Railroad to take him to Baltimore. From Baltimore, the Western Maryland Railroad would take him to Rocky Ridge, the southern terminus of the Emmitsburg Railroad.[156] At Rocky Ridge, the stationmaster could be hired to take him and his belongings to Mount St. Mary's Seminary and College.

Mount St. Mary's[157] was an oasis of Catholicism in the United States. Founded in 1808, it was part of the blossoming of Catholicism and the expansion of the Catholic Church that took place under the watchful eye and careful planning of Archbishop John Carroll from his headquarters in Baltimore, the heart of Catholic Maryland. From its beginning, Catholic Maryland held a special place on the landscape of then-British America, and its role in the birth and growth of Catholicism in the United States, after the founding of the new nation, was a major factor in the style and form of the Catholic Church in the United States. Emmitsburg, very early in the nation's history, became the hub of an intense and dedicated Catholic community, thanks to the labor of a number of émigré priests and a handful of former Jesuits, the future Archbishop John Carroll among them.

In 1692, during a period of religious intolerance in Maryland and the outlawing of Catholic worship, a small group of devout Catholics under the leadership of William Elder had moved westward in their state to a fertile valley in the shadow of the Blue Ridge Mountains. There, they established a community where they could worship freely and raise their families in a Catholic setting. They settled in the shadow of a promontory that they named Mount St. Mary's.

For decades, the community was served by itinerant priests who passed through the territory: Mass was celebrated in private homes, babies were baptized, young folk married, and funeral rites were celebrated for the dead. In 1739, William Elder built himself a new home with a house-chapel attached, which became the place of worship for the families of the valley. The Elder home-chapel became known as Elder Station and was the resting place for priests traveling farther west to Kentucky or Tennessee.

After the American Revolution and John Carroll's appointment as first bishop of the new nation, Bishop Carroll sent a request to Paris for priests of the Society of St. Sulpice. They came in 1791 and founded St. Mary's Seminary in Baltimore[158] for the training of priests for the growing Catholic population. This was the seed from which Mount St. Mary's Seminary and College would spring.

In 1791, an émigré priest from France, John Dubois, arrived in Norfolk, Virginia. A refugee from the terrors of the French Revolution, he offered himself to serve the American mission. Taking English lessons from Patrick Henry, who was highly regarded by all who knew him, Father Dubois showed himself to be a dynamic and innovative pastor of souls. As soon as his talent and zeal were recognized by Archbishop Carroll, he was assigned to replace an aging Jesuit at Frederick, Maryland, with missions at Hagerstown and Emmitsburg. One of his missions was also to the Catholics at Elder Station, where the number of families had grown into an energetic and active community.

In 1805, with the influx of new priests, Father Dubois was assigned exclusively to Emmitsburg and Elder Station.

The parishioners were so delighted with their energetic priest that both communities, Catholic and Protestant, cut logs off the side of the mountain and built a two-room home for the priest. His next step was to point out a spot farther up the mountain where he would build a church. It was from this church, with its panoramic view of the whole valley, that Father John Dubois set his mind to greater things.

In his zeal and astonishing foresight, he recognized that there were sons from the Catholic families in Emmitsburg and the surrounding towns with no access to higher education, and among them there might be young men who could be recruited for the Catholic priesthood. His first idea was a college where these young Catholic men could study. But the idea grew into something more original and unique: a combination seminary and college, with the seminarians teaching classes at the college and the college itself serving as a seedbed for vocations to the priesthood.

The "Mount," as it came to be called, not only educated future priests and bishops in all parts of a growing United States but also several generations of doctors, lawyers, statesmen, and professional men of every description – even an Associate Justice of the Supreme Court. Its reputation for intellectual excellence and genuine devotion to religion was outstanding, and every September at the opening of the scholastic year, hundreds of alumni returned to take part in the opening celebrations.

Mount St. Mary's

Eddie arrived at Mount St. Mary's in the fall of 1904, in time for the opening event of the school year, the annual Barbecue Day[159] on October 19, and the annual influx of alumni on the same day. His formal introduction to the college was the annual retreat for the "boys," as the collegians were called, and the formal opening of classes a few days later. His board and tuition were paid by his uncle, Thomas Larkin,[160] and on October 1, 1904, he was enrolled in the college records as "Master Edw. J. Flanagan," with a scholastic record second to none in the college.

The annual Barbecue Day was a grand opening of college and seminary activities, a day of games, track runs, musical events, humorous drama, and just plain fun. It was a time for new students to become acquainted with faculty and fellow students and to be broken in to their new way of life.

Not only was the setting of Mount St. Mary's stunningly beautiful, with the Blue Ridge Mountains watching over the valley like a sentinel, but the seminary and college communities also were unique, with a teaching faculty that served both, and the seminarians acting as prefects and religion teachers to the collegians. It was a plan frowned upon in Rome, but in 1904, the arrangement had provided so many outstanding priests and bishops for the country that the arrangement was tolerated.

Not only had the founder of Mount St. Mary's, Father John Dubois, become Archbishop of New York, but his three successors – Archbishops John Hughes, John McCloskey, and Michael Corrigan – were all graduates of Mount St. Mary's. The school had also provided bishops for many of the major dioceses of the country. One of the most notable was Archbishop William Elder of Cincinnati, a great-grandson of the founder of Elder Station. The bonds of the Mount, with the hierarchy of the country, were deep and lasting and its reputation for turning out priests outstanding in learning and holiness was legendary.

When Eddie arrived at the Mount, there were about 500 students in the college and seminary. Sports were huge and some of the best athletes were seminarians. Soon after his arrival, a group of seminarians left for Cincinnati to provide the choir for the funeral of Archbishop William Elder, an alumnus of the Mount. There was always a coming and going by bishops and priests to the Seminary, and in two years, Eddie would become familiar with many of the major figures in the American Catholic Church.

Baseball, football, and basketball games were scheduled throughout the year with local area colleges such as Georgetown, Johns Hopkins University, and Gettysburg College. Periodically, there were excursions to Baltimore for sports events or pleasure and to Washington for historical reasons. Handball was also an active sport and Eddie, enrolled as a collegiate and working toward a bachelor's degree, soon became known as the best handball player on campus. He also became a member of the Glee Club when it was organized a few months after his arrival. He joined the Chapel Choir and the Sodality of Our Lady. The setting and the environment were in keeping with his deepest desire and aspirations, the beginning of the fulfillment of a dream he had dreamt since boyhood. His road to the priesthood seemed dead ahead.

His curiosity about his new country drew him into conversations with his classmates. One of them was a seminarian from the Archdiocese of New York, John A. Harris, who would precede him to Dunwoodie Seminary. Another of his classmates, James J. Walsh, became one of the founders of the Maryknoll Missionary Society.

Eddie found much to occupy his free time at Mount St. Mary's. There was skating on St. Anthony's Lake and musical programs of high quality in which his rich baritone voice was heard often in the Glee Club and Chapel Choir. There were sleighing parties and frequent visits by priests, bishops, alumni, and a colony of Mexican seminarians that added a touch of the exotic to the student population. There was the presence of the religious community of Mother Elizabeth Ann Seton and the memory of her astonishing pioneer work in Catholic education almost a century before. Eddie was surrounded by a unique Catholic culture, rich in memory and in the achievements of pioneer priests who had left their mark on the emerging Catholic Church in the United States.

But he was and remained the student. Eddie immersed himself in his studies, which expanded his mind considerably. He did not allow himself to be distracted by the flurry of activities at the college. There was a oneness of mind about his application to study and his immediate goal: admission to Dunwoodie Seminary as a candidate for the priesthood of the Archdiocese of New York. This was the goal that was uppermost in his mind, and this desire would almost burn him out as he had scarcely begun his journey. But it also sharpened his vision of what it meant to be a priest and riveted in his mind the conviction that this was his God-given destiny.

Eddie's reading was not only of the serious books of philosophy he had to master. He waited eagerly for every episode of the *Adventures of Sherlock Holmes* that came off the presses and delighted in the exploits of this master detective.[161]

Christmas vacation found him returning to Nellie in New York[162] and to his colony of relatives in the East Village, where he heard the news the Flanagan family was preparing to migrate to the United States. Nellie had convinced John and Nora Flanagan that opportunities for their children were greater in the United States than in Ireland. The entire family was preparing to make the trip.

Eddie returned to Mount St. Mary's after the Christmas holiday in time for the mid-term exams. In April, the Mount was visited by Cardinal Gibbons of Baltimore, who gave the students a few days extension of their Easter vacation. On Easter Monday, there was a student visit to Frederic, rich with the history of the American Civil War. Cardinal Gibbons returned for the Commencement of 1905, and young Eddie again returned to New York City, perhaps in the company of John Harris, who had graduated that year and would be entering Dunwoodie for the next scholastic year.

In the fall of 1905, James, Delia, and Teresa arrived in New York from Ireland,[163] and were the guests of Jane Cox, their aunt, who had been so welcoming to Eddie when he arrived the year before. After Nellie's visit to Ireland in 1904, it had been decided that the rest of the Flanagan family would emigrate to the United States, where opportunities for the children and the stability of the family were assured. Michael Larkin and his brothers were prosperous contractors, and the Irish community in the East Village not only gave newcomers temporary residence, but also offered their homes as boardinghouses for those who had not yet married. The word throughout Ireland was, "In America, every man is a sovereign," and this word brought thousands of new Irish immigrants to New York City. Many of these Irish immigrants had moved west, where as "gandy-dancers" they laid the rails of the Union Pacific Railroad as it snaked its way from the Midwest to the Pacific coast. The railroad had also platted many towns along its route where many of these Irish immigrants settled, along with immigrants from other European countries where civil and religious liberties were restricted.

Father Patrick Flanagan, ordained in 1904, had preceded his brother to the United States and was serving an Irish community as assistant pastor of St. Agnes Church in South Omaha, Nebraska. His first assignment had been to the Irish community of O'Neill in northeast Nebraska, where Eddie himself would one day begin his priestly career.

Eddie was scarcely nineteen, but mature for his years, and his intellectual browsing was shown when he gave a talk at a meeting of the college Temperance Club on the book, *Work-house John's Sermon*.[164] "Work-house John" was John Micklebourth, one of the founders and advocates of the English work-house, so despised by Dickens. It was a rare book to find in 1906. It is clear that the care of the poor was on Eddie's mind as he browsed through libraries to inform himself on anything that threw light on the problem.

On April 21, 1906, John and Nora Flanagan, with son Michael and niece Lenore Norton, disembarked from the *S.S. Caronia* onto the docks of New York City.[165] Nellie, and no doubt other members of this extended family, were there to greet them. Eddie was not there, as he was in the middle of preparing for his final examinations at Mount St. Mary's and for graduation in June, but probably received the news by letter or by telephone.

Arrangements had been made with Thomas Maurice Mulry, now president of the Emigrants Industrial Savings Bank, for a home for the family on East 20th Street.[166] But they probably went immediately to the house of Jane Cox for a family reunion and to rest from their long journey. John Flanagan was seventy years old and Nora was fifty-four. Travel on an immigration ship was wearisome and long. Nellie's plans for the family were finally carried out and the whole Flanagan family, with the exception of Mary Jane and Kate, was now in the United States facing a new country and a new way of life.

Susan, twenty-four, was a nurse, taking care of elderly relatives. Nellie was thirty-two and would now help her parents and her sisters and brothers get settled in their new home. James was twenty-six and could easily find work with his uncles' contracting business. Delia was twenty-two, her education completed, ready to start a new life in a new country. Teresa was fifteen and would continue her schooling, most probably at the parish school, and fourteen-year-old Michael would join her.

Eddie's last year at Mount St. Mary's was ending and he would now have a home to return to after finishing college. Before him was Dunwoodie Seminary in nearby Yonkers, so his family would be close during his seminary days. The center of their religious life would be St. Ann's Church on East 12th Street, where the pastor, Father Thomas Myhan, had already met the young Flanagan.

Eddie graduated from Mount St. Mary's College on June 20, 1906,[167] with an A.B. degree that qualified him for entrance into Dunwoodie Seminary as a seminarian for the Archdiocese of New York. He was only nineteen, the youngest student ever to graduate from the Mount.[168] In later years, his only expressed regret would be that he had not misbehaved a little,[169] which would have qualified him for entrance into the "Mountaineers," the name given to students who had misbehaved and were required to climb the local mountain in retribution, reciting long lines of poetry.

On leaving Mount St. Mary's, Eddie requested a Letter of Recommendation from the college president, Father Dennis Flynn,[170] to the rector of Dunwoodie Seminary, Father James Driscoll. Father Flynn wrote:

June 26, 1906

Very Rev. James Driscoll, D.D.

Reverend Sir: Mr. Edward Flanagan, a recent graduate of our College, has applied to me for a letter. It gives me pleasure to state Mr. Flanagan's conduct and application were at all times completely satisfactory. He has shown most positive indications of a vocation to the sanctuary.

As we do not give letters to students, this letter is sent to you.

Wishing Mr. Flanagan every success, I am very sincerely yours,

– D. J. Flynn, Pres.

His conduct and application had indeed been satisfactory. Eddie had distinguished himself in the study of Latin and Greek and had received Second Highest Honors in Composition and English. He received high praise for his speech in the college Elocution Contest, which was always part of the graduation celebration. He took as his topic, "The Gaelic Revival,"[171] which was reaching its peak in Ireland with the founding of the Abbey Theater and the work and writings of William Butler Yeats and a host of other writers, poets, and artists. The movement for Home Rule was also exploding throughout Ireland, and Irish emigrants to London, like George Bernard Shaw, Oscar Wilde, William Allingham, and Brian Stoker, were the toast of London society,[172] sparking an explosion of literary genius unparalleled since the age of Dickens. Eddie's bonds with his native country would always be strong and he drew heavily on his own Irish roots to shape his concept of the priesthood.

Mount St. Mary's was not only Eddie's introduction to his new country, with trips to historic sites in the area and long conversations with his classmates, but also the first time he faced the issue of racism and the social remnants of slavery. Evidence of this was all around him, in the slave quarters of many of the old local houses as well as in the former slaves who were an important part of the Emmitsburg community. It is clear from his later statements that Eddie was shocked and troubled by this seeming contradiction in the American experience. His efforts to overcome it in his founding of Boys Town would be a glorious page in American social history.

For the last time, young Eddie took the train from Rocky Ridge to New York City, his college degree in hand, as he prepared for his next meeting with Archbishop Farley. James, Delia, and Teresa had been living with their aunt, Jane Cox, before the arrival of John and Nora Flanagan, and were now on East 20th Street with the rest of the family. Susan, who had finished nursing training, was caring for their uncle, Michael Larkin, who was not well. Young Michael and Teresa were enrolled in St. Ann's School on East 12th Street.

As soon as he arrived in New York, Eddie reported to the pastor of St. Ann's Church, Father Myhan, to arrange for his entrance into Dunwoodie Seminary. He also met again with his cousin, Thomas Mulry. Since Archbishop Farley was out of town, they soon both wrote letters to the Vicar General of the

Archdiocese, Monsignor Joseph Mooney, recommending Eddie's acceptance to Dunwoodie.[173] By the end of the summer, he was accepted for entrance as a candidate for the Archdiocese of New York.

The summer for Eddie was a time of family gatherings, long talks with mother and father, and spending time with brothers and sisters. There were visits to relatives, especially to the home of Jane Cox, the older sister of his mother, Nora. St. Ann's Church was the hub of the cultural center of the East Village,[174] close to Astor Place, Cooper Union, and Cooper Square. It was the heart of the religious and devotional life of the Irish community, with an active Catholic school, religious organizations like the St. Vincent de Paul Society, and religious and devotional events that were the lifeblood of the Catholic community.

As the summer wore on, Eddie made visits to the seminary in Yonkers, where he would meet for the first time, the rector, Father James Driscoll, and Father Francis Duffy, one of the professors at the seminary. Both would have a powerful influence on Eddie.

During the summer, Eddie also became more familiar with his colony of relatives in the East Village. His uncles, Michael, Patrick, and Thomas Larkin, were successful contractors in New York City and well known to the pastor of St. Ann's Church. The pastor was something of a spiritual father to the Irish immigrants in the East Village and admired their large families and their intense devotion to their religion. Another uncle, William Larkin, the youngest of the brothers, had a daughter, Sister Mary Celestine, a Sister of Charity.[175]

Aunt Jane Cox was something of a mother hen to her relatives arriving in New York from Ireland. Her home at 208 East 10th Street became a mecca for family members arriving in New York. Besides her brothers, Patrick and Thomas, she had housed a variety of Flanagans, Larkins, Byrnes, and Allens in her home, which became a tribal boarding house for new arrivals from Ireland.[176] Patrick and Thomas had a special place of honor in her home and became sort of grand-uncles to the younger members of the Larkin clan. Thomas had even paid the seminary expenses for Eddie at Mount St. Mary's.

Dunwoodie

St. Joseph's Seminary in the Dunwoodie section of Yonkers was the dream and achievement of Archbishop Michael Corrigan, the predecessor of Archbishop John Farley for the Archdiocese of New York. Founded in 1896 with much fanfare and careful planning, it was the pride of the Archdiocese and the hub of a growing Catholic culture in the northeastern United States.[177] Until 1906, the seminary was under the direction of the Congregation of St. Sulpice, headquartered in Paris. But in the year young Eddie Flanagan entered, the seminary was completely in the hands of Archbishop Farley and the Archdiocese of New York.[178]

In ten short years, Dunwoodie had developed into an intellectual center for American Catholicism, second only to the Catholic University of America in Washington, D.C. Its staff of professors, carefully handpicked by Archbishop

Corrigan and Father Driscoll, were first-class scholars in their fields and the educational status of the seminary was remarkable for a Catholic community that was still considered missionary territory in Rome.

Eddie entered Dunwoodie conscious of the seminary's reputation for intellectual excellence and intense spiritual training.[179] He started on the tenth anniversary of Dunwoodie's founding and his first days were marked by tenth-anniversary celebrations. The student enrollment was 124, 113 of whom were seminarians for the Archdiocese of New York.[180] The roster of professors included both American and European scholars in every major field laid down in Canon Law; some, like Francis Gigot in Biblical Studies and Gabriel Oussani in Semitic Languages, had a world-wide reputation. The most popular teacher in the seminary was Father Francis P. Duffy,[181] who would become the special friend, tutor, and mentor of young Eddie during his first year of seminary training.[182]

At Dunwoodie Seminary, Eddie joined fellow seminarian John Harris, whom he had known at Mount St. Mary's. Eddie was entering a first year of philosophy, mandated by Canon Law, as the first step in a six-year program of seminary training. Another year of philosophy would follow and then four years of theology.

In 1906, the annual tuition was about $200, with minor expenses for books, travel home, and personal items. However, Dunwoodie had a policy of accepting any qualified student for the priesthood, regardless of his ability to pay: "No knowledge or non-payment gets beyond the Treasurer's private records and as a result no distinctions or embarrassments have been made or felt at the seminary."[183]

Eddie found that life in a seminary was vastly different from life in a college, even a college attached to a seminary, like Mount St. Mary's. Father Francis Duffy, soon to take on the direction of Eddie's studies himself, described a student's first days at Dunwoodie:[184]

"The first twenty-four hours a student spends in the seminary are devoted to putting in order the room that has been assigned to him, arranging about his classes, finding out about the order of exercises, meeting old friends, and making new ones. At the end of that time, he finds himself suddenly launched into a week's retreat, during which silence and meditation, spiritual reading, the recitation of the office, and conferences from professors tend to give him a proper idea of the seriousness of life and the importance of the step he has taken. After this, it is a positive relief to find an opportunity of putting good resolutions into practice by setting down to the regular work of seminary life. Week follows week, unbroken except by the Wednesday holiday and the Sunday and holiday services. Before Christmas, examinations are held to test the knowledge acquired during the term."

From the age of fifteen, Eddie Flanagan was a student and a singularly exceptional one. But his first year at Dunwoodie would test not only his scholastic ability but also his very determination to be a priest. He had scarcely taken his first steps of formal training when he had to face the prospect of crushing defeat, something neither his mind nor his idealism were quite prepared for.

The studies were intense, the spiritual training demanding, and the personal commitment exacting. The seminary was a huge religious community, dedicated to the highest ideals of Catholic priesthood, with a corps of well-trained and dedicated teachers intent only on fashioning young men for a life of service to the Church. The discipline of the seminary and the schedule of activities reflected this goal.

Father Duffy thus described the seminarian's daily routine at Dunwoodie:[185]

"At 5:30 every morning, winter and summer, the persistent bells jangle out their call to a new day's work. Immediately afterwards, one of the students on each corridor knocks at the doors of his comrades and wakes them with the reminder of what the day's work ought to be, crying 'Benedicamus Domino,' to which comes the response, 'Deo Gratias.' And then, 'Laudetur Jesus Christus,' and 'In Aeternum.' The now-awakened student dresses himself, and if there is time, steps into the chapel for a few minutes to say a good morning prayer to the Lord before meditation. At 6 o'clock all repair to the meditation halls, and a half hour spent in the saying of morning prayers and the making of a meditation. Then all attend the Holy Sacrifice of the Mass in the beautiful chapel of the seminary, and those who receive Holy Communion remain for a Thanksgiving Mass. The students retire in silence to their rooms to make their beds and prepare for the day's classes.

"Breakfast is at 7:30 a.m., two hours after rising, and after breakfast, the solemn silence which had prevailed since 8:30 the preceding evening is broken by recreation. After 8:15 all retire to their rooms to prepare for class, which is from 9 o'clock until 10. Then follows an hour of study, an hour of class, and fifteen minutes of free time. Afterwards all go to the chapel to read a passage of the New Testament and make a particular examination of conscience. Dinner follows at 12:30, then Angelus in the chapel and recreation until 2:30. There is a half hour of study at 2:30 and then class for an hour. Then after a half hour of recreation, comes the 'Long Study,' from 4:15 to 6:15. The beads are recited in private and supper follows at 6:30.

"Then the Angelus in the chapel, recreation until 7:45, study or class until 8:30, and spiritual reading in common for half an hour. At 9 o'clock all meet once more in the chapel for night prayers. After prayers, the sweet familiar hymn 'Adoro te devote' is sung, and then, after some time in private devotion to the Blessed Sacrament, each student silently passes to his room, there to read his Bible or make a short spiritual reading, prepare the points of meditation for the following morning, and prepare for his night's rest. At 10 o'clock the lights are extinguished throughout the house."

This almost monastic schedule and environment appealed to Eddie Flanagan's deepest instincts and rooted in him a contemplative spirit that had been growing since his long hours tending sheep and cattle on Leabeg. It rooted in him a sense of the magnitude of God, which never left him, even in his most active years.

Several times Eddie expressed a regret for not following that instinct into a deeper and more personal solitude.[186]

To his classmates, he was distinguished only by his quiet manner[187] and intense curiosity about American life. Later, a classmate, Aloysius Dineen, who succeeded Father Francis Duffy as chaplain of the Fighting 69th, described his impression of Eddie:[188]

"In those days, Flanagan was still a raw boy. He was not a loudmouthed fellow, but a very thoughtful one. His eyes could look right through you and never see you when he was busy in his dreams. And I can tell you this – no one in Dunwoodie during the brief time he was there would ever have voted Flanagan the most likely to succeed. I think the majority view would have been that he would wind up as a pastor of some little country parish, where the world would never hear from him."

In his studies at Dunwoodie, Eddie came under the influence of Father Duffy, professor of Philosophical Psychology and Logic at the Seminary, both classes being part of the philosophy curriculum. Father Duffy's influence on the seminarians was massive. "His popularity with the students did not come from his fawning over them… he constantly pushed them to excel in their studies." His talents were manifold, "student, teacher, writer, priest, pastor, preacher, lecturer, citizen, and patriot."[189] He drew out the best in his students, but recognized their own individuality and tried to help them cultivate their own priestly skills, encouraging them to think for themselves. He had a scholarly and critical mind, open to the new winds blowing through the Church, and the need to be thoroughly Catholic but thoroughly contemporary as well.[190]

Father Duffy's success as a pastor when he left the seminary faculty embraced the whole city of New York, and as one commentator noted at the time of his death, he made the whole of New York City his parish. He walked through the city as if he owned it. His holiness and closeness to God were transparent, a quality he passed on to his students.

Before joining the Dunwoodie faculty in 1898, Father Duffy volunteered as a chaplain for the army during the Spanish-American War. The war was over before he could carry out his plan, but after its end he became chaplain to the army troops at Montauk Point in New York who were suffering from typhoid fever. He caught the disease himself and was hospitalized for several months before joining the Dunwoodie faculty.

But it was his overwhelming kindness to any and all, to the town drunk and the homesick seminarian ready to leave the seminary, that endeared him to all. It was also Eddie's good fortune that Father Duffy knew Ireland. He knew its history, its literature, its patriots and martyrs, its saints, and its struggles for freedom. Even before the Easter Rising of 1916, Eddie knew by heart the names of Pearse, Plunkett, and MacDonough, and the other thirteen heroes who were taken out and executed. Eddie's friendship with his teacher and mentor would last until Father Duffy's death in 1932.

At Dunwoodie, every Wednesday was a free day, but the students were expected to do more than fill their free time with recreation. They were expected to visit patients in local hospitals; it was part of their training. Eddie took to it like a fish to water. In fact, he volunteered for the worst assignment: visits to the tubercular wards of these hospitals, which were overcrowded, seldom visited, and reeked with the stench and smell of this dread disease.[191]

The popular word for the disease was "consumption," and only a few bold people ventured into these wards, even to visit close relatives. These were the most neglected patients, housed in havens of despair, where people died in solitary loneliness wondering whether their next cough would show "pearls or rubies" – harmless phlegm or the blood that signified death. Eddie very soon learned their vocabulary of despair, not realizing that he would grapple with that same despair as his own lungs weakened under the strain of his studies and his devotion to this work of mercy.

He walked into the tubercular ward of his first hospital, the lone attendant passively watching him as he observed its double row of cots stretched out before him. Eddie would later write that the faces of the patients were "as white as the sheets on their beds."[192] He was speechless, but gradually his speech returned as he passed by their beds, answering their questions and seeing their faces light up at his words. He returned again and again to these rooms of darkness, finding cheering words to say, happy to see the laughter on their faces and the hope in their eyes as he walked in the door, pen and paper in hand, calling each one by name. He wrote letters for them, providing stamps from his own small supply of money, and talked and joked with them, becoming a smiling face and cheering voice to them, bringing news to them from the world outside.[193]

He told them about a world that was closed to them, how the grass was green and the flowers were blooming in the warm spring or dying in the autumn cold. He described the sound of streetcars and horse and buggies on the streets and the voices of people at baseball games and in department stores. It was the "outside" they wanted to hear about, the things that normal people say and do, the weather and the changes of seasons.

"My gift of narration then, I fear, was meager. But I tried to tell these sufferers what the color of the parks is in May and how a flower looks against a green lawn. All the faces in the rooms were turned towards us,"[194] he would later write.

In later years, he further described his impression of these days: "If I had not become interested in anything else, there was work enough for me to have done all the rest of my life, just in visiting condemned, terminal cases in hospitals for the poor. Anyone who wants to go to work for God can start there, writing letters for the desperate and helpless. And others can write letters to them. There is no more heart-rending hour than mail time in some of our hospitals. They lie there, helpless for the rest of their lives – and never get a letter. This world is full of careers for people who are willing to help. Every hospital, every asylum, every orphan home is a want ad for a position with the Lord, doing

His work. And the pay lies in helping to bring someone a little moment brighter than the rest."[195]

This first experience of bringing joy to others was infectious and it stayed with Eddie for the rest of his life. He never considered it a duty or some obligation to those less fortunate than himself. Instead, it was the sheer happiness of making others happy, of relieving some misery, and creating "bright moments" in someone's bleak and hopeless life. To say that this became a passion with him is an understatement; it became the thrust of his whole existence, something he began to glimpse in the pages of *Oliver Twist*, *Great Expectations*, and *Nicholas Nickleby*, in which a world of human misery was first revealed to him and the need to relieve that misery.[196] That one of the most graphic images in one of those books was that of a homeless child on the London streets, illustrated in all its pathos, shows that a seed was sown early for the adventure that became Boys Town.

Eddie's health had always been fragile. When Nora Flanagan heard of his visits to the tubercular wards, she feared for his health. When he first began his studies of Greek, Latin, and French under Father Hughes at the age of twelve, she would find him wandering around the house in the middle of the night, fast asleep, muttering his Latin lessons.[197] She saw the same intensity in him now, worried that he was studying too hard and that the visits to tuberculosis patients might be a hazard to his fragile health. As a child, he was often the victim of wracking colds. As the cold winter began to set in, she knew that his coming and going to and from the hospitals would soon weaken his resistance and she begged him to take better care of himself.[198]

Eddie saw little of his mother during this first semester so her concern for him could be expressed only by letter. Seminarians were free to go home only during Christmas and Easter vacations, but he might have dropped by the family's new home on East 20th Street on visits to the hospitals, although this is unlikely because of the strict discipline of the seminary. His sister Nellie, who must have seen him during this time, remembered that he would beg or borrow extra cash for stamps and stationery.[199]

Besides the Wednesday visits to hospitals, his time was spent mastering his subjects and preparing for the mid-term examinations before the Christmas vacation.

There are indications that he visited a doctor at this time, most probably in the infirmary of the seminary, where doctors could be consulted from time to time by the seminarians. It may have been a cough that brought him there or the concern of Father Duffy or one of his teachers that he did not look well. He was told that he might not finish the year if his health deteriorated further. There was even the suggestion that he might consider going west for his health.

But his visits to the hospitals and the tubercular wards continued. He wrote letters to friends and relatives for money to buy stamps or other conveniences for his patients, most of whom had become his close friends. Eddie saw that he was the only relief in the desperate lives of these people. He could not and would not abandon them in their misery. His words on the subject make this clear: he had taken on the work of an angel of mercy and saw this as almost the equal of his own vocation to the priesthood. It seemed that he was envisioning a culture where the poor and homeless were not neglected and where suffering people like his "patients," as he called them, were treasured, cheered, and comforted. It was an astonishing concept that would grow with the years until he had to face another kind of misery and another kind of neglect. When he began to see that all things were possible (and later, in that singular work that was to become Boys Town), Eddie's only limitations were his own efforts.

This kind of discovery dominated his first days in the seminary, discoveries that he did not find in books but which became part of his inner conviction and practical memory. The streets of New York spoke to him as the streets of Omaha would speak to him when a tornado hit the city and jobless men roamed streets and back alleys, hungry and desperate, not a hand raised to help them. It was this lack of practical Christianity that would sadden him to his dying day, as he searched his own soul for the solution to human misery. At Dunwoodie, he was laying down a program for himself and a vision of human worth that would dominate his whole priesthood.

Edward Flanagan (front row, second from right) and his older brother Patrick (front row, first from right) arrive at New York City's Ellis Island aboard the *S.S. Celtic*, 1904.

3

The Darkness of Defeat

Disaster at Dunwoodie

As Christmas approached at Dunwoodie, Eddie Flanagan was looking forward to a home visit and a Christmas holiday with his family, his first since he'd left Ireland.

The family was settled in a home on East 20th Street and Second Avenue in the East Village, surrounded by relatives, their home address forty blocks from St. Patrick's Cathedral. There had been visits back and forth by members of the Larkin family since it had been over forty years since Nora Flanagan had seen her sister and brothers.

In seminaries, and Dunwoodie was no exception, the seasons of Advent and Lent were spiritual highlights of the year, with more concentration on things sacred and on personal spiritual renewal.[200] Often there were special events like a Christmas Oratorio in New York City during Advent or a special exhibit of religious art. It was not only the cultivation of priestly skills that the seminary encouraged but also a love of music and the arts. Just before Christmas, the first semester exams were held[201] and, with these over, the seminary prepared for the exodus of its army of seminarians to their homes, most of them in the New York area.

A small number of seminarians were from outside the New York area, from places as far away as Savannah, Georgia, and Nashville, Tennessee. With the mid-term exams over, it was a good time to relax and forget the books, and some of them would remain at the seminary during the Christmas holidays. Many were undoubtedly invited to the homes of a classmate for the holidays and firm friendships were formed that lasted a lifetime.

Christmas began with the traditional Midnight Mass at the seminary. At mid-morning there was a trip to St. Patrick's Cathedral in Manhattan for the Solemn High Mass of Christmas,[202] with Archbishop Farley presiding. Vacation did not begin until after High Mass in the Cathedral. The trip to the Cathedral from Yonkers brought Eddie closer to his parents' home on East 20th Street, which was some distance from the church. Eddie mounted the steps of the Cathedral with Dunwoodie's 124 seminarians, some of them scheduled to take part in the ceremony as acolytes.

There was standing room only in the huge Cathedral. The seminarians had to stand, jammed together in one corner. Eddie found himself backed up against an open steam radiator, the hot pipes against his back and spine. The Mass was long, and his whole body was hot from the heat of the register.[203] When Mass was over, he followed the other seminarians to the door of the Cathedral, as each bade the others goodbye for the holidays. He stepped out into a howling blizzard and started walking to the family home in the East Village. Fighting the wind and wading through deep snow, Eddie made his way to his parents' house, about forty blocks away. It was a long and treacherous walk, the snow biting into his face and the cold wind hitting him on every side. Once at his destination and inside the house, the exhausted young man began to cough, his whole body shaking and trembling. The family gathered round, fearing the worst.[204] Relatives were called, and the next morning, Eddie was rushed back to the seminary and put right to bed. Later in the day, his condition was worse and he was too weak to get out of bed. Roommates bundled him in overcoats and carried him to the seminary infirmary. His condition was so bad, John and Nora Flanagan were called; they were told their son had double pneumonia. They were warned he might not recover and that his lungs could be irreparably damaged.

Long consultations were held with doctors and the seminary director. It was decided that Eddie should stay in the infirmary until his health improved.

Eddie had passed his first semester exams and he was determined to keep up with his other classes. But now he was told he had paid a high price for passing his exams and that his lungs had a touch of tuberculosis. One of the doctors consulted was Father John Brady, a member of the faculty who also was a licensed physician. Eddie was told he needed months of rest and that the risks of continuing to attend classes were too great.

His body had always been frail. His work among the sick had worn him out. When the cold of the blizzard struck his frame during the long walk to his family's house, his body did not have the strength to resist. When his parents came to see him again, they were shocked at his appearance. He was wracked by a cough that shook his whole body. Eddie was told he needed a complete rest and that he was lucky to be alive. Studies were out of the question for at least a year.

Eddie later returned to his parents' home for a few weeks, but his restlessness was so great that the doctors permitted him to come back to the seminary infirmary. There, his advisor and confidante again was Father Duffy, who had overcome a debilitating sickness himself after serving as a chaplain for army troops in Cuba. Father Duffy knew how much Eddie wanted to be a priest. Every afternoon, he visited Eddie and every afternoon there was serious talk about his health.

Over three months, under the careful care of the seminary doctor, Eddie's condition improved. Father Duffy warned him recovery would be slow. Eddie's lungs, which since childhood had never really been strong, had taken an almost fatal beating and only complete rest and limited activity would restore his health. Eddie learned a long patience and a quiet endurance as Father Duffy watched and waited.

In mid-semester, after consultation with the doctors and the seminary rector, it was decided that Eddie could continue his studies privately for two hours a day, with Father Duffy as his teacher and mentor. For the next two months, he was able to keep up with the other students in his class, and in early May,[205] he was permitted to return to class. "Just don't overdo it," was the stern warning.

But gradually, in his eagerness to pass his critical first-year exam, he lengthened his hours of study, sometimes hitting the books until late in the night. Soon, his wracking cough returned, and as his examination approached, the spasms grew worse. Bedridden and exhausted, he took his end-of-the-year exam, barely able to speak above a whisper. But the effort was too much for his weak lungs, and when the doctors examined him, they told him he would have to leave the seminary for at least a year. Father Duffy agreed.[206]

It was a crushing blow to Eddie and he did not know what step to take next. The family was now together, mother and father and all of the children, except Mary Jane and Kate, who had remained in Ireland, and Father Pat, who was in Omaha. The doctors had recommended a healthier climate, where the air was purer and there was plenty of sunshine. Father Pat wrote from Omaha that Eddie should come west, where he could recover his health and then make plans for himself. It was with a heavy heart that Eddie returned to his family's home, wondering what the immediate future held for him.

Reluctantly, a family council was held at the Flanagan home. It was decided that Eddie would go west, to Omaha, where his brother Pat was a priest of the diocese. Nellie preceded him there[207] to act as Father Pat's housekeeper, as she had for many of her Larkin relatives. Now she could nurse her younger brother back to health.

It was presumed that Eddie would be back at Dunwoodie after a year of complete rest.

Omaha

Omaha had been established in 1854 when the Kansas-Nebraska Act opened what had been the Indian territories to settlement. Speculators from Council Bluffs, on the eastern side of the Missouri River, crossed over in ferryboats and platted a new city on the western bank of the river. The city quickly became the gateway to the West, the headquarters of the Union Pacific Railroad,[208] and a resting place for those traveling to California and other points west. By 1907, the city was a fast-growing metropolis of 120,000, of which 25,000 were immigrants. The city was a hub of growing businesses, educational centers, and economic empires, the most notable of which was the Union Stockyards that challenged like centers in Kansas City to the south and Chicago to the east.

Omaha was a booming railroad city, the railroad bringing in workers, speculators, and immigrants by the thousands. In the Diocese of Omaha, ethnic churches were already being founded to accommodate growing numbers of Irish, Italian, Polish, German, Czech, and Croatian families that were beginning a new life on the plains. Some of these churches were in the city itself, but others were scattered across the small towns that were springing up in northeastern Nebraska.

Omaha was also an open city, the throbbing heart of several smaller towns growing up in its orbit. The most notable of these was South Omaha, where a steady flow of immigrants was beginning to settle in with all the problems of a diverse and expanding population. It was an open city in the sense that crime, sleazy business practices, and moral depravity were endemic to the city. Omaha was ruled by a political boss named Tom Dennison,[208] with an undercurrent of economic and political corruption that young Father Flanagan would have to face when he chose to become a priest of the streets after the drought of 1913.

Omaha also was the site of Creighton University, a Jesuit university in the center of the city, and of St. Joseph's Hospital, whose devotion to the poor of the city was legendary.[209] When Eddie arrived, the new St. Cecilia's Cathedral was under construction on the west edge of the city and Omaha was fast becoming a city of Catholic Churches.[210]

Eddie was met at the Omaha Union Station by his brother Pat and his sister Nellie. Two years before, Pat had begun a four-year appointment as Director of St. James Orphanage in Omaha and Nellie had come west to act as his housekeeper. Eddie would stay with his brother until his health improved and he could return to the seminary. There were long talks with his brother and sister about his seminary studies and Pat decided to take in hand his brother's seminary training.

Soon after his arrival, Pat brought his brother to meet the Bishop of Omaha, Richard Scannell, who, like Pat, had studied for the priesthood at All Hallows College in Dublin.[211] After several conversations with the bishop, it was decided that Eddie would be released from the Archdiocese of New York and become a seminarian for the Diocese of Omaha. When the release arrived from the Archdiocese of New York, it included a copy of Eddie's scholastic record. This frail young man was an outstanding student, and as the summer wore on and Eddie's health improved, the Bishop made a monumental decision. Eddie would go to Rome to study.[212]

When the news was received by the Flanagan family in New York, it was decided, perhaps at the suggestion of Father Pat, that the whole family would transplant to Omaha. The first to head west were Teresa and Michael, who were still in school. Teresa enrolled as a boarder in Mount St. Mary's Academy in

Omaha and Michael was sent to St. Mary's Academy in O'Neill, Nebraska. St. Patrick's Church in O'Neill had been Father Pat's first parish assignment and had a boarding school as well as a day school.

A few weeks later, on July 4, 1907, John and Nora Flanagan, James, Susan and Delia, and Nora Norton arrived in Omaha, making their home at 1504 South 29th Street in a magnificent frame house that would hold the whole family.[213] Once the family was settled, James found work as a steamfitter, Susan found work as a nurse, and Delia found work as a clerk for Hayden Brothers. Once again, the family was together.

In spite of his health problems during his year at Dunwoodie, Eddie's scholastic record was remarkable. When Bishop Scannell, no mean scholar himself, received the record from the Archdiocese of New York, he knew he had a gem on his hands. Since he and Father Pat Flanagan were both graduates of All Hallows College, they had much to talk about in their casual meetings. Father Pat had always looked after his younger brother. He had accompanied Eddie to school when Eddie entered Drimatemple at the age of five and had helped him to academically skip three years of primary school. When Pat was home from Summerhill College, the tutoring continued. After Eddie entered Summerhill, their summers, six in all, were spent together while Pat was at All Hallows. When Eddie arrived in New York, it was Pat who came east to advise his brother about canonical procedures for becoming a seminarian for the Archdiocese of New York. It was also Pat who encouraged relatives to give moral support to their young cousin in his journey to the priesthood.

As the summer wore on, with his family around him, Eddie prepared to make the long journey to Italy. When he began his trip to Rome, classes had already begun at the Gregorian University where he would be studying so there was no room for him at the North American College where American seminarians resided, the famous House on Humility Street.[214] Arrangements were made for him to reside in Capranica[215] College, the national seminary for Italian students.

This was to be the longest trip Eddie Flanagan had made. And rather than crossing an ocean to a colony of relatives who would greet him with open arms, he was entering a new and different culture, surrounded by people speaking a totally different language, with classes exclusively in Latin taught by professors who spoke no English. It would be an introduction to a larger world and an immersion in the history of Catholicism, a privilege granted to few students for the priesthood.

In August of 1907, less than three months after arriving in Omaha, after a complete rest and the joy of being united with his family, Eddie sailed for Italy from the port of New York. He arrived in Naples and made his way to Rome and Gregorian University.

Rome and More Heartbreak

Capranica College was the residence for Italian seminarians in the Holy City, the Italian counterpart of the North American College for Americans. Its official title was "Almo Collegio Capricana," and it was one of the most important ecclesiastical institutions in Rome, with a long and illustrious history.

It was founded in 1457 by Cardinal Domenico Capricana for the poorer young men of Rome who lacked the means to provide for their ecclesiastical education. That education was spiritual, intellectual, and cultural, one of the unique efforts before the Council of Trent to provide well-educated and holy priests for the city of Rome and its environs. It had been the breeding ground of bishops and popes, two of the most illustrious of the latter being Giacomo della Chiesa, the future Pope Benedict XV, and Eugenio Pacelli, the future Pope Pius XII. It had a unique relationship with the Gregorian University, where most of its seminarians studied, and to the Academia Ecclesiastica, the diplomatic corps of the Holy See. Many of its graduates served the Church in the Roman Curia or in diplomatic posts around the world.

Soon after his arrival, Eddie struck up a friendship with Enrico Dante,[216] a future cardinal and master of ceremonies for Pope Pius XII. Special bonds were born between those who studied together in Rome and those bonds usually lasted a lifetime. In later years, on Father Flanagan's visits to Rome, there was always a meeting with his friend, who would reside in Rome for most of his life.

In spite of his sickness at Dunwoodie, Eddie had passed his first year in that seminary with flying colors. At the Gregorian, he was registered for Dogmatic Theology, Moral Theology, Church History, and Hebrew.[217] His facility in languages was notable and he was fluent in French, Italian, German, Latin, and Greek. It was at the Italian seminary of Capranica College that Eddie further developed his Italian, since he was the only American there and was forced to use the knowledge of Italian he had learned at Summerhill College.

Classes at the Gregorian began on November 4. This would be Eddie's introduction to the larger world of the Catholic Church. The bond of unity was the Latin of the lectures and the one faith that bound the students together.

A student's day at Collegio Capranica began with early Mass, with breakfast afterwards. Classes at the Gregorian began at eight and continued through the morning and afternoon, with time out for lunch and a short siesta, when everything in the city seemed to stop dead. Class assignments were heavy and much time was spent in the library consulting texts from original sources or current textbooks. At Capranica College, where he lived, Eddie often studied until after midnight, still bent over his books.

Eddie's classmates were from every major country in the world and from some that were merely names on a map. They were of every race, color, and national background. Eddie may have learned here that people of different nationalities, races, and languages could work and study together for a common purpose.

Eddie's first month was spent just getting used to his new surroundings, getting to know his fellow-students from the United States, becoming accustomed to classes in Latin, and writing letters home. Also, the Gregorian University was not far from St. Ignatius Church, where the bodies of the young Jesuit saints, St. Aloysius Gonzaga, St. John Berchmans, and St. Stanilsaus Kostka, were buried. Eddie's devotion to young saints had always been very strong, and later, when Dowd Memorial Chapel was built at Boys Town, he would enshrine their memory in the stained-glass windows that graced the chapel.

In November, soon after classes began, the Roman winter set in with its biting cold, penetrating dampness, and freezing rains. Eddie's rooms at Capranica were cold and unheated, and soon the winter dampness started to creep into his bones.[218] The classrooms at the Gregorian were also cold, and before the month was out, his cough returned and he began to experience other ailments. On free days, he walked with other seminarians to the churches of Rome, to St. Peter's for special ceremonies, and to historic sites like the Roman Forum and the Coliseum.[219] Soon the swelling in his ankle started to bother him, and his cough wracked him as he tried to sleep or listen to lectures. He lost weight and soon was too sick to attend classes.

He avoided the doctors, for he knew too well what their decision would be. But after Christmas in the Holy City, he collapsed and the verdict of the doctors was unanimous: "You have to leave Rome. You'll be dead if you don't."[220]

Farewells were painful and the thought that he might not be able to continue his studies anywhere cast a dark shadow over his whole future. What would his family think and what would the bishop think? With his future uncertain and his life seemingly in shambles, Eddie collected a few books together, and with a few souvenirs from Rome for his family, prepared to leave the city. But he would not travel alone.

On January 28, 1908, Eddie left Rome for Naples. A day later he boarded the *S.S. Cedric*[221] for New York in the company of a chef from the Collegio Capricana, Attiliano Di Giovenale,[222] whom he had befriended during his stay there. The chef was enroute to Cincinnati, Ohio, and Eddie agreed to accompany him on the trip. The trip lasted almost two weeks, and on February 10, Eddie arrived in New York and stayed in the parish of a Father Kelly in Brooklyn before taking the train for Omaha.[223]

In Omaha, he joined his family on 1504 South 29th Street[224], their home life now an American version of the home in Leabeg. The family had settled into life in the city, and the older children – Susan, James, and Delia – had found work, James as a steamfitter, Susan as a nurse, and Delia as a clerk at Hayden Brothers. Soon after his arrival, the family moved to a larger home at 2776 California Street.[225]

In Eddie's long talks with John and Nora Flanagan and Father Pat, it was decided that Eddie would forget about the priesthood for the time being. It was important that he recover his health if his studies were to continue. He began to eat regular meals and slept late each day. He put down his books and went for long walks. He lounged in the sun, and on bad days he spent hours talking to his mother, who was glad to have him close after so many years away.

Eddie was puzzled by his setbacks to becoming a priest, but he would not accept defeat, even when others hinted that his efforts were useless. It is probable that he consulted Father Duffy in his agony, for Father Duffy too had faced a death-defying sickness as a young priest.

From the age of fifteen, Eddie was a student, and a singularly exceptional one. But he had scarcely taken his first steps of formal training when he had to face the prospect of crushing defeat, something neither his mind nor his idealism were quite prepared for. He found himself superbly equipped for his chosen vocation and fired with strong ideals, but again and again, three times in three years, his health broke and he had to accept almost complete failure. That the suffering and anguish of those years tempered in him that gentle toughness inherited from family life there can be no doubt. It also concentrated him on that inner world of thought and feeling that is the heart of priesthood, a lonely eminence and spiritual solitude that stayed with him until the day he died.

That experience made him independent and decisive, and gave a cutting edge to his mind and manner that set him apart even in the Flanagan clan. This intense concentration of mind and energy upon his own inner world gave him just a touch of the contemplative. He acquired a strength and a stability of spirit that helped him face even more severe defeats later in life. His final defeat in Rome came when the freezing cold and penetrating dampness of the Eternal City struck his body and withered his spirit at a time and place that made the whole experience cruel, meaningless, and spiritually incongruous, turning him in on himself, giving him an inner strength born of sheer desperation. He clung to his hope for the priesthood and he refused to be beaten down or turned back. He learned discipline and a ponderous patience.

Now he was told to rest, to take it easy, to take long walks, and to build up his strength by wholesome meals and plenty of sleep. Not far from his home on California Street was St. John's Church,[226] the parish church attached to Creighton University, just down the street. With missal in hand, he went to daily Mass, walking the short distance to the church and spending hours in prayer.

In the spring, the family doctor, A.W. Riley,[227] examined Eddie and shook his head approvingly. The rest, the regular hours, and fresh air had performed wonders. The doctor advised him to get himself a job, something not too strenuous, but something to occupy his time. Father Pat agreed and warned him to forget about the priesthood until he fully recovered his health and God gave the word. Eddie found a job as an accountant with the Cudahy Packing Company in Omaha,[228] and for a whole year walked to the Cudahy office at 13th and Jones Streets. This was their distribution warehouse where the butchers and grocers of Omaha and Council Bluffs could pick up their orders of meat.

His fellow workers noticed that Eddie carried his missal with him to work and it was clear that he attended Mass before coming to work. They joked that Eddie always had to say his prayers before he could do his additions.[229] He was often asked if he still thought he could be a priest.

"This is only a detour," he told them. "We'll see where it leads."

At first, it was not clear where it would lead. But he tackled the balancing of books the same way he tackled his studies and soon found himself fascinated with the business methods of a large corporation. Cudahy was a huge financial empire,[230] expanding rapidly, dealing with millions of dollars, with financial transactions that were intricate and massive. Fascinated with a world far beyond his own interests and experience, Eddie developed new skills and a knowledge of business methods that would later make him say: "If we can do it for beef, we can do it for boys."[231]

Soon he was appointed chief accountant for the Omaha office. (In later years, he would be grateful for this business experience.) He kept at this regimen for a whole year, and in the summer of 1909, another family council was held. The doctor's reports were good and Eddie's determined patience had wrought miracles. He was strong and sturdy and eager to go back to his studies. The question was, where?

New Possibilities

In the Austrian Tyrol near Innsbruck there was a university whose reputation for scholarship was unsurpassed and where some of the finest students for the priesthood were trained. It was surrounded by mountains, the high Tyrolean Alps, and in that rugged countryside the air was clear, brisk, and healthful.

Father Pat was the first to suggest the site[232] during the family council at the Flanagan home at 2776 California Street. John, Nora, and perhaps other family members were present, but Father Pat had the final word. Like Leabeg House, the whole family lived there, except for Michael and Nora Norton, who were both away at school.[233] It was decided that Eddie indeed would go to Innsbruck, but his health would have to be carefully monitored and provisions made for a program of study that would not be a threat to his health in the future.

Bishop Scannell had been consulted, but he may have been hesitant to take on the expenses of a student whose health had failed three times and might fail again in the future. It was agreed that the family, in particular Father Pat, would be responsible for Eddie's travel and university expenses. The diocese would take over his seminary expenses when he received clerical tonsure and entered the ranks of the diocesan clergy.[234]

Eddie was ecstatic. At twenty-three, he was already a veteran of setbacks and suffering, but his determination to be a priest never wavered. Now he would be a student at one of the great universities of Europe, where scholarship was prized, surrounded by landscapes and a history that would enchant him for the rest of his life.

The first step was acceptance at the university, where German was the spoken language and where his official documents had to be sent. An initial letter requesting entrance to the university generated a return mailing of papers to be signed and a request for Eddie's scholastic record, his formal application, and an official letter from Bishop Scannell. Eddie's scholastic record indicated he had taken six semesters of philosophy and one semester of theology.[235] But Canon Law was clear; he had to complete eight semesters of theology to graduate from the university and for ordination to the priesthood. It was a tough study schedule and Father Pat was worried that it might again tax Eddie's strength and endurance. He would have to make sure his brother would not again find his studies a health hazard.

Correspondence with the university indicated that Eddie would be given some leeway in his classes. He did not have to attend classes, but would be free to study at his own initiative. He could take examinations when he felt he was ready and could live in quarters where healthy meals were provided. It was a rare and unusual privilege, but it was clear that the university prized scholarship and Eddie's scholastic record spoke for itself.

In the summer of 1909, Eddie Flanagan was twenty-three years old and his theological studies had been interrupted three times: twice during his year at Dunwoodie and a third time in Rome. His determination to continue his studies for the priesthood and his patient waiting until his health improved impressed everyone, especially his fellow workers at Cudahy. They were humored at the way he plunged into his job as an accountant and mastered the skills of what seemed to him at first an arcane craft. His application was intense and thorough. Eddie would reflect in later years that it was the accounting skills he acquired at Cudahy that helped him lay the foundation for the practical skills involved in the founding of Boys Town.

It is not surprising that Eddie enthusiastically tackled the practical tasks that came his way on his journey to the priesthood, gaining insights he would need in his future work. At the age of eighteen, at Mount St. Mary's College, curious about the plight of the poor he had discovered in the writings of Charles Dickens, he made a study of one of the founders of the English workhouses, John Micklebourgh. Micklebourgh's only claim to fame was a sermon he gave to the Corporation of Cambridge, in the parish church of St. Andrew on January 27, 1750. It was such an obscure piece of writing, printed at Cambridge in 1771, that it is surprising that young Flanagan even knew of its existence; how he found out about it and where he obtained a copy is still a mystery.

Eddie also voraciously read anything that would throw light on his future work. Something of the zeal of Father Michael O'Flanagan, one of his mentors at Summerhill College, possessed him, since that priest became deeply involved in the Irish battle for independence, even serving as vice president of Sinn Fein, the revolutionary party. There was no need for such extreme actions for the Irish in the United States, but Eddie saw a lifetime of work in the plight of the poor in the streets of New York, in the tubercular hospitals of the city, and later in the streets of Omaha as a newly ordained priest.

When Eddie arrived in New York from Omaha in 1909, as was his custom whenever he traveled east, he visited the Larkins and the Coxes in the East

Village. (One of his cousins, Mary Larkin, the daughter of his uncle, William Larkin, was a Sister of Charity, and one of Father Flanagan's first Masses as a newly ordained priest would be at the Grace Institute where she taught for many years.) His visits to his relatives over, with perhaps a visit to Father Duffy at Dunwoodie, Eddie boarded a ship for Europe.[236]

The Flanagan family in Omaha, Nebraska, circa 1908: (front row, left to right) Edward, John (father), Michael, Honora (mother), Father Patrick; (second row, left to right) Delia, Theresa, James, Nellie, and Susan.

Seminarian Edward Flanagan (middle) with his classmates in Innsbruck, Austria, 1912.

Edward Flanagan (standing, second from left) and a group of fellow seminarians put on a play at the Royal Imperial Leopold Francis University, Innsbruck, Austria, circa 1912.

4

INNSBRUCK

New Horizons

The Royal Imperial Leopold Francis University of Innsbruck is set in the Tyrolean Alps of Austria, in the city of Innsbruck at the foot of Brenner Pass, used by the ancient Romans in their conquest of Germania and Gaul. The original college from which the university grew was founded by St. Peter Canisius, the Jesuit missionary to central Europe in 1562, at the request of Emperor Ferdinand I of Austria. From its beginnings, it was under the direction of priests of the Society of Jesus. In 1669, it became a stadium universale when courses were expanded to those of a full-scale university.

The city of Innsbruck, the capitol of the Austrian state of Tyrol, is in one of the most beautiful mountain settings in the world. In the first century, the Romans conquered the Celtic inhabitants of the area, establishing the Roman province of Vindelicia, which included territories north and south of Brenner Pass. In the fourth century, they established an army post there to protect the important commercial road from Germany into Italy, a critical economic lifeline for the Roman Empire. The city is set on the Inn River, with its origin in a bridge over the river, from which the city got its name. In Roman times, the area became a retirement site for soldiers of the Roman Empire. Soldiers were forbidden to marry during their military service and found the valleys of the Austrian Tyrol an ideal place to settle and raise a family after their service ended.

Enroute to Innsbruck aboard a ship of the Holland American Line,[237] Eddie made a tour of cities along the way. It is clear from his own remarks that he enjoyed his new freedom and was determined to profit from these visits. The ship docked at the Port of Rotterdam, the largest in Europe, with hundreds of ships in the harbor from every major country in the world. The sight of the harbor itself was breathtaking and it was from here that Eddie would begin his journey across Germany to Austria. Before leaving Rotterdam by train, he visited the Zoological Gardens and, as was his custom, the churches of the city.

| 63

The railroad line across Germany to Innsbruck passes through Cologne, Frankfort, Heidelberg, and Stuttgart. Eddie stopped at Cologne and Heidelberg. In Cologne, it was the great cathedral, over 600 years in the making, that attracted him, with its Shrine to the Three Kings; in Heidelberg, it was the university, made famous in song and legend.

Arriving in Innsbruck, he made his way through the maze of streets that led to the University, with the steeple of the Jesuit Church in the distance to guide him. This would be his parish church for his three years at Innsbruck: close by was the Nikolai-Haus, the residence hall for the seminarians. Here he met the rector, Father Michael Hofman.[237] Like Father Francis Duffy at Dunwoodie, Father Hofman would have a profound influence on Eddie, who would always cherish the memory of this remarkable Jesuit.[238]

Once settled in his quarters, there was the business of assignment to classes, directions to libraries and university offices, and meetings with the registrar regarding the payment of his tuition. The records of the university indicate the name and address of his father, John Flanagan, described as a "kaufman," a laborer, living on California Street in Omaha. The records also show that Eddie's spoken language was English and that he was entering the university as a student of theology.[239]

On October 6, the day after he arrived, Eddie registered for his classes; as agreed upon earlier, he would not have to attend classes but could study privately, perhaps under the supervision of Father Hofman.[240] Father Pat, Eddie's brother back in Omaha, would have been worried by his schedule of subjects, nine in all.[241] But there was no need to worry. Out of the darkness and defeat of his black years, Eddie came to this university high in the mountains of the Tyrol, a place in later years he would consider a near paradise, with all the idealism that had been pent up in his battered spirit ready to burst into flame, and he worked with a calm and determined demeanor.

Among his classmates were Vilmos Apor, a future bishop of the Diocese of Gyor, one of the martyrs of the Ukraine, and Konrad von Preysing, a future Cardinal Archbishop of Berlin and an outspoken foe of the Nazi regime.[242] (The Canisianum, a new residence hall at Innsbruck, would become known as a seedbed and training ground for scholars and priests outstanding in holiness and heroic leadership, some of whom would become martyrs and foes of totalitarian regimes.[243])

It is difficult to assess how great an impact Innsbruck had upon young Eddie. His remarkable mind, unhampered by ill health and completely free from the regimentation prevalent in other seminaries, recovered and strengthened a vision of the priesthood that was unconventional and bold. His contemplative bent found joy in his theological studies and drew from them a sense of identity that shattered any hesitation or fears that still clung to him from his dark years of defeat.

Hours alone on mountaintops (he became an expert mountain climber and even joined an Alpine Mountain-Climbing Verein) nourished in him a deep sense of prayer, and the freedom and personal solitude of those years made him happier and more contemplative than before. He would always have a peculiar attraction for high mountains and monastic solitudes. At one time, Eddie even became convinced that his vocation was to be a Trappist monk. His contemplative gifts became tools for a rich priesthood and it was in the vastness and nourishing peace of the Tyrol that the seeds were planted for the daring projects and experiments that led to Boys Town. The qualities of leadership he consistently showed in later years (and the irritating "impracticality" that made him the despair of some of his contemporaries) were the fruit of a theological vision, ruthless and raw, acquired in the Innsbruck years.

In Edward Flanagan, the scholarship and brilliant intellect were always hidden under the humanity and compassion of the apostle. He was never known for his knowledge of theologians and schools of theology. All his learning turned to love and to deep wells of kindness and compassion. However, when the occasion demanded, Eddie could bring forth from the arsenal of his mind knowledge, facts, and forceful reasonings shot through with pragmatic sense that guided all of his work.[244] Moreover, he clothed his theology in the humane literary tradition of Dickens and Canon Sheehan, so his scholastic prowess was often hidden from even his closest friends.

The tranquility of these years never left him. The vision of Eddie's priestly work acquired at Innsbruck was the driving force of his whole genius. He always had a fondness for well-written books, especially of biography and history, which captured an idealism similar to his own. He treasured the life or words of any man whose aim was a genuine nobility of life. It was this solidly Christian naiveté, profoundly theological and prophetically pragmatic, that was sometimes not understood by men of a more practical cast of mind. His insight and intuition escaped them.

It was at Innsbruck that Eddie acquired what might be called a "theological vision" of his work as a priest, a vision drawn from the richest sources of the Catholic tradition, strengthened and buttressed by exposure to minds that were, for him, at first only names in history. There in the quiet and serenity of the Tyrolean Alps, he drew upon insights into human behavior and human nature from rich theological sources of a Patristic and Thomistic renaissance.

The Patristic renaissance was based chiefly on the seed studies of the early Church Fathers by John Henry Newman,[245] whose writings at the time had become classical, with names like Athanasius of Alexandria, Basil of Caesarea, and Gregory of Nazianzus, the most prominent. These three in particular had created on the foundation of a rich Greek classical world, a Christian culture of astonishing richness and depth, where a Christian vision of human worth and possibility inspired social and educational experiments that transformed the Roman and Byzantine world.

Far more significant, because it was closer to Eddie in time, was the revolution in theology brought about by Pope Leo XIII in his restoration of

St. Thomas Aquinas[246] as the author and propagator of a humane intellectual tradition, with insights into the roots of human behavior and motivation unparalleled in the history of human thought. The Second Part of the Summa Theologica[247] is a masterly exposition of the internal workings of the human mind: What motivates, what hinders, what develops, what colors, what enlightens, what darkens, and what determines human behavior. Then, what strengthens, what assists, what directs, what supports, and what saves human behavior from making dangerous and unhealthy choices.

Eddie's training in psychology, in the deepest and most penetrating meaning of the world, was far superior to anything available in any university of the day. "The Treatise on Man"[248] in the First Part of the *Summa Theologica* and the Second Part on human behavior have never been surpassed by any other thinker, before or since. It is clinical in its examination of human behavior in the whole range of human choices and vividly demonstrated the height of human excellence and the depths of human depravity. It was the first major study of what might be called "normative anthropology."

Eddie had been introduced to this rich theological and philosophical tradition by Father Duffy at Dunwoodie.[249] But in the quiet of Innsbruck, unhindered by bad health or outside distractions for three full years, he could plumb the depths of that tradition and make it his own. Like his patron, St. John Bosco, he would have a vast and unprecedented knowledge of the adolescent boy from his experience in the streets. From his valuable research later on the men of his Workingmen's Hotel (thousands of broken men whose childhoods had been shattered by homelessness and neglect), he would have a well-pondered and intellectual understanding of the workings of the human psyche, long before Freud, Jung, or Adler came on the scene with their theories and insights. From the heart of his own work, he would be equipped to critique them and draw from whatever valid insights they could throw upon his own work. Another key figure in his studies at Innsbruck was Father Michael Hofman,[250] rector of the seminary and a professor of Church History at the University.[251]

The Canisianum

Eddie fell in love with the Tyrol – its mountainous peaks, its heady air, its sports, its taverns. During his first two years, he was housed in an overcrowded seminary, the Nikolai-Haus. But a new residence – the Canisianum – was under construction some distance from the University. Eddie would live there for the remainder of his time at Innsbruck.[252] His brother, Father Pat, realized Eddie's immersion in study had weakened and almost destroyed his health. So he and the family provided money for excursions into the Tyrolean countryside, into the small quaint villages of the region, and into the taverns where the students gathered after classes for rousing good times.

A later account described the social scene this way: "String music in the corner, and the loud banter of students hugging the bar in a centuries-old taproom. Some men in bare-kneed, green-jacket Tyrolean costume, other garbed in seminary black; these future priests listened while the more worldly young men teased a barmaid… they raised their steins in diurnal, ritualistic toasts to Elsa; traditionally, each student with his own stein, with his name lettered in gilt, and when not in use it would hang on a peg in the wall."[253]

Thus did the young American remember his golden days at Innsbruck. He always sat in his favorite table in the corner, with other theological students. They were often deep in discussion about the issues of the day, rising for the traditional toasts and then discussing the deep worlds of Descartes, Nietzsche, or Hegel, or the latest news from Rome where the Modernist crisis was the talk of the Church.

Eddie found in Tyrol a religious atmosphere much like that in Ireland, with shrines at crossroads and in the fields. Religion was part of the daily life of the people. They crowded into the great church of Innsbruck on Sundays, feast days, and during the seasons of Advent, Christmas, Lent, and Easter. Any afternoon, he could catch the orange-painted streetcar and make a tour of the city. Sometimes the seminarians would spend hours in their black cassocks and clerical hats strolling through the streets by quaint shops and an occasional tavern, stopping into churches on the way for Vespers or an hour of prayer. In one of the churches, the Maximilian, were the tombs of Archduke Ferdinand and his commoner wife, one of the romantic legends of the region.

Although study was the order of the day, the lifestyle was frugal. Eddie's room was like the room of a monk, with straight-backed chairs, a small dresser for clothing, a bed with a straw mattress, and an oil lamp. At first, diet was a problem, for Austrian food was heavy and greasy and plentiful. Wanting to keep their American student healthy, the seminary authorities, perhaps at the urging of Father Hofman, provided Eddie with a special diet.[254]

Besides being careful about the food he ate, Eddie found it was also important for him to participate in suitable recreation. Much of his free time was spent hiking with an alpenstock, the typical Alpine walking staff, and climbing mountain roads with fellow students, surrounded by the unmelting snows of the great Alpine peaks like Sattelspitzen, Seegrubenspitzen, and Hafelekai. The students also biked, discussing the religious and philosophical questions they would face in coming examinations. Sometimes they would stop by a herdsman's hut or a shepherd's high chalet, where hospitality was the rule. Here, Eddie would regale his friends with an Irish song or ballad in his rich baritone voice.[255]

He became a member of a mountain-climbing Verein and sent home pictures of himself dressed for the Schutzenfest – green velvet pants, short leather jacket, and a pointed hat with the cocked feather and turned-down brim. He also mastered the art of yodeling and took part in student theatrical productions, including an American minstrel show where he appeared in blackface as the redoubtable Mr. Bones.[256] "I have learned to yodel," he announced in one letter, "and have even picked up a dance step or two – folk dances, that is. We seminarians sit together in the student beer taverns in our own special corner and carry on serious discussions in theology, with the singing going on all around us. And such singing! These people sing all the time and put their whole hearts into their songs."

The letters came often and the Flanagans were happy for him. Eddie was at last on the way to the priesthood.

He made many new friends, among them future bishops who in later years would remember Eddie Flanagan with great affection. One was Konrad von Preysing, from Munich. He arrived in Innsbruck a year before Eddie entered the seminary. (Many years later, when Father Edward Flanagan was on a mission for the United States government to postwar Europe, the priest who was his friend at Innsbruck was by then the Cardinal Archbishop of Berlin.)

Early in the summer of 1910, Eddie and a fellow student, Frank Abts, rented bicycles and set out for nearby Bavaria to see the production of the *Passion Play* in the village of Oberammergau. The trip would take twelve hours, over steep hills and mountainous country. When they were ten miles from the village, coasting down a steep hill, young Frank ran into a team of horses and was seriously injured when one of the animals stepped on his chest. Eddie helped him to a nearby hospice and bandaged his wound. Frank continued the journey by bus, and Eddie pedaled on alone, spending the night at Ettal Monastery, close to Oberammergau.

Eddie arrived in the village in time for the *Passion Play*, which played to a packed house. Frank also was there, having spent the night at the home of a local butcher.

The *Passion Play* at Oberammergau was the highlight of Eddie's three years at Innsbruck. Performed on an open stage by more than 700 performers, it was accompanied by music and lasted eight hours. It was the most stunning theatrical performance he had ever experienced. Afterwards, Eddie and Frank met Anton Lang, the actor who portrayed Jesus, and Eddie purchased from him a huge, hand-carved crucifix that he would treasure for the rest of his life.

The two students returned to Innsbruck by bus. It took Frank several months to recover from his accident. After graduation, he would establish a medical practice in Cincinnati, Ohio, and he and Eddie would remain close friends until Frank's death in 1940.[257]

Priesthood at Last

During his first summer at Innsbruck, Eddie became a member of the Deutscher und Oester-reichischer Verein, a mountain-climbing club. He often took a camera on their climbs, and sent home photos of him and his classmates standing on the summit of Mount Brandjoch, or of himself, nattily dressed, looking toward the summit of the mountain.[258]

The photos that accompanied his letters home also were of the churches and cathedrals in Austria, Germany, and Switzerland he had visited, attended Mass in, and prayed in. Eddie's religious devotion was high as he visited historic sites he had read about and the shrines of saints who at one time were only names in the liturgical calendar. It was an experience of faith as well as of history and it rooted in him the historical and geographical nature of his religion, and the art, architecture, and works of beauty that it had inspired.

Each year, Eddie's health would weaken under the stress of studies. Then, when vacation time came, he would build up his stamina again at the expense of his brother, Pat, who paid the bills while Eddie toured Central Europe and Switzerland, drank and bathed in famous spas, and rested in the shadow of the Alps.[259] Eddie had learned to balance his devotion to study and the care of his health. As he grew taller and stronger, Eddie's confidence in his vocation grew and he began to see some meaning in the dark days of sickness and despair.

There were sleigh and sled rides into snow-filled crevices and ravines, boat rides up the Rhine River, and excursions to nearby cities like Prague, Salzburg, Munich, and Nuremberg. There seemed to be either a mischievous glee or a solemn seriousness to Eddie's demeanor as he stood with classmates for an official photo or class picture. His classmates were from every part of Europe, ancient in their faith and their loyalties. He was part of a brotherhood and a community of comrades, all set on the high goal of priesthood, each looking to an unknown future, building bonds that would last a lifetime.

As Eddie's time at Innsbruck was coming to an end, there were letters home informing the family of the date of his return, final examinations, the celebration of "dry Masses" monitored by a senior priest, and time set aside for a private retreat and consultations with University authorities on documents to be sent to his home diocese. There were also last nights at the local tavern with fellow students, with the fun and frolic that was part of those gatherings, and final songs and farewells to celebrate the approaching end of their years of study.

One of the most touching traditions of the Canisianum was a farewell banquet held at the end of each scholastic year for the Americans who were to be ordained to the priesthood. It was planned and sponsored by the "American Exiles," the undergraduate American seminarians, as a parting tribute to their fellow countrymen. The speaker for the occasion was always an American priest who was an alumnus of the University. There were speeches, toasts, American food, music, and a touch of melancholy for those "exiles" left behind.[260]

The farewell banquet was intended to relieve some of the homesickness that is part of every student's experience in a foreign country and to bring a touch of America into the lives of these young men who were so far from home. The seminarians honored that night would soon be returning home, the oil of consecration still fresh on their fingers and a joy on their faces as they were called "Father" for the first time. It was a parting none of them would forget.

"We stand for the last time together,
Hand in hand, face to face, heart to heart.
A day may divide us forever,
We'll sing one more song ere we part.
As friends when the banquet is ending,
Stand closer to give one last cheer,
So tonight let our voices all blending,
Ring out our last song loud and clear."[261]

Edward Joseph Flanagan was ordained to the priesthood on July 26, 1912, in St. Ignatius Church in Innsbruck.[262] The ordaining prelate was the Bishop of Brixen, Franz Egger. Edward's ordination was the climax of four days of ordinations at the University; he was ordained to the Subdiaconate on July 21, to the Diaconate on July 25, and to the priesthood on July 26.[263]

In a class of one hundred, Father Flanagan was chosen to celebrate his first Mass the next day for his fellow seminarians at the Canisianum, an indication of the great respect and affection his classmates had for him. Father Hofman was at his side for this momentous occasion for the young priest.

After a last breakfast with his friend and mentor, Father Flanagan and Father Edward Myers, another newly ordained priest from the United States, took the train to Munich, where they celebrated their second Mass. Then it was onto Berlin, and then to Hamburg. In Hamburg, Father Flanagan boarded the *S.S. Cincinnati* for New York.[264]

It was a two-week crossing and he could relax at last after the excitement and mild confusion of the ordination and his final days at Innsbruck. He had said goodbye to friends and classmates from all over Europe, and had packed away gifts for members of his family, together with souvenirs of the most remarkable three years of his life: a Tyrolean hat, a stein with his name engraved on it, and the hand-carved crucifix he had purchased at Oberammergau. He also brought back dozens of photos of himself climbing dangerous Alpine peaks with his university friends.[265]

In New York he was met by his sisters, Nellie and Susan, who had come east as a welcoming committee for the family. A whole colony of relatives – aunts, uncles, and cousins – crowded into the parish church his family attended when they lived in the city, the Church of St. Ann's on East 12th Street, for his first Mass in New York. His second Mass in New York was in the parish of his uncle, William Larkin, whose daughter, Sister Mary Celestine, was a cousin and friend. Out of courtesy to her, his third Mass was at the Grace Institute where she taught. There, he celebrated Benediction of the Most Blessed Sacrament for her community.[266]

After visits with relatives in the East Village, and undoubtedly a visit with Father Francis Duffy,[267] Father Flanagan was off to Nebraska. He would later write: "I immediately left for the west, after about a week in New York, accompanied by my two sisters, arriving in Omaha where I was reunited with my parents and members of my family after a long separation of over three years."[268]

His first Mass in Omaha was in St. John's Church, the parish church of his parents, and the following Sunday he celebrated his first Solemn High Mass at Holy Angels, a new church his brother, Father Pat, had founded in the west part of town.[269]

During Father Flanagan's two weeks with his family in Omaha,[270] he had long conversations with his brother. The brothers had been close all of their lives and the bond of their priesthood drew them even closer. Pat had been at Edward's side through encouragement and advice, as well as through financial support, during his brother's journey to the priesthood, and it seemed something of miracle that the days of darkness and defeat were over and young Eddie's goal of becoming a priest had been reached. Family bonds were still very strong and family gatherings were frequent, as they had been at Leabeg.[271]

Soon after his arrival in Omaha, Father Flanagan received his first parish assignment from the Bishop's office. He would be the assistant pastor at St. Patrick's parish, serving the Irish community in O'Neill, Nebraska. The church was Father Pat's first parish assignment after his arrival in Omaha in 1904.[272]

First Assignment

"At that time I knew practically nobody in the west, as I had always lived in the east since coming to this country… neither did I know many of the priests of the Diocese, so… Father Cassidy, my future pastor, was just another name,"[273] Father Flanagan would later write.

O'Neill was located in Holt County, in the northwestern part of the diocese, about two hundred miles from Omaha. Access to the town was chiefly by train, the Chicago and Northwestern Railroad, because the roads in that part of the state were rough and unpaved.

The assignment was memorable for many reasons. O'Neill was a community of Irish settlers, many of them newly arrived from their home country, others brought to Nebraska after the Civil War through the efforts of General John O'Neill, an Irish patriot active in the Fenian Movement.[274]

O'Neill was one of the leaders of Irish immigration and the settling of Irish immigrants in the western United States. In 1873, he traveled to Lincoln, Nebraska, to explore the possibilities for a settlement in northeast Nebraska on lands offered to him by several large landowners. His chief concern was to make Irish immigrants landowners, something they had been denied in their home country. The first settlers who arrived in 1874 faced all of the difficulties of pioneer life: platting the town, assigning plots of land to arriving families, building homes and a church and school, and laying the beginnings of county and town government. So primitive were the conditions that many did not stay.[275] But a second wave of settlers in 1875 began the serious business of establishing Holt County and the town of O'Neill.[276]

One of the first efforts of the settlers was to establish a Catholic parish as the center of their religious life, since many had come to the United States to escape religious persecution in Ireland. General O'Neill had promised the settlers a priest, and from the very beginning of the settlement, the General was in correspondence with the recently appointed head of the Nebraska Vicariate, Bishop Michael O'Connor. After a canonical visitation of the O'Neill community by a priest of the Vicariate in 1877, a temporary church was started and a first pastor was appointed.[277]

General O'Neill continued his efforts to settle Irish immigrants in the west, and several other Irish communities in Nebraska were founded by his efforts: Greeley, Wisner, Spaulding, Atkinson, O'Connor, Emmet, and Ewing. But O'Neill City, as it was first called, was the hub of these settlements. The general's arrangements with the Union Pacific Railroad, with its center in Omaha, brought thousands of Irish "Gandydancers" to build the lines of the railroad west, and many of these railroad workers and their families became the first settlers of these Irish towns. At O'Neill's death in 1878, the work was carried on by the Irish Catholic Colonization Association, headed by Bishop John Ireland of St. Paul, Minnesota, and Bishop O'Connor of Omaha. By 1900, O'Neill was a thriving city with a church and a school, a resident pastor, a community of Franciscan Sisters, and a growing population.[278]

In 1912, when young Father Edward Flanagan was given his assignment to O'Neill, Monsignor Michael Cassidy, the pastor there, was one of the most revered priests in the Diocese of Omaha. According to Father Flanagan's testimony, he was "a noble, religious, saintly, and prudent pastor," who left the young priest pretty much to himself in carrying out his pastoral duties. Monsignor Cassidy must have recognized the sterling quality and vast learning of his young assistant, and, except for small talk at meals and passing in the hallways, their conversations were few. "I learned from him," Father Flanagan wrote later, "the meaning of meditation in the life of a priest."[279]

But the quiet, meditative demeanor of Monsignor Cassidy was deceptive. In 1912, he was fifty-nine years old, several years past his prime. Ordained in 1878 by Bishop O'Connor, he was one of the pioneer priests of the Vicariate of Omaha. He was stationed at Columbus, Nebraska, in 1879, working with another pioneer priest, Father John T. Ryan, in a parish that stretched from Fremont in eastern Nebraska to eastern Wyoming. That same year, he was sent to be the founding pastor of the church in Rawlins, Wyoming, with a parish that covered half the state, including what would later become Yellowstone National Park. Monsignor Cassidy was always on the road, serving Catholics scattered over frontier territories that had known only Indian tribes, sometimes following in the footsteps of the indomitable Father DeSmet, S.J., the "Blackrobe" of Indian fame. In this assignment, Father Cassidy, a man of learning and deep spirituality, showed himself to be an innovative and resourceful pioneer pastor, laying the foundations for the Diocese of Cheyenne, Wyoming, which was established in 1887, the year after his assignment to O'Neill.[280]

In O'Neill, Monsignor Cassidy replaced his cousin, Father John T. Smith, who in 1877 had become the first resident pastor of the O'Neill parish. During Father Smith's nine-year tenure, he fashioned a wild, pioneer people, scattered over the wilderness of Holt County, into a thriving Catholic community with its own church, the beginnings of a Catholic school, and a strong civic pride that made O'Neill the social and economic center of northeastern Nebraska.[281]

Father Flanagan was not Monsignor Cassidy's first assistant pastor. In 1904, when Father Patrick Flanagan arrived in Omaha from Ireland, his first assignment was as an assistant to Monsignor Cassidy. O'Neill had been a training ground for several young priests who would later show remarkable leadership in the growth of the diocese. The city of O'Neill was a long way from Omaha, but it was not just a name on a map. It was a beehive of activity for a young priest eager to begin his priestly service.

Father Flanagan's parishioners were scattered over several hundred square miles of prairie country, with small farmsteads and small colonies of settlers in remote parts of the county. There was a parish school to attend to, along with the nuns who staffed it. There also were children to be taught and the rounds of parish duties. Three outlying missions were attached to the parish; Father Flanagan could visit one by train, but the other two were far off the railroad line, one twelve miles away and the other twenty, and he had to visit them once or twice a month, in good weather or bad.

Every Sunday, Father Flanagan would rise before dawn, offer Mass at St. Patrick's, wait for a team of horses to be sent over from a local livery stable, and then drive a wagon to one of the distant missions. In the winter, there was the howling wind and blowing snow, and he often would arrive at his destination with his hands and feet numb from the cold. Sometimes, he was driven off the track by the blinding snow. After Mass during each visit, there was a hot meal to send him on his way.[282]

Life was difficult and bleak for many of the families he visited.[283] Father Flanagan appeared among them with his half-scholarly air and with a bit of the seminary detachment about him. He baptized their babies, buried their dead, and officiated at the weddings of their young folk. Some were prosperous, but many were poor. The winter's bite drove some to near hunger and others to a physical wretchedness he had never seen. For himself, Father Flanagan had a few books not worth selling and few dollars. Their sadness was his.

It was a rigid and rugged discipline, a priestly experience he considered priceless. It opened to him the vast world of the priesthood, its unique opportunities, and the power of the priestly presence.

But all was not bleak and burdensome at St. Patrick's in O'Neill. Two years before Father Flanagan's arrival, a grand church building was completed and dedicated with a large gathering of bishops and priests. The church, a magnificent structure, one of the grandest in the diocese, was the realized dream of the pastor, Monsignor Cassidy. St. Mary's Academy, staffed by Franciscan Sisters, was flourishing as the center of Catholic education in the area, and would later become a boarding school for Catholic boys and girls.[284]

There were also teaching chores, religion classes for children, the celebration of major feast days like All Saints and Christmas, the training of altar boys, visits to the sick in hospitals, and officiating at baptisms, weddings, and funerals.

But Father Flanagan's service in O'Neill was short-lived. Early in March 1913, just before the annual celebration of St. Patrick's Day, the major parish celebration of the year, he received notice from the Bishop's office that he was being transferred. His new assignment was St. Patrick's Church in Omaha; the pastor there was the remarkable Father John T. Smith, who had founded the O'Neill parish and left his mark on that community.[285]

For the Flanagan family, it meant that Father Flanagan would be close to home and that, except for Mary Jane and Kate, the whole family would be in Omaha.

Edward Flanagan in mountain-climbing attire, Innsbruck, Austria, 1909.

TOP: Seminarian Edward Flanagan (back row, left) with fellow seminarians in Innsbruck, Austria, circa 1911.

RIGHT: Seminarian Edward Flanagan (kneeling at bottom left) feeding pigeons in Venice, Italy, circa 1912.

LEFT: Portrait of the newly ordained Father Edward Flanagan, 1912.

BOTTOM: Father Flanagan with parishioners at his first parish assignment at St. Patrick's Church in O'Neill, Nebraska, 1912.

5

The Mission to the Men

Omaha

Omaha's St. Patrick's Church was one of the centers of Irish life in the city.[286] Father John T. Smith, the pastor, was one of the pioneer priests of the diocese, taming wild frontiersmen who invaded the territories and laying the foundation for a huge development of Catholic life in Nebraska and Wyoming.

Unlike his cousin, Monsignor Michael Cassidy, Father Smith was neither quiet nor meditative. At St. Patrick's in O'Neill, he had fashioned a wild, scattered colony of Irish settlers in Holt County into an active, devout, and dedicated Catholic community. At his second assignment in far-off Cheyenne, Wyoming, he prepared the way for the establishment of the Diocese of Cheyenne in 1887.[287]

When Father Flanagan arrived in Omaha in 1913, Father Smith was a sick man.[288] It was Holy Week and as the new assistant pastor, Father Flanagan's first Sunday Mass at St. Patrick's was on Easter Sunday, May 23. It would be a memorable date for both him and the city.

Around 6 o'clock in the evening, a violent tornado struck Omaha[289] with such destructive power that one-third of the city was destroyed. It came from the southwest, crossing the city diagonally, striking the most densely populated residential districts, the poorer dwellings in the lowlands, and the most beautiful homes on the hills. The path of the tornado through the city (was) from two to six blocks wide and four and a half miles long.[290]

Father Flanagan had been in Omaha less than a week.[291] Now he was thrown into human tragedies and human suffering on a scale he never could have imagined: husbands without work or a means to work; families without fathers; the sick and bedridden in hospitals; children and old people who needed to be cared for and comforted. It was a massive human tragedy and the novice priest plunged into it with a skill, compassion, and determination that foreshadowed the years ahead, when he would become a legend in the city.

His charity and meager salary were stretched to the limit, but Father Flanagan became innovative. He gathered friends and family to help him. He made friendships with civic leaders and prominent citizens, business executives, doctors, lawyers, and neighborhood societies. But this was only a beginning. It took months to reclaim the damaged neighborhoods and comprehend the loss of life. Whole blocks had been torn out of the city's structures; commercial centers and homes had to be rebuilt. It was the first time Father Flanagan had been thrown into this kind of massive tragedy, this terrible loss of life, and this monumental upheaval and dislocation of thousands of families.

The morning after the tragedy, he was out with a friend, the mortician Leo Hoffman,[292] picking up the bodies of the dead in a wagon and making arrangements for their decent burial.

The tornado left Omaha in shambles.[293] One hundred fifty-five people were killed, hundreds of people were made homeless, hundreds of others filled the hospitals, and scores of men were out of work, unable to support their families. The young priest was busy well into the summer, learning a new kind of pastoral work, quite different from his experience at O'Neill.

Omaha was an industrial city, and the tornado heightened a common problem in a city of that size. Poverty was rampant. ("I found want and neglect in proportion to the population," Father Flanagan later wrote in a memoir.[294]) Because of its location, many itinerant workers headquartered in the city each winter, waiting for the warm-weather months when they could make their living planting and harvesting crops.[295] The harvest hands remained a little longer, until the yellowing fields of Kansas called them to work.[296] Others came looking for work in the stockyards, packinghouses, and railroad terminals. There not being enough jobs for all, hundreds were turned away.

The tornado and another untimely blow from Mother Nature only worsened those conditions, turning the city into an economic wasteland.

That summer, a blistering heat wave devastated farms and wheat fields throughout the Midwest, leaving hundreds of the itinerant farm and harvest workers without jobs when they left Omaha for their seasonal work. With no money and no place to stay, they poured back into the city in droves. Many stood in hopeless little groups on street corners, often stopping by St. Patrick's Church for assistance.

St. Patrick's was a workingman's parish, with an active St. Vincent de Paul Society. As families and unemployed fathers turned to the church for assistance, Father Flanagan was there to help them.

The priest quickly became familiar with these harvest workers, walking among them and talking to them about their needs and the uncertainties of their lives. He had for support the members of the St. Vincent de Paul Society who met every week to look after the needs of the poor. This organization became his right hand in the parish's service to the poor.

The workers drifted into the city from early spring to late summer, and could be seen congregating and sleeping in alleys, tired and hungry, with desperation on their faces and no food in their stomachs. During the winter months, the need increased and the parish continued to assist them. This massive unemployment was new to Omaha, which was already stretched to its limits in the aftermath of the tornado. City officials found themselves with few resources to offer this army of homeless unemployed.

"They were not bums or hoboes, unaccustomed to working," Father Flanagan would later write. "They had been used to paying for their needs with the money they earned. I saw them at first in small groups, loafing on certain corners. I have never seen more hopeless-looking men. Each day brought more and more of them into the city… as summer waned, more and more returned to the haunts which in other years welcomed the harvesters. But this year, there was little welcome, because the harvesters had no money.[297]

"Gradually, they began calling at the rectory. They did not ask for money. From ten to fifteen were coming to our door daily. My small income could not possibly have covered their needs, had they asked for money."[298]

In the beginning, Father Flanagan would scrape together whatever food was available for them, calling upon his family and friends. He worked out an arrangement with a local grocer so the men could get coffee and food to prepare mulligans.[299] He tried to find them jobs, but there was little work to be found, and as the summer went on, his anguish became almost too much to bear. It reminded him of the tubercular patients he had visited in the New York hospitals as a seminarian, and he felt helpless in the face of such massive human need. The young priest, still with something of the seminary detachment about him, watched the growing crisis as lonely, hungry men rang the rectory doorbell day and night.

"I became more and more concerned about their fate, and began inquiring among my friends as to the best means of helping all these down-and-out men…." he wrote. "Everywhere I went I saw them, in small groups or in large groups. They were discontented and dejected. Winter was coming on and they would have no shelter.

"One day I met a friend of mine and we discussed the situation at length.

"'Father,' he told me, 'you haven't seen half of the picture. There are hundreds of these men sleeping in old coal bunks on the other side of town. They haven't any blankets, and it is getting pretty chilly these nights.'

"I couldn't believe that these men had no other shelter but coal bunks, and my friend saw my doubt.

"'If you have any time Sunday afternoon, Father, we'll walk down there and I'll show you that it is true.'

"And this friend proved to me that all he had said was not only possible but true. I saw hundreds of these itinerants milling around, trying to get settled for the night. A few were hovering over a mulligan or a cup of black coffee. Others did not have even that amount. They were trying to arrange for the night. The coal bunks gave them little shelter."[300]

Father Flanagan pondered and prayed, and read his Dickens and published works coming off the presses, works like John Spargo's, *The Bitter Cry of*

Children, and Jane Addams', *Twenty Years at Hull House*. His mind was searching for fresh ideas and innovative models that had worked for others. He decided to plunge into the deep with no money, no resources, little sympathy for his concerns, and a few members of the St. Vincent de Paul Society to help him.

"If you have any money in your treasuries at a time like this," he told them, "it's a mortal sin when so many of your fellowmen are in such dire need."[301]

The drought drove Father Flanagan into the streets. The seminary detachment left him, and as August moved into September, they saw him on Thirteenth Street and near the barges by the river. As the despair of the men deepened, his sense of helplessness became overwhelming, and he told his sister Nellie and his brother Father Pat that his anguish was almost too much to bear.

Finally, as the chill of autumn began to hit the streets, he found an old garage on a side street of the city, spread straw on the floor, and told the men, "You can sleep here."[302] It was a makeshift solution, but it took some of them out of the cold. He saw the looks on their faces each time he came among them, each one clinging to the hope he would be able to help them. "These men, although from nearly every state in the Union, were bound together with a common bond of need," Father Flanagan would later write. "One could not help one without offering to help to all. I saw this and it settled a plan that had been formulating in my mind for some time.[303]

"After I had gone home (one) night I worked out a temporary plan that would give these men at least a clean place to sleep, (and), if possible, I meant to see that they had food."[304]

His plan was to open a shelter for the men, but he had no idea how he could do it. It was just a germ of an idea, and he began searching the streets of Omaha for a place where they could stay. He could not let these men be exposed to the weather when winter set in. Nebraska winters were cold and windy, and it was already late in the fall.[305]

Father Flanagan talked it over with Father Smith and Bishop Richard Scannell, who told him to go ahead with his plans, but not to expect financial assistance from the parish or the diocese. Organized relief also was out of the question; no agency in the city was equipped for this kind of massive unemployment and homelessness.

The First Hotel

A short time later, good fortune smiled on Father Flanagan.

"On what is now the site of a postal station, there was an old tumbled-down structure which had in its better days been a hotel," he later wrote. "It had not been occupied for some time. Nevertheless, I looked upon it as the answer to my needs. To me at the time, it was a wonderful hotel. I went through every part of it and found there were twenty-five to thirty rooms which could be used, after they were renovated. The roof in places had given way and water poured in whenever it rained. Hence, there was little plaster left on the ceilings.

"These handicaps did not daunt me. I do not know just why I chose this old place, except that it was unoccupied, and hence I could get it for little or no rent. I had no money of my own, and I mean no money. The small salary paid an assistant pastor was barely enough to meet the necessities he needed. The little I had left over went to a grocer friend's bill for the orders of food for the hungry harvesters."[306]

He laughed at his own impracticality and reveled in it. The fate and suffering of the poor and disadvantaged, after his experience as a young seminarian in the tubercular wards of the city hospitals of New York, was central to his thinking, and the fate and suffering of such people was always on his mind. It burst into flame as he wandered through the old hotel and saw it as a unique solution to the suffering of the homeless men. "As I proceeded with my plans," he wrote later, "I became fired with an enthusiasm equal to that which had gripped me when I first found suffering and loneliness in a New York hospital."[307]

There was something bottled up inside of him that came to the surface and spurred him into action. In his plan to start a "hotel," a rather novel idea at the time for a shelter for the homeless,[308] the seed was being laid for a future in which he would turn the world upside-down to carry out his own unique vision of humanity.

Father Flanagan would later describe the transformation of the Burlington Hotel in almost playful terms. "I gathered around me a group of men and told them what I was doing. They were more enthusiastic than I was, and no work was too hard or any day too long for them when they were helping me to get the hotel ready for occupancy. We did all the… repairing ourselves, and among those men were some who were experts in almost every kind of work.

"We made a few improvements in the building itself. Most of our efforts were put in on cleaning it up and in making it as comfortable as possible. We realized this was only a temporary refuge, but at that it was a palace to the men who, at best, had only a coal bunk to sleep in. I had told my men that just as soon as we could see our way, we would find larger and better quarters, and this so pleased them that they immediately began planning with me for those halcyon days."[309]

As they worked alongside each other every day, Father Flanagan became friends with these men, and as they worked and talked, he learned the stories of their lives. These were hardworking men, but some had become bitter because of their inability to find work and support their families. Some struck out against the country and a government that seemed helpless to assist them in their need. But often there was gold beneath the bitterness, and once on their feet, they became co-workers with the priest in his parish and in his work for the homeless.

Salvaging the faith and family of some of these men gave the young priest deep satisfaction for the labor he had taken on in their behalf. He saw that without his help, many of them would have drifted from their religion, from their family life, and perhaps into deeper pits of despair from which they might not have recovered. He wrote of one of them: "His changed attitude toward everything gave me no end of courage and hope. One can always wonder what might have happened to him had he drifted a little longer."

When the heavy work of cleaning and remodeling the hotel was complete, he and his men turned their attention to furnishing it. "Local lumberyards gladly contributed pieces of lumber, and our men made tables and benches for our 'lobby,'" he wrote. "Their pride in these homemade pieces was wonderful. Friends helped us in donating beds and bedding and other furniture we could use."[310]

Their total expense was $150, but friends made up for the deficit, and he wrote exultingly: "We moved in… free from debt."[311]

And just in time. It was November when the hotel was ready for occupancy, and the first week, fifty-seven men moved in. With deep satisfaction, Father Flanagan remarked: "We were like a large friendly family." That was the concept. The nature of the work "demanded cooperation and… the give-and-take of family life." Labor and care of the house was organized and all the work was done by the "guests."

No one was ever turned away; they made room even for the weary stranger who wandered into the hotel in the dead of night. Every man was a one-man welcoming committee to anyone who sought shelter in the hotel. Amazingly and providentially, there were all kinds of talents among the men, so many had the training and experience needed to run the shelter.

There were more plusses to this kind of arrangement. "In the evenings, we sat around the lobby, visiting in groups," Father Flanagan would later write. "Had I been wise then, I should have been busy keeping a daily account of the stories of success and failure, of despair and hope, which were told whenever these men gathered together."

The hotel was open twenty-four hours a day. Since his duties in the parish required his presence most of the time, the young priest managed to spend evenings with the men. When he left late at night, one of the men took over as night clerk. Another guest took over in the morning for the day shift.

With the opening of the Burlington Hotel,[312] Father Flanagan's genius for organization emerged. "In order to make our hotel more than a mere shelter or stopping off place, we immediately established in one corner of the lobby, an employment bureau," he later wrote. "This gave a job to another man. He became an employment clerk. In order to have jobs available, I went out and contacted personally many of the employers of the city. All of them were generous in giving my men work. We found that the housewives of the city were also willing to cooperate with us and give our men day work that needed to be done from time to time… many calls came in every day for help."[313]

But he realized that these itinerant workers had a genuine pride in themselves and were not about to merely live off the charity of others. It was agreed that from their meager salaries, each man would pay the hotel ten cents for a bed and five cents for a meal. There was a law of honor among the men, and the men themselves enforced that law rigidly. "Only occasionally did I find a 'chiseler' who tried to horde his dollars and let the others bear his part," Father Flanagan would later recall.

What the priest had established was a remarkable community-within-a-community that went beyond the social graces of helping the indigent, but drawing upon the goodwill, talents, and sense of oneness of the larger community. This was most evident in how food was provided: "From the first day, we provided a meal every day, because housing these men without providing them in some way with a little food was only solving part of their problem. The packinghouses were willing and helpful cooperators and provided us with good meats for stews, soups, and other dishes. The local bakeries gave us day-old bread, and wholesale vegetable and fruit houses added their share of provisions."[314]

The operation was makeshift at best, but it kept hundreds of men out of the streets and gave them the experience of returning to something like a home after a day's work. But as spring arrived, the farm laborers began to leave, and in the middle of the summer, the itinerant harvesters packed their knapsacks and took to the road.

During all of this, Father Flanagan's experience with Father Smith was quite different from his experience with Monsignor Cassidy in O'Neill. Father Smith was something of a scholar and an intense conversationalist. He liked to carry on debates and discussions at mealtimes, testing the knowledge and intellectual prowess of his young assistant or any other young priest who happened to be present. Their meals were intense intellectual bouts, the older priest grilling the younger priest on arcane theological questions, or making him defend some casual remark he had made in the course of their conversations. These conversations would even take place when the bishop was present for Confirmation or some other diocesan affair, and the other young priests of the diocese delighted in these theological round tables in which the pastor of St. Patrick's was always the main attraction.

But their table conversations revealed a lot more about Father John T. Smith. He had inherited a poor and run-down parish, deeply in debt, the parish buildings, both church and school, merely frame structures. The parish was in the middle of the skid row section of the city, where incomes were low and poverty rampant. In spite of this, he had managed to pay off the debt, and in 1910, built a magnificent church, one of the finest in the city. But as his young assistant soon learned, he was a very sick man. In two years, Father Smith would be dead.

The Second Hotel

But from Father Smith and his work, Father Flanagan gained confidence and inspiration. All Father Flanagan had initially planned for was a temporary shelter. Now he knew the men would be back when winter returned and that he would need a larger place for them to stay.

Again, he went on a search of the city. This time, he found what he was looking for at the corner of Capitol Avenue and Thirteenth Street.[315] Called Livesy Flats, it was a large rooming house, four stories high, with a basement.[316]

With the help of a few hangers-on who had remained through the summer, he moved tables, benches, and other furniture to these new quarters. It was a grand improvement and would hold hundreds more men. Father Flanagan gave it the pretentious name of "The Workingmen's Hotel," for that was what he intended it to be: a new and larger shelter for the itinerant workers who came into the city after the farm and harvest work was over. He was sure the men he had housed in the Burlington Hotel would bring many more occupants with them as news of his shelter spread among other workers.

Livesy Flats took several weeks to remodel and furnish, with the help of the summer occupants, the St. Vincent de Paul Society, and the groups of business-men and housewives who had become the priest's steady helpers and patrons. There were five floors of rooms to furnish with beds and bedding, and tables and chairs, and the building needed a thorough cleaning. It was an immense undertaking, and with the opening of the hotel at the end of the summer, the city began to take notice of the young priest who was transforming the welfare system of the city. For the first time, Father Edward Flanagan was on the front pages of the local newspapers.

Friends, benefactors, and supporters of Father Flanagan and his work soon scheduled a huge benefit for the new hotel in the Municipal Auditorium. Three thousand people attended and the sponsors were able to hand Father Flanagan a check for $1,500 to support his work.[317] The influx of men into the hotel, which kept them off the streets, and, in some cases, out of the jails, impressed the city leaders, and Father Flanagan was lauded for his work. The hotel now was not just a refuge for the jobless farm and harvest workers, but a haven for homeless men of every kind. It, like the Burlington Hotel, provided food, lodging, and an employment service, which made a significant contribution to the economy of the city.

In November 1914, when the farm workers and harvesters returned to Omaha, they had money in their pockets. The number of "guests" who filled the hotel caught the attention of the local newspapers, who sent feature writers to cover the story. The reporters interviewed some of the men and the hotel was recognized as an important addition to the city's welfare system. The newspaper coverage also brought a new wave of homeless men to the hotel, and there were times when Father Flanagan sheltered a thousand men in one night.

But running the new hotel demanded an even tighter organization than that at the old Burlington. It was larger, provided rooms and meals for hundreds of men, and needed someone to regularly occupy the employment desk, since many of the itinerant workers needed jobs during the winter. Help also was needed to collect food for the meals and man the kitchen. There were other services that had to be provided. Some men were sick and in need of medical care. Expenses grew with the increased occupancy and local doctors and hospitals were called upon to take care of urgent cases. Small groups of local women contributed to the needs of the men. And Father Flanagan's friends and family continued their support.

But Father Flanagan soon found that the new hotel was attracting another kind of occupant. These were the bums and hoboes who did not work and did not want to work, the down-and-outers, the drunks, and the drug addicts. With their arrival, serious problems started to arise.

"In that first year at the old hotel, we had little need for discipline, except the ordinary rules of routine," he later wrote. "But when we took in a class of man who never works and never intends to, our problems became more complex.

"We set up as quickly as possible a set of rules and regulations in which my old 'guests' helped with suggestions and warnings. If we were to house a thousand men who just walked in off the road, we would necessarily have to have some form of government."[318]

Many of the older residents were shocked by the new occupants, and even warned Father Flanagan that they might be a danger for him.

"You had better reserve one floor or part of a floor, Father, for the drunks and dopes," one of his harvesters wisely suggested. "There'll be a lot of them along as soon as the weather gets colder." The harvester was right. Winter sent these men scurrying for shelter.

"We equipped the basement for them, and some of the men nicknamed it the Lower Regions, and it carried that title as long as we had the Workingmen's Hotel," Father Flanagan would later write. "Wasted fragments of men drifted into the Lower Regions every night: former professional men, businessmen, workers whom life had left disillusioned… they sought escape in drink and dope."[319]

As the harvesters had warned the priest, the men in the Lower Regions were a constant source of violence and danger. "Their characters were depraved and they were indolent and cared little for what became of them," Father Flanagan remembered. "Many were experienced in crime and had done time in jails and penitentiaries."[320]

But even in light of these challenges, Father Flanagan again showed his remarkable gift for organization and compassion. Nothing was done to make the men in the Lower Regions feel that they were only being tolerated. Just like the other guests, they had the run of the services provided and their quarters were kept spotless by a well-organized corps of moppers, dusters, and sweepers. The priest understood that the environment in which these men lived contributed mightily to their morale, and, in his own words, "cleanliness helps build hope and confidence in hearts filled with despair, or broken with sorrow and disillusionment."[321]

In February 1915, Father John Smith died and was replaced by Father Peter Gannon,[322] in whom Father Flanagan found a remarkable friend and mentor. Father Gannon was the founding editor of the diocesan newspaper, *The True Voice*, and was a friend of bishops and archbishops who often visited Omaha just to visit with him. As editor of *The True Voice*, he became an active participant in the affairs of the Catholic Church in the United States and, often, was an outspoken critic of these affairs. He was learned and well-informed and generous, and young Father Flanagan, scarcely two years out of the seminary, found him a joy to work with. Their conversations were perhaps less intense than the young priest's conversations with Father Smith. But both pastor and assistant were bright of mind and deeply dedicated to the work of the priesthood, and Father Flanagan thrived on his association with this remarkable priest and editor.

Some evenings, before he left for his parish, Father Flanagan would man the hotel's night desk until someone came to relieve him. From there he could welcome the strangers who came through the door, some of them entering timidly, as if they were afraid of the greeting they would get, and others brash and bold, desperately trying to hide their embarrassment at their down-and-out condition. The night clerks had been trained never to embarrass the incoming guests, regardless of their appearance or how shabby their clothes were.

One evening, a young man of about thirty came through the door; the air about him indicated he was not a drifter or a bum off the streets. He had a certain dignity, and although his coat was shabby and worn, it was clear it was an expensive coat that had seen better days. His head was tucked down into his coat, and he walked back and forth at the edge of the room, as if he were not sure that he was really welcome.[323]

"I went over to him and welcomed him to our hotel and offered him what we had of food and drink," Father Flanagan later wrote. "He shook my hand warmly and thanked me. There was something about his bearing which distinguished him from the average drifter."[324]

The next morning, Father Flanagan offered the man the job of night clerk and he willingly accepted. He quickly showed he was able to handle the daily and nightly guests who came through the door and could recognize who should be housed in the Lower Regions and who was to be given a room elsewhere. Often in the evening, he and Father Flanagan would talk. Finally, one evening, when they were alone in the lobby, the man opened up.

"I suppose, Father, you think it's funny I've never told you who I am or where I came from," the man said.

Father Flanagan assured him it was not, and also explained that he never embarrassed the men by inquiring about their lives.

"Well, I am going to tell you," the man continued. "I happen to have a title in Hungary as a count. My father and mother both come from titled families. After I graduated from the university, my father gave me a trip to America 'to round out my education,' he said. I guess he was right. This trip has rounded out my education.

"You know, Father, my country is entangled in this mess in Europe, and my father is right in the middle of the whole business. At first I was able to get word through to him, and I got a few letters back from him. But now that's all over. We haven't been able to get word to each other for several months.

"My money ran out, and I had no one to go to. So I had to take to the road. I heard about your hotel a couple of weeks ago, and I headed for Omaha."

"You're welcome to stay here as long as you like," Father Flanagan told him.

Hungary was in the middle of the First World War and the dissolution of the Austro-Hungarian Empire. That Empire had dominated the politics of Europe since the time of Bismarck. Noble families lost their titles and their status and many were reduced to poverty in the new Europe that was emerging. Father Flanagan was quite familiar with the young man's situation, since he had been in touch with former classmates and professors from Innsbruck, which was at the center of the political upheaval that was going on.

The "Count," as Father Flanagan called the man, was a welcome guest of the hotel, and he proved himself to be a valuable asset, in particular by his protective concern for Father Flanagan.

A few days after the Count's arrival, a huge man named Pete came to the hotel. He was tall and full-muscled, with hands like hams. When sober, he was gentle as a puppy and followed Father Flanagan around, eager to help in any way. He eventually became the handyman of the hotel, and his great strength was appreciated when there was heavy work to be done.

One night, however, he returned to the hotel with a flushed face and bleary eyes, dead drunk and offering to take on anyone in the place in a fight. The other men knew his strength and backed away. The Count was at the desk, watching the scene unfold. When Pete approached Father Flanagan, the priest held his ground and stepped forward to direct him to the Lower Regions. Pete picked up Father Flanagan as he would a sack of grain, lifted him high in the air, carried him outside, and threw him over a fence.

The men in the room rushed forward, subdued the drunken man and pummeled him to the ground. The next morning, Peter was embarrassed and contrite as he apologized for his behavior.

The incident made the Count realize the danger Father Flanagan faced as he walked freely among the men at all hours, sometimes even going to the Lower Regions. Some were psychopathological cases, men who resented Father Flanagan and held him responsible for their troubles. The hatred of these bitter, sick-minded men often ran deep.

The Count often warned Father Flanagan about this danger, but the priest took little notice.

One night when the Count was on duty and Father Flanagan was getting ready to leave, the telephone rang. It was a call from someone who was sick and wanted to see the priest. As he took down the address, the Count told Father Flanagan, "That's a rough part of town. I'd better go with you."

"That's not necessary," Father Flanagan said. "No one would harm a penniless priest on a sick call." But the Count insisted, and Pete said he would go along, too.

The call led the three to a hotel, which was actually an old dilapidated rooming house in a run-down part of the city. The three men entered the dingy lobby, the Count and Pete close to the priest as they approached the clerk on duty.

"One look at the clerk should have told me that something was wrong, but bent on my duty, I took no heed," Father Flanagan said later.

Father Flanagan asked for the room of the person who had called, giving the clerk the name. The clerk gave him a room number and told him, "If you go up there, you go up alone."

"I began to explain to him that priests always make their sick calls alone, but that my friends had accompanied me out of courtesy," Father Flanagan said. With a bound, the Count was up the stairs, the desk man shouting after him that the priest had to go up alone. As the priest followed the Count and reached the top of the stairs, the Count rushed back to him and took his arm. "Get out of here, Father," he said. "It's a trap. The people in that room are trying to frame you. This is not a hotel, it is a dive. We have to get out of here right now."

Father Flanagan later recalled: "I began to protest, still feeling that he did not understand that a priest must answer a sick call, regardless of the danger. In no uncertain way, he took my arm and we hurried down the stairs and out of the building."

"It just didn't look right to me," the Count told the priest. "They knew you'd answer a sick call, that was part of their plan. God knows why they'd pick on you."[325]

Then one evening in 1917, when Father Flanagan arrived at the Workingmen's Hotel, the Count was gone. The United States had entered the war raging in Europe, and the Count's homeland had been defeated. It may have been his concern for his parents and family that moved him to leave. Also, he was an enemy alien since Austria-Hungary was part of the Dual Alliance and had sided with Germany in the war. Father Flanagan never heard from him again. "He was my oasis in the midst of a desert of forgotten men," he would later write.[326]

The men in the Lower Regions were dangerous and there were strict rules about their coming and going, rules that Father Flanagan and the other night clerks strictly enforced. There also were strict rules on alcohol. No alcohol could be taken to the Lower Regions and a man who was drunk had to sit in the lobby until he was sober. The men in the upper rooms were there to help Father Flanagan or the night clerk handle any drunk who came in late at night.

Many of the drunks were con artists of the first order, and could be persuasive with a glib tongue and impeccable manners. One evening, Father Flanagan was off his guard, and a man talked the priest into letting him leave after the ten o'clock curfew. After he left, Father Flanagan was sure he would return drunk, weaving through the door. But the man returned stone sober. Suspecting there was a bottle somewhere on the man, the priest searched him, pocket by pocket, like the expert "frisker" he had become. The man stood beaming in front of him, ready to return to the Lower Regions, when Father Flanagan reached up and knocked the hat off his head. A bottle of White Mule tumbled to the floor.[327]

With the United States' declaration of war against Germany in April 1917, the Workingmen's Hotel was almost emptied, as many of the homeless and jobless men took advantage of the call to arms and a regular paycheck. But the rooms were soon filled again as news of the hotel spread throughout the Midwest and over the underground communication lines of hobo jungles. The news promised a paradise in the middle of Omaha, where you were housed and fed, given a clean bed to sleep in, and even provided medical treatment if you needed it. The place was run by a kindly priest who never asked questions and treated you like company.

Many of the new arrivals, the priest soon learned, were former executives of corporations, doctors, lawyers, businessmen of every description, and some fathers and husbands who had broken their family ties, and for various reasons, had taken to the road. Some who had commanded others in their business or profession became the priest's close associates in the work of running the hotel, keeping it solvent and directing others in its upkeep. Some stayed a few days and others stayed longer. It was often the norm to house 500 men in one night.

Father Flanagan was fully aware of the new kind of occupant that now occupied his hotel. Most of them were over thirty and had spent many years just drifting. They willingly took part in the work required to keep the hotel running smoothly, from making beds and sweeping floors to washing windows and acting as the desk clerk. Father Flanagan would later describe the average occupant of the hotel:

"I saw a bit of almost every nation in the world wander into that hotel. They mingled in our humble lobby, which offered a friendly welcome to those who were barred from other hotels. Proud men and humble men, the weary and the broken and (some) bitter remnants of (humanity)."[328]

Father Flanagan sat with them in the evening and listened to their stories, which were as varied as the men and as colorful as their backgrounds. This introduction to a rare kind of underground culture, hidden from the eyes of most Americans, was an eye-opener for the young priest. It was a culture of lost men, and as he began to take notes and compare stories, he discovered that one theme ran through all of them: Their problems had started in their boyhood.

"I listened to old men in rags tell me… how and why they had failed. I heard middle-aged men recount the first missteps they had made. Later, I compiled these notes… I had records of over one thousand men… their life stories. At nights, I would go home and read these, milling over them and worrying about them."[329]

Something of the scientist awoke in him as he compared stories and digested the facts he had recorded. Each tale led to a dead end, and the stories of Dickens he had read as a boy came rushing back to him. The description of Coketown in *Hard Times* sounded astonishingly like the description of many of these men's boyhood homes: poverty, neglect, physical abuse, childhood anger at their living conditions, and the urge to get away, to get away from everything. None of them had come from a loving and caring family; all were victims of parental neglect or broken homes, or homes where a parent had died or deserted the family. The story was always the same.

Father Flanagan paged through books on the subject, like *London and the London Poor* by Henry Mayhew, a study of poverty in Great Britain written in 1850, and the powerful lesson of *Oliver Twist*, in which a change of environment and the care of a loving parent had changed the whole direction of a boy's life. He saw that as a seismic change in the future of that child. Why was there no similar seismic changes in the lives of these men? It was a question that haunted him day and night.

The Burlington Hotel, the first shelter for men opened by Father Flanagan in Omaha, Nebraska, 1915.

Father Flanagan stands in the doorway of the Workingmen's Hotel (Livesy Flats) in 1916.

6

THE FIRST BATTLE FOR BOYS

Homeless Boys

One night in the summer of 1917, a boy sauntered into the Workingmen's Hotel, went to the night clerk's desk, and asked for a room for the night. The lobby was full of old men, and as the boy entered, every eye in the room was upon him. Father Flanagan noticed the sudden change in the room when the youngster entered and thought perhaps that these worn-out men saw something of their own boyhood in him. The boy had about him an air of sophistication, as if he were accustomed to this kind of life, and an adolescent toughness of manner that was almost humorous.[330]

He looked about 14, and Father Flanagan called him over. They sat down at a table to talk, away from the others in the room. When Father Flanagan asked him where he was from, the boy told the priest it was none of his business and that if he couldn't have a room in the hotel, he would go elsewhere.

"You're welcome to anything I have to give you," Father Flanagan told him. At that, the boy loosened up and began to talk, mentioning a town not far away. At first he refused to give his name, but after some coaxing, he revealed that he was Bob Harper.

"I want you to have a room by yourself, Bob," Father Flanagan told him. "You can stay here as long as you wish, and if I can help you in any way, just let me know."

As soon as the boy was in bed, Father Flanagan sent a telegram to the chief of police in the town the boy had mentioned, asking if the chief knew a Bob Harper who had run away from home. Then he left for the night for his parish.

When he arrived at the hotel next morning, the boy was gone. Apparently, he thought the priest had asked too many questions and wanted to get away before anyone was up. There was a telegram waiting for Father Flanagan from the chief of police the priest had wired. The message said the boy had run away from home and that his mother, a widow, was heartbroken that he was gone.

Thinking that the boy could not have gone very far, Father Flanagan began searching the neighborhood. He found the boy eating in a restaurant close by, in the company of a tough group of men. At first the boy tried to talk tough. But Father Flanagan told him his mother was worried about him and finally convinced him to return home. The boy returned home, but kept in touch with Father Flanagan for the rest of his life.

Another young arrival at the hotel was a twelve-year-old who came in asking for the "man in charge" and wanting a room for the night. There was no telling where he had come from; he was just a homeless boy who came in off the streets. Father Flanagan took him in, provided a warm bath and a good meal, and got him a bed for the night. With the help of a local welfare society, he was later able to find a good home for the boy.[331]

While those boys left an impression on Father Flanagan, it was a third youngster who spurred him into action.[332]

The boy had been living in an empty packing box behind an abandoned warehouse. His father had enlisted in the army and had died, not in the war, but during the influenza epidemic that struck the country. With the father gone, the mother deserted the boy, and for weeks he just wandered the streets of Omaha, each night making his way back to his packing box shelter. No friends or relatives had come forth to help him and he was purely and simply alone and homeless. To survive, he begged for food at the back door of restaurants. One day, he returned to his packing box only to find someone had carted it away. Some man on the street told him he might find a room in Father Flanagan's hotel, and he showed up later that day.

The boy was not more than eight or nine years old. Father Flanagan made sure he had a warm bath and a hearty meal. It was late in the evening and the priest had to leave for St. Philomena's Church, which he had been transferred to in July 1916. But before he left, he told the night clerk, "That boy will never be hungry again or without a place to sleep... not if I am alive to prevent it."

"Why don't you start a home for boys?" the night clerk replied. "There's hundreds of kids like that one upstairs in this city."[333]

Other boys arrived at the hotel as the summer wore on. Some were orphans whose fathers had died in the war. Some had been in reform schools or had been in minor brushes with the law. Most were from ten to fourteen years of age, somewhat toughened by their experience of fending for themselves on the streets, sometimes in the company of older men. Father Flanagan made sure the boys were housed in rooms far from the men in the Lower Regions; this gave him a chance to talk to them and learn their stories. As he listened, he found their stories to be strikingly similar to those of the older lost men who inhabited the hotel. The priest decided to look into the juvenile problems of the city.

A New Approach

Father Flanagan found there was no provision for homeless boys, boys who wandered the streets without supervision, with no place to go. Curious, he began visiting the juvenile courts, listening to cases that came up every day and getting a vivid picture of the juvenile justice system. He found that it was heartless and unconcerned about the plight of the boys, the conditions under which they lived, and the dangers they faced in their aimless existence. He found that judges were sending little boys to reform schools[334] and he watched in horror as boys were led in, in the company of an officer, pronounced guilty of some minor offense or simply of just being homeless, and then sentenced.[335] No friend or relative came forward to plead for the boys or take responsibility for them.[336]

This was different from the underground culture that existed with the old men. These were boys, without homes or parents, seeking out an existence in the streets, living on the edge of violence, with no future but the streets and alley ways and open highways for the rest of their lives. Some found shelter in hobo jungles and moved from city to city in empty railroad cars, where they often met older men who hardened them in their way of life and taught them the skills needed for survival as vagrants and vagabonds.

Sometimes, after a court hearing, Father Flanagan asked permission to talk to the boys, a permission easily granted since he had become a well-known advocate for the poor and homeless. The boys opened their hearts to him and he listened to their stories. These boys were fodder for the lost men of tomorrow. Each time he left the courts, he asked himself how he could help these boys and prevent them from becoming like the men who came to his hotel.

"I began comparing their stories with the stories the men had told me of their boyhood," he later wrote.[337]

The pattern was the same: youthful truants; their first act of petty thievery; their arrest by an officer; appearance in juvenile court; then more serious offenses and more jail time; then hardened criminals, taking to the road. His hotel was full of men who had followed the same path as these boys, but no one was there to help them in the beginning. What if someone had stepped in after their first juvenile offense? What if someone had interceded in their lives before they took to the road and began a useless existence?

And then the sudden realization: *"I've been working at the wrong end of their lives!"*[338]

It was here that Father Flanagan began to reconstruct his concept of his work in the streets. In some sense, his work had failed. But not entirely. His hotels had at first provided a home for the hardworking fathers and husbands who followed the harvest west and north each year, and most of them were with their own families. Occasionally, they did stop by the hotel just to renew their friendship with the priest or assist him in running the hotel in some way. Many would remain his friends for a lifetime, and down through the years, as he met them again, their gratitude for him and admiration for his work never waned.

But the new occupants were something quite different. His hotel had become a refuge for men off the streets: tramps, bums, and hoboes of every description, vagrants off the railroad cars and highways, drug addicts and alcoholics, all looking for a bed for the night and a free meal, only to begin again their odyssey into nowhere the next day. His hotel did not live up to its name. "It was neither a hotel nor for workingmen," he wrote later. "It was a refuge for the down-and-outer men, loafing in the city during the daytime and sleeping in the parks at night."

He saw a new work looming up before him: "I saw that this waste of lives was preventable."[339]

That was driven home to him after he visited a condemned prisoner in the Nebraska State Penitentiary. Men in prison would often ask for him, either because they had heard about him or because some had stayed in his hotel themselves before being sent to prison. (The scene is dramatized exactly in the opening scene of the movie, *Boys Town*, where Spencer Tracy, as Father Flanagan, visits a man who is condemned to die. "One understanding friend when I was twelve years old and I would not be here, Father," the prisoner says. "It's too late now."[340])

Father Flanagan began to haunt the courts, talking to judges[341] and juvenile authorities. He could not imagine anyone with an ounce of judgment sending small boys to reform schools. His heart bled just thinking of the injustice. He wished he had a home to offer those boys who were sent away to a reform school simply because they were homeless. "This caused me more than one sleepless night," he wrote. "There was simply no place for them to go."[342]

One judge told him: "You're right, Father. These boys don't need punishment. Most of them need three square meals, a clean bed, and someone interested enough in them to take care of them and give them an education. But what am I to do? They come in here after a little trouble, and where am I to send them? I can't send them home. In most cases, that would be to send them back to more trouble. Some of them don't have any home. What can I do, Father?"[343]

Suddenly, after taking the judge's words seriously and doing a little research on the matter, the priest came to one firm conclusion: "The fault is in the system."[344]

He began an intense study of the juvenile justice system. He checked on the records of boys who had been in reform schools and were free again. None of them had profited from their time in a reform school.[345] In fact, they had become hardened and bitter at how they were treated there. Not only that, they were reform school graduates, they had a prison record, and nobody would give them jobs. He began to see the reform school as a school of crime.

These are his exact words: "Many fine young boys were sent up for minor delinquencies. They were associated with older and more criminally inclined boys for a period of eighteen months. Their association was of the most intimate type. Without the aid of religious training, the boys had little incentive to improve... I do not think any effort was made or could be made to isolate the boys into... age groups, or to keep those who had developed vicious habits from the cleaner-type boy. The braggart-type of boy delights in telling the more innocent boy of the various kinds of immorality he has explored and finally brings him down to his own level. These boys are then returned to society at the expiration of their sentence, but wiser in the ways of sin and depravity."[346]

There was some flaw in a system that would label young boys as "criminals" and then introduce them to a prison system that would make adult criminals out of them for sure. Father Flanagan wanted to make an extensive study of the relationship between children and crime. In this he was a pioneer, for the subject had scarcely been touched by experts and specialists in crime and criminology. And from the very beginning, what he found differed radically from most studies on juvenile crime.[347]

Father Flanagan's true pedagogical genius is seen in this study. Because it is here, in the year the United States entered the First World War, that his findings would overturn most clinical studies on the subject. He outstripped them in the depth of his perception of the juvenile mind and the careful conclusions he came to in the realm of juvenile psychology.[348] The Flanagan mind was a unique combination of theological vision, an uncanny grasp of pragmatic possibilities, and the courage and ingenuity to explore those possibilities.[349]

He saw the progression from boyhood to manhood in the broken men of his Workingmen's Hotel and he sensed that something was lacking that might have made a difference. With a boldness unprecedented at the time (Jane Addams' Hull House was a close contender),[350] Father Flanagan created a religious, educational, and social model from a small body of empirical data that was interpreted in a markedly different way from others in the same field. He saw clearly, as his vision of Boys Town moved toward becoming a reality, the failure of almost every other model on the horizon, and he rejected most of the conclusions on the youth problem that were articulated in the professional journals of the time.

So Father Edward Flanagan had not only a vast and unprecedented experiential knowledge of the adolescent boy from his experience on the streets and from his valuable research on the men of the Workingmen's Hotel, where he sheltered thousands of broken men whose boyhoods had been shattered by homelessness and neglect, but also a well-pondered and intellectual knowledge of these boys, long before Freud, Jung, or Adler came on the scene with their theories and insights. From the heart of his own work, he was equipped to critique these youngsters and draw from them whatever valid insights they could offer.

Because Father Flanagan was open to the valid insights and demonstrable conclusions of any genuine human science, he could learn from a wide variety of experts in any professional field and was not closed to correcting some of his own conclusions, when there was ample scientific evidence to warrant it. However, he had developed a highly critical mind and he knew how to separate the true from the false, the credible from the doubtful.

Father Flanagan immersed himself in contemporary studies of the subject, his interest now sharpened by his experience in the juvenile courts. His cousin,

Thomas Maurice Mulry, had revolutionized Catholic social work in New York City, and in the country as a whole, by allying himself with Jewish, Protestant, and even civic organizations to face the growing problems of poverty and youth crime brought on by massive immigration to the Eastern seaboard. Mulry had been the prime mover in the reorganization of Catholic Charities in New York and was the head of the city's St. Vincent de Paul Society, which was the main vehicle for the charitable work of the Archdiocese of New York. It was his letter, at the time he was president of the Emigrants Industrial Savings Bank, that assured Edward Flanagan's entrance into the archdiocesan seminary in Yonkers. Before his death in 1916, Mulry's leadership served as a shining example of collaboration on a large scale to address social problems that were of a common concern to all. It was an example that Father Flanagan was fully aware of.[351]

During his walks from St. Philomena's to the Workingmen's Hotel, Father Flanagan carried with him contemporary studies of the specialists in the field of children and crime. He studied case histories of delinquent boys who had become violent criminals and made himself familiar with the new theories of criminology. He pored over the books of other pioneers in the field, collating his own findings with theirs.

Father Flanagan was particularly impressed with the scope of the work of one man and the major role he was playing in the field of juvenile justice. Judge Benjamin Lindsey of Denver, Colorado,[352] was a pioneer in the establishment of the American juvenile court system and his work exactly mirrored some of the goals Father Flanagan had set for himself: take the child out of the criminal justice system and have laws enacted that would benefit indigent families. Judge Lindsey also was a leader in the abolishment of child labor.[353] In later years, the two men would meet[354] and collaborate in passing child protection laws and other measures to benefit youth.

The scope of Father Flanagan's studies was astonishing, given the short time he worked on them. In the summer of 1917, he was ready with facts and figures, and the latest research in the field, when he decided to challenge the juvenile justice system of Omaha, Nebraska.

What Father Flanagan began to realize was that he faced something resembling a massive social collapse. It wasn't just a juvenile problem but a family problem, a parental problem, a social justice problem, a problem of employment and the economic instability of family life and the poverty in which many families had to live. He found in the work and writings of Judge Lindsey an echo of his own convictions on the root causes of juvenile crime. This passage in particular told the whole story:

"Criminals are born and criminals are bred... I found no problem of the children that was not also a problem of the parents. The young bud was blighted by the same corruption that infected the twig, killed the branch and ate the heart out of the trunk... the dependent and delinquent children who came into my court came almost wholly from the homes of dependent and delinquent parents, who were made such by the hopeless economic conditions of their lives... I could not do my duty towards the children without attacking the conditions that deformed the lives of the children."[355]

A Growing Ministry

Father Flanagan continued to be a familiar figure in Omaha's courts and soon became friends with the judges.[356] They would often invite him into their chambers after the court sessions to discuss some of the cases and were amazed at his knowledge and his insights. They discussed new ways to handle the problem of juvenile crime and some possible solutions. The priest soon became an advocate for the youngsters who were brought into the courts; he continued to talk with them and listen to their stories, and sometimes convinced the judges to go easy on the sentences of these young offenders.

The first boy who was released to him was not the typical boy in trouble. He was fourteen, from an Italian neighborhood, and was very bright. He spoke both English and Italian, and had become something of an interpreter for his parents, who spoke only their native tongue. Although they were immigrants, his family was not poor, and he was doing well in school. He was brought before the court for a long list of petty thefts. Both Father Flanagan and the judge agreed that the boy did not belong in a reform school and he was released into Father Flanagan's custody, who gave him a room in his hotel. In a short time, the teen was returned to his parents.[357]

Meanwhile, Father Flanagan was searching his mind for some way to help other boys who came before the courts and keep them out of the reform school. He thought that a parole system might be a solution. He talked this over with the juvenile judges, and they agreed to give it a try. They would parole boys to the priest and he would be responsible for their behavior, with the assurance they would not be back in court again.

Parole would give boys in trouble another chance, something Father Flanagan felt the courts had denied them. The judges were quick to see a solution to their own problems. No one really wanted to sentence a boy to a reform school, but until then there had been no other options. The first boys paroled to the priest were from good families and who were in trouble for the first time, usually a minor offense of stealing or breaking in, perhaps because they were egged on by bad companions. But as Father Flanagan left the court with this first group of boys, he had no idea what to do next.

"We had no place to meet, except in the city parks, or on a street corner," he wrote later. "But I must see the boys regularly, so we arranged to meet one evening a week. At this time, we discussed what the boys had been doing for the past week and the boys knew that I had to make a report to the judge on their conduct. It was up to them to make the report satisfactory.

"It was remarkable that these boys entered into our contract with full cooperation. They knew that I had in a sense guaranteed their good behavior, and it would embarrass me before the judge if they broke their word to me. They sensed my interest in their welfare, and knew that I was their friend and big brother."[358]

By their association with Father Flanagan, these boys were soon out of trouble, and he had the gratitude of their families for rescuing them from reform school.

This was not the case with the next group paroled to him; these were boys from one of the toughest neighborhood in Omaha. This is Father Flanagan's account of their story:

"They were used to gathering on a certain street corner after dark and engaged in telling filthy stories, and made insinuating remarks about passersby. They became so bold that they were a real nuisance. Most of their older brothers had graduated from such a gang into participation in crime. Everyone in the neighborhood was disgusted with them… good parents in that district were in constant fear of their boys being enticed into this gang. Membership in it was almost a certain passport to some penal institution.

"Finally, a number of this gang was brought into juvenile court for some offense. There was little that could be said for the boys. They had earned a bad reputation… public opinion was against them. They were known as 'bad eggs.' The judge would have little recourse except to send them to a reform school.

"I had heard of the boys and their escapades, yet I believed they were victims of their surroundings, more than really bad boys. I was in the courtroom the morning they were brought up for trial. I saw the seven of them come in. They were frightened nearly to death. That was a good sign. The boys were not hardened."[359]

After the list of the boys' offenses were read, Father Flanagan boldly asked the judge to parole the group to him.

"Father," the judge objected, "do you know what you are taking on yourself?"

"Yes, Your Honor," Father Flanagan replied. "I know the neighborhood and the temptations these boys have. I have investigated the background of most of these boys and I believe I can help them."

"You're asking for a man-sized job, Father," the judge warned.

"I know it, Judge, but I believe in these boys."

Father Flanagan later wrote gleefully in his memoirs: "And I got the seven of them!"[360]

As he left the courtroom, all eyes were upon him, with people shaking their heads in sympathy and disbelief. "Tough kids from Sheelytown![361] That priest doesn't know what he's getting into."[362]

The boys were twelve to fifteen years old. They knew they were in trouble and that they had escaped the full weight of the law for their offenses. As they came out of the courtroom, they crowded around Father Flanagan. What was going to happen next? Was this priest going to take them to his hotel where he would watch over them like a hawk? What was he going to do with them?[363]

The group left the courthouse and walked to a nearby vacant lot. There, Father Flanagan sat down with them to talk about their future plans.[364] He knew they all had homes they could return to, but some were homes where the parents let their kids run wild with no supervision. If they merely returned home, they would simply drift back into the first gang that welcomed them, he thought.

The priest did not mention what had happened in the courtroom or why they were there. He just told them they would meet at this vacant lot three evenings a week. They would make up games to play, go on hikes, and just have a good time together. He later wrote:

"Here was a gang with all the potentialities of good. They were just as eager to enter into wholesome activities as they had been to follow the bad. As subtly as I could, I explained to the boys what this chance meant to them, and how all of us had to cooperate. We talked of baseball; we discussed their schoolwork and they told me what they liked best. Each one was enthusiastic about sports, and like most boys, preferred baseball in the summer and football in the fall.[365]

"Quickly we laid out a ball diamond, since it was summertime. It was no time until we had attracted other boys who wanted to get in the ball teams. We were all set. The corner gang was all over. We were ball players now. I managed to get my boys together for a little talk, before or after the games, and I saw that each one was doing his part not to break faith with me."[366]

Much to his surprise, he found that he had become something of a mother hen, baseball coach, and truant officer. The vacant lot soon became a baseball diamond, and he found himself excited about the direction these young lives were taking. "I was never so interested in anything in my life. I had thought that my hotel was about the most wonderful experiment anyone ever made, but these boys proved I was wrong. Here I was working on new clay. They had their lives before them."[367]

It was his first real experience of education, education in the deepest sense: drawing out from the young their interests, their talents, their dreams, all the good that was inside of them, and their hopes for the future. It was shaping the clay before it had become hardened, molding the character before it was twisted out of shape.

From that moment, Father Edward Joseph Flanagan knew what his life's work would be: **It would be molding these young lives into a manhood that would not be wasted.** He saw in the faces of each of these boys the faces of the men for whom it was too late. But it would not be too late for these boys. There was an intense excitement about what he was learning and what he was doing. He was priest, friend, teacher, Father Confessor, and the leader of a "gang." He deliberately gave the group that name. But it was a gang intent on good and he found that these seven boys were proud to be part of it.[368]

Father Flanagan would soon find that he was overloaded with responsibilities. He was still the assistant pastor at St. Philomena's with Father James Stenson and was still responsible for running his hotel. He had men who could fill in for him during the day, but at night he had to be there himself. So he developed a new plan for his boys. He hired a "coach" for them, a young man in the neighborhood who was good at sports and enjoyed working with boys. This coach filled in for

Father Flanagan when he could not meet with the boys. The young man organized them, first into teams and then into an athletic club. More boys joined the teams, keeping them off the streets as well. It was a happy solution to at least a small part of the juvenile problem in the city and the city began to take notice.

The boys were encouraged to go to their church regularly, and from the beginning of Father Flanagan's work, there was no distinction of creed, race, or color, a hallmark that remained. In fact, "no distinction of race, color, or creed" was the masthead on his correspondence, much to the anger and distress of many people in Omaha.

With help of his coach, Father Flanagan's athletic club met three times a week. When fall came, football replaced baseball. When winter came, he got permission to use an old abandoned building and moved the group inside for indoor sports. The results were outstanding: None of the original seven ever returned to the juvenile courts.

In his memoirs, Father Flanagan would write down this conclusion and his conviction, which was radically different from that of many of the studies of juvenile crime he had read: "My brief experience with these boys proved to me that no boy is so bad he cannot be helped. While there are many boys who are left to drift until bad habits are deeply rooted, there is always some way to reach the good that is in them, if the proper approach is made. My assistant and I succeeded also in getting the boys to whatever church they belonged. The religious and moral influences were the greatest bulwark they had. Outside their dreary homes they found a star to which they could aspire."[369]

Soon, the judges were gladly handing over individual boys to the priest, as well as groups of boys from time to time. He found that once he had a boy's confidence, the boy would do anything to not disappoint his new friend. This appeal to a boy's personal honor gave him an interest in his own welfare and in his own future.

From his wide reading on juvenile crime,[370] Father Flanagan found that the experts in the field[371] were able to sound the depths of the evil in an adolescent boy. But none, except for himself and Judge Lindsey, were tapping the depths of goodness in these young offenders. He found that the instinct for good in these boys was far greater than the instinct for evil, but tapping into that positive instinct required more than his casual meetings with them. "Many of them were weak-willed, and their environment was their constant temptation," he later wrote. "They were easily led by others, and occasional meetings would not solve the problems of many of them, and keep them out of further trouble."[372]

A complete change of environment was needed, an environment he would have to create. More and more youngsters were paroled to his care. In spite of parish duties including Mass, confession, pastoral duties, and all the activities of societies and sodalities of the Church, he never refused a request from the bench. What troubled him most was that it was all so haphazard as there was no structured or systematic way of caring for them. The park bench remained the meeting place. The time had come to venture into the deep.[373]

Laying the Foundation

To carry out his new plan, Father Flanagan talked about his ideas with his friend and pastor, Father Stenson, knowing it would require his leaving parish work for good and devoting himself to the boys full time. He then asked for an appointment with the new bishop of Omaha, Jeremiah Harty, who had arrived in Omaha in December 1916 after the death of Bishop Scannell. In Bishop Richard Scannell, Father Flanagan had lost a great supporter of his work with homeless men, with his Workingmen's Hotel serving as a shining example of the diocese's concern for the poor and helpless.

Jeremiah Harty possessed the title of Archbishop, a title he gained from a ten-year assignment as Archbishop of Manila in the Philippines.[374] There, he established schools and churches, founded orphanages, built a new seminary, brought in the Good Shepherd Sisters to staff a refuge for the poor,[375] and fought the government of President Theodore Roosevelt over its administration of the islands. He had been the bishop of Omaha for over a year and was well aware of this dynamic young priest who had turned the city upside-down in his work with homeless men.[376]

When Father Flanagan revealed his plan to found a home for homeless boys, Bishop Harty willingly gave his permission,[377] congratulating him for turning his attention from homeless men to the more serious problem of homeless boys. But he reminded the priest that he would have to find his own resources to finance the work; the diocese was already supporting an orphanage and its finances were stretched to the limit. At Father Flanagan's request, the bishop freed the priest from his parish work so he could devote his time to this new venture,[378] with the understanding that the Workingmen's Hotel would be turned over to others, most probably the St. Vincent de Paul Society, which had been a close collaborator in founding the hotel.

In November 1917, Father Flanagan got together with friends and supporters in the home of Arthur Mullen, an old friend from the tornado recovery days when Mullen was secretary of the Nebraska Tornado Commission.[379] Mullen's wife[380] had been a supporter of the priest's work from the beginning and had organized women's groups to help him in his work with homeless men.[381] The purpose of the meeting, Father Flanagan told them, was to discuss opening a refuge for homeless boys. Again, he was willing to launch out into the deep with no resources, no finances, no place to begin the work, and no idea of how he was going to proceed. But those who knew him had watched as Father Flanagan visited the courts. They knew he had met with boys on street corners and in vacant lots, and that many of them were beginning to call themselves "Father Flanagan's boys."

Father Flanagan knew he couldn't do enough through periodic meetings with his "gang." These boys desperately needed constant concern, attention, and guidance, something resembling devoted parents and a "family" environment where he could get to know them individually, show them personal interest, and help them to overcome their troubled past.[382] (There are indications Bishop Harty was also concerned about boys in the streets and may have called a meeting himself in the home of a parishioner known for his involvement in public affairs.)

Father Flanagan left the meeting in the Mullen home with a new mandate, a mandate to found a home for these boys. He thought about their needs for a long time and began to search for models that might help him in his work.

"I found orphanages, of course, in practically every city. And in the larger cities, several. But the orphanage was maintained for the younger children and for infants. I discovered also that there were sectarian homes for boys, such as the ones lodges maintain, which are open only to the sons of members… I could not find an example of a home for boys which admitted a homeless and neglected boy without some string attached. I visualized a home where these older boys would be gathered together, be given care, education, and training, be taught how to work and how to play and form a community of boys happy in the knowledge that they were no longer homeless."[383]

Even at this time, something resembling a town for boys was like a seed in Father Flanagan's mind. But the kind of home was not the immediate problem; the problem was how to take the boys off the streets. He had to find them a home.

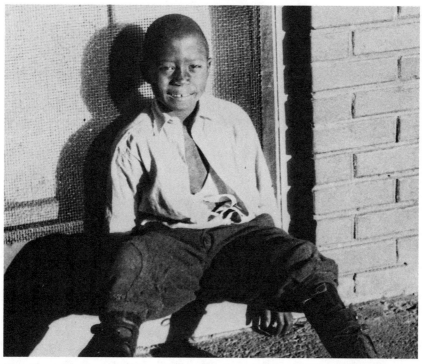

From the very beginning of his ministry to help homeless boys, Father Flanagan went against the societal norms of the day and welcomed youngsters of all races, religions, and cultural backgrounds.

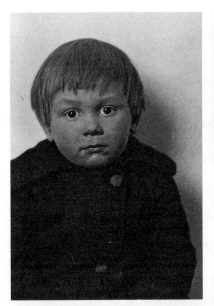

Father Flanagan would quickly discover that the problem of juvenile homelessness affected boys of all ages, and that they usually roamed the streets – hungry, lonely, and dressed in rags.

7

THE HOUSE ON 25ᵀᴴ AND DODGE

Welcoming the First Boys

Father Flanagan approached his new project with no illusions about the tremendous difficulties involved. There was simply no precedent for what he wanted to do and his resources for doing it were nil. He had no money, not even his $25-a-month priest's salary. He was still in charge of the Workingmen's Hotel, and that was filling up every night with men off the streets. After leaving St. Philomena's Church[384] with the blessing of Father Stenson, he set up a room for himself at the hotel. Then he started to scout the city to find a home for his boys.

In late November 1917, he got on the streetcar at 13th Street and Capitol Avenue with his friend Leo Hoffman, whose mortuary stood on the corner of 24th and Dodge Streets. Hoffman had been a prime partner of Father Flanagan in his work with homeless men; the two had met after the tornado that struck the city in the spring of 1913. Hoffman was the president of the St. Vincent de Paul Society, which had helped the priest set up his two hotels, and he often accompanied the priest on trips through the city.

As the streetcar turned from 13th Street onto Dodge and began climbing the hill toward the mortuary, a few passengers recognized the young priest and struck up a conversation with him. Father Flanagan told them he was looking for a house for homeless boys, and asked them if they knew of anyone who had a place to rent. One of the passengers pointed to a young lady and said, "That lady works for a real estate agent. Maybe she can help."

The young lady was Catherine Shields,[385] and when Father Flanagan asked about a house, she told him, "There is one available on this very street and we can stop here and look at it, if you like."

The three got off the streetcar at 25th Street and entered the two-story structure, just up the street from Hoffman's mortuary.

The house was known as the "Byron Reed Building," and it had been vacant for a long time. It was clear that it had seen better days, but it was well-built and sturdy, with ten rooms and high ceilings. Plenty of room for an army of boys.

"The rent is $90 a month," Miss Shields told the priest, "and I have to have the money in advance."

"I'll have the money for you tomorrow morning," he told her. "Draw up the papers."

He was back the next morning at Miss Shield's real estate office with the $90 for the first month's rent on the house.[386]

Since the rental marks a critical point in the founding of Boys Town, the question of who gave Father Flanagan the money has been raised many times over the years. The priest revealed only that it was "a friend." But those who knew him well were sure they knew who that friend was.

For many years, Father Flanagan's closest friend was Henry Monsky, an Omaha lawyer and a fighter for social justice, with a zeal and determination not unlike that of the priest himself.[387] Monsky was a leader in Omaha's Jewish community, and in later years served as the head of the Jewish philanthropic organization, B'nai B'rith. A remarkable man in his own right, Monsky was already a national figure in the battle against anti-Semitism, racism, and all forms of injustice.[388] It is not known when they met, but in a tribute to Monsky in later years, Father Flanagan revealed that he knew Monsky as "a boy, a student, and a young lawyer,"[389] which would mean they met in 1907 or 1908, when young Flanagan first came to Omaha.[390]

In 1915, Monsky was three years out of law school and a partner in the law firm of Monsky and Burke. At the time, Monsky was also a juvenile probation officer and was himself deeply involved in the problem of homeless boys; it is probable that Father Flanagan was already consulting his friend on legal matters, so the interests of the young priest and the young lawyer became intertwined very early.

After the founding of the home for boys, Monsky would become the personal lawyer of Father Flanagan and Boys Town.[391] Monsky's law office was in walking distance of the house on 25th and Dodge and the Workingmen's Hotel on 13th and Capitol.

Obtaining the money to rent the house was only the beginning. "After I had borrowed the money to pay my first month's rent, I explained my plan to Mrs. E.W. Nash, who gave me $2,000 and several others made substantial donations,"[392] Father Flanagan later wrote.

Now the task was to prepare the house for occupancy. As they had in his work for men, friends and relatives came together to help. The women's organization, under the leadership of Mrs. Arthur Mullen,[393] went through the home with broom and bucket, sweeping and mopping floors, hanging curtains on windows and pictures on walls. Furniture and bedding was gathered, and long lines of people carrying kitchen utensils, towels and rugs, dishes and kettles, clothing for the smaller boys, and even food for the pantry formed outside the home. Father Flanagan's brother, Father Pat, furnished benches and kneelers for a small chapel, and, as if to solemnize the importance of this next step in his work, Father Flanagan hung in the chapel the crucifix from Oberammergau[394] he had brought with him from Innsbruck.[395]

Father Flanagan would later describe the home's look on moving day.

"The result was a weird conglomeration of attic castoffs. Nothing matched anything else. The chairs around the dining room table represented a half dozen ages and designs in furniture making, from a broken-down Duncan Phyfe forgery to a Macy basement special. The meager supply of chinaware, the knives and forks and spoons, formed a rag-bag, a junk box of kitchen equipment. So, too, on the second floor; a chaotic jumble of beds, cots, blankets, and spreads brought to orderly usefulness in the dormitories."[396]

With the house furnished,[397] and after a month of sweeping, cleaning, and preparing rooms, the home was ready for its first young residents. Father Flanagan went to the court, where a judge released two young juvenile offenders to him.[398] He also gathered three other boys off the streets who had been members of his original "gang."[399]

On December 12, 1917, there was a solemn opening of the home. Archbishop Harty dedicated the small chapel,[400] bringing with him three Sisters of Notre Dame to assist the priest in his work.[401] Two were professed nuns and the third was a novice, on loan from the Notre Dame Motherhouse in Cedar Rapids, Iowa.[402] Besides Father Flanagan's own presence in the home, there would be the motherly presence of the nuns.[403]

The first five "boarders" reacted well for boys eight to ten years old. Once they had met the nuns and deposited their few belongings on their beds, they set out to explore the house, from cellar to attic. By dinnertime, they were comfortable enough with each other that an argument broke out between two boys over who would have a bed by the window. The nuns had to yank the two apart.

All the boys were full of questions: Were other boys coming? Did they have to go to school? Would there be time for play? The priest was overwhelmed by their eagerness and their liveliness. "Yes, there'll be a school," he told them. "Yes, there will be time for play. Outside, if the weather is good. But you have to stay out of the streets."

It was new, he wrote in later years, with unexpected problems and joys.

There were problems like keeping the house swept and clean, washing clothes and dishes, making beds, and washing windows, more tasks than the nuns were able to attend to. Father Flanagan's sister, Nellie, and his mother, Nora, who lived not far away on California Street, would come and make the place tidy for the boys, hanging the clothes out to dry, mending shirts and pants, and getting the boys to brush their teeth and comb their hair. For his mother, who had raised eleven children, these tasks were easy to handle.

But the home's population grew much faster than the priest expected. By the end of the first week, fifteen boys were in the house. And before the year was out, there were thirty. It was now truly a "family" of boys, and Father Flanagan soon realized this work would be radically different from his work with the men. He was now the "father" of a growing brood. He sat down to put some of his thoughts into words. From those words would come, within a few short weeks, the first edition of the *Boys' Home Journal*,[404] where a record of his work would be chronicled month by month and year by year.[405]

For the first six months, Father Flanagan did not live at the home on 25th and Dodge. He kept a room at the Workingmen's Hotel and would take the streetcar each day to the home or walk the distance.[406] On weekdays, he would celebrate Mass in the small chapel, and on Sundays would offer Mass just down the street at St. Mary Magdalene's Church, where the pastor, Monsignor Bernard Sinne, was a close friend.[407] From the very beginning, he started to write letters to garner support for his work, but he found that interest in a boys' home wasn't as high as for his work with the men. The boys on the street had become something of a menace in the city, and few people saw any other solution to the problem than sending them off to the reform school in Kearney, Nebraska. Even some of his fellow priests thought him unwise in trying to salvage these tough kids who traveled in gangs and roamed the streets at night.

Early Days

"My five boys were like the first men who helped get the hotel ready – they were great little assistants," Father Flanagan later wrote. "I can still see them trying to help me in many ways beyond their years, always eager to do more than they could, filled with enthusiasm at this new venture and the prospects they had of a home."[408]

This was a different kind of community from that of the men, and it took Father Flanagan time to adjust to the difference. The boys' needs were vastly different and he began to realize that founding a home for boys made him responsible for more than giving them shelter and food.[409] What impressed him was the infinite details of caring for children, their unlimited wants and needs, the tender care required for these wounded and helpless waifs, the painful memories that had to be erased through loving care and affection. Still, there was the need for firmness and discipline in their upbringing. Father Flanagan could only fall back upon his experiences from his own home and upbringing, and often referred to his own upbringing and the love and devotion of his own parents.[410]

But he discovered very quickly that his boys' home was also a place of high jinks and mass confusion as the house filled with more boys. There was not only high-spirited play and the rough-and-tumble antics of boys on the run, but also brotherly rivalries, the testing and teasing of newcomers, the bullying of younger boys by older boys, and the harmless games concocted on a moment's notice that sent feet flying and evoked peals of laughter. At times, it was all Father Flanagan and the nuns could do to keep the home from exploding into a madhouse of play as boys went screaming through the house, intent on outrunning or outdoing one another. In the first days, he would often retire to his room at the Workingmen's Hotel worn out and exhausted.

But there were other problems as well. Where to get the food to feed this growing army of boys? Where to find hats, shoes, and clothing for boys of every size, from ages ten to fifteen? How to occupy them during the hours from rising to sleeping? How about school?

During the first few weeks the home was open, food was scarce. But suddenly someone would arrive with day-old bread from a bakery or a sack of groceries from a store. The women of his family, who lived only a few blocks away on California Street, would suddenly arrive with fresh fruit and vegetables, canned goods from some family's kitchen, or something one of them had freshly cooked.

Much to his surprise, the boys kept coming. Most were sent by the courts, but some arrived on foot as news spread that there was a boys' home in Omaha. By Christmas, the house was a jumble of beds and cots on the floor, and a jumble of voices at tables set for meals, with boys jockeying for a place as the nuns brought the food. Sometimes the food was sparse, and this was especially true on the first Christmas morning.

The boys had talked of holiday turkey and there were high hopes that tables would be piled high with food. When Father Flanagan arrived from Mass at St. Mary Magdalene's Church just down the street, there were questions about "turkey with all the trimmings." He could see the disappointment on their faces as the day wore on and nothing in the way of a feast arrived.

"A friend had given us a barrel of sauerkraut the day before Christmas, and with some boiling meat, bread, milk, but not butter, we called it Christmas dinner," he later said. "Humble as it was, I found that it was a better Christmas dinner than most of the boys ever had."[411] The boys pitched in, full of good cheer. In fact, good cheer was everywhere as this little army in cast-off clothing – a variety of hats, shoes, and shirts – sat around the table, warm and comfortable, with no worry about tomorrow.

Soon after, Father Flanagan was out with Leo Hoffman, visiting local pastors or principals of nearby public schools to enroll his boys in classes. The boys left each morning in their hand-me-down clothes, the easy butt of jokes by other students. Central High School, the finest public high school in the city, was just down the street and easily accessible from the home.

"Four of our boys attend Holy Family School; four received their transfer to Central School; and the others receive their schooling at the home," he later wrote.[412] Father Flanagan's gift for organization soon had the boys sorted out according to their age, religion, talent, interests, family background, previous schooling, and personality traits. His experience with the homeless men, of setting up of an employment office in the hotel, and the detailed organization necessary for housing as many as 500 men a night served him well. But a house full of boys was vastly different from a hotel of homeless and jobless men.

Father Flanagan was always alert for special gifts and talents in the boys: "We have a second Caruso in our midst in the person of Alfio, but Alfio is getting a bit peeved over the appearance of another musical star, John...." The priest also had presented the boys with a pair of donated boxing gloves: "The lads are hard at it, training every evening, that in the near future they may be able to give the donor a strenuous contest."[413]

From the beginning, he took the boys on walks through the city, down Dodge Street to the moving traffic and the sites on 16th Street in the center of town. Sometimes, they stopped at stores or ice cream parlors for an afternoon treat.

"Like every boy, our boys delight in pleasurable recreation," he later wrote. "Among these recreations, the moving picture show is one greatly sought after. Our boys, too, have a keen appreciation for the movies. We satisfied that craving, as we try to satisfy all their boyish, lawful desire for pleasure. After a leisurely stroll through town on one of those rare, mild days this winter graciously granted us, we wended our way to the 'Muse,' where the historical tale, *The Crisis*, was displayed in picture. (Having read Churchill's, *The Crisis*, in the very town where the scenes are depicted, Father Flanagan was able to explain the historical facts to the boys.) 'When can we go again?' was the unanimous utterance, and proved how anxious they are for many repetitions of such treats."[414]

His rag-tag collection of boys soon had tongues wagging in Omaha. People were asking: How could this priest, with no money in his pocket and no visible means of support, accomplish anything for the good of the city? Besides, he had a hotel that filled up every night with drunks and vagrants, which was enough of a danger to the city, as men came off the roads and railroad cars into the heart of the city, without adding to it a refuge for young hoodlums.

It was here that the young priest decided to publicize his work. In February 1918, less than two months after the opening of his home, the first issue of Father Flanagan's *Boys' Home Journal* came off the presses,[415] a slick, magazine-sized publication notable for four items on the front cover: a photo of the priest and his first boys' home staring at the reader; a notation that read, "With the approbation of Most Rev. J.J. Harty, D.D."; a banner across the top that read, "Published monthly in the interest of Father Flanagan's Boys' Home, Workingmen's Hotel, and Charity in General"; and an audacity that noted, "Price 10 cents."

Besides informing the city about his home and his work, publishing the *Journal* also provided a healthy daily activity for some of the older boys.

Father Flanagan was still desperate for money and the boys continued to come, one or two from the courts, a few just off the street. Here is how he described his plight: "Our Home for Boys has been open not fully two months, and still we have it filled almost to capacity. We have now about 25 boys. There is no difference between these boys and those in a well-regulated home. They eat, sleep, and play, and enjoy God's fresh air just the same as other boys."[416] This was the first time he laid down the philosophy and policy of what would eventually become Boys Town: boys of all races, colors, creeds, and ethnic backgrounds were welcome. He would never waver in this policy, even under the most strenuous public outcry or intense private criticism.

Father Flanagan would send his "street hoodlums" throughout the city, mingling with the army of newsboys already there, to sell the *Journal* on street corners and at local churches.[417] It provided the public with detailed knowledge of his work for the boys and for the homeless men who still haunted his Workingmen's Hotel. The priest already had in his hands Jane Addams', *Twenty-Years at Hull House*, with its vivid and detailed descriptions of Addams' work for the poor of Chicago. He hoped to accomplish the same thing with his *Boys' Home Journal*.

The first issue accomplished three things. It gave a detailed description of the citizens of the city, the women in particular, who supported his work. It welcomed others to the effort; on the first page, he penned this invitation: "Anyone who wishes to get in touch with the work may come at any time to the Boys' Home, at 106 North 25th Street, and we will be glad to show what we have, and what we are doing." It also described the boys in residence there, with a stirring defense of his work and his methods.[418]

There also was a report of his work to benefit homeless men, with these astonishing statistics: "Within the past two years, ending December 31st, 1917, we have had 46,374 lodgings at the Hotel, and of this, 25,990 were free lodgings. We served a total number of 18,283 free meals during that time. In addition to this, clothes and shoes were given to many in need of them. To help men who are actually in need has always been the policy of this institution, and we have endeavored to do this in a quiet and conservative manner, ever having before our minds the idea of Constructive Charity, to help men to help themselves. In this way, we have endeavored to be of some assistance to our grand City, of which we are proud to be citizens, ever alive to the problem of Charity, which a progressive City must face."[419] This served as an answer to Father Flanagan's critics, with facts, figures, and detailed descriptions of his work and the motives behind it. (He had already given notice to the men at the Hotel that it would be closing in June of 1918 and that he would be devoting himself exclusively and completely to the homeless boys on the street. On the same page as his report on the Hotel, he had a description of the Boys' Home and its work.)

Something Father Flanagan learned from the very beginning was the importance of accountability in dealing with the public, both his supporters and his critics. He had learned from his experience as an accountant at Cudahy about balancing books, adding figures, and producing financial reports. His former fellow workers at Cudahy may have taken notice of this, for in the second issue of the *Journal* in March 1918 was a huge, bold-faced ad with the text: *Compliments of The Cudahy Packing Company*.[420]

In fact, the *Journal* was paid for by classified ads from every major company and professional service in town: doctors, lawyers, banks, laundries, bakeries, funeral homes, etc. Within a few weeks, with the help and support of his Women's Committee, Father Flanagan had canvassed the city for ads. The business skills he had developed at Cudahy were put to work in these first days at 25th and Dodge, and he later would exclaim, "If they can do it for beef, we can do it for boys."

But he also realized that the boys needed more than walks through the city and occasional outside entertainment. He rounded up a collection of musical instruments so the boys could form something resembling a band. On his orders, the nuns supervised the evening sessions for study and homework, and he was insistent that each boy show progress in school and hold sacred the time for study. He knew that personal achievement was essential to a boy's sense of personal worth and that the development of a boy's mind had to keep pace with his physical growth.[421]

In each issue of the *Journal*, there was news of this growing community of boys and the emergence of something quite different from the traditional orphanage.

- "In less than three months, our number of boys has reached the thirty mark."
- "Boxing and wrestling are on a backburner, now that the marble season is on."
- "Our vocal geniuses are still very modest. At some future date, no doubt, they will give our friends a real musical treat."
- "A number of boys have something up their sleeves. They are imbued with the idea that they establish a local government for their own betterment."

It was clear that Father Flanagan was delighted with his boys, and, in spite of his financial worries, he was finally in his element: the priest, the teacher, the educator, something more than a father to his boys as his interest in them was more than just keeping them out of trouble and off the streets. He saw them working and playing, making this house their home, each one making his unique contribution to this unique "family."

On Sundays, some boys scattered to the Protestant churches and syna- gogues in town[422] while the Catholic boys attended Mass in the Home's small chapel. From the beginning, boys of every race, color, and creed were welcomed, a policy that put Father Flanagan at odds with some of the "better" families of the Omaha.

Racism had been part of the city's history from its founding. Race riots and ethnic clashes regularly broke out as German, Polish, Irish, Greek, Czech, Italian, and Croatian families emigrated to Omaha. In 1917, African-Americans made up a small part of Omaha's population, and segregation of the races was the rule. African-Americans, unfortunately, were despised by most Omahans and violence against them was not uncommon.[423]

But Father Flanagan was adamant in his policy of inclusion, even when it turned many of the prominent families in Omaha against him. He had a keen memory of the oppression of the Irish under British rule in his home country, simply because of their nationality and their religion. He refused to compromise his religious and moral principles for any social or personal advantage. Racism, especially toward the Jew and the African-American, was part of the American culture of the time, something that saddened and angered him. When he encountered it in actions directed at his boys, he responded with an anger that shook or shamed the culprits. For that reason, in later years, neither Boys Town's football teams nor the Boys Town Choir would play or perform in the South.

Compassion and a Growing Ministry

"During these months in this first Home, I learned a great deal about caring for children. I had among the boys two little fellows whose father had died and the mother deserted them. Our house got pretty cold in the middle of the night, and it was on one of the coldest nights that winter that I heard one of these little boys crying. I got up to see what the trouble was and found the younger one was suffering from an earache."

Father Flanagan found that the boy was crying for his mother, who always rocked him when his ear hurt. He realized that, besides the earache, the boy missed his mother and the tender care she had given him. He spent the rest of the night with the boy, applying hot towels to the aching ear and rocking him as his mother might have done. Toward morning, the boy fell into a sound sleep and when he awoke later in the day, the earache was gone.

The priest was constantly searching for ways to make the boys happy, and it occurred to him that every boy wanted a dog. He had one when he cared for the sheep and cattle on the Leabeg estate in Ireland, and he would never walk those fields without a dog at his heels. Several of the boys had even asked for one.

Father Flanagan would later recall a fateful meeting: "One afternoon, I met a friend on the street, and in the course of our conversation, he said, 'Father, you don't happen to want a nice collie pup, do you? I imagine those kids would like to have a dog. I have a dandy one at my place. If you want, you can come and get it.'

"But this friend lived clear on the north edge of the city, about fifty-five or sixty blocks from my Home. Automobiles were a real luxury then, and naturally, I did not have one. My only means of transportation was the street car.

"I told the boys about our good fortune and they begged me to get the pup the next day."

Father Flanagan took the streetcar out and picked up the collie pup, intending to take the streetcar back. But as he boarded it, he was told that a city ordinance prohibited dogs on streetcars. So, tucking the pup under his arm, he set out on the five-mile walk back to the Home. Several hours later, he trudged in to be met by thirty screaming boys who had waited supper until he returned. The dog, who the boys named Carlo, became not only a pet but a protector, often chasing wayward boys away from the street or barking when a streetcar came in sight.[424]

Support for the Home was meager. There also was much criticism of Father Flanagan's work from those who still looked upon homeless boys as little criminals, a danger to the community and not fit to associate with other children in the city. At his insistence, his boys were admitted to the local schools, but they were treated as outcasts by the other children. Some of them were behind in their studies and often had to stay away from school because they were sick. Desperate, Father Flanagan tried to reach out to his critics in the March issue of his *Boys' Home Journal.*

He wrote about "The Boy Whom Nobody Wants," using his first catchword to describe his work and describing such a boy and why he must be given a chance.

"The *boy whom nobody wants* is, as a rule, a troublesome little fellow, who is full of tricks and boyish pranks, and, I am sorry to say, often lacking in the qualities of a lovable boy. He is a boy who is difficult to control by those who cannot understand him, and cannot take time to learn. He is deceitful and perhaps dishonest, in small things, but not entirely devoid of conscience. The latter is just a little blunt and stunted, because it has never had a chance to grow through moral training. His appearance is not, as a rule, attractive, and he may show signs of wear and tear of great negligence. On the whole, he is not the type of boy that everyone might care to pick up and bring into a good home."

Near at hand was the St. Vincent de Paul Society, which had taken over and managed the Workingmen's Hotel until its closing later in the year. Father Flanagan also could depend upon a dedicated staff of women, the Women's Committee of the Boys' Home. They found ways of raising money for the Home through bake sales and soliciting contributions from friends, and helping the nuns with cleaning, cooking, washing, and sewing.

Father Flanagan knew the kind of boy he was dealing with, and as more cots began to occupy the floors, corners, and closets of the Home, he began to look around for a larger space, where there was room for play with no danger from the streets, where he could have his own school, and where he could house a hundred boys or more. He had planned a money-making event in January, but the city calendar was too crowded. So he planned it for April,[425] with the help of his Women's Committee and his friend and collaborator, Leo Hoffman.[426]

His hope was to raise $10,000 and he explained why in the March issue of his *Journal*: "Our present quarters are entirely inadequate, and the demands on the Home are so great, we cannot do justice to the work unless we can secure larger and better equipped quarters." He was desperate, and with Leo Hoffman at his side, he began to ride the streetcar through the city, looking for a new home for his boys. Catherine Shields, who had found him his first home, was no longer in the city. She had married a soldier, Jim Dannehy; he was on duty in Virginia and she was there with him.

The new Home they eventually found was on South 13th Street, a two-story building on nine acres of land, with rooms for a hundred boys, open areas for gardens, a baseball diamond, and plenty of room to run and play. When Father Flanagan first heard of the place and was told the rent was cheap, he thought there might be something wrong with the building. But he soon learned why the building was available at a low cost. It had been the center of German-American activities in the city, and after the declaration of war on Germany in April 1917, no one would rent it.

The new Home would provide more than just larger quarters. It would give the priest the independence and autonomy he needed to carry out his own vision of his work. He had made a study of other institutions and other models for child care and disagreed with most of them or saw them as inadequate for the task of fashioning the young. A later biography would describe his research this way: "He searched orphanages and other homes for children, examining their strengths and weaknesses. Every institution he examined had limitations on the class of children they would help. Homes that were operated by fraternal lodges, for example, were only open to boys who fit narrow criteria. Orphanages were maintained only for younger children or infants. There were no homes for adolescent boys that he could use as a model."[427]

Father Flanagan was searching for a new concept and a new educational tool, and his concept of the homeless boy was almost breathtaking in its implications. He saw the boy as a citizen in a state of formation, but already possessing dignity and rights. The German-American Home was the first step in creating an atmosphere where this boy could experience his own unique self, using an array of personal gifts and possibilities to shape his own future. The *Boys' Home Journal* gave Father Flanagan the opportunity to test these concepts and put them into words,[428] and the new Home would provide the setting for carrying out his vision.

The German-American Home was a godsend, and when Father Flanagan told the boys they were moving, a mighty cheer erupted from the more than thirty youngsters. He told them they could now have their own school with their own teachers, their own baseball teams, and their own band. But first the building had to be cleaned up, new furniture had to be brought in, floors had to be swept, and windows had to be washed. For this he turned to his women helpers and the St. Vincent de Paul Society and soon a huge army of workers descended on the place.

Then he sent his "newsies" to the street corners and the entrances of churches and public buildings to spread the good news.

Three of his biggest supporters were his former pastors: Father Gannon of St. Patrick's, Father Stenson of St. Philomena's, and Father Sinne at nearby St. Mary Magdalene's. Father Flanagan had celebrated Mass each Sunday for Father Sinne at St. Mary Magdalene's, but now had to tell his friend that his work required his presence at the new Home full time. He and Father Sinne had a special bond. Father Sinne had himself studied at Innsbruck University and it was he who had first suggested that young Eddie Flanagan study there. Father Gannon used the diocesan newspaper, *The True Voice*, to publicize Father Flanagan's work in the Catholic community, and articles appeared from time to time as the work progressed. Father Stenson was Father Flanagan's confidante and advisor, to whom he turned for advice and counsel.

The publicity and moral support were badly needed. Since Father Flanagan had taken in the first five boys the previous December, 200 boys had passed through his care. Some had been returned to their families after a short stay; for others, he found families that were willing to take in a boy, with the priest carefully monitoring the new home situation. He was always desperate for food, money, and clothing, and the *Boys' Home Journal*, with its list of needs, often brought in boxes and baskets of needed supplies. The Women's Committee often surprised him by finding new sources for help and assistance, and its members and the local newspapers,[429] especially *The Omaha Bee News*, kept the public informed about his activities with timely articles and current reports on his work.[430]

Father Flanagan also kept in constant touch with the juvenile authorities and probation officers as new boys in trouble were brought before the courts. Some were from families that had recently immigrated and spoke little English. Father Flanagan's command of European languages, especially Italian, German, and French,[431] broke down a lot of barriers of communication with these boys and their parents. Massive immigration had brought hundreds of families to the crowded neighborhoods of Omaha and South Omaha, where they squeezed into small tenements, their children roaming the streets day and night with little or no supervision. At one time, half the boys in his home were from the crowded Italian neighborhoods;[432] and at other times, Polish boys from Sheelytown or Irish youngsters from his old parish filled his rooms.

The house at 25th and Dodge Streets had been the arena in which Father Flanagan began to combine his social, educational, and pedagogical principles to fashion the vision of his work that would guide him for the next thirty years. There was a definite theory behind his work, but it was a theory seen in the work itself. It involved the creation of an organism rather than an organization and mutual education on a large scale, where the influences for good were so many that very few boys who fell under his influences did not come off the better for it.[433]

It was the careful molding of individuals by individuals in a mutual give-and-take that eventually would become Boys Town. Some detected no system at all in his work, and others were severely critical of the slogan he made famous ("There's no such thing as a bad boy"), crediting him with mere platitudes, if not rank sentimentality. But Father Edward Flanagan was no mean scholar and he approached his work with a thoroughness and intellectual acumen known only to a few. He discussed his views with anyone who wanted to listen, and those who listened were professionals and educators in their own right. According to one of them, Dr. Franz Plewa,[434] who would later come to Boys Town from Alfred Adler's Child Guidance Clinics in Vienna, Father Flanagan was that rare human specimen who appears only once or twice in a lifetime, the intuitive genius, and Boys Town would embody the totality of his pedagogical vision.

Father Flanagan saw every boy as the raw material for greatness. He saw what was possible, and somehow that rubbed off on the boys who came to him.

He made it impossible for a boy to get into trouble, the positive peer pressure always driving a boy in the opposite direction. Eventually, he would give the boys a "town" of their own, something of pride and personal possession, of which each one was a vital part. He understood the meaning of community, of belonging, and of a contrived culture where education was total.

In contrast to most educators, he did not just devise a system of education or found an institution. He created a culture, a culture where the values he cherished and the goals he wanted his boys to have were the living currents of that culture. He was not merely trying to solve a social problem, and most social scientists did not understand him. He abhorred the casework mentality of most social workers, and instead depended upon the organism to work, which it did, miraculously, surprising even himself. Boys Town was mutual education in a planned environment where undefinable forces were at work, the undefinable influence of person on person, where freedom and individuality were prized.

The educational system that Father Flanagan drew on was as ancient as his homeland and pre-dated every other system in Europe. Whether he reflected on it or not, he never indicated, but it was reflected in his work. The ancient Irish system of fosterage[435] was unique in the ancient world and became part of the Celtic monastic system when Christianity arose in Ireland. It was based on a huge respect for the innate originality of each child and began by establishing the child in total freedom. It was gentle, immersed the child in play, and drew out of the child's own inner genius its own rich and unique potential. The system always centered around one beloved figure who gathered his charges around him and fashioned bonds with them that lasted a lifetime.

In his work for boys, Father Flanagan was determined to break the back of the educational system that said education must be forced, that morality was taught chiefly by fear of punishment, and that education could flourish only in a system of constraints and strict discipline. He knew that was not true from his own home experience and he knew it was not true from the Gospel of Jesus Christ. His educational system came from the Gospels, but he backed it with a support system that touched every base in a boy's personality. He embodied his principles in a living culture, a culture of his own making, drawing upon a humane tradition that had achieved miracles in the past and had transformed whole peoples, leaving behind a rich cultural legacy.

What Father Flanagan saw as he entered upon his work in the house on 25th Street was a social crisis, in which the homeless child was almost a surplus commodity; a religious crisis, in which character was molded by restraint; and an educational crisis, in which mass education was the norm. He rejected all of these, and inaugurated a social, religious, and educational revolution that took the world by storm, making his work famous and the name "Father Flanagan" a household word.

His most significant insights were that human beings are fashioned by culture, that the human person develops its full potential in an atmosphere of freedom and total acceptance. These two insights, coupled with the Christian conviction that the Gospel must not be forced, either in its propagation or in its development, gave Boys Town a measure of success that drew the admiration of educators the world over.

The first Home for Boys at 25th and Dodge Streets in Omaha, Nebraska, 1917.

Some of the earliest residents of the Home came from the streets and courts, 1918.

8

THE GERMAN-AMERICAN HOME

Room to Grow

On June 1, 1918, the city witnessed a strange caravan of trucks,[436] cars, and wagons heading first down Dodge Street[437] and then south on 13th Street into South Omaha, where the German-American Club was located. South Omaha at the time was a bustling community of stockyards and packinghouses, of German, Italian, Polish, Lithuanian, and Czech neighborhoods, with their own social clubs, churches, businesses, and restaurants. A prosperous commercial and civic center in its own right, it had been annexed by Omaha three years earlier. Now these two hubs of business activities were joined by streetcar lines, with streetcars moving continually between Dodge Street in Omaha to L Street in South Omaha.[438]

The German-American Home was a huge building, two stories high, with a full basement and dozens of rooms. It had been vacant, used only for occasional dances, but now it was ready for the army of boys that invaded it that first day of June. There was plenty of room for play, for baseball and volleyball, for planting gardens; a full nine acres, bordered in the back by a small forest of trees that stretched down to a park below. Because of the large spaces inside and out, it beckoned to something more than crowded bedrooms and games of hide-and-seek on the front lawn of the boys' original dwelling.

The first provision was to find space for a new chapel and to solemnly place the Oberammergau crucifix over the altar. As the boys arrived in the cars and trucks, rooms and beds were assigned, the kitchen and dining room were furnished, and rooms were set aside for Father Flanagan and the Notre Dame Sisters who had come with him. Also, some rooms were designated as classrooms and furnished with desks and blackboards. No boys would be sent to school outside the home; now they would have a school of their own. Cheers erupted as Carlo,[439] the beloved collie, was given a tour of the Home, with plenty of room to run and play in the back yard.[440]

Father Flanagan also had another plan for the new house; it would later be described this way: "As they carried their belongings over to the new home at cockcrow, the priest carried in his pocket a strange list, not an inventory of belongings, but of youngsters, homeless boys whom he had recently been forced to turn away because there was no room. These would be the first cases considered for the new home. Thirty were accepted the first week. The population of the home jumped in that brief time to more than a hundred."[441]

The new, larger Home required a bigger staff, a more careful organization of the boys, the planning of activities, and the hard business of raising funds to meet the massive, growing needs of a hundred residents. "We had no money – no nothing – we were living in a fool's paradise,"[442] Father Flanagan would later say.

He organized something called the "Boy Savers Society,"[443] the first of his many associations to generate support for the Home.[444] The names of donors began to appear in the *Boys' Home Journal* and the city soon became dotted with support groups that not only provided a trickle of financial support for the Home, but also a variety of gifts and services for the boys.[445]

Soon after, Father Flanagan also received new mobility – the husband of his sister, Susan, Dr. J.R. Dwyer, gave him a car of his own.[446] Until now, his only form of transportation was the city's streetcars, although from time to time a friend or neighbor would drive him around in a car. The gift was fortunate, for no sooner was he in the new Home than parents in trouble began calling him and letters began to arrive from courts and social workers all over the Midwest asking that boys be admitted to his Home.

Activities at the Home took off right away. There was room on the nine acres for gardens, and it wasn't long before the boys began planting potatoes, carrots, and other vegetables. But no vegetables grew right away, and they had to work at it for a year or so before they could grow produce for their meals.[447] Father Flanagan talked to a local musicians union, which sent musical instruments to the Home so a band could be formed. The priest also talked to one of the local baseball clubs about furnishing uniforms for his boys, and soon games were scheduled at the Home, the boys dividing into teams of "Blues" and "Whites."

The Home's first dairy was started when friends presented Father Flanagan with a wonderful cow. The problem was that no one knew how to milk a cow. The boys thought that one cow should supply enough milk for the whole Home. An elderly neighbor, upon learning of the priest's predicament, came over and taught some of the older boys how to do the milking. Whenever the boys milked the cow, many of the others would stand around and admire the process and then proudly carry the pail of milk to the kitchen, every night and every morning."[448]

It was here, as boys continued to arrive every day, sometimes alone, on foot, or in twos or threes, that Father Flanagan began to reflect on exactly what he was trying to do. He did not intend to give temporary shelter to homeless boys, sending them on their way when they had been fed and clothed. He had to give them a life, a foundation for the future, where they could grow into the men they were intended to be before the tragedy of their lives could pull them down. This meant he had to know each boy individually and had to surround that boy with an environment for growth, where he could use his gifts and talents in a community of equals, each boy cherished, treasured, and recognized for his own worth. The concept of a town for boys had not yet come to him, but the German-American Home became a laboratory where he began to explore all the possibilities and tools of education that would lead to that concept. He also realized from the moment he set foot in the door of this second Home that it was totally inadequate for what he wanted to do. The place was not his, and the owners could raise the rent at any time or tell him they needed it for some other use. He began to look around for a place he could really call his own.

Meanwhile, the boys kept coming.[449] He was in the new Home scarcely a week when they started to arrive from all over the Midwest.[450] Word had spread through all the surrounding states there was a new boys' home in Omaha, and soon, the floodgates opened. Father Flanagan was overwhelmed by phone calls from mothers pleading for help for their sons and juvenile authorities eager to place some troubled youth in his care. He was simply not organized for this kind of massive need, and quickly realized he needed some kind of a staff and assistance in running the home.

Not long after Father Flanagan took over the German-American building, the women of the neighborhood held a meeting to discuss how they could help. A delegation informed him of the creation of a Mothers' Guild, whose sole purpose was helping to care for his boys.[451] And they meant it, washing, ironing, and mending clothes.[452] There were twenty in the group, and their work quickly eased the operation of the home.[453]

Also fortunate was a timely visit from Catherine Dannehy (formerly Catherine Shields), the young lady who had helped Father Flanagan rent the house on 25th and Dodge. She had returned to Omaha after her husband, Jim Dannehy, finished his military service, and had taken a job with an insurance company. Several of her friends had told her about Father Flanagan's new Home, and curious, she came to visit him, hoping to sell him an insurance policy. He was short of funds, but she convinced him that he had better start building up equity for his Home so he would have something to fall back upon when funds were short. He bought the policy,[454] and then pointed to his desk and empty office: "I have no stenographer, no bookkeeper, no mailing list – all I have is boys. I need a secretary. Why don't you go to work for me?"[455] Mrs. Dannehy turned him down at first, since it would mean a large cut in her salary. But finally, at his persistence, she agreed. (The insurance policy was stored away, but it proved to be a boon later when the Great Depression hit the country.)

"I could tell you a hundred stories of the lean years," Mrs. Dannehy wrote later. "How many trips to the bank a certain insurance policy made so Father Flanagan could meet food bills and other expenses."[456] Her advice was well taken, and from that day forward, the priest began to look for ways to build up equity for his Home. And she was there to keep his books, write his letters, and watch the house fill up with boys. Among that correspondence were form letters she began to write and send out by the hundreds to people in Omaha and the surrounding towns. Little by little, financial support began to trickle in. But it was never enough to fully meet the Home's growing needs. Mrs. Dannehy would work for Father Flanagan for a year, putting his affairs in order, handling his personal and business correspondence, and beginning a file on each boy who entered the Home. When she left him for the birth of her first child, he had a well-organized office and the start of a mailing list for his *Boys' Home Journal*.

Help often came from totally unexpected sources. As soon as new boys arrived, neighbors would come over to offer assistance.[457] Some brought food or clothing; some worked on putting the place in order. One neighbor brought Father Flanagan his first typewriter, and, before Catherine Dannehy started her employment, some neighbors wrote letters. Others became part-time coaches for baseball, football, handball, basketball, and track competitions. The Home had two sets of boxing gloves and matches were held on one of the back lots. A local music teacher offered to train the boys to play their odd assortment of musical instruments, and the first Boys' Home Band was formed. The ladies' group hosted card parties, and sometimes dances were held right in the Home's hall.[458]

Word of Father Flanagan's desperate need for funds eventually reached those in the city who had sponsored fundraising events for his Workingmen's Hotel. They came in twos and threes, and sometimes in large groups, drawn by the publicity about the Home in the city's newspapers and the sight of these boys selling their *Boys' Home Journal* on the streets of the city. A group of his first visitors was from the women's group he had met with in the home of Mrs. Arthur Mullen at the request of Archbishop Harty, when he was preparing to launch his project for boys.

They left mightily impressed,[459] with the promise that support would come.

Stories of Heartache

"I had no one to fall back upon for financial help. I had obligated myself to my superior to 'pay my own way.' So a great deal of my spare time was spent trying to solve my financial problems," Father Flanagan would later write. "But in some way God did provide for us month from month, for I was able to meet the monthly obligations, even when my boys numbered one hundred fifty.

"No sacrifice seemed too great to make for my boys, who depended on me to provide for them. Time proved that there would be many sacrifices to make, but also that the boys were worth it. I was surprised at the number of applications that I received from isolated communities. Homelessness and neglect are not confined to any one place."[460]

Father Flanagan often recounted harrowing stories of neglect and cruelty to children, parents deserting their children, children facing every kind of violence, and, in one case, the murder of a boy's mother. You can almost feel the heartbreak and horror in his voice as he told the stories.

"I remember distinctly the case of the three Koch boys, fifteen, fourteen, and nine years old when they came to us. One extremely hot afternoon, some of my smaller boys and I had been having a story hour under the trees in the yard. I looked up and saw three barefooted boys coming up the street towards us. They were looking timidly at the buildings. They did not seem to notice us sitting nearby in the shade.

"They stopped outside the door and were standing there when I came over to greet them. I was not expecting any boys that day, but I learned to expect homeless boys whenever they arrived. Later on, when my work was better organized, this changed.

"Such neglected little fellows I never hope to see again. The only clothing they had on their slender bodies was a ragged pair of overalls and a tattered shirt, each. The oldest boy was carrying some kind of a sack on his back. I took them into my office and brought them something to eat and drink. They were almost famished. The boy dropped the knapsack on the floor. Something inside it clicked. We talked for a little while, and finally he opened the sack. There, in the bottom, lay a few little trinkets. They had been brought by their parents from their homeland in Europe. Worthless baubles, but they were priceless to these poor boys. They would not part with them."[461]

Father Flanagan had heard about these boys, who lived elsewhere, and had asked the court to put them into his care as soon as he heard their tragic story. But no one had told him when they would arrive in Omaha. The sight of these three boys walking up the street, alone and unattended, shocked him and he was even more shocked when he heard their whole story.

"The father and mother were living on a ranch in the northwestern part of this state," he would later recount. "For some time they seemed to be happy with their three boys. Then the mother began leaving home for a week or two at a time. Perhaps she was driven by the loneliness of life on that isolated ranch, or by the poverty she endured year in and year out. The father was, no doubt, a nervous and impetuous man. On the mother's last trip away from home, the father took sick and developed a high fever.

"Fearful of what his sickness might prove to be, and conscious of the care and responsibility of the three boys, he fretted himself into a serious sickness. The mother returned to find her husband in this condition. Argument and quarreling ensued. The mother finally told him that when she left again, she would never return.

"Incensed by the challenge, the father got out of bed and went out to the stable and got a piece of harness on the end of which was a heavy buckle. He returned and attacked his wife, beating her into unconsciousness before the eyes of his three boys. She died there a few minutes later. The crazed man, not knowing what to do, picked up the body and took it out to the hog lot. That night he buried it there.

"The boys were wild with fear and apprehension. They wondered what would become of them. The father cautioned them to secrecy. He also told them to tell anyone who inquired about their mother that she was 'away.' Since she was known to be gone at times before, he thought that this would not arouse suspicion.

"But his plan did not work. Rumors began going around, and finally one day the sheriff came out and started asking questions. He sensed something wrong, and in searching the place, came across the newly dug grave. Then the truth came out.

"The father pled guilty, and was sentenced to life imprisonment. But nothing was done about the three boys who were left on that lonely ranch. Finally, their plight was discovered and the newspaper took up their cause. I wired the judge in their county immediately that I would take the boys and care for them until they were able to take care of themselves. And they walked in just as they were, ragged and barefoot that hot July afternoon."[462]

Such horror stories were common, and Father Flanagan began to fill up his files with the stories of these boys as he had the stories of the homeless men. They were a chronicle of neglect, abuse, and human suffering that made everything he was doing worthwhile. The term "homeless boy" began to take on a new poignancy and a new meaning, and with an eloquence that Omaha had not known before, the priest began to trace his "Romance of the Homeless Boy" in writing and in speeches that reached beyond Omaha and Nebraska. It was not just boys off the street now. It was any boy without a home, and Omaha became a mecca for boys from places as far away as California and New York.

"One winter evening a few months after the Koch boys came, one of my boys called and told me there was a woman in the office who wanted to talk to me," Father Flanagan later wrote. "I went to the office and a young woman greeted me. I saw little boy who looked about eight years old sitting on a chair. He did not get up, but I thought no more of that.

"The woman proceeded to tell me about their plight. The father had deserted them, she said, and she could not care for the boy. She begged me to take him and give him a home, and promised her help as far as she could.

"I took the boy,[463] and the mother went out into the night, never to return, or to inquire about the boy. To this day I do not know what became of her.

"I returned to the office and asked the little fellow to come with me. He was still seated. Then I saw that he could not rise. He was totally crippled.[464]

"He was left in my hands, and I had to do what I could for him. He spent several months in local hospitals, under the care of the best orthopedic surgeons we had in Omaha. As he grew older, braces were placed on his weak legs."[465] (The young man later finished the Home's commercial class and got a job as a private secretary. He walked with the aid of only a cane.[466])

One evening, Father Flanagan received a phone call from a woman who had left her two sons with him. She phoned from the railroad depot and told him, "You've got my two boys at your Home and I'm leaving Omaha. There's no use trying to carry on any longer. Father, I have a baby that's a year and a half old and I just left her with a woman who's in the basement of an apartment on the southwest corner of Twenty-Fourth and Douglas Streets. If you want to take care of my baby, you can have her."[467]

Father Flanagan tried to reason with her, but she was adamant: "You have my permission to take her, but don't lose any time."

Something in the woman's voice warned him that something might be wrong. He headed to the address in the Model T Ford that had been given to him by his brother-in-law, Dr. Dwyer. The address on Douglas Street was not far from his former Home at 25th and Dodge. When he reached the apartment, he found his way down a dark stairway into an even darker basement. In a room, in the light of an old coal-lamp, he saw an old woman sitting in a worn-out chair beside a bare, board table. There were no other furniture in the room. She held a baby in her arms and was rocking back and forth, crooning to the child. When she saw the priest, she shrieked, "No! You can't take this baby away from me. I'm going to keep it."

"No," Father Flanagan said. "The mother has instructed me to take the baby and take care of it."

The old woman was determined to keep the child, so he took from his coat pocket a policeman's badge which had been given to him by the local police. "I am an officer of the law," he said, "and I order you to give me that baby."

She hesitated for a moment, then handed over the child to Father Flanagan, who hurried out of the building. When he reached the German-American Home, he gave the baby to the nuns. Sometime later, he was able to place the baby with a local family.[468]

There were other stories that seemed to be right out of penny dreadfuls, with characters to match. Father Flanagan would recount them to others or write about them later.

"Take the two who came to the Home following their attempt to invade Mexico. These lads had resolved to capture the notorious bandit (Pancho) Villa... the pair, fourteen and fifteen years old, had actually organized a band of some twenty-five youngsters from their town on the banks of the Rio Grande. They had, a little at a time, stolen food, guns, and ammunition from their families and neighbors and from hardware stores. All the supplies were cached under a livery stable. But other activities of the boys had riled the police... so the boys decided they dared not delay their 'invasion' any longer.

"When twilight came to the banks of the river, they 'borrowed' a motor-boat which they renamed *The Buzzard*. Under cover of darkness, they loaded their supplies. The night was clear and cold as twenty-five boys crowded on board and finally, in the deep early morning, the would-be conquerors of Villa set sail.

"Half an hour later, a United States Customs boat drew near and hailed, upon which the two leaders of the 'invasion' shot full speed ahead.

"The fantastic chase lasted more than an hour. Sometimes, the Customs men's bullets sprinkled in the water around them. Finally the boys realized they were being driven out to the open waters of the Gulf and decided there was nothing to do but surrender. 'We agreed,' the two leaders said later, 'to run up the white flag.'

"Most of the children involved were given suspended sentences and allowed to go home in the custody of their parents. But the two leaders, against whom public sentiment ran highest, were headed for real punishment."

Reading about the case in the papers, and checking into the facts, Father Flanagan sent word to Texas that he would be willing to take the two boys into his Home.

"I have read," he told the authorities, "that you believe these two boys to be bad. I don't see that you can help them very much, if you think that. They are not bad; they are victims of a fallacy that deceives many older persons – the misguided belief that a good end can justify a bad means. Those lads felt like the knights of old – and Villa was the dragon they set out to destroy. And that is true whether they knew about knights and dragons or not."

The authorities replied in a telegram that they were glad indeed to send the two would-be generalissimos away. In fact, the wire added, the two boys were already on their way. During the months they remained at the Home, these boys were never in trouble, nor were they afterwards. With their own backgrounds re-established, they would, at length, be returned to their families.

It was this uncanny ability of Father Flanagan to see the deep-seated motives of these youngsters and articulate them in terms that anyone could understand that astonished educators and juvenile authorities. He seemed to be able to place himself inside the inner workings of the boy and identify with his character and the reasons behind his choices. What is even more remarkable is that while the priest never approved of the means the boys were using, he saw that most of the time, their goals were good; usually, the child was trying to extricate himself from some real or perceived evil.

"Some time ago, a fifteen-year-old boy was taken into the Home. His parents were dead and his only living sisters, to whom he was nothing except for the money he could earn… nearly worked the child to death," Father Flanagan would recall. "He was a timid shadow when he came, but he soon brightened up under the influences of congenial surroundings. One day he saw one of his sisters come through the gate, on a visit to the Home. When we went to look for him, he was nowhere to be found. His sister stayed a while, but finally had to go home without seeing him. It was late that night when we found him, five miles away. He had run as far and as fast as he could go, because he was afraid she would take him away from us."

Building a Better Boy

Most of the boys were behind in their schoolwork, and the first order of business always was to give each one the individual attention that was necessary to help him succeed in school. Teacher volunteers were brought in for the summer, and the Mother Superior of the Notre Dame Sisters[469] sent two extra nuns to help with the work. Father Flanagan's niece, Lenore Norton,[470] who had just graduated from St. Mary's Academy, also helped with the summer school program.[471]

With his own school, and with the help of the Mother Superior and a number of well-trained teachers, Father Flanagan put his education program on a solid footing, so that in the fall, each boy could begin classes at his grade level. With a special grant from one of the patrons of the Home, the priest established a Manual Training program,[472] as a supplement to the Home's scholastic program. He began to see that most of his boys would not go on to college and needed to develop practical employment skills that would prepare them for a variety of trades in the labor market.

In this, Father Flanagan was not just trying to solve the social problem of boy gangs and homeless boys in the streets. Instead, he was inaugurating a huge educational complex, comprising a home, school, sports, workshops, music and the arts, song, dance, films, drama, and the presence of those who excelled in all of these activities as models of what his boys might achieve. He wanted his boys to experience the best in all these fields, and soon his Home became a stopping-off place for the great and famous who were passing through the city. He had his secretary, Catherine Dannehy, watch the newspapers for musical, drama, and sports events that were scheduled in the city, and he contrived to obtain tickets to these events for groups of boys or those who excelled in any of these skills.[473]

Professional men in the city began to take notice of the priest and his work, and several offered their skills to assist him. Doctors and dentists[474] offered their services gratis. His friend, Henry Monsky, became his legal advisor. The priest became familiar with bankers, since he would often be knocking at their doors for extensions on loans. The St. Vincent de Paul Society, headed by his close friend and confidante, Leo Hoffman, brought its services to his aid in countless ways.

To develop the talents of his boys, Father Flanagan also brought in coaches, musicians, actors, entertainers, and tutors, letting the boys' imaginations run wild. Soon there were musical performances by the boys, intense competitive sports, boxing matches, comedy routines, sing-alongs, and story-telling. There were boy singers, boy musicians,[475] boy actors, and boy orators.[476] The huge hall on the first floor of the Home became the recreation center where performances occurred. Baseball became the chief competitive sport and pick-up teams from the Home began challenging teams from local schools. As the boys' names and faces began to appear in the *Boys' Home Journal*, Father Flanagan was thinking of other ways to share the treasures he had with the outside world.

Support for the Home came in drips and drops: five dollars here, ten dollars there, each donation recorded in the *Journal* together with the name of the donor. Neighbors brought food, women's groups sponsored dances and card parties in the great hall of the Home, and his "Boy Savers Society" brought in a trickle of money from hundreds of members. Still, it wasn't enough, and the priest spent many a sleepless night wondering how he would pay for food, fuel, clothes, and the monthly rent. The donations would later be described this way: "Support still came chiefly from small gifts sent in (by) an increasing number of donors, augmented by sums earned through the sale of the *Boys' Home Journal*. Some of the clothing came in gift boxes, invariably second-hand, repaired on the spot by the Mothers' Guild. Much of the food was donated by local trades-people, as were shoes and shirts. A department store would send out several gross of shirts."[477]

Money was always tight. The war in Europe raged on and no one knew how long it would last. The Home's supply of coal was low and might not last through the upcoming winter. As the number of boys grew, so did the need for clothes and new shoes, to say nothing of winter coats and boots. The needs were endless and Father Flanagan wrote in desperation to his benefactors: "In addition to the demands that the war makes on us, we have other great responsibilities, which we must not overlook or neglect... We have cared for some three hundred boys since the Home opened last December, and the influence and moral training which these boys have received have put a ray of hope into their neglected little souls, and many of them today are out doing their part and are making good... I know, kind reader, if you were to know our needs and the scanty means we have to care for them, you would assist us. We will leave the matter to your judgment to decide what you will do to help us in caring for these 'lads that nobody wants.'"[478]

He would soon find out that not everyone in Omaha considered his work in that positive light, and that many, including perfectly decent citizens, thought of his Home as a refuge for mini-criminals and street hoodlums who were probably a danger to the neighborhood and would be better off in reform schools. But the boys kept coming. Anytime of the day or night, they would walk up the street from the railroad cars they had been riding or from cars that had picked them up on a street or highway. One arrived from Iowa with a tag around his neck that read, "Father Flanagan – Omaha."[479] And it was not unusual for the priest to receive a phone call with the message, "Bus depot calling... we have a boy for you."

Some of these boys had been in serious trouble with the law. Others were destitute orphans. Neither creed nor race had any bearing on whether a boy was admitted, and all were treated equally in the Home. There were bitter critics of such tolerance. A few referred to it as Father Flanagan's "Reform School" for young thieves. Others criticized the policy of white, Chinese, and Negro[480] boys living together without segregation.

"If God intended people to be all the same," one Omaha politician demanded, "why did he make them of different colors?"

"And could you tell me – what is the color of the soul?" was Father Flanagan's reply.

White and yellow and brown, they kept on coming, some without training or education of any kind.[481] Their stories were varied and different. From every city and state in the country, from every race, religion, and ethnic background, each one a sad story of rejection, abuse, or neglect, and each child, it seemed, was a gem to be polished. Most boys could not believe they were coming to a Home where they would be fed, clothed, cared for, and cherished. The experiences of their young lives had embittered some of them, and it took weeks and months for them to realize they had found a real home.

Father Flanagan met one boy who stepped off the train at Omaha's Union Station barefoot. The priest asked, "What did you do with your shoes, son?"

"Shoes?" the boy replied. "I never got any shoes."

On the way to the Home, Father Flanagan stopped at a shoe store and bought the boy a sturdy pair of shoes. The priest helped the boy lace his new shoes and he was delighted with the gift. But trouble started when he tried to walk in them. He hopped, he jumped, he stumbled, but the boy simply did not know how to walk with shoes on. With passersby on the street stopping and staring, Father Flanagan led the boy the several blocks it took to reach the Home.[482]

When Father Flanagan first moved his boys to the German-American Home, the building was the temporary place of worship for St. Rose's Parish, established in May 1918. The church's Czech pastor, Father Francis B. Tomanek, was living in the building. The pastor continued his residence after Father Flanagan and his boys arrived, and continued to say Mass each Sunday for parishioners in a large auditorium-size hall that had been converted into a church. This was convenient for the new occupants since it gave the Home a ready-made chapel. Later in the year, when Father Tomanek became ill and was confined to a hospital, Father Flanagan took over the parish duties,[483] paid off the parish debt, and left the parish in sound financial condition for the next priest.[484]

Desperate Times

With the Home desperately short of money and more boys arriving, there seemed to be a shortage of everything. The rent had to be paid each month as well as the coal bill, and Father Flanagan, knowing that his *Boys' Home Journal* reached the homes of the rich and the poor of the city, as well as the offices of businesses that advertised in the publication, sat down and wrote a begging letter in 1918, one of many that would be written over the years. It was simply entitled, "Our Needs:"[485]

"The beautiful Fall weather is upon us, and the glorious September sun with its ruddy morning light, suffusing nature with a scarlet cloak, reminds us of the approach of a long, cold winter. We like the sunshine and its flowers, and our boys love to play in these days of sunshine, bare-footed and thinly clad for greater comfort. But the coming of winter weather makes us feel sad, not that we do not love the brisk, cold days, with their balmy air and the beautiful white garment that envelopes nature, and I am sure our boys long for the time when they may coast 'the long, long trail' leading down into the woods, but other thoughts fill the minds of those who have to supply the needs of those boys during the long, cold winter.

"We are reminded of the fact that our Home must be heated, and that coal is expensive. This is an extra expense. Through a great deal of saving, we have been able to buy enough coal to last probably two months. After that is gone, only God can tell when or how we can get the rest. Our boys will need warm clothes and good shoes. We have about forty boys at the Home, and out of that number, only about ten are provided for, by their parents. The others we must care for, and it is no small item to buy shoes and clothes for so great a number, and besides, buy groceries and meat.

"We have cared for some three hundred boys since the Home was opened last December, and the influence and moral training which these boys have received have put a ray of hope into their neglected little souls…. Our Home is surely in need. We are striving our best to get one hundred cents out of every dollar. These dollars are not spent for salaries, but for groceries, meat, clothes, shoes, light, rent, and coal, etc…. We would be most pleased to receive second-hand clothes and shoes, which we will be glad to repair, that our boys will be kept warm during the cold winter."

In the same month this appeal was written, the country and the world was struck by the second wave of the Spanish flu epidemic of 1918.[486] Hospitals were filled and gatherings of people were forbidden because of the danger of spreading the disease. Doctors and nurses were in short supply, and the Nebraska State Board of Health ordered the closings of all public meeting places, all schools, all churches, and all theaters.

Father Flanagan's Boys' Home, too, was struck by the epidemic, and twenty boys were down with the disease, five of them close to death from pneumonia. The Home was turned into a hospital, attended by Dr. J.R. Dwyer and the Notre Dame Sisters.[487] One boy, Joseph Guerin, died from pneumonia,[488] the first death in this small community. He was the oldest boy in the Home and something of an older brother to the rest of the boys. Six of the boys acted as pallbearers. It was a sad day for the family of youngsters.

It was here that Father Flanagan began to draw on his experience as an accountant at the marketing offices of the Cudahy Packing Company. His job there, first as an 18-year-old inexperienced clerk, and then as the chief accountant, opened to him the world of business and marketing and the skills that were necessary to market a product. He had thought those years were simply lost to him, but as the boys grew in number and his financial resources shrank, he reached back to them to bring his work for boys to the attention of the public.

His first opportunity came in June 1919, when he had been at the German-American Home for just one year. The war was over and people were beginning to gather in parks and stadiums for recreation, sports, and just a good time. He planned a public picnic day at a renovated park in the Benson section in the north part of the city. Krug Park had amusements, rides, an ice cream parlor, a roller coaster, a dance pavilion, and even a hot air balloon. The picnic would be open to the public and it would be Father Flanagan's first chance to show off his boys.[489]

The outing was widely publicized in the local newspapers and in letters to the patrons of the Home, as well to every Catholic parish in the city. The entrance of the boys to the park was later described this way:

"The boys of the Home, accompanied by some twenty-five others who were formerly at the home, and who had been invited by Father Flanagan to be his guests for the day, started from the Home for the park at 9 a.m. in a procession of automobiles, generously provided for the occasion by a number of prominent citizens, and in this manner journeyed through the business section of the city to the park.

"Dressed in neat, light-colored shirt waists or blouses and knickerbockers, every pair of shoes gleaming like polished steel or white as chalk could make them, heads covered with fanciful military style chapeau, every little chap looked and acted his best, and as they progressed through the streets of Omaha were the recipients of as much attention and applause as is usually given to a popular military parade."[490]

Father Flanagan was really proud of his boys on their first official public outing. They had their pictures taken by the admiring crowd, and then were let loose to roam the park and take advantage of the rides and other attractions. Then, in the priest's own words: "Ladies from all sections of Omaha had assembled by streetcar and auto, each laden with baskets and packages of good things to eat… the finest coffee was made and served on the grounds, as well as delicious lemonade, ice cold ginger ale, pop, root beer, etc. as well as oranges, candies, fancy cakes and cookies and ice cream for the boys."[491]

It was an all-day affair, with games, sport events, races of every kind, and prizes for all the winners. And, there was an added attraction, which Father Flanagan later described: "The Columbia Girls' Club, Joan of Arc, and St. John's Sodality young ladies each attended the picnic in a body, and also generously contributed to furnishing lunches for the boys…. At the close of the evening sports,[492] the boys were gathered up and conveyed back to the Home in the manner in which they had come, a tired but happy bunch, having had one of the most enjoyable outings of their young lives."[493]

The outing was the crowning achievement of the priest's first year at the new Home, binding the boys together in something resembling family ties. Watching his boys in their daily activities, the pure fun of their Krug Park outing, the eagerness with which they welcomed new boys, and their genuine pride in the Home made him realize that he had an untapped resource for spreading the news of his work throughout the city right in front of him.

His *Boys' Home Journal* by this time had a wide circulation, chronicling the life of the Home and the activities of the boys, not only in reports, articles, and biographies of the young residents (sometimes authored by the boys themselves), but also in photos by a master photographer, Louis R. Bostwick, whom Father Flanagan had met when the Home was on 25th and Dodge.[494] Father Flanagan had hired Bostwick to take a photo of the Byron Reed Home before the boys occupied it. Now he had hired him to chronicle the lives of the boys and the Home's activities in photos that could appear in the *Boys' Home Journal* as well as in local newspapers.

Father Flanagan was not unfamiliar with the photographs of Jacob Riis in his *How the Other Half Lives*,[495] with its graphic photos of life in the slums of New York at the turn of the century, and he knew that a picture often speaks louder than words.[496] Bostwick's photos were remarkable in telling the story of the homeless boy, capturing the charm and innocence of the boys themselves,[497] and providing a photographic calendar of the Home's life and activities.[498]

Three years later, when Father Flanagan penned the first edition of *The Romance of the Homeless Boy*, it was Bostwick's photos that captured the attention of the public and splashed the story of this lost generation of American children in newspapers all over the country. It brought Father Flanagan to the attention of others in the field of juvenile justice, like Judge Ben Lindsey[499] of Denver, and a host of concerned authorities throughout the United States.

With the success of the outing at Krug Park, Father Flanagan began appearing with his boys at public events like parades, holiday celebrations, ethnic festivals, and parish activities, with the boys dressed in festive and seasonal outfits. His boys were so popular with the people on the streets that he realized the boys themselves were the best publicity for the Home.[500]

He also began to see his *Boys' Home Journal* as the chief tool of public relations for the Home as well as a tool of teaching, a pedagogical instrument to instruct his boys in everything from good manners to habits of the heart. He knew the boys read the *Journal*, passed it among themselves, contributed articles for its wide readership, and sometimes saw themselves portrayed in its pages.

Drawing upon memories of his own childhood, Father Flanagan held a regular "story hour" for the boys, retelling the stories he heard from his own father while in the fields tending sheep or cattle, or around one of the fireplaces in the Leabeg house. He explained to the boys how these stories had fired his own imagination, together with the stories of Dickens, Scott, and Macauley when he was older. Storytelling, he knew, was the oldest form of teaching, in almost every culture. In Ireland, it was the tradition of the Seanachai,[501] the itinerant story-teller, who passed on the religious and cultural heritage of the Irish people, as well as the filid, the writer who preserved the memories, the music, the myths, and the legends that were passed on from one generation to the next.

With rare insight and foresight, Father Flanagan developed a program of elocution[502] for the boys, with results that pleased and surprised him. Some of them, like Master Jack O'Connor,[503] the boy actor, developed rare acting skills. Other boys took to public speaking with an ease, alacrity, and eloquence that made him realize that his boys had hidden talents that could be put to good use.

The Long Road to Overlook Farm

In April 1919, when he and his boys had been at the German-American Home less than a year, it was clear to Father Flanagan that the Home was really too small for his needs, as the number of boys continued to multiply and its capacity was stretched to its limits. He could see that his army of boys was eager for work and play, some of them walking and lounging around in groups, or just tramping in pairs, talking, restless in the periods between tending to the gardens and an occasional baseball game. "One year's experience," he wrote, "has shown that (this place) is far too limited in its resources and accommodations to meet the ever-growing needs of this institution, and even now, with some seventy boys at the Home, it is filled to about capacity."[504]

As the priest began thinking of other solutions for housing his family of boys, he hit upon the idea of finding a farm where the boys could work and where there would be plenty of room for expansion. He talked over his idea with the older boys and sounded out his friends and associates who had followed him thus far. He often drove his Model T Ford, alone or in the company of Leo Hoffman or some other member of the St. Vincent de Paul Society, out to the edge of the city, looking for suitable sites. He also consulted bankers and real estate agents who knew land values and could tell him the cost of what he was looking for. This is how he described it in the *Boys' Home Journal*:

"The only practical solution to the housing problem therefore seems to be that of securing a moderately sized farm, within a short distance from Omaha, upon which could be erected suitable buildings to be developed as needed, and at this farm could be conducted both mental and manual training for these boys."[505]

Father Flanagan and his advisors came up with a figure for what a suitable farm might cost. It was a figure way beyond his current means, but something to be hoped and asked for. "To secure such a farm and the necessary buildings and equipment would require an outlay of approximately $75,000," the priest later wrote. "At first glance this seems like a large sum of money, but if one person in a hundred of the populations of Nebraska and Iowa contributed one dollar each, the amount would be fully subscribed."[506]

It seemed like an impossible dream. But he had tackled such dreams before and so he went looking for a piece of property that he and his boys could call their own.

His problem was there were too many boys and too little money. Lengthy articles began to appear in local newspapers about his boys and the Home,[507] with reporters coming to interview him or one of his staff. Catherine Dannehy was busy writing letters to donors, asking for donations or thanking those who sent money or gifts,[508] the names and amounts appearing in the pages of the *Journal*. Father Flanagan also busied himself with what he considered to be important public relation activities: writing descriptive articles about the boys for the *Journal*,[509] accepting new boys from the courts or from homes where they were not receiving proper care,[510] arranging for sports activities,[511] directing the planting and harvesting of fruits and vegetables,[512] and scheduling entertainment for his boys, either at the Home[513] or at local church festivals.[514]

But in spite of these massive concerns and the constant worry about paying the bills, he kept the idea for the farm uppermost in his mind, in the pages of the *Journal*, and in his conversations with the professional men of the city.

In June 1919, Father Flanagan was appointed a member of the Public Welfare Board of Omaha.[515] He was now a well-known part of the city's life, and his work and experience with helping boys began to earn him national recognition. Also in that month, he was invited to address the National Catholic Hospital Association in Chicago to speak specifically about his success with homeless boys.[516]

Two months later, on August 5, 1919, he achieved a quiet milestone of his own, becoming a citizen of the United States of America. He was now officially an American and was determined to do everything he could to help the children of his adopted country.[517]

His search for a new site for the Home continued through the summer months, and in mid-August, after spending much time calculating facts and figures, he laid out in the *Journal* a plan for raising the needed funds. He asked for pledges from the little-known as well as the famous, from the prosperous as well as the less endowed, from his high-salaried friends at banks and corporations to his neighbors next door. He had a long list of benefactors, from the lady in South Omaha who mended the boys' stockings to the Mullens and the Nashes, who sent large checks periodically when his funds were low. It was his heartfelt appeal to the hearts and pocketbooks of the city of Omaha: "How splendid and satisfying it must be to any one possessed of an abundance of this world's goods, to be able to have their intentions fulfilled with regard to any charity, while they are still in the flesh, and not to wait until after their death, or rely upon others or the intent of their legal will being carried out, as they would have it, after they have entered into eternal rest."[518]

His new plan was as innovative as it was necessary. He skillfully mentioned the names of persons of wealth who lived in other cities, who did not wait until their deaths to share their wealth for philanthropic causes, who "have chosen to perform their good works while they may have knowledge that their desires will be fulfilled in every respect, not leaving it to others to put their own interpretation upon the same."

Then he brought in the "big guns," as if to say: "There is something right here in your own backyard that needs your help and you are blind not to see it.

"It is the ardent desire of Father Flanagan, in fact, his life and purpose, to establish a real Home for his boys, and not to be dependent any longer than absolutely necessary upon rented quarters. As any business man can readily comprehend, the vagaries of the real estate market are many and uncertain, and a Home of this character, if it would develop its true purpose, must have above all, a permanent and abiding place – one that it can call its own."[519]

He spoke to his business and professional friends in their own language, laying down a master plan for exactly how much he needed and what he intended to do with the funds he was raising, and undoubtedly drawing upon his experience as an accountant, knowing that such plans were essential to the growth and prosperity of a company:

"With the object of raising the necessary money with which to purchase a plot of ground within easy reach of the heart of Omaha, though it may be in an accessible suburb of the city. To build thereon a suitable structure to combine all the essentials of an institution of this character, such as dormitories, classrooms, workshops or rooms for manual training, dining hall, and chapel, $85,000 to $100,000 is necessary.

"To start this fund, the following table has been devised:

Benefactors are Asked to Pledge

1	$10,000	$10,000
3	5,000	15,000
5	2,000	10,000
10	1,000	10,000
20	500	10,000
25	200	5,000
50	100	5,000
100	50	5,000
200	25	5,000
500	10	5,000
1000	5	5,000

For a total of $85,000"[520]

Father Flanagan had done his homework and he had now taken the task of providing for his boys into his own hands. Other plans would arise as the Home grew and the need for more funds became more desperate.

But his appeal fell on deaf ears as other events captured the public's attention. Race riots had hit the city in the wake of ethnic tensions and ethnic violence, and in September, an African-American man, William Brown, was falsely accused of attacking a white woman. Brown was dragged out of the jail and lynched, and his body was burned by an angry crowd outside the courthouse in downtown Omaha.[521] There was also wide city discontent with the political bossism of Tom Dennison,[522] and the previous corrupt administration of his puppet mayor, James (Cowboy Jim) Dahlman. Brothels and gambling houses were common in the city, especially in the Third Ward in downtown Omaha controlled by the Dennison machine.[523] This was not the healthiest moral atmosphere for a Boys' Home, and Father Flanagan's motivation for moving the Home to the country quickly extended beyond just country air and farm gardening.[524]

The immediate response to his appeal was disheartening: one subscription for $150, two subscriptions of $100 each, one donation of $20, two for $10, and one for $2.[525] Nothing really came of the appeal and so no land was acquired. The priest realized he had to offer the public something concrete, and so his search for a farm site continued.

Father Flanagan was able to show his sense of humor at the failure of his appeal, as well as his knowledge of the tricks and vagaries of the money market, in his next editorial of the *Journal*, again drawing upon his experience as an accountant at the Cudahy Packing Company ten years before: "The casual reader of the more or less prosaic pages of this periodical may have noticed that we made a plea for financial assistance in our August issue, and even burned the midnight oil in working out an equitable plan for financial assistance, to suit, as we thought, all purses, fat and lean – but maybe it's the recent hot spell, or absence from home – at any rate, the building fund has NOT increased by leaps and bounds.

"Now if we were financiers such as the late George Fitch[526] used to tell about, we might rapidly increase our building fund, either in hot or cold weather, after the following manner, which George related,[527] was about the way the average financier turned the trick.

"If a financier had a dollar and needed two, he would use the dollar as a first payment on a $10 bill, and would bond the bill for a $20 gold piece and would charge $5 for doing this. Then he would sell the option on the $20 gold piece at $17, for one dollar down, to forty-five people, and then would dispose of half an interest in the entire transaction for $150, two dollars down, and the rest payable in short-term notes."[528]

(The "hot spell" could have referred to the weather, but it also could have been a not-too-subtle reminder of the violence mentioned earlier that had broken out in the city that very month, a city-wide riot that ended in the murder of William Brown, and the near-lynching of the newly-elected mayor who tried to stop the violence. It was a sad commentary on the moral climate of the city.[529])

This little editorial, entitled "If We Were Financiers,"[530] must have surprised and unsettled Father Flanagan's friends in the financial and professional community, who realized they were dealing with a sharp business mind, someone who was savvy in worldly matters and with the trade secrets of the financial community. It is Father Flanagan at his best: caustic, witty, and bold, with a pen dripping with satire and irony.

His success in this kind of journalistic banter was born out by the fact that in the next issue of the *Journal*, he announced the purchase of the farmland he was looking for at a price he could not turn down, even though he had to borrow money to cover the cost.

It seems that friends had come to his rescue and lent him money to buy twenty acres north of the city, in the Florence area of Omaha. It was called Seven Oaks Farm and it cost $14,000.[531] Of that, friends had provided $2,000; Father Flanagan had borrowed the remaining $12,000, putting himself deeply in debt. Perhaps the insurance policy he had bought from Catherine Dannehy was part of the collateral for the loan, or perhaps a banker was willing to advance him the money on the strength of his fundraising efforts. Whatever the reasons, the farm was purchased, and he immediately had an architect draw up plans for building on the site.

"Our newly acquired farm has given us new hope and greater ambitions; the farm, however, is not ours yet," he later wrote. "We borrowed almost all the money to pay for it, and our indebtedness is $12,000. If we had this debt off our mind, we could begin figuring on our building.... Our new Home should have a capacity of one hundred fifty boys, and were it not owing to our present limited quarters, we would have that number in our Home now."[532]

In high spirits over the acquisition, Father Flanagan sent out word to subscribers, benefactors, and a long list of contributors that he had almost crossed the Rubicon. He had his own piece of land and he could make plans for the future. First, a building to house at least one hundred fifty boys and then barns and outbuildings where they could learn trades and practical skills. Then gardens and fields of wheat and corn, and livestock, making the Home self-sufficient and the boys entrepreneurs in their own right. There would be baseball, football, basketball, and boxing teams, with gymnasiums and fields for play, and printing presses and barber shops where special skills could be learned, with a choir and a band and everything else that a town should have.

He made himself familiar with demographic studies, court documents, and sociological reports on the youth problem in towns and cities, both far and near, and he came to one solid conclusion: He needed a town of his own, where all boys, homeless or in trouble, could come, something that existed solely for the needs of boys, the boys that nobody wanted, the seed for a grand and glorious future.

The lease for the German-American Home was for two years and would expire in December 1919. Father Flanagan had already received word from the owners that the lease would not be renewed and the Home would have to be vacated. In desperation, Father Flanagan made a lengthy plea in the December issue of the *Journal* for funds that would allow him to begin building on the Florence property. "Our little farm in Florence has a most beautiful site, and the only drawback now is sufficient funds to justify the building of a Home."[533] (December also marked the second anniversary of the founding of the first Home on 25th and Dodge.)

In December, Father Flanagan also lost his devoted secretary, Catherine Dannehy, who was expecting her first child.[534] She had organized his office for him, started the record-keeping he so desperately needed, and carried on his vast correspondence.[535] (She would return from time to time, both to the German-American Home and when the Home moved to Overlook Farm. She would later recall her eventual return to his employment: "Then one night in 1930 I heard a knock on the door and there he was again. He asked me if I could come back to work. I went back and stayed there" until he died in 1948.[536])

In the fall of 1919, Father Flanagan had asked an architect to put pen to paper, and the drawing of the first proposed building for the new site appeared on the front cover of the December issue of the *Boys' Home Journal*. It was a huge structure, three stories high with a full basement, larger and more spacious than his Workingmen's Hotel on 13th and Capitol. The drawing was surrounded by sketched branches of holly leaves, as if to hint that this would be the Christmas present he and his boys were hoping for.

But again, the support did not come, and the priest also suddenly realized that the twenty-acre Seven Oaks Farm was too small to sustain a population of one hundred fifty boys. Subsequently, in early 1920, he sold the farm to the Notre Dame Sisters for $14,000, the price he had paid for it.[537] With the money from that sale, he made a down payment on a larger tract of land in Florence known as Forty Acres.[538] He moved the cows and the chickens and other livestock from the German-American Home to the Florence property, hired two men to care for the farm, and later sent some of the boys by streetcar to help the men with the chores. There were fruit trees on the property and room for gardens, and so that spring and summer, the Home had a regular supply of fruits and vegetables.[539] Part of his dream was realized; he had a farm for his boys.[540]

A month before acquiring Forty Acres, Father Flanagan had received the notice that the lease for the German-American Home would not be renewed and the building would have to be vacated in February 1920. This brought about a crisis for his small community; there was no place for him and his boys to go. In desperation, he spoke to Archbishop Jeremiah Harty. In the February issue of the *Boys' Home Journal*, on the second page, appeared a photo of the Archbishop in his full episcopal robes, with an appeal from him for funds to build a new Home for the boys.

"Two years ago," Archbishop Harty wrote, "the Reverend Edward J. Flanagan placed before me a project for a Boys' Home. I approved of the plan. It began by receiving into a rented house 8 boys committed to his care by the Juvenile Court, because they were homeless and thought to be incorrigible.

"But Omaha was growing fast and with its growth grew the problem of caring for more neglected boys. Father Flanagan opened his door to other waifs and then to others until he housed and fed one hundred of them. In his good work he made no distinction of race or color or religion. They were boys whom nobody wanted except Father Flanagan. They were boys who, if allowed to drift along, would likely become a menace to society. Yet being boys, they would, if properly trained, develop into good men and safe citizens. Indeed, under Father Flanagan's guidance and the care of the ladies known in religion as the Sisters of Our Lady, many of these boys have been placed in families, where they are 'making good.'

"At present the Father Flanagan's Boys' Home is the rented building at 4026 South Thirteenth Street. The owners of the property have given notice to Father Flanagan that he and his boys must vacate the premises by June first. Hence he must build a house for them; he therefore appeals to the public for funds to build and to carry on his work in which all citizens should take an efficacious interest, if they desire to live in a better Omaha."[541]

Opposite the Archbishop's appeal was Father Flanagan's "levels of giving" plan for raising the money: Burses, $5,000 each; Founders, $1,000 each; Honorary Members, $100 each, and Associate Members, $50 each.

In the same issue was a letter from Omaha Mayor Edward P. Smith,[542] together with a picture of the first major donor to the boys' new Home, Mrs. E.W. Nash,[543] who opened the building campaign with a gift of $10,000. Within weeks, Father Flanagan had received a second major gift from Mrs. Ben Gallagher,[544] who had visited the Home several weeks before and spent an afternoon with the boys. Both of these donors were widows of two business pioneers of Omaha, Edward W. Nash and Benjamin Gallagher, respectively.

These two gifts became the talk of the business community and a delegation of businessmen decided to visit the Home.[545] Father Flanagan's caustic and witty editorial in the *Boys' Home Journal* after the failure of his first appeal showed his familiarity with the inner workings of the business community, as well as his cynicism about those who held the purse strings of rich corporations.[546] He had hinted that greed was the motor and motivation of business practices, and that the welfare and good of the Omaha community played no part in business practices. The city was already saddled with a corrupt political machine that had lost favor, as well as the mayoral election, and the new mayor, Edward P. Smith, now ruled the city.[547]

As a result, the major representatives of the commercial and business world of Omaha were now making tracks to Father Flanagan's Boys' Home, and the priest's description of their visit in a later *Journal* editorial was almost gleeful:

"Some weeks ago, a few of Omaha's businessmen expressed a desire to come down and see our boys. These few brought with them others, and the result was that our boys had a most enjoyable evening taking dinner side by side with great men. The contrast between those eighty boys and our guests on that evening was indeed a revelation of the progressive spirit of our times. These men seemed to enjoy themselves in our poor quarters… as if they were seated in a most gorgeous dining room at some great banquet in company with other great and illustrious men. They listened with as much deference and respect… to the simple stories of the boy's life, his years of neglect, and his appeal for a chance in life with other boys, all told by the boys themselves, as if they were an audience to some great silver-tongued orators….

"A visit to the Home made out of these men enthusiasts for the cause of the neglected boy. They feel that, as men better circumstanced, it is their conscientious duty to cooperate in every way towards this worthy work, and they pledged their support, financial and moral, in building a much-needed and permanent Home for these boys."[548]

But Father Flanagan had not lost his dismay at the uninhibited lust for money and power among the well-to-do, and this dismay got the better of him as the expiration of his lease on the German-American Home got closer and closer.

"Wealth to most people is a dangerous enemy," he wrote in the editorial. "Without being conscious of its insidious influence, they permit it to glorify them in the scarlet cloak of pompous worldliness, of an exaggerated and, oftentimes, domineering influence, using that power of money which a mere accident may have invested them in, to the detriment of the cause of God's chosen ones – the poor and the suffering. Such people lack the light of religion to reveal to them their great responsibilities, and fall short of their greatest stewardship."[549]

Dickens could not have expressed it better, and Father Flanagan was raising the rallying cry in an Omaha bursting at the seams with widespread prosperity, political corruption, and racial violence, amid massive poverty and unbridled wealth. He had a promise of civic and financial support from prominent business-men of the city, but Father Flanagan knew that such support often was only in words or on paper, and came with admonitions about the mixture of races and creeds in his Home or the fact that many of his boys were from the courts. His editorial ended with remarks aimed specifically at his recent visitors:

"Thank God there are such people in the world as Mrs. Nash, who will foster with more than her advice such noble work of Christian Charity."

Fortunately, the response from the businessmen was more than just advice. Letters of support from the heads of local corporations began to appear in the *Boys' Home Journal*,[550] and its pages began to fill with new ads from local busi-nesses, expanding the size of the publication from sixteen pages to twenty-eight. Payment for these ads was a welcome source of income for the Home.

With something of wit, something of humor, and something of brazen audacity, Father Flanagan had swayed others into his way of thinking and turned their world upside-down, with an eloquent appeal to their own better interests. The major companies of the city not only displayed ads in his *Journal*, but also took up his challenge to their investment practices, that an investment in the future of these homeless boys would bring greater benefits to the city of Omaha than any other investment.[551] He was not appealing to their charitable instincts, or what he called the *"Oliver Twist* appeal"; instead, he was talking about hard cash and the return on hard cash. This began to make sense to a number of hard-headed businessmen who were captivated by his logic and the way he dismantled, before their very eyes, the lust for gold that was the secret engine of their financial enterprises.

Father Flanagan could see heroism in the little boy off the streets and in the girl selling tickets at the movie theater. But what set him apart was his ability to see heroism in men immersed in the pursuit of wealth and to use their own logic and their own self-interest to enlist them in a nobler cause, making them heroes in spite of themselves.

The initial gifts of Mrs. Nash and Mrs. Gallagher, and the support of the business community of Omaha, triggered a flood of donations. What had been $1 and $5 gifts became gifts of $10, $25, and $50, and in some cases, even $100 and $1,000. News was getting around about the heroism of this young priest, less than ten years out of the seminary, sleeping on a castoff iron frame bed, moving in the most dangerous parts of town to rescue the homeless,[552] welcoming the unwanted and the rejected children of the city, his name on the lips of bums, vagrants, and tramps in every hobo jungle across the country. His *Boys' Home Journal* was reaching thousands, with detailed stories of his boys and their unique Home, and juvenile courts from Baltimore to Seattle were familiar with his name.

Further support came from the Omaha Chamber of Commerce, which recognized his unique contribution to the city: "Our investigation shows that the institution is a very worthy one and is doing great work in this city and should be supported by the citizens of Omaha."[553]

There were success stories. Some boys returned to their parents when their home situation improved, since Father Flanagan was very reluctant to separate a boy from his family.[554] Some boys who showed an aptitude for farming or some other skill were placed in the care of a farm family or a family where a boy's skills could be used and developed.[555] Some of the older boys who showed an aptitude for higher studies entered colleges.[556] Some boys were adopted by families that were willing to provide a home for them.

With the launch of the building campaign to re-establish and enlarge the Home on a tract of land in North Omaha, and with the growing support of the business community,[557] Father Flanagan wrote yet another editorial for his *Journal*, outlining in great detail the reason for the fund drive and the need it would be meeting. It was the Magna Carta of his work, and was addressed to every subscriber of the *Journal*, to the businessmen who filled the publication with ads, and to the public who bought it from his "newsies" on street corners or at the door of local churches. Entitled simply "Building Fund," the editorial appeared beside a photo of one his boys dressed in suit, white collar, and tie, with a bowler hat in his hand.

"Great interest is being manifested in the building of a much needed Home for our poor boys. Most encouraging reports on the progress being made toward that end are coming to us every day. We feel certain that the good friends of this Home will see to it that, as soon as the final plans are completed, a spontaneous response will result.

"Father Flanagan's Boys' Home is filling a great need in the middle western country. It stands alone as an institution which cares exclusively for the homeless and neglected boy. God alone knows of the hundreds and hundreds of such boys, who, without the influence of such a Home, would become a menace to society and a blot on our citizenship. It will be a blessing for society that such a Home be provided to them to make for better citizenship. That this be efficiently accomplished, cooperation is needed. We who are engaged in the work can only give ourselves to it. Money we have not, but with the financial support of all those who see the real good being accomplished, the great object can be easily obtained.

"Let us not forget the policy of the Home. Every boy who is homeless, or through neglect, has wayward tendencies, and is in need of care and supervision, is welcome at our Home. Religion, nationality, or even color[558] are never brought into question, neither is there any interference on the part of those directly in care of the boys, in matters of religion. The broad policy of attending to the boy's needs, giving him an education, teaching him the great meaning and responsibility of patriotism, are matters that are of vital importance to such boys, whose minds, oftentimes through neglect, have become deranged and must be trained along the channels of right thinking and right doing, that they become good and useful members of society.

"Our Home in the past two years has been taxed to over-crowding, and still we are unable to care for all the indigent boys. Had we a Home that could shelter at least two hundred boys, we would then be in a position to refuse no worthy case. With our contemplated project, this will become possible. You, good friends, will undoubtedly answer the call of these boys at this time. They need a Home just as other boys, and they ask you to help with your money to build this Home for them. Will you do this most needed act of charity? The boys need this Home now, not a year from now, and that they may have it, they need your money. Please do not put it off; it is easy to forget when men are busy with so many things. God's blessings will be a sufficient recompense for what you may do in this hour of need, and the consciousness of having helped a poor boy who was down, to a higher and better life will surely be a great happiness to you.

"Will you, please, write that check today?"[559]

It was indeed a critical moment. Without the funds to proceed, he would have to close the Home and put the boys out on the street. He would have to turn away hundreds of boys on the brink of beginning a wasted life.[560] He would have to refuse boys from the courts and see most of them condemned to life in a reform school. He would soon be out on the street if the owners of the German-American building insisted on ending his lease. He needed more time, and began to think of other possibilities for raising funds and publicizing his work.

The first was to put his Home on a firm legal and corporate basis. Until then, it had been the private venture and work of one lone priest, with a variety of helpers, supporters, benefactors, and generous neighbors, with canonical authority from his ecclesiastical superiors. But he was solely responsible for the success or failure of the Home. He had in Henry Monsky a good friend, advisor, and legal counsel, and as he often declared, Monsky was his personal lawyer. They had both worked together with the courts to address the serious problem of homeless boys and juvenile crime in Omaha. So with Monsky's help, Father Flanagan had Articles of Corporation drafted and a Board of Directors[561] selected for "Father Flanagan's Boys' Home, Incorporated," putting into legal form, for the first time, his mission and the purpose of his work: "The object for which this corporation is organized shall be to equip, maintain, and conduct in the city of Omaha a home for indigent and wayward boys, to support and educate boys in said home, and to equip and prepare them to lead useful lives."[562]

It was a modest description of what would soon become a social and educational revolution.

A Second Chance

Fortunately, the owners of the German-American Home relented and renewed the lease for another year. But there still was not enough money to build on the Forty Acres property. Money was coming in, but not in large enough amounts to finance a new building. The architect's drawing of the building appeared in every issue of *Boys' Home Journal*, sometimes with a small boy standing in front of it with the caption: "The Greatest Need... Will His Dream Come True?" The building would cost $300,000. At the rate funds were arriving in response to appeals in the *Journal* and from small money-making events in parishes and in the city, it would take ten or fifteen years to generate the necessary funding. He and his boys did not have that kind of time.

Father Flanagan was using the money that was coming in to pay for the Forty Acres property, which had gardens, a few outbuildings, and fruit trees, and provided housing for the older boys who could work on the farm.[563] In the pages of the *Boys' Home Journal*, he kept the public up-to-date on the Home and the progress of the Building Fund. It was simply a time of waiting for money to come in and things to happen.

His boys were restless, asking when their new Home would be ready. To distract them, he outfitted them in holiday dress[564] and accompanied them to festivals and fairs and civic holidays,[565] or organized marble tournaments, boxing matches, and intramural games.

"After a long and dreary winter of a shut-in monotony as a protection against the cold, snow, and rain, our boys are almost beside themselves with joy at the coming of the beautiful sun shining into our poor quarters to cheer us all with a new hope," the priest wrote. "For some time now, they have been enjoying the outdoor exercise, playing marbles, practicing on the small terrace for the ball team, and romping around on the young green grass....

"Our much discussed Farm Home is still not a reality and is the general topic of conversation among the bigger boys, who have had the privilege of visiting the Farm and working there on Saturdays. They speak in glowing terms of the place to the others, and are constantly asking: 'When do we start the New Home, Father?' Little do they know of the difficulties and disappointments that are met with every day in connection with this matter, and how difficult it is to interest men of wealth to this project. Money is the first essential and, that we may build to care for our present needs, almost Two Hundred Thousand Dollars are needed. Fifty Thousand have already been subscribed and our farm is now, thank God, and thanks to our benefactors, out of debt."[566]

Even in this time of uncertainty, there was a certain security. Father Flanagan was out of debt, he could depend on a devoted and well-trained staff, and he had a house full of talented boys who wanted to do something. But he knew he had to make his work better known throughout Nebraska and the surrounding states. So he decided to begin a fund-raising tour through Nebraska and Iowa, giving talks in each town and bringing some of the boys with him.[567] It was the beginning of what became known as "Father Flanagan's Circus." But it was not a circus of clowns, trapeze artists, and wild animals. It was a circus of talented young actors, musicians, dancers, comedians, singers, and acrobats, all boys from the Home. It started modestly with five carefully selected boys,[568] but soon became an entire traveling troupe that resembled a miniature carnival.

It was a time and an opportunity for Father Flanagan to share the astonishing results of his work with a wider audience through entertainment.

One of the first groups he had organized in the Home was the Boys' Home Choristers, who sang not only at the Home but in public performances as well. With donated musical instruments, some of the boys also formed a small band. At first, they just entertained the Home's other residents but later began to play in public parades and civic holidays. The Home's "Boy Actor," Master Jack Connor, the hit of the Krug Park outing, entertained at the Home and at other festivities, appearing in the pages of the *Journal* as something of a celebrity.

Ahead of the tour, letters, posters, and flyers were sent to a number of towns in Iowa and Nebraska with information that donations for the Home would be accepted at every performance. Father Flanagan was sure he had something worthy of the Schubert and Orpheum vaudeville circuits.

The idea for this traveling show had come from a visitor to the Home two years after it had moved to the German-American building. The visitor was Dan Desdunes, a native of New Orleans who had come to Omaha in 1904 and been hired by the Omaha Chamber of Commerce to organize and train an official band of musicians to play at civic occasions. Impressed with Father Flanagan's work, and aware of the priest's desperate need for money, Desdunes offered to train the Home's boys for a city-wide minstrel show that would draw public attention to the Home's mission. The show would be presented in January 1921,[569] and would be a huge success.

The tour planned for Nebraska and Iowa in 1921 was a wild idea, and was the seed of the great circus wagon caravan that over the next few years would take the boys across the Midwest, with horns blowing, flags flying, and crowds gathering to watch this talented group of youngsters perform. These tours pre-dated the promotional efforts of the Boys Town Choir, which would perform in the great theaters of the country over future decades, and the Boys Town football team, which would travel across the country to compete against well-known schools, from New York to San Francisco.

It was fortunate at this time, when he had obtained an extension of his lease on the German-American Home, that Father Flanagan welcomed a collaborator and associate who would stay with him until the day he died. Patrick Norton, the son of the priest's sister, Mary Jane, had come to the United States in 1913 when he was fifteen. After finishing high school at Creighton Prep in Omaha, he completed his education at colleges in Indiana and New York. He was twenty-two years old when he arrived back in Omaha, just in time to accompany Father Flanagan and his boys on their great tour of the Midwest. Norton became the manager of the troupe, and during the next few years, would become Father Flanagan's assistant, business manager, baseball coach, musical director, and general handyman.

On their first Midwest tour through Nebraska, Iowa, and Minnesota, Father Flanagan, Norton, and the boys who accompanied them traveled in a small cars. Norton would go ahead and make arrangements for the events in auditoriums, church basements, and sometimes in the open air. (Father Flanagan had done a traveling show on a smaller scale in 1920. That first tour was such a huge success that the Knights of Columbus offered to sponsor another tour of Nebraska later that year, with each Council in the state sponsoring the troupe in their own town.[570]) While those tours were successful,[571] they did not yield the financial bonanza Father Flanagan had hoped for. They also took him away from the Home for weeks at a time, and his absence was felt by the boys and his staff.

The new year of 1921 opened with plans for another Charity Ball,[572] but also brought some most distressing news. The owners of the German-American Home gave Father Flanagan an ultimatum: He must vacate the building by April. The priest begged for more time, but the owners refused.[573] Desperate, and without the funds to build his proposed home on Forty Acres,[574] he had to create a temporary solution to his housing problem.

He thought he had found it in a former Presbyterian seminary. It was located in north Omaha, at 3303 North 21st Street (well within the city limits), but it could provide temporary quarters for his more than one hundred boys. However, when the news got out that an army of homeless boys was invading the neighborhood, opposition to the move was loud and vociferous.[575] A committee of concerned citizens met to protest the move and word spread across the city that the families in the area, as well as churches and businesses, did not want Father Flanagan's "little criminals" in their neighborhood. Twenty residents signed a resolution and presented it to Archbishop Harty. In part, it said: "The resolution in no way condemns, but recommends, the work being done by Father Flanagan for the one hundred twenty-five boys he has in his home... we deem it not for the best interests of the community, nor of the boys' home to have an institution of this kind located there."

There apparently also was the fear on the part of the eleven Protestant churches in the area that the Home would be used as a proselytizing center for the Catholic Church. The resolution gave no reasons "why the churches and residents of the community do not want this home located in the seminary buildings."

In response, Father Flanagan "deplored the action of the churches and the residents in condemning the sale of the seminary... The institution is not a reformatory, but a harbor and refuge for the boys, most of whom are from poor homes or are orphans, and not the incorrigible type... There has been no complaint from residents in the neighborhood of the present establishment against the boys, and the reason for moving is that the present lease expires April 1 (1921)... The home is not teaching the Catholic or any sectarian religion to the boys."[576]

This opposition, and the reasons given, made Father Flanagan reflect more clearly about the future of the Home. It really was time to get out of the city and find a place where he had complete control of the Home and its environment.

There was not only a gross misunderstanding of the purpose of the Home on the part of the citizenry in Omaha, but also the mistaken notion that his boys were really miniature criminals and teenaged hoodlums, despised by many in the city and considered a dangerous influence in any neighborhood. Also, his mixture of races, colors, and creeds was anathema to many of Omaha's "better" families, who saw the Home as a first step toward miscegenation and the mixture of the races abhorred by a population that was not above lynching a black man in public (and that had, in fact, murdered a black citizen in that manner not two years earlier). It was a prejudice the priest found difficult to overcome and which he fought against in word and in writing.[577]

The controversy brought reporters to Father Flanagan's door and he told them: "The objectors are undoubtedly conscientious, but they are protesting against something they know nothing about. They call my school a reformatory. It is not. There is only one reformatory in the state, at Kearney. My home is a home in every sense, as well-regulated and well-disciplined as any Christian home in Omaha."[578]

Father Flanagan realized that the resolution was prompted by those who saw no reason for such a home. They did not see the kids who walked in off the road, with no place to go, no place to eat, and no place to sleep. He told the reporters of his excursions into the back streets and deserted haunts of the city to rescue some youngster who had no place to live, and how he would drive in the middle of the night to some back alley where some homeless boy was hiding.

"Only two weeks ago I was called to Sixteenth and S Streets at midnight to care for a little lad who had climbed into a clay bank for shelter. His father was serving time in the state penitentiary for murdering his mother. If he had been left in that clay bank that night, he would have been picked up a frozen corpse the next morning."[579]

So he accepted the inevitable, informing the owners of the German-American Home they would have to tolerate him for only a little while longer. Then he went looking for a site far away from the city, far from residential areas and troublesome neighbors.[580]

Ten miles west of the city, he found exactly what he needed.

It was called Overlook Farm, and when he saw it, he knew that, except for the price, it was the solution to his problem of providing a permanent Home for his boys. It was on West Dodge Road, 160 acres surrounded by other farms as far as the eye could see. He consulted a real estate friend, Joseph O'Keefe, and was told it might be possible to buy the land. The owners, O'Keefe told him, were David Baum and his wife, Ann. The selling price: $100,000.

With O'Keefe and a few other interested friends, Father Flanagan drove out to the farm in early May, 1921. After introducing himself to the tenant farmer, Dan Cattlett, the priest and his group made a tour of the property. Cattlett told them he had fifty-five acres of corn, and twenty-five acres each of alfalfa, clover, timothy, and oats. There were fourteen acres of pasture land, and the farm was well-stocked with cattle, horses, pigs, and chickens. In his most roseate dreams, Father Flanagan could not have envisioned a more ideal location for a permanent Home for his boys. Previous owners had landscaped the property, planted trees, and built essential roads. There were already thirteen buildings on the property, including a small, frame farmhouse, barns, piggeries, and other structures. Before the tour was over, Father Flanagan had decided to purchase the land, although he had no idea where the money to pay for it would come from.

Father Flanagan certainly didn't have $100,000; perhaps, there was $50,000 in his Building Fund. His budget for taking care of the immediate needs of the Home was tight, and, if he was able to purchase the property, the $50,000 would have to be used to make the buildings on Overlook Farm ready for occupancy by his army of boys.

When he arrived back at the Home, he called all of the boys together, as was his custom when he wanted to discuss anything that had to do with their welfare. When they were all gathered, he described to them the beautiful and fertile farm he had just visited. He told them about the fresh air there, the fruit trees, and fields of corn, alfalfa, and hay. He told them it was the place he had been looking for, a place where they would have plenty of room to play and exercise, where they could make all the noise they wanted without disturbing anybody, where they could build a community that would be the envy of every boy in America. By this time, the boys were cheering so loudly that his words were being drowned out.

What he did not tell the boys was that he did not have the money to buy Overlook Farm.

Where he would get the $100,000, he did not know. He only knew that he had to have that farm and that it was the only hope for continuing his work. Otherwise, his boys would be out on the streets again and thousands of other boys would have to take to the streets and the highways. As he thought of the thousands of men he had housed in his hotel, he knew he simply could not let this happen.

His later commentary on his discussion with the boys indicates his dilemma and the fierce determination with which he faced it:

"One evening at supper time I asked (the boys') opinion… their interest alone gave me the courage to go ahead with the new plans of obtaining the farm, and there building a permanent Home for all my boys. Not only for those who were with me at that time, but for the homeless boy of the future as well." The priest was thinking not only of the present, but of generations of boys to come. He could not let this opportunity go by without making sure of that future. It was all or nothing at all.

Father Flanagan's next step was to visit Dan Gaines, one of the members of the Home's Board of Directors. Gaines was the vice-president of the State Bank of Omaha, and was something of a financial genius who had advised the priest on financial matters and had a vital interest in his work. What Father Flanagan did not know was that Gaines and David Baum were partners in the ownership of numerous farm properties in Iowa and Nebraska. Overlook Farm, however, was not one of them. Gaines told Father Flanagan that Baum was a shrewd businessman. He also said the fact that Father Flanagan had little cash on hand for the purchase was "irregular, but he'll (Baum) listen to what you have to say. Then, he'll tell you his terms and – he'll not change them."

Baum's office was on the floor above Dan Gaines' office. Father Flanagan went upstairs, and after exchanging a few pleasantries, he told Baum he had come to purchase Overlook Farm.

Baum asked one question: "Why?" Father Flanagan explained his work in great detail – his work with the boys off the streets and from the courts, what he had accomplished already with little cash and little resources, his crowded quarters, the predicament that new boys were coming day and night, and his lease was expiring. Baum listened, mentioned the price of the property was $100,000, and asked if that was what the priest was prepared to pay.

Father Flanagan explained that he had a little money in reserve, but would need it to build temporary quarters for his boys once they moved to Overlook.

"In other words, Father Flanagan, you have no money, and yet you wish to purchase this property at the figure I just quoted to you?" Baum asked.

"Precisely," Father Flanagan replied. "However, I do have some property in Florence – forty acres that I would like to have you consider as part-payment for the property."

"Yes, I'm familiar with that tract of land…," Baum said. "But if you want that property as much as you say, I'll accept your forty acres in Florence as a down payment on Overlook Farm."

Father Flanagan could scarcely believe his ears. Then he asked, "And the balance?"

"That you can pay me with a series of installments," said Baum.[581]

Delirious with joy, Father Flanagan left Baum's office. The miracle had happened. He could scarcely believe it; it had happened so swiftly, so unexpectedly. One hour earlier, everything was up in the air and now he had his farm. Everything he had dreamed of and planned for his boys had come true. He could build a permanent home for hundreds – for a thousand – boys and not one would have to be turned away. Now he could carry out his master plan for the homeless boy that he had been hammering out in his mind ever since that boy in the box had wandered into his hotel. It came from his innate reverence for the uniqueness of each individual boy and the unlimited possibilities he saw in each one of them.

He instructed Joseph O'Keefe to draw up the papers for the purchase of the land and informed Archbishop Harty of the purchase.[582]

Then he called another meeting of the boys to tell them the good news.

One of the boys with Carlo, the collie pup who was the Home's first pet, circa 1918.

ABOVE: The boys took great pride in their dogs and held an annual dog show, circa 1930.

LEFT: Over the years, the boys collected a wide variety of pets, usually dogs donated by well-wishers, 1920s.

Father Flanagan and his boys at the Home's second location, the German-American Home at 4206 South 13th Street, Omaha, Nebraska, 1918.

A group of boys dressed for church on the front steps of the German-American Home, 1919.

On Sunday mornings, some of the boys would sell the *Father Flanagan Boys' Home Journal* outside churches, circa 1920.

Father Flanagan celebrates Mass at the German-American Home, 1920.

The boys and Father Flanagan welcomed Eamon de Velera (front row, second from right) who would go on to become the first president of the Irish Republic, 1920.

Father Flanagan and the boys gather for a photo on the front steps of the German-American Home, 1921.

9

OVERLOOK FARM

It is clear from his own words that Father Flanagan considered Overlook Farm a gift of Divine Providence, so astonishing was its ideal setting, its natural beauty, and its possibilities for development. On his first visit, he could see that it fit into his plans with amazing accuracy. Father Flanagan was convinced that he had been handed a gift at a time and moment when he was ready to venture out into the deep, with a clear understanding of the critical importance of what he was doing. This was Father Flanagan's description of Overlook Farm when he first saw it:

"A twenty-minute ride along West Dodge Road brings the visitor to the attractive gateway, set in an even box hedge which borders almost the entire farm.

"Row on row of gorgeous pink, red, and white peonies are massed against the choice shrubbery which lines the winding, gravel road. The flaunting yellow of the Japanese fig, the green fretwork of the weeping mulberry, the unfamiliar outlines of dozens of different trees seldom seen in Nebraska bear testimony to the art of the landscape gardener who planned and planted there for a wealthy grain man, more than twenty years ago. Because of financial losses, he did not build the palatial country home he planned, and the neglected boys of America will have the advantage of the $25,000 he expended in beautifying the place.

"Every fruit tree which will grow in this climate can be found among the eighty-nine varieties of trees on 'Overlook Farm.'[583]

"Five varieties of grape vines, spreading luxuriantly over lattice-work trellises, add to the attractiveness of the fruitful acres. And as though it had been planned in the beginning for a boys' paradise, cunningly built bird houses peek out of dozens of different places."

It was on Decoration (later Memorial) Day, in late May of 1921, that Father Flanagan brought a group of boys to visit Overlook Farm. A later account of the visit said, "Excitement among the boys was at fever pitch... everyone clamored for a chance to go there first. Father Flanagan led them out in small groups to watch the roads being laid and construction started on the temporary housing."

(One of the boys, Al Witcofski, would later remember his first days at the farm: "There were just like those old barracks you had in the army. The two buildings on the south were dormitories; that's where we slept. The one at the end was the rec hall, and there was a classroom and a chapel. They had a folding door down the middle so they had two classrooms and the altar at the end. The fourth building was the Dining Hall and the kitchen at the end. And in one was where we separated the milk."[584])

It took all summer to lay new roads and renovate the buildings for occupancy. This is Father Flanagan's description of what he wanted: "In the new Home, I hope to be able to offer my boys, who range in age from 4 to 17, a complete grade school course, a high school course, a commercial course, and their choice of the following trades: tailoring, plumbing, wireless, automobile repairing, and electricity."[585]

When the school year ended, four of the older boys went out to Overlook to spend every week helping with the renovation of the buildings. On their return on Sundays, the others gathered around them asking questions. Father Flanagan promised a picnic on the property for all the boys before the summer was over, so that even the youngest boy could get a taste of the place.

The progress was noted this way: "Buildings within the quadrangle... were completed late in September. Workmen were lining the walls with flaxlinum and finishing the interiors with plasterboard. Other structures, including the laundry, bathhouse, and staff residence, were almost finished. Stoves had arrived and were ready to be installed when the contractor informed Father that the place would be ready for occupancy on October 15."[586]

The waiting had been a worry. Winter was coming on and if the move had been delayed another month, cold weather and perhaps a snowfall would have made it hazardous. Besides, the former occupants of the German-American Home were eager to take possession of their building again, and they were again pressuring Father Flanagan to vacate the building.

According to later writings, Father Flanagan was "no less anxious than his boys to make the long-contemplated move. He made frequent trips to the farm site, there to encourage workmen and supervise preparations that were being made to receive his boys. Each time (he) returned from a trip to the farm, he would be surrounded by scores of children, who tugged at his coat sleeves and pleaded for news of when they would be taken to their new Home in the country."[587]

News soon got around the city that Father Flanagan had found a new site for his Boys' Home, and those who had expected (and perhaps wished) that the priest would soon run out of resources were astonished at the news. Many were happy that the Home would now be out of town, far away from the streets of the city, and those who had prophesied that the priest was a wild-eyed visionary with no practical gifts and poor financial judgment to boot, were perplexed by his success.

There were those in the city, however, who had recognized his greatness from the beginning, who admired his compassion for the poor and homeless, and who had applauded his efforts to improve the welfare system of the city by taking homeless and jobless men off the streets. He was a close friend of judges and juvenile authorities who saw something of genius in his work for boys and had cooperated with him in getting boys off the streets. The city had come to his rescue several times before with fundraising events and neighborhood campaigns. Father Flanagan was also a respected member of the city's Welfare Board. It was known that juvenile authorities in other parts of the country had consulted with him and that judges in states as far away as Maryland and California had placed boys in his keeping. Only recently, his boys troupe had met with the most prominent juvenile judge in the country, Judge Benjamin Lindsey of Denver, Colorado, and the judge had praised Father Flanagan's work as an outstanding example of a city's concern for its youth.[588]

With the renovation of the Overlook Farm and the buildings underway, Father Flanagan turned his mind to his final plan for the property: building a new residence that would house 200 boys. A photo of the proposed residence had appeared in the pages of the *Boys' Home Journal* for over a year. (He had at first planned to build it on the forty acres of farmland in Florence.) The cost was estimated at about $300,000 and the need was immediate.

After the turmoil in the city over his plan to occupy the former Presbyterian Seminary on North 21st Street and the shame the uproar from local residents had brought on the city, there were those in Omaha who were eager to make amends to the priest. There also were those who were equally ashamed of the prejudice that had arisen because of his acceptance of boys of every race, color, and creed. Father Flanagan had struck back in the pages of his *Journal* and in the local newspapers, explaining that his boys were not hoodlums and that the race prejudice of the city was something that he simply would not tolerate.

Fortunately, there were several prominent citizens of Omaha who felt the same way, and with the announcement of the purchase of Overlook Farm, a Building Committee was set up to plan and direct a building campaign for Father Flanagan's Boys' Home.

With Archbishop Jeremiah Harty as Chairman, Father Flanagan as Secretary, and Dan Gaines, the priest's banker friend, as Treasurer, the Committee comprised more than two dozen of Omaha's finest citizens: men and women, businessmen, bankers, doctors, lawyers, educators, philanthropists, and clergymen and clergywomen, all noted for their charitable and civic activities. In an editorial in the *Boys' Home Journal* announcing the purchase of Overlook Farm, Father Flanagan recognized the Building Committee:

"A campaign is now underway for the raising of $300,000 necessary to erect and equip a new building by popular subscription, and the following committee has been formed: Dan W. Gaines, W.J. Coad, Paul Gallagher, Arthur Smith, Leo A. Hoffman, George Brandeis, Jim Hanley, Rabbi Frederick Cohn, Otto A. Barmettler, Francis Matthews, Henry Monsky, Gene Melady, Mrs. Louis Nash,

John Hopkins, Walter Head, John D.C. Creighton, Ben Gallagher, Paul Martin, Robert Trimble, Ward Burgess, Mrs. E. W. Nash, James Kinsler."

The publicity director was Morris Jacobs, a publicity and advertising man who was a close and dear friend of Father Flanagan. Jacobs and his public relations skills would remain at Father Flanagan's side long after the campaign was over.[589]

The architect for the new building, J.M. Nachtigall, had preliminary blueprints for the new structure drawn up, and the Committee announced that ground would be broken on July 5 that year.

Father Flanagan expected the campaign to raise the needed funds within two months. But it soon became clear that it would take more than two months to raise $300,000. Excavations for the foundation of the new building had already begun, with some of the older boys helping with this part of the project. They would arrive every Monday morning to work on the renovation of the older buildings, work on the new foundation, and then return to the German-American Home on Friday. Father Flanagan was on the property almost every day and would sometimes bring some of the younger boys with him.

The campaign, however, never fully got off the ground, and it became clear that a tighter and more carefully monitored organization was needed to raise the required funds. Poorly advised, the original Committee had hired a fundraising organization, whose purpose was to make money on the project and to take its cut of the funds raised first. So it was decided that the city itself would run the campaign. Under Henry Monsky's leadership, the cream of Omaha's business community came together, holding planning sessions throughout the city over the next four months. The new plan was to make the campaign a city-wide appeal, with every home in the city being asked to make a financial contribution to the new Boys' Home. The leader and prime mover of the campaign, chosen as chairman of the Executive Committee, was J.D. Davidson, [590] who had carefully watched Father Flanagan's work for boys. Davidson had been impressed with the fact that the priest welcomed boys of every race, color, and creed, and that the nonsectarian nature of the Home made it an important asset to the civic and commercial life of the city. Davidson's fundraising skills were well-known, and he had been the driving force in a campaign for the civic and recreation center known as Aksarben.

Davidson took the challenge. There was some criticism, but he laughed it off, bringing with him prominent members of the business and professional community. Under his leadership, the campaign did, in fact, turn into something of a city-wide crusade, appealing to a wide range of potential donors, including businesses, churches, universities, civic organizations, Jews, Protestants, Masons, small grocery stores, Boys Scouts, and women's clubs. Two men who joined the campaign would work closely with Father Flanagan for many years: Morris Jacobs, the head of a publicity firm who took on the task of making the campaign a hot news item, and Francis P. Matthews, who would later become Supreme Head of the Knights of Columbus and the U.S. Ambassador to Ireland.

Moving Out and Moving In

"In October of 1921, I gathered my flock around me, loaded them (with all the furniture, etc.) into trucks, and we moved to Overlook, the mecca of our dreams," Father Flanagan would later write.

"For months, they had talked and dreamed – Overlook – Overlook – Overlook. Will we ever get there? Every boy who was fortunate as to visit the farm, prior to moving day, was plied with questions as to how it looked, what was being done, and above all, 'When do we move?'[591]

"We secured a few big trucks which first moved our earthly possessions. Several of the older and larger boys came out to the Home to receive the furniture and be on hand as overseers, then returned to the town to get the boys. There were 150 in our family then, and all of them crowded into the trucks, (and) a living, wiggling, singing caravan of homeless boys moved out of the city to Overlook Farm, the first real home many of them had ever had. They piled out of the trucks and were like young deer turned loose in the forest. Many of the boys had never been on a farm before…. In a few hours every foot of the farm was explored, and re-explored. I can still see these little boys running here and there, wondering, no doubt, if this were really true, or if it would suddenly vanish from under them."[592]

Looking around, Father Flanagan had a chance to reflect on his good fortune: "That was a memorable day. I had an entirely different feeling from the one I experienced the day my men moved into the second hotel. Here was a possibility of growth and development, here was young life, and here we could take root and build for a definite future."[593]

The move took several trips. First the larger furniture, then tables, chairs, beds, school desks, books, clothes, and kitchenware. Then, sports equipment, Father Flanagan's records, papers, books, and files. Then the altar, vestments, sacred vessels, and the Oberammergau crucifix. Finally, Carlo the collie, who was reluctant to leave, but was lifted bodily and placed on a truck.[594] It took more than half a day, but no one wanted to quit as rooms were furnished, bedrooms assigned, and a tour was made of the property by all the boys.

On the last trip, as Father Flanagan drove through the stand of birch trees that lined the main entrance, he was greeted by the shouts of boys who were already there, running beside the truck and telling of their explorations of their new Home. They crowded around the truck, making it impossible for him to get out, until one of the more astute older boys rang the bell for supper and the excited boys made a bee-line for the dining hall.

Father Flanagan set up residency in an old garage on the property,[595] but the primitive conditions did not disturb him. He had his new Home.[596]

He was, in fact, gleeful. It was as if a huge, almost unbearable burden had been taken off his shoulders. He could not have remained at the German-American

Home any longer. He had to turn away boy after boy, ten in one month, and, as the numbers multiplied and funds dwindled, he was almost in despair. His pleas in the *Journal* and in letters to supporters had become more and more insistent.

The Presbyterian Seminary fiasco had unnerved him, but it had geared Father Flanagan into action, since he realized for the first time that his Home would never take root in the city. He needed a place of his own, where in total freedom and with space for all the boys' needs, he could build his village as he was beginning to envision it, a village of boys, for boys, built by boys. Here it was, laid out before him, almost like a master-plan, in the scattered buildings and with one hundred and fifty boys running wild over the countryside.

Housed in their ramshackle quarters, with trees and an abundance of flowers bursting all around, the boys considered their new Home a paradise. They could wander the fields by two and threes, as boys do, shimmy up trees, pitch stones into the small lake on the property, play throw-and-toss with baseballs or footballs, and organize hurry-up games of baseball, with one boy at bat and five or six in the field.

The property stretched from West Dodge Road on the north to Pacific Road on the south, with what would later become 144th Street as the western border. The 160 acres were about one-fourth of the 640 acres that constituted a square mile of land.

Father Flanagan and his boys had no sooner settled in when his *Boys' Home Journal* invited the public to visit Overlook Farm. Plans for the Building Fund Campaign were still in full swing and he wanted the people of Omaha to see what their money was buying. Even though the boys were in temporary quarters, the foundation had already been dug for the new main home building where they would eventually live. In a two-page spread of the *Journal*, complete with a photo of his army of boys, the invitation read: *"We Invite You to Visit our New Home at OVERLOOK FARM, and see –* [597]

Our 125 boys.
Our 160 acre farm (one of the finest in Nebraska).
Our site for a $300,000 building to house boys.
Our cows, horses, sheep, pigs, and chickens.
Our new temporary quarters.

When–	Where–	How–
We are always open.	*Ten miles west of*	*Take Fremont Bus*
You are always welcome.	*Omaha Post Office*	*Line, get off at*
	on Dodge Street.	*Overlook Farm.*

On the back cover of the same issue, there was a picture of a boy in tears under the title, "The Waif," with these words: "The boy pictured here is only one of an average of ten that are turned away from Father Flanagan's Home because all the rooms of the Home are filled. A drive will start November 14th to raise $300,000 for permanent buildings. The homeless boys are now housed in wooden structures at Overlook Farm, the new site of Father Flanagan's Boys' Home."[598]

The boys were fortunate that the former manager of the farm, Dan Catlett,[599] had stayed at the farm to help them. He soon gathered a crew of boys around him and they began planting gardens, since they would have to grow much of their food themselves. Boys were also assigned to milk the cows for the Home's supply of milk and butter. There was an intense rivalry among the boys to milk the cows, but one of the boys won out and the other boys would watch as pails were filled and then carry them to the kitchen.

No sooner were the boys in their new quarters than "tag boys" started to arrive. Most were from Omaha, but others came from farther away. They were called tag boys because some father or mother who, for various reasons, could not take care of their children, would put a tag around their boy's neck with necessary information about the boy and send him to Overlook Farm. Although it was crowded, Father Flanagan managed to find room for these newcomers. But he had to turn down some applications and many boys were put on hold until the new living quarters were completed.

When the move to Overlook took place, the traveling troupe of seven boys under the direction of Dan Desdunes was away. So when they returned, these boys found themselves in new quarters, and also enjoyed a brand-spanking new band room to play and practice in. Those seven had played in over a hundred towns in the Dakotas and Minnesota, and were recognized as minor celebrities wherever they went.[600]

Showing Off Their New Home

In response to the invitation in the *Journal*, groups of visitors soon began to arrive at Overlook Farm. They came to noonday luncheons, served by the boys, while other boys acted as traffic cops and tour guides of the farm. These were not casual trips, but well-planned outings that gave the civic clubs of Omaha and members of the Building Committee an opportunity to see firsthand what the city was being asked to support. Not only did they observe Father Flanagan's boys in their new juvenile habitat, but they also were entertained by the Home's talented young singers, orators, actors, and musicians. "Considering that our Farm is ten miles from Omaha, and reached only by automobile, coupled with the fact that a few of the days were far from ideal, it was indeed an agreeable surprise to us in the number (that) attended the luncheons," Father Flanagan would later write of the outings. "On several occasions, it was necessary to set a 'second table,' even with our dining room seating 125."

This mass exodus of the Omaha Women's Club, the Advertising Selling League, the Concord Club, the Kiwanis Club, and the Campaign Women of Omaha to Overlook set the stage for the official launch of the Building Fund Campaign on November 14.[601] Several visitors were journalists from the local newspapers, and on the opening day of the campaign, this article appeared in the pages of the *Omaha World-Herald*, written by a reporter who had visited the Home on one of these civic outings:

"The campaign which opens today to raise $300,000 for a home for Father Flanagan's boys is one of the biggest and worthiest movements to which Omaha has ever devoted itself. It is because Omaha has come to know Father Flanagan as a very remarkable man, who is doing wonderful work, that this city has organized to raise for him a sum adequate to the needs of the noble cause to which he has given himself....

"And Father Flanagan's presence, if he shows up, causes no subdued hush, no sign of embarrassment. For he is their pal, their friend, their father. He fits them like an old shoe. The kindly sympathy and affection that well from his heart, that shine in his eyes, are the love for which every normal boy is hungry – the love which most of these boys had never known until a merciful providence threw them into the good father's arms.

"You go away from Overlook Farm with a lump of gratitude in your throat for the fine and true service that is given to those who need it most. Father Flanagan is able to take care of 500 boys at a time instead of less than 200. Especially do you feel keenly what it will mean to the unfortunate boys who are turned away daily because there is no room for them, though they have no other earthly home.

"And you realize, too, what it will mean to society. It is a work of building clean manhood that is going on out there. It is a character university whose attendance is constantly shifting. No boy is kept there longer than is necessary to give him the right footing for right living.... As each passes out into the world, another takes his place. It means the rescue of thousands of boys, fitting them to fill an honorable and useful and happy place in the world, who otherwise (most of them), would become flotsam and jetsam on the tides of life. It means the building of homes rather than additions to penitentiaries and asylums. It means a growing attendance at the church of all faiths, a diminishing line before the police judge each morning. It is indeed the love of a homeless waif that is for sale in Omaha this week."

Father Flanagan was back in Omaha for the opening of the campaign on November 14. He had opened a small office at 514 South 13th Street and it was from there that he took care of the business of the Home until his new quarters were completed.[602]

When the campaign kicked off, excitement was at a fever pitch as the appeal became a door-to-door dynamo, with someone visiting 14,000 homes across Omaha, and boys with collection buckets in downtown Omaha, their small band playing on street corners or in some local park. Men and women also passed the buckets around the city; one group was even called the "Women's Bucket Brigade."

These bucket brigades invaded not only homes in every section of the city, but also restaurants, stores, night clubs, pool rooms, even speakeasies. Bootleggers, gamblers, bums, and crooks in the backwash of Omaha's business section threw their coins and dollar bills in the buckets.

One account described the campaign's attention-getting methods: "J.D. Davidson and others agreed that the main thing was to get the public's interest at once, even if they had to set off firecrackers in the streets. They did not go that far, but they did go down to the railroad yards and buy a batch of signal flares. They started out their first meeting at night, parading the dark streets, with their freight-yard torches. Crowds would follow them to a corner; there would be a few rousing songs, a few shorts talks. Then – the main speaker of the night would stand up – tall Father Flanagan.

"'Three boys a day are turned away from Overlook Farm because we have no room for them,' the priest would say. 'I tell you, gentlemen, many a time I have wept as I saw a boy turned away, carrying his grip, his head bent low, beginning his journey back – to where? He has no home, he has no friends; his home is the streets and alleys and unclean hovels where criminals are made.'"

The priest's sales pitch always worked, and his picture graced the cover of the *Boys' Home Journal* in January 1922, when the campaign was at its height.

The plan also called for enlisting some of the boys themselves into the campaign and several of the "boy orators" and "boy actors" of the Home gave talks at gatherings around the city. Charles Kenworthy was the star of this team, and his face and voice became a regular feature of the campaign.

Mayor James Dahlman, J.J. Boucher (a rival who spoke against the mayor in the political campaign the previous spring), and Henry Monsky also talked at the street meetings. The Boys' Band played, while other boys held the red fire torches.

The campaign was announced in churches, both Catholic and Protestant. In local theaters and on the main streets of Omaha, fund-raising sessions were held, and the whole city seemed to come alive for the campaign.

Improving Life on the Farm

Life at Overlook Farm was far different from the cramped quarters and limited space of the German-American Home, which was close to a busy street and the daily rush of cars and buses. When the exploration of their new Home had made them familiar with its newness and its vastness, the boys still had to make their new quarters livable, and make provisions for the ease and comfort of one hundred fifty residents, many of whom were unfamiliar with life on a farm.

A well had to be dug for running water. Early on, waking in the morning meant the boys had to splash cold water on their faces, a daily reminder of their primitive condition. Also, their latrine was an open pit between two unsteady walls, open to the sky and the winter's cold. But soon the buildings would be outfitted with toilets and bathrooms.

There were chores, and every boy, except the youngest, was expected to feed the hogs, clean out the stables, and care for the animals – pigs, cows, sheep, and horses. Other tasks included husking corn for the table, planting strawberries, and splitting and piling wood to be burned on the cold winter nights.

One of the boys later recounted the early days at Overlook:

"When we built our frame buildings, we expected that we would probably have to spend at least one school term in them so arrangements were made for school rooms, trade workshops, dormitories, a chapel, and living quarters.

"Life on the farm… was different from anything we had ever known. The tasks around the Home took up part of the boys' time. When they were finished, they had ample time to play. Discipline was simple. There was growth and development all around us. The boys worked in the gardens and the fields, as well as those who helped with the animals, and those who helped with the animals saw life and hope on every hand.

"We soon laid out the permanent site of the athletic field, and smoothed out a portion of the field for a baseball diamond."

It was a fierce and grim lesson in self-preservation, but it bound the small community of boys together. Father Flanagan shared in the early hardships, housed in an old garage that was open to the weather, with rats for company and little comfort of his own.

With winter coming, there was also a need for warm clothing, quilts, and blankets for the 200 boys who were now running and romping across the farm every day. Clothing had to be mended, and the younger boys were quickly outgrowing their battered shirts, trousers, socks and shoes, mittens, and underwear. When word went out, the women of Omaha came in droves, a dozen at a time, to assist the nuns in their work of cutting, patching, sewing, and mending, and to bring homemade quilts and blankets.

Not long after the boys were settled in their quarters, a reporter from the *Omaha World-Herald* again visited the Home and gave his impression of this stalwart band of youngsters: "They take possessive pride in the plain and rough wooden barracks, which constitute their temporary quarters. They attach themselves in such a confident and friendly way to the visitor, drag him breathlessly about to see our pigs, our cow, our harvested corn, our coal supply, our chickens, and our asbestos lined smoke house – our individual wash basins and toothbrush cups, our cleanly kept cots, our bandstand, our playhouse, our mess hall – it's all ours. They are young men of property, these boys, with a place in the world and work to do. They are partners in, as well as the great beneficiaries of, a great enterprise."

It was plain to see that Omaha was at last beginning to open its eyes to Father Flanagan's presence and the grandeur of what he had accomplished with this army of boys off the streets, their pride in each other, some never having had a home of their own or anyone, parent or otherwise, looking after their welfare.

So successful was the city-wide campaign that in less than six months after the move to Overlook Farm, ground was broken for the new five-story main building. It would include classrooms, a dining hall, a gymnasium, a dormitory, a chapel, and an infirmary.

But just as quickly as the new building was underway, money again began to run out. The builders had to be paid and the boys had to be fed. Father

Flanagan may have had friends among prominent people in Omaha who were working hard to raise money for the new building, but the ordinary folk who provided the staples for the boys' three daily meals were not so generous. Bills from grocers piled up and trucks loaded with food often had to turn back for Omaha due to lack of payment. There were many days when the boys' dinner and supper comprised what was left in the kitchen from the previous meal.

With his fertile mind and his pocketbook stretched to their limits, Father Flanagan went out on a limb again for new sources of income. Impressed with the Women's Brigade, which had swept through the downtown and the inner city raising funds as part of the Building Campaign, he hired two of its members – Zaida Dimond and Gertrude McCarthy – as field agents who would scour the country raising funds.[603]

He also looked to his Mothers' Guild to set up a laundry and take care of the weekly and monthly care of the boys' clothing. Then there was the problem of providing shoes for 200 boys. This was solved by bringing local cobbler Rudolph Kotek to the Home. Kotek trained some of the boys in his own trade, and as a master violinist, entertained them with his music on many otherwise-dull evenings.[604]

It was Father Flanagan's ability to see the good and the possibilities for good in a boy that was the heart of his genius. The wide range of ages of his boys meant they had different educational needs. Also, some were college material and others needed skills that only a trade school could provide. So the priest invited men and women with a variety of skills to teach the boys singing, dancing, acting, elocution, and how to play sports; present classes that would prepare them to attend colleges and universities; provide training for trades like animal husbandry; and teach manual skills like pottery and woodworking. He taught his boys day and night that their only limitations were in their own efforts, and many went on to fulfill his words in their lifetime achievements, in which he took genuine pride.

Slowly, too, the farm began to grow and the boys began to behave like cowboys out on the range, the whole Home becoming a place of learning as the boys gained new skills and became adept at riding horses, milking cows, and shearing sheep. The new main building with room for 200 boys gradually filled the horizon, and strangers from the city came to gawk, some bringing needed food or clothing. Familiar figures like Henry Monsky and Morris Jacobs could often be seen chatting with Father Flanagan, and the Mothers' Guild would bring mended shirts or trousers or some special dessert for the holidays.

Some of the first buildings to be built in the midst of all the chaos of turning old shacks into living quarters, dormitories, and classrooms resembled Noah's ark; three buildings housed chickens, geese, ducks, pigeons, and rabbits. There, the boys gathered to feed the animals and watch them grow; some animals became food for the tables and some were sold to local farmers or families as pets.

Other outbuildings were transformed into a gym, a broom factory (the boys ran a small broom business that brought in a little income),[605] a carpentry shop, and a shoe shop. There was a horse barn and a corn crib, and a huge recreation hall where the boys could gather for games of all kinds and entertainment presented by the boys themselves. Also, there were living quarters for the nuns and a special building for the chapel.

Just getting settled in their new Home was something of an adventure and just plain hard work. Animals had to be fed and their stalls or coops had to be cleaned daily; eggs were collected from hen houses and milk from the cows. One of the first boys who tried to milk a cow started on the wrong side and got his pail kicked out of his hands, the milk spilling all over amid the laughter of his comrades, who lifted the boy from the ground and accompanied him to the other side of the cow.[606]

Life on the farm revealed itself to be vastly different from city life. It meant getting up early for chores, knowing where to spread the straw or hay in the stables, getting to know the needs and temperaments of animals, learning about the variety of fruit trees and when their fruit was ripe for picking, laying out the gardens, and knowing where to set up facilities for sports, like a handball and tennis court, a baseball diamond or two, with a track for running.

Father Flanagan watched in mild amusement as the business of organizing and running a farm shifted to high gear, with the boys taking on new chores and skills, and the older boys teaching the younger ones, and everyone feeling a part of this new adventure called Overlook Farm.

The first winter at Overlook presented many challenges. The buildings were cold and drafty. And once news of the new facility spread, applications poured in from all over the country. Father Flanagan had to turn most of them down, but boys who came in off the road and new "tag" boys were allowed to stay.

The first winter also brought its own new activities, including skating on the small pond on the property, harvesting and storing ice from the Elkhorn River, and converting one of the larger rooms into a movie theater on Sunday evenings, which sometimes drew attendees from miles around.

Father Flanagan saw the boys taking pride in their chores, and writing about it in the *Boys' Home Journal*.[607] And when the chores were done it was "Hi Ho" to the baseball[608] diamond, where the Gobblers played the Garden Gang, or to the handball court and marbles fever. There was hay to be mowed and taken in for the cattle, a laundry to be equipped, a well to be drilled for water, all occupations that were new and necessary.[609]

As for Father Flanagan's physical condition, the strain and excitement of moving to Overlook and running the Building Campaign took its toll. And the cramped quarters he lived in did not help. Exhausted from these great efforts,[610] the priest resigned from the Omaha Welfare Board, of which he was a leading member, and decided to concentrate on his fast-growing population of boys. Even with the success of the campaign, money always seemed to be scarce and

Father Flanagan realized he was the director of an amazing experiment that would demand his full time and attention.

Meanwhile, developments in the world outside Boys Town that commanded his attention had also taken their toll. One example was the negative decision of the U.S. Supreme Court in the 1918 child labor case, *Hammer vs. Dagenhart*. The decision had been a keen disappointment to him and he had commented on it in the *Boys' Home Journal*.[611] There was nothing that provoked his ire more than injustice to children, and child labor was one of the greatest of these injustices.

In 1921, Father Flanagan purchased Overlook Farm west of Omaha; the farm would eventually be transformed into the Village of Boys Town.

When the boys moved from the German-American Home to Overlook Farm, the younger boys rode in rented trucks while some of the older boys walked the twenty miles to their new home, 1921.

Father Flanagan, at far left, lines up his boys from youngest to the oldest at their new Home at Overlook Farm, 1921.

In the summer of 1921, four new wooden buildings to be used as dormitories, classrooms, and a dining hall were constructed at Overlook Farm.

10

'THE WORLD'S GREATEST JUVENILE ENTERTAINERS'

A Unique Traveling Show

Father Flanagan and his boys were now solidly in the public eye, settled in their tight little community on the western edge of Omaha. But the Presbyterian Seminary incident and the public uproar over moving his diverse group of boys into that neighborhood had stirred up his ire, and he realized that despite all of his efforts, the public's perception of the homeless boy had not changed at all. As he watched his boys acting and behaving as miniature adults, claiming their new Home at Overlook and embracing the warmth and bonds of friendship that had grown among them, he thought there still had to be some way to change that perception.

"I realized that I might continue for years to tell people that these boys were not criminals, and were not bad, but to most that would mean little. They would go on with their prejudices," he later wrote. "My immediate problem was to break down this prejudice, and create a genuine interest in the welfare of all homeless and neglected boys. I had the feeling if the public could see and know these boys, they would quickly change their opinions only too quickly.

"But how was I to do this?"[612]

Then he hit upon a brilliant idea.

"Back in the German(-American) Home in Omaha, we had established a band, which was now flourishing," he wrote. "This band provided the germ of the idea I had in mind. We would organize a show with the band as the nucleus and take that show to the people. The boys in the show would be representative of boys in my Home. When the people saw them and talked with them, they would have as good idea what my other boys were like, too."[613]

His entrepreneurial skills came alive as he saw the public relations possibilities. He announced the plan to the boys and there was a lot of shouting and clapping. Some of the boys had already accompanied him on his speaking tours, and had been warmly welcomed wherever they played. What he envisioned was an old-fashioned minstrel show, like the one the Home's current bandmaster, Dan Desdunes, had orchestrated two years before, but bigger, with all the humor, high jinks, and buffoonery that was part of the minstrel show tradition.

Competitions were held to find the good singers and actors, and those with musical and oratorical skills,[614] with bandmaster Desdunes becoming as excited as the boys. A motley crew of the band appeared on the front cover of the February 1922 issue of the *Boys' Home Journal*, resplendent in their ragtag hats and coats, and instruments in hand. Father Flanagan's commentary read: "This month's cover shows our band which is now being trained by Mr. Dan Desdunes. We have not yet been able to buy uniforms for the boys, but hope to have sufficient funds before the first day of May, at which time we are planning on making a trip through the larger towns of Nebraska. When one remembers that six months ago not a boy in this band read or played a note of music, one realizes the whole-hearted way in which the boys have responded to Mr. Desdunes' wonderful efforts."

As soon as school was out in May,[615] rehearsals began and continued for weeks until it was clear the troupe was ready. The band instruments were old and battered, but the boys made do. Twenty-five boys were selected for the traveling troupe, and Father Flanagan sat down to plan their itinerary, their means of transportation, and the rules for life on the road.

Travel by cars and trains was out of the question. "In 1922, the roads in this section of the country were doubtful," Father Flanagan later wrote. "Paving, except for short stretches immediately outside of the cities, was unheard of. Graveled roads were still a luxury… automobiles, besides being too expensive for us, would not provide the living quarters for the boys. This was a large problem when you took twenty-five boys on the road. Likewise the trains would not be satisfactory because our itinerary took us to small towns and cross country where train service would be slow and impractical.[616]

"There was only one other course open to us. That was a horse-drawn vehicle… I had discussed the plan with a friend in Omaha and he suggested that we get regular show wagons… so show wagons they were.[617]

"I negotiated for four of these large, ponderous wagons, especially constructed for our purposes. Three were for the boys and the fourth was a property wagon, in which we would carry band instruments, baggage, show property, and utensils for cooking… then we turned our attention to getting horses…."[618]

Father Flanagan then hired an advance man to route the show. The first leg of the tour, planned for central and southern Nebraska, and starting in Bennington, just northwest of Omaha, was announced in the *Boys' Home Journal*: "We now have a band of thirty-two pieces that any school in the West would be proud to possess. On May 1st this band will start to tour the States through the summer months and thus help raise funds for their permanent home which is now being built on Overlook Farm."[619]

Each boy was outfitted with two pairs of khaki pants, two pairs of shoes, two pairs of coveralls, six pairs of stockings, a raincoat, and a cap.

Excitement grew as eight stout horses arrived at Overlook, where there was scarcely enough building space to house them. For the professional touches, the wagons were painted bright red to catch the attention of the crowds as they entered the towns, and across the sides of the wagons, in large letters, was printed "Father Flanagan's Boys' Shows."

The preparation of the wagons took days, and by early June all was ready: twenty-five boys in their colorful uniforms, the horse-drawn wagons proclaiming who was coming to town, and advance notices in each town of the arrival of Father Flanagan and his boys.

"The wagons were finally loaded – seats were built for the boys to sit on... then the big horses with their shining harnesses were led out and hitched up," Father Flanagan wrote. "There was a jingle and brilliance about the harnesses that gave us the feeling that we were starting on some glorious venture."[620]

The whole community of boys turned out for the departure of the troupe. Bandmaster Desdunes wore his striking band uniform, as colorful as the boys' uniforms. Father Flanagan and Pat Norton took their places inside one of the wagons, and shouting, clapping, and stomping of feet resounded as the wagons started out. "The spirit of all the boys remained behind as we pulled out of the yard. The shouts followed us down the road until they died in the wind."[621]

Their first performance was in Bennington, five miles from Overlook, over narrow dirt roads. The wagons arrived as planned at about four in the afternoon, in time for the matinée show planned for the village's children. According to Father Flanagan's careful planning of the tour, that would leave the evening performance for the adults, from whom he expected a generous response to the boys' performance. The priest later described that show this way:

"The curtain went up that night at 8:15, but an hour earlier, the house was packed. We could hear the murmur of voices in the audience beyond the stage, and several outbursts of clapping told us they were anxious to have us begin.

"Naturally, I was concerned over this first show. All of us wanted it to succeed for several reasons. It was an experiment. On its success depended this campaign to win friends for the homeless boy and break down the old prejudices against him.

"Eagerly I watched the show proceed, and I listened carefully for the applause, which came after each act with almost deafening certainty. The boys reacted wonderfully under this approval. They took the cue and put on a perfect performance. I was astonished to note that they did not skip a line, needed no prompting, and really put on their acts better than they ever did at rehearsals.

"When the final curtain fell, their friends called the boys back again, until finally we left the curtain up and the twenty boys remained on the stage and acted as a reception committee... these boys who a few months before had few, if any, friends in the world were suddenly transported into the heart of their first public."[622]

What surprised the priest was the amazing talent of the boys. It was his conviction that each boy had talents, skills, and unlimited possibilities that had to be drawn out of him, and that it was that experience of his own self that gave a boy a sense of self-worth and confidence in his own future.

Satisfied that the remainder of the trip would be a success, Father Flanagan returned to Overlook Farm, leaving Pat Norton in charge of the troupe.[623] He was eager to oversee the continuing construction of the new Main Building that would hold two hundred boys and to attend to the needs of the boys left behind: "There were many things that demanded my personal attention every day."[624]

The program for the first musical tour was remarkable for the talents of its ragtag collection of boys off the street and a tribute to the teaching skills of Desdunes, who came out of a tradition of New Orleans musicians that produced Louis Armstrong and a whole generation of jazz greats. The boys' musical selections were a hodgepodge of old favorites, with plenty of room for high jinks and comedy routines Desdunes had cribbed from the Vaudeville circuit and circus clown acts.

....

MINSTREL SHOW [625]

Interlocutor . . . . Bernard Warden

Humpty Dumpty . . . . Overture
By the Company

Little Johnny Green . . . . Comic Song
Johnny Gilbert

Juanita . . . . Love Song
Henry Wiebelhaus

Freckles . . . . Kid Song
Frank Newton

Old Irish Mother . . . . Sentimental Ballad
Charles Brehm

Brown Jug . . . . Laughing Song
Oscar Flakes

Ode to Our Father . . . . Finale
By the Company

....

All the boys got their bows, but the favorite of the show was the Drum Major, an African-American youngster named Oscar Flakes,[626] who charmed the crowd with his wit, his antics, and his sheer exuberance. Later, Father Flanagan often traveled with the troupe, and Flakes remembered him and the value of his presence well: "He was a beautiful man. He was mother, father, everything to a young boy. He would wrestle with us, run with us, horse ride with us, do anything a youth would care to do… shoot marbles with us."[627]

In spite of all the good times, however, Flakes also would have stark memories of places where the troupe was not welcome because of the racial mixture of the boys, and especially how the African-American boys were singled out as targets of prejudice.

Flakes would later describe one such incident that happened in South Dakota on the second tour of the troupe:

"We had come in the nighttime, late. When the morning came, we got up. Father Flanagan was with us then. Anyway, we boys gave our order of what we wanted for breakfast and one of the boys would take it to the restaurant and put the order in. At that time there weren't too many hotels that had their own dining room. In this particular instance, we got ready to go. I most generally brought up the back end because I liked to window shop and trail along behind. So when I came into this restaurant, the fellow said that he wanted the little colored boy to eat in the kitchen. Father asked him why. He said, 'Well, we don't serve any colored people in this town.' 'Okay,' Father said, and we all went to the kitchen.

"And the man said, 'I don't mean all of you, just the little colored boy.' And Father turned around and said, 'Well, if the boy can't eat out there and we can't eat in here, then we don't eat here at all.' He turned around and he left the food… they had a table all set, and everything, the food was all cooked and waiting for us… and he walked out."[628]

During the boys' performance that evening, the man from the restaurant came and gave Father Flanagan $500. During the rest of their stay in that town, all of the boys ate in the dining room.

As the first musical tour continued, everything went smoothly for the next few weeks. Night after night, the boys would play a town, then pack the show back into the wagons and start off for the next town. As they neared a town, local boys would gather én masse to welcome them, and later would march behind the departing wagons as they rolled away.

Along the way, the boys had plenty of opportunities to visit ice cream parlors, play games, and go swimming. Some of the boys became so badly burned from the sun that they had difficulty playing their instruments, and one lad was forbidden to do any more swimming because he swallowed too much water.

There was success after success after success, and those left behind at the Home eagerly awaited news from the troupe. But the success did not translate to financial gains, and weeks into the tour, the troupe ran out of money.

Then, in a town in western Nebraska, the troupe ran into a totally unanticipated problem. In every place they had played so far, they had been met at the edge of the town by boys and adults, and sometimes town officials, who were happy for their arrival.

But this particular town was different. There was no welcoming group; in fact, there was no one to meet them. When Pat Norton left his wagon to look into the situation (someone from the town had to lead them to where they would perform), it soon became clear why. From one of the buildings on the edge of town came the mayor, the local sheriff, and two or three others. Norton walked toward them but was ordered to halt as he approached.

"We don't want any niggers or Catholics in this town," he was told, "so take your wagons and get out of here!"

Norton, shocked and aware of what was happening, backed away. He knew that the Ku Klux Klan was active in rural Nebraska, that crosses had been burned on the front lawns of the homes of Catholics, and that a Catholic church in Orchard, in northeast Nebraska, had been burned to the ground. The wagons turned around, and as the mayor and sheriff watched from a distance, they headed back toward a small town they had just passed through. When they got there, Norton telephoned Father Flanagan and explained their situation.

"We are broke and our food supply is gone," he told the priest. "Our agent was driven out of town and this was our last engagement."

Father Flanagan visualized the situation and responded.

"It would be a dreadful expense to bring my boys in that distance, with such slow travel methods, without any performance enroute...; I left for the 'front' immediately," he would later recall. "Our funds from all sources were at ebb tide. Our new building was under construction and this work took every dollar we could raise, outside the actual maintenance of the Home. One thing was certain, I had to rescue the stranded little showmen, for the weather was extremely hot by this time, and the boys and the horses could not endure this indefinitely."

When he arrived at the town where the troupe had sought refuge, he found a sad and dejected group: tired, hungry, and with twenty-five boys and eight horses to feed before the long journey home. But this crisis brought out a boldness and an ingenuity that surprised even him.

As they started moving again, new possibilities on the road home loomed up before him. At town after town, even though funds were low, the boys were eager to perform.

"It was a lucky thing for us that it was summer, even though the heat was extreme," Father Flanagan later wrote. "For food was cheap and lodging simple, with cots and four large wagons in the caravan. When we arrived at Harvard, Nebraska, which is about 150 miles from Omaha, we had $7.50 as our sole operating fund. It was about noon when we pulled in."[629]

The little town of Harvard had never been treated to a traveling road show, so arrangements were made for a performance in the only hall in town, a room over the town fire department. Afterwards, the boys were treated royally by the citizens of the town. With $15 in their pockets from their show, they were on their way next morning, still miles from home. But the boys were never undaunted by the heat and the travel, and gave a band concert in every town they passed through, resting at the end of each day on the edge of town or in someone's back yard.

After two weeks of making ten to twelve miles a day, the troupe reached a small rise in the road south of Lincoln. As they trudged on through the morning, the gray walls of the state prison loomed up before them. After stopping outside the gate, Father Flanagan went inside to talk to the warden, who was a friend. (The priest had often been called to the prison to meet with some inmate who had asked to see him; usually, it was one of the men who had passed through his Workingmen's Hotel.)

"I left the boys in the wagons and sought the warden's office. Mr. Fenton was there and welcomed me warmly. After I told him that I had twenty-five boys outside, he hurried out to meet the young troupers."[630]

The warden suggested that the boys might like to entertain the men in the prison that evening. Then, realizing the boys had not eaten all day, he led the hungry crowd to a nearby patch of cantaloupes that were ripe for eating.

After devouring the cantaloupes, the boys gathered for perhaps the strangest concert they would ever give; in Father Flanagan's words, "a group of unfortunate boys singing Gounod's 'Ave Maria' before five hundred convicts. Most earnestly they sang, lost in the music. The criminals, murderers, rapists, underworld creatures of every breed, were deeply stirred by the threnody of young voices lifted in praise of purity and goodness and motherhood.[631]

"I am sure that Warden Fenton never realized what he had done for me and my hungry boys that day…. When we pulled out of Lincoln a little later next morning, we felt that the road home would be short… we pulled in at the gates of Overlook Farm, penniless, tired, but ever so much wiser in matters pertaining to the road show."

A Second Tour

On the whole, the tour had been a rousing success.

People had been charmed and delighted by these boy entertainers, and Father Flanagan received dozens of letters with questions about the Home and the boys. So a giant publicity campaign was launched to inform the public about the priest's work, including the production of a short film about the Home and the lives of the boys. The boys who were in the traveling troupe became the "stars" of the film, since they were already familiar to the audiences for whom they had played. "We wanted the public to get a bird's eye view of the whole Home, with our troupers as factual evidence,"[632] Father Flanagan said.

There were other surprises. Along with the letters, large checks began to arrive in the mail. Father Flanagan had a long conference with Pat Norton and some of the older boys. Even with some of the bad experiences of the first tour, they decided they would try again, and Dan Desdunes began rehearsals.

But this time they would travel by train. Almost flat broke, Father Flanagan borrowed some money from a friendly banker in Omaha and began looking over maps of the Midwest.

"I was seriously considering another itinerary, with different methods of travel," the priest said. "If we could map out a trip through larger towns and cities, which would be reached easily by train, our next trip would not only be more successful, but be much easier on the showmen. [633] I arranged for the services of an experienced advance man and we made plans for an entirely different routing, which would take the troupe to larger towns and the schedule was such that the boys would have uninterrupted rest."[634]

The troupers were so eager for another trip, Father Flanagan decided to take advantage of their enthusiasm and plan a trip for the fall. Since school was critical to the boys' future and to their development, he arranged for an experienced teacher to go along with the troupe. The boys could have their class sessions in the mornings on the train. Since their shows were in the evening, none of them would have to miss school.

The whole Home was excited as the troupers prepared for their second trip, this time north to the Dakotas and Minnesota, with their first engagement at Vermillion, South Dakota.

"That trip on trains was far different from the ones in circus wagons," Father Flanagan later wrote. "We rode comfortably on good trains from town to town, never missing an engagement in the three months we were out…. We played all the principal towns in the two Dakotas, in parts of Minnesota and the north and western parts of Iowa… and closed on December 22, 1922, with every member of the troupe anxious to get home for Christmas."[635]

This second tour was a rousing success, and with good reason. What Father Flanagan did not immediately realize was that news of the boys' first traveling show had reached every town they visited during the second tour, making him and his boys legends.

The story of the stranded circus wagons during the first tour had hit the local newspapers of those towns and the bigotry of one small town had been the talk of breakfast tables and coffee klatches. And the image of innocent waifs singing "Ave Maria" to hardened criminals in their chains almost brought some to tears. During that second tour, in every town, the boys sang and danced to packed houses, and in several places, local boys asked to join the troupe or just sing or play with the band.

One night after a show, as the boys were getting ready for bed in their bunks, there was a knock on the door. One of the boys opened the door and there stood a little boy, ragged and hungry-looking.

"Could I see the man with the black hat?" the little boy asked.

"Bring him in," Father Flanagan said.

The boy was eight years old. As Father Flanagan took his hand, the boy asked, "Can I go on the train with the other boys?"

The priest asked the boy where he came from and what he heard shocked him. This little fellow lived with another little boy in a shack close by. The boy then took the priest to the shack, where the pair shared a dirty old bunk and sold newspapers on the streets for money to live on. After checking with the local authorities, Father Flanagan decided to take the boy with him.

"He had told me the night before that I would find him on a certain corner the next morning. After all necessary arrangements were made, I went for my new boy. He spied me coming almost a block away and came running to meet me.

"He said, 'Kin I go with you?'

"I told him he could. From then on he was my boy."[636]

As the tour continued, the boys made friends wherever they went; some even returned after graduation to settle in the towns that had welcomed them. But it was the effects these tours had on the local people that impressed Father Flanagan. His instincts had been right: Just let the public see what his "homeless" boys were really like, in all their exuberance, talent, good manners, and sheer lovability, and support for his work would grow. The marketing skills he had learned in the offices of Cudahy and Company were paying off, and his comment on this connection became famous: "If they do it for beef, we can do it for boys."

A Joyous Homecoming

Christmas of 1922 was more than just a homecoming for the boys of the traveling tour. New boys had arrived at the Home, old friendships were renewed, the tour boys and the boys who had stayed at the Home compared grades, and groups of boys gathered in corners and on the playing fields to hear news of the tour from those who had made it a success.

"I had all I could do to keep my little band intact," Father Flanagan later wrote. "Friends wanted to take my boys, adopt them…. These people gave me their names and addresses, which I took home with me. In every case possible, we sent them later the little trouper they wanted… some other boy then filled his place in the show."[637]

The priest also saw timid boys blossom in their contact with the larger world. "The educational value of meeting people, of talking with them, and of playing before large audiences, had had its effect on the plastic minds and hearts of my boys."

There was also a healthy competition among the boys. They saw that those who worked harder at their skills and developed their talents replaced those who took their position in the troupe for granted.

By the time the troupe returned to the Home, the new Main Building was completed. A mighty exodus began, from the ramshackle shelters the boys had been living in without running water or bathrooms to what seemed to them a grand hotel with room for more than two hundred boys. There were sleeping quarters, a kitchen and dining room, classrooms, offices, and even a small chapel.

The Home had become respectable, and prominent visitors were common. The traveling troupe had made the Home famous all over the Midwest and the small movie about Father Flanagan and his boys had been shown in movie theaters and social clubs for miles around.

Upon their return, Father Flanagan also made a decision on future travels by the troupe: "After a series of trips by train on regular day coaches for short trips and Pullmans for longer jumps, I decided to get our own railroad car, equipped so we could live in it… it would provide our boys with better accommodations, and insure them several hours of rest. In fact, it would be our home on wheels."[638]

Father Flanagan also was surprised that the talents of those who stayed at the Home had blossomed in their new environment. The boys sensed that Overlook was a test of their survival and they were quickly molded into a close-knit family; as the troupe went on the road, the others kept the home fires burning. They watched as a small village began to grow up around them; old buildings were torn down and new ones were added, along with playing fields, a printing press, and a makeshift movie theater. Older boys had pitched in to help with the construction of the new Main Building, which now dominated the community's landscape with a promise of great things to come.

At the Christmas break, in his office in the new Main Building, Father Flanagan began to gather statistics on his five years of taking in boys. From that first day in December 1917, when he started with five boys, until Christmas of 1922, he had sheltered 1,364 boys of 20 different nationalities from 21 states; 986 came in off the streets, 354 had been placed by the courts, and 24 were "tag" boys; 91 were Catholics, 918 were non-Catholics, and 55 were Jewish.

As winter turned into spring, planting time, the constant care of animals, the clearing of ground for gardens, the construction of storage bins and makeshift kitchens for the canning of fresh fruits and vegetables, and the assigning of chores for every boy who was able dominated the Home's activities. The smaller boys were simply allowed to entertain themselves in the wide open spaces that seemed to stretch endlessly.

By the arrival of the second summer, the care and upkeep of the farm had become a well-organized and carefully planned program, with duties assigned as described in this report in the *Boys' Home Journal*:

"For the month of June, our reports show that we received 4,800 quarts of milk from our cows and every quart was consumed by us boys. We have slaughtered three calves this month, and still have two more to go…. Anthony Burnett and Edward Cole seem to like this kind of business when it comes to skinning the calves.

"It keeps our dairy barn boys busy milking cows and keeping the dairy barn clean…. Willard Carr reports that the flies are bothering the cows during milking time…. We have 13 milking cows and they sure keep the boys busy…. Virgil Magers has charge of the creamery and it surely keeps him busy washing the separator, cooling the milk, and washing the milk cans."

It was also a time when the nearby communities where the boys had entertained began to take an interest in this amazing community on their doorstep. They came not only with gifts but also with planned outings for "Father Flanagan's boys," as they were now called. An occasional visitor was Archbishop Harty, who had watched this wild experiment of one of his priests with praise and adulation, and who knew the difficulty of initiating new pastoral projects from his years as Archbishop of Manila, where he broke precedents and alienated not a few by his own innovative pastoral projects.

What the priest had also discovered, and something that would become an important part of his Boys Town pedagogy, was the healing power of music and the keen sense of accomplishment in the mastery of an instrument or of singing skills that became the heart of the boys' repertoire. That was part of the reason for hiring Dan Desdunes in the first place, and the power of music on his boys was evident from the moment they received the battered and worn out instruments for their first band.

For many it was the first, and sometimes the only, personal accomplishment they achieved, and one or two went on to make a name for themselves in the world of music.[639]

From the beginning, Father Flanagan's work had been a family affair. His mother and sisters had helped with outfitting his first Home on 25th and Dodge Streets and had pitched in at the German-American Home. His brother-in-law had provided the priest with his first automobile, which gave him a mobility he had lacked before. The arrival of his nephew, Patrick Norton, took much of the administrative burden off his shoulders and provided his boys with something of a guardian angel and big brother figure.

In August 1923, Father Flanagan's father died.[640] It was a great loss; his father had been the backbone of his strength from his earliest years, a hidden influence that had shaped his character and his knowledge of his Irish heritage. His father had been his first teacher, taking him at the age of four into the great outdoors of the Leabeg estate to help care for the sheep and cattle, sharing the skills of farming and caring for the land, and expanding his knowledge of matters of character and conscience and the history of his origins.

"My father would tell me many stories, stories of adventure, of the struggle of the Irish People for independence," Father Flanagan wrote. The literature and lore of his native Ireland and that intense spirituality that saw God hovering over everything were lessons which had never left him, even in his darkest hours.

Soon after, Father Flanagan's mother moved to Overlook Farm to care for her son and to make his motherless youngsters her own. She was joined by her daughter, Nellie, who would remain with her brother as a cook and housekeeper for the rest of his life.

Another welcome addition to the staff at that time was Father Hugh Gately, the pastor of the parish in nearby Elkhorn, who took up residence at Overlook Farm while continuing to serve the Catholic community in Elkhorn. Father

Flanagan's staff now consisted of his mother and sister; his nephew, Pat Norton; Father Gately; three Sisters of Notre Dame; Dan Desdunes, the music director; and Dan Catlett, the farm manager.

Father Gately was the first of many priests who assisted Father Flanagan through the years. He not only was a dear friend of Father Flanagan (they had probably met in Rome during Eddie Flanagan's short stay there in 1907), but had also preceded Father Flanagan as the assistant pastor at St. Patrick's Church in Omaha. His presence made it possible for Father Flanagan to be away on speaking engagements and trips with his boy entertainers. Father Gately also was Irish, shared Father Flanagan's love of sports, and was something of a coach to the boys. It is clear that Father Flanagan delighted in his company.[641]

The "World's Greatest Juvenile Entertainers" prepare for a tour of Nebraska, 1922.

Three former circus wagons, painted bright red, carried the boys and everything they needed to put on a show in communities across the Midwest, 1922.

LEFT: A young member of the traveling show troupe, 1922.

RIGHT: Joseph Pivonka was orphaned at age four and came to the Home for Boys when he was eight. He survived the Spanish Influenza pandemic, and starred as the show troupe's first alto, 1922.

Father Flanagan loved music and organized a band for the boys in the Home's early years, 1924.

The boys' band welcomed legendary bandleader John Phillip Sousa (center) to Omaha, 1926.

11

THE ROMANCE OF THE HOMELESS BOY

A Home, A Community

The success of Father Flanagan's speaking tours, touching dozens of cities throughout the Midwest, and the even greater success of his traveling troupe,[642] convinced him that the world was ready to learn even more about his boys. He began what can only be called a marketing plan for introducing his boys to the public, with the theme of what he termed "the romance of the homeless boy." Each boy had an *Oliver Twist*-like story, with the darkness and light that Dickens could bring to life with his masterly pen and "the principle of Good surviving through every adverse circumstance."

Father Flanagan's first act was an imitation of life: hiring a master photographer to chronicle the life of his boys in much the same way photographic genius Jacob Riis had presented the lives of the poor of New York City in his visual studies of the slums, *How the Other Half Lives*.[643] The priest had learned much from Riis, and as a young seminarian at Dunwoodie, had seen the same poor in his visits to the tubercular hospitals of New York and his walks through Hell's Kitchen. His partner in this plan to change how the world looked at homeless boys was Louis R. Bostwick,[644] who had begun to work for Father Flanagan when the first boys arrived at the Home on 25th and Dodge.

Bostwick's first photos had been simply historical, a photographic record of the boys as they came (some in the most miserable of condition), and then portraying them at work and at play, and in their daily round of activities. Bostwick had created a photographic history of the Home's earliest days, but his photos were more than casual shots of boys at work or at play. The personality of each child seemed to burst out of each photo, and over the years, almost 600 of these glimpses of the boys' lives filled the pages of the *Boys' Home Journal* and local newspapers. With these photos, the image of the homeless boy began to change as Father Flanagan relentlessly sought to show, by word and graphic illustration, the sheer goodness that poured out of his boys and the unlimited possibilities of their future. Bostwick's most striking and memorable photos lent powerful images to Father Flanagan's work with the boys of all ages who wandered in off the streets.

Besides finding a way to present his boys to the world in a positive, hopeful light, Father Flanagan faced other challenges. For example, what were the boys to do after they graduated? A few had found homes with local or farm families after leaving the Home, but Father Flanagan became reluctant to continue to "farm out" boys. Oftentimes, these boys were placed with a farm family in the spring, used as a farm hand or cheap labor, and brought back in the fall, no better for the experience.[645]

But there were several placements that proved to be golden opportunities for the boys involved, and some went on to become successful businessmen, college graduates, doctors, and lawyers in their own right. One was Henry Sutti, who became the first former Boys Town resident ordained as a priest. He would study with other graduates[646] at Conception College in Missouri and then join the Jesuits to spend the rest of his life in British Honduras.[647]

Right from the beginning, Father Flanagan recognized that not all of his boys were destined for college and the classics, and so his educational plans also included a trade school, where boys could be trained in a variety of skills that would prepare them to enter the workforce when they graduated. It was this thrust toward self-sufficiency that motivated him to express a strong conviction many times, in many ways: In this country, your only limitations are in your own efforts.

Another problem he faced was the race question. Father Flanagan rejected with a passion racial prejudice of any kind. Differences, he said, are enriching, not divisive, and to the shock of many in the general public, black, white, Native American, Asian, and Mexican boys lived together, worked together, played together, argued and fought together, and even took showers and swam together. Most remained close friends for the rest of their lives.[648]

Father Flanagan was building a community of friends, aptly described as the "City of Little Men," and when its story would later splash across the screen in the movie *Boys Town*, the whole world would take it to heart. The priest worked from a religious and educational genius, rare even in the Catholic Church, and the roots of that genius transcended the common image of him as a kindly padre who just wanted to take kids off the street and give them a decent home.

It was for a good reason that as a youngster, he had devoured the writings of Dickens and Macaulay, and the stirring poetry and novels of Sir Walter Scott, and had later added to his pedagogical repertoire the works of John Henry Newman, St. Thomas Aquinas, and the Patristic legacy of the Catholic Church. The force that drove him also resounded somewhat in the novels of Canon Patrick Augustine Sheehan, who was more than a literary oddity among the Irish priests of his day.[649] Sheehan was a close friend and confidante of Supreme Court Justice Oliver Wendell Holmes, Jr.,[650] and showed himself as the intellectual equal of that remarkable jurist, whose interests ranged over the whole landscape of modern thought and practice.

Father Flanagan's mind was literally a dynamo of growing insights and convictions about religious education in particular. He insisted that the first effort in education of any kind must be the development of character,[651] since without it, every human gift is wasted. (This was later indicated in his reaction in 1946 to the orphanages and workhouses of his native Ireland that were mistreating children and using them for their own financial advantage.[652])

His study of the problem of the abuse of children – in families, orphanages, so-called "reform" schools, the courts, and child labor – drew him into the problem of juvenile crime and juvenile justice. Together with Judge Ben Lindsey of Denver, he became almost the sole voice in a cause that affected a large portion of the population centers of the United States. Shocked and dismayed by such studies as John Spargo's *Bitter Cry of Children*[653] and Judge Ben Lindsey's *Children in Bondage*,[654] he rushed into the cause with an eloquence that filled the pages of his *Boys' Home Journal* and reverberated in the speeches and talks he gave before club meetings, women's groups, and public gatherings.

In 1925, the first publication of Father Flanagan's campaign to change the public image of the homeless boy, aptly titled, *The Romance of the Homeless Boy*,[655] was released. It was lavishly illustrated with Louis Bostwick's photos of the boys and contained detailed information on the eight-year history of the Home, which was still called "Father Flanagan's Boys' Home." (The name "Boys Town" and the concept of the Home as an experiment in self-government would come a year later. Also under that concept, educational plans included classrooms, study halls, and a library as well as a trade school that offered a variety of skills like pottery, barbering, auto mechanics, and printing. The Home would also continue its musical tradition with a band and a boys choir.)

Father Flanagan realized with some dismay and anticipation that he was creating a new youth culture, a novel experiment in communal living involving boys of many races, religions, ethnic backgrounds, and nationalities. The move to Overlook Farm had begun ten years, at home and on the road, that defined Father Flanagan's work long before it was embodied in the community of Boys Town. These were years of intense activity for the priest as he spoke throughout the Midwest, accompanied by boy orators,[656] or at events in Omaha, where he had served as president of the Omaha Welfare Board, or on occasional trips with his boy entertainers as they traveled as far away as California and New York.

Father Flanagan also tapped into new methods of communication for gaining public support for his work, including radio and film documentaries.[657] In September 1925, he began a weekly series of talks on WOW radio in Omaha, often accompanied by one of his boys, "Johnny the Gloom Killer." These talks became a regular feature of the station, and Johnny the Gloom Killer became one of the first stars of this new medium. Father Flanagan's Boys' Band also became a regular feature of the program.[658]

A New Name and Self-Government

In 1926, the boys voted to change the name of the Home to "Boys Town,"[659] and the concept of a real community of youngsters, run by the youngsters, began to grow. Up to now, the Home had been run as an extended family, older boys looking after younger boys,[660] with Father Flanagan's mother, Honora, his sister, Nellie, and his nephew, Pat Norton, taking an active part in its operation. Another sister, Susan, and her husband, Dr. J.R. Dwyer, looked after the health of the boys. But in March 1926, Father Flanagan's Boys' Home became Boys Town and the concept of self-government was introduced.

The germ of self-government came from the boys themselves: "Plans are being consummated for the organization of a club at Father Flanagan's Boys' Home. The suggestion came from one of the boys, who submitted an outline of the plan. Every boy in the Home is keen for it… We should have a constitution and by-laws and a definite objective. Father Flanagan and his associates believe that such a club could be developed into a very helpful organization, in fact one that might practically conduct all the affairs of the Home."[661]

(The Knights of Honor had been organized and developed earlier by the boys to keep order at the Home and help Father Flanagan with its operation.[662] It was an early experiment of self-government, with a mayor and commissioners to oversee and supervise the life of the boys in various areas of responsibility like safety, activities, and finance. While the experiment percolated for some time, as the Home and its activities grew, the Knights of Honor had no real authority.)

After weeks of meetings, brainstorming sessions, the sharing of ideas, help from the outside, and intense discussion among the boys, the simplest rules for an election were laid down by Father Flanagan: "Each candidate will have a certain amount of printed matter… none may spend money, marbles, knives, or anything else for the expenses of the campaigns. Neither may they give anything to anyone for voting for them. (No political corruption here.) Each candidate, however, may have one campaign manager."

Thirty-two boys ran for office. The term of office for mayor and the commissioners would be six months. Council meetings were to be held once a week, with each commissioner handing in a report on the activities in his area.

Omaha's mayor, James Dahlman, and several other city commissioners were delighted to take part in this mini-election on the edge of their city, and the first election went off with flags flying, youthful campaign oratory, and boys undoubtedly taking sides in the campaign. In the end, William Roach was elected as the Home's first "unofficial" mayor.

Father Flanagan's introduction of self-government to his boys was an important milestone in the development of the Home. However, it would not be until 1935, when Boys Town was recognized as an incorporated village of the State of Nebraska, that the system of self-government and its offices (mayor and commissioners) would be considered legal and official. That did not diminish the importance of the concept of the boys having a strong voice in the decisions affecting how Boys Town operated, both as a home and a community, in the 1920s and early 1930s.

Father Flanagan's Boys' Home had come of age.

Even with those triumphs, the finances of the Home continued to be fragile. Father Flanagan's major concern was a $103,000 mortgage that would come due in April 1927. Knowing that his work was now known and admired in all parts of the country, he sent out a widespread appeal in 1926:

"Our indebtedness consists of $103,000.00 bearing 6% interest in the form of bonds which were sold to complete our building. These bonds will come due next April. Our struggle in the past years to carry on the work here, to feed, clothe, and educate our large family of homeless boys, (has been so great) that I have been unable to set aside any money to pay off our indebtedness."

In his desperation, he added: "If I could get 100 persons to pay $1,000.00 each, this would be one way of paying it."

Despite his optimism, the financial burdens of running the Home, in reality, were beginning to overwhelm him. He was also burdened with the fact that he had no high school. The schools in the city were too far away and too expensive for the boys, and so he was desperate. All he wanted was for his boys to have a chance. "They are bright and ambitious boys, and I know they will grasp any opportunity to work and work hard for board and room and clothes if some good people would take them into their home," he wrote.

It was the sudden realization that he was running out of resources that deeply distressed him, and boys were still banging on the doors to get in.

Aware that his speech tours and his boys' entertainment circuits had made a lot of new friends for the Home, Father Flanagan made a radio appeal on WOW in Omaha, no doubt with oratorical help from Johnny the Gloom Killer. The speech was long and filled with a sense of dejection at the heavy prospects of not being able to meet his obligations and possibly having to close the Home:

"This indeed has been a worry that would break down the constitution of any man were it not for the encouragement I receive from the friends of the Home from time to time. Such a burden would have sapped all the vitality out of me and made me a fit subject for an insane asylum, but God has given me courage to continue, even though at times only dark clouds encircled the horizon of that Home."

To stir up more interest, he sent his boys' band through Nebraska and Iowa and then took his entertainment troupe to California. By the start of school in the fall of 1926, several of his eighty graduates had found homes in Omaha so they could begin attending high school in the city.

But debt still loomed over the Home.

Father Flanagan found his plan for a solution just after Christmas of 1926. The plan had something of a public relations flavor about it, and the idea may have come from his friend and publicist, Morris Jacobs, who visited frequently. This was the announcement in the February 1927 issue of the *Boys' Home Journal*:

"Everyone at Overlook Farm… is very enthusiastic over our 'Burn the Mortgage Campaign,' which will be held from the 4th to the 14th of April. We all realize what a tremendous task this is, to raise One Hundred and Three Thousand Dollars by that time, but we know, too, that it can be done, if the friends of the homeless boys will rally around us and each one do his part."

That others besides Father Flanagan had a hand in this project is evident in the organization that took place to cover territories inside and outside the Omaha area. Every town and city in the state was covered and his weekly radio programs were beefed up to reach thousands more. The Home's programs were the most popular on the two Omaha radio stations, WOW and WAAW, with one sponsored by the Woodman of the World Life Insurance Company and the other by the Omaha Grain Exchange. Now that the financial needs of the Home had been developed into an identifiable campaign, everyone in the civic and business community of the city and state threw their hat in the ring.

Money began to come in, in drips and drops at first. Then, a huge surprise: the governor and the mayor got into the act with public endorsements of the campaign. The governor wrote, "The drive for funds that will buy the match to burn the mortgage, I trust, will be liberal and warmhearted."[663] The mayor added, "It is an enterprise that claims the assistance of every man and woman who reckons the worth of the boyhood of America at its proper value."[664]

The concept of the *Romance of the Homeless Boy* had reached the state-house and the holders of power in the city! Father Flanagan's work had come of age, and in less than ten years, he had conquered the city, the state, and the regions beyond. At last, his voice was one to be reckoned with by those in the seats of power.

In spite of the deep disappointments of the early days, his work had finally captured the heart of Omaha. It also had begun to change the racial prejudice of the city, with his work for boys of "every race, color, and creed" being recognized as a huge step forward in humanitarian concern. It would not be long before he would be recognized as one of the world's outstanding humanitarians.

The response of the city's newspapers to the campaign was indicative of this new public awareness of his work.

The *Omaha World-Herald:* The Boys at Overlook Farm

In a few weeks Father Flanagan's Boys' Home will launch a campaign to raise a little more than 100 thousand dollars in cash to pay off the mortgage on Overlook Farm. That campaign is going to cause a lot of men and women to dig freely and gladly and deeply into their pockets – for Father Flanagan's Boys' Home represents the kind of charity that commands public respect and gratitude.

The home is chock-full of boys, black, white, and tan, of many different creeds, of many different nationalities. They come from many communities. In the home, they find friendship, wise and tender supervision, good food, comfortable living quarters, and an opportunity to develop their individualities and make the best of themselves. Many of them, without the home, would be kicked and cuffed about the world, and would fall into those associations that make for evil. Given a home at Overlook Farm, they find it easy to develop the qualities of self–reliance and the strength of character that make good citizens.

When the mortgage burns – and it will be burned – Father Flanagan and his aides will have a load lifted from their hearts, and their work will be made that much less difficult. The boys will know that this community is sympathetically interested in their welfare and that will encourage them.

The Omaha Bee News: Boys or Dollars?

Which is worth more in this world, a boy or a dollar?

No hesitance as to the answer to that question. Now comes another. What about the boys who are deprived of homes, left to shift for themselves? To meet the adversities and hardships of a world they know nothing about, and (for which) they are not prepared either physically, mentally, or morally.

They must be cared for by somebody, if they are to be given a boy's right to grow up under proper conditions, to be well-trained for a man's place in the world. No boy is an orphan by choice. When he is deprived of parents, loses father or mother, or both, and is set adrift, he is the victim of one of life's saddest tragedies.

Ten years ago, Father E.J. Flanagan was a young priest assistant at one of the largest churches in Omaha. He noted the need for a home for boys and set about to provide for the need. It was a dream, maybe, but he brought it to a glorious reality. Overlook Farm, west of the city, a sightly location, with a great building, is the outcome of that dream. In eight years, 1,955 boys have been cared for in Father Flanagan's Home. Of these, 1,263 have come from Nebraska, the others from thirty different states and one from Canada. Of them, 1,230 have been non-Catholic and 725 Catholic. In December 1917, he had five boys in an old wooden building downtown. Today he has over 200 in a fine modern, fireproof structure.

Just a hint of what has to be done. But it has taken money to do this, and Father Flanagan's Home is supported by voluntary contributions. A mortgage of $103,000 is coming due and must be cared for. Hence the appeal that is being made for funds to support this noble work. It should not be in vain. Of all the institutions supported by public or private contributions in Omaha, none is more worthy.

Cast the problem up in your own mind. What is more valuable to you, a boy or a dollar? Answer it as you will, the reply must be in favor of Father Flanagan's Home.

The good will cheered Father Flanagan's heart; such an outpouring of love and concern for his work! He could live from day to day on the edge of bankruptcy, put up with the incessant and demanding needs of his boys, spend weeks on the road spreading word of his work, and battle with banks and creditors, if he could keep his doors open and his little village prospering. What he came up with in desperation was now tapping a source of income that could continue long after the mortgage was paid and burned, and generate income with no strings attached.

It would create a new kind of bond, not a bond that paid interest to the buyers but one that brought money in with no monetary dividends going out. It was a new form of investment, and was touted in large letters in the *Boys' Home Journal* as "The Finest and Safest Investment," described simply as "Bonds of Happiness," with the only payoff being "Dividends of Smiles." Strangely, it worked and there was a clamor for these "Bonds of Happiness" all over the Midwest.

The Invention of a Unique Man

In 1927, a residence was completed for Father Flanagan[665] at Overlook and he, his mother, and his sister, Nellie, moved in. Other family members also helped at or visited the Home. The priest's younger brother, Michael, a professional singer, entertained the boys with an occasional concert[666] and various nephews and nieces dropped in from time to time. There also were visitors from Ireland; Father Flanagan had stayed in close contact with his home country, as Irish independence became a reality after the 1916 Easter Rising and the establishment of the Irish Free State in 1922.

Nephew Pat Norton had been his right-hand man since arriving at the German-American Home in 1920, providing support and assistance through all the major crises of the early years. Norton traveled with the entertaining troupe from 1920 to 1928,[667] and later would become the first postmaster and then business manager of the Home.

As the Home grew, the *Romance of the Homeless Boy* was manifested in many ways; there were boy orators and boy actors, boy violinists,[668] boy singers, boy farmers,[669] boy bakers,[670] boy chefs,[671] boy engineers,[672] and boy horsemen, as well as an all-boy band and orchestra. With the new freedom and space Boys Town provided, the skills of the boys seemed to multiply.[673] Besides learning how to play baseball, football, basketball, and handball, they also excelled at farming, planting, harvesting, and storing and preparing food. The Home even had a corps of boy journalists,[674] boy firemen, and starting with the self-government elections of 1926, boy politicians.

The intellectual reach of some of the boys surprised the priest. Two started their own in-house newspapers,[675] and his boy orators were eloquent speakers who could hold listeners spellbound on radio and on the road. Young entertainers like Oscar Flakes and Charles Kenworthy were almost national figures, spending their years at the Home packing in crowds during road shows from

Ohio to California. The leaders in the self-government system often called in the mayor of Omaha and other city officials to advise them on governance and the proper procedures for electing public officials.[676]

Father Flanagan's approach to child care and teaching was noted for providing a maximum of freedom and a minimum of discipline, in radical contrast to other systems being used at that time. ("No walls," he said. "You don't wall in your own family.") There was, in fact, a definite theory behind his work and it involved creating an organism rather than an organization. It was a system of mutual education on a large scale, where the influences to do good were so numerous that very few boys who came under Father Flanagan's care did not come off the better for it.

That was his genius. It was the careful molding of individuals by individuals, in a mutual give-and-take that was Boys Town. Some detected no system at all in his work, and others were severely critical of the slogan that made him famous ("There are no bad boys...."), crediting him only with mere platitudes, if not rank sentimentality. But Edward Joseph Flanagan was no mean scholar and he approached his work with a thoroughness and intellectual acumen known only to a few. He would discuss his views with anyone who wanted to listen, and those who did listen were often professionals and educators in their own right. One of them was Dr. Franz Plewa, who came to Boys Town from Alfred Adler's Child Guidance Clinics in Vienna, Austria. Dr. Plewa described Father Flanagan as that rare human specimen and intuitive genius that comes along only once or twice in a lifetime, and Boys Town embodied the totality of his pedagogical vision.

Father Flanagan saw every boy as the raw material for greatness; he saw what was possible, and that somehow rubbed off on the boys who came to him. He made it impossible for a boy to get in trouble by surrounding him with peer pressure that leaned in the positive direction. He gave lost boys a "town" of their own, a place where each individual played a vital role and could take pride in and a personal possession of its accomplishments. Boys Town was the invention of a unique man who understood the real meaning of family, of belonging, and of a contrived culture where acceptance was total.

What he saw as he entered his work was a social crisis in which the homeless child was almost a surplus commodity; a religious crisis in which character was molded by restraint; and an educational crisis in which mass education was the norm. He rejected all of these, and inaugurated a social, religious, and educational revolution that took the world by storm, making Boys Town world famous and "Father Flanagan" a household name. Not everyone could say what the name symbolized, but people came from all over the world to find out.

Father Flanagan's most significant insights were that human beings are fashioned by culture, and that the human person develops his or her full potential in an atmosphere of freedom and full acceptance. These two insights, coupled with the Christian conviction that the Gospel must not be forced, either in its propagation or its development, gave Boys Town a measure of success that drew the admiration of educators the world over.

In less than ten years, the priest had gathered around him men and women of every race, religion, profession, and political conviction who saw and sensed something culturally miraculous in what now was being called the "City of Little Men." Father Flanagan's friend, Morris Jacobs, who was a police reporter when he met the priest in the city courts, commented that, "Boys Town is not an institution… it's a factory… a factory making good citizens on the principal of the assembly line."

Soon, national figures began to join the chorus of praise for what was growing as a cradle of democracy on the edge of Omaha: Babe Ruth,[677] who had grown up in an orphanage; Tom Mix;[678] John Philip Sousa; two Nebraska state senators, George W. Norris and Robert B. Howell; and even President J. Calvin Coolidge, Jr., whom members of the boys' band had met on one of their tours through the Black Hills when Coolidge was vacationing there.

Father Flanagan's radio programs, featuring the Home's band and Johnny the Gloom Killer, continued to spread the word about Boys Town all over the Midwest, garnering letters from listeners. Most letters contained money, with notes of congratulations on Father Flanagan's work. This was a new source of income, and each letter was answered with additional news about what was happening at the Home.

There was the booklet, *The Romance of the Homeless Boy*, massively illustrated with photographs by Louis Bostwick that depicted the life of the boys, from farm work and band practice to baseball and books, and the happy faces of kids who had once roamed the streets, without a friend or a home. Now, they had both.

TOP: Many boys hitch-hiked their way to Boys Town, 1930s.

LEFT: A Depression-era photo of how boys often arrived at Boys Town, dirty and dressed in tattered clothing.

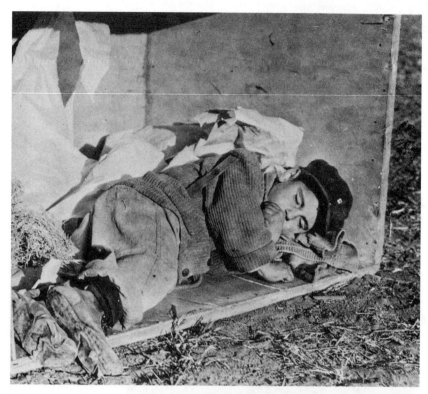

ABOVE: This powerful image of a boy living in a piano crate helped increase awareness about Boys Town's work.

RIGHT: Many photos of boys in the streets symbolized the desperate need for a refuge like Boys Town for America's homeless children.

During the 1930s, the Home used this "Homeless Boy" image to draw attention to the plight of destitute youth.

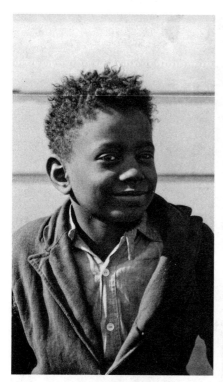

TOP LEFT: From the earliest days of his Home, Father Flanagan accepted boys of all races, boldly challenging racial bigotry and the societal norms of separation and inequality.

TOP RIGHT: After being admitted to Boys Town, boys would clean up and be photographed wearing a new suit of clothing, 1930s.

During Boys Town's first ten years, many boys walked hundreds of miles to reach the Home, carrying their meager belongings in a paper sack or a bed roll.

12

THE ANATOMY OF JUVENILE CRIME

Life on the Streets

Like his friend and mentor, Father Francis Patrick Duffy, whose parish was more out of the Bronx and Hell's Kitchen than a church and rectory, Father Flanagan preached a practical theology that was straight out of the streets. First, it was in his work for jobless men, then in[679] his exhaustive study of the men off the street whose early lives mirrored those of his boys.

Father Flanagan's first encounter with life on the streets was certainly when he read the novels of Charles Dickens as a boy while watching his father's sheep. The lessons of *Oliver Twist, Hard Times*, and *Nicholas Nickleby* were riveted in his mind, and even moved him in his college days (when he was barely nineteen) to make a study of English workhouses. He was familiar with Jacob Riis' photographs of the slums of New York, first published in 1890, which brought shame to the whole city and was a visual portrayal of the helpless poor, many of them children roaming the streets or living in the most degrading of human circumstances. In these images, Father Flanagan also saw the power of an image.

It may have been Riis' graphic portrayal of the life of the poor in *The Way the Other Half Lives* that moved Father Flanagan to hire Louis Bostwick to chronicle the life of his boys and to change forever in the public's mind the image of the homeless boy.

Finally, it was in his experiences with the kids in the streets of Omaha. (Father Flanagan had seen street youth in Sligo, at Summerhill College, where they begged for money, and on the streets of Hell's Kitchen in New York, during his seminary days at Dunwoodie.)

His first real shock came when he met his first boy off the streets, a nine-year-old who had been living in a box behind a department store in Omaha. This made him realize there were dozens, maybe even hundreds, of such boys living in the same circumstances. That homeless nine-year-old planted the seed of an idea: "These boys need a home."

But the stigma of the youthful criminal was still on these boys. The public was convinced that these homeless boys were mini-gangsters on the loose, the kind of boys who would be made famous on movie screens as the "Dead End Kids" or the "Bowery Boys," always in trouble, ready to break in, rob, steal, and terrify the neighborhood. Knowing his boys, and all that was in them – the friendship and camaraderie and sheer goodness that flowed out of them – Father Flanagan began to make a study of the juvenile mind. Basing it on a wide range of empirical data and raw materials that he had right before him at Boys Town (which was unavailable to most scholars in the field), he came up with some startling conclusions.

He had made a similar study of 2,000 of the men who inhabited his Workingmen's Hotel after the harvest workers left; he had been warned by those workers that his hotel would now attract a different kind of guest. He learned to his own sorrow and bitter experience that they were right, and in one memorable case, it almost cost him a public embarrassment that might have ended his efforts for these lost men.[680] Many of them ended up in prisons. (The opening scene of the movie Boys Town is an accurate portrayal of the fate many of them met.)

Father Flanagan's realization that he was working at the wrong end of these broken men's lives was the catalyst that sparked his mind when he first saw boys in court. It led to nights of reading the latest research on the juvenile problem and to him joining forces with Denver's Judge Ben Lindsey, who had almost singlehandedly created the juvenile justice system as part of the court system of the United States. It was this compassion for lost youth that drew the two men together, and their collaboration became one of the great binding of minds in a pioneering effort to change how children were treated in America's judicial system.

(In Great Britain, the effort started a little earlier thanks to the writings of Charles Dickens, though it wasn't until 1933 that child labor was outlawed in that country. In the United States, child labor wasn't outlawed until 1941.[681])

When Father Flanagan arrived in Omaha in 1913, the city was the gateway to the West. For over half a century, pioneers, Indian scouts, gold seekers, cattlemen, and wave after wave of immigrants had passed through it, first on wagon trains that crossed the prairies or came up the Missouri River from St. Louis, and later, as railroad lines were laid, on trains of the Union Pacific Railroad, headed west to California and Oregon. Omaha was growing fast, expanding west from the Missouri River, and from its center to the north and south, making it the largest city between Chicago and San Francisco.

With this growth came all the problems of a larger city, with brothels and bars and gambling dens springing up where the city met the river. There were closed neighborhoods of Italian, Irish, Polish, Bohemian, German, Greek, Jewish, and Scandinavian immigrants, most of them poor, their residences grouped around churches and synagogues. There was corruption in city government, with a powerful political machine that had ruled the city since the turn of the century.

For all its pioneer flavor, the city had come into its own with the lavish Trans-Mississippi Exposition in 1898. The Exposition brought thousands of visitors to Omaha and sparked a civic and commercial development that made many of its citizens not only rich and prosperous but also patrons of the arts, education, and civic enterprises that created some of the city's most durable institutions. The economy of the city was based primarily in the stockyards of South Omaha, which employed thousands, and the meat-packing industry that rivaled those of Chicago and Kansas City.

When Father Flanagan started his work for homeless men, the city was awash with jobless immigrants, most of whom were unable to speak English. Poverty was rampant in their ethnic neighborhoods, and hundreds of men sought work in the stockyards and packinghouses.

The city was controlled by a political machine headed by Tom Dennison,[682] who manipulated his office for his own purposes, and from his headquarters in the city's Third Ward, encouraged open vice, shady business practices, bawdy houses, and underworld activities that gave Omaha the reputation of being a crime city.

There was a "respectable" and prosperous element in the city that ignored the massive immigration poverty and kept aloof of the activities of Tom Dennison and his cronies. These families, most of them in the business community, were deeply embarrassed by the growing social problems: the poor, the huge immigrant population, and then, this priest reminding them there was a juvenile problem and that is was the responsibility of the citizens to save the youth of the city.

With a combination of wit, humor, and brazen audacity, Father Flanagan was able to trap others into his way of thinking, eventually turning the city of Omaha upside-down through his unconventional appeal to their better instincts. The major companies of the city not only started displaying paid ads in his *Journal*, but also responded to his challenge that their investment in the future of these homeless boys would bring a greater benefit to the city than any other investment. He was not appealing to their charitable instincts or to what he sometimes called the "Oliver Twist Appeal." He was talking about hard cash and the return on hard cash, and this began to make sense to hard-headed businessmen who were captivated by his logic and his ability to dismantle, before their eyes, the lust for gold that was the engine of their financial enterprises.

After many years of laying this foundation, Father Flanagan and his boys were now often in the news, and he was often in the courts. The courts had been the beat of a well-known police reporter named Morris Jacobs, who was also a close friend of Henry Monsky. In 1921, the year Father Flanagan moved his boys to Overlook Farm, Jacobs teamed up with Leo Bozell to found the public relations firm of Bozell & Jacobs and took on Father Flanagan and his boys as one of their clients.

Jacobs visited Overlook Farm often, observing the utter dedication of Father Flanagan to his boys.[683] He and Father Flanagan became close friends and

Jacobs was impressed by the priest's work for boys and the skill with which he changed street boys into responsible citizens.

Father Flanagan went about his work with the tenacity of a hard-headed businessman, showing that a small investment could reap huge results. Bozell & Jacobs had a publicity man represent Boys Town for the rest of Father Flanagan's life.[684] They suggested that Father Flanagan retire his *Boys' Home Journal* in 1939 and helped inaugurate its successor, *the Boys Town Times*, which would quickly have a tremendous circulation around the world.

It was Father Flanagan's ability to see the goodness in every boy who came to him that was the touchstone of his genius, and it was his skill in drawing that goodness out that opened wide the door of each boy's future. He somehow gave them a sense of their own worth, and communicated to them that their only limitations were their own efforts. His pedagogy was experiential, rather than homiletic, and he learned from the constant rough-and-tumble and close-knit association with boys of every of race, color, and creed that differences were enriching, not divisive. This lived experience was Boys Town, even before Overlook Farm became an incorporated village and each boy became not just an inhabitant but a citizen.

From the time that nine-year-old boy wandered into his Workingmen's Hotel and he realized that boys were on the streets making trouble, Father Flanagan took a clue from Charles Dickens and tried to grasp how "the purest good may not be drawn from the vilest evil,"[685] and how a boy was still a boy, whatever evil may become attached to him.

He was well aware that young criminals did exist, and, like Dickens, he had to dig deeply into juvenile crime to find out why and how it lured poor youngsters into its web.

There, lurking in the carefully crafted prose of Dickens was the insight: Change the environment and you change the boy. If the environment brings out the evil, then someone had to provide an environment that brought out the good. But Father Flanagan had to look carefully at juvenile crime in all its deformity, in all the human wretchedness out of which some of these boys came – the squalid poverty and the shocking circumstances that dulled their consciences and shaped their behavior.

"I enriched my own experience tremendously in these trooping years," he later wrote. "I found that the problem of the homeless boy was not confined to any one section or any particularized sized town or city. While conditions were aggravated in congested areas in cities, they were not peculiar to these areas. There can be just as much abuse of homeless and neglected children on farms and in small towns, as far as the individual child is concerned, as in any city.

"I took advantage of these travels to study the law governing juvenile offenses, and found to my amazement that they were, in most cases, very similar to those affecting adult crimes. In many states, these same laws are still operating. Every now and then, the public is shocked when a child commits what is termed a major crime. Whether he is ten or eighteen years old, he is classed as a criminal, and the law says he must pay the penalty of his crime behind prison bars and high walls."[686]

Then there was this salient observation: "Rarely does any community in which such a crime occurs take into consideration the environment and home conditions which contributed to this child's delinquency. This child is to be punished, in most cases, for his neglect."[687]

Turning over in his mind the experience of those "trooping years," when the Home was gradually becoming a community of boys, Father Flanagan gravitated more and more to the roots and causes of juvenile crime, and found them in the one place one would least expect: the juvenile court system. He found it in a case that resembled in its stark tragedy a page out of Victor Hugo's *Les Miserables*, something he considered unbelievable, inexcusable, and almost criminal.

"It was but natural that my interest in the fate of neglected boys who came into conflict with antiquated laws would be ever widening," he would say. "My attention was attracted to prominent cases which got into the newspapers in other states, as well as my own."[688]

One of those newspaper reports concerned two boys, one seven and the other nine. Like Victor Hugo's hero, these two young boys were arrested for breaking into a grocery store. They were brought before the court, convicted of a crime, and sent to a juvenile prison. They had been living with their mother, whose husband had deserted her, leaving the family with no means of support. She often left the boys at home alone, and they survived as best they could. One evening, they went searching the back streets and alleys for something to eat. Finding an open door into a grocery store, they entered, saw food all around them, and began to eat. A night watchman making his rounds caught them devouring the food. He called the police.

In his first real attempt to challenge the juvenile justice system, the priest appealed to the governor of the state for the release of the boys.[689] But he was informed that the boys must pay for their crime and were not fit to associate with other children in an orphanage or youth shelter. Father Flanagan appealed to the governor again,[690] but received an even less-courteous refusal. Then he offered to accept the boys at Overlook Farm. But the governor was adamant.[691] Finally, Father Flanagan made a public issue of it. The story reached the newspapers and the boys were removed from prison and placed in a home for dependent children.[692] The priest suddenly realized the value of public exposure and the power of the press.

Judge Ben Lindsey[693]

As more and more horror stories reached Father Flanagan, he came to the realization that the juvenile justice system, as far as youth were concerned, was in need of a vast overhaul.[694]

No child, whatever his age or the circumstances of his offense, was exempt from the brutal arm of the law. He made his own study of the juvenile justice system and found only one voice that resounded with the same indignation as his own, that of Judge Benjamin Lindsey[695] of Denver, whom his boys had met at one of their shows in Colorado.[696]

When he began his law career in 1900, Lindsey fought the policies and politics of the court system in Colorado and soon became known as the "Kids' Judge." He fought for a juvenile justice system that treated children as children, looked into the child's home situation, and kept them out of adult prisons.[697] Like Father Flanagan in Omaha, he had to fight a statewide political machine that held both city and state government hostage, and corrupt Democratic and Republican parties that carefully controlled candidates for public office and the courts, and opposed any efforts at social or judicial reform. By an accident of history, Lindsey was appointed to fill the unexpired term of a county judge and made a name for himself as he tried to bring about reforms in the judicial system.[698]

Right away, he became the target of the "Big Boss" organization of the city of Denver, which manipulated the courts and the government of the city to favor whom it willed. This stirred up Lindsey to call the organization, in his own words, "a Beast." In 1910, he went public with his reform campaigns with a publication of the same name, *The Beast*.[699]

Through his friendship with Jacob Riis, whose book of photographs of the New York slums, *How the Other Half Lives*, brought the plight of the poor to national attention (and in particular, to the attention of then-New York Police Commissioner Theodore Roosevelt), Judge Lindsey joined a group of nationally prominent persons working toward reform of the welfare system and the end of child labor. Among these national figures were Jane Addams,[700] Florence Kelly,[701] Julia Lathrop,[702] Samuel McCone Lindsay, Paul U. Kellogg,[703] and Homer Folks.[704]

In 1904, Theodore Roosevelt was elected president of the United States and was introduced to Benjamin Lindsey by Riis, beginning a lengthy association between Lindsey and the president. Roosevelt endorsed Judge Lindsey's basic principles of the juvenile court movement[705] and recommended that such a code be adopted by Congress for Washington, D.C.

Through his friendship with Judge Lindsey, Father Flanagan joined this generation of social reformers and opponents of child labor, and became a vocal critic of the juvenile justice system and a major player in the movement to reform the system in Nebraska and in the nation as a whole.

Father Flanagan later wrote, "It is almost unbelievable that this most vicious system could still be in use in a civilized nation."[706]

Like Judge Lindsey,[707] Father Flanagan decided to fight the system. From his research, which began when he first stood before a judge asking that a boy in trouble be paroled to his custody, the priest knew the law did not take into account the boy's age, the circumstances in which he lived, the details of his home life, or the supervision he received from adults. His detailed description of one of his first efforts to help children in trouble – the case of the two boys caught stealing food from a grocery store – illustrated the complete insensitivity of the law to the circumstances that drove poor and hungry children to break the law:

"The first one of these cases in which I tried to help boys was that of Donald and George Shetron, seven and nine years old, respectively.[708] These two little children were arrested in Missouri for robbing a grocery store. They were not only accused of the crime, they were convicted of it.

"Let us take a look at their childhood. The father and mother had quarreled for some time previous to their separation. Soon after the younger boy was born, the father deserted and disappeared from the community. He was never heard of afterward.

"When he had been the head of the family, they barely eked out an existence. But with that small income gone, the mother had nothing to turn to. She was incapable of earning much herself, and if she were to be gone during the day, she had no one to leave her children with. This was the problem most common with those who need help.

"Finally, the mother gave up the struggle. She paid little attention to the boys, both of whom were of school age now. They shifted for themselves as best they could. They were ragged and hungry most of the time.

"But even children will not starve to death without some final effort to get food. Donald and George made that effort. One evening, they were wandering streets and alleys in search of something to eat. They had had no supper. They came upon a back door of a store that was open. The smells from the inside told them that it was a grocery store. They went in.

"Here at last they had landed in the realm of plenty. There was food all around them. Far more than enough for their supper.

"The night watchman making his rounds heard a noise in the store, and investigating, found the little boys. He arrested them and charged them with breaking and entering. The law, seeking revenge on the boys' neglect, convicted them and sent them to a juvenile prison. There they were associated with boys twice their age who had much experience in wrongdoing."

By making the case public, Father Flanagan got the public on his side. Finally, the outcry became so great that the boys were placed in a home for dependent children.[709]

Father Flanagan learned by bitter experience that the youth problem was a high-stakes game, with lives at risk and the future of thousands of youth in the balance. His words came sharp and decisive, and were sometimes caustic. He knew the critical importance of the public forum and the power of the spoken word. When he began his work for boys, it was the insensitivity of judges and juvenile authorities, and their inability to see the harm that was done by poverty, homelessness, and neglect, that stirred Father Flanagan into action, then fired his mind as he put pen to paper.

Father Flanagan discovered early that he was matching wits with principled and unprincipled occupiers of power. They were judges, state officials, and governors, many of whom were merely bureaucratic managers and occupiers of office, shaped by political pressures and the demands of the electorate. He learned to appeal to that electorate, and it was the electorate that became his ally in his battle for homeless youth.

Eddie[710]

Father Flanagan's study of the anatomy of juvenile crime boiled down to two factors: environment and motivation. He proved their impact as boy after boy graduated from Boys Town, not only with skills learned in the classroom and workshop but also with skills learned from living in an environment of freedom and total acceptance.[711] Father Flanagan's experience with eight-and-a-half-year-old Eddie was indicative of his genius: His conviction that good often lurks under what seems to be a deeply ingrained evil, his refusal to strike back with punishment as a remedy for bad behavior, and his revolutionary theory that evil genius can be turned into a genius for good by the simple application of unremitting kindness. As he told Eddie's story, he often boasted that this boy was his toughest nut to crack:

One winter night, Father Flanagan got a long-distance phone call from a Sheriff Hosey in Virginia.

"Father Flanagan," the sheriff asked, "do you have room for another boy?"

"Where is the boy now?" the priest asked.

"He's in jail," the sheriff said. "He's a desperate character – robbed a bank, held up three stores with a revolver."

"How old is the lad?" Father Flanagan asked.

"Eight and a half," the sheriff replied.

"He's what?" asked Father Flanagan.

"Don't let his age fool you, Father," the sheriff said. "He's all I said he was – and more. Will you take him off our hands?"

"If I can't handle an eight-and-a-half-year-old boy by this time, I'd better quit," the priest said. "Bring him out."

Three days later, the sheriff and his wife arrived in Father Flanagan's office with their prisoner, a pale little fellow with a smirk on his face. He was scarcely taller than the priest's desk, with "frowsy dark hair dangled over the pinched face, sullen brown eyes shut beneath long, dark lashes."

"We had to bribe him with cigarettes all the way out here," the sheriff said as he handed Father Flanagan a packet of papers. "He's nothing but a little gangster. I wish you luck with him because you're going to need it."

As Father Flanagan walked to his desk with the packet in his hand, he tapped the boy on the head and said, "I'm sure that Eddie's a good boy."

"To hell I am," Eddie replied, never taking his eyes off Father Flanagan. There was a hardness in the boy's voice that belied his age and size, and the priest thought he had never seen such a mixture of the comic and the tragic in one so small. Then, thanking the sheriff and his wife for bringing the boy, he dismissed them and turned to Eddie.

Motioning for the boy to sit down, he took a sheaf of papers in his hand and began to read the report. There was no last name; the boy was just called "Eddie." He was born in a slum near the docks of Newport News, and lost his father and mother in a flu epidemic when he was four. He wandered through waterfront flats, surviving as best he could as he went from table to table, living like a pet puppy, sleeping in dark corners or under open staircases.

Looking up from the report, the priest studied the boy. He sat silent and still, head lowered. Without looking up, he took a cigarette paper and a sack of tobacco out of his pocket. Cowboy style, he rolled a cigarette, lit it, and blew a cloud of smoke across the desk. His eyes flashed as he looked up at the priest, as if daring him to do something.

"This is your home now, Eddie," Father Flanagan said. "This whole place is run by boys. A boy mayor, a boy city council, boy policemen. You'll like it here."

"Where's the jail?" Eddie asked. "That's where you'll probably put me."

"No jail," said Father Flanagan. "You're going to take a good bath, get some supper, and tomorrow you can start school. You and I can become friends. It's strictly up to you. Eddie, I know you're a good boy."

Eddie's answer came in one shocking syllable.

When Eddie was gone, taken in hand by two of the Home's boys, Father Flanagan studied the report further. Eddie had spent his life on the streets, eking out an almost animal-like existence. Hardship had made him cunning and resourceful. At eight, he was the leader of a gang of boys, some nearly twice his age, and he led them in petty neighborhood crimes that he planned carefully, giving orders like a mob boss. When he was challenged by some of the older gang members to do something besides give orders, he managed to rob a bank, sneaking his undersized body past tellers who were busy at their windows, and stealing two hundred dollars from an unattended cashier's cage. In disbelief, the gang told him he was a phony because there was no news of the robbery in the newspapers.

So Eddie started a one-man reign of terror, and the front pages of the newspapers were soon full of stories about him. Finally, he walked into a candy store, gun in hand. The little old lady who ran the store grabbed him by the hair, shook the gun out of his hand, and called the police.

Eddie was caught.

The morning after his arrival at Boys Town, Eddie swaggered into Father Flanagan's office, his hair cut and neatly combed, a note in his hand. The note read: "Father Flanagan, you say there is no such thing as a bad boy. What do you call this one?" It was signed by one of the nuns. Eddie had come into her classroom, and after sitting quietly in his seat for about an hour, started parading up and down the aisle, swearing, knocking books to the floor, and then throwing an inkwell at the nun.

Eddie stood in front of Father Flanagan, sullen as ever.

"I still say that you're a good boy," the priest said.

"To hell l am," said Eddie before walking out of the office.

People began to wonder if Father Flanagan had finally met his match – a truly bad boy.

Eddie made no friends with the other boys or his teachers. Most of his spare time was spent looking for a chance to run away. He stood at the edge of the baseball field, muttering, "Kid stuff," and wandered around the village like some lonely stranger. For the first six months, he didn't laugh or cry once or show any emotion except complete boredom.

"Does he learn anything?" Father Flanagan asked the nuns.

"He's learning more than he lets on," one nun told him. "He just seems eaten up by hate."

"I'll have to throw away the book on this one," Father Flanagan said. "I'm going to try spoiling this little devil with love."

The priest took the boy to dozens of second-rate movies, and they shared hot dogs, hamburgers, candy bars, ice cream, and soft drinks. Every day, Father Flanagan would have Eddie come to see him, and every day the priest would repeat again and again, "Eddie, you are good boy." And Eddie would trounce out of the office.

Eddie did begin to fish a little at the lake, but there was no smile on his face when he pulled in a trout. The whole of Boys Town watched this tug-and-pull between the priest and the boy. Only once during this experiment of total kindness did the boy almost crack. As they were crossing the street after seeing one of those second-rate movies, Eddie was looking the other way when he walked into the path of a huge truck. Father Flanagan reached out, grabbed him by the seat of the pants, and pulled him to safety. The boy looked up at the priest, and for one brief moment, something akin to gratitude flickered on his face. Then he turned his head and said nothing.

One morning, after one of their escapades in the city, Eddie came for his daily visit with Father Flanagan and announced to Catherine Dannehy, the priest's secretary, that he wanted to "have it out with Father Flanagan." She announced him and he walked into the office, went straight up to the desk, and shouted, "Father Flanagan, you're a phony!"

This time, Father Flanagan was the one who was tough. "You better prove that Eddie, or shut your mouth."

"Okay," Eddie said. "I just kicked the nun in the shins. What do you say about that?"

"I still say that you're a good boy."

"You know that ain't true. You keep on lying and you know it's a lie."

Father Flanagan looked straight at the boy. "Eddie, you are smart enough to know when a thing is really proved. What is a good boy? A good boy is an obedient boy, right?

"Yeah!" Eddie said with smirk. "Always does what teacher tells him."

"Well, that's all you've ever done, Eddie. But you have had the wrong teachers – wharf bums, petty gangsters, dockside bullies. But you certainly obeyed them. You've done every dirty rotten thing they ever taught you to do. If you would only obey the teachers at Boys Town the way you obeyed those teachers, you would be a good boy!"

For a long moment, Eddie just stared at Father Flanagan, not saying a word. Suddenly a great load seemed to lift from the boy's face. He squinted his eyes as if he understood something for the first time. Father Flanagan's words were like an exorcism, driving out all the devils deep inside. At first he looked dumbfounded. Then a glimmer of sheer downright relief came over him and he began to cry. Slowly, he edged himself around the side of the priest's desk. Father Flanagan opened his arms to receive him. Probably for the first time in his young life, Eddie was crying. And when he was cried out, he turned and walked out of the room.

Father Flanagan sat there, astonished that such an obvious piece of logic, and all the love that went with it, had done the trick.

Boys, Prison, and the Law

Father Flanagan's travels with his boys had taken him to all parts of the country, and he found that the problem of the homeless boy was not confined to the larger cities. "While conditions were aggravated in congested areas in cities, they were not peculiar to those areas," he wrote. "There can be just as much abuse of homeless and neglected children on farms and in small towns."[712]

That was the shock – abuse, neglect, and homelessness was a national problem, and almost a national crime.

Judge Lindsey's *The Beast*[713] had pinpointed the root of the problem: the failure of city councils and state legislatures to recognize that children were not adults and that the real root of the problem was parental neglect. But the more insidious cause also was laid out in Lindsey's book in all its graphic detail: political corruption at the state and city level. That was true in New York City, as Jacob Riis' photos illustrated, and it was just as true in rural towns and villages where mayors and sheriffs often conspired to run their communities as their own private preserves.

Lindsey's book broke down the corruption in great detail, and the book itself almost became a handbook about political corruption at the highest level. But it was Father Flanagan's personal experience of this corruption in almost every state and city that he visited with his boy entertainers[714] that shocked him into starting his own campaign against the system, since the most innocent victims were children, usually boys.

Father Flanagan studied in particular the laws and practices affecting children. "I found to my amazement that they were, in most cases, very similar to those affecting adult crimes," he said. "In many states, these laws are still operating. Every now and then, the public is shocked when a child commits what is termed a major crime. Whether he is ten or eighteen years old, he is classed as a criminal, and the law says he must pay the penalty for his crime behind prison bars and high walls.[715]

"It is almost unbelievable that this most vicious system could still be in use in a civilized nation. Instead of helping such a child to become re-established in society, the state laws add further burdens on his weakened shoulders, and give additional backgrounds to live down. In most cases, his fate is sealed."[716]

Father Flanagan's anger was evident in his words, and there came a firm determination to work, if need be, at the highest levels of government to get rid of this "beast" and to use every store of intellectual, moral, and political currency at his disposal. He fought numerous battles, starting with the Shetron boys in Missouri.

"Everyone knows, who understands boys, that a child of ten, twelve, or even sixteen, who makes a serious mistake usually has been robbed of proper guidance, and the distorted little brain, through neglect, does things which society terms criminal,"[717] he said.

He found himself fighting for individual boys, which brought him into ugly confrontations with state officials and juvenile authorities who did not share his conviction about the patently "bad boy" – the boy who had killed or committed some other crime of violence. To them, the Flanagan conviction was criminal neglect, and they resented this "soft-hearted priest" who could hurl hard words into their faces and whose learning and logic could be phrased in language that slashed at their dignity. Father Flanagan stripped the juvenile problem to its naked reality and his fierce reasoning made him a terrible adversary.

(In the 1938 movie, *Boys Town*, Whitey Marsh was a kid who got in trouble because he had no family or adult supervision and was an easy candidate for Boys Town. But it was the boys in the reformatory in the movie's sequel, *Men of Boys Town*,[718] who Father Flanagan went out of his way to fight for, and in many cases, brought to Boys Town. In hand-to-hand combat with judges, governors, and juvenile authorities, he showed himself to be a master sociologist, psychologist, and educator.)

Several times, Father Flanagan went out on a limb for a boy, bartering with a governor or a judge to allow him to take those boys to Boys Town, if only for a short stay. Usually, a bond was demanded beyond what the priest could provide. For this, he would sometimes call on his many friends in the business community or his public relations associates at Bozell & Jacobs. But usually, he turned to his personal lawyer and friend, Henry Monsky, whom he had known since Monsky was a student at Central High School in Omaha and later a law student at Creighton University. Monsky obtained his law degree the same year Father Flanagan was ordained to the priesthood and returned to Omaha for his first parish assignment. Monsky had been at his side since the beginning of his work for boys off the street, and their interest in youth who were in trouble was identical.

It was Monsky who had provided the $90 the young priest used to rent his first house for boys at 25th and Dodge Streets, and who constantly called on his well-to-do friends in the professional and business community to come to the priest's rescue when funds began to run out. Monsky's son, Hubert, would later tell of his father's conversation with Father Flanagan when the priest was in Iowa trying to get a boy released to him; the boy had shot his drunken father as the father was beating his mother. Father Flanagan posted a $25,000 bond on an account that did not exist and then phoned Monsky to make the bond good.[719]

"Eddie, what trouble are you in now?" was Monsky's usual reply. He would then take steps to make the bond good so another boy in trouble could go to Boys Town. It was this wide collaboration with the business community of Omaha, after the priest had convinced them an investment in troubled youth was good business, that Father Flanagan could count on as Overlook Farm became Boys Town and his success with troubled youth began to receive national attention.[720]

One case that broke the back of the old juvenile justice system that Father Flanagan and Judge Ben Lindsey sought to dismantle made history in the legal annals of Nebraska. It was a case of "boys being boys" in a small town in western Nebraska, where a group of boys on the prowl, playing hooky from school, wandered along a railroad track outside of town and ran across a discarded coat in a ditch. Going through the pockets, they found a gun, and decided to play cops and robbers. One of the boys, named Donald, picked up the gun and pointed it at his buddy, just as he had seen it done in the movies. "Bang! Bang!" he said as he pulled the trigger. The gun exploded, and the other boy fell to the ground, dead.

The other boys ran and Donald threw the gun away when he saw his buddy was hurt. In something requiring heroic strength in a nine-year-old, Donald half dragged, half carried his wounded buddy into town, pulled him upstairs to a doctor's office, and told the doctor in boyish fashion; "Somethin's happened! Somethin's happened!"[721]

Nearly hysterical, Donald rushed to where his mother worked in a local store. He had killed his friend, he told her. Within minutes, the news was all over town and it seemed there may be violence as people gathered in backyards and on street corners. The boy's mother began to worry for his safety. Next day, the local newspaper carried the story and the news of one boy killing another even reached the Omaha newspapers.

A coroner's inquest was held soon after and the shooting was declared accidental. But the whole town was aroused and the mood grew dangerous. Word reached the mother that the older brother of the dead boy was out "to get Donald."

News of the shooting also reached Lincoln, the state capital, and a woman from the state Welfare Department was assigned to investigate the case. After talking to Donald and his mother, and discerning the mood of the town, she told the mother there were threats being made against her son's life and he was not safe in the town. The Welfare Department worker advised the mother to get the boy out of town until the proper authorities could look into the case.

Father Flanagan's troupe had often played in that part of the state, and the priest's boys and his Home were legends in these small towns. Donald's mother and Donald took the train to Omaha and were at Father Flanagan's door the next day.

"I was sitting one afternoon in my office... when a mother with a little boy tapped at my door," Father Flanagan later wrote. "I asked her to come in and timidly she entered. The little son followed. The mother poured out her story. 'They want to kill my boy,' she said. 'I had to bring him somewhere, so I brought him to you.'

"I told the mother that I would keep the boy until I looked into the case, and since I always worked with the courts, I would take the boy back if the court so ruled. I would assume full responsibility. She left to stay in a nearby town with relatives and asked me to keep her informed about what developed.

"After the mother left, I had a long talk with Donald. In his childish way, he told me the story... yet in the heart of that little boy there was no crime, no taint of murder. He had killed a pal while he was playing. He suffered from that knowledge as only a child can suffer."[722]

Father Flanagan recognized this was a test case. A boy was caught in the tentacles of the law, helpless and alone. It called for immediate action. He called his co-workers together and laid the case before them. They all agreed that this case was a perfect example of why their community of boys existed, and that even if it meant taking legal action, they would do everything possible so that Father Flanagan could take custody of the child, who was plainly a victim of someone's neglect.

Father Flanagan then called Henry Monsky, his friend and lawyer, who advised him to accompany the boy back to his home and act in his defense. The priest girded himself for a big fight.

"Immediately I got in touch with the county attorney from which the boy and mother had fled. I told them I had the boy... that since I always cooperated to the fullest extent, I would bring Donald to his hometown whenever the court asked me to."[723]

Father Flanagan found that the county attorney was bitter and incensed because the boy had been taken out of his jurisdiction. He held that the mother was trying to escape from the law, but did not realize that perhaps the boy's life was in danger.

"I had given the mother to understand that my Home was not a refuge for those escaping from justice, and that I would abide by the rulings of the court in her county."[724]

It is clear from Father Flanagan's account in his memoirs that this case was a turning point in his fight against the laws governing youthful offenders of the law. Rather than a quest for justice, he sensed a passion for revenge and that something resembling mob rule often determined the outcome in the courts. But he was encouraged in this case because "the attitude of the county attorney changed somewhat when he knew that I would produce the child when the court willed. I was taking a gambling chance on winning custody of this little boy, because of the animosity of the community and the nature of the accident."[725]

Father Flanagan turned all of his attention to the boy, who was now alone. He knew, given the mass confusion surrounding Donald, that it was no time for him to be left alone.[726] The priest decided to take the boy home by train, a distance of about five hundred miles, almost to the western edge of the state. He decided to travel at night, just so Donald could get some needed rest and so that he could get to know him better.

"I didn't want Donald to sit at the train window and think of what he was going back for, nor to await with dread and fear coming back to the town from which he was a little exile."[727]

Here is his very long account of the trip, the events that followed, and the touch of greatness that his work with boys had brought him to. His description of their ride together is almost like something out of Dickens and he must have sensed that this was another *Oliver Twist*-like story, but in real life, not in fiction. It was not only a deep paternal instinct that he had developed for these troubled boys, but also a tenderness that pulled at his heartstrings for these young lives, bewildered and broken by events beyond their comprehension.

"I dressed my little companion in a nice suit… anyone who could look at him and say he was a murderer would be laughed at."[728]

"Donald clung to my hand, as if he wanted protection on this strange ride. Night fell around us and Donald soon fell asleep with the motion of the train. I knew he would be lonely during the night, so we had berths across the aisle." (That may have brought back memories of the small boy at the 25th and Dodge home, crying for his mother in the middle of the night and Father Flanagan sitting up all night to comfort him.)

The scene was quite touching, as he remembered it.

"During the night, I heard him tossing and knew he was awake.

"'Father?' It was a timid little call.

"I got up and looked in on him. He was sitting up in bed with a frightened look on his face.

"I'm here, Donald. Don't worry."

"'Father, you won't leave me, will you?'

"No, I won't leave you. I'll be right here. It will soon be morning and then we'll have a nice breakfast."

They arrived at the courthouse in the county seat and the judge, the county attorney, and officials from the boy's hometown were waiting for them. The judge and county attorney were disturbed that the mother had run off with the boy to escape justice, and Father Flanagan could do nothing to change their minds. The county attorney, the priest noticed, "was ready and willing to exact his pound of flesh."[729]

The county attorney read the charge and its punishment: murder in the first degree and commitment to the state reformatory until he was twenty-one years old. "If it were not for his age," Father Flanagan would later recall, "he would ask that the boy be sent to the penitentiary for life."[730]

The boy was sworn in, put on the stand, and interrogated as if he were an adult. At this Father Flanagan interrupted, reminding the court this was a juvenile case and that the interests of the child should come first. He insisted that any questions that were to be answered should be referred to him. Then he came out with a blast that turned the whole case around, and in some sense, put the county attorney on trial.

"My purpose in being here is in the interest of this child. I refute the charges made by the prosecuting attorney and I deny that this child is a murderer. I know that he is neglected and therefore, Your Honor, I appeal to you to turn this boy over to me. I am willing to abide by your decision in this case for I know that it will be just. I know you want this boy to have a chance."

The county attorney, apparently surprised by this eloquent defense of the boy, chimed in that the boy was a criminal and a murderer and that he deserved punishment according to the full extent of the law.

It was seldom that Father Flanagan had shown his anger in public, but this time he turned on the county attorney: "Do you in your heart believe this child is a murderer? Look at him! Do you see anything in that little face that looks dangerous to society? I admit he is a victim of environment and neglect. But he is not a criminal."

Then he reviewed the facts of the case.

"Murderers do not drag their victims to the nearest doctor. They shoot to kill. This child and his pal were playing. Do you think that if he intended to kill that child, he would have then taken him to a doctor, pleading with that doctor to save his life?"

Turning to the judge, he pounded home his point.

"Your Honor, you may have a son. Perhaps he is a grown man. But once, he was a child as this blue-eyed child is now, whom your county attorney wishes to call a criminal. This accident could have happened to your boy, when he was playing Indian. Would you call him a criminal or a murderer? Would you send him to a reform school until he was twenty-one?

"You know you wouldn't. I admit the boy needs care and supervision. He has been neglected. If he is permitted to go on as he has, he may become a dangerous man. I am here, ready and willing to take full responsibility for this boy, and give him that care, education, and training which he sorely needs. I promise it will not cost the county one cent."

The whole atmosphere of the courtroom changed dramatically after this outburst. The judge was in tears. Donald was crying. The county attorney was wilted. Father Flanagan knew the boy was his.

There was a long silence in the courtroom as feet were shuffled, and it took a few moments for court to come to order and the trial to continue. An official report of the trial had to be drawn up, recorded, and signed. The case would have to be entered according to the usual court procedure. But Father Flanagan's task was not finished. No record of the boy's "offense" must enter the official records; if it did, he would be marked for life and his good name would be destroyed. That would affect his whole future.

But the county attorney also was not finished. He proposed that the charges he had made against Donald remain on the records and that the boy be "paroled" to Father Flanagan. Again, Father Flanagan countered.

"Someday," the priest said, "this boy may return here, who knows, perhaps the graduate of a law school. He may be running for the office of county attorney. I do not want to be so negligent that any opponent can come to these records and find something which might be used against him. It is unfair to any boy who has already had more than his share of burdens to carry, to leave a record behind him which will, in any way, be detrimental to him. I want this boy's past to be buried and forgotten."

"You may write the record, Father," the judge said quietly.[731]

Father Flanagan's final words concluded this piece of drama that shook the Nebraska law community and forever changed the state's juvenile justice system.

"The case was closed for all concerned.[732] Never in my life do I remember being so spent as I was then. I bundled up my little charge and left the courtroom."[733]

Boy Tramps Found Worthless Lot, Willing to Be Leeches

New York.—(Special.)—An investigation made among boy tramps, whose numbers have been greatly increased by the depression, has shown that most of them are not worthy of pity but rather of social worry. M. . Lapento, writing to The Times, says:

I was very much interested in the pictures in your rotogravure section of the so-called "homeless boys" now roaming the country. In the summer of 1927, being interested in the boy Scouts and for my own satisfaction, I made a journey of some 8,000 miles up and down this country to see for myself the condition of these homeless boys." I traveled with them, slept and ate in their jungles and got to know them really well.

The majority had left home for the greater glamor and adventure of traveling about the country on other people's money and sympathy and to get something for nothing." Most of them came from middle-class families and had left home of their own free will and still had the homes to return to. Most of them are slackers and think the world owes them a living. I remember when about fifteen of us were given supper by a Minnesota farmer on condition that we would work in the grain fields next day at $3 a day. That night we slept in the barn and in the morning there were three of us, because the others had sneaked off in the night.

Last summer at my camp six miles below Bear mountain I found a jungle of them on my property, all young, robust fellows who thought they had the world by the tail. I offered them work about the camp and, out of nine, two accepted. They did indifferent work for a couple of hours, stole my watch and money and fled. We immediately surrounded the jungle and gave the remaining homeless boys" a good, solid, old-fashioned licking. The two others were caught by some of my boys and given the same "cure."

What is to be done with these boys? is asked. They should be gathered up by the local authorities and forced to do some honest-to-goodness hard work like the rest of us. But, of course, this is such harsh treatment for these "poor, weak, homeless boys," and so we'll carry these youthful slackers on our backs!

Priest Wants Boy Tramps Instructed, Not Put in Prison

Omaha, Nebr.—(Special.) — Making a plea for a definite program of constructive help to fit the army of nearly two million wandering and misfit boys of the nation for independent citizenship, Father E. J. Flanagan, founder and director of Father Flanagan's Boys' home in Omaha, has prepared a series of radio addresses to be given over KFAB in Omaha each Sunday at 1 o'clock.

Father Flanagan, who has cared for more than 3,000 homeless, abandoned boys in the fifteen years he has devoted to this work, believes that the millions of dollars now being spent on punishing these boys after they have committed some crime could be used more effectively in preventing the crime.

MIRACLES DISCUSSED FOR GEMMA GALGANI CAUSE

Vatican City.—Cardinals belonging to the Sacred Congregation of Rites held a preparatory meeting at the Vatican Oct. 25, to examine the miracles proposed in the cause for the beatification of Gemma Galgani, who died at Lucca, Italy, in 1903.

Father Flanagan was very good at garnering press coverage to draw attention to the plight of homeless children and to publicize the Home's work and the need for financial support from the community.

BOY VAGABONDS HELD ON THEIR WAY WEST

Lads, 11 and 13, Joined Fortunes After Meeting in Chicago.

BUMMED WAY ON TRAINS

Joe Osterfi, 11, of Toledo, O , and Cody Columbus, 13, of Parkes Prairie, Minn., met in Chicago Thursday morning and after exchanging greetings and learning that each was on his way out into the world, leaving behind him a comfortable home, joined hands and turned their faces westward.

They boarded a box car in Chicago railroad yards about 4 Friday afternoon. Both were hungry at the time. In the car they found some hard bread which they ate with great relish. Cody had been without food for two days, he told his new companion, Joe.

The freight train stopped in the Webster street yards in Omaha at 9 Saturday morning. The hard bread had done little toward satiating their hunger. So they approached the first pedestrian they saw and asked him for a meal. He questioned them. Then he turned them over to Police Officer Pat Payne who took them to Central police headquarters and delivered them to juvenile authorities.

Juvenile authorities took them to Riverview home where they were given baths first, then big meals.

Admitting they were more comfortable than they had been at any time since they left their homes, the two lads told their story last night.

Joe did most of the talking. Cody was downcast and tearful. He didn't want to talk and couldn't hold back the tears when questioned.

"I met Cody in Chicago", began

Father Flanagan could cite numerous articles and stories that described the conditions homeless boys lived in as he advocated for what was needed to save them.

DENVER POST—DECEMBER 2, 1931

FAMILY ANTAGONISM MAY DRIVE CHILD TOWARD LIFE OF CRIME

Social Workers, Courts and Police Meet Protest From Delinquent Children, 'I Would Rather Die Than Go Home'—Sympathy, Love Needed.

(By LOUISE T. LAZELL.)

The juvenile courts, pastors, social workers and even the police sometimes meet with the protest from a delinquent child, "I would rather die than go home." Family antagonism has often driven the child out into the streets for companionship, and that companionship has led the child into criminal practices. Yet the members of his family feel no guilt; they do not hold themselves responsible for the situation in any way, and show neither pity nor love for the wayward member.

Harshness or neglect on the part of parents often makes such children defiant and suspicious toward the whole world, and they must be carefully re-educated by trained teachers before they can be either happy or useful members of society.

Education in human relationships is still left to parents and guardians and not checked up in any way unless the child becomes a public charge. Then the damage has been done, and the child instinctively places the blame where it is deserved by saying that he would rather die than go home. These are the stronger characters among abused and neglected children. Other pathetic mites still cling to the ones who beat and abuse them, knowing no other standard for parents and giving affection and trust even where they are no longer deserved.

Father Flanagan described why children became homeless on numerous occasions, imploring the public to help families before they broke up and put more children on the streets.

Poor Fear Cold, Give Tots Away

Children's Institutions Report Rush of Parents of Omaha and State to Rid Selves Of Young.

Unwillingness to Have Children Face Destitution With Them in Wintry Months Impels Sacrifices.

Parents in Nebraska are actually giving away their children.

This fact became known through a survey of children aid societies in Omaha today. The Nebraska Children's Home society, 502 McCague block, has received 22 children so far this month and has already placed 11 in homes, while the remaining 11 who have been given up by their parents are awaiting disposal, according to the Rev. R. B. Rolls, state superintendent of the society.

Six a Month.

The Children's Home society ordinarily receives an average of six children a month.

"The last two weeks show that home conditions in some families in the state will be difficult this winter," declared the Rev. Mr. Rolls. "The fact that we have received 22 children needing homes so far this month means that parents fear to face the winter in destitution with their children."

Rev. Mr. Rolls is looking for homes for six boys, from babes to 3 years of age, and five girls ranging from 4 to 13 years in age. Many of the cases coming to the attention of the Nebraska Children's Home society are pitiful. A mother who was left a widow yesterday appealed to Rev. Rolls to find a home for her only little girl.

Alone in World.

"I'm left alone in the world without any money," she cried, "and know I'm too weak to work this coming winter. I won't be able to even keep my little girl with me. I must find her a good home."

Father Flanagan's Home for Boys has received applications for board and room for children at the rate of 40 a day for the past two weeks. Father Flanagan, head of the insti-

Almost at Limit.

"We are almost at our limit now," he declared. "We have 110 boys and expect to be overcrowded before winter sets in. Applications have doubled in the last two weeks. It seems parents dread to face the music this winter and they're getting rid of their children now. The common plaint is, 'We can't support 'em.'"

"Some parents give their children away without so much as a parting kiss," Father Flanagan said. "Others leave them tearfully."

Refuses Ten.

Father Flanagan said he had to refuse to take in 10 children last week on account of lack of accommodations. He will move from his present quarters at 4206 South Thirteenth street to Overlook farm, on the West Dodge road, in three weeks.

"Then we'll be able to take in more boys," Father Flanagan said.

The priest is relying upon prayer and charity to weather the storm of the coming winter. "We're living from month to month now and don't look for trouble until it comes."

Orphanage Crowded.

St. James Orphanage in Benson is filled almost to capacity with babies that have been given up by their parents. More babies have been taken in at the orphanage during July and August than at any other time in the history of the institution, according to the mother superior of St. James.

Preparations are being made to receive more children during the coming winter, it was stated. The institution is caring for 180 babies now and is placing them in homes as rapidly as possible to make room for more destitute children.

Father Flanagan often advocated for poor families with children that received no assistance.

13

HARD TIMES AGAIN

Good and Bad News

In the summer of 1929, money was tight, the boys were numerous, and there were 275 requests for admission to Boys Town. The debts were piling up and it seemed that the sheriff and a bank foreclosure might be shutting down the Home at any time. Amid all this, Father Flanagan's largest graduating class was ready to be sent into the world.

It was clear Boys Town was crowded. Some of the barracks that had served as the boys' primitive living quarters and indoor activity spaces were now almost falling apart and their danger as potential fire-traps was a constant concern. In fact, fires had broken out in some buildings[734] several times and there was the constant fear that a small fire might spread and result in a major tragedy.

Besides upgrading living facilities, one of the most critical needs at that time was a new trade school.[735]

"Each boy at our Home is taught a trade[736] so that he will be able to care for himself when he leaves our Home and we do not want our boys to work in fire-traps which would be condemned if officials of the county ever saw our buildings," Father Flanagan wrote. "And in the winter these buildings are so cold that we have to stop our trade school to keep the boys from freezing.[737] In these same buildings, the boys have their band room, exercise room, and their meeting hall."[738]

The other major need was an administration building and adequate space for sports activities like baseball, football, track, basketball, swimming, and handball.[739]

The fact was the place was not adequate for the number of boys who lived there, their education, and their activities. Boys Town had come of age and was now ready to move into high gear to accommodate the growing number of boys who wanted to live there.

Father Flanagan was getting desperate, but the news was not all bad. He had come a long way from the early days of the Home. Over the years, nationally known figures like boxing champions Jack Dempsey and Jim Corbett[740] visited the Home on their way through Omaha. Major League ballplayers Babe Ruth and Lou Gehrig were also among the famous visitors, which placed Boys Town on the front pages of every newspaper in the country. (Ruth stopped by several times[741] since Boys Town probably reminded him of his own years at a boys' home in Baltimore, where he learned to play baseball under the tutelage of one of the religious brothers who ran the school there.)

There were also reminders that more than just years were passing. Father Flanagan's great friend, supporter, and keen observer of his work, Archbishop Jeremiah J. Harty, had died in October 1927.[742] Father Flanagan felt the loss keenly since Archbishop Harty had been with him from the start[743] and had seen his work grow from five boys on 25th and Dodge to a real community of youngsters that drew national attention. The Archbishop was an innovator himself and had ruffled many feathers during his years as Archbishop of Manila, where he saw the need for Catholic schools, even appealing to Pope Pius X to order reluctant religious congregations to come to the Philippines. Archbishop Harty had also authorized the founding of Father Flanagan's Boys' Home Corporation, with himself as Chairman, to give a solid legal vehicle for the work, and to ensure it was more than a one-man project.[744]

In June 1929, the boys lost their beloved bandmaster, Dan Desdunes,[745] who had offered his talents and services to Father Flanagan when the priest and his boys were at the German-American Home in South Omaha and the priest was desperate for help in getting his boys involved in wholesome activities. Desdunes, a master musician in the jazz tradition, had trained and drilled the boys with second-hand instruments and, under his direction, the Home's band became something of a national institution. From those earliest days, the band was featured at all fundraising events and Desdunes was their leader as the "World's Greatest Juvenile Entertainers" covered the Midwest in their horse-drawn circus wagons, and later traveled in their own private railroad coach as far away as New York and California. For the boys, it seemed to be the end of an era. For Father Flanagan, it meant the loss of a close friend and collaborator who had helped him put the homeless boy on the map.[746]

But the Home forged on. At a meeting of the Home's Board of Directors,[747] with the new bishop, Joseph Rummel,[748] now a member, the decision was made to go ahead[749] with the construction of new buildings, and architects soon started drawing up plans.[750]

By October 1929, the new buildings were going up – the much-needed trade school, a new gymnasium, a faculty center for the Home's growing staff, and new baseball and football fields. The boys now would have baseball and football fields, a track, and a new gym and basketball court. The construction made the landscape look like a tornado had hit the property, but by April 1930, Overlook Farm had the appearance of a small village.[751]

Father Flanagan again was head-over-heels in debt (this time more than $200,000), a gamble he could take thanks to the insurance policy Catherine

Dannehy had sold him ten years before.[752] And there was more good news. By a stroke of luck, Gene Moriarty,[753] a protégé of Knute Rockne of the Fighting Irish of Notre Dame, had signed on as sports director after scouting for a place to get experience in coaching. The future of athletics at the Home looked good, and the new coach predicted a red letter year, with sport facilities going up and the boys eager to play. At last, too, Father Flanagan had a handball court, where he could enjoy his own personal sport and introduce the boys to a skill he had mastered in his Sligo days.[754]

The priest could also reflect and take pride in knowing that in the twelve-plus years since those five boys romped through the house on 25th and Dodge Streets, 2,500 boys had passed through his care. In the spring of 1930, he would have his largest eighth-grade graduating class[755] (the highest grade the boys could complete at that time), with his boys scattering to the four winds. Over the years, many would return to the Home with a wife and children, or just stop in as they passed through Omaha. Most kept in touch by letters.[756]

The Home's radio programs with Johnny the Gloom Killer were among the most popular and listened to broadcasts throughout the Midwest[757] and had generated the National Gloom Killers Club, with a projected membership of 25,000. Will Rogers, who consented to be the club's president,[758] was a visitor, as were Paul Whiteman, who entertained the boys with his orchestra, and band-leader John Philip Sousa. Sometimes Father Flanagan and his band[759] met guests at the train station, providing a welcome that made newspaper headlines.

In the December 1929 issue of the *Boys' Home Journal*, Father Flanagan wrote, with a bit of sadness and a bit of nostalgia: "There will be 12 candles on the birthday of the Home, December 12th. It will be our 12th birthday. I remember our first Christmas dinner – it consisted of mostly a barrel of sauer-kraut that somebody had given us. I remember going around a few days before Christmas time asking for a few dollars from friends so those boys in our Home would have something to eat and decent clothes for Christmas."

That recovered memory had become something of a legend every new boy had to hear.

New Setbacks

The next two years would be difficult ones for Father Flanagan and Boys Town. His travels and his labors had worn him out. His work in the courts, sometimes requiring him to go halfway across the country to help a boy in trouble, had tested his endurance, his physical stamina, and his health, which had never been strong. He had never fully recovered from the physical break-down he had suffered in his first two years of theology education, in Dunwoodie and in Rome, and the broken-down living quarters he had to live in when he first moved to Overlook Farm were not the healthiest of environments.[760] He now had his mother, Honora, and sister, Nellie, to look after him, but they knew too well the years had taken their toll on him.

The first great setback came soon after Father Flanagan had signed the papers for the new buildings that would expand the Home's education and sports facilities. (He was deeply concerned about the education of his boys, who were able to complete only the eighth grade at the Home. He was more eager than ever to have a high school, which would make education at Boys Town resemble that of a small college. A high school facility would be built in a few short years, and the presence of its older students would give him close collaborators in running the Home.)

On March 2, 1930, a Sunday morning, the gas tank on a tractor backing out of a shed adjoining the power plant exploded, spreading flames to two adjoining buildings. Hearing the explosion, several boys raced to the burning building and rescued six horses from their stalls. Then they rushed into one of the other burning buildings, removing clothing and cots. One boy, Adolph Lopez, threw the electrical switch in the power house, thus cutting off the electricity and preventing arriving firemen from being electrocuted. Six Omaha fire companies rushed to Boys Town and all was mass confusion as the whole town of boys arrived at the scene, trying to help in any way they could. Seeing the flames spreading, the boys formed a bucket brigade to protect other buildings. It took three hours to subdue the flames. The power house, granary, and horse barn were destroyed; the loss was especially great because the power house housed the laundry, the tailor shop (with the Home's supply of clothing), and the machine shop.

The total loss was over $50,000, which insurance would cover. But the fire, coming when it did, with new boys arriving and graduates preparing to leave, was a fierce blow to the boys' morale. It would take time to replace the buildings. In April, the front cover of the *Boys' Home Journal* showed Father Flanagan viewing the ruins, and he expressed his feelings in his editorial page, thanking all who had come to the Home's assistance, especially the Omaha-area fire departments:

"The loss that we suffered by this fire is a great calamity to us," he wrote. "Damage that amounts to $50,000 to $60,000 would be a great loss to any institution, commercial or otherwise, but to us who started without a cent of money twelve years ago, and who have since by tireless and ceaseless labor struggled to give refuge to homeless and abandoned boys, this loss is calamitous indeed... that which has been destroyed will be rebuilt...."

The fire had destroyed much of the boys' baseball equipment, so spring training was slow to get started. But the baseball fields, track,[761] and new gymnasium were nearing completion. New activities were blossoming and sprinters were already practicing on the new track. The trade school, with its print shop and carpenter shop, was up and running.[762]

By this time, Boys Town was a national institution, and once the news of the fire hit the newsstands, donations again started to pour in. The front pages of the *Omaha World-Herald*, the *Omaha Bee*, and the *Omaha News* provided shocking headlines and vivid images of the destruction, and the accounts of the extraordinary heroism of the boys made for wide editorial comment.[763]

With graduation that year,[764] eighteen of Father Flanagan's older boys left the Home, most of them destined for high school while living in private homes.[765] Again, he was losing the oldest and most experienced of his youthful collaborators, and each graduation left its mark on the mood and atmosphere of the place. The 1930 graduates were soon replaced by eight new boys,[766] with others arriving throughout the summer.

Still another blow was the death of Father Flanagan's youngest brother, Michael. Known in Omaha for his singing voice and musical talent, Michael had often entertained the boys with private concerts at the Home. He was deeply beloved by the boys and was a member of their own Father Flanagan Celebrity Quartet, and as such, was almost a member of the Boys Town family.[767]

Amid these setbacks, Boys Town's national audience was growing, with sports figures, Hollywood stars, writers, musicians, and even cartoonists joining the chorus of admirers. Some added their own skills to publicize Father Flanagan and his work. A favorite cartoon figure of the time was "Skippy," the creation of cartoonist Percy Crosby, whose character would soon be made famous in a movie starring Jackie Cooper. Crosby sent a cartoon for publication in the *Boys' Home Journal*. It showed Skippy kicking the dust and saying, "Well, when ya feel like this there's nothin' like talkin' it over with Father Flanagan."[768] It was one of the first tributes to grace Father Flanagan's office wall, joining photos of Tom Mix, Babe Ruth, Lou Gehrig, and other celebrities who had visited Boys Town.

By the early 1930s, Boys Town was on the map and continued to draw prominent visitors to Omaha, who always took a detour to tour what had now become known as the "City of Little Men." Boys Town was especially popular with politicians, who liked to be seen shaking Father Flanagan's hand. (A few years later, one of them happened to be New York Governor Franklin Roosevelt,[769] who was running for President in 1932. During a campaign trip, Roosevelt and his wife, Eleanor, stopped at the Home while passing through Omaha,[770] and the candidate and Father Flanagan became fast friends.)

In fall 1930, something that seemed like a miracle to Father Flanagan and his boys was the completion and dedication of the new buildings.[771] Two thousand guests, including the governor,[772] attended the dedication, with Bishop Rummel presiding. Father Flanagan's friend and confidant, Henry Monsky, also was on hand as president of the Home's Board of Directors, and the boys pulled out all the stops in greeting their visitors. Johnny the Gloom Killer, now as famous as Amos and Andy with radio audiences, presented greetings in the name of the boys[773] and the boys' band played with unusual verve, knowing they were the celebrities of the occasion.

As the little village continued to grow, it was clear the Home would need more room. "Our original 160 acres no longer supplied the increasing needs of the Home," Father Flanagan wrote. "It did not supply nearly enough pasture space on which to graze our cattle, which were so necessary to obtain a proper meat, milk, and butter supply for our boys. Neither did it give us enough acreage for grain, corn, potatoes, and vegetables. Each year we had to buy large amounts of these."[774]

So with Catherine Dannehy's insurance policy in hand, Father Flanagan made the rounds to the banks. Obviously, there were questions about extending the Home's mortgage. But the priest had an answer: "I took it upon myself, with the best wishes of every boy at the Home, to visit the banks… I explained to them our needs of the present and our dreams of the future. I told them that the homeless boys and I would work night and day to pay for this farm." A bank was convinced to lend additional money to the Home, no doubt with the help of phone calls from prominent members of Boys Town's Board who had hopped on the Flanagan bandwagon after seeing him in action and witnessing the stunning results of his work, the national names now associated with the place, and the growing little village just ten miles from the city.

So the village expanded south, more than doubling in size to three hundred sixty acres and becoming more and more self-sufficient with additional land for gardens, crops, and cattle. It was truly becoming a town, and several years later, it would be recognized as a municipality in its right. It was also evident that the world was watching this grand venture.

A Needed Rest

In early summer 1931, Father Flanagan entered St. Catherine's Hospital in Omaha for a sinus operation. When he returned home, it was clear he was in no condition to continue as the Home's director. One afternoon, in his office, he slumped over his desk. He managed to make it to his home, a short distance away, and Nellie got him to bed and called a doctor (most likely his brother-in-law, Dr. J.R. Dwyer). Dr. Dwyer called in other doctors and they bluntly explained the priest's condition to his family: He was suffering from the breakdown they had often predicted. His lungs were weak and he would need at least six months of complete rest away from the Home, away from his work, and away from Omaha.[775]

With the country in the middle of the Great Depression, Father Flanagan was concerned about the financial state of the Home. He was occupied by the care and training the boys were receiving in their new trade school, as well by a burst of new activities that came with the opening of the new sports facilities. He argued with his doctors for hours, reluctant to leave when the Home had taken on a new mortgage and new boys were banging on his doors to get in. The doctors insisted that he rest. Bishop Rummel agreed,[776] and assigned Father Flanagan's brother, Father Patrick Flanagan, pastor of Holy Angels Church in Omaha, as the Home's temporary director.[777]

Father Flanagan had often been advised by the Board of Directors to take a vacation,[778] but the work at the Home was so pressing that he would leave only for business reasons or to rescue some boy who was in trouble with the law. His experience with the law and the courts made him doubtful that any boy would get a fair hearing. He had his staff comb the newspapers for news of boys in trouble and he did not hesitate to travel to distant places if he became aware of a boy who needed his help.

When the doctors continued to insist he take at least a six-month rest and recuperation, reluctantly, he consented.

The place chosen for him was Mercy Hospital in faraway Denver.[779] The day he left, his boys lined up at the gate to shake his hand and wish him well.

The main reason for the breakdown of his health was the financial crisis in which the Home again found itself.[780] It was constantly on his mind, even as he lay sick and helpless in Denver. News reached him that an $87,500 mortgage payment was due; if it was not raised immediately, the Home would have to close.[781]

With a heightened sense of urgency, appeals again went out in the *Boys' Home Journal*. Father Patrick took over his brother's radio program to beg its wide audience to come to the rescue of the Home once more.[782]

From his sickbed in Denver, the founder himself penned a desperate appeal that went out to every name on the Home's list of benefactors and appeared in the September issue of the *Boys' Home Journal*.[783] He was seeing his life's work crumbling around him and the fate of thousands of homeless boys put at risk.[784] It was perhaps the lowest period in the Home's history and he knew it. He had finally come to the end of his resources and his brother's radio appeals became even more desperate.[785]

Within two months, everything would change as he was plunged into the most notorious case of his lifetime, a case that would make him an international celebrity.

Boys Town residents formed bucket brigades during the Dust Bowl years to save their vegetable gardens, 1933.

ABOVE: Father Flanagan's health occasionally slowed his efforts to care for his boys and advocate for the plight of homeless youth. Here, two boys cheer him up with a gift of flowers.

RIGHT: The Home suffered a deep personal loss when Dan Desdunes, the charismatic bandleader hired by Father Flanagan to develop the musical talents of the boys and organize fundraising road shows, died in 1929.

Because of the drought, we have had no harvest---
Our Cupboard Is Nearly Empty

200 HUNGRY GROWING BOYS ARE ASKING FOR YOUR AID.

A good part of our food supply has always come from our gardens and our fields. Last spring we planted more than 15 acres of gardens, 19 acres of potatoes and 110 acres of small grain. But an exceptionally dry summer caused us a complete loss of many thousands of dollars of potential food produce. About 100 acres of corn resulted in partial loss.

Because we have no harvest, what our Home will use this year must be purchased. This means we must have money—money which must come from our friends, for we get no help from church, city, state, federal relief or community chest. As the picture shows, we have already bought some food supplies with money which generous friends have sent us. May we count on you for help?

Please Send Your Contribution to---
Father Flanagan's Boys' Home
Omaha, Nebr.

At the height of the Great Depression and Dust Bowl droughts in the early 1930s, Father Flanagan made desperate appeals for public support to keep Boys Town open in the *Boys' Home Journal.*

Boys Town youth Johnny Rushing became known to thousands of radio listeners as "Johnny the Gloom Killer" as the Home broadcast its message of hope to a national audience.

14

The Battle For Boys II: Herbert Niccolls

The Case of Herbert Niccolls

In August 1931, Herbert Niccolls was a twelve-year-old, wandering the streets in the middle of the night, hungry and on the prowl. He had escaped from an oppressive, uncaring home life. A pistol he carried in a holster made from scraps of an old boot made him feel important and safe, away from his grandmother, who would lock him in his room without supper.[786]

A later police photo taken after he was caught would show him in a tattered shirt and overalls, feet bare, a little fugitive on the run.[787] Passing a grocery store, he'd seen cigarettes through the window. He tried the door, but it was firmly locked. Sneaking around to another glass-paneled door, he smashed the window with the butt of his gun, reached in, and undid the lock. Entering, he saw a whole store worth rifling; not just food but tobacco, candy, gum, and anything else he could stuff in his pockets, including cash from the registers. He picked up a paper bag and went after the cigarettes and gum first.

As he was filling the bag in the dark, he became aware that others were in the store. Hearing voices, he dropped the sack on the floor and scurried to the back of the store. Then a voice rang out. It was the local sheriff from Asotin County, Washington, John L. Wormell, who had been warned that someone had broken into the store. "Come on out!" the sheriff shouted.[788]

No answer and no movement in the back of the store. The sheriff shouted again, "Come on out!" Over the barrel of his pistol, the Herbert could see the sheriff, silhouetted in the moonlight as he came closer. "Come on out before someone gets hurt!"

Suddenly the store lights flashed on and the boy could see the sheriff clearly. He aimed his gun carefully and pulled the trigger. The sheriff pitched forward and fell. Two other men – one of them a deputy sheriff who had accompanied the sheriff into the store – rushed forward, ducking for cover as the sheriff fell. The other man rushed out into the street and shouted to a passerby that the sheriff had been shot and that he should go for a doctor.

Revolver in hand, the deputy shouted for the shooter to surrender. "Come out, or I'll kill you!" There was a long pause. Then, from behind a barrel where he was hiding, the boy threw his gun onto the floor and stepped out into the open. The deputy grabbed the boy by the shoulder and shouted, "Why did you do this?" They stood over the body of the sheriff, a bullet hole visible above his right ear.

"I was told to," Herbert said as he was handcuffed and led away. "Bill Robinson put me up to it."[789]

Thus began the strange story of parental neglect, a boy's wild imagination, and a tragic escapade that turned a city and state upside down and drove a governor from office.

News of the sheriff murdered by a twelve-year-old boy hit every newspaper in the country, and the small town of Asotin, Washington, soon began to fill with reporters from the larger cities of the state. One of them took a photo of Herbert, barefoot in his shabby overalls, and it quickly was on front pages everywhere.

Herbert claimed that he had broken into the store on the advice of Bill Robinson, who had driven the boy from Robinson's property when he was on the prowl for food. Robinson soon joined the boy at the jail, claiming he had no part in the break-in and declaring his innocence. Crowds began to gather outside the jail, and with the threat of mob violence imminent, the deputy sheriff hurried both Herbert and Robinson into his car and drove to the county seat, away from the angry crowd that was shouting to hang the boy.[790]

Herbert and Robinson were turned over to the sheriff of Garfield County, in Pomeroy, the county seat, for safe keeping. Then the grilling of the boy began. Under rigorous questioning, Herbert admitted that Robinson had nothing to do with the murder, that he was the lone culprit, and that in the darkened store, he had fired his gun to kill. "If I didn't get him, he would have gotten me," was his explanation.[791] Robinson was set free and returned home to Asotin, and the morning newspapers carried the story as it had poured from the lips of the twelve-year-old confessed murderer.

In a new suit of clothes, the boy was later returned to Asotin for trial, with reporters crowding into the courtroom and citizens of the town becoming celebrity-conscious. The prosecutor, Elmer Halsey, had spent days developing a strong case against the boy-murderer, and since he also acted as the county coroner, he had a firsthand knowledge of the case and had made extensive inquiries of all persons associated with it. The trial had to wait until the circuit judge, Elgin Kuykendall, could work it into this schedule. Meanwhile, Herbert's grandmother had told the judge the family could not afford an attorney. So Judge Kuykendall appointed two lawyers, John C. Applewhite and Edward Doyle of nearby Clarkson, to defend the boy. Another attorney. A.G. Farley, who had met the boy in Pomeroy, also offered his services.[792]

The trial opened on October 26, 1931. The courthouse was packed, with reporters from the news services shouting questions at Herbert as he walked from a car to the courthouse. With all eyes in the courtroom on him, the boy was led by his lawyers to his chair, cameras clicking and fingers pointing all the while.

As the trial began, Herbert fell asleep and remained asleep for the rest of the morning. Prosecutor Halsey gave the jury a history of the boy. His homeless existence as he went from a children's home to selected families, repaying his hosts with petty thievery. His violent outbursts. He stole a car and broke into a safe. And when he was about to be sent to the state reform school, his grandmother intervened and he was put in her care.

Then began what Halsey described as a violent campaign of youthful crime. He said Herbert burglarized a post office, stole cars with abandon, and broke into homes and stores, making himself the town's holy terror. He was taken to church, but stole from the collection and set fire to the church. He was sent to the reform school. When paroled, he continued his ways as a petty burglar, stealing anything he could get his hands on. Eventually, he got his hands on a gun.

As if to dramatize the final result of this spree of youthful crime, the prosecutor declared to the jury: "He shot Mr. Wormell, and the pistol was found with the hammer back, indicating that he was ready to shoot again."[793] Halsey then urged the jury to bring in a verdict of guilty to honor the memory of the murdered sheriff.

The defense had its time in court, with Herbert's main attorney, Edward Doyle, ending his arguments this way: "With an insane father, with a mother fear-stricken because of poverty, without food enough to satisfy a growing boy's appetite, Herbert's twelve-year experience gave him a distorted view of life."[794]

At noontime, with a break for lunch, the judge turned the case over to the jury.

After just three hours of deliberation, the jury delivered its verdict to the judge in a full courtroom. The judge asked the accused to stand and Herbert stood up. "Do you have anything you wish to say?" asked the judge. "Nothing," Herbert replied.

Then the judge read the verdict: Guilty of murder in the first degree.[795]

The Boy and the Priest

"I was a patient in a Denver hospital when I first read of Herbert's case in the Denver papers."[796]

This was how Father Flanagan described the start of his fight for a boy that made national headlines and helped make Boys Town an even more visible center of juvenile justice reform. It is ironic that the priest became aware of the case while convalescing in the original home territory of Judge Ben Lindsey. But Lindsey had departed from Denver and Colorado, and would become a major player in the juvenile justice system in California,[797] where he and Father Flanagan would eventually be involved in the Whittier School affair in 1940–1941.[798]

Father Flanagan had been in Denver only two months when he read about Herbert Niccolls in late October. In his eyes, it was a classic case of parental neglect and lack of adult supervision. But the court and the governor of Washington state saw it differently.

What enraged the priest at first was the age of the boy and the court's decision to consider sentencing him to life imprisonment. It was the utter inhumanity of sending a twelve-year-old boy to prison that stirred him into action. Thus began a tug-of-war that made headlines, concentrated the attention of the nation on juvenile crime, and further brought the name of Father Flanagan to national and international attention.

"I sent a night-letter (dictated to a nurse) to the authorities in Asotin, and requested a speedy reply at my expense,"[799] Father Flanagan would later write. Next day, a detailed account of the case appeared in the newspapers, and Father Flanagan wired the boy's attorneys, asking what he might do to obtain the boy's release to him.[800]

In his hospital bed, Flanagan watched the clock. On the West Coast, it was one hour earlier, but surely by now his message had been received. He heard footsteps, and then a nurse stepped into the room, a telegram in her hand. Her face was solemn as she handed it to him. It was too late, the attorney wrote. His offer had been received an hour after the boy had been sentenced. He was already on his way to prison. Again the nurse sat at his side with her steno book and pen. Father Flanagan would write to Washington Governor Roland Hartley.[801]

It would be four weeks before the governor would reply.

The priest immediately checked himself out of the hospital and left for Omaha. "I could not remain longer in the hospital,"[802] he said as he prepared for another battle with the courts and with another governor over the fate of a boy. He had scarcely reached Omaha when he was in the headlines, the press recognizing that something resembling a battle of the titans was about to be waged.

In Omaha, the priest immediately took to the radio[803] to publicize the fate of the twelve-year-old boy in Seattle and to stir up public interest in what he considered a grave miscarriage of justice. His words, splashed under headlines throughout the country, sounded the alarm about a defective court system that tried juveniles in criminal courts and the barbarism that would send a twelve-year-old boy to an adult prison:

"Herbert was brought to trial, and a jury of twelve men sat in judgment against him. This was no juvenile court proceedings. Herbert was tried and sentenced just as any adult murderer would be…. Society must protect itself against a twelve-year-old boy who slept while the jury deliberated."[804]

Father Flanagan carried on the fight from his radio platform in Omaha, as well as in the newspapers. His first blast was in response to a statement from a state official, Kenneth Mackintosh, a candidate for the office of Supreme Court

Justice in Washington. A reporter from the *Seattle Post-Intelligencer* had asked him, "What does the Honorable Judge Mackintosh think about sentencing a child to life in prison?"[805]

"The boy had previously shown a criminal tendency," Mackintosh told the reporter, "and should have been removed from contact with society before he committed this murder. He undoubtedly will always be a criminal – a constant menace to society. It is reasonable to expect that at some future time he will again be at liberty… Life under our present system means only a few years in the penitentiary. He should have been hanged."[806]

Enraged by Mackintosh's statement, the priest issued a statement of his own that was picked up by newspapers around the country: "It is a statement without mercy or gentleness… to pronounce judgment… upon a mere child, a victim of society. What a travesty of justice to commit a twelve-year-old boy to life imprisonment and to speak of hanging him, when all of the other crime commissions, special enforcement societies, and government prosecutors congratulate themselves upon sending such an arch criminal as Al Capone to jail for eleven years."[807]

In desperation, Father Flanagan appealed to Judge Kuykendall for help, but the judge told him it was too late. He then appealed to Clarence Long, the warden of the penitentiary, who gave the same answer. But Long had his doubts about the wisdom of sending a mere child to a prison for adult criminals; Herbert could only come out worse. Judge Kuykendall had called Long about making provisions for the boy murderer, and Long was determined to do something.

Now Father Flanagan's last hope was with Governor Hartley. The priest had written to him days after Herbert had been sentenced, saying, "I have been deeply moved by the conviction and imprisonment of Herbert Niccolls, the boy murderer, who is now serving a life sentence in a penitentiary of your state. It is pathetic that a child so young must meet the fate of the worst adult criminals."[808] The priest had asked that the boy be paroled to him for residence at Boys Town. "Were it not that we have had considerable experience in the caring of real problem boys during the past fourteen years, I would not attempt to ask for such a parole. My experience has taught me that through the influence of our Home, where kindness, love, and an understanding interest in these boys' problems play such an important part, I am certain our Home can bring to this forlorn and dejected boy, hope, and future success."[809]

As Father Flanagan was to find out, Governor Hartley would brook no challenge to his authority, and he was as adamant about keeping the boy in prison as Father Flanagan was about getting him out. But much to his surprise, Father Flanagan found there was a whole country of supporters that backed him in his conviction to bring Herbert to Boys Town.

He also did not know that the news of him leaving a sick bed in Denver to fight for a youngster in Washington State had hit newspapers all over the country, and, he would find out later, all over the world. Letters poured in, first from nearby states like Missouri, Wisconsin, and Minnesota, and then from the state of

Washington itself and from every corner of the country. Some came with money for the cause and for the Home, and Father Flanagan knew that he had struck a nerve in many people's convictions about what had become his life's work.

One letter from Washington was notable. It was from Mrs. Armene Lamson, a child psychologist in Seattle, and a remarkable woman herself. Mrs. Lamson had started a free parental clinic in Seattle, where poor families could obtain medical help. Her letter indicated huge support for Herbert Niccolls' cause. "I've been approached from many sources in our state for an opinion about the offer you make," she wrote. She asked for more information about Father Flanagan's work for boys, saying, "You have my interest as well as my good will and admiration for the work you are doing."[810]

Father Flanagan wrote back a vivid and detailed account of Boys Town and his work that had impacted a whole generation of homeless boys. Describing what turned boys who were in trouble into good and honest citizens, he explained that the temptation to crime "would get nowhere if he (the troubled boy) knew he had a home and friends. Every child at Overlook Farm is made to feel that this is his home, and that he must live up to the fine things expected of him, and whenever possible, he must achieve something worthwhile for his alma mater, whether it be on the football field, in the classroom, or in the performance of daily duties about the home. Surely there can be no more glorious work than saving boys and making men."[811]

Father Flanagan grasped this first note from Washington state as a sign of support, since his appeal to the judge in the case and Herbert's attorneys had been of little help. Other letters from Washington would follow, urging him to continue his fight.

Yet there still was no word from the governor. So the priest again took to the airways. His talks were carried by radio stations from New York to California, including those in Washington, and by some as far away as Texas and Canada. On November 12, his voice reached into thousands of homes and the response was electric. His challenge to Governor Hartley was unmistakable, and his final words in that broadcast laid out his case carefully before the public: "In consideration of this boy's pitiful condition and the injustice done him by a cruel society, Father Flanagan's Boys' Home of Omaha, Nebraska, has petitioned Governor Hartley of the State of Washington to parole this boy to our institution for boys and turn him over to me to receive that care and training that has been denied him during the twelve years that have comprised his short life."[812]

Father Flanagan had set the stage for his ultimate public fight. Delivered in his melodic brogue, he invoked his audience's sentimental feeling for their own young, calling on their gratitude to God. The priest had dealt Hartley a swift blow the governor would hold against him forever.[813]

The speech brought a deluge of letters to the governor, delivered by the bagful at the State House. But Hartley was determined that he would not be influenced by a soft-hearted priest from Nebraska. His authority was absolute;

Herbert Niccolls was imprisoned in a maximum security prison for his crime – and he would remain there.

The broadcast also brought letters from concerned Washington citizens who invited Father Flanagan to Seattle to carry on his fight for Herbert. Before he left, the priest received a phone call from his friend, Morris Jacobs. Jacobs was a partner in the public relations firm of Bozell & Jacobs, which had taken on Boys Town as its free client. Jacobs had planned a publicity campaign for Father Flanagan's trip to Seattle, and he offered to contact the radio and newspaper services in Washington and in states along the way to publicize the priest's anticipated meeting with Governor Hartley. He also assigned a member of the firm's staff, Nate Jacobs (his brother), to accompany Father Flanagan and stir up interest about the priest's plan to bring Herbert Niccolls to Boys Town.

But the involvement of Bozell & Jacobs did not end there.

They contacted every newspaper nationwide and invited every major civic organization in the country to join the fight to save Herbert. Letters again poured into the governor's office, urging him to parole the boy to Father Flanagan. They came from the American Legion, the Federation of Dads Clubs, hundreds of Parent-Teacher Associations, and child welfare groups across the nation. Jacobs had even alerted Henry Luce of *Time* magazine, Walter Winchell, the nation's most-listened to voice, and William Randolph Hearst, with his powerful chain of newspapers.

It seemed that Father Edward Flanagan from Boys Town and his campaign to save a twelve-year-old boy from life imprisonment had the whole nation's attention. As his train drew out of Union Station in Omaha, on its long trip west, plans had been made for his cause to be taken up by prominent public figures who had visited Boys Town or endorsed his work. Among these were Will Rogers, Babe Ruth, Jack Dempsey, Admiral Byrd, John Philip Sousa, Tom Mix, and many others in the public eye.

Governors in states along the route of his trip joined in the chorus, as well as the president of the Boys Scouts of America.

As his train sped west, Nate Jacobs brought word that Oliver Morris, editor of the *Seattle Post-Intelligencer,* had not only run news stories publicizing Father Flanagan's trip but also had arranged for a reception and dinner for the priest when he arrived in Seattle. The event was to be held at the Washington Athletic Club, with the cream of Seattle's business and cultural community in attendance. Father Flanagan would not have to worry about a place to stay, since the Washington Athletic Club would become something of a campaign headquarters as he awaited his meeting with Governor Hartley. In light of the rebellion right on the governor's doorstep and with public pressure rising on all sides, Hartley penned a gracious letter of welcome to his adversary from Nebraska.

With headlines touting this battle of titans, Nate Jacobs decided Father Flanagan would not go directly to Seattle, but would instead detour through Portland. There, he would meet for lunch with his friend, Will Rogers, who would make a public statement of support for Father Flanagan, and then meet with the governor of Oregon.

In Portland, Father Flanagan stepped from the taxi and was whisked away to the Benson Hotel. Within a few minutes, Rogers came down the marble staircase to warmly shake his hand.[814]

The following day, after he and Rogers had visited with the governor of Oregon, Father Flanagan was back on the train, heading north toward Seattle. Rogers rode along with him as far as Tacoma, where he would set sail for Manchuria to become a war correspondent.

"Rogers took a note pad and pen and scrawled down the message that would be sent to newspapers across the country: 'I have known Father Flanagan for many years and he is a very fine man and has a wonderful boys' home. I know that Herbert Niccolls will be a better man with Father Flanagan in charge.'"[815]

Seattle

In Seattle, Father Flanagan stepped off the train a national celebrity.[816] When he came into sight, cheers went up from the hundreds of people who had gathered to greet him. Armene Lamson, accompanied by Oliver Morris of the *Seattle Post-Intelligencer*, hurried the priest into a car for the quick trip to the Washington Athletic Club, where his talk was to take place.

With Father Flanagan's arrival in Seattle, Mrs. Lamson was sure the governor would now relent. The huge crowds that greeted the priest were only part of the public pressure, since both radio and newspapers had heralded Father Flanagan's coming. Hartley had been invited to the dinner at the Washington Athletic Club but declined. Instead, he sent a brief note that read: "Welcome from the people of the State of Washington."

After a short rest, Father Flanagan, with Mrs. Lamson and her husband at his side, entered the hushed reception room, filled with guests who were eager to meet him. After the reception and dinner, he rose to give the words everyone had gathered to hear.

"I have not come as a critic, but as a citizen to offer my humble home as a solution to this problem," he began. He advised for continued pressure on the governor on behalf of the boy "languishing in prison, the boy who never had a father's protection or a mother's love…. If you have an institution in this state where the boy can be saved for society, then let him go there. If not, I want to take him to my Home.

"Of the three thousand boys we have had there, none ever took another false step. And we have had boys who were much more of a problem than I believe Herbert Niccolls to be. If the good governor would give this boy a chance – he has never had one – I personally will supervise his training and education."[817]

The applause after his words was deafening. Many came to him for more than a handshake, offering him the support of their business or corporation. Others went even further. Representatives of the American Legion wired the governor to inform him that the Legion's 30,000 members favored the boy being paroled to Father Flanagan. Civic, fraternal, and religious groups with one voice agreed: The boy should go home with Father Flanagan.

After the reception and dinner, and round after round of congratulations and handshakes, the priest was rushed off to radio stations to broadcast his message to a wider audience. Then he settled down to wait for word from Governor Hartley.

It came in the form of a telegram brought to his door by a bellboy: "Will be at Washington Hotel, Seattle, tomorrow afternoon at four o'clock. Roland Hartley, Governor."[818]

The next day, moving through a swarm of reporters at the hotel, Father Flanagan walked upstairs to the governor's suite.

A half hour later, he came downstairs and announced: "Governor Hartley gave me a most sympathetic interview and I am convinced that he has Herbert's best interests at heart. He told me that he made an investigation of my school and he understands what it stands for and what I am after. He said he will give me his decision soon."[819]

However, the governor would not let Father Flanagan meet with Herbert.

Father Flanagan promised the governor he would make no public statements that would embarrass his administration. After a few days of hoping to hear from the governor, Father Flanagan decided to go on to Los Angeles, where he would wait for Hartley's answer. There, Morris Jacobs had arranged for Father Flanagan to meet William Randolph Hearst, who had already defended the priest in the pages of his many newspapers.

On the day of his appointment, Father Flanagan sat in Hearst's spacious office at the *Los Angeles Examiner.* Hearst leaned back in his chair and listened carefully as the priest recounted Herbert's sad life. Then he asked what he could do.

"If the governor declined to help the boy, an editorial supporting the release of Herbert to Overlook Farm would be a great help," Flanagan told him.

"Consider it done," Hearst said.[820]

Before leaving Los Angeles for Omaha, Father Flanagan sent a telegram to Governor Hartley, urging him to hasten his decision and release Herbert to him in time for the Christmas holidays.[821]

Back in Omaha, Christmas came and went with no word from Hartley. In the meantime, Morris Jacobs was keeping up the pressure on the governor. He was staying in touch with *Time* magazine's Henry Luce and with Walter Winchell, whose columns covered the nation. Letters continued to pour in from every part of the country, and Father Flanagan was constantly on the radio, urging that letters be sent to Seattle advocating for the release of Herbert Niccolls.

After four weeks of intense waiting, the governor's decision finally arrived. But instead of granting Herbert's release, Hartley turned the whole case upside-down, with screaming headlines attacking Father Flanagan and his efforts on behalf of Herbert Niccolls.[822]

"As per my understanding with you in Seattle, November 22nd last, I am giving you herewith the result of my investigation into the case of Herbert Niccolls, boy slayer of Sheriff John L. Wormell of Asotin County, Washington at one-thirty a.m. August 5, 1931.

"Because of the youth of this boy, his case attracted nationwide attention and furnished opportunity for sensational newspapers to wring the heartstrings of highly emotional and sympathetic people. Special writers were dispatched to the ordinarily peaceful town of Asotin, where Herbert was photographed in his working clothes, better to give character to the exploitation that was to follow.... Sympathetic people, particularly those far removed from the scene of the crime, were stirred by these subtle misrepresentations and persuaded that the boy was being dealt with inhumanely and that a grave injustice had been done.

"It is deplorable, Father Flanagan, that a man of your training should have overlooked the propriety of making due inquiry concerning the facts and the responsibility imposed upon the officials of the State of Washington in dispos-ing of situations involving the rights of citizens, before injecting yourself into this case. This courtesy was due the officials of this State and the officers of Asotin County who met a most serious responsibility with courage, intelligence, and wisdom. The implication that the citizens of Asotin failed in their responsi-bility to this boy show how far afield newspapers and other agencies that have concerned themselves with this case have gone.

"In my judgment, nothing in recent years has taken place so detrimental to the youth of our land as the melodramatic publicity and exploitation which attended your trip to the State of Washington and the request to have this boy turned over to your institution.

"In the light of facts, it is evident the jury and trial judge showed discrimination and wisdom in placing this boy where he would be legally restrained pending further study to determine his ultimate ability to take a place in society.

"You entered the case, seizing the opportunity to direct nationwide attention to your boys' home, facilitated by the sensational publicity that had accompanied the trial. The people whose sympathies had been stirred by the newspaper accounts of the trial viewed your appeal as an act of mercy that no state or governor would deny.... What a happy situation – Father Flanagan needed the newspapers as a vehicle to supplement his appeals; the newspapers needed Father Flanagan in his role of humanitarian.

"For weeks, misleading and false statements went out through the press, from the pulpit and from... radio stations, over which you appealed to an entire nation to help get this boy, urging that the governor be overwhelmed with letters. Many people throughout the nation, misinformed by you and the newspapers, responded to this urge. Not a word of consolation or sympathy was extended to the bereaved family of the sheriff who was killed in the performance of his duty – seven brothers and sisters, a wife and four children, entirely forgotten."

To support his decision, Hartley gave his own interpretation of the case and of Herbert Niccolls, his character and family life, and the circumstances that led to the crime:

"Contrary to published reports and radio broadcasts, Herbert Niccolls was born... in an average religious farm home, received the sympathetic affection of the average child from his parents, is not an orphan, and has never been abandoned.

"Herbert's complex has baffled his parents, other relatives, institutions, and a generous friend who took him from the Idaho Industrial School into a home of refinement and luxury, where he was given every advantage, including schooling, instruction in music, and association with two wonderful children. It was hoped that, under careful supervision, he would emerge with a degree of dependability that would enable him to again be safe at large. All of these influences have failed.

"The case of Herbert Niccolls also presents a legal aspect which precludes turning him over to your home or to any other agency outside the State of Washington. Any action permitting the removal of the twelve-year-old-boy from the State of Washington would be tantamount to giving him complete release. Apparently many persons do not realize that the moment Herbert stepped outside the boundaries of this state, he would be free. If his relatives wanted him back in Idaho, or wished to take him to some other state, there would be no legal obstacles to overcome. Legal authority over the boy could not be vested in you or in any other agency outside this State by Executive Action.

"From the indictment contained in your telegram to me dated December 1st, one would be led to believe that this State was a wild African jungle with no institution or facilities for caring and helping the wayward to regain the privileges of citizenship. Our people and our institutions rank with the finest in the Republic. Our hearts are warm. Herbert Niccolls will never suffer from neglect while he is the ward of this commonwealth.

Then, the governor's final decision:

"According to expert testimony which is well corroborated by the boy's history, Herbert Niccolls is at present, unsafe to be at large. This case is the responsibility of the State of Washington. The Chief Executive would be derelict in his duty should he undertake to transfer his responsibility to the agency of another state.

"In view of all these facts, your request for the parole of this boy cannot be considered."

The hardheartedness and unbending determination to keep the twelve-year-old in prison cemented Father Flanagan's determination to carry on the fight for Herbert Niccolls. No sooner had the governor's decision hit the newspapers and airwaves than Father Flanagan's phone began to ring. Governor Hartley's decision and his personal attack on the priest and his motives became the stuff of headlines and editorials across the nation. Hartley had made his letter public and Father Flanagan decided to reply in kind. The governor's accusation that he had used the trial of Herbert Niccolls to gain publicity for his

Home for Boys had to be answered and his reply also hit the next day's newspapers. It was clear that a war was on:

"Governor Hartley is within his honored province as chief executive of the State of Washington when he denied the parole of Herbert Niccolls, the unfortunate twelve-year-old murderer.

"But when he deplored my efforts and cast insinuations upon my sincere motives in trying to obtain the boy's release, he stepped into the gutter of ward politics.

"Gov. Hartley made the statement that well-corroborated experts advised him that Herbert is beyond being saved. As a student of sociology and with fifteen years of experience in handling wayward boys, I am interested in knowing from whom the governor obtained this advice.

"What a pity and a shame that Gov. Hartley should base his opinion on such evidence when students of sociology are aware that heredity is a minor influence on a child and that environment is the chief influence that determines character.

"Herbert's environment, and not heredity, prompted him to do the things that led to the tragic day when he pulled the trigger and killed a peace officer. What Herbert, who is little more than a baby, did and what he is today, is not because of his true heart and mind, but it is the result of poor home environment and bad influence on his first twelve years of life.

"Father Flanagan's Boys' Home needs no publicity. I was surprised that such attacks would come from the executive mansion of the State of Washington. To me it sounds like the… mutterings of a whipped political boss.

"I can't believe that it is Governor Hartley himself making such a venomous and undeserved attack upon me and our institution, but that he has been ill-advised; and if he has not, then in my humble opinion he is making Herbert Niccolls a political football. What a Christmas for Herbert!"[823]

The effect of this battle between priest and governor was electrifying, with the whole country solidly behind Father Flanagan. But Father Flanagan was in for another surprise. Morris Jacobs appeared at his door the next morning with newspapers in his hand, early editions of the Hearst newspapers. In each was an editorial written by Hearst himself in support of Father Flanagan and his request for custody of Herbert Niccolls:

"In upholding the sentence of life imprisonment for a boy of twelve, Governor Hartley said that the experts had advised him that the youth is beyond being saved, and when Father Flanagan asked for the boy's release and offered to care for him and train him, the governor stated that the purpose of the request was to obtain nation-wide publicity for Father Flanagan's Boys' Home.

"That insult was the small-minded politician speaking the only language that such politicians understand…. They cannot understand anyone doing anything for any other reason.

"Father Flanagan has no such motive. He is a high-minded and splendidly worthy man, conducting a greatly needed and very greatly beneficial institution, and it is an outrage that he should be attacked and his motives questioned simply because he happens to disagree with Governor Hartley on the proper treatment of degenerate youth.

"According to the very best sociological and penalogical thought, it is Governor Hartley who is old-fashioned and reactionary and unchristian, if not uncivilized, and it is Father Flanagan who is modern and progressive, following alike the gospel of Christ and the light of modern thought and civilization.

"While the governor is still floundering in the dark ages of punishment as the only cure for crime, the priest sees the light of modern scientific criminology as a gleam of light to the world."[824]

Hearst's editorial made headlines, generating letters of support by the hundreds to Father Flanagan. Christmas was scarcely over when the priest received a telegram from Armene Lamson in Seattle, informing him that the governor's decision had only generated more support for Father Flanagan's plans for Herbert Niccolls and that stinging editorials had appeared in Seattle newspapers condemning Hartley and demanding an investigation of his handling of the cases of other juvenile offenders.

Governor Hartley was in trouble with his own people. Oliver Morris, editor of the *Seattle Post-Intelligencer*, wrote to Father Flanagan that the governor's "abysmal ignorance of modern scientific methods of treating juvenile crime has cooked his goose in politics. I don't think he can be elected to anything again. So your trip has accomplished one good for the state… On the whole, your effort to get the Niccolls boy has been highly successful. It has centered the attention of the whole nation on the archaic methods of treating child offenders and has made a big man out of you and a small one indeed out of Gov. Hartley… Public opinion is with you and we will have a new governor within a year."[825]

It was as if a battle cry had been sounded in Seattle and throughout the state. In this, Father Flanagan saw a glimmer of hope that the governor's decision could be overturned if more facts about the case became public.

In all of the activities surrounding the trial, Herbert Niccolls himself had not been consulted or given the chance to tell his side of the story. In his reply to Morris, Father Flanagan suggested that all the facts surrounding Herbert's case be brought to light.

"I think it would be a splendid thing if Mrs. Lamson would write the story of the Herbert Niccolls case…," the priest wrote. "It would be most important that all the facts be brought out in his case… The defense attorney, Mr. E.J. Doyle… would be very happy, I am sure, to give all those details. It seems that the governor and the prosecuting attorney have accused this child of crimes that have not been proven. The commission of those crimes did not come up, but have been used since then in statements detrimental to the boy's character… as a sustaining argument against his parole. I refer to the statements that he put a bomb under the church when the congregation was inside and stole money from the collection… Think of a little twelve-year-old boy, helpless and alone and unable to fight back these accusations, and think of the cruelty and sportsman-ship of a prosecuting attorney and governor making statements such as these."[826]

It was clear that Father Flanagan had thoroughly studied the facts of Herbert's case and its documentation, a skill that began when he made studies of the 2,000 men who had inhabited his Workingmen's Hotel. All of the details of the trial were handed to him by the boy's attorneys; other documentation was sent to him by Morris Jacobs and others who were concerned about the case.

Aftermath

When 1932 dawned at Overlook Farm, Father Flanagan was deluged with letters from people who were outraged at Governor Hartley's decision to send a twelve-year-old boy to prison for life. Editorials like those of William Randolph Hearst supporting Father Flanagan appeared in newspapers across the country, and Armene Lamson in Seattle was preparing an article on the Niccolls case for the *Seattle Post-Intelligencer*. The governor himself was flooded with letters from angry citizens demanding his resignation.

One of the governor's biggest problems was not being able to explain the pardon and release he had granted to two other murderers, both eighteen years old. The pair had killed a policeman while committing a robbery, after a long series of auto thefts, burglaries, and holdups. Caught and imprisoned, they overpowered a guard and escaped, but were recaptured. After only four years in prison, Hartley pardoned them and they were released.

However, the public was up in arms. To make clear that he let the punish-ment fit the crime in the case of Herbert Niccolls, Governor Hartley made public the case of Walter Debuc, a teenage murderer who, on the governor's orders, had been executed on April 15, 1932.

In July 1931, Debuc, then sixteen, and Harold Carpenter, thirty-five, robbed and killed eighty-five-year-old Peter Jacobsen. Jacobsen was found bludgeoned to death and Carpenter was arrested two weeks later in Yakima with $3,000 in cash and Jacobsen's pocket knife in his possession. After Debuc was convicted and sentenced to death, there were petitions to have his sentence commuted to life in prison. But Governor Hartley refused. He had decided he wanted the public to know that he would not be soft on teenage murderers, and he used this stand to support his refusal to release Herbert Niccolls to Father Flanagan.

Even in the face of the bad publicity surrounding Herbert's case, the governor was adamant. His refusal to stop the execution of Walter Debuc, in retaliation for public criticism, was only the first act in his response to his critics and to Father Flanagan's stinging reply to his own letter. He decided to go public with his appraisal of the Herbert Niccolls' case to justify the boy's sentence and his consequent action, but his letter of explanation was aimed at Father Flanagan himself. It included his correspondence with the priest and the governor's response, and a tissue of lies about the boy's home situation and upbringing. At Father Flanagan's suggestion, Mrs. Lamson began a public letter in reply to the governor's letter[827] and the priest invited her to visit Omaha and Boys Town.

Bozell & Jacobs made arrangements for Mrs. Lamson's trip, whose purpose was not only to visit Boys Town but also to begin a national tour of women's groups to rally support for the plight of Herbert Niccolls. Her appeal to women voters in Omaha, Washington, and Detroit made national headlines[828] and she returned to Seattle ready to continue her campaign against the governor.

Back in Seattle, she was able to obtain a meeting with the governor, where she pleaded Herbert's case. The governor was nervous during the whole interview. She did wring from the governor permission to visit Herbert and wrote a detailed account of her visit for Father Flanagan.

By the end of the summer, Mrs. Lamson finished her public letter to Governor Hartley, entitled "An Answer to Governor Hartley's Letter Regarding the Case of Herbert Niccolls." It was sent to the 100,000 subscribers of Father Flanagan's *Boys' Home Journal,* and its publication was timed to influence the Washington primary election in September, with hopes that a new governor would look more kindly on the fate of Herbert.

The letter was a public indictment of the governor's actions and his use of his office to carry on something resembling a personal vendetta against a child in trouble. It also accused him of distorting the facts of Herbert's home life and upbringing.

The effects of the letter were devastating for Governor Hartley. *Time* magazine gave the issue a national audience. Hartley's party turned against him, and the courts demanded that his books be released for public examination.

In the end, Hartley's political career was ruined, and Herbert Niccolls remained in prison and was not released to Father Flanagan's care. But the battle between the priest and the governor shone a harsh, bright light on the plight of the vulnerable, disenfranchised youth of America. (Herbert was pardoned by Governor Clarence Martin after serving ten years in prison, and went on to live a crime-free life. He died in 1983.)

Boy Killers---Will History Repeat?

ROBERT TEMPLEMAN, fifteen, who slew his brother, and in whose behalf child psychologists and juvenile court advocates moved to save him from what they called the "bungling" in the case of the state's other boy slayer, now in the penitentiary at Walla Walla.

HERBERT NICCOLLS at fourteen, at the time he slew a peace officer, whose trial in 1931 on first degree murder charges aroused child welfare groups, who claimed he was a case for mind specialists and juvenile experts rather than for the criminal law. He was given life.

NEW DEAL FOR YOUNG SLAYER IS DEMANDED

Child Clinic Head Declares Fate Of Templeman Shall Not Parallel Niccolls Case

Mrs. O. F. Lamson, head of Seattle's child clinic, who enlisted child and welfare groups of the state in behalf of Herbert Niccolls, fourteen-year-old Eastern Washington slayer, yesterday announced that the same groups would oppose any effort to repeat the handling of the Niccolls boy in the case of Robert Templeman, fifteen-year-old Buckley slayer.

Mrs. Lamson wrote a letter to Judge Fred G. Remann of the juvenile court of Pierce County at Tacoma, in whose custody the Templeman now is, praising him for his statements regarding his preliminary analysis of the case and "enlightened handling of the matter to date."

'NO NICCOLLS CASE'

"We do not want to repeat the Herbert Niccolls case," Mrs. Lamson told the Post-Intelligencer. "The Templeton boy is entitled to intelligent handling, and the case should be kept in the juvenile court, not turned over to the prosecutor and the criminal courts, as was Herbert Niccolls. The boy should be carefully studied and all background and facts carefully investigated before action is taken, and we are sure Judge Remann will see that this is done.

"We did not criticize the judge in the Niccolls case. He was held to a cut and dried procedure under the criminal law when the case was turned over to the prosecutor. The mistake was made in ever letting the case get into the criminal courts. You cannot secure justice for a child in the environment of the criminal courts and the penitentiary. There is no leeway in the criminal law—everything is handled under rigid rules, and individual study and handling of children cannot be had."

IN FIRST DEGREE

The Niccolls boy was convicted of murder in the first degree and sent to the penitentiary for life. Subsequent efforts failed to have him paroled to Father Flanagan's famous boys' industrial farm in Nebraska. There, child welfare groups held, he could have been educated and prepared for life under a self-help and discipline program that has redeemed and sent back into society, as safe citizens, scores of boys who otherwise would have been criminals.

Herbert Niccolls killed John L. Wormell, sheriff, at Asotin, Wash., when the peace officer discovered him while he was hiding in a store at night, allegedly to burglarize the place.

Father Flanagan often took up the cause of boys who were accused of murder. He felt they could be saved, and asked the courts to release them to Boys Town's care.

Herbert Niccolls' mugshot, from the Washington State Penitentiary, circa 1931.

OMAHA BEE-NEWS-OMAHA, NEBR., NOV. 27, 1931

FATHER FLANAGAN RENEWS MERCY DEMANDFOR BOY SLAYER

'SEES RED' AT LIFE TERM FOR LAD

SEATTLE POST-INTELLIGENCER
NOVEMBER 19, 1931

Warm Welcome Is Planned For Father Flanagan

Friend Of All Boys To Be Given Reception At Washington Athletic Club

By R. B. BERMANN

Their imaginations kindled by the spectacle of a man embarked on a 2,000-mile journey for the sake of a child he has never seen, Seattle men and women prepared yesterday to give an enthusiastic welcome to Father E. J. Flanagan, nationally recognized expert in juvenile rehabilitation.

Father Flanagan left Omaha for Seattle yesterday to try to persuade Gov. Roland H. Hartley to parole to him Herbert Niccolls, twelve-year-old boy recently sentenced to life imprisonment for the killing of John L. Wormell, sheriff of Asotin County.

Due Tomorrow

Accompanied by Nathan E. Jacobs, a member of the staff of Overlook Farm, where he has given more than 3,000 boys a new start in life, Father Flanagan will arrive in Seattle at 2:20 tomorrow.

Overlook Home Head Asserts Every State Should Have Rehabilitation Policy

LOS ANGELES, Nov. 27.—"Every boy is entitled to his natural birthright—and you'll never find this in a penitentiary or reformatory.

"Proper environment makes good men out of bad boys. Yet there are thousands of little boys behind prison bars today, being methodically ruined, who need only proper home surroundings."

Such were some of the observations Thursday of Father Edward J. Flanagan, head of the famous Overlook Farm home for boys at Omaha, Neb., who come to the Pacific coast on an errand of mercy.

Father Flanagan is attempting to have Hubert Niccolls, 12-year-old slayer of Asotin, Wash., paroled to his school. The boy, convicted of shooting Sheriff John Wormell, was recently sentenced to a life term in the Washington state penitentiary at Walla Walla.

Efforts of Father Flanagan for an opportunity to rehabilitate the boy slayer have aroused nationwide interest.

The noted "boy saver" arrived here from Seattle for a few days' rest while awaiting final word of Governor R. H. Hartley on the parole plea, which is said to be backed by thousands of prominent

OMAHA WORLD-HERALD
OCT. 30, 1931

AVERS BOY KILLER SHOULD BE HANGED

Bu ther Flanagan C Home to Hubert Niccolls.

Walla Walla, Wash., Oct. 30 UP.—As 12-year-old Hubert Niccolls began a life sentence in the Washington penitentiary for murder, an offer to reform the boy came today from a priest at Omaha, Neb., while a member of the Wickersham crime commission declared the youth should have been hanged.

At Seattle, Kenneth McIntosh, member of the Wickersham commission and former justice of the state supreme court, said:

"The boy undoubtedly always will be a criminal, a continued menace to society, and it is reasonable to expect that at some future time he will again be at liberty. 'Life' under our present system means only a few years in the penitentiary. He should have been hanged."

Defense counsel announced that Father E. J. Flanagan, who conducts a boys' home at Omaha, had

The Herbert Nicholls case and Father Flanagan's intervention to save the boy was a major story in newspapers around the country.

THE BATTLE FOR BOYS II: HERBERT NICCOLLS | 251

15

Boys Town, Nebraska

A Growing Community

The national publicity generated by the Herbert Niccolls case made Father Flanagan and Boys Town known worldwide, and even more boys came to the Home. Some walked, some came by train or bus,[829] and some were sent by judges who saw Boys Town as a new solution for boys who had broken the law. Father Flanagan's labors for boys in trouble with the law, and the work of Judge Ben Lindsey, had awakened the courts to the true nature of juvenile problems, and new laws were enacted for the care of youth who came before them. The pioneering work of Judge Julian Mack of Chicago,[830] who had established the first juvenile court in 1899, also was being followed by more juvenile courts across the nation. The success of Judge Mack's determined efforts for juvenile justice and the support systems he organized became the model for the whole country.[831] But as Father Flanagan had discovered in his experiences with Missouri, Nebraska, and Washington, the courts were not working in most states, and boys were still being sent to adult prisons or reformatories, places where they emerged more highly skilled in criminal ways.

In November 1932, Father Flanagan received a visit from Franklin and Eleanor Roosevelt during Roosevelt's campaign for president.[832] This began a friendship between the priest and the Roosevelts that would last until President Roosevelt's death in 1945. At the time of the visit, the Great Depression that followed the Stock Market Crash of 1929 was at its height and money was scarce everywhere. Still the Home managed to survive, and the insurance policy Catherine Dannehy had sold Father Flanagan in the early years of the Home provided needed cash on many occasions.

In the 1930s, a boy usually stayed at the Home through eighth grade. Then, provisions were made for him to join a family and enter high school elsewhere.[833] For boys who were not preparing for high school, a Commercial School was set up at the Home,[834] where they could learn a variety of skills and trades.[835] This kept some of the older boys on campus to help supervise the younger citizens. These older boys proved to be a stabilizing factor, and as high school classes were added, one year at a time, something resembling a self-government system began to emerge, with older boys looking after the younger boys[836] and directing many of the Home's activities.

In his work, Father Flanagan was determined to break the back of an educational system that said education must be forced, that morality was inculcated chiefly by fear of punishment, and that learning could flourish only in a system of constraints and strict discipline. He knew this was not true from his own experience and he knew it was not true from the Gospel of Jesus Christ. His educational system came from the Gospels, but he backed it up with a support system that touched every base in each boy's personality. He embodied his principles in a living culture, a culture of his own making, drawing upon a humane tradition that had achieved miracles in the past and had transformed whole peoples, leaving behind a rich cultural legacy.

What Father Flanagan saw as he entered upon his work was a social crisis in which the homeless child was almost a surplus commodity, a religious crisis in which character was molded by restraint, and an educational crisis in which mass education was the norm. He rejected all of these and inaugurated a social, religious, and educational revolution that took the world by storm, making Boys Town world famous and the name "Father Flanagan" a household word. Not everyone could say what that word symbolized, but people came from all over the world to learn what the symbol stood for.

"It is not enough to see that what has been called an underprivileged child is given food, warm clothing, and a clean bed," Father Flanagan wrote. "An Army commissary can do as much. No! More than food, clothes, and shelter, what those lads have been deprived of is a mother's tenderness, and a father's wisdom, and the love of a family. We will never get anywhere in our reform schools and orphan asylums until we can compensate for that great loss in such lives.

"And what does that mean? It means that you will have to develop a new class of social workers, not merely distinguished for their professional training, but, more important, consecrated to the great, the soul-lifting task of bringing tenderness and solicitude and understanding and motherly interest, if you please – a doting interest, if you don't mind – to the little affairs of desolate children."[837]

The priest's most significant insights were that human beings are fashioned by culture, and that they develop their full potential in an atmosphere of freedom and total acceptance. These two insights, coupled with the Christian conviction that the Gospel must not be forced, either in its propagation or in its development, gave Boys Town a measure of success that drew the admiration of educators the world over.

With an influx of boys of every age and background, Father Flanagan's housing and educational resources were being strained to their limits,[838] his sports activities were multiplying, and there was an explosion of skills and individual interests[839] as this army of boys began to shape and express what was fast becoming a unique community. It was more than a school, since it occupied each boy's waking hours, and it was more than a protective institution, since it was run by the boys themselves.[840]

Father Flanagan had reasons to rejoice at his success. His eighth-grade graduates were placed in homes where they could finish high school,[841] and those who graduated from high school went on to higher education,[842] most of them being remarkably successful.[843] Letters from these "former boys," as they were called, filled the pages of the *Boys' Home Journal*, and it was always a gala event when one of them returned for a visit.[844]

With a community of boys surrounding him and with more arriving as others departed, Father Flanagan often reflected on the miniature culture he had created. From the time the first boy came into his Workingmen's Hotel and he became aware of boys being in trouble with the law, he had to draw on his own pedagogical tradition and the elements of home, family, and school that had fashioned his own life.

In the Omaha of his day, Father Flanagan's educational vision included the black child, an outcast in the urban vision of the time, where a mounting racial crisis would explode twenty years after his death, shattering the complacency of the city that ignored the injustice of its civic and educational policies. His most dedicated supporter was not a Catholic layman or a prominent Catholic family whose wealth might have underwritten his labors. It was Henry Monsky, a Jewish lawyer and fighter for social justice who was the head of B'nai B'rith. What Monsky also recognized was something rabbinical in Father Flanagan's aphorisms and insights, a Talmudic wisdom that the priest drew from his Irish heritage, summed up in his classic saying, "There's no such thing as a bad boy." This was the hand of hope that the priest held out to every boy whose life he touched, the redemptive grasp he had of his priestly mission, and the unflagging confidence in the strange role that had been thrust upon him.

The variety, talents, and character of this new influx of boys astounded and cheered Father Flanagan, and he filled his *Boys' Home Journal* with page after page of detailed accounts of each new arrival. Most of these boys were not in trouble with the law and few had ever seen a courtroom. For various reasons, they had been deserted, left homeless, or left to fend for themselves.

The flood of boys was so great in the summer of 1933 that the Home was bursting at the seams, and there was a great need for some kind of internal organization to plan and oversee activities. Several of the boys who had been away at high school or college had returned to the Home for the summer, and acted as "big brothers" for the younger boys who filled the dormitories and crowded into the dining hall for meals. But something even greater in scope was necessary.

In June 1933, the Home took the first step toward official self-government with the election of a Student Council. The start of the council's work was described this way: "The purpose of the council is to give the boys a voice in the government of the Home, and the making and enforcing of rules and regulations… Nine boys were chosen to sit on this council with Father Flanagan and representatives of his staff… The installation of the officers of the council took place on May 13… Each member of the council gave a short talk."[845]

Father Flanagan's comment on this first step solidified the Home as something more than a protective institution for homeless and wayward boys: "With this new arrangement, each boy is conscious of having a part in the government and in solving the problems that arise from day to day," he said. He and his staff would act only as counselors, and "the boys will preside at the meetings."[846]

The Home began to take on the character of a real town when the boys also decided to start their own newspaper.[847] The Home already had a print shop, and printing had become one of the favorites among the many trades offered to the boys. The print shop also printed the *Boys' Home Journal*, keeping the publication's thousands of subscribers up-to-date on what was happening in this City of Little Men.[848]

Father Flanagan's total vision of his work found its full expression in the Home as a real town for the boys and in the boys as citizens, rather than wards or inmates of an institution. The boys were in a state of growth and formation, but already possessed dignity and rights. This concept was at work very early, when Father Flanagan's collaborators were pitifully few in numbers and the older boys were responsible for the younger boys. Now it was gaining structure and purpose.

The town concept arose just as the priest's hopes of finding homes for his boys began to dwindle. Boys who were adopted in the spring often were returned in the fall. Also, his continuous appeal for foster parents went mostly unanswered.[849] In June 1933, Father Flanagan found himself with nine eighth-grade graduates and no homes for them to go to so they could continue their education in high school. That fall, though, a high school freshmen class was added to the curriculum,[850] and a sophomore class was added for the 1934 school year.[851] And the boys were staying longer so the older boys could take on more responsibilities.[852]

On the sixteenth anniversary of the founding of the Home, Father Flanagan sat down and counted the number of boys who had passed through his care so far. The total was 3,478, with these designations: Charity: 2,836; Court: 601; Tagged: 41. It seemed to be time for the Home to take a new direction.

Shaping a Generation through Leadership

In the summer of 1934, Father Flanagan began writing a chronicle of his work.[853] His Home had become much more than a temporary refuge for boys who were homeless and in trouble. He was beginning to fashion a whole generation of remarkable young men in an atmosphere of acceptance, freedom, and the development of talents and interests of which none of them were aware.

His chronicle was also an account of his own journey, along with these boys, and the power of love, acceptance, and the stretching of one's possibilities to its limits. Something of the prose of Dickens began to flow from his pen and characters as real and as colorful as Oliver Twist, the Artful Dodger, and Wacksford Squeers erupted on every page.

There was a totality to his work that only gradually dawned on him, and that totality demanded a self-sufficient village *of* boys, *by* boys, and *for* boys. The possibilities – and the responsibilities – of creating such a place kept him up nights thinking about it.

His Home was a family, but richer and more diverse than any other family. Why shouldn't the younger boys profit from the knowledge and experience of the older boys, just as younger children do in any family?

He realized his boys' village had to be a real village, and that "Boys Town" had to be something more than a clever name. Already it was more than a school; it was a carefully planned, self-sufficient community of amazing diversity, age, and variety, with talents galore.[854]

In the fall of 1934, at Father Flanagan's request, the U.S. Postmaster General approved the establishment of a post office on the Boys Town campus,[855] with Pat Norton as postmaster. This gave Boys Town a postal destination – "Boys Town, Nebraska" – which was recognized by the United States government.[856]

Obtaining the post office address of "Boys Town, Nebraska" coincided with the seventeenth anniversary of the Home's founding (December 12, 1934), and at a celebration, Father Flanagan made a startling announcement: Now that Boys Town was an official, legal village, it was going to have a legal government in which the boys were the government, freely elected by the other boys – a government of the boys, by the boys, and for the boys.[857]

The announcement was greeted with cheers from the boys, and within hours, the "Build the Boys Town" party and the "Help Our Town" party – junior versions of the Republican and Democratic parties – were organized. Soon after, mini-conventions were held to select candidates for the positions of mayor and a council of commissioners.

Christmas was overlooked that year in the rush of politics as each party organized its program and chose its candidates. The "Build Boys Town" party chose seventeen-year-old Tony Villone as their leader and candidate for mayor. The "Help Our Town" party chose Joe "Chief" Renteria. The election date was set for January 15, 1935, so that the New Year would open with a mayor and village officials legally in place.[858]

With the two parties well-organized and candidates carefully selected, each party went into huddles, closed-door meetings, and electioneering to ensure that their goals would be well-known to the electorate, from the youngest Boys Town citizen to Father Flanagan and his staff.

Boys Town had not seen such excitement since the Home moved to Overlook Farm and the boy entertainers returned from their nationwide performances. It marked a new era in the history of this City of Little Men, and soon the local papers were chronicling the event. Outsiders eagerly watched as this miniature drama unfolded and the national newspapers soon picked up the story and gave it widespread coverage.

Its status as a town was not the only thing that was new about Boys Town. A new auditorium and gymnasium had just been completed, giving the boys a basketball court, a swimming pool, and room for other indoor sports activities.

The new gymnasium served as the polling place for the election, as described in this account:

"Shortly after 7:30 in the evening, all the boys gathered in the new gymnasium building. At the far end of the auditorium, three voting booths had been set on the stage. In an orderly line, the 200 boys filed up. First they were checked on a list by judges to make sure they were entitled to a printed ballot. Then they went single file into the voting booths."[859]

It was also decided that adult staff members, including Father Flanagan, should vote. The priest's ballot was delivered from his sickbed, where he was recovering from a cold. After what seemed like an eternity as the ballots were counted, the new and first official mayor of Boys Town was announced: seventeen-year-old Tony Villone, representing the "Build Boys Town" party.

Amid wild cheering, Joe Renteria, the spokesman for the losing party, added just the right touch for the occasion, congratulating Mayor Villone and the BBTers on their victory. Stepping to the front of the stage, he raised his hand for silence.

"Boys, we lost. But that doesn't mean we aren't going to give the new commission all the support we can," he said. "After all, the chief interest of us all is the future welfare of our city. We've got to work together. We're going to work together."[860]

The boy journalist reporting the incident added in his story: "The 'Chief's' beau geste was cause for more spirited cheering."

Almost at once the Home took on a new character, with the mayor assigning his commissioners their areas of responsibility. Their titles were not just for show. These boys were to govern Boys Town according to the duties that were laid out: Police. Public Safety. Parks, Health, and Hygiene. Buildings. Public Works. The office of mayor also was more than just a title. Responsible only to Father Flanagan, the mayor was to keep order, enforce discipline, and punish offenders. A court was set up with the mayor and council members as judge and jury, respectively. It was a grand experiment that introduced mere boys to the serious responsibilities of self-government.

The opening of Boys Town's first U.S. Post Office in 1934 brought needed local and national attention to the village.

Tony Villone (LEFT) was elected Boys Town's first official mayor in 1935, besting his opponent, Joe Renteria (RIGHT), who had a goat as his campaign mascot.

All of the boys, from the youngest to the oldest, were allowed to vote in Boys Town's first official elections. Father Flanagan started the elections to teach the boys about citizenship and democracy, and give them a voice in how the Home was run.

16

THE MOVIE, *BOYS TOWN*

Early in 1937, John Considine, Jr.,[861] a major producer at MGM Studios in Culver City, California, saw an item in the *Los Angeles Times* about the election of a boy mayor in a Nebraska village called "Boys Town."[862] Curious about the name of the town and the "boy mayor," he phoned Father Flanagan, thinking a story about a village of boys with a duly-elected mayor might make a good motion picture.[863]

"Send out your writers," Father Flanagan told him, curious about the inquiry and wondering what Hollywood might do with the story. MGM chose four of its top writers to work on a storyline: Dore Schary,[864] Eleanor Griffin, Thomas Meehan, and O.O. Dull. Schary and Meehan were commissioned to come up with their versions at the studio, while Griffin, Dull, and a fifth member of the team, William Rankin, were sent to Boys Town.[865]

When the trio arrived at Boys Town, Father Flanagan told them, "If you are planning to weave a sentimental plot around the name Boys Town – if you intend an 'Oliver Twist' orphanage picture, I'd rather that it never be made."[866] He made it clear that he would be a fierce critic of any storyline they came up with, and also demanded final approval of the screenplay.

"Boys Town is not an institution," he told them. "It is a township where fine little men live, work, study, and play. If you can capture such a Boys Town on the screen, I sincerely believe you will have a great motion picture, as dramatic and packed with romance as any you might produce."[867]

Taken aback by this frank appraisal of the project, Griffin and Dull remained at Boys Town for ten days to immerse themselves in this "City of Little Men," as Boys Town came to be called at MGM. They mingled among the boys, talked to them, saw them at work, at play, at school, and on the playing fields, and even wondered if some of the boys might appear in the film in minor roles.[868]

It was clear to Eleanor Griffin that Father Flanagan was eager to have the story of his work reach the screen. But there was a problem and a need for haste. Father Flanagan's work was in the public domain. If word got out that MGM was considering making a movie based on his work, some other studio could take up the idea, change the names and locale, and create a fictional version of Boys Town.[869] It was important for MGM to quickly come up with a script that Father Flanagan could accept.

Oddly, Father Flanagan had demanded no payment for the use of his story as a motion picture. He accepted a token one dollar for MGM's right to his story, in the hope that the studio might come up with something suitable. He knew the value of publicity and had used it in his own way to spread the word about his work. Very early, he had started broadcasting his weekly radio programs and had sent his boys on the entertainment circuit to make his work known across the country

But a movie!

Father Flanagan's doubts about such a movie, however, were well-founded. This was no love story, and there would be no lead actress in the cast. It would all depend on the script, the actors who were chosen, and the story itself. To ensure the studio had a firsthand account of his work, he gave the writers a copy of his own memoirs, *His Lamp of Fire*,[870] which he had written three years earlier.

On their return to California, the MGM writers got to work on a storyline, and several versions passed between Hollywood and Boys Town. Father Flanagan rejected each one. The studio was deeply concerned and feared the priest would lose interest. And, thousands of dollars had already been spent on the project. Finally, John Considine commissioned Dore Schary[871] to come up with a story idea that would satisfy Father Flanagan.[872]

Schary worked on his idea over the Christmas holidays of 1937–38, and presented it to Considine on January 6. Recognizing Schary's story as the best yet, and the one that was sure to please Father Flanagan, Considine sent Schary to Boys Town to confer with the priest.[873]

As he prepared for a dinner meeting with the priest, Schary was not sure what kind of man he would encounter. "When I arrived," he later wrote, "it was bitter cold. I found myself to Father Flanagan's home, but I was practically frozen, and also deeply concerned about how to behave with a Catholic priest. Father Flanagan joined me in a moment or two and relieved my chill and my tensions by offering a long drink of straight Irish whisky.[874] After we had two of these generous appetizers, I was warm and captivated by this tall, craggy priest who spoke with a slight brogue but with no affectation.[875]

"He didn't look a bit like (Spencer) Tracy, but he had Tracy's charm, his smile, and twinkle."[876]

Schary's last remark summed up his hopes for the movie: "He's going to be a cinch to catch on film."

Schary was deeply impressed with Father Flanagan and with Boys Town. The priest, in turn, was pleased with what Schary had written and they spent the next evening together in quiet and intense conversation. "Later, at the hotel," Schary wrote, "I spent two or three hours writing some of my impressions of this interested and committed man... the story elements flowed quickly and surely."[877] Schary was sure he had a hit on his hands, but thought the centerpiece of the movie should not be the boys but the priest. His job now was to "catch him on film." The whole concept of the movie had changed; the film would concentrate on Father Flanagan.[878]

Before Schary left to return to Hollywood, Father Flanagan suggested that Spencer Tracy might be considered for the lead role.[879] Tracy had played a priest in the hit movie, *San Francisco*, with Clark Gable and Jeanette MacDonald, and Father Flanagan had been impressed with his portrayal. Tracy was in the running for an Oscar for his role in the 1937 film, *Captains Courageous*, but it was well-known that he did not want to be typecast.[880] And his bouts with alcohol made him somewhat unpredictable. Besides, the priest's role in *Boys Town* did not seem suitable for an Oscar winner, unless – and this had already struck Schary – the movie was about the man.[881] With the whole centerpiece of the movie changed, Schary now would have to convince Hollywood. The dinner discussion inspired the writer to make Father Flanagan the main character in the screenplay; his script would evolve into a biographic, a picture about a man committed to goodness and benevolence.[882]

Back at MGM, Considine was not hard to convince and he commissioned Schary to work on a screenplay with Father Flanagan as the major figure.[883] Within two weeks, the final screenplay was well under way and Considine ordered Schary back to Boys Town, accompanied by Jack Ruben, the director chosen for the movie.[884] The two immersed themselves in "the City of Little Men," and the studio was already planning a documentary on the film with that title in anticipation of the movie. The publicity wheels were beginning to turn.

Schary and Ruben were enchanted with this miniature village of boys, and they wandered the campus with a sharp eye for anything that could be incorporated into the film. They observed Father Flanagan at close range and got a feel for the setting of the movie. The town was filled with drama, and they began to shape some of the boys they saw into characters for the movie. They studied the give-and-take of the boys themselves, upon which much of the movie would be based, and began to flesh out characters from real-life situations.

The movie would be an ensemble of MGM's roster of child stars, with Mickey Rooney heading the cast in his first major starring role. Tracy had not yet been approached for the leading role of Father Flanagan since the priest had been only a minor character in the first versions of the film's storyline. Tracy was critical to the movie's success; it was an MGM principle that star power was the main attraction for a movie, and Tracy's star power had been proven through a string of earlier movies, including *Fury*, *San Francisco*, and *Captains Courageous*.[885]

Schary and Ruben were captivated by the setting of the movie as they moved among the boys and visualized their screenplay coming alive. At one point, they watched a basketball game with the boys wearing rag-tag uniforms; they quickly phoned MGM to request that the studio provide new uniforms for the boys.

They were also quite taken with two of the younger boys, Andy and Jimmy Cain,[886] who were brothers whom they thought might play characters in the movie. Schary and Ruben invited Father Flanagan and the boys to Hollywood[887] to test the boys' acting skills.[888] It was also agreed that Morris Jacobs would accompany Father Flanagan and the brothers to the MGM studio,[889] since it was important that any news of the coming movie filtered back to Omaha to generate local publicity.[890]

Already a shrewd hand at the art of publicity, Father Flanagan knew the value of the Boys Town story – to Hollywood and to Boys Town itself. He accepted a $5,000 fee for the film rights with the understanding that a successful motion picture could be worth hundreds of thousands of dollars to the Home.[891] Jacobs envisioned a promotional plan that reached out to national and international media outlets to spread word of Father Flanagan's work for boys to the whole world. Jacobs had been associated with Father Flanagan since the priest's first days in the juvenile courts, when Father Flanagan begged judges to release boys in trouble into his custody, and was one of the first to realize the potentially international scope of his work.

On February 1, Father Flanagan and Morris Jacobs arrived in Culver City, California. From that moment, Jacobs became Father Flanagan's "front man" in his trip to Hollywood.[892]

It was on this trip to the MGM Studios that Father Flanagan met Spencer Tracy for the first time.[893] It was the beginning of a warm friendship and the two carried on an intense conversation about Tracy's portrayal of the priest.[894]

"All actors," Tracy told Father Flanagan, "do everything possible to live their part – to be the very image of the person they are portraying. But few actors, Father, have the opportunity of being confronted by that person."[895]

What Father Flanagan saw in Tracy was a consummate actor already at work. He would later write of their conversation: "As he talked, I could feel his eyes upon me, studying my every little mannerism: the way I sat in the chair, the way I talked, the way I pushed my hair back from my forehead. I knew he was studying me – the man he was to become – as searchingly as I studied him. I knew almost what was running through his mind."

Father Flanagan also met with studio head Louis B. Mayer, Mickey Rooney,[896] and many of the studio's other major stars.[897] He was shown a first version of the screenplay, and had other long conversations with Tracy about the actor's role in the film.

Andy and Jimmie Cain did not get speaking parts in the movie.[898] Unfortunately, it seemed they could not act and so the part one of them might have played – the character of "Pee Wee"[899] – was given to child actor Bobs Watson,[900] who came from a family of child actors.

On returning home, Father Flanagan's remarks on his visit to MGM were only laudatory. He had seen the massive planning and concern for detail that went into the production of a movie, and his impression of the stars, the producers, the writers, the cameramen, and the whole army of skilled men and women who planned and created movies drew his highest praise. "I found, in Hollywood, not the frivolous, gilded sort of existence I had been led to expect from reports oral and printed, but a hard-working, sincere group of men and women working in a comparatively new but powerfully effective medium,"[901] he would later say.

Soon after his return home from California, Father Flanagan's mother, Honora, died on March 21, 1938, at the Omaha home of her daughter, Susan Dwyer. For many of Boys Town's older boys, Mrs. Flanagan had been the only mother they ever known, and her presence among them, along with her daughter, Nellie, created a feeling of family for the boys who had none. Her funeral was in St. Cecilia's Cathedral in Omaha, with her two priest sons as celebrants.

A Movie Moves Forward

MGM studio was convinced it had a hit on its hands after Father Flanagan's visit, and John Considine took charge, putting John Meehan and Dore Schary to work on revising the screenplay of *Boys Town* to focus on the priest, not the boys. To accomplish this, Meehan and Schary returned to the original work of Eleanor Griffin, merging her story of the roots of the original Home for Boys with the later tale Schary developed about the most incorrigible boy Father Flanagan ever met.[902]

Considine faced another challenge. Jack Ruben, the director of the movie who had accompanied Schary on the visit to Boys Town, was diagnosed with a serious heart disease and was taken off the picture.[903] Considine had to find a replacement and his choice was a noted director of children's films whose record of hits was legendary. Norman Taurog[904] had directed Jackie Cooper, his nephew, in *Skippy*, and had just finished the childhood classic, *The Adventures of Tom Sawyer*, one of the major hits of 1938. Choosing Taurog ensured that *Boys Town* would be a major production and it led to another decision by Considine: He and Taurog would go to Boys Town on their own, since it had now been decided that the picture would be filmed "on location" there.[905]

On May 3, Considine sent Father Flanagan a copy of Dore Schary's latest version of the screenplay. Father Flanagan responded by inviting Considine, screenwriter John Meehan, director Norman Taurog, and Spencer Tracy to Omaha for a conference on the script. Tracy, who was already busy studying the script for his first scene with Mickey Rooney in the movie, declined.

The Considine-Taurog visit cemented the bond between Hollywood and Father Flanagan, with both men looking to the Irish priest as something of a spiritual father. Taurog admitted as much, even though he was not a Catholic.[906] There was something about the wit, wisdom, and solid moral character of the founder of Boys Town; Father Flanagan's unashamed love of every person he met endeared him to everyone.

MGM's publicity for the film began soon after. With on-location shooting at Boys Town, the studio began planning a trip to Nebraska for its film crew and stars. It was an unprecedented decision, but Considine and others felt the setting for the movie had to be Boys Town itself, even though a replica of the town's main building would be built at the studio for certain exterior shots when the crew returned to MGM.[907]

Frank Whitbeck,[908] head of MGM's publicity department, also joined the company, specifically to look after Tracy, who was known to be difficult during on-location shooting. Whitbeck also would gather material for a short documentary on Boys Town entitled, *The City of Little Men*,[909] which is what Boys Town was being called by the studio.[910] This documentary would introduce the public to Boys Town and Father Flanagan, who had made his first film appearance in two staged scenes in which his philosophy and the purpose of Boys Town were graphically portrayed.

With telegrams[911] sent from the studio to Father Flanagan[912] requesting a minimum of publicity for the trip,[913] sixty-one people from the studio boarded the train bound for Omaha.[914]

But the arrival of the stars, director, and film crew in Omaha became a city-wide sensation,[915] with local newspapers touting the event as a celebration for the whole city.[916] The Hollywood contingent was housed in the local Hotel Fontenelle, which was crowded with visitors, mostly teenage girls, who were eager to get a glimpse of the folks from Hollywood.

The evening of their first day in Omaha, the stars of the movie were welcomed during a reception at the Omaha Theater.[917] Father Flanagan appeared onstage, introducing Tracy and Rooney as well as the minor players like Frankie Thomas, Gene Reynolds, Sid Miller, and Bobs Watson to the audience. Next morning, cast and crew headed for Boys Town, followed by a curious public eager to see Hollywood at work so close to home.[918]

MGM had also sent producer John Considine, Jr.[919] to oversee the production. Father Flanagan would be on hand, along with the young citizens of Boys Town, their mayor, and other city officials.

As the boys welcomed Hollywood to their city,[920] it at first seemed like Boys Town had been invaded. One of the boys would later describe it this way: "Up the driveway they came… ten cabs full of them… everyone was terribly excited… the cabs stopped one by one in front of the office building, and pretty soon lots of people were milling around all over the place… Just then a cab drove up and Mickey Rooney,[921] Spencer Tracy, and a fat man got out. We had met Mickey[922] and Spencer the day before, but this was the grand opening and we made as much noise as we could. Mickey[923] yelled back at us and shook hands with as many kids as he could…."[924]

Within hours, Boys Town became a vast movie set as the crew took over, identifying places where the cameras would roll and where all the equipment would be stored for easy access. Taurog seemed very much at home in this city of boys.[925] Curious boys stood around watching, one or two with pens in hand to record the event for the *Boys' Home Journal*.

"Most days, the crew began setting up the first shot at dawn. Owing to the heat, the company usually wrapped up by mid-afternoon, when cast and crew packed up and headed back to Omaha. Each day's exposed film was air-expressed overnight to Hollywood. The rushes returned the next day for Taurog and Considine to view."[926]

The minor boy stars – Frankie Thomas,[927] Gene Reynolds,[928] Sidney Miller,[929] and Bobs Watson[930] – mixed in well with the Boys Town citizens and left a positive impression as child movie stars. Tracy became something of a father figure to the boys, and many of them corresponded with him after he returned to Hollywood. One of the boys, Tony Villone, Boys Town's first mayor, wrote glowing accounts of the Hollywood experience.[931] After his graduation, with the help of Frank Whitbeck and Spencer Tracy, Villone was hired by MGM's art department and worked at the studio until its dissolution years later.

Boys Town's citizens, from the mayor to the youngest boy, took part in the making of the movie,[932] some appearing in crowd scenes and some as ordinary citizens of Boys Town, creating a realistic backdrop to scene after scene.[933] Father Flanagan insisted that the boys' normal activities should go on as usual, unless they were called to be part of a scene. This often happened during working hours, and an army of boys would descend upon a set, warned cautiously not to disturb the scene. A hushed silence would follow.

The boys' recollections of the filming is a story in itself. They were as curious as the rest of the world about the story of Father Flanagan and their City of Little Men. They could not get much of the storyline from the few scenes being played out in their village, and so, coming in small groups, they waited for opportunities to watch the filming or talk to the director, crew members, or Tracy and Rooney.

For the most part, the normal life of the Home went on as usual. But the boys were always eager to be part of the unusual goings-on around them. One boy described those days this way:

"It was mutiny, us having to work every morning while they were shooting scenes right outside the window, but our afternoons were mostly free, and we sure made up for lost time. The first chance… we set out to get the dope on Mickey Rooney. He was lying under a tree waiting to shoot a scene with Bobs Watson, Pee Wee in the movie… Mickey thought Boys Town was swell, and he wanted to know if it was true, like in the picture, that we had our own mayor and commissioners who ran the town just as they pleased…. We asked Mickey to tell us the story of the picture. He had hardly begun when a man who turned out to be Norman Taurog, the director of the picture, called him to get ready for the next scene."[934]

There was absolute silence while the cameras were rolling, but the boys crowded around these strangers when scenes were finished or a day's work was over. Another boy wrote:

"While Frankie Thomas was wiping the heavy pinkish grease paint off his face, he told us the way he understood it. 'The picture was to begin with Father Flanagan as a young priest, running a hotel for bums and drunkards who had no home. After Father realizes that he can't help men who have fallen so low, he starts his place for homeless boys. The going is pretty rough at first, but with the aid of a friend who thinks Father is crazy (but never refuses to help him), the home gradually succeeds.'"[935]

Most of the boys knew little about Father Flanagan's early work with the men off the street, and his first work for boys was now over twenty years in the past. So they gathered eagerly around those who would dramatize the story of their unique village.

On the first or second day of shooting, the boys were delighted to hear that the next day's scenes would feature the village, with them in it. There were scenes in the boys' dormitory, the dining hall, the boxing ring, and on the road that led into Boys Town. Every boy took part, appearing with Tracy, Rooney, and the other boy stars. Father Flanagan watched, sometimes from the window of his office or just off to the side, wearing his straw hat or chatting with Tracy or one of the other actors.[936]

The filming of the picture in their own town was an experience in filmmaking.[937] School was out during the summer months, but there was work to be done, in the homes and on the farm. The boy reporter of the *Boys' Home Journal* was quite observant, eager to instruct his boy readers in the art of motion pictures.[938]

Besides standing on the sidelines, Father Flanagan hosted Tracy and Rooney for dinner, joked with Watson,[939] who began to look up to Father Flanagan as his idol, and chatted with director Taurog between takes. Rooney could play slapstick and high jinks when off camera, but with Father Flanagan around, he was a bit awed and always on his best behavior.

The young actors, basking in the glow of working with Tracy[940] and Rooney, under the firm direction of a master director like Taurog, saw in Father Flanagan someone who was far away from cameras and publicity, and perceived a warmth and friendliness in the priest that had nothing to do with their status as actors. "He took an interest in me," actor Gene Reynolds observed, and others made similar remarks.

The priest stood aloof from the making of the movie, trusting the experts, whom he had studied well, to do their job. One photo shows him with a seated Tracy as the actor studies his lines, a crew in the background preparing for the next scene.[941]

Food for the actors and crew was catered and spread out on folding tables. As one of them described it: "We ate Santa Monica Seagulls... chicken, but not very good chicken."[942]

At the end of each day of filming, the cast and crew took hired cabs for a trip back to the Fontenelle Hotel, where young girls waited for the Hollywood boys. Each actor or crew member had vouchers for dinner and the evenings often were spent studying lines and preparing for the next day's shooting. On Saturday nights, more attention was given to the girls. Mickey Rooney led the way, sometimes with more than one girl on his arms.

The Fourth of July came midway through the filming, and Father Flanagan threw a party for the Hollywood visitors and boys. It was another time for getting to know each other and sharing experiences as the movie progressed.

The ten days of the filming passed swiftly, but the presence of two major stars in this community of boys and the experience of moviemaking brought something magical into this City of Little Men. It was clear that Boys Town would never be the same after this Hollywood invasion.

Both Boys Town and Hollywood entered into a world larger than their own, and from that summer forward, the world would make its way to Boys Town. It started with the crowds who came each day to watch the filming, sometimes as many as 5,000. The people of Omaha, who long ago had taken Father Flanagan and his boys to their hearts as they watched the beginnings of this unique community of boys, flocked to see the strangers from Hollywood. (Unfortunately, the crowds of onlookers that showed up every day to watch the filming caused severe damage to the grounds and Father Flanagan was forced to use most of the $5,000 he received from MGM for repairs.[943])

For Father Flanagan's boys, most of them unknown and never in the spotlight before, it was mass confusion to find themselves the objects of interest and concern, both by these people from Hollywood and the public from Omaha that seemed fascinated with all the attention given to this unique town on the edge of their city. As filming ended and the army of celebrities left, the village settled back into a somewhat normal existence, the whole town excitedly looking forward to the finished product and their place in it.

As one boy wrote:

"It was really swell having those Hollywood people around, and we sure hated to see them go. We knew it would be dead as a doornail around Boys Town after they left... Spencer Tracy gave us an ice cream party one night, and he had *Test Pilot* shown for us, too. Besides that, they promised to get Tony Villone a job at the MGM studio when he left Boys Town."

On a personal level, some boys made friendships with the Hollywood notables that would last a lifetime, and letters would be exchanged over the years between boys and their newfound friends.[944]

A Big Omaha Premiere

Upon returning to California, director Taurog sped up the pace of his work. He began to film the prologue scenes, encompassing the first forty-five minutes or so of the movie. Rooney and the other young actors who went to Boys Town were put on a three-week hiatus while a new group of boys depicted the early days of Father Flanagan's work in 1917 and established the reasons and issues behind his founding of the first Home for Boys.[945]

After completing the final scenes, plans were quickly made for the release of the movie. But there was one major problem: Louis B. Mayer's vocal concern that the movie would not appeal to the general public.[946] After intense sessions with Rooney, perhaps a word or two from Tracy, and strong objections from Taurog and Considine, Mayer relented and invited Father Flanagan and Archbishop James Hugh Ryan of the Omaha Archdiocese to Hollywood to view the final product, hastily packaged in its final version by Considine, Schary, Griffin, and Taurog.

Once convinced of the marketability of the movie, Mayer planned a grand reception and luncheon for Father Flanagan and Archbishop Ryan. Taking note of the Catholic background of the movie, and with the subject of the movie being a guest of the studio, Mayer invited a roster of Catholic stars whose devotion to their religion was well-known, including Don Ameche, George Murphy, Maureen O'Sullivan, and Dennis O'Keefe. Film clips of the movie were shown at the luncheon, along with the documentary, *The City of Little Men*. Father Flanagan and the bishop then viewed the finished *Boys Town* in private after the luncheon.

When the studio planned the world premiere for Washington, D.C., Nebraskans protested, and Father Flanagan used his leverage to make Omaha the site. As soon as word reached town that the priest had secured the premiere for Omaha, elaborate arrangements got underway.[947]

When the day of the premiere of the movie finally arrived, crowds gathered at Omaha's Union Station to welcome Father Flanagan, who was accompanied by the stars of the movie, Tracy and Rooney, as well as John Considine, Maureen O'Sullivan, and Frank Whitbeck.

A throng of 7,000 people greeted the travelers, cheering the great humanitarian who had captured the admiration of all the world through his work with homeless boys. The welcoming committee included Mayor Butler and other Omaha city officials, as well as Boys Town Mayor Jack Farrald and his city commissioners. There was music and excitement, and each celebrity was asked to say a few words to the assembled masses.[948]

Tracy's biography would later describe the scene this way: "The company of fifty-eight was the biggest, by far, ever to hit Nebraska. When they arrived early in the evening of the twentieth-fifth, several thousand jammed Omaha's Union Station to catch glimpses of Tracy and particularly Mickey Rooney, who had just become the hottest thing in pictures."[949]

After the rousing welcome from the huge crowds at the railroad station, Father Flanagan retired to his office, where several weeks of work awaited him. Then he met with his boys, the mayor, and the commissioners to declare the next day "Premiere Day." Omaha joined in the celebration by letting Farrald and his commissioners take over the city.

Later, the first issue of the new *Boys Town Times* announced, "Premiere Scores Big Hit – Thousands Jam Omaha Streets For Big Event." The whole city of Omaha, it seemed, had turned out for this tribute to their own "City of Little Men" and the now-internationally known priest who had made it possible. They knew, with Father Flanagan surrounded by Hollywood royalty, that the whole world was aware that Omaha was his home.[950]

The Boys Town Times reported: "Father Flanagan, touched by emotion, stood before the crowd and told them how happy, how thrilled by the great honor which had come to him… and the huge crowd arose to its feet and cheered until it seemed the roof of the theatre must come off."

In the summer of 1938, a film crew from MGM Studios descended upon the village to film the motion picture, *Boys Town*.

Father Flanagan with Bobs Watson during the filming of the movie *Boys Town*. Watson played "Pee-Wee" in the movie.

Stars of the *Boys Town* movie arrived for the film's Omaha premiere on a Union Pacific train. Omaha's Union Station was decorated with movie-related images for the event.

Thousands of people gathered outside the Omaha Theater to watch the arrival of stars and special guests at the *Boys Town* premiere on September 7, 1938.

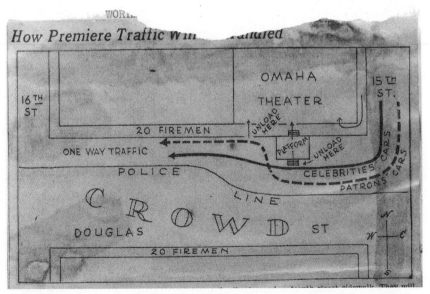

The *Omaha World-Herald* newspaper published a diagram of traffic flow for the premiere of *Boys Town* at the Omaha Theater.

17

BRICK AND MORTAR AND MORE BOYS

An Ongoing Need

Despite the tremendous success of the *Boys Town* movie, telling the story of Father Flanagan's work on the silver screen had the opposite effect of what was expected. In fact, it almost plunged Boys Town into bankruptcy.[951]

Donations dropped off, [952] over a thousand new boys sought admission, and another expansion of [953] the village became an immediate necessity. Henry Monsky,[954] Flanagan's friend and advisor, wrote to Louis B. Mayer of MGM Studios and suggested that, with the success of the movie and huge profits for the studio, Boys Town's share of the profits might be considered. Mayer replied that he would take it up with the corporation.[955]

Since the population of the town had increased considerably due to the movie and the publicity that attended it,[956] there was a desperate need for new housing. The Main Building, where the boys had lived, took their meals, slept, and attended classes since its construction twenty years earlier, was totally inadequate. Digging deeper into his own resources and counting on the growing interest in his City of Little Men, Father Flanagan made plans for four new apartment buildings, each to house one-hundred fifty boys, and a new dining hall in the center of town. The cost of the expansion was approximately $1.5 million, and would triple the capacity of the Home.[957]

Father Flanagan explained to anyone who would listen that expansion was critical: "I'm going into debt for the whole building program, as has been done ever since the institution began more than twenty years ago. I am well aware that it would be much easier to sit back and reject applications with the excuse that the Home is full, but it is impossible for me to do that."

The priest could not turn down these youth, most of them boys without families, or kids living on the streets or the highways, going nowhere. Boys Town had to expand and that expansion would cost money.

But the Herbert Niccolls case had gained Father Flanagan national and even international attention, and his talks all over the country had made him a household name. One person who was listening was John Considine, Jr., the producer of the *Boys Town* movie and now a dear, close friend of Boys Town and its founder.

Considine's interest in Father Flanagan's dream had brought him to Boys Town to oversee the filming of the picture, and he took a special interest in the town's future, staying behind with his wife after the movie's premiere to host an ice cream party for the boys. He also hired buses to take Boys Town citizens to a special showing of the film. But his interest in Boys Town and its future did not stop there. He was concerned that the movie gave the impression of a prosperous Boys Town; in reality, he knew the movie almost broke Father Flanagan financially and that MGM and Hollywood had a hand in the financial crisis the priest was now facing.

After a number of talks with Father Flanagan and personal experiences with the scope and quality of the priest's work, Considine returned to Hollywood, to MGM in particular, to come to the rescue of Father Flanagan.

His first effort was to convince Mayer, the head of MGM, that Father Flanagan and his boys should receive more from the success of the film than the $5,000 the Home initially received. Mayer agreed and decided on a special event to highlight MGM's generosity and honor Father Flanagan and his role in the success of the movie.

Mayer planned a dinner in Hollywood for Father Flanagan and his bishop. MGM sponsored the event and involved some of the most important people in Hollywood – including prominent Catholic stars of the day. At the dinner, Mayer announced[958] that MGM would donate a building for the expansion of Boys Town at a cost of $250,000.[959] Present at the dinner were Spencer Tracy and Mickey Rooney, stars of the film, and everyone from MGM who was important.[960]

MGM was not the only company that got into the act; a whole roster of Hollywood notables began to plan events to bring public attention to the needs of Father Flanagan and his boys. One of the first of those events would bring part of Boys Town to Los Angeles.

It was announced that a football game would be played between Boys Town and Black-Foxe Military Academy in Los Angeles, a school attended by the sons of many Hollywood stars. As the Boys Town team got ready for the trip west, newspapers began to tout the match: "The Boys Town football team will travel to Los Angeles to play a benefit football game with the crack team of the Black Foxe Military Academy on November 26th. The Military Academy boasting one of the best teams on the coast, is run by Maj. Foxe, President, and arrangements for the game were made by John Considine, producer of 'Boys Town.'"[961]

Considine's plan was to have the receipts from the game (and other Hollywood events supporting the Home) go into Father Flanagan's Building

Fund. There was even talk at MGM of producing a sequel to the movie, with proceeds also going to the building fund.

All of Hollywood,[962] turned out in support of Father Flanagan as his Boys Town warriors defeated Black Foxe Military Academy, 20–12.[963]

During the game, a cheering section composed of Bing Crosby, Robert Taylor, Al Jolson, Darryl F. Zanuck, and Lucille Ball, and led by Considine, rooted for Boys Town. Bobs Watson, who played Pee Wee in the film, led a distinctive cheering section made up of the entire Watson family, all professional cinema stars, all rooting for Boys Town.[964]

Father Flanagan's effect upon the Hollywood community was quite remarkable. He was not a creation of Hollywood, and his devotion to the poor and helpless was more than just the theme of a motion picture. Tracy put it into words, an encore to an amazing performance that earned him a second Best Actor Academy Award: "The utter selflessness of the man, yet in mind and manner not only bright, but brilliant in his grasp of the human condition and in his insight into the innate goodness in everyone he met."

Don Ameche was inspired to imitate Father Flanagan in response to Boys Town's invasion of Hollywood. He gathered seventy underprivileged children from all over the city and treated them to the game, with the help of Hollywood giants like Myrna Loy, Norma Shearer, Clark Gable, and Bing Crosby. That was followed by a Thanksgiving dinner they would never forget.[965]

New Supporters and a New Chapel

In the wake of his astonishing reception in Hollywood and Boys Town's stunning victory over Black Foxe Military Academy, Father Flanagan began receiving invitations to speak from all over the country. At the same time, he began receiving even more letters from boys seeking admittance to Boys Town, and from judges and other state officials recommending the acceptance of some boy. The boys' letters were heartbreaking,[966] echoing the plea of the boys depicted in the movie and its documentary, *The City of Little Men*: "Will you take me, Father? I have no place to go."

With the movie, Boys Town had suddenly become something of a national institution, with individuals and organizations wanting to be a part of Father Flanagan's mission to save homeless children. One of the first was the Fraternal Order of Eagles, which wrote to Father Flanagan offering to provide one of the new buildings needed at Boys Town.[967] In 1939, Father Flanagan appeared before the Grand Aerie of the Fraternal Order of Eagles, composed of representatives of all subordinate units of the Order. After hearing the priest, the Order voted unanimously to build an additional dormitory to cost $135,000, which would house more than twenty-five percent of the village's population.[968]

The need for expansion remained critical as the *Boys Town* movie was shown throughout the country and around the world, even in the Vatican and Ireland. Requests for admission of boys rose sharply wherever the film was screened and invitations for Father Flanagan to speak often came from the same places as those requests. But buildings take time, and the four new residences and new dining hall would take a year or two to complete. Meanwhile, Boys Town awaited an influx of new citizens.

The expected growth in population meant expanding the Home's teaching staff, and Father Flanagan began a search. He found what he wanted in one of the great teaching orders of the Catholic Church, an order of teaching brothers that had schools in several major cities. They were the Brothers of the Christian Schools, popularly known as "Christian Brothers."[969]

With students from fourth grade to seniors in high school, the priest knew he also needed to overhaul and expand his educational system. The upper floors of the original Main Building would house the school. Five hundred boys would fill those classrooms and the Christian Brothers would serve as their experienced and dedicated teachers, covering every grade and every subject.

The brothers would also serve as prefects in the high school apartments, providing spiritual guidance and monitoring out-of-school activities. It was a huge step forward for Boys Town and for the education of Father Flanagan's boys. Some students would concentrate more on the Trade School, where a number of trades were offered, but each would also graduate from Boys Town with a honored diploma that would open many doors after graduation.

When the *Boys Town* movie opened in New York City, record numbers of people turned out to see it. Among them was Miss Mary Dowd, whose interest in Father Flanagan and Boys Town inspired her to see the picture over and over again, each time accompanied by her friends and acquaintances.[970]

Miss Dowd wrote to Father Flanagan, asking for a meeting and explaining that she had a brother who had died and had expressed the wish to do something for young boys. She thought this might be an opportunity to carry out her brother's wishes. After several letters were exchanged, Father Flanagan met with Miss Dowd while on a speaking tour to New York and explained his expansion program: the new dormitories for five hundred boys, a dining hall to match, and bigger facilities for sports, recreation, and music, including a band and a choir.

Impressed, Miss Dowd asked if the village had a suitable chapel and what it might cost to build one. Deeply pleased, the priest told her he would get information to her upon his return to Nebraska. It was something he had not planned for, but the possibility delighted him. Back at Boys Town, he met with architects to assess the size of a chapel and sat down with the Leo Daly Company of Omaha to determine the cost.

Later, Miss Dowd visited Boys Town, met with Archbishop Ryan and the architects, and attended Mass in the tiny room that served as a chapel in the Main Building. It was so cramped and small, and so unworthy of Father Flanagan's dream of the place, she was overjoyed to make a gift of a new chapel.

The summer of 1939 heralded many changes and milestones. The arrival of the Christian Brothers[971] would turn the former living quarters into a first-class education center, with a library to match. The new apartment buildings were going up fast and workers had already begun to clear the land for the new chapel.[972] The pages of the *Boys Town Times* were recording the rise of a new Boys Town.[973]

Then there was good news from Hollywood. John Considine had been working hard for Father Flanagan and Boys Town, and had convinced his studio to produce a sequel to the first film, again starring Spencer Tracy and Mickey Rooney.[974] And the studio would pay Boys Town $100,000 to make the new movie. This was a huge surprise and a great relief to Father Flanagan, who was still searching for income to pay for the expansion of Boys Town.

As buildings were completed, boys moved in and even the Boys Town government took on a new stature. The elected mayor and commissioners were in charge of the new apartments, and real self-government was at work. Headlines and articles in the *Boys Town Times* reported the explosion of new activities, as the City of Little Men entered a new era.

The apartment system became the working model of the new Boys Town. Older boys, many of whom were first-class athletes, were put in charge of each apartment of twenty-five boys, and quickly became mentors and role models for the younger boys. This "big brother-little brother" relationship also enabled the older boys to pass on their interests and skills to the younger boys.

By 1939, the Village of Boys Town had expanded to include four new dormitories for the boys and a new dining hall. The Chapel of the Immaculate Conception (Dowd Chapel) was under construction (far right).

In 1948, a major construction program initiated by Father Flanagan that would double the size of the village was underway.

When the construction program was completed in 1950, the high school boys moved into their new cottages and schools. Boys Town's population grew to over 900 boys, ages nine to eighteen.

18

THE WHITTIER SCHOOL[975]

Two Suicides

On August 11, 1939, the lifeless body of thirteen-year-old Benny Moreno[976] was found in the "Lost Privileges" section of the Whittier School for Boys in Whittier, California. Moreno's suicide immediately made headlines throughout the state.[977]

In July 1940, Edward Leiva,[978] a seventeen-year-old Mexican boy, committed suicide at the school as well.[979] The deaths of these two boys touched off a storm of controversy about the school and its practices,[980] which eventually drew Father Flanagan into the controversy. The priest expressed his most vocal condemnations of reformatories and their penal systems, in particular California's juvenile justice system, and the physical abuse that was an essential part of their correctional methods. And the fact that most of the boys sentenced to the Whittier School were of Mexican or African-American background hinted at policies that were based on racial prejudice.[981]

When Father Flanagan learned of Leiva's death, he was so shocked that, in response to a request of Frank Scully,[982] president of the Hollywood Humane Society, he sent an article by telegram to the *Los Angeles Examiner*. The article, entitled "Suicide As An Escape From Brutality,"[983] roundly condemned the reform school system as an act of cruelty to young offenders that created the hopelessness and helplessness that led them to suicide. He also wrote there was "no need for me to describe the mental attitude of fear which grips the heart and mind of a boy who chooses suicide rather than submit to the punishment and the brutality of guards."

It seemed that the whole West Coast was overcome by horror at the tragic deaths of Benny Moreno and Edward Leiva. Father Flanagan's voice was one of the first to be heard, and he struck out with an eloquence that left no doubt of his fierce condemnation of the reform school system and the inborn effects of the system:

"Such is the system of reform schools – such to a great extent the punishment which causes boys to commit suicide rather than suffer the consequences of the lash, or the lonely confinement in the hole, on bread and water, or to bake in the field under the burning sun like the galley slaves of old goaded on by a brutal guard."[984]

His words of pent-up anger came easily, directed at the adults in state houses or locked prisons who drove young boys to suicide inside their locked cages. And it may have been this experience of brutalized youth that brought about the decision in the movie, *Men of Boys Town*, the sequel to the original *Boys Town* movie, to include graphic scenes from one of those youth prisons.

Opposition was immediate and fierce. Two members of the Board of Trustees of the Whittier School, [985] one of them a monsignor, sent Father Flanagan scathing letters in response to his article in the *Los Angeles Examiner*. But everyone, from John Considine, who knew the priest well, to other public figures urged him to turn his efforts to the Whittier School scandal and to bringing justice to the youth there. What was at stake was in the public interest, and what was being demanded in screaming headlines was a denunciation of the juvenile justice system of California.

Also being questioned after the death of two young boys was the competence of those who made the laws, the actions of those who enforced them, and care and concern for youth in state institutions.

Father Flanagan's article in the *Examiner* was reprinted in the August 23, 1940, issue of the *Boys Town Times*, with this opening explanation:

"In an article written at the request of the *Los Angeles Examiner* and reprinted in this issue of the *Boys Town Times*, Father Flanagan dramatically indicts the reform school system exemplified as the Whittier State School (California), scene of two inmate suicides within one year."[986]

Father Flanagan was ready for a fierce battle, and he received urgent letters from people in high places to challenge the Whittier School and the state of California, based on the shining example of what he had accomplished at Boys Town.

"I have for the past 25 years condemned reform schools as unnecessary schools of torture and schools of crime...," he wrote. "These reform schools do not reform. They turn out young fellows steeped in the poison of revenge – trained in the red lore of criminal anecdotes – young fellows with the determined resolve and knowledge to seek vengeance on a society so stupid as to punish and cure."

His words came hard, and brought the issue of the Whittier School to national attention.

He also received a number of hate letters, claiming that he was defending little gangsters who were caged up in their cells where they belonged. He answered some of them. But he waited to see what would happen in the wake of the bad publicity about the school. The bad publicity was so massive that the governor of California, Culbert Olson, demanded a report on the policies of the school from the head of the State Departments of Institutions, Dr. Aaron

Rosanoff. Dr. Rosanoff responded by writing a lengthy defense of the school[987] and its policies.[988]

There were public interviews with present and former inmates of the school, as well as with the parents of the two boys who had committed suicide. In consequence, several current school employees were fired amid accusations of using cruel and inhuman tactics toward several generations of boys. Finally, the California Congress of Parents and Teachers got into the act and demanded that the governor appoint a committee to carry out a thorough investigation of the Whittier School.[989]

Under pressure from the press and parents' groups, and in light of the dozens of interviews with several generations of boys who had passed through the school, the governor appointed the committee, to be headed by Judge Ben Lindsey of the Superior Court of California. Lindsey chose as his two associates Helen Mellinkoff, a sociologist from Beverly Hills, and Ernest Caldicott, the pastor of the Unitarian Church in Los Angeles, both of whom were active in social causes.[990]

Their investigation took four months. The 167-page report that followed recounted the criminal horrors of the Whittier School administration.[991]

This was the committee's conclusion:

"It is evident that Whittier needs a complete revised program... the preponderance of evidence compiled in our report proved conclusively that the damage done at Whittier is attributable to lack of interest, lack of knowledge, or both, on the part of those who are vested with authority and responsibility. The change necessary at Whittier must necessarily be a drastic one."

This was the committee's recommendation:

"Three highly trained, courageous individuals should be summoned to California as soon as possible. One should be borrowed from the Department of Justice at Washington... one from the Osborne Society in New York, and the other should be Father Flanagan of Boys Town. These three persons should make a checkup of the facilities of Whittier and then formulate a workable program for the school."

The governor's response was to send a telegram immediately to Father Flanagan, as he began to act upon the committee's recommendation.

It was December 20, 1940.

By New Year's Day 1941, a copy of the Whittier School Report compiled by Judge Lindsey and his colleagues was in the hands of Father Flanagan, with this notation from Frank Scully: "To Father Flanagan, the living proof of 'it can't happen here,' with affection and admiration on behalf of the Lindsey Committee and the Hollywood Humane Society."

Father Flanagan read the 167-page report in utter disbelief.

Six days later, he received a letter from his old friend, Judge Lindsey. "We are very hopeful that the Governor will be able to follow our recommendations," the judge wrote. "I understand that he has had some communication with you and that you are willing to serve if His Excellency, my friend the archbishop, will consent."[992]

Father Flanagan also received a letter from FBI Director J. Edgar Hoover,[993] urging him to accept the governor's request that he head the committee.[994]

The New Year also brought with it something to distract the priest momentarily from the Whittier School Report of Judge Lindsey and the distressing news it held.

The dedication of his new chapel was the crown and centerpiece of his expansion project. For the size of the village – a collection of about a dozen buildings – it stood out like a cathedral. In February, Father Flanagan was in Los Angeles to discuss with MGM the second movie about Boys Town. But he had heard no final word from Governor Olson about the Whittier School.

Progress was slow as officials in charge of the Whittier School delayed action, even though some of those who were directly responsible for the school were fired. From January to March, the governor took no action to carry out the recommendations of the Lindsey Committee. Several of the boys at the school tried to speak out, and one of them was beaten for testifying against the guards at a court hearing on the case. And boys were still trying to escape the school.[995]

It was clear that those in charge of the boys at the school would do everything possible to delay action. But the public was getting impatient. Headlines were screaming for something to be done.

Girding for Battle

In early March, an article appeared in the pages of the *Los Angeles Examiner*, with the headline, "Why the Delay?" [996] and this added comment: "Whittier is still under the management of a discredited but unchastened administration. The *Examiner's* exposures and the unanimous public indignation can only reveal the conditions at Whittier, condemn and deplore them, and insist on drastic reforms. All that is needed is the go-ahead signal from the Governor. When will you give it, Mr. Olson?"

On March 25, Judge Lindsey, impatient with the delay, wrote a letter to the governor demanding immediate action. Father Flanagan was again planning to be in Hollywood for conversations with MGM about the second Boys Town movie, and was invited by Judge Lindsey to meet with the governor about the Whittier School and carrying out the recommendations of the committee.

Apparently, the governor was being pressured to ignore the Lindsey report, or to simply delay taking action. Lindsey, wanting the governor to act at once, wrote:

"I wish you could confirm these appointments as soon as possible. I have a letter from Father Flanagan today saying that he will be here at the Beverly Hills next week, April 1st and 2nd. I wish you would address a letter at once to him at the Beverly Hills Hotel informing him of his appointment on the Committee and your intention to go ahead with it. He has been very kind in helping us and in expressing his willingness to serve, but in the letter I received today he seemed a bit discouraged and wondered if anything further is to be done. So, please, in any event, get in touch with him so that he will have your letter by April 1st."

It was evident that two forces were at work: those who demanded change, and the legal and corporate structure of the state that was determined that no change would take place in the policies of its reform schools.

But since there also was national pressure for change, the governor reluctantly sent a telegram to Father Flanagan at Boys Town:

"Informed that you will be in California. If possible would like to meet with you and Judge Lindsey in Sacramento. Will you please advise me if this would conveniently fit in with plan for your trip here?"

Father Flanagan gave an immediate reply:

"Your wire reached me last night on my return from Chicago, and I thank you for your invitation… I expect to be at the Beverly Hills Hotel from April 1st to 3rd… Thanking you, dear Governor, for your fine good will and hoping that the splendid committee you have seen fit to choose will accomplish much good in the management of those unfortunate children."

The newspapers, especially the *Los Angeles Examiner*, which broke the story, continued to demand action by the governor.[997] Judge Ben Lindsey and his colleagues were impatient with the delay, and the Lindsey committee's plan for the renewal of the Whittier School was in the headlines. It was clear that the governor was reluctant to act, since action involved important members of his administration, in particular Dr. Aaron Rosanoff, Director of the State Institutions and a key player in the administration of the Whittier School. Dr. Rosanoff was responsible for appointing the director of the Whittier School and he and his associates were quick to defend the school, its employees, and its policies.

When Father Flanagan arrived in Los Angeles, the governor sent him a telegram at the Beverly Hills Hotel:

"I am appointing you, Mr. William Cox of the Osborne Association,[998] and Mrs. Helen Mellinkoff as a Committee of three to examine into and formulate a working program for the school… Please acknowledge this appointment and when you will be able to go ahead with this work."[999]

The choice of William Cox was no surprise. The Osborne Association was a pioneer in prison reform and was nationally known for its innovative efforts on behalf of those in prison and their families. The governor's move to invite two nationally known authorities on prison reform gave the impression that he was taking the issue out of politics and putting it in the hands of professionals who were known nationally for their work in this area. By doing so, the governor hoped to silence his critics.

This is what everyone had been waiting for and again the headlines reflected that. Father Flanagan found himself torn between the work to be done at Boys Town and the fate of the imprisoned boys of the Whittier School. But now the priest's answer was clear.

"I accepted," he said later, "as soon as the Governor indicated I could be of help and I had read the Lindsey Report. The Lindsey Report, which Governor Olson gave me in Omaha, urged certain radical changes in the school. Certainly no time should be lost in making such changes."

Father Flanagan was now busy on three levels. The expansion of Boys Town required his immediate attention as new buildings were being finished and boys arrived to fill them. There was also the work of implementing a new educational system, which demanded new classrooms for a new generation of boys, and assigning the new and larger duties of the mayor and the commissioners.

At the Whittier School, his plan was to make immediate changes to create, if not a new Boys Town, at least an approximation of the Boys Town system. Then he would leave Pat Norton to work out the details in cooperation with the state officials in charge of California's juvenile justice system.

But it seemed to be a losing battle from the start.

First, most of the men (over a hundred of them) who were responsible for the brutal system of control over the school were still in charge, and their control over the boys was absolute. And their huge salaries were also at risk. In the middle of this controversy, Dr. Rosnaoff, the man in charge of Whittier and its policies, demanded a huge increase in his salary, almost daring someone to challenge him. In fact, Dr. Rosanoff seemed to be the chief obstacle to any change in the Whittier School administration.

Father Flanagan had met briefly with his fellow committee member, Helen Mellinkoff, and with Judge Lindsey to outline his plans. On his arrival at Whittier School with Pat Norton, Father Flanagan's action was swift. He fired the superintendent of the school, E.J. Milne, appointed Norton in his place,[1000] and announced: "No physical punishment, no cells, no Lost Privileges Cottage."[1001]

Newspaper headlines announced the changes.

The biggest shock in the story was the number of employees at Whittier: one hundred five staff members to care for two hundred thirty-two boys. It seemed that the Whittier School existed not for the care of boys in trouble, but for the employment benefits of friends of Dr. Romanoff.

Father Flanagan was very frank in his statements on this abuse of privileges: "The crux of the situation," he wrote, "is that 232 boys are kept there to provide livelihood and position for 105 persons on the payroll." It seemed that in every direction the investigating committee turned, it encountered opposition and blocking tactics from the persons who felt their jobs were endangered. The priest had stumbled upon the one reason why his efforts and those of his committee would fail.[1002]

Soon, the third member of the governor's committee arrived to join Father Flanagan and Mrs. Mellinkoff in their investigation of the Whittier School. William B. Cox, director of the Osborne Association in New York, was an authority on prisons and youth problems. After an intense investigation of the school, the three would make a detailed report to Governor Olson.

Their report was not long in coming and was direct:

"In compliance with your instructions to Rt. Rev. Monsignor E.J. Flanagan, Mr. William B. Cox, and Mrs. Helen Mellinkoff to formulate a program for the Whittier State school, the committee devoted considerable time and study to the problems and existing conditions at Whittier. After due deliberation, the committee recommends complete reorganization of all departments at Whittier School. Towards that objective the following specific recommendations are made at this time so that immediate action may be taken and a new program started."

The changes included:

1. Changing the name of Whittier.
2. Requiring a psychological and psychiatric examination for all members of the staff to determine their fitness for specific assignments with children.
3. Setting qualifications for candidates.
4. Reorganizing the school to serve the needs of the boys and not the personal advantages of the staff.
5. Setting up vocational and educational programs for the benefit of the boys.
6. Providing a full-time physician to the school.
7. Making religious and moral training available to the boys.
8. Providing a playground and recreational facilities.
9. Developing a merit system to recognize good behavior.
10. Establishing a student government.

Their final recommendation was almost a cry of despair in light of the conditions they found at Whittier:

"Your committee thoroughly believes that unless a new virile rehabilitative program is developed at Whittier, then it would be far better to enlarge and strengthen the Parole Department, release all the children, discharge the entire official personnel, close the institution, and sell the property."

There it was in plain English, a full report on the disastrous state of the Whittier School and the means to correct it.

With his task done, Father Flanagan left for Boys Town, leaving Pat Norton, Mrs. Mellinkoff, and Cox[1003] to carry out the changes the governor had requested. Cox was ready to replace Norton as superintendent of the Whittier School,[1004] when needed, so that Norton could return to Boys Town, where he was critically needed as the Home entered a new era.

Cox's name was already in the headlines as "the new head of Whittier school."[1005] It was the governor himself who had urged Cox to help re-organize Whittier, and Cox had agreed even though he was critically needed at Osborne Association, whose work for youth was nationally known.

Planting the Seed

What the committee did not know was that Dr. Rosanoff, in his capacity as head of the State Departments of Institutions, had already tied the hands of the governor's committee from taking any action or making any changes in the administration of the Whittier School.[1006]

Four days before the committee's report to the governor, on April 18, 1941, Dr. Rosanoff had written a three-page letter to Patrick Norton, Whittier's acting superintendent.

Detailing the legalities of California law, he said that any changes the committee made in the policies of the Whittier School would be "disapproved and revoked" by his office, and that any changes they recommended to Governor Olson could be declared unconstitutional.[1007]

With this blow to the committee members' ability to make necessary changes at the school, Norton, Mrs. Mellinkoff, and eventually, William Cox,[1008] left the Whittier School, keenly shocked and disappointed at the governor's inaction.[1009] They felt betrayed by the State of California and its unwillingness to make changes in its reform school system.

The rejection by the state of California, through its ignorance, intrigue, and invincible ill will, of the Osborne Association and Father Flanagan, with his wealth of experience in the care and treatment of troubled youth, was a shock and an embarrassment.

Father Flanagan never fully recovered from his failure to help the battered and beaten boys of Whittier School. He felt betrayed by the governor and was shocked at the brutal and unfeeling tactics of state officials in their treatment of the troubled youth. But he expressed one small hope that California itself would turn on its state officials and create new laws to protect the young.

"I accepted the Governor's invitation in good faith, feeling that it was a challenge… to make it possible for those unfortunate, unloved, and unwanted children… to be given a program that would enable them to go back to a normal society better men for their enforced stay at Whittier…," he would say. "I have not lost faith in the people of California to rally to this crying need for a new deal at Whittier."

That faith was not misplaced. No sooner were the locks returned to Whittier School and the fate of young Californians in trouble sealed by the application of outdated laws than other voices began to be heard. A small army of educators and legislators decided to do something about the Whittier School and the troubled youth of the state. Their action began to create new laws to protect the young of California and new institutions to enforce them.[1010]

Within weeks of Father Flanagan's departure, California introduced the Youth Corrections Authority Act,[1011] a first step in gaining control over the reform schools of the state.[1012] In 1942, in a direct response to Dr. Rosanoff's control over Whittier, Whittier School was removed from his jurisdiction, with this statement of purpose:

"A committee of concerned legislators, judges, lawyers, social workers, psychiatrists, and others across the state, came together to propose legislation aimed at overhauling Whittier School.… Rather than building the institutions on the principles of punishment and retribution, the new plan focused on rehabilitation and reform."

When completed, the Youth Corrections Authority Act[1013] went before the California legislature, where it was passed unanimously. It then went to Governor Olson, who promptly signed it, less than three years after the deaths of Edward Leiva and Benny Moreno.[1014]

An assessment of the Act's impact almost echoed Father Flanagan's efforts and convictions:

"For the first time we have an agency which can give an overall picture of youth crime and youth delinquency; for the first time we have an agency which can make every facility, both public and private, which exists within the state, available in every country, to every court, and to every man and woman; for the first time we have an agency which can consistently promote standards of casework and of personnel and of institutional and agency programs; for the first time we have an agency which, with a minimum of red tape, can treat offenders as individuals; for the first time we have an agency which can promote a worthwhile delinquency and crime prevention program on a statewide basis."[1015]

Whether Father Flanagan knew it or not, the seed had been planted, the seed of compassion and concern for youth in trouble, dramatized on screens all over the world by the movie *Boys Town*. The second film, in progress, would include scenes in a reformatory that was similar to Whittier. And Whittier was certainly on his mind when he heard about "Industrial Schools" in his native Ireland and soon found himself fighting a similar battle with Irish authorities.

Father Flanagan was back at Boys Town in time for the graduation of 1942, sending another senior class into the world. And in June of that year, he found himself with a new assistant priest, Father Francis Schmitt, who would leave his own mark on Boys Town as director of the Boys Town Choir.[1016]

THE NEWS, LOS ANGELES, CALIF.
July 31, 1940

Whittier boys trained for independent living

(This is the second of two articles on what goes on at Whittier State School for Boys, and why.—Ed.)

By W. W. FERGUSON

Life at Whittier State School for Boys begins shortly after sunup in the summer, before sunup in the winter.

That median point in time is 6 a. m.

The older boys get their breakfast at 6:45 a. m.

They are served cafeteria style and seldom take more than 15 minutes to eat. They can take all they want, but there are no second helpings. The catch is, a boy is supposed to eat all he takes. There is no penalty for breaking this rule, but the boys themselves enforce it pretty well.

By 8 o'clock the 525 inmates of the school are either in shops, classrooms or at work on the 40 acre farm. The 109 instructors and assistant superintendents are about their instructing and superintending.

At noon the younger boys are fed first and at intervals of seven minutes, the whole student body. Seven teachers—four high school and three of primary grades—supervise the school work. Courses are adjusted to the occupational status of the student.

When a student enters he is first quarantined in the hospital ward. When he is certified in perfect health he is given a choice of training in 20 occupations. They are:

Farm work, printing, laundry work, shoemaking, tailoring, garage work, care of power machinery, painting, woodworking, storekeeping, barbering, flower and vegetable gardening, instrumental music, cooking, baking, auto shop work, plumbing, bookkeeping, dental assistant and hospital orderly.

George Bessler has taught baking at Whittier State for 33 years. Many of his former pupils hold high jobs in the baking industry. His star pupil, after finishing a postgraduate course in the chemistry of foodstuffs, has just been made superintendent of a big flour mill in Milwaukee.

Practically any student Bessler recommends can get a good job in a bakery.

Ted Raile, athletic supervisor, was once an instructor in swimming at the University of Southern California. He was a letterman on the football team at Brigham Young university. No student can graduate from the Whittier school without becoming a pretty good swimmer, eligible as a nautical lifesaver.

Robert van Vorst is the psychologist on duty at the school. It is his job to grade the mental efficiency of its inmates.

"Three or four," he said, "are of an intelligence quotient equal almost to genius. Ten or 12 are of the order of 125, which should enable them to finish college without much effort. The average intelligence of the boys at the school, however, is about 90. Normal is 100, of course."

It is in this aberration from normal that the problems of his school lie, Superintendent Milne believes.

"No normal boy would want to run away from this school," Milne said. "If all of the children we get were normal we would have no trouble with them at all.

"From our probation reports we know that most of the boys come from subnormal homes. Few of them have any natural incentive for finishing school and regular jobs are hard for boys under 18 to get in California because of employment and insurance laws.

"These boys we are trying to fit for independent living when they are dismissed from school. That they have succeeded in so many instances is an indication of our success."

Such a successful student is Mark Tapscott, 17, currently the president of Paramount Honor club, highest group in the self governing structure of the school.

Mark is a trumpeter in the band and has a job awaiting him when he graduates. He is a brilliant student and popular with schoolmates and faculty alike.

The impression a casual visitor to the school gets is that the inmates are well fed, well cared for and intelligently instructed.

One can't get away from the fact that there is no fence around the school grounds.

LOS ANGELES EXAMINER — August 1, 1940

School Brutality Told by Witness

For five minutes a 12-year-old inmate of Whittier State School for Boys was forced to grovel on the ground and bury his face in dirt as "punishment" for doing what he had been told to do!

One of the most outrageous incidents of cruelty yet to come to light as a result of public demands for a far-flung inquiry into conditions as the Whittier institute, this was revealed here yesterday by a witness to the barbarous act.

He is Frank L. Sage, 38-year-old flying instructor, who long has carried in his mind the inhuman treatment of the youngster and now "wants to relate it in detail when an expose probably would do the most good."

Formerly a newspaper circulation manager in the Whittier district, Sage had occasion to visit the Whittier State School several times a month.

TELLS OF INCIDENT

"On this occasion," the flying instructor related, "I was standing on the grounds, watching the 'Lost Privilege' squad getting their exercise under direction of this guard, whose name I now have forgotten.

"A little Mexican boy, about 12, walked up to us and told the guard that one of the supervisors had ordered him to report to the squad."

With that, he continued, the guard turned to the lad with a snarl on his lips and commanded:

"'What the b—— have you been up to now?'

"Without waiting for an answer, the guard, Sage said, grabbed the boy by the hair and delivered an unmerciful "rabbit punch" to the back of his neck, directing a stream of profanity at the youthful offender.

BURIED IN DIRT

"'Now, you little ——,' Sage quoted him as saying, 'get over there by that tree (pointing) and rub your dirty face into the ground until I tell you to stop!'

"'That's the only way to handle 'em here,' he said, turning to Sage.

Although sickened at the guard's brutal act, Sage said he managed to control himself from "punching the face off that big guard." The only thing that restrained him, he said, was that he was on state property and feared he might be charged in some way with interfering with the duties of an institution guard.

"For about 5 minutes," he continued, "I saw that little boy with his face down in the dirt. I got out of there before I lost all control of my temper."

A few days later, he said, pointing out that the incident referred to occurred about four years ago, he was on the grounds when he again accosted the same guard.

In "show-off" manner, the guard for no apparent reason singled a boy out of a group on the playing ground and "gave him the worst cussing out I have ever heard," Sage said.

"I've heard this guard use language so profane that it wouldn't be tolerated in the lowest water front dive," Sage declared.

He said that a little later he brought the subject up when talking to one of the women employed at the institute, and was told that "you are an outsider and have no idea of the difficulties we're up against here in handling so many boys like this."

LOS ANGELES EXAMINER — July 30, 1940

Solitary for Boy Flayed by Judge

Solitary confinement cells at Whittier State School, in which two boys have committed suicide, are fit only for hardened criminals.

This denunciation of the methods of punishment at the school, now under fire, was voiced yesterday before the luncheon meeting of the Federation of State Societies by Judge M. Hartmann, for 18 years on the Circuit Court bench in St. Louis, Mo. and for three years a juvenile judge.

"The doors leading to the solitary confinement cells should be battered down," he declared.

"The purpose of juvenile institutions is for correction, not punishment. The cells are the grossest kind of punishment.

"Those are intended for hardened criminals. Putting a child in solitary makes him vicious —and a subject for San Quentin."

California's Whittier State School for Boys was a reform school where brutal conditions led two boys to commit suicide in 1939 and 1940. Father Flanagan and others intervened, eventually leading the governor to appoint a committee to run the school.

Father Flanagan Responsible For Many Changes For Better In Reform Schools Of Nation

True Voice 1948

Father Flanagan believed a boy who had made a mistake needed to be understood and helped rather than punished. Uncompromising in his criticism of the reform school, he was largely responsible for many changes to be found in the modern industrial training school.

In 1941, when the bodies of Benny Moreno, 13, and Edward Leiva, 16, were found hanging in the "Lost Privilege Cottage" at Whittier, California's governor asked Father Flanagan to come to Whittier to investigate and make recommendations.

A committee headed by Father Flanagan asked that the name of the school be changed to California School for Boys. It also was recommended that staff members be scientifically tested to see if they were competent to deal with children, that religious training be instituted, that a democratic system of administration similar to that at Boys Town be set up, and that vocational training be started and playground facilities be increased.

Father Flanagan himself turned the key in the lock of the "Lost Privilege Cottage." Boys no longer were marched in lock step from place to place under armed guards. All boys were put on their honor and given freedom of the grounds.

This change had hardly been made when some fifty boys ran away, but more than half of them returned voluntarily, despite the fact that this new freedom was yet an innovation to them.

It is needless to say that Father Flanagan, who never believed that a stronger padlock makes a better boy, soon won the respect of the boys at Whittier. Through his efforts a new program was adopted. Instead of punishing the boy inmates, by forcing them to eat from a bowl on the floor with their hands tied behind them while doing the "snake crawl," as had been the practice, love and understanding were used to win their confidence and co-operation.

Today this California institution is one of the best of its kind in the nation. It has a constructive program of character training based on humanitarian principles and is administered by qualified personnel. Similar changes have been made in other state institutions through the influence and initiative of the Boys Town founder.

By 1948, the press was covering the positive results of Father Flanagan's efforts to change or close America's reform schools.

19

THE WAR YEARS

The Japanese attack on Hawaii's Pearl Harbor on December 7, 1941, sent a shock wave through every community in America, including Boys Town. In fact, Father Flanagan found himself with a rebellion on his hands as the whole senior class crowded into his office, demanding to join the Army and get into the war. They were led by Mayor Jimmy Ross,[1017] a native of Honolulu, who had inspired the others to join him. "I'm from Honolulu," he told them. "That's my hometown and I want to defend it."

"So do we," the others exclaimed. "We want to join Jimmy Ross!"

It took some time for Father Flanagan to talk them out of it.

"Get your diplomas," he told them. "You won't get very far in the Army without a high school diploma."

The war fever was on. Faced with this eagerness to get into the war, the Christian Brothers[1018] set up special summer programs for boys who wanted to graduate early so they could enlist. In the coming months, former boys would be seen walking across the Boys Town campus in Army, Navy, and Coast Guard uniforms and the *Boys Town Times* was filled with photos of these visitors greeting Father Flanagan.

Boys Town also felt the absence of Pat Norton, the priest's nephew and closest associate, who joined the Army. Norton had been at Father Flanagan's side since the Home's earliest days and had shared experiences in its development that no one else had. In many ways, he could almost be called the co-founder of Boys Town.

Meanwhile, the village's new buildings were filling up with new boys, and the new Dowd Chapel stood out like a crown of the new expansion. The community also had become a tourist attraction, with large groups of visitors seeking tours, especially on weekends and holidays, and boy guides organized to welcome them.

While the war, and eventually news of the boys who were serving in the armed forces, dominated his thoughts, Father Flanagan still was steadfast in his responsibilities of running Boys Town and caring for its young citizens. Planning for future events was underway and major developments were unfolding at Boys Town.

A huge celebration was being planned for December 12, 1942, to mark the 25th anniversary of the Home's founding. With the expanded school program, the high school's course offerings were better preparing students to continue their education at a college or university. Father Flanagan's concern for every boy's future was real and personal, and he had scholarships on hand, not only for state and local universities but also for a host of other schools across the country.[1019]

For those boys who were not academically minded, there was the Trade School, where they could learn a variety of marketable job skills, from barbering and auto mechanics to ceramics and radio repair.

Father Flanagan's interest in music and sports as ways to personally enrich the lives of his boys and help them build character moved him to make two major decisions. First, he directed his new assistant priest, Father Francis Schmitt, to create a Boys Town Choir.[1020] And in 1943, the Home hired Maurice "Skip" Palrang as its sports director and coach.[1021]

Palrang became available because he was retiring as head football coach at Creighton University, which had terminated its football program. In the years to come, with Boys Town tripling its population, Palrang would coach Boys Town teams to a string of victories that would make the Home famous as the Notre Dame of high school football, producing Hall of Fame of athletes who would be talked about for decades at alumni gatherings.[1022] Football wasn't the only sport where Palrang-coached athletes shined, as he also developed star athletes in track, basketball, boxing, and tennis. Some would go on to make names for themselves in the Olympics and at universities around the country.

Father Schmitt, meanwhile, was making musical geniuses of his choir boys and their voices,[1023] and the Boys Town Choir would soon be performing throughout the country, rivaling the fame of the Vienna Boys Choir, with whom they were sometimes compared. Their singing also highlighted the Sunday and feast day Masses at Boys Town, and Father Schmitt used their vocal talents to draw to Boys Town nationally and internationally famous names in the world of music, like Flor Peters, Roger Wagner, and Jean Langlais.

A Personal Loss

The morning of December 7, 1941, was one Father Flanagan would never forget. When the Japanese attack on Pearl Harbor began, four of his boys were stationed there: William Debbs and George Thompson were aboard the *USS Oklahoma*, Donald Monroe was on the *USS Arizona*, and Walter Clark was aboard the *USS West Virginia*.

In the attack, the *Oklahoma* and the *Arizona* were sunk by bombs and torpedoes, and Debbs, Thompson, and Monroe were killed. Clark survived, but his ship was badly damaged.

In a letter to Father Flanagan, Clark described the Japanese attack:

"At 7:50 a.m. death and destruction came out of the sky... the ship caught fire and was blowing up. Other ships in the harbor were also hit by this time. The gun I was on didn't get many rounds out. But instead I helped fight fires and care for the wounded. I had several friends killed and I sure hated that. But most everybody lost friends here."

The attack brought the United States into World War II, and as more of Father Flanagan's boys entered the service as the war escalated, the telegrams bearing terrible news arrived more frequently at Boys Town. The priest had boys fighting in the Pacific and in Europe, and many, scarcely out of their teens, were dying in battle.[1024] With the help of his secretary, Catherine Dannehy, he began a huge letter-writing campaign,[1025] reaching out to boys like Billy Capps and Bob Paradise in the Philippines; to Porky Burns in Sicily, who was on his way to Italy; to Bob Wiskochil on Wake Island; and to dozens of others as he received word of their whereabouts. Sadly, some were killed before his letters reached them – Burns in Italy, Capps on Bataan, and Wiskochil in a Japanese prison camp.

When he got news of Burns' death, Father Flanagan asked Byron Reed, his business manager, for the grim total so far.

"Fifteen," Reed answered.

Each time the news of another boy lost came to him, the priest would sit quietly at his desk. Mrs. Dannehy and anyone else in the room would quietly leave, closing the door gently behind them.[1026]

Soon the number had reached nineteen, and Father Flanagan often was seen in his new chapel at four or five in the morning, kneeling, deep in prayer, as the burden of the losses weighed heavy upon him.

That burden was so heavy because these boys knew him as the only father they'd ever had. They were as much a part of him as he was of them. He had known some of them since they were nine or ten, and had watched them grow, graduate, and leave. And now some of them were gone.

Father Flanagan's pain was evident in a letter he wrote to the mother of one of his boys who was killed in combat: "I know something about loss. Boys Town has lost 19 wonderful boys and perhaps you may think these boys are not as close to me as they would be to a natural father. They are very close and I feel the loss of each and every one deeply."

The hurt also was in the treasured memories of his boys, enduring the hard times, building Boys Town, planting crops and milking cows, boys realizing their talents and skills, on the road, selling Boys Town to the world. Boys governing their unique city, competing on the football field, sometimes in tattered uniforms, trouncing teams from larger and better equipped schools. One by one, his Boys Town family was dying, and it was making him an old man before his time.

A Boy Who Survived

Even before the war started, Father Flanagan had kept in touch with many of his boys who were already in the military. Judging from the letters between them, the bonds were close. The boys were deeply grateful for what Boys Town had done for them and they carried a sincere personal affection for Father Flanagan. Some of those boys would later become heroes on the battlefield.

One was Bob Paradise. The heartbreaking drama of Paradise's wartime ordeal would keep the priest on his knees in intense prayer for more than three years, from Paradise's capture by the Japanese on the Bataan peninsula in the Philippines in April 1942, four months after Pearl Harbor, until October 1945, when he arrived at Fort Lewis in Tacoma, Washington, after three years as a prisoner of war.[1027]

Paradise had come to Boys Town in 1932 and had graduated in December 1938. He entered the military soon after graduation and was serving as a surgical technician in the Army Medical Corps in the Philippines when the war broke out. The Japanese attacks on Hawaii, the Philippines, and other American strongholds in the Pacific were part of their master plan to destroy the United States' capability to stop Japan's conquest of the Far East.

By destroying or heavily damaging U.S. forces, the Japanese would be free to invade Australia and gain control of the region, militarily and economically. The Philippines, then a territory of the United States, were a prime target because of America's extensive military presence there, which equaled that of Hawaii.

On December 7, the Japanese attack on Clark Field in the Philippines came several hours after Pearl Harbor was attacked. As in Hawaii, the damage was extensive; 100 American bombers and fighters were destroyed. When the Japanese invaded, the garrison's 75,000 American and Filipino troops, Paradise among them, took to the jungles of Bataan, where they continued their resistance.[1028]

The fighting was fierce and Paradise was kept busy caring for the wounded; many died in makeshift hospitals because medical supplies and food were in short supply.[1029] The daily routine of artillery barrages, bombing from the air, and ground attacks quickly took their toll on the Allied forces.

The makeshift hospitals where Paradise worked were crammed full of injured men, who occupied every square foot of space. Surgical teams competed with each other to see which one could handle the largest number of patients.[1030]

On February 8, 1942, Paradise wrote a small note to Father Flanagan: *"(Somewhere in Bataan). Censorship is strict so I can't write much. Here we are in the middle of a war. And all is o.k. Don't worry."*

But Father Flanagan was worried. The Japanese invasion of Bataan and the neighboring island of Corregidor dominated the headlines, and there was no further word from Paradise. As the enemy closed in, he had taken to the jungles of the Bataan peninsula with thousands of others to carry on a fierce battle with the Japanese forces. Finally, exhausted and demoralized, with soldiers dying of malaria, dysentery, and beriberi, the American commander, General Jonathan Wainwright, surrendered his army to the Japanese on April 9, 1942.

About 75,000 men were listed in the Allied forces on Bataan when the surrender came. They were tired and weak from living for months on a starvation diet. Many were wounded or were suffering from tropical diseases and fevers. They were glassy-eyed scarecrows, struggling just to take the next step.[1031]

Now, their Japanese captors were forcing them to walk the sixty-five miles to a prison camp. It was the start of what would become known as Bataan Death March, a trek during which thousands of men died, some from their wounds and illness and many from being shot or bayoneted by their ruthless Japanese guards.

"I saw at least seven men killed within 500 feet of their destination," Paradise would later write. "The march had taken six days but even when they were in sight of their goal, if they fell, they were dead. The ones I saw die were killed by bayonets and swords. There were 22,000 men who didn't make it."

At one point, Paradise rebelled, attacking a guard while trying to protect a fellow soldier from being beaten. "About six Japanese soldiers grabbed me and beat me unconscious," he would recall. He was left for dead, "but two American doctors dragged me to their tent. I had a skull fracture, a broken arm, a broken shoulder… but I recovered."

In January 1943, Father Flanagan learned that Paradise was alive.[1032] It was by way of a small, fill-in-the blanks postcard sent to Father Flanagan from the Japanese Imperial Army. It read: "I am interned in Taiwan. My health is usual. I am working for exercise. Please see that your health is taken care of. My love to you. Bob Paradise."

But the message was not from Paradise. When the Japanese discovered that Paradise was a Boys Town boy, they began to write letters in his name to Father Flanagan, using the priest's international celebrity to give the world a false impression that American prisoners of war were receiving good treatment.

From 1943 to 1945, Father Flanagan continued to receive these types of glowing letters from Paradise, describing how well his captors were treating him. Father Flanagan would always respond by sending news from Boys Town and a copy of the *Boys Town Times*, with no suspicion that the letters were just a charade. (After his release, Paradise would explain: "Shortly after I came to Camp Karenko, I was visited by several Japanese intelligence officers. They asked me if I was from Boys Town and if Father Flanagan was a famous person in the United States. I answered yes to both questions and that was when they started to write the letters.")

Paradise was moved several times during his three years in captivity, enduring the horror and suffering of men dying all around him, and some-times fighting back at the risk of being killed. Finally, in the fall of 1945, he and the small group of men who were still alive in his camp were freed by American troops.

Paradise's joy at being rescued was somewhat tempered as charges of spying and threats of a court martial were initially directed at him. "It was those propaganda letters," he later explained. "Some people in the army took them seriously. But Father Flanagan convinced them I was not the kind of guy who would write something like that."

On October 19, 1945, Paradise arrived in Seattle and was moved to Fort Lewis to recuperate. From there, he sent a telegram to Father Flanagan, saying he was safe and would be coming to Boys Town for a visit soon.

"Thank God for Bobby," Father Flanagan exclaimed when he received the good news. "Our prayers have been answered."

The city of Omaha and Boys Town gave Paradise a hero's welcome when he finally made that visit. "When I stepped off the train in Omaha, a band started playing, and I rode with Father Flanagan through downtown Omaha," Paradise would recall. "It was amazing."

For Father Flanagan, it was a testament to the sheer heroism of his boys, forty of whom had died in the war, on every major field of battle.

On the Home Front

Despite the hardships the war years brought to Boys Town, there were some high points for Father Flanagan and the boys to celebrate. For the 25th anniversary of Boys Town's founding in December 1942, former citizens from all walks of life – many of them in the military – wrote or visited. There also were complimentary letters from commanders or shipmates who had known a former boy who had been killed on the battlefront. Friends like Henry Monsky who was with Father Flanagan from the Home's earliest days, were there, and President Roosevelt sent a letter that was read at a special anniversary banquet for the boys:

Dear Father Flanagan:

Hearty congratulations on the completion by Boys Town of twenty-five years of constructive service to American citizenship. In innumerable ways the value of your work has been demonstrated during the past twenty-five years, but in no respect more than in the splendid contribution being made by former young citizens of Boys Town now serving valiantly in the country's armed forces. God bless and prosper this noble work.

But while the anniversary celebration pleased him, Father Flanagan's health had become a problem, as it always had prior to critical moments in his life. Soon after, he was in the Mayo Clinic for a sciatic condition, a leftover from his handball days when the game was his only form of recreation. His age was catching up with him, but he refused to slow down.

Whenever he was home, he scheduled weekly Sunday morning conferences with his boys in the main auditorium. Sometimes it was to introduce a visiting former citizen, or to talk about the early days of Boys Town. Other times, it was to congratulate a newly elected mayor and commissioners or to resolve a local issue, like smoking, that had arisen among the boys.

Smoking was a common problem and a major offense, and at one point it had become so prevalent that Father Flanagan, with the help of his mayor and commissioners, simply confiscated all the matches in Boys Town. But much to his surprise (and hidden amusement), one little fellow named Pedro was still smoking. Curious about where he got his matches, the priest secretly followed Pedro one day, and discovered he was lighting his cigarette from the vigil candles in the chapel!

Years later, on his way to Japan to assess the care of war orphans at the request of President Truman, Father Flanagan stopped off in Guam to visit some of his boys stationed with the Army and Navy there. One of the sailors was Pedro.

Greeting him, Father Flanagan said, "Pedro, you are a sight for sore eyes. Have a cigarette on me." Pedro's astonishing reply? "Sorry, Father. I haven't smoked since I left Boys Town."

Then there were the unusual ways Father Flanagan would challenge the boys' other bad habits, like cheating.

In the Home's early days, marbles was one of the boys' favorite games. Every boy played marbles, a pastime with a terminology all its own: Aggies. Keepsies. Knuckle Down. Playing For Keeps. And a dozen more phrases that kept the game alive for years.

There was one little fellow who everyone knew cheated when he played marbles. One day, a concerned Father Flanagan called all the champion marble players into his office.

"Do you have any marbles?" he asked them.

"Sure," they said.

"How many?" the priest asked.

"Millions!" they said.

"Will you give them to me?" he asked.

"Sure, Father," they said, curious about what he would do with them.

Father Flanagan found they were not exaggerating. They brought in marbles in boxes, cartons, bags, crates, even in a barrel, stacking the supply in a corner of his office.

Then the priest called in the boy who was cheating. "These are yours, dear," he told the boy. "You can take them away."

Welcoming Others in Need

Father Flanagan was well-known for his generosity and his habit of helping anyone he saw in need. Any drifter passing by Boys Town knew that if he stopped in, Father Flanagan was good for at least a twenty dollar bill.

So it was not surprising that Father Flanagan went into action when he received a call for help from several Japanese-Americans after President Roosevelt issued Executive Order 9066 on February 9, 1942.[1033]

The order called for the immediate imprisonment of Japanese-American citizens in special internment camps located along the West Coast. From Washington to California, thousands were forced out of their homes with scarcely the clothes on their backs and herded like cattle into the hastily built camps as if they were prisoners of war and enemies of the United States.[1034] [1035] In Los Angeles,

30,000 Japanese-Americans were moved to a holding center at the Santa Anita racetrack in May. These were loyal American citizens, born in the United States, with no ties of loyalty to Japan. Many were professionals, doctors and lawyers, with family and business ties and deep roots in their local communities.

Many of them had children in the Maryknoll Grade School in East Los Angeles, called Little Tokyo because it served chiefly the Japanese and Japanese-American families in the area. Some parents of these students appealed to the Maryknoll Fathers, who ran the school, for help. This was soon after the Whittier School scandal, in which Father Flanagan's advocacy for the school's residents had made headlines in Los Angeles. Father Hugh Lavery,[1036] the head of the Maryknoll Grade School, suggested that the parents contact Father Flanagan, who had contacts in the government and with President Roosevelt himself.

Two Japanese-American women – Lily Okura and Margaret O'Brien Takahashi – wrote to Father Flanagan, expressing their deep desperation for help. Mrs. Okura was the wife of Pat Okura, a UCLA-trained psychologist and a prominent and well-known member of the Los Angeles Civil Service Commission.

Father Flanagan immediately responded, his return letters inviting them to come to Boys Town and offering housing and employment. Their move to Nebraska could occur as soon as their new status was submitted and cleared with the proper authorities.

Marilyn Takahashi, who was six at the time, would later describe her family's response upon receiving Father Flanagan's letter:[1037]

"My father got a truck to load mattresses, bare necessities. He drove 3 days and 3 nights without sleeping, only stopping for fuel. He made this decision because at the first stop he was questioned whether he was Japanese. He could feel this was dangerous so he answered he was Chinese, got back in his truck, and continued driving.

"In the meantime, my mother, younger sister, baby brother, and I boarded a train for Omaha. It took about 2 or 3 days to get there. It was night when Father Flanagan came to the train depot to pick us up. He came with a bag brown paper bag full of candy…. Then he took us to a hotel in Omaha to stay for the night until he could locate us closer to Boys Town. He put us up in an old farmhouse on the edge of Omaha.

"Eventually Father Flanagan brought in more families…. After a year or two, Father Flanagan built a number of brick houses."[1038]

Pat Okura was hired as a resident psychologist at Boys Town, where he and Lily would remain for seventeen years. In his later years, Okura became nationally known for his leadership in civil rights.

Personally, Father Flanagan was shocked at the nation's treatment of the Japanese-Americans. It reminded him of how his countrymen had been treated under British rule in Ireland, and how the Black and Tans – former English soldiers – had been sent in to enforce British rule in 1919, when the Irish were fighting for their political freedom.

By the end of 1943, ten Japanese-American families were working at Boys Town, some as gardeners, some as staff, and some as farm hands. Their children attended school at Boys Town[1039] and graduated with other Boys Town citizens.

During the war years, Boys Town also was a stopping-off place for other Japanese-Americans who were seeking jobs in other parts of the country, courtesy of Father Flanagan's generosity.

A Different Challenge

Father Flanagan was often challenged on his view that there is more good in troubled boys than bad. At times, he had to face difficult questions in the face of obvious criminal behavior. For example, two boys who came to Boys Town had killed their stepfathers; the stepfathers were beating the boys' mothers in a drunken rage. Both youngsters were released to Father Flanagan. One remained at the Home and graduated; the other was placed in his care for one year, then committed a crime and was imprisoned for twenty-five years. The priest fought judges, governors, and other state officials over the fate of such boys, and he made headlines when he brought them to Boys Town.

But one case stood out above the rest because it brought down upon his head the accusation that he encouraged crime, overlooked obvious criminal behavior, was soft on murderous intent, and was insensitive to the victims of such crimes. Oddly, the case that brought him face-to-face with the justice system was not even about young boys, but involved two teenaged sailors from the Naval Air Station in Foley, Alabama.

Their names were Murice Shimnick and Joseph Leemon. Bored by military life, they decided to go AWOL, rob somebody, and have a good time with the money. They started hitch-hiking outside Meridian, Mississippi, and were picked up by Thomas Boykin, a former sheriff, who was on his way home to his wife and children. Shimnick slugged Boykin with a blackjack and the car stopped. The pair drove the car off the road and dragged Boykin into the woods. To stop him from yelling, they cut his throat and took his money. Shimnick later explained the crime: "We stayed in Mobile awhile. Then we came to Meridian where Joe had an aunt. We planned to rob someone and take his car, but we had no intention of killing a man. Boykin just happened to be the one we picked to rob."

The two were eventually apprehended, convicted after a quick trial, and sentenced to death in the electric chair.

When Father Flanagan heard about the case, he took a deep interest in the young men, mainly because of their ages; both were nineteen years old, scarcely out of high school. He also looked into their home life, discovering both were from excellent Christian families. He was keen in recognizing factors that were overlooked by others in youthful criminal behavior. In this case, one of those factors was their military training.

"The training which they received and which was destined to make them strong, iron men – a training to fit them for combat service with a dangerous enemy – this training did something to these boys…," Father Flanagan would later say. "In ninety percent of the cases… the result is as desired, but apparently in a small percent of the cases, it reacts to the detriment of the one receiving the training."

In his words, "the depravity to which they have sunk has undoubtedly been brought on by reason of their youth and environment while engaged in the service of their country."

This was not sheer guesswork. The country was at war and sailors and soldiers were being trained how to defeat the enemy in combat. Father Flanagan was convinced that these two young men were the victims of the military training that had taught them how to kill, but had not provided the moral training that had to go with it.

The priest wrote a letter to the governor of Mississippi,[1040] pleading for the boys' lives.[1041] Receiving no answer, he traveled to Mississippi the day after Christmas in 1944.

The governor invited Father Flanagan to dinner, and afterwards, they spent several hours in conference. After their meeting, Father Flanagan told the press: "I came down here on my own initiative and at my own expense to bespeak a word on behalf of two youths who committed a terrible tragedy that is unexplainable. I realize the responsibility of the governor and the many requests made on him to see that justice is done." The next day, the governor announced that he would not commute the boys' sentences and that their executions would proceed.

Father Flanagan knew his words and efforts to save these two young men would result in wholesale condemnation, public and private, of what he was trying to do. "An eye for an eye and a tooth for a tooth" was still the public response to criminal behavior, especially in a case of murder of an innocent person.

But he saw that in this case, the military training that was designed to prepare Shimnick and Leemon for combat in a war against a ruthless enemy had given these two teenagers a warped view of the world, triggering something inside them and turning them into killers. He knew from personal experience a hundred times over how boys had been twisted out of shape by their environment and he had known young boys who were so warped by their environment that they stole and sometimes killed.

Even in the face of criticism, Father Flanagan's instinct for Christian mercy was overwhelming, as he explained in a letter to a fellow priest:

"I wanted to have a commutation of sentence to imprisonment instead of the electric chair. I lost out on my appeal and I was surprised to know and hear of the uncharitableness of most people down there – both Catholic and non-Catholic – and their desire to have those lives snuffed out immediately – so different from the spirit of Christ."[1042]

When he arrived back at Boys Town, he found a letter waiting for him from Joseph Leemon, who wrote:

"Before you receive this – no doubt but what I'll be executed, but I want to thank you for your efforts towards saving my life. I deeply appreciate what you did. Father Flanagan, I am happy to say I have made peace with my God. I have no fear of death."[1043]

Father Flanagan received letters of criticism from many who told him that the executions were none of his business. He responded by saying, "Christ did not come to earth to punish the wicked. He came to teach. He came to show his love for suffering and sinful humanity. He came to lift up the human race from its lethargy of sin and its suppressed state of slavery under Satan. Who are we that we should cast the first stone against a fallen man or a fallen woman."

Most shocking to the priest was the public's passion for revenge and its failure to understand how these two young men had used the military skills they were taught to kill another human being for their own personal advantage. These young men were simply unplanned victims of a nation at war. In a letter to the parents of Murice Shimnick, Father Flanagan wrote:

"The strange thing I found in my meetings with people down there, and particularly the intelligent people, was that everyone wanted these boys to be electrocuted. I didn't find one, outside of the Catholic priests, who felt that life imprisonment should be given them. I fear for that kind of revenge. It is destructive. It is dangerous. It is the kind of thing that destroys security for the future – for peace. It is the kind of thing that begets a miscarriage of justice, which makes for brutality and bestiality, revenge, punishment. In other words, Christ is not permitted to enter the picture, and these are the people who are constantly talking about religion and Bible study and Bible class and Church. But... there is no religion in their hearts.

"I returned a broken man in spirit because of my failure, but I am happy that I tried. I would do it all over were it necessary."[1044]

For Father Flanagan, who knew the heart of a boy better than anyone else, it was the training of conscience in the adolescent years that made the difference and was the key to a boy's success. It was what turned a teenager around and made him a responsible adult. Somehow this was lacking in Murice Shimnick and Joseph Leemon, and they had been transformed into trained killers through their military training.

Little did the priest realize that he soon would be facing an even greater challenge: his condemnation of a whole nation, his native Ireland, on its treatment of youth and on the responsibility of both Church and State in the care and education of children, especially the lost children in the country's child care institutions. It would be a battle in which he would shake his native Ireland in a voice heard round the world.

Former Boys Town citizens George Thompson (ABOVE LEFT), William Debbs (ABOVE RIGHT), and Donald Monroe (RIGHT) were killed in the Japanese attack on Pearl Harbor on December 7, 1941.

During World War II, alumni servicemen like Bob Henderson would send their pictures to Father Flanagan, who displayed them in his office.

Cecil Stoughton, a former Boys Town resident who served as a military photographer during the war, eventually would become the official White House photographer for President John Kennedy and President Lyndon Johnson.

During a wartime visit to a military base in South Dakota, Father Flanagan met Boys Town alumnus Lee O'Hern, who was driving the jeep.

Francis Fox was just one of hundreds of former Boys Town citizens who served in uniform during World War II, representing all branches of the military.

Sgt. Kenneth Woodside, awarded a Purple Heart after being wounded in the Marshall Islands, returned to Boys Town to visit Father Flanagan.

Navy Seaman William Pettit returned home to Boys Town to say hello to Father Flanagan.

Joe Ortega, one of Father Flanagan's boys, would name his plane the "Spirit of Boys Town" during the Korean War.

20

SUFFER THE LITTLE CHILDREN

A Worldwide Concern

In August of 1944, Father Flanagan wrote a letter to President Roosevelt about the need for international concern for children in Europe and Asia amid the horrors of World War II.[1045] It said, in part:

"When the war has been won on the battlefields of Europe, there will be literally millions of orphaned children left homeless, destitute, and abandoned. There will be many whose fathers have not returned, and whose mothers have been victims of atrocities, or who have perished through various natural or unnatural causes. There are others who will be fatherless, but whose mothers will not be able to properly provide for them.[1046]

"If these children are neglected, they will constitute a very serious problem in the immediate future and in the years to come... It will be a long time before war-torn Europe will be able to properly care for these war orphans."[1047]

It was time, Father Flanagan thought, to share Boys Town with the world, especially a world where so many children were at risk. He saw a need for an international effort. He was aware that other Boys Towns were springing up around the world, and was in touch with authorities in India[1048] and other countries that were considering Boys Town projects. The two movies about Boys Town had gained him an international reputation, and he had entertained visitors at Boys Town from many of the major nations of the world.

Roosevelt wrote back, thanking Father Flanagan for his interest and insight, and also mentioning that the United Nations, a new organization in development, was aware of the problem and had set up its own vehicle to face postwar problems – the United Nations Relief and Rehabilitation Administration. The president promised to send Father Flanagan's letter to those in charge of the program.[1049]

Roosevelt died in April 1945. But when the government turned its concern and attention to the children of war-torn Europe, Roosevelt's successor,

President Harry S. Truman, called upon Father Flanagan to help coordinate those efforts.

Father Flanagan's ongoing concern had always been to help more children, which moved him to continually make plans for a "new," bigger Boys Town. For years he had such a plan on his wall, and curious boys would often ask about it. "That's your new home," he would tell them. That "new home" included a new high school, cottages for 500 high school boys, a new administrative building, a reception center, a dining hall, a trade school, a music hall, and a movie theater.[1050]

The current Boys Town would become home to 500 grade school boys, who would have their own living quarters, dining hall, and school. With these two connected communities, Boys Town would be able to care for a thousand boys.

To many of the boys of that time, it seemed an impossible dream. But in the spring of 1946, ground was broken for the new Boys Town, with eager boys looking at plans for the new buildings and trying to visualize what their new home would look like.

This was the "town" Father Flanagan had envisioned since he and his boys left the German-American Home for Overlook Farm in 1921. Now, the farm's whole square mile of land would be used, turning the small community into a real "town."

Along with the Home's physical growth, Father Flanagan also began to expand his staff. Most notably, he began to bring in other specialists in youth psychology. One was Dr. Franz Plewa from Vienna, an associate of Alfred Adler, the eminent child psychologist. When Hitler invaded Austria, Plewa and his wife[1051] had fled because Mrs. Plewa was Jewish. The couple settled in England, and Plewa wrote to Father Flanagan, who invited them to come to Boys Town.

A Return Home

If the Whittier School incident publicly brought out Father Flanagan's concern for abused children and his willingness to battle for their rights, then his experience with the Industrial Schools of Ireland in the mid-forties brought out his genius for identifying those rights and his determination to make them an essential part of a nation's laws.

Besides looking at the laws of various states in the United States relating to reform schools[1052], he had been taking a good look at the laws that governed youth institutions in his native Ireland.

In the Republic of Ireland, there were more than fifty "Industrial Schools," a comprehensive name for children's institutions that were staffed by members of religious orders, both men and women. Among others, the Irish Christian Brothers, the Presentation Brothers, and the Rosminian Order were in charge of institutions for boys, and the Sisters of Mercy, the Sisters of Charity, and the Oblates of Mary Immaculate were in charge of institutions for girls.[1053]

The juvenile institutions of Ireland, like those of Great Britain and its colonies and former colonies, were based on the Borstal system,[1054] which used punishment, repression, and the suppression of individuality[1055] for the sake of control. Moreover, the Borstal system was the source and financial backbone of the religious orders that ran the institutions, and challenging the system would have repercussions, not only in Dublin, Belfast, Limerick, and Cork, but also in Rome. It was the Whittier School on a larger scale.

The Industrial Schools system was brutal and physical punishment was common.[1056] Boys and girls were beaten,[1057] deprived of food, and sometimes clothed in rags. They were controlled by fear, and made to feel that they should be grateful to the good clergy members for taking care of them. And it was well-known that only a pittance of what the government paid these religious orders was spent on the children.

This was Father Flanagan's assessment of these "training schools":

"Most of the training schools in Eire are conducted by the Christian Brothers,[1058] and confidentially, they are not doing a very good job. They are supported by the government and they run institutions – and you can capitalize every letter of that word 'institutions.' There is no home life, no individual training... I have visited some of these institutions – one of the largest at Artane, Dublin – and I left sick at heart. I intend to make a more minute study on my visit in June. I hope at that time to have an opportunity of talking with... the Archbishop of Dublin. I want to show him some of the pictures of Boys Town and the basic philosophy on which Boys Town is founded and perhaps we might get an invitation to establish a unit in Eire."[1059]

The problem was with the religious orders themselves; their prosperity depended upon money from the government and they were directly responsible for how the children were treated. In some Industrial Schools, the children were put to work – tending the farm, caring for pigs and cattle, or working in the laundry or kitchen. Child labor was the order of the day.[1060] Moreover, as Father Flanagan found in his visits to Ireland, and in his conversations with bishops and government officials, no one in authority, in both the Church and the State – bishops, religious superiors, and government officials – was disturbed by the treatment of children in their Industrial Schools, which treated all children as miniature criminals. Father Flanagan hoped to bring about change in two ways: first, by giving both the Church and the State a new model of youth care, and second, by replacing the Borstal system in every Industrial School with the Boys Town model.

Wherever he went in Ireland, he found that he was praised and listened to as Father Flanagan of Boys Town, an Irishman who made himself famous throughout the world through his labor for troubled and homeless youth in Omaha, Nebraska. He was almost as famous as a movie star in the minds of the public. But many in the government,[1061] believed he had no right to challenge the system of youth care in Ireland.

(In fact, it would take another fifty years for the case to be taken up by the Irish government, when the Borstal system of child care was revealed in all its horror, cruelty, and inhumanity,[1062] and revealing that only one man – Father Flanagan of Boys Town – had challenged it.[1063] It was clear to Father Flanagan that the original concept of Borstal was to apply the criminal justice system of Great Britain to the care of children. It was this distorted and unlawful application of the word and practice of Borstal that Father Flanagan rejected as part of the child care institutions of Ireland. But he could not convince the government or the bishops that the concept and practice should not apply to children. It took the scandal of inhuman brutality toward children in Ireland, unearthed by the Commission to Inquire into Child Abuse of 1999 and the Ryan Report of 2009, to reveal and legislatively correct the terrifying effects on several generations of children in Irish Industrial Schools.)

Father Flanagan's efforts in Ireland in the 1940s began with an inquiry to a friend, Father Thomas Collins, an Irish priest who was working in Nevada to improve that state's reform school policies. Father Collins had some connection with an important member of the Irish government, the Speaker of Parliament, Frank Fahy,[1064] and Father Flanagan wanted to get in touch with the Welfare Department of Ireland to discuss youth care in Ireland. He also wanted to talk to the Prime Minister of Ireland, Eamon de Valera, and the Archbishop of Dublin, John McQuaid, about starting a Boys Town in Ireland.

In previous visits to Ireland, Father Flanagan had been made aware of the penal nature of Ireland's Industrial Schools, and he had visited two of them – Artane[1065] in Dublin and St. Joseph's in Letterfrack.[1066] He was not impressed with what he saw and condemned the Borstal system outright, in words that left no doubt about his judgment of how Ireland treated its children:[1067] "From what I have seen since coming to your country, your institutions are not all noble, particularly your Borstals, which are a disgrace."[1068]

Since he had received numerous requests to found Boys Towns in India,[1069] Australia, and China,[1070] he decided to do something about Ireland.

"I am wondering if the Dublin authorities might be interested in establishing a Boys Town somewhere in Eire…," he wrote. "I do think we have something that will develop homeless and abandoned children along more constructive lines than what is now being accomplished."[1071]

He also expressed his assessment of the Industrial Schools he had visited: "I understand that the unfortunate boy who finds himself homeless or abandoned… is cared for by commitment to a training school. These training schools are conducted by the Christian Brothers. I visited Artane in Dublin and also the one in Galway and must say I was not well impressed with either place. I am afraid that the curse of institutionalism has fallen on these institutions. The children who go there are taught a certain amount of trade, but their individuality and their spirit are snuffed out."

Father Flanagan decided to make a lecture tour of Ireland to inform the Irish people about Boys Town, about the cruel state of their institutions for children, and about his willingness to found a Boys Town in their country. He hoped the cry for change would be so great that the government itself would make changes in the system and invite him to open a Boys Town. He had met Eamon de Valera, the Irish Prime Minister and almost sole creator of modern Ireland, when De Valera visited Omaha in 1920 (when the priest and his boys were residing at the German-American Home), and he thought he had cemented a friendship.

Because of that, the priest was hopeful: "I am sure Mr. De Valera and Sean O'Kelly, whom I also know, would be interested in at least a conference on the matter," he wrote. "I have very much to do in Ireland along these lines and I hope that I can accomplish what I set out to do."[1072]

Sean O'Kelly was the president of Ireland, the second in command to the Prime Minister, and Father Flanagan hoped to convince the leaders of both the State and the Church to accept the Boys Town model of youth care.

What he was setting out to do was to publicly challenge, with the full force of his international personality, the treatment of children in Ireland's youth institutions. He would do this by taking his case to the Irish people, from Belfast to Dublin, and he would visit the children themselves, from the Milltown Industrial School in Northern Ireland to Artane, Letterfrack, and Carriglea Park in the south. He was prepared to launch a tremendous effort to bring Boys Town to Ireland as his first step in bringing Boys Town to the world.

But he would not go alone. His older brother, Father P.A. Flanagan, pastor of Holy Angels Parish in Omaha, would go with him, and they would first visit their hometown of Ballymoe.

Prior to their departure, Father Flanagan wrote to his nephew, Dr. Edward Staunton, the son of his sister Kate:

"Father P.A. and I expect to leave here right after graduation, which is the second of June, and will leave by plane for New York. We will leave New York on the seventh of June at 4:00 p.m., and will arrive the next morning, Saturday, at the eighth, at 9:15 A.M.…. I would like to have you make arrangements with some taxicab company – I think the Flanagans of Ballymoe have such – so that we will be able to have transportation during the four weeks we will be in Eire (Ireland)." (Father Flanagan had given up driving years earlier because of his age and health, and in Ireland, he would have long distances to cover.)

On June 8, 1946, the brothers arrived in Dublin and were met by Kate, nephews William Staunton and Edward Norton, and a delegation from Edward's old school, Summerhill College in Sligo.

Father Flanagan had four weeks to turn Ireland upside-down.

In his hometown of Ballymoe, he was welcomed like a returning conquering hero.[1073] A procession of cars met him at Fuerty, a few miles outside of town, and escorted him into the village, where a huge crowd had gathered. An army of hundreds of children surrounded his car as bonfires blazed and huge banners proclaimed, "Welcome!"

At Ballymoe and at Roscommon, he was surrounded by friends, relatives, and well-wishers, old classmates from Summerhill College and parish priests from the region. There were invitations for him to speak at everything from local fundraisers to youth clubs. He did accept a few offers to dinner, where he talked about Boys Town and his reasons for coming to Ireland.

Father Flanagan had his share of important and influential friends in Ireland, some in the government and some professional people who knew him well and knew why he had come. He had written to several about his trip and had asked for suggestions about where he might go and whom he might speak to in preparation for face-to-face visits with the heads of government. Many shared his view of Ireland's Industrial Schools and the mistreatment of children by the religious orders that staffed them. James Sheil, of Irish Cinemas Ltd. in Dublin, had arranged lectures for the priest in Dublin, Cork, and Limerick, and meetings with the local bishops. Dublin would be his star appearance, where he would meet with the heads of government as well as with the most important religious figures in all Ireland, the Archbishops of Dublin and Armagh.

His most attractive offer to speak was from Belfast, where the Gaelic Athletic Association was sponsoring a Youth Week that involved hundreds of young people from all over Northern Ireland. Four lectures had been scheduled for him, plus a Youth Parade, press interviews, and a visit to one of North Ireland's Industrial Schools.[1074]

Newspapers, especially the *Irish Independent*, publicized Father Flanagan's visit and kept him on the front pages from the day he arrived. He was a celebrity and he knew it, and he intended to use his celebrity to banish the Borstal system from Ireland and replace it with the Boys Town model.

Everywhere he went, hundreds lined the streets to get a look at him. In several cities, the *Boys Town* movie was shown to mark his arrival. Everywhere he traveled, he was vocal about the fate of children in government schools, which he openly said "were simply prisons for the young and a disgrace to the nation."

Father Flanagan was amazed at the size of the crowds that met him. As he approached Belfast, 50,000 people lined the two-mile route into the city. The local bishop met him, and they rode in an open car surrounded and escorted by 3,000 members of the Catholic Youth Group. Young people were everywhere, hundreds of them, shouting, singing, and welcoming this priest who was the pride of Ireland and the pride of the world.

In Belfast, five days had been set aside for his visit, with youth parades, press interviews, two major talks, and a visit to the Industrial School at Milltown. He would say later that he was sickened by his visit to Milltown, where little boys offered him gold medals to give to his boys at Boys Town, all the while surrounded by the trappings of a strictly run, oppressive reform school. "Reform schools have nothing to offer in the line of reform," he said later. "It is detention and punishment all the time." He added that it seemed to be Charles Dickens' *Oliver Twist* all over again.

Wherever he went, he recounted how Boys Town had started to large crowds who hung on his every word: "With a borrowed $90 and five boys – two from the juvenile court and three homeless – I founded my first home for abandoned, neglected, and homeless boys."

They also listened as he described his boys and the care they received. There was the nine-year-old who wandered into his Workingman's Hotel; the boy had been living in a packing box after his father died and his mother deserted him.

"I gave him a bed for the night and realized, this boy needs a home. That's how it all started," the priest said. He told them about his boys who had died in the war, forty of them, and about one who survived the Bataan Death March and came back to talk about it. He told them about Eddie, the toughest case he ever had, and about his new Boys Town that would house a thousand boys.

He talked about his work and its purpose: "My aim was to take these future citizens before their thinking and habits had become fixed and help them, by proper care and training, to become happy, useful citizens. The success in working with these boys, and the public response in support of my efforts, are proof of the wisdom of this procedure."

Father Flanagan made it clear in all of his talks, public and private, that he wanted to bring Boys Town to Ireland. But not everyone welcomed this mission. He gravely offended the Irish political establishment and his public statements on the country's juvenile penal system, including Industrial Schools, reformatories, and Borstals, caused extreme discomfort to the all-powerful Irish Catholic Church hierarchy that ran these institutions, as well as the State that was not ready to take responsibility for them.

When Father Flanagan spoke out, the Irish government itself opposed him and the silence of the Catholic hierarchy was massive, even though many local bishops attended his lectures. What he hinted at was a cover-up, by the State and the Church, of the true conditions in their children's institutions. He had visited several and had a firsthand knowledge of these abuses.

A Bold Challenge

After his well-publicized visit to Belfast, Father Flanagan was prepared for either absolute silence or fierce opposition during his visit to Dublin. At first, he was kindly received in Dublin. But that changed very quickly. Bishops, priests, and government officials attended his lectures at the Theatre Royal and Mansion House, and some even chatted with him before his talks. But it was their absolute silence on the issue of how children were treated in the country's youth institutions that angered him and encouraged him to speak more boldly.

In a long and detailed account of the treatment of children in the Industrial Schools, he told them: "A child cannot be reformed by lock and key, and fear will never develop a child's character." He called the Borstal system, which was primarily based on fear of punishment, "a scandal, un-Christlike – and wrong."

This hit the front pages of the *Dublin Evening Herald*, and his lectures became the talk of the city.

After Dublin, his public views on the treatment of children became an embarrassment to both the government and the Church. Father Flanagan talked privately with the bishops of Waterford, Limerick, and Elphin, and also with the Cardinal Archbishops of Dublin and Armargh, who were the chief religious authorities in all Ireland. One word from them and the whole character and behavior of the religious orders in charge of Ireland's Industrial Schools could change. But it was clear to him from their discussions that none of them saw any reason to change.

Father Flanagan also met with both Sean O'Kelly, the president of Ireland, and, as he had hoped, with Prime Minister Eamon de Valera. (No one knows what his conversation with de Valera accomplished and the priest never talked about it. At the time, de Valera was in the midst of negotiations for Ireland's admission to the United Nations, and so any meeting with Father Flanagan would have been cursory at best.)

His final talk, at the Savoy Cinema in Cork, ended with him telling the crowd of his bold efforts to bring Boys Town to Ireland: "From what I have seen coming to this country, your institutions are not all noble, particularly your Borstals, which are a disgrace."

Then he challenged them: "You are the people who permit your children and the children of your communities to go to these institutions of punishment. You can do something about it – first by keeping your children away from these institutions!"

The whole audience rose, shouting, cheering, and applauding him out of the theater.

Father Flanagan had spent less than a month in Ireland. The newspapers had covered his visit, as well as his views on Ireland's Industrial Schools and their penal system.[1075] But despite all his efforts to bring real, lasting change to the country's child care system, he left Ireland deeply disappointed and determined to return.

Not Backing Down

When he arrived back in New York, Father Flanagan was met at LaGuardia Airport by reporters from *The New York Times*. They asked him to explain his remarks about Ireland and its treatment of children. Eager to face the issue head on, he went into great detail on the massive cruelty of the Irish Borstal system, especially in its violence toward children.

"The brief stay did not permit me to visit all of Ireland's penal institutions. I did visit some; in addition to this, I learned of conditions from the lips of others. I was saddened to find that physical punishment is still used as an accepted form of punishment.

"There is the case of a fifteen-year-old lad at Glin who was brutally flogged. He is one of the few who have been able to escape after such beatings so that their mistreatment might be exposed. The signed statement of the doctor who examined the welts on his back states that they were 'such as would be produced by a leather thong.'[1076]

"Punishment administered with the rod, the cat-o-nine-tails,[1077] and the fist, is horrifying to most people. They can see it for what it really is – an expression of revenge carried over from the stages of a primitive society.

"Advocates of physical punishment are usually intolerant of constructive educational methods. Kindness is considered as sentimentalism or mollycoddling. They brag of being of the 'old school,' which uses 'stickology' instead of psychology."

His words were a devastating condemnation of the Irish penal system in all of its forms, but most especially, of the country's children's institutions. These institutions were run by religious orders under the surveillance of the bishops of the country, who seemed ignorant of, or completely insensitive to, the suffering of the children under their care.[1078]

"I also have the statements of two educated men who had knowledge of the Borstal at Cork a few years ago and who assert that the boys there feared a school that was run without imagination and where punishment was severe," Father Flanagan continued. "Flogging and other physical punishments wound the sense of dignity which attaches to the self. The result of such negative treatment is that the boy comes to look upon society as an enemy. His urge is to fight back, not to reform. Brutality breeds brutality.

"Avoiding facts and appealing to clichés and individual prejudices is as futile as trying to settle a dispute by seeing who can shout the loudest. Little is gained unless argument leads to inquiry.

"My prayer[1079] is that the Christian people of Ireland will see the conditions as they are and that they will take such action as they themselves may choose in attacking this problem, which can be solved only through deep religious faith in the fatherhood of God and the brotherhood of man."

Then he spoke boldly to the Irish people themselves.[1080]

"What you need over there is to have someone shake you loose from your smugness and self-satisfaction and set an example by punishing those who are guilty of cruelty, ignorance, and neglect of duty in high places…. I wonder what God's judgment will be with reference to those who hold the deposit of Faith and who fail in their God-given stewardship of little children."

The response from Ireland to Father Flanagan's statements was a bombshell. Ireland's Minister of Justice, Gerald Boland, blasted Father Flanagan for "offensive and intemperate language about conditions of which he has no firsthand knowledge."

The priest's statements were a personal blow to Boland because he, as Minister of Justice, was responsible for the country's reformatories for young men. Father Flanagan's accusations were that the nation's Industrial Schools for children were places of suffering and mistreatment, and Ireland's reformatories for boys were "a disgrace to the nation." This struck hard at the very concept of "justice" for the whole of Ireland. (In his criticism and condemnation of Ireland's Industrial Schools for children, Father Flanagan also condemned reform schools in the United States, like the Whittier School in California, for their neglect and mistreatment of young boys.)

The Irish newspapers covered Boland's response to Father Flanagan this way: "Strong criticism of some of the views expressed by Monsignor Flanagan of Boys Town during his recent visit to Eire was made in the Dail last night by Mr. Boland, Minister of Justice…. His attention had been drawn to criticism of the prison and Borstal systems in this country, reported to have been by Monsignor Flanagan during his recent visit, published in Irish newspapers, and to similar criticism made on his return to the United States, which were published in the New York press."

Boland was asked if he was aware of American press reports that Father Flanagan had stated physical punishment, including the use of the cat-o-nine-tails, the rod, and the fist, was used in reform schools in Ireland and Northern Ireland. Boland answered that he "was not disposed to take any notice of what Monsignor Flanagan said while he was in this country, because his statements were so exaggerated that I did not think that people would attach any importance to them. When, however, on his return to America, he continued to make statements of this kind, I feel it is time for someone to reply."

Father Flanagan's remarks to *The New York Times* also would become a topic of conversation in the Dail Eireann, the Irish Parliament. James Dillon, a member of Parliament, remarked that, "Monsignor Flanagan turned up in this country and went galumphing around to tell us what a wonderful man he was and the marvels he had achieved in the United States. He then went back to America and published a series of falsehoods and slanders."

Father Flanagan "managed to gravely offend the Irish political establishment… his public statements on the country's juvenile penal system, including Industrial Schools and Borstals, caused extreme discomfort to the all-powerful Catholic Church's hierarchy, who were responsible for most of these institutions, as the State was not ready to take responsibility for them," Dillon said.

Once he had returned to Boys Town, Father Flanagan replied to Boland.[1081]

"I can only suggest that the honorable Mr. Boland visit the institutions which I visited to convince himself of the truth of my statements. If trying to help forgotten boys in reform schools and prisons, whether in Ireland or the United States, is intemperate and offensive, I'll have to plead guilty.

"It is not my intention to enter into controversy with the Honorable Jerry Boland, Minister of Justice of Eire, who questioned my statement that the reform schools and prisons of Ireland are 'a disgrace to the nation.'

"The Honorable Mr. Boland questions my right to speak regarding a situation of which he says I have no firsthand knowledge…. While in Ireland, I visited the Borstal in Belfast, and prisons and reform schools in Dublin, which are the chief penal institutions in the two countries. I also talked with people who gave me firsthand information of existing conditions to supplement my own observations.

"During my visit to Ireland, I many times pointed out to the people that prison conditions were a disgrace to the nation. My statements were received with applause by the people who knew that my criticisms were true. Ireland, because of its Christian faith, is a great country, and great work is being done for youth by athletic associations and social clubs. However, the Borstal system, which prevails in both Northern (Ireland) and Eire (Ireland), and which is based on physical punishment for the inmates, is hardly in keeping with the high ideals of a Christian nation.[1082]

"I do not believe that a child can be reformed by lock and key and bars, or that fear can ever develop a child's character. Those who inflict physical punishment on a child are not psychologists, and therefore cannot possibly tell the reactions of a child in the particular case. I have always spoken out in defense of youth, and I have worked towards bringing a more enlightened system of caring for those unfortunate boys who have got into trouble.

"The institutionalization of little children in great factory-like places, where individuality has been and is being snuffed out, with no development of the personality... and where little children become a great army of child slavery, in workshops, making money for the institutions which give them a little food, a little clothing, very little recreation, and a doubtful education.... How in the name of God could a man like Mr. Boland justify his stewardship of these helpless children through the island of Eire, when he is faced with all the information that has come out through the papers since last July – criticisms which I have justly made."

The response to Father Flanagan's reply to Gerald Boland stirred up public interest in Ireland's penal system and the care of children in the Industrial Schools. Ireland's newspapers entered into public dialogue on the subject. Father Flanagan himself continued his attack on the nation's penal system and its Industrial Schools through lengthy articles in Irish newspapers. It was clear that the newspapers and the people backed Father Flanagan, and he was determined to keep on with the battle.

He intended to return to Ireland after he had gathered certain and detailed information about the Irish penal system and the treatment of children in the country's Industrial Schools. He wrote to several people who were willing to gather this precise and exact information for him. In a series of twenty letters, he built up a clear and factual exposition of the abuses of the Irish Borstal system and its effect on the lives of several generations of children, teenage boys, and imprisoned adults.

Over time, Father Flanagan carefully collected letters from people in Ireland who had alerted him to the fate of children in the country's orphanages, and who had invited him to Ireland in the first place. Two of these contacts were James Sheil, the manager of the Theatre Royal in Dublin who had arranged for the priest's Dublin appearances, and Martin McGuire, a counselor from Limerick who had arranged for his lectures in Limerick and Cork. They provided story after story of abuses he had never dreamed of, but which would be described in detail in the Commission to Inquire into Child Abuse of the Irish Government in 1999, and in the Ryan Report which followed in 2009. The Commission's reports on the Christian Brothers' Industrial Schools at Artane and Letterfrack, which Father Flanagan had labeled as major offenders, were shown to be worse and far more destructive to children than the priest had described after his visit to Ireland.

Father Flanagan was determined to return to Ireland and face leaders of both the Church and the government, and with detailed information he gathered from many sources, he wrote to the Irish government asking permission to visit a number of penal institutions in Ireland.[1083]

But before he could carry out his plan to return to his native country, he received an invitation for another mission from another source. General Douglas MacArthur, who had been appointed as Supreme Commander of the Far East after World War II, asked for his help to solve the problem of orphaned and homeless children in post-war Japan and Korea.

At that moment, all of the priest's other plans were set aside.

On his 1946 tour of Ireland, Father Flanagan visited a number of children's homes.

Father Flanagan talked with local children in Ballymoe, near where he grew up.

Father Flanagan met with several local boys in Ennis, Ireland. The *Boys Town* movie had made Father Flanagan a celebrity in his home country, and people flocked to see him.

Father Flanagan (standing, right) and his brother, Father Patrick Flanagan, stopped in to see their sister, Kate Stoughton (standing), and her family in the siblings' hometown of Ballymoe.

Father Flanagan posed in front of St. Croan's Church, his childhood parish in Ballymoe, County Galway, during his visit to Ireland in 1946.

21

The Far East Assignment

A Special Mission

Father Flanagan's Far East assignment began with a letter from Father Michael McKillop, a Maryknoll priest stationed in Japan, on September 3, 1946, just a few weeks after Father Flanagan's return from Ireland.

"I have been asked to inquire of you personally, if you would consider accepting an invitation from the office of the Supreme Commander... to give the Welfare Officials the benefit of your long years of experience in boys work...," Father McKillop wrote. "The aftermath of the war in Japan has left the country faced with major social problems, not the least of which is the problem of young boys uprooted from their homes, wandering around the country, disinterested in aught save the present urgency of food, clothing, and some place to call home."[1084]

The Supreme Commander in postwar Japan, General Douglas MacArthur,[1085] had run into a problem. After the mass destruction of World War II in Asia, thousands of children were left homeless, without parents or a means of survival, wandering the streets day and night without supervision. They were becoming a menace and a danger to themselves as a result of the terrible war that had destroyed family life in Japan. In the face of this crisis, General MacArthur called upon the one man who was world-famous for rescuing lost children from the streets and making first-class citizens out of them.

Prior to the war, there were few homeless and abandoned children in Japan. In the close system that characterized family life in Japan, there was always a relative who would take care of a homeless child. But now, Japanese family life was non-existent.

It was a challenge Father Flanagan could not refuse. However, he was scheduled to appear at nearly thirty lecture engagements over the next six months. In his response to Father McKillop, Father Flanagan said the situation could be remedied for the good of the children in question:

"You can see from this schedule that I am booked up to the middle of February. Notwithstanding this, dear Father, if the Office of the Supreme Commander thinks that I have something to offer the underprivileged youth of Japan, I will immediately cancel all of my engagements…. I would appreciate your advising as soon as possible the decision of the Office of the Supreme Commander, so that I can make the necessary arrangements and leave whenever that Office wishes me to leave – and remain for as long a time as that Office will consider my stay essential."

The possibilities of this invitation astounded him, and gave him much to prepare for and ponder. A whole nation of youth, boys and girls, without homes. Whole families torn apart by a cruel war and the aftermath of two atomic bombs. A whole nation and every family in turmoil, with no central government to address the postwar crisis.

From the Supreme Commander's Office in Japan came a reply that brought Father Flanagan some relief. There was no hurry – an invitation for March or April of 1947, six months away, would be sent to Father Flanagan from the Supreme Commander's Office. It would give the Japanese authorities time to line up some of their proposed projects for dealing with the war orphan situation. There was also a special note of good news from Father McKillop: "I have asked our own men in Kyoto, the Maryknoll Fathers, to look over some property in their prefecture with the view to starting a work similar to your own splendid work at Boys Town… perhaps a Boys Town in Japan?"

A Boys Town in Japan could be the beginning of Father Flanagan's dream of establishing Boys Towns around the world – in China, India, and Australia, and perhaps one day, even in Ireland.

Over the next six months, the priest's busy lecture schedule took him from Washington, D.C., to Boston, to Chicago, and twenty other places around the country. Meanwhile, he made plans for his trip to the Far East. Byron Reed, Boys Town's public relations director and the priest's close friend, would accompany him on the mission.

Father Flanagan wrapped up his lecture series on February 13, 1947, and returned to Boys Town to await his travel orders from General MacArthur. They came on March 25 from the War Department in Washington, D.C.:

"The following named individuals, Experts, are hereby directed to proceed by air on or about 7 April 1947, from Boys Town, Nebraska to Fairfield-Suisun Army Air Base, California, for further movement by air on or about 8 April 1947 to Tokyo, Japan and such other places in Japan as may be necessary for the accomplishment of this mission, for the purpose of giving professional advice to the Japanese government in matters of child welfare programs presently being developed, on temporary duty for approximately eighty-five (85) days…

NAMES
Right Reverend Monsignor Edward J. Flanagan, Expert, $30.00 per day
Mr. Byron Reed, Expert, $15.00 per day"[1086]

What Father Flanagan did not realize was that his time in Japan would be the most intense and satisfactory of his whole life as he tried to put a nation back on its feet, domestically, economically, and spiritually, while rescuing generations of abandoned and homeless children, and restoring the family as the foundation and future of Japanese life. That he did it almost singlehandedly was the greatest feat, to Reed, who accompanied him, and to General MacArthur and the Japanese royal family who watched him do it.

Ironically, he had just come from a nation that did not want him to rescue children who were being abused and mistreated in its youth institutions, and that almost threw him out of the country for trying. The invitation from General MacArthur to help save the children of Japan was a breathtaking opportunity to carry out Father Flanagan's suggestion to President Roosevelt that something be done for the children of war-torn countries after a destructive war.

Father Flanagan also had his own plans for the trip. Boys Town graduates serving in the armed forces were scattered over the whole world, and word went out to bases in places like Hawaii, Guam, Johnston Island, and other Pacific outposts that Father Flanagan was coming to Asia and wanted to meet with "his boys."

A stop in Manila was memorable. After word of his arrival was announced, the whole city showed up to greet him. He was met at the airport by the mayor of Manila and by the military heads of the Army, Navy, and Marines (no doubt on orders of General MacArthur). Father Flanagan had planned to stay in Manila for only two days, but ended up staying for six. It was front-page news for Manila's dozen daily newspapers.

Manila was special to Father Flanagan; two of his boys had perished during the Bataan Death March after the fall of the Philippines, and memories of the war were all around him. One of his boys, Joe Galle, a recent Boys Town graduate and now a Marine, accompanied Father Flanagan on his tour of the city and was at the airport when the priest and Byron Reed left for Tokyo. Father Flanagan left behind the blueprints for a Boys Town in Manila, which became a favorite project of the city's mayor.

Lifting a Broken Nation

"Upon invitation of the Secretary of War, at the request of General MacArthur, I came to Japan and Korea to act as a consultant in child welfare and institutional care and training."[1087]
— Father Flanagan, 1947

As soon as Father Flanagan stepped onto Japanese soil from the C-54 that carried him from Manila to Tokyo, he was accepted by the Japanese people, not merely as an individual, but as Father Flanagan, a Catholic priest who was greatly interested in the welfare of children.

The first order of business was to hold a press conference at Radio Tokyo, thus announcing his arrival and his purpose for coming to Japan. That was followed by a luncheon with General MacArthur and Mrs. MacArthur, and members of the Catholic clergy who were welcoming him to Japan.

Father Flanagan was greatly impressed with General MacArthur. "He is a great Christian gentleman. He is a great statesman, scholar, and soldier – he is one of the great living Americans," the priest said.

The next three days were spent with various U.S. military officials and representatives of the Japanese government, who explained the scope of his mission, the extent of his labors, and the utter destruction he would see in city after city.

Father Flanagan would find his work to help the homeless, abandoned, and neglected children of post-war Japan to be the most intense, heartbreaking, and difficult experience he'd ever known. In every city and village of two highly populated countries, Japan and Korea, his efforts at times seemed hopeless in the face of the millions of children without a home or family.

These are the dire wounds of war he faced:

"Sixty-six major cities, including Hiroshima and Nagasaki, had been heavily bombed, destroying 40 percent of these urban areas overall and rendering 30 percent of their populations homeless. In Tokyo, the largest metropolis, 65 percent of all residences were destroyed. In Osaka and Nagoya, the country's second- and third-largest cities, the figures were 57 and 89 percent.[1088]

"At Hiroshima, on the bright clear morning of August 6, 1945, thousands were killed, more thousands were fatally injured, and the homes of a quarter million people were destroyed, within seconds of the falling of a single bomb."[1089]

In Nagasaki, "a brilliant flash had illuminated the sky, followed by an explosion equal to 21,000 tons of TNT. With searing heat and an annihilating force that defies imagination, the blast tore through the factories, shops, and homes, carrying unprecedented levels of radiation that penetrated the bodies of human beings and animals. An estimated 74,000 people were killed, and another 75,000 were wounded."[1090]

Father Flanagan had never experienced the culture of war. He had left Ireland before the Easter Rising, the coming of the Black and Tans, the British invasion of the country, the imprisonment and slaughter of its young men, and the occupation of his homeland. He was unprepared for the massive destruction of Japanese cities, the annihilation of total populations, the millions of children lost to their families and forced to eke out an existence where starvation was normal and family life non-existent.

The priest's 40-day itinerary included visits to the Japanese cities of Tokyo, Kanagawa, Kyoto, Osaka, Nara, Takatsuki, Kobe, Fukuoka, Nagasaki, Kure, Hiroshima, and Sendai, and the Korean cities of Seoul, Kaesong, and Pusan. He knew his health was not stable, but there was a job to be done for millions of children and an entire nation that might be deprived of family life, perhaps for another generation. Reed, his traveling companion, would take notes for Father Flanagan's final report to General MacArthur and for an article for the *Omaha World-Herald*, after their return to the states.

The physical state of postwar Japan was almost impossible to describe when Father Flanagan arrived there. Hiroshima and Nagasaki had been obliterated by atomic bombs, and the cities hadn't begun to recover from the terrifying effects of such massive destruction. The cities' residents were still in something of a daze, with the horror of defeat and destruction all around them, and they welcomed the priest almost as an angel from heaven on a mission of mercy.

Father Flanagan found himself busy from the first day, meeting with both American and Japanese officials, collaborators, and co-workers at every stop and encountering a mixture of problems that at times seemed insurmountable. The schedule would be described this way in "Father Flanagan's Child Welfare Report" of his trip:

"Orientation conferences were held with local Military Government officials and with those Japanese officials with whom they had made previous arrangements. The procedure followed on these tours entailed visitations and inspections of three to six orphanages, homes, institutions, and schools every day, followed by round table discussions with local welfare workers, governmental officials, educators, women's club leaders, and interested public-minded citizens.[1091]

"In each city he (Father Flanagan) visited, he would first confer with American military government teams, then with Japanese government officials. This would be followed by a tour of child welfare institutions, sometimes five or six a day. He would then confer with American military teams and Japanese government officials.

"In each city (fifteen in all), he would conclude his visit with a public talk to as many as five thousand people, from every branch of Japanese society, including educators, women's clubs, and university students."[1092]

Father Flanagan's talks were always about the children. The fate of these children was in his hands, and he saw them everywhere, as noted in his report:

"The children ran the streets and alleys and railroad stations, begging and stealing. Paralleled with this were numerous children coming from homes which, by reason of economic conditions, could not provide adequately for members of the family. And they encouraged their children to go on the streets and solicit candy and cigarettes from members of the occupation forces; such items procured were used for black marketing to assist the family in bartering for daily necessities."[1093]

This is why he was called here – for the sake of the children, and especially for the boys, many of whom had run away from orphanages and homes where they had been placed. Most of the orphanages had little food to support these boys, and their detention there was very different from their traditional Japanese lives. Father Flanagan also found that child labor was common – in one institution, he found fifty boys working eight-hour days, six days a week, making farm implements. In another, boys ages eight to fourteen were making bicycle lamps.

While he witnessed the horrors of the aftermath of the war wherever he went, Father Flanagan also was enthusiastically greeted by large crowds of children and adults, bringing mounds of freshly cut flowers as a token of their appreciation for his coming to Japan. Most were familiar with the Boys Town from the movie, and were eager to see the real Father Flanagan in person.

In many areas, he found heroism in the midst of tragedy and sacrifice in the face of need. In Osaka, he met a young woman who was caring for twenty children who she found wandering the streets. A woman in Tokyo was caring for sixty children she found at railroad stations. He found other adults who gathered boys off the streets, and there was talk of establishing Boys Towns all over Japan and Korea.[1094]

Toward the end of his visit, Father Flanagan returned to Tokyo for a number of meetings that were recorded in his report:

"After visiting Nagasaki and Hiroshima, where Father Flanagan had the opportunity of seeing firsthand the effect of the atomic bombs, and talking with Jesuit priests in Hiroshima who lived to tell of the bombing, we returned to Tokyo for a week, at which time Father Flanagan addressed a series of National Welfare Conferences. During this week Father Flanagan was invited to the Imperial Household for an audience with Emperor Hirohito and the Empress…. Father Flanagan did most of the talking during his audience with the Emperor and Empress. He explained his purpose of his mission to Japan…. The Emperor leaned forward in his chair, a broad smile on his face."

In a private meeting on July 7, 1947, Father Flanagan presented his report, "Children of Defeat," to President Truman. The priest recommended that a foster home system be created and that American occupation forces help educate the Japanese people about this concept. He also called for tighter regulations of orphanages to make it impossible for racketeering to occur under the guise of aiding helpless, starving little children.

Father Flanagan welcomed any opportunity to talk to children on his travels through Asia.

Father Flanagan spent time with several boys herding goats at a Japanese orphanage. Having grown up in a rural setting, Father Flanagan was always interested in the agriculture of the areas he visited.

On his humanitarian tour of Asia in 1947, Father Flanagan inspected numerous orphanages, where he was greeted by their young residents.

At a Boy Scout rally in Tokyo, Father Flanagan met the future Emperor Akihito of Japan.

Father Flanagan held a press conference to discuss the plight of the homeless and orphaned children in Japan during his 1947 tour.

Father Flanagan entertained some children with stories at a Japanese orphanage.

22

THE MISSION TO EUROPE

Austria and Germany

Still tired and scarcely recovered from his experience with the orphaned children of Japan and Korea, and the shock of seeing the wartime destruction of so many Asian cities, Father Flanagan left New York City on March 5, 1948, aboard the *Queen Mary*, bound for Southhampton, England. Accompanied by his nephew, Pat Norton, it was the beginning of a mission requested by President Truman to assess how children were being cared for in post-war Europe.

A week later, the two men left London on a U.S. Navy plane that took them to Frankfort, Germany. Then it was off to Vienna, Austria, and a foray into the Russian-controlled zone where the Catholic Church was barely tolerated.[1095] They found Vienna in shambles, the city's cathedral destroyed, and the work of the Church hampered by constant Russian interference. Father Flanagan visited with Cardinal Innitzer, then met briefly with military authorities and made plans for a three-week stay in Austria. With his headquarters in the Bristol Hotel,[1096] he met with religious and military authorities, and began visiting schools, hospitals, factories, prisons, and private homes to gather detailed information about the state of the children of postwar Europe.[1097]

There were unforeseen problems. In his meeting with Socialist Youth Leaders, who were heavily indoctrinated in Marxism, Father Flanagan stated his opposition to the Communist government's political education of the young, realizing that much of Austria[1098] was still under heavy Communist influence. To reach a wider audience, he held press conferences and spoke on the radio, as his work became better known. It appeared that a Communist takeover of Europe was inevitable after the war, which soon became evident in Poland, Hungary, East Germany, Bulgaria, and Romania. Father Flanagan's discussions with the Communist youth leaders, Peter Strasser and Paul Blau, on St. Patrick's Day made news and were topics of concern in his discussions with the leaders of the Catholic Youth Movement.[1099]

Because Father Flanagan was touring Europe as the personal representative of the president of the United States, his concern for youth and Communist influences was taken seriously. His press conferences and radio talks were carefully prepared and reached a large audience. Young people, ages fourteen to twenty-one, were being openly recruited by the Socialist Party. The imminent Communist takeover of Europe would mean the loss of over a million Austrian youth to the Communists. The problem, as he saw it, was huge.[1100]

To address these concerns, Father Flanagan called a conference of the leaders of the national and city youth organizations and the lay leaders of the Catholic Youth Movement to discuss the dangers to Catholic youth in Austria. He also discussed the problem with Cardinal Innitzer, since the future of Catholicism in Austria was at stake.

But the greatest problem was the displaced children.[1101] In Austria, after the war, the Soviets had moved quickly to set up a Communist state and to ensure that displaced children were denationalized and educated as citizens of that state. In 1948, the United Nations passed a Convention on the Prevention and Punishment of Genocide and equated the denationalization of children with genocide. Father Flanagan had come to Europe on the heels of that Convention, and part of his problem in Vienna and in Austria was to undo the effects of the Soviet's efforts to denationalize Austrian children. It was his stature as a priest, an educator, and the founder of Boys Town that gave credence and acceptance to his mission. Beginning in Vienna, he made the whole of Austria his domain, knowing the Communist government was aware of his presence and his efforts.

As part of a united effort to counteract the Soviet influence in Austria and Germany,[1102] and to also undo the harm to German youth from Nazism,[1103] he clashed with both Soviet and German officials. The number of children in trouble and extreme danger was overwhelming: nearly 300,000 children in Vienna and more than a million in all of Austria.

The challenges of the mission to Europe seemed insurmountable.

During his 1948 tour of Austria and Germany, Father Flanagan and General James Powell inspected a mobile library as several German children looked on.

Father Flanagan attended a presentation on German youth programs while visiting the U.S. Air Force headquarters for Europe.

Just as he had in Asia, Father Flanagan visited numerous orphanages on his 1948 tour of Austria and Germany.

This is the last photograph ever taken of Father Flanagan. Several hours after this briefing in Berlin on the living conditions of German youth, the beloved priest passed away on May 15, 1948.

EPILOGUE

'THE WORK WILL CONTINUE...'

By Thomas Lynch,
Boys Town Director of Community Programs

As the nations of Europe and Asia began to rebuild following the devastation of World War II, they were faced with the momentous task of caring for large numbers of homeless, orphaned, and neglected children. The American government turned to Father Flanagan, asking him to first tour Asian countries and report on the conditions of the children and how they could be helped.

In 1947, Father Flanagan had traveled throughout Japan, Korea, and the Philippines for two months, meeting with hundreds of government officials, visiting children's homes, and evaluating conditions. Upon his return to the United States, he had presented his report, "Children of Defeat," to President Harry S. Truman at a White House meeting. Soon after, the priest was asked to begin a similar tour of Europe.

Father Flanagan accepted the assignment even though he was still exhausted from his trip to Asia. He commented to a few close companions that he believed if he went on this new mission, he would not live to see his beloved Boys Town again. But he knew the children of Europe's war-torn countries needed help. On March 5, 1948, he sailed from New York aboard the *Queen Mary* to Southampton, England, and then flew to Austria.

In Europe, Father Flanagan spent long days traveling and attending meetings that lasted late into the evening. The strain became evident when Father Flanagan collapsed after saying Easter Mass in Vienna, but he refused to cut back on his schedule.

Before retiring for the night on May 14 in Berlin, Father Flanagan discussed with a colleague the thoughts he planned to share the following morning with General Lucius D. Clay, the U.S. military governor of Germany.

Sometime during the night, Father Flanagan began to complain of chest pains. He was rushed to the 279th Station Military Hospital, where he passed away at 2 a.m., after receiving the Sacrament of Anointing of the Sick.

The news of Father Flanagan's death was flashed around the world. In the Village of Boys Town, his boys heard of their leader's passing from a radio bulletin.

The boys immediately gathered in Dowd Memorial Chapel to pray for Father Flanagan. President Truman sent this message:

"He has left a living monument in the countless boys who are today honest men and upright citizens because of his benign influence in the inherent goodness of human nature."

From all over the world, letters and telegrams of condolence and sympathy flooded the village, many addressed to the boys who had lost their "father." Boys Town alumni from all over America returned "home," joining the long, solemn procession of current residents who filed by Father Flanagan's casket to say their last good-bye to the beloved priest who gave them a second chance when no one else would.

So many mourners converged on Boys Town for his funeral service that two Masses were conducted in Dowd Memorial Chapel, where Father Flanagan's remains were laid to rest in the former baptistery.

Several days after the funeral, President Truman visited Boys Town to pay his respects to the children and to lay a wreath on the tomb of Father Flanagan. Inspired by the vision of Father Flanagan, Boys Towns were eventually established in eighty-nine other locations around the world.

Today, the Home for Boys founded by Father Flanagan more than one hundred years ago is one of the largest child and family care organizations in the country, impacting the lives of over two million people every year. Father Flanagan's ministry and mission to save children and heal families not only has been maintained but has grown, thrived, and changed the way America cares for those in greatest need.

None of this would be surprising to the dedicated champion of children's causes. Not long before he left on his fateful trip to Europe, Father Flanagan was asked if his work would be able to endure in his absence. Prophetically, he replied, "The work will continue, you see, whether I am there or not, because it is God's work, not mine."

Somewhere in a German town the stars rolled back their doors;
And hands that molded seas and suns reached down and folded yours.
Deep in the wings of God you slept, tired and weary so.
You were one of earth's greatest and someday the world will know.

— By Father Clifford J. Stevens

In Berlin, a memorial service was held for Father Flanagan at the Holy Rosary Church. Following the service, his remains were flown back to the United States.

Former Boys Town residents served as pallbearers to remove Father Flanagan's casket from a plane after its arrival at Eppley Airport in Omaha, 1948.

In Japan, children read tributes to Father Flanagan during public memorial services that drew thousands of citizens, June 1948.

At Boys Town, two funeral Masses were held in Dowd Chapel for Father Flanagan. One was for the public and the other for the current and former residents of the Home.

Father Flanagan's body laid in state for several days. Over 25,000 people filed past his casket, including many of his current and former boys.

Father Flanagan was laid to rest in a small vestibule off the main entrance to Dowd Chapel. Thousands of Boys Town youth have visited his tomb over the years, drawing inspiration and strength to change their lives for the better.

ENDNOTES

Chapter 1: Lad of Leabeg

1   This ancient capital of the Kingdom of Connacht was located close to a contemporary site, Rathcroghan, near the Roscommon town of Tulsk.

2   Cf. "The Train," translated by Thomas Kinsella, Oxford University Press.

3   Birth Records, Castleplunket, County Roscommon, entered 6 August, 1886, #177.

4   There is no indication of when John Flanagan became manager of the Leabeg estate, but according to the marriage license of John and Honora Flanagan, he was residing at Leabeg at the time of their marriage on February 8, 1871. Her place of residence is given at Ballygalda.

5   Parish records, St. Croan's Church, Parish of Ballintubber, Ballymoe, Ireland, July 18, 1886.

6   The grandfather was a "herd," something of a veterinarian, who was accustomed to attending the birth of calves and lambs. He had undoubtedly used the same warming technique for the small bodies of lambs whose lives seemed in the balance.

7   Unpublished manuscript of Gilson VanderVeer Willets from interviews with Father Flanagan, 1943.

8   Irish genealogical records: Website: family trees.genopro.com/tonylarkin/family/John Flanagan and Nora Larkin-frm.

9   "The old-fashioned home with its fireside, companionship, its religious devotion and its closely-knit family ties, is my idea of what a home should be." From an article by Father Flanagan in *Perfect Home Magazine*, Stamats Publishing Company, Cedar Rapids, Iowa, November, 1947, pg. 3.

10 Father Flanagan's own words: Letter to Father Michael O'Flanagan, April 26, 1942. Boys Town Archives.

11 A ceili (pronounced kay-li) is a gathering of family, friends, and neighbors for music, song, talk, story-telling, dancing, and just plain fun. Often, an itinerant seanachai was the reason for the gathering and, in the 19th century, serious talk about Irish traditions and freedom. The name has taken on a new meaning in recent times and is often simply the occasion for a concert and dancing with music of a ceili band.

12 Cf. Note 8.

13 Honora Larkin, Edward Flanagan's mother, was descended from the Galway branch of the Connacht Larkins. Her father was James Larkin and her mother was Mary Garvey. Her father was born in 1803 and died on September 11, 1893, in Ballygalda. Her mother was born in 1809 and died on November 12, 1885, most probably at the Flanagan home at Leabeg. Honora Larkin was one of ten children and her brothers Michael, William, and Timothy emigrated to the United States, where they became successful building contractors in New York City. Some members of her mother's family, the Garveys, also emigrated to New York and were visited by young Edward Flanagan when he arrived in the United States in 1904. Honora Larkin's branch of the Larkin family came from Clontusterk in Galway. Her Larkin ancestry links her to the Muintir Lorcan Siol nAnmchadha Ui Maine sept, which was prominent on both sides of the Suck River in Galway, Roscommon, and Offaly. After the Norman invasion of the 13th century, the sept was confined to what is now the Diocese of Clonfert, in east Galway, the ancient territory of the Hy Many. The Larkin clan was early associated with the monastery of Clonmacnoise in Offaly, and were protectors and guardians of the tomb of St. Ciaran, founder of Clonmacnoise. The clan is noted for its many scholars, priests, and religious figures, and this tradition may have had some influence on Edward Flanagan in his choice of the priesthood.

14 *Annals of the Four Masters*, under the year

1231; English translation by Down Connellan, The Irish Genealogical Foundation, Kansas City, Missouri, 2003, pg. 53.

15 "According to the tradition in of the County of Roscommon, the territory in which O'Flanagan was chief extended from Belangare to Elphin, and the O' Flanagan resided at Mointeach." *Annals of the Kingdoms of Ireland*, by the Four Masters, pg. 48, footnote.

16 *O'Hart's Irish Pedigrees*, by John Hart, 5th edition, 1892, Appendix VI, #2: Roscommon. Also, *Fairbairn's Crests*, by James Fairbairn, Thomas C. Jack, Publishers, Edinburgh.

17 *The Life and Writings of St. Patrick*, by Most Rev. Dr. Healy, Archbishop of Tuam, M.H. Gill & Sons, Dublin, 1905, Chapter 10, pgs. 207-208.

18 John Brady, *Ballymoe: Mogha na gCrann*, Ballymoe, Ireland, 2005, pg. 13.

19 John Brady, "A Sense of Ballymoe in 1904"; talk given on May 22, 2001, on the occasion of the visit of a delegation from Boys Town to Ballymoe and Leabeg.

20 Cf. Note y.

21 John J. Brady, op. cit.

22 Finbar McNamara, President of the Ballymoe Boys Town Association; talk given at the homestead of Father Edward Flanagan on November 9, 2007, on the occasion of a visit to Ballymoe by Father Steven Boes, National Executive Director of Boys Town; Dan Daly, Ph.D.; John Mollison; and William and Linda Swindell from Boys Town; and Mickey and Jan Rooney from Hollywood, California, to erect a statue of Father Flanagan in the town.

23 Ibid.

24 *Roscommon Herald*, July 13, 1886, "Evictions in Keshcarrigan."

Also, *The End of Hidden Ireland*, by Robert James Scally, Oxford University Press, 1995. The story of evictions from the townland of Ballykilcline in County Roscommon, from 1836-1847, of people from ancestral homes they had occupied for centuries. The tenants ignored the eviction notices, began a rebellion against the evictions, and sued the British Crown. The rebellion lasted over ten years and the only response of the Crown was to offer to pay the expenses of the tenants to North America. When the famine struck in 1845, the townland was deserted, both from hunger and from sheer exhaustion after their long struggle against the Crown.

25 John Brady, op. cit.

26 Cf. Note 7.

27 "My father would tell me many stories... stories of adventure, of the struggle of the Irish people for independence." Father Flanagan, article in *Perfect Home Magazine*.

28 *Annals of the Four Masters*, under the year 1552; English translation by Owen Connellan, Irish, Genealogical Foundation, Kansas City, Missouri, 2003, pg. 432.

29 *The Fenian Movement*, by T.W. Moody, Editor, 1968.

30 "Boulavogue," a song commemorating the Irish Rebellion of 1798, with its heroism of a small band of Irishmen, but a tragic defeat and loss of life of the Irish fighters.

31 *Father Flanagan of Boys Town*, by Fulton and Will Oursler, Doubleday & Co., 1949, op. cit., pg. 30.

32 "Three times a day I would travel over those immense lands of Leabeg – you have no idea what it was like –with dangerous bogs on the north and south – as I traveled through those vast fields, mostly without shoes, saying my Rosary as I went along, and other times, as I grew older, reading one of Dickens' novels." From a letter of Father Flanagan to Father Michael O'Flanagan, 1942. Boys Town Archives.

33 *Father Flanagan of Boys Town: A Man of Vision*, by Hugh Reilly and Kevin Warneke, Boys Town Press, 2008, pg. 17.

34 Willetts, op. cit., Chapter 2, pg. 31.

35 *Father Flanagan of Boys Town*, by Fulton and Will Oursler, Doubleday & Co., 1949, pgs. 27-28.

36 Ibid.

37 The novels of Charles Dickens opened his mind to a world of poverty, human misery, and neglect that would stay with him to the end of his life. Dickens' novels were written not only as stories to be read, but to bring

about change in the English society of his day. "Almost immediately on his return to London, he began *Nicholas Nickleby*; in one sense a return to the picaresque narrative of *The Pickwick Papers*, with a large cast of itinerant characters, but into it Dickens poured all the harsh comedy of social suffering, which had transradiated the pages of *Oliver Twist*. He knew now what it was to acquire power – power over the reader, certainly, but also power over the world. He had been attacked as a 'radical' in the established newspapers for his fulminations in *Oliver Twist*, but his exposure of the Yorkshire schools in *Nicholas Nickleby* led to the closure of many of them. The 'infant bastilles,' in the words of one contemporary periodical, were quite exploited." From *The Life and Times of Charles Dickens*, by Peter Ackroyd, Hydra Publishing, New York, 2003, pgs. 51-52. Father Flanagan learned many powerful lessons from Charles Dickens, in particular the need to publicly expose social evils and the power of publicity to eradicate these evils. His public exposure of Ireland's "infant bastilles" in 1946 closely resembles Dickens' exposure of the Yorkshore schools in *Nicholas Nickleby*, with the same results – public outcry at the exposure of the evil.

38 Willetts, op. cit., Ch. 2, pg. 19.

39 Oursler, cf. Note 30.

40 Oursler, op. cit., pg. 28.

41 Oursler, working notes for *Father Flanagan of Boys Town*. "There were as many as 150 cattle and perhaps as many sheep."

42 The National School was established as a replacement for the Model School. The Model School was established in 1831 for the public education of Ireland for children of all religions. Catholic children who attended Model Schools did not get instruction in their religion. The outcry from the Catholic Bishops, who wanted complete control of the education of Catholics, was so great that the National School was established as a compromise: It could be used for Protestant and Catholic religious education. When the Model Schools were established, Catholic bishops forbade any Catholic child to attend them and their orders were universally obeyed. The establishment of the National Schools saw the end of the Hedge Schools. Cf. "Parliamentary Papers by Great Britain Parliament, House of Commons, 1870: Royal Commissions of Inquiry, Primary Education in Ireland," pgs. 183-723. Published by Her Majesty's Stationery Office. Also, homepage.eircom.net/-modelschool/page 2-3.

43 The schools were carefully monitored by the Department of Education for the quality of teaching, the performance and qualifications of teachers and monitors, adherence to the established curriculum, the number of children attending, and the results of examinations for teachers and monitors. A report on the number of children attending the Drimatemple School in 1886, the year of Edward Flanagan's birth, listed 169 boys and 176 girls, but this was certainly never the number attending classes. It was simply the names of those children who attended continually, sporadically, or even only one class. Cf. "The Fifty-Ninth Annual Report of Commissioners of National Education in Ireland, Mr. Mielwaine, for Roscommon, March 19, 1887, Dublin, Alex Thom & Co., pgs. 87-95.

44 Ibid.

45 There were seven levels for the Primary School, two years for infants (ages 4, 5, or 6), and six levels for children 7 through 13 or 14. Normally a child was promoted to a higher grade at the beginning of the school year, but attendance was often so irregular that some children were kept in the same level for a second year. When all six levels were completed, the student was given a Leaving Certificate. Those completing Primary School often did not continue on to Secondary School, and left school altogether. For more advanced students, especially those continuing on to Secondary School, there was an advanced year added to the 5th level, with the 6th level devoted to immediate preparation for Secondary School. The subjects of the Primary School included Irish, English, Arithmetic, Music, Physical Training, Drawing, Nature Study, and Geography, and for advanced students, Algebra and Geometry, with religious instruction on every level. Written tests were administered in Irish, English, and Arithmetic at the completion of the Primary Course. Cf. *Irish Education: Its History*

and *Culture*, by John Coolahan, Institute of Public Administration, Dublin, 1981. Chapter One: Primary Education.

46 "Report of the Council of Education as Presented to the Minister of Education: 1) The Function of the Primary School, 2) The Curriculum," Dublin, published by the Stationery Office, PR-2589, 19th century, no date.

47 Reilly & Warneke, op. cit., pg. 15.

48 In the vicinity of Roscommon and Sligo alone, there are these monastic ruins: Inchmore (5th century), Drum Lias (5th century), Athlone Abbey (5th century), Inismore (480), Craobhgrellain (525), Drumcliff (580), Inishmurray (6th century), Roscommon Abbey (6th century), Clontiskirt (6th century), Doshan (6th century), Inch-Mac (6th century), Eadal-ruim (6th century), Cluan Caerpthe, (6th century), Achonry (6th century), Eala Irium Abbey (6th century), Kilmalton (6th century), Caille (590), Emleach fada (575), Drum-otha (7th century), Kil-Garbon (7th century), Killukin (637), Easdara (635), Boyle Abbey (1161), Roscommon Holy Trinity (1215), Holy Cross (1229), Kilmore (1232), Kilruisswe (1250), Sligo Abbey (1252), Clonshanvil (1385), Banada Abbey (1423), Ballindune (1427), Killtullaagh (1441), Tulsk (1448), Clooney Meaghan (1488). Cf. *The Church of Erin: Her History, Her Saints, Her Martyrs, Her Monasteries and Shrines*, by Rev. Thomas Walsh & D.P. Conyngham, D. & J. Sadlier, New York, 1885, pgs. 867-868.

49 Cf. *Isle of Saints: Monastic Settlements and Christian Community in Early Ireland*, by Lisa M. Bitel, Cornell University Press, 1990.

50 Ibid., pgs. 860-869.

51 *The Flowering of Ireland*, by Katharine Scherman, Little Brown & Company, Boston, 1981, pg. 123.

52 Ibid., *Virgilius of Salzburg*, pgs. 283-287. Dicuil, *Geographer and Astronomer*, 770-814 A.D., pgs. 289-291.

53 Poets that flourished in the early days of Ireland: Becc mac Luiddech (5th century), Brim ac Bairchid (5th century), Dubtach moccu Luair (5th century), Senchán

Torpéist (c. 560–647), Luccrerth moccu Chiara (fl. 600), Laidan of Corcu Duibhne (7th century), Blathmac mac Cu Brettan (fl. 750), Mael Ruain of Tallaght (8th century), OEnagus Celi De (c. 800), OEngus mac Oengaoba (c. 800), Orthanach ua Coellamae (fl. 800), Colman mac Leneni (d. 604), Adomnan (704), Fiann Mainistrech (1056), Irard mac Coisse (pre-980), Marcus of Ratisbon (1149), Cinead O hArtucain (died 975), Flann file of Ronan (022), Uallach ni Muimnechaid (died 934).

54 *A Celtic Miscellany*, translated by Kenneth Hurlston Jackson, Penguin Books, 1971.

55 *Early Irish Communion Vessels*, The Irish Treasure Series, by Michael Ryan, the National Museum of Ireland, Dublin, 2000.

56 *The Treasures of the National Museum of Ireland*, 7.

57 Caelius Sedulius, 5th century, "Carmen Paschale."

58 *Carmina Gadelica: Hymns and Incantations*, collected by Alexander Carmichael, Lindisfarne Press, 1992.

59 *1000 Years of Irish Poetry*, edited by Kathleen Hoagland, The Devin-Adair Company, 1947.

60 *Columb's Other Island: The Irish at Lindisfarne*, by Gareth W. Dunleavy, The University of Wisconsin Press, 1960.

61 Scherman, op. ct.

62 Cf. Note 7.

63 Willets, op. cit., Ch. 2, pgs. 16-17.

64 *Echoes of a Savage Land*, by Joe McGowan, Aeolus Publications, 2006, pgs. 166-168.

65 Cf. Note 7.

66 *Peig: The Autobiography of Peig Sayers of the Great Blasket Island*, translated by Bryan McMahon, The Talbot Press, Dublin, 1974. Also, *The Irish Tradition*, by Robin Flower, Lilliput Press, 1994.

67 *Ireland*, by Frank Delaney, Harper/Collins, 2005.

68 Marianus Scotus, the founder of the Irish monastery at Regensburg, Germany, in 1067. He was the creator of hundreds of "books of Kells" and illuminated manuscripts: manuals, psalters, commentaries on the

Bible. His monastery of St. James in Regensburg was the motherhouse of a federation of twelve monasteries extending through the heart of Europe. These monasteries, for five hundred years, evangelized, educated, brought new agricultural methods, and stabilized the economies of the emerging nations of Europe, and were religious and educational centers for the peoples of those areas. Thus Arnold Toynbee: "The period of Irish cultural superiority over the continent and over Britain may be conveniently dated from the foundation of the monastic university of Clonmacnoise in Ireland, circa A.D. 548, to the foundation of the Irish Monastery of St. James of Ratisbon (Regensburg), circa 1090. Throughout those five and a half centuries, it was the Irish who imparted culture, and the English and continentals who received it."

69   Cf. Note 29.

70   John Scotus Eriugena, one of the Irish scholars at the court of Charlemagne, 810-867 A.D. A philosopher of genius who introduced the Greek writings of the Pseudo-Dionysius of the Areopagite to the West. He was one of many Irish luminaries in the Frankish court.

71   St. Columbanus, monastic founder, scholar, educator, and intrepid Irish saint, 530-615 A.D. One of the Irish *peregrini* who evangelized continental Europe after the Barbarian Invasions, his monasteries of Luxeuil in France and Bobbio in Italy became huge religious and educational centers that pre-dated the rise of Benedictine monasticism on the continent.

72   Some of these others were: St. Fridolin (Burgundy and Switzerland), St. Gall (Switzerland), St. Fursey (France and Germany), St. Fiacre (France), St. Kilian (Germany), Dungal (Italy), Donatus (Italy).

73   Cf. *The Irish Educational Guide and Scholastic Directory*, 1883-84, Secondary School Curriculum, Dublin, John Mara, Printer & Publisher.

74   *The Rediscovery of Ireland's Past: The Celtic Revival: 1830-1930*, by Jeanne Sheehy, Thames & Hudson, London, 1980.

75   At his graduation from Mount St. Mary's College in 1904, he read a paper entitled, "The Gaelic Revival." *The Mountaineer*, student publication of Mt. St. Mary's College & Seminary, Vol. 12, pg. 279.

76   Oursler, op. cit., pg. 30.

77   Also known as St. Columba, 527-597 A.D., Monastic founder and Prince of the Ui Neill. The finest product and fearless propagator of Celtic Monasticism: Wrapped up in the mystique of the Celtic tribal traditions, poet and bard, Latinist and Scriptural sage, versed in a vast body of Celtic literature and lore, student of the classics, schooled in the lore of the filids and bards, a lyric and epic master of peerless skill, musician, and musicologist, heir to the throne of Tara and founder of countless monasteries, in particular, Derry, Iona, Durrow, Kells, and Drumcliff.

78   Real name, Lorcan Ua Tuathail: 1128-1180 A.D., son of a tribal chieftain, Murtagh O'Toole, prince of southeast Kildare. Monk and Abbot of Glendalough, Archbishop of Dublin. Fought the Anglo-Norman invasion of Ireland. Died in exile in Normandy.

79   Irish martyr: 1625-1681 A.D. Archbishop of Armagh, during the days of intense persecution of Irish Catholics during the reign of Charles II. He was arrested and convicted of high treason and executed at Tyburn in 1681. He had ancestral roots in Edward Flanagan's Roscommon.

80   Irish martyr, bishop of Mayo, died in 1578, during the reign of Elizabeth.

81   Priest-hero of the Battle of Boulavogue, whose story is told in the song, "Boulavogue," often sung around fireplaces and at ceilis.

82   In later years, when he was a student at Mount St. Mary's College in Emmitsburg, Maryland, at the age of nineteen, he gave a talk to the student body on "The Gaelic Revival," with a remarkable knowledge of recent Irish history and literature.

83   Cf. *Saint Andrew Daily Missal*, by Dom Gaspar Lefebvre, O.S.B., Abbey of St. Andre, Bruges, Belgium, English edition, The E.M. Lohmann Co., St. Paul, Minnesota, 1947.

84   According to the priests who worked with him at Boys Town, he was always to be found early each morning at prayer in the chapel, before any of them arrived, and this

was his habit of many years and perhaps for a lifetime. Cf. "The Oral History of Monsignor Peter Dunne," a priest of the Archdiocese of Omaha who worked with Father Flanagan during the four years before he died.

85 From a conversation with the author three months before Father Flanagan left for Europe at the request of the United States government, and from statements of priests who worked with him at Boys Town, e.g. Monsignor Peter Dunne.

86 "The Hovering of God: The Poetry of Celtic Monasticism," by Clifford Stevens, *The Desert Call*, August 1989, pgs. 21-22.

87 "Carmina Gadelica: Hymns and Incantations," collected by Alexander Carmichael, Lindisfarne Press, Hudson, New York, 1994.

88 *1,000 Years of Irish Poetry*, edited by Kathleen Hoagland, The Devin-Adair Company, 1947. Also, *A Celtic Miscellany*, edited by Kenneth Hurlstone Jackson, Penguin Books, 1971.

89 The testimony of Ed Flanagan, Father Flanagan's grandnephew from Omaha, who visited Summerhill College and found the school record of young Eddie Flanagan in the archives of the college.

90 Finbar McNamara, a local authority in Ballymoe and Roscommon, told me that the suit was not a "store-bought" suit, but was custom-made by a local tailor named Lyons in Castlerea. The shop where the suit was bought went out of business a long time ago, but he pointed out the spot in Castlerea where it once stood. The 1901 Irish Census lists a Patrick Lyons in Castlerea as a tailor, so it is most probable that Eddie Flanagan's new suit of Donegal Tweeds was bought at Patrick Lyons' shop.

91 There was a burse of 500 pounds established by the Diocese of Elphin for boys entering Summerhill College. The board and tuition per annum in 1901 was 31 pounds, which was not an excessive amount for a herd family at that time.

92 *Irish Hunger*, compiled and edited by Tom Hayden, Roberts Rinehart Publishers, Boulder, Colorado, 1997. *The Great Famine: Ireland's Potato Famine: 1845-51*, by John Percival, Viewer Books, New York, 1995.

The Irish Famine, by Peter Gray, Harry N. Abrams, Inc., New York, 1995.

93 "More than 80 percent of Irish Emigration in the nineteenth century was to the United States"; *In Search of Ireland's Heroes*, by Carmel McCaffreu, Ivan R. Dee, Publisher, Chicago, 2006, pg. 177. More than 4 million persons emigrated. They were young and of working age, from 1840 to 1887 and after.

94 *Young Ireland*, by Dennis Gwynn, Cork University Press, 1949. *Young Ireland*, by T.C. Sullivan, The Kerryman Ltd., 1945. *Young Irelander Abroad: The Diary of Charles Hart*, edited by Brendan O'Catholic, Univ. Press.

95 *The Manchester Martyrs: The Story of a Fenian Tragedy*, by Paul Rose, Lawrence & Wishart, 1970.

96 *Douglas Hyde*, by Janet Egleson Dunleavy and Gareth W. Dunleavy, University of California Press, 1991. *Young Douglas Hyde: The Dawn of the Irish Revolution and Renaissance: 1874-1893*, by Dominic Daly, Rowman & Littlefield, Totowa, N.J., 1974.

97 Jeanne Sheehy, op. cit.

98 *Ireland and the Classical Tradition*, by W.B. Stanford, Irish Academic Press, Dublin, 1976.

99 "The broad characteristics of Irish emigration are these: The population of the country fell from 8 million on the eve of the Famine to 4.4 million in 1911. More than 4 million persons emigrated. They were young and of working age; from 1850 to 1887, 66 percent, and after 1887, 80 percent, were in the fifteen-to-thirty age group. Most were sons and daughters of farm laborers and small farmers. Six counties, all in the west, provided about half of the migrants; on the receiving end, 85 percent went to the United States, and three quarters of those lived in seven states as of 1900. Most were literate, and in most cases, spoke English and Irish Gaelic. When they left, they were unmarried and traveled as individuals, whether men or women. In the post-Famine migration, family groups probably accounted for no more than a third of the migrants. Nearly all were Catholic. Since few had any capital, vast numbers were financed by remittances

or prepaid tickets from relatives or friends already in North America. Steamships out of Liverpool and Firth of Clyde began stopping at Londonderry, Cork, and Galway in the late 1860s, and by the 1870s, Queenstown (now Cobh, which is Cork's harbor and Moville, near Derry) surpassed Liverpool as one of the main Irish embarkation ports. Steerage fare to the United States reached $8.75 in 1894. Private philanthropy, local governing boards, and American railroads all subsidized immigrants." *Crossings: The Great Transatlantic Migrations: 1870-1914*, by Walter Nugent, Indiana University Press, 1995, pgs. 50-51.

100 The American Wake, roots web/ancestry. com/-irlker/wake.

101 Ibid., quotation from text by Ray Marshall.

102 "Come Back to Erin," was written for someone who had emigrated to England, but it expresses the bonds between those leaving Ireland with those they left behind, and the sadness and sorrow associated with an "American Wake."

103 Susan emigrated to America to become a nurse, and later, in Omaha, married a doctor, T.J. Dwyer.

104 Susan would become a nurse and apparently had this in mind when she left for the United States. The education of their children was very important for John and Nora Flanagan and they saw all of their children educated.

105 The generosity of Catholic Ireland in supplying priests for the missionary countries of the world is truly astonishing. All Hallows College is a stunning example of that generosity. Cf. *The Missionary College of All Hallows: 1842-1891*, by Kevin Condon, C.M., Dublin, 1986.

106 *Sligo: Land of Destiny*, by Joe McGowan, Cottage Publications, Donaghadfee, North Ireland, 2004. *Echoes of a Savage Land*, by Joe McGowan, Aolus Publications, 2006. *In the Shadow of Benbulben*, by Joe McGowan, Aolus Press, 1993.

107 *The Diocese of Elphin*, edited by Francis Beirne, The Columba Press, 2000, pg. 315. *Diocese of Elphin: An Illustrated History*, by Francis Beirne, 2007. *Sligo and Its Surroundings*, by Tadhg Kilgannon, pgs. 149-150.

Summerhill College website: summerhill. ie.html.

108 *The Green Flag: A History of Irish Nationalism*, by Robert Kee, Penguin Books, 1972.

109 Catholic Emancipation had come in 1829, when the terrifying policies of the English government toward the Catholic Church and its priests began to wane and, although the suffering and oppression of the Irish people continued under stringent laws, Mass houses and churches were built where the Catholic religion was practiced openly and without government interference. But the heroic lives of its priests were remembered and became part of the legend of Ireland. Passages like this were read around Mass Rocks and hearth fires, and young Eddie Flanagan must have listened to them often as a young boy: "When Ireland had to choose between the torture and death of Calvary and the soft ease of earth, led by her priest sons, she fearlessly set her feet upon the Way of the Cross... her priest was classed with the wolf, and legally could be killed on sight. 'No priest to be left in all Ireland' was the order. The high-cliff saw them bound back to back, and pushed to death on the black rocks below; trapped in the Mass cave, they died in the reek and smoke; sold to the slave trader and transported, they worked till death under the lash of their owner; from end to end of the land, their bodies swung in the shadow of the 'priest's tree.' Every gallows in the country shook as priest after priest climbed the ladders at the bidding of their would-be exterminators. But transportation, prison, torture, death – all were of no avail. It was death for a priest to be found in Ireland, and death for a father to send his son out of Ireland to be trained as a priest. Yet, no sooner did one fall than another sprang to take his place." From *The Soul of Ireland*, by W.J. Lockington, S.J., The Macmillan Company, New York, 1920, pgs. 103-104.

110 *Father Hand*, by Rev. John MacDevitt, M.H. Gill & Sons, Dublin, 1885. *The Missionary College of All Hallows: 1842-1891*, by Kevin Condon, C.M., All Hallows College, Dublin, 1986.

111 There were other emigrants from Ireland at this time, whose motives were not economic or religious, but literary, artistic,

or political, who sought a larger stage for their talents and interests. Their destination was chiefly England, although some emigrated to Paris or Switzerland, like James Joyce. The emigrants to England left their mark upon the cultural landscape of London, in particular: George Bernard Shaw, Oscar Wilde, William Butler Yeats, John Lavery, and in some respects, Charles Stewart Parnell. They had been preceded by a generation of Irish scholars, writers, artists, and poets who found the political and cultural climate of Victorian England more to their liking than the oppressive political climate of Ireland. Cf. *Conquering England: Ireland in Victorian London*, by Fintan Cullen and R.E. Fosters, National Portrait Gallery, 2005.

112 *Father Michael O'Flanagan: Republican Priest: The Story of His Life and Extracts from His Speeches*, by C. Desmond Greaves, Connolly Association, 1954.

113 Oursler, notes for *Father Flanagan of Boys Town*, Boys Town Archives.

114 "He (Bourke Cochran) came to Summerhill College at Sligo to give a talk to the students at the College. He was an alumnus of the same college many years before when it was located at Athlone. He was in his day the great silver-tongued orator of America, and well do I remember the theme of his lecture, which was 'Success and Life.'" Father Flanagan to Gilson VanderVeer Willets, contained in notes for his unpublished manuscript. Boys Town Archives.

115 We know the names of some of the members of his class and the names of some of his professors, besides Father Michael O'Flanagan. His classmates were John Conry, John P. Devine, Patrick Doherty, Andrew Dooley, Matthew Galvin, William Gilbert, James Keenan, Thomas Kieran, Daniel Carney, Albert Neumann, Patrick Nicholson, Denis O'Connor, and Peter O'Leary. His professors were Bartholomew Kelly, Bartholomew Currid, and Thomas Carney. Cf. Census Records of 1901, Sligo County, Mail Coach Road Townland. The Census Record also lists John McCormack two years ahead of Edward Flanagan.

116 *The Irish Educational Guide and Scholastic Directory: The Secondary School Curriculum: 1883-84*, by John Mara, Printer &

Publisher, Dublin. Also, *Irish Education: Its History and Structure*, by John Coolahan, Institute of Public Administration, 1981. "Chapter Two: Secondary (Intermediate) Education."

117 "His marks at Summerhill placed him at the top rung of his class. For sports, in his freshman year, he started out for track, but sprained an ankle which had always been weak, since he had twisted it years before in the fields back in Leabeg. So he returned to his one favorite sport – handball." Oursler, op. cit. pg. 38.

118 "There was the night when he found a classmate, a boy called Mac, packing up. Mac had sneaked out behind a building and had a puff on a cinnamon cigarette. They were sending him home in disgrace. Eddie remembered his experience with the old clay pipes. Had John Flanagan known about that escapade, it would have meant a spanking for Eddie, but it would not have been a major crime. To be sent home from school, like Mac, was an earthquake in a boy's life." Oursler, op. cit., pg. 35.

119 Perhaps he would have been reminded of this scene from Dickens' *Hard Times*: "In the hardest working part of Coketown, in the most innermost fortifications of that ugly citadel, where Nature was as strongly bricked out as killing airs and gases were bricked in, at the heart of the labyrinth of narrow courts upon courts, and close streets upon streets, which had come into existence piecemeal, every piece in a violent hurry for some one man's purpose, and the whole unnatural family, shouldering and trampling, and pressing one another to death, in the last close nook of this great exhausted receiver, where the chimneys, for want of air to make a draught, were built in an immense variety of stunted and crooked shapes, as though every house put out a sign of the kind of people who might be expected to be born in it, among the multitude of Coketown, generically called 'the Hands' – a race who would have found more favor with some people, if Providence had seen fit to make them only hands, or like the lower creatures of the seashore, only hands and stomach – lived a certain Stephen Blackpool"; Chapter 10.

120 The scene may have recalled this passage from *Oliver Twist*: "I confess that I have

yet to learn that a lesson of the purest good may not be drawn from the vilest evil. I have always believed this to be a recognized and established truth, laid down by the greatest men the world has ever seen, constantly acted upon by the best and wisest natures, and confirmed by the reason and experience of every thinking mind. I saw no reason , when I wrote this book, why the very dregs of life… should not serve the purpose of the moral… in this spirit.… I wished to show, in little Oliver, the principle of Good surviving through every adverse circumstance and triumphing at last"; Preface to the Third Edition.

121 Oursler, op. cit., pg. 38.

122 It was also rumored that he took up boxing and also excelled in this. At Boys Town, boxing became one of the competitive sports he always encouraged.

123 "It is a strange coincidence that I should be present at his first public appearance that he gave in the Town Hall of Sligo, and I think you will remember that occasion, and also to be present at this last public concert in Concert Hall, Chicago." Father Flanagan to Father Michael O'Flanagan on September 21, 1939. Boys Town Archives.

124 "Geoffrey Austin," "The Triumph of Failure," "My New Curate," "Luke Delmege," "The Blindness of Dr. Gray," "Clenanaar," "Lisheen," "The Intellectuals," and "The Graves at Kilmorna."

125 Canon Patrick Augustine Sheehan, 1852-1913, Parish Priest of Doneraile in County Cork. Cf. *Canon Sheehan of Doneraile*, by M.P. Linehan, The Talbot Press Limited, Dublin, 1952. Also, *Canon Sheehan of Doneraile*, by Herman Joseph Heuser, Longmans, Green & Co., London, 1918.

126 Canon Sheehan, at the height of his fame as a writer, became friends with U.S. Supreme Court Justice Oliver Wendell Holmes, Jr. They met at the home of Lord and Lady Castletown, who resided at Doneraile Court in County Cork, and were parishioners of Canon Sheehan. Their correspondence from 1903 to 1913, the year of Canon Sheehan's death, reveals a rare friendship and a surprising identity of interests. Cf. *Holmes-Sheehan Correspondence: Letters of Justice Oliver Wendell Holmes, Jr. and Canon Patrick Augustine Sheehan*, edited by

David Burton, Fordham University Press, 1993. They also show the breadth of knowledge and wide intellectual interests of the Irish parish priests of the time, something that became an essential part of Father Flanagan's formation and outlook.

127 *The Roman Catholic Church in Ireland and the Fall of Parnell: 1888-1891*, by Emmet Larkin, The University of North Carolina Press, Chapel Hill, 1979.

128 Oursler, op. cit., pg. 38.

129 *Sligo: Land of Destiny*, by Joe McGowan, (paintings by Anne Osborne), Cottage Publications, Donaghadee, N. Ireland, 2004, pg. 44.

130 *Omaha World-Herald*, October, 1960, obituary of Monsignor Patrick A. Flanagan.

131 Willets, op. cit., Ch. 2. pgs. 19-20.

132 Passenger list, *S.S. Campania*, Feb. 20, 1904, Queenstown to New York.

133 *The Irish Educational Guide and Scholastic Directory: 1883-1884: Program for Examinations for 1884*, by John Mara, Printer & Publisher, pgs. 34-50.

134 Willets, op. cit., Ch. 2., pg. 9; also Oursler, op. cit., pg. 39.

135 Oursler, op. cit., pg. 38.

136 Cf. Eddie's letter to the Rector of Dunwoodie Seminary, pg. 57.

137 Father Flanagan explained to Gilson VanderVeer Willets his thinking on his decision to leave Ireland for study in the United States: "He reasoned, quite correctly, that Ireland was a very small country and a very religious country, and that the number of men who, like himself, aspired to be priests, was far more than the country could support. Also, it seemed reasonable that a priest, who was educated in America by Americans for Americans, would be better qualified for a lifework in this country, than one who had been educated in Ireland and then sent overseas for the inevitable ten years of missionary service." Willets, op. cit., Ch. 3, pg. 10.

138 Cf. *Ireland: A Concise History*, by Maire and Conor Cruise O'Brien, Thames & Hudson, New York, 1999, pgs. 128-129.

139 National Archives, 1911 Census, Leabeg, Drimatemple Parish, County Roscommon;

the entry reads: "1911 Census, Leabeg, William Hanley, 21, Catholic, herd, single, born Co. Roscommon, (Landholder, G.W. Blake Kelly of Dundermot),"

Chapter 2: The Immigrant

[140] Passenger list, *S.S. Celtic*, arriving at New York on Aug. 27, 1904. Their destination was listed as 208 East 10th Street in New York City, which was the address of Jane Cox, the older sister of Nora Flanagan. Nellie is listed as "housekeeper," so she was probably assisting her aunt with the housekeeping for her four daughters and her uncles, Patrick and Thomas Flanagan, who also lived at this address.

[141] *Roscommon Herald*, Aug. 14, 1886. "The Earl of Kingston evicted 100 families on Arigin Slopes"; "Thousands were evicted in the western counties."

[142] *Lord Randolph Churchill: A Political Life*, by R.F. Foster, Clarendon Press, Oxford, 1981, pgs. 376-377.

[143] *The Roman Catholic Church and the Plan of Campaign*, by Emmet Larkin, Cork University Press, 1978.

[144] "Sister Celestine reported that the young Ned Flanagan showed up at their house in Manhattan from Ireland with $10 in his pocket and a note from his mother saying he should go to his cousins Larkin." Personal communication from Tony Larkin, founder of the Larkin & O'Donoghues website, and distant cousin of Edward Flanagan.

[145] The four brothers were Michael, Patrick, Thomas, and William. Michael Larkin lived at 240 East 15th Street and was a well-known and beloved member of the New York Irish community. His wife, Ellen, had recently died and Michael was living with his son, James, and James' family. Michael, Patrick, and Thomas had emigrated to New York soon after the Great Famine of 1845. The brothers were in their early twenties when they left Ireland, and a younger brother, William, joined them later.

[146] The older sister, Jane, arrived in the United States sometime after 1851, already married to Thomas Cox, and they settled with their children at 208 East 10th Street in New

York City, the heart of the New York Irish community. It was to her home that the other members of the Larkin and Flanagan families came when they arrived in the United States. Her home became what the Irish families called "a rambling house," where members of the extended family and neighbors gathered for mutual support and comfort and for festive celebrations that strengthened family bonds and softened the sharp feeling of alienation in a strange and different country. Her house at 208 East 10th Street was built by James Mulry, an uncle of Thomas Maurice Mulry, who leased lots on East 10th Street in 1867 from a certain Hamilton Fish, apparently for relatives and others arriving in New York after the Great Famine. This was most probably part of a project of the Emigrants Industrial Savings Bank to provide housing for incoming immigrants from Ireland after the Great Famine of 1845, when millions of Irish families were emigrating to the United States.

[147] "The Emigrants Industrial Savings Bank, at a special meeting of its Board of Trustees, held at the bank, No. 51 Chambers Street, Manhattan, on March 16, 1916, unanimously adopted the following memorial of its late President, Mr. Thomas M. Mulry: 'Thomas M. Mulry died at his home in New York City on March 10, 1916. He was elected a Trustee of this bank on December 12, 1901. He served as a member of the Executive Committee during the years 1904 and 1905. He was elected President of the bank in January 1906. For more than ten years until his death he served continuously in that office'; 'When Mr. Mulry entered its Board of Trustees, he was celebrated among the varied groups of citizenship of this great city in the charities which have made it famous. He gave to the bank the service of a devoted and able advocate of the charity which it particularly serves, the fostering of thrift among the people'; 'He was progressive and wise in considering new methods. He was courageous in carrying into action the results of his careful thought upon the bank's affairs and its circumstances. He brought to them an experience of more than thirty years in large business in this, the city of his birth. He was particularly skilled in

the management of many men of every condition'; 'He found the bank already a leader among the great savings banks of the world. His death finds it the largest of all institutions of its kind. The banking house which he first founded has given place to another tenfold as large'; 'His personality gave to this bank an asset of the greatest value. His integrity, his wisdom, his charity were known throughout the nation. His character was gentle and humble. He was beloved by all, whom he met in the course of his duties. His advice and assistance were sought by the great and the powerful and by the lowly and the weak alike.'" *The New York Times*, March 12, 1916.

148 Cf. *Thomas Maurice Mulry*, by Thomas Francis Meehan, The Encyclopedia Press, Inc., New York, 1917.

149 "In dealing with the Society of St. Vincent de Paul... the cardinal, like Archbishop Corrigan, leaned heavily on Thomas M. Mulry who was the most representative Catholic layman of his time in New York. He was an able, vigorous, and industrious man of sound practical judgment and wide vision. He was also a deeply devout, charitable, and self-effacing man who sought none of the distinctions that came his way and used them only to promote the numerous good works he found time to help. He was educated in the parochial schools, the LaSalle Academy on Second Street, and at Cooper Union. He then joined his father's successful contracting business and later became president of the Emigrants Industrial Savings Bank"; "Mulry joined the Society of St. Vincent de Paul at seventeen and was an active member until his death. He was a lifelong advocate of close cooperation among all charitable groups, Catholic and non-Catholic alike, and was the first Catholic member of the Charity Organization Society, founded in 1882 to bring such cooperation about. The C.O.S. helped to coordinate activities of 138 charitable groups, including the city department of Public Charities and Correction. He was on the New York State Board of Charities, was President of the National Conference of Charities and Correction, and in 1909, was one of the committee of three appointed by President Roosevelt to organize the first White House Conference on Children. Cardinal Gibbons thought him one of the leading Catholics in America. Cardinal Farley thought him the leading Vincentian and Archbishop Hayes described him in 1919 as 'One who had done more in the interest of Christian Charity than any other American layman in his generation.' His own happy family life – he was one of fourteen children and had thirteen of his own – deepened his constant interest in any and all aspect of child welfare and he was a tower of strength to many child-caring institutions." *A Popular History of the Archdiocese of New York*, by Monsignor Florence D. Cohalan, United States Catholic Historical Society, 1983, pgs. 236-237.

150 *Dunwoodie: St. Joseph's Seminary, Yonkers, New York*, by Thomas J. Shelley, Catholic Classics, Westminster, Maryland, 1993.

151 The letter was dated September 17, 1904, less than a month after Edward Flanagan arrived in the United States. The address on the letter is 208 East 10th Street, the address of his aunt, Jane Cox, where he was staying with his sister, Nellie.

152 Cohalan, op. cit., pg. 211.

153 Cf. Letter to Dr. Driscoll.

154 Cohalan, op. cit., pgs. 219-220.

155 Mount St. Mary's College, Students Register, 1904-05, #182.

156 *A Short History of the Emmitsburg Railroad*, by W.R. Hicks. Also, *The Emmitsburg Railroad*, by George W. Wiremans. Information about the Emmitsburg Railroad was provided by the website of the Emmitsburg Historical Society, and by detailed information of railroad services from New York City to Emmitsburg, by George Delaplaine, President and Publisher of the *Frederic Newspost* of Frederic, Maryland.

157 *The Story of the Mountain: Mount St. Mary's College and Seminary, Vols. I & II*, by Mary M. Meline and Edward F. X. McSweeney, *The Weekly Chronicle*, Emmitsburg, Maryland, 1911.

158 *The Premier See: A History of the Archdiocese of Baltimore, 1789-1994*, by Thomas W. Spalding, The Johns Hopkins University Press, Baltimore, 1989, pg. 23.

159 *The Mountaineer*, the student publication of Mount St. Mary's College and Seminary, Vol. XII, No. 2, November, 1904, pgs. 39-41.

160 College Account Record of "Master Edw. J. Flanagan," Oct. 4, 1904, totaling $170.00 paid by Mr. Thomas Larkin, which covered $150.00 for board and tuition, $5.00 for doctor, $5.00 for gymnasium, and $10.00 for books.

161 Personal communication of Father Flanagan to author, December, 1945.

162 "The following remained at the College during the holidays: Carmody, Starr, Ferry, Finch, Jordan, Gu Brown, Freeman, C. Reilly, 'Josh' Smith, John Tierney, P. Milligan, W. Milligan, Munoz, O'Neill, Paniagus, L. Gomez, Charles Molina, E. Seltzer, Juanes, Andrade." *The Mountaineer*, Vol. XII, 1904, pg. 112.

163 Ellis Island Ship Database, Nov. 3, 1905, White Line Ship Cedric, passenger list numbers 93, 94, 95.

164 *The Mountaineer*, Vol. XIV.

165 Ellis Island Ship Database, April 21, 1906, White Line Ship Caronia, passenger list numbers 702, 703, 704.

166 Oursler, op. cit., pg. 48.

167 *The Mountaineer*, Vol. XIV.

168 "A few interesting facts about Father Flanagan during his years at the Mount: 'Arrives in 1904 and at the age of twenty was the youngest member of his class; Received his A.B. degree from the Mount on June 20, 1906; Academic honors included: Second highest average in composition, distinguished in Latin, Greek, and English, and honors in the college's Elocution contest for his speech, "The Gaelic Revival"; Member of the Glee Club, College Choir, and the Sodality of the Blessed Virgin Mary; Recognized as one of the best handball players on campus,'" Newsletter, Mount St. Mary's College, Summer 2009.

169 Oursler, op. cit., pg. 44.

170 Boys Town Archives.

171 *The Mountaineer*, Vol. XIV, pg. 279.

172 Cf. *Conquering England, Ireland in Victorian England*, by Fintan Cullen and R.E.

Foster, National Portrait Gallery, London, 2005.

173 Boys Town Archives.

174 "St. Ann's was a blend of a fashionable residential area and a civic center. It contained Astor Place, where the first church stood, and Union Square. Both Cooper Union and the Academy of Music were within its boundaries." Cohalan, op. cit., pg. 144.

175 Sister Celestine Larkin was a member of the Sisters of Charity in New York City, and remembered that, as a young girl, young "Ned" Flanagan, as he was known to his New York relatives, arrived at her home in 1904 with $10 in his pocket, and a note from his mother introducing him to her relatives in New York.

176 New York City Federal Census, June 9, 1870, page 24, Enumeration District, 359. Jane Cox, age 50, is listed as living on East 11th Street in Manhattan, married to Thomas Cox, and their children, Bridget, Patrick, Mary, Bella, and Ann. Also living at this address are her brothers, Thomas and Patrick Larkin. Listed as also living at this address are: James Allen, son of her sister, and a cousin, Thomas Byrne; New York City Federal Census, June 1, 1900, Borough of Manhattan. Jane Cox, age 70, listed as living at 208 East 10th Street, with her four daughters, Bridget, Mary, Bella, and Ann. Also listed at this address are her two brothers, Thomas and Patrick Larkin, and three other persons whose names are not readable, undoubtedly recent relatives from Ireland.

177 Shelley, op. cit., pgs. 72-91.

178 Ibid.

179 "This same concern (for intellectual excellence) led to a tightening of admission requirements before Dunwoodie was three years old. In 1899, Archbishop Corrigan agreed to give the faculty complete control of admissions.... Henceforth the entrance examinations was a two-day affair, involving written and oral questions, in English, Latin, and mathematics, with the Archbishop himself serving as one of the oral examiners," Shelley, op. cit., pg. 107.

180 *St. Joseph's Seminary, Dunwoodie New York: 1896-1921*, by Arthur C. Scanlan, United

States Catholic Historical Society, New York, 1922, pg. 112.

181 Cf. *Duffy's War: Fr. Francis Duffy, Wild Bill Donovan, and the Irish Fighting 69th in World War I*, by Stephen L. Harris, Potomac Books, Inc., 2006. A vivid picture of this remarkable priest, known chiefly as Chaplain of the Fighting 69th in World War I, and whose statue stands on Broadway in New York City. Also, *Chaplain Duffy of the 69th Regiment*, by Ella M. Flick, The Dolphin Press, Philadelphia, 1935.

182 Cf. *Father Duffy's Story: A Tale of Humor and Heroism, of Life and Death with the Fighting Sixty-Ninth*, by Francis P. Duffy and Joyce Kilmer, George H. Doran Co., New York, 1919.

183 Scanlan, op. cit., pg. 183.

184 Scanlan, op. cit., pg. 208.

185 Scanlan, op. cit., pgs. 207-221.

186 Father Flanagan's remarks to the author, February, 1948, on a visit to New Melleray Abbey, Dubuque, Iowa, where the author was in his first studies for the priesthood. Father Flanagan remarked that he had a dream of entering such a monastery before he died.

187 This is how the seminary authorities described him: "Nice decent Irish boy, kindly and friendly, obedient regular – talent only fair and not very good formation – works well – on the whole v. satisfactory – nice family – nice little gentleman but delicate in health, nervous about his condition – health – just fair in talent, visits too much – too many questions to ask of confreres."

188 Oursler, op. cit., pg. 45.

189 In 1919, in the pages of his *Boys' Home Journal*, Father Flanagan wrote this tribute to Father Duffy, who was on the frontline of the war in Europe: "Major Duffy, chaplain of the 165th Infantry, A.E.F., and formerly chaplain of the famous old fighting 69th, New York National Guards, which was part of the Army unit, is believed to be the only army chaplain who was promoted from the rank of lieutenant to major without serving as captain. Father Duffy is greatly beloved in the army for his many good qualities of head and heart, and has received the Distinguished Service Cross from General Pershing and the Croix De Guerre from the French government for conspicuous bravery on the field of battle"; *Boys' Home Journal*, March, 1919, pg. 8.

190 Shelley, op. cit., pg. 225.

191 The poor in hospitals were only part of the poverty in the slums of New York at this time. It is known that as a young seminarian, he was appalled by the poverty, youth gangs, and human degradation that he witnessed in the city. Cf. *How the Other Half Lives: Studies among the Tenements of New York*, by Jacob A. Riis, Charles Scribner & Sons, 1890.

192 This is his full account of his entry into his first tubercular ward: "'This way please.' A group of young men, we were scarcely more than boys, followed the hospital attendant down the long corridor; 'The wards are in the wing at the end of the hall,' the attendant informed us. It seems to me that she was leading us down a long dark tunnel. Did friendless sick people have to lie in these dark wings?, I asked myself. When we reached the end of the dark tunnel, the attendant indicated the directions we were to take to find the wards we had asked to visit"; "It was our first mission to the poor and lonely sick, and I know that I had rehearsed many times the little speech which I had supposed I would give when I entered the ward. Gradually my eyes took in the long rows of white cots. Faces almost as white as the pillows on which they lay, turned toward me. There wasn't a bit of color in the entire room. White, broken only by the shadows around the sunken cheeks and eyes. An almost continuous coughing told me that I was in a tubercular ward." *His Lamp of Fire*, by the Rev. E.J. Flanagan. Unpublished manuscript, pgs. 1-2.

193 *His Lamp of Fire*, pgs. 1-3.

194 Ibid., pg. 3.

195 Oursler, op. cit., pg. 47.

196 He found it hard to understand the lack of simple kindness in those who ran social institutions or those responsible for the care of the poor. It was this heart-breaking experience that made him even more determined to be a priest and to get involved

in some kind of social ministry. It was this inborn compassion for the poor and suffering that drove him in his first parish assignment in Omaha to get involved in the lives of the jobless men who roamed the streets of Omaha after a drought in 1915. He seemed to sense that if he were to carry out his vision of priesthood as service to the larger human community, he would have to work outside the normal parish structure. This ability to identify with the suffering of others and to identify them as "other selfs" was the passion behind his work and that fired his determination to change the world he lived in.

197 Oursler, Outline Notes.

198 Oursler, Outline Notes, pg. 11, #29.

199 Oursler, Outline Notes, pg. 10, #26.

Chapter 3: The Darkness of Defeat

200 Scanlan, op. cit., pg. 208.

201 Ibid., pg. 208.

202 Ibid.

203 Oursler, op. cit., pg. 48.

204 Ibid.

205 On May 31, 1907, this notation was made in the student records of St. Joseph's Seminary under the name Edward Flanagan: "(1906-7 One year phil) nice decent Irish boy kindly & friendly, obedient regular – talent only fair, & not. V gd formation, works well – on the whole accent gd: . . . Nice family. L. nice little gentleman but delicate in health, nervous about his condition but just fair in talent, visits too much, too many questions to ask of confreres." This notation was made when young Flanagan had been advised to leave the seminary for health reasons. Boys Town Archives.

206 Oursler, working notes for *Father Flanagan of Boys Town.*

207 Willets has a different reason for Nellie going west: "While Director of St. James Orphanage, Father 'P.A.' contracted double pneumonia. He was a very sick man when he finally sent word to New York asking his mother to come west for a visit. Mrs. Flanagan was unable to travel at the time, so in her place, she sent Nellie, who came to

Omaha and helped nurse her brother back to health." Willets, op. cit., Ch. 3, pg. 22.

208 *Political Bossism in Mid-America,* by Orville D. Menard, University of America Press, 1989; *The Old Gray Wolf, He ain't what he used to be: Tom Dennison's Omaha: 1900-1930,* by Harl Dalstrom.

209 Cf. *Impertinences: Selected Writings of Elia Peattie, A Journalist in the Gilded Ages,* edited with a biography by Suzanne George Bloomfield, Chapter I: "Early Omaha: With Works of Charity: St. Joseph's Hospital and the Good Sisters Who Do Its Work."

210 Cf. *A History of the Catholic Church in Nebraska: The Church on the Fading Frontier,* by Henry W. Casper, S.J., The Bruce Publishing Company, Milwaukee, 1966; *History of the Catholic Church in Northeast Nebraska,* by Stephen Szmrecsany, The Catholic Voice Publishing Company, 1981.

211 Szmrecsany, op. cit., pg. 7.

212 Willets, op. cit., Ch. 3, pg. 35.

213 Omaha City Director, 1908.

214 Cf. *The House on Humility Street,* by Martin Doherty Longnans, Green, 1944.

215 Archives, Archives of Omaha.

216 Oursler, op. cit., pg. 60.

217 Archives of the Gregorian University, Rome, for the Academic Year, 1907-08. Matriculation Number 006687. His professors were Father Hermanius van Laak, S.J., Dogmatic Theology; Father Januarius Bucceroni, S.J., Moral Theology; Father Fidelis Savio, S.J., Church History; and Father Henry Fismondi, S.J., Hebrew.

218 Oursler, op. cit., pg. 69.

219 Ibid., pg. 60.

220 Ibid., pgs. 69-70.

221 Passenger list, *S.S. Cedric,* arriving in New York from Naples, Feb. 9, 1908.

222 We know his name from the passenger list of the *S.S Cedric.*

223 Father Flanagan's Memo, a copy of which was given to the Ourslers for their book together with this explanation: "While at the College Capranica in Rome, the chef was an Italian whom some priests wished to get into this country as a cook. When

Father left Rome, he brought this man with him to America. The man settled in Cincinnati and after many years working for the Father in Cincinnati, he left to cook for a private family. He left the private family to work for a museum. In 1943, he was 65 years of age. All those years, the friendship between Father Flanagan and the Italian chef has been very strong. They visit each other frequently. Sometime after his arrival in America, the Italian's girlfriend was brought to this country and they married. They had four children. When the oldest one was three years old the mother died. The father brought up the two girls splendidly. The two girls are married to Ph.D.s, and the two boys are in the Army. The Italian knew Frank Abts, who was a Cincinnati doctor." The Memo was given to the Ourslers when they visited Boys Town before Father Flanagan left for Europe in 1948 and contained the following information:

- 1908: January 28 – Left Rome with Mr. _____.

- January 29th – Sailed from Naples, second-class in stateroom for two aboard *S.S. Cedric*, White Star Line, 21,000 tons.

- February 9th – Arrived in New York.

- February 9th – Father Kelly's home in Brooklyn, New York.

- February 11th – Mr. _____ arrives in Cincinnati.

Apparently, Father Flanagan could not remember the Italian chef's name, and kept it blank.

224 Omaha City Directory, 1908. The Directory lists the following residents of 1504 South 29th Street: John Flanagan, Nellie, Susan, James, Delia, Edward.

225 The 1909 Omaha City Directory lists their residence as 2776 California Street.

226 Notes dictated by Father Flanagan on August 17, 1943, to Gilson VanderVeer Willets, notes for Chapter 4, page 47 of Willets' unpublished manuscript. Boys Town Archives.

227 Oursler, op. cit., pg. 71.

228 Ibid., pg. 72.

229 Oursler, op. cit., Ch. 7, pg. 73.

230 "In 1887, Michael Cudahy and his brother, Edward, with the help of Philip Armour, started a meat-packing business in Omaha, the Armour-Cudahy Company. Within the next two years, the Omaha plant grew to 1,500 employees with a payroll of $700,000 and boasted sales of over $13 million." *Impertinences: Selected Writings of Elia Peattie, a Journalist for the Gilded Age*, University of Nebraska Press, 2005, pg. 65.

231 Ibid., pg. 74.

232 "While I was with the Boys' Home on 25th and Dodge Streets, and as there was a scarcity of priests, I assisted my friend, Monsignor Bernard Sinne, Pastor of St. Mary Magdalene's Church. Monsignor Sinne was a great friend of mine, and in fact, it was through his advice and counsel that I was privileged to go to Innsbruck, as he was a former Innsbrucker himself." Notes dictated by Father Flanagan to Gilson VanderVeer Willets, August 23, 1943.

233 Omaha City Directory, 1909.

234 This is indicated by the fact that the diocese started paying for his expenses at Innsbruck only in 1911, an expense of $345.00, a debt Father Flanagan had to pay after ordination, together with the expenses of his trip to Rome and for his residence at Capranica College. Omaha Diocesan Records.

235 Edward Flanagan's record of classes, Innsbruck University Archives.

236 Willets, op. cit., Ch. 2, pg. 38.

Chapter 4: Innsbruck

237 Willets, op. cit., Ch. 3, pg. 42.

238 "He always spoke fondly of his... years at the Canisianum in Innsbruck. He held the memory of Father Hofman in special affection, for to him he could always go when discouraged." From *Boys Will Be Boys: A Memoir of Boys Town*, by Msgr. Francis P. Schmitt, Ares Publishers, Inc., Chicago, Illinois, 2000, pg. 38.

239 Students records, University of Innsbruck, list number 73, Boys Town Archives.

240 Oursler, op. cit., pgs. 78-79.

241 Included were classes in Dogmatic Theol-

ogy, Canon Law, Church History, Moral Theology, Pastoral Theology, and Homiletics. While in Innsbruck, he also became fluent in German.

242 Among his classmates were Vilmos Apor, a future bishop of the Diocese of Gyor, one of the martyrs of the Ukraine, and Konrad von Preysing, a future Cardinal Archbishop of Berlin and an outspoken foe of the Nazi regime.

243 Other notable priest graduates of Innsbruck were Josef Frings, future Cardinal and Archbishop of Cologne; August von Galen, Cardinal and future Bishop of Munster; Adam Stefan Sapieha, Cardinal and future Archbishop of Krakow; Joseph Slipyj, Cardinal and Metropolitan of the Ukrainian Catholic Church; Myroslav Ivan Lubachivsky, future Cardinal and Archbishop of Lviv; and two other Ukrainian martyrs: Blessed Nykyta Budka and Blessed Andrew Ishchak.

244 Cf. Boy Guidance, by Rt. Rev. Msgr. Edward J. Flanagan, 1948, in manuscript for Boys Town's Hall of History.

245 "Instruction in the Study of the Fathers of the Church in the Formation of Priests," Congregation for Catholic Education, November, 10, 1989, published in L'Osservatore Romano (English Edition), January 15, 1990. Also, "Newman and the Study of the Church Fathers," by Thomas McGovern, Homiletic and Pastoral Review, February, 1992, pgs. 8-18.

246 Pope Leo XIII, Encyclical "Aeterni Patris," August 4, 1979.

247 Summa Theologica, I-II, Questions 6-21.

248 Summa Theologica I, Questions 75-89. Also, At the Origins of the Thomistic Notion of Man, by Anton Pegis, The Macmillan Company, New York, 1963, and Thomistic Psychology, by Robert Brennan, O.P., The Macmillan Company, New York, 1943.

249 Cf. Shelley, op. cit., pg. 128.

250 Willets, op. cit., Ch. 3, pg. 42.

251 Other professors teaching at the University at the time were: Hugo Hurter, whose father was the historian Friedrich V. Hurter. Hugo had studied at the Germanium in Rome and held a doctorate in Philosophy

and Theology. He taught Dogmatic Theology. Also Joseph Muller, Anton Straub, Johann Stofler, and Hieronymus Noldin.

252 Reilly & Warneke, op. cit., Ch. 2, pg. 29.

253 Oursler, op. cit., Ch. 8, pg. 77.

254 Oursler, Working Notes, Ch. 9, note 14.

255 Oursler, op. cit., Ch. 8, pgs. 79-80.

256 Ibid.

257 Willets, op. cit., Ch. 3, pgs. 36-49.

258 Photo collection, Boys Town Archives.

259 Willets, op. cit., Ch. 3, pg. 44.

260 "Farewell Banquet of the American Exiles to the Ordained Members," by Rotholz, Tirol, June 10, 1924.

261 Ibid.

262 "He returned to Innsbruck only a few weeks before he died, and the rector told me how he had made his way through the rubble of the war of the war-scarred collegiate church to point out exactly where he had lain during the Litany while receiving Orders." Schmitt, op. cit., pg. 38.

263 Archives, Archdiocese of Omaha.

264 Notes dictated by Father Flanagan to Gilson Willets, 17 August 1943.

265 Oursler, Working Notes, Ch. 10, notes 1-3.

266 Ibid., note 23.

267 In 1912, Father Duffy was pastor of Our Saviour's Church in the Bronx and not on the faculty of St. Joseph's Seminary in Yonkers. In 1914, he became chaplain of the famous Fighting 69th Regiment of World War I and was the most decorated chaplain in the history of the U.S. military. Cf. Duffy's War: Fr. Francis Duffy, Wild Bill Donovan and the Irish Fighting 69th in World War I, by Stephen L. Harris, Potomac Books, 2006. Also Father Duffy's Story: A Tale of Humor and Heroism, of Life and Death with the Fighting 69th, by Francis P. Duffy and Joyce Kilmer, George H. Doran Company, 1919.

268 Ibid.

269 Ibid.

270 Ibid.

271 Omaha City Directory, 1912.

272 Notes of Father Flanagan to Gilson Willets.

273 Ibid.

274 Ibid. General John O'Neill was one of the most colorful, flamboyant figures in 19th century American history.

275 "The town of O'Neill had no special drawing card to lure settlers into the area. There were no valuable mineral deposits, the land was hard to farm and suffered from wind erosion and drought, and access to the region was by ox-drawn wagons over virgin prairie. In short, there was no easy road to success except the lure of cheap land and the idea of a fresh start." From *O'Neill, Nebraska: The First Quarter of a Century,* by Gregory R. Passewitz, master's thesis, University of Omaha, August, 1973.

276 *History of the Catholic Church in Nebraska,* by Henry Casper, S.J., Vol. III, *Catholic Chapters in Nebraska Immigration,* Part I, Chapter 1, "O'Neill – The Man and the Place," pgs. 3-34.

277 *100 Years of Faith,* unpublished history of St. Patrick's Church in O'Neill, Nebraska.

278 *History of St. Patrick's Parish, Holt County, Nebraska,* by Monsignor Michael Cassidy, unpublished.

279 Notes of Father Edward Flanagan to Gilson Willets, 1943.

280 Ibid., Note 33.

281 Willets, op. cit., Ch. 4, pgs. 11-13.

282 Ibid., Ch. 4, pgs. 15-17.

283 Cf.. *Omaha Sun,* May 5 , 1977, pg. 16A: "Father Flanagan: rural priest."

284 Cassidy, op. cit.

285 Willets, op. cit., Ch. 4, pg. 18.

Chapter 5: The Mission to the Men

286 *His Lamp of Fire,* by the Rev. E.J. Flanagan. Unpublished manuscript, Chapter II, pg. 15.

287 Notes dictated by Father Edward Flanagan to Gilson VanderVeer Willets, August 23, 1943.

288 "In 1913, while Father Smith was still pastor, another priest came to St. Patrick's as an assistant. The young priest had a magnetic charm that drew parishioners to him. The descriptions received of Father Flanagan were: 'kind,' 'caring,' 'understanding,' and 'a dear, dear priest.'" History record of St. Patrick's Church, Omaha, Nebraska, pg. 8.

289 *Picture Story of the Omaha Tornado Disaster of Easter Sunday Evening, March 23, 1913... the most terrible destruction of human life and property from a tornado in the history of the United States,* by Louis R. Bostwick, Baker Brothers Engraving Company, Omaha, Nebraska, 1913.

290 *The Easter Sunday Tornado of 1913,* first published by the *Omaha Bee* newspaper in 1913, Modern Reprint Series, 1998, River Junction Press, 1998, opening page.

291 *Omaha's Easter Tornado of 1913,* by Travis Sing, Arcadia Publications, 2003.

292 Leo Hoffman, a co-worker of Father Flanagan in his work, was founder and president of the Omaha council of the St. Vincent de Paul Society, which was active in many parishes, including St. Patrick's. It was to Hoffman and the Society that Father Flanagan first turned in his work for the jobless men and for the setting up of his two hotels.

293 *Swept By Mighty Waters,* by Thomas H. Russell, Chicago, Laird & Lee, Publishers, 1913.

294 *His Lamp of Fire,* by the Rev. E.J. Flanagan. Unpublished manuscript, pg. 4.

295 Ibid.

296 Ibid., pg. 5.

297 Ibid.

298 Ibid. pg. 6.

299 "Works out deal with grocer to give some of men 'food orders' to take away and prepare for themselves. Flanagan chipped in from his small pay, so some of men were able to get coffee and food to prepare mulligans." Ourslers' Research Notes to Ch. 11 of their book. Boys Town Archives.

300 Ibid., pgs. 7-8.

301 Personal communication: Al Joyce, a St. Vincent de Paul member who helped Father Flanagan find shelters for the jobless harvesters, 1960.

302 Ibid.

303 *His Lamp of Fire*, pg. 8.

304 Ibid., pg. 9.

305 "I opened my first Working Men's Hotel in a building known as the Burlington Hotel, in November 1913. I had to repair this old building with the aid of my men to make it livable. This building proved entirely inadequate for the demands made upon it by the guests, and so I looked around the following spring (and) found that the Livesy Apartments were available, which consisted of about 100 apartments – about four stories and a basement.

"This place I renovated with the aid of my own men and some expert plumbers, and I transferred my Working Men's Hotel in July, 1914. Here I remained until the summer of 1918, but meanwhile I opened the Boys Home on 25th and Dodge Streets on December 12, 1917, and ran both institutions for about five or six months." Notes dictated by Father Flanagan, August 17, 1943. Boys Town Archives.

306 Ibid., pg. 9.

307 Ibid., pg. 10.

308 "Burlington Hotel for Workingmen's Home," *Omaha World-Herald*, December 8, 1915, pg. 11.

309 Ibid., pg. 11.

310 Ibid., pgs. 13-14.

311 "Father Flanagan started his first Workingman's Hotel on Eleventh Street. It was a place for the unemployed and the people of the street to come for a place to sleep. Father Flanagan ran the hotel, but the people of St. Patrick's helped with furnishing money, linens, food, and clothes. They also helped to clean the hotel. When asked, they worked 'because Father Flanagan needed help.' He seemed to invoke the best that people had to give."

312 By some of the men, especially those who simply drifted in off the streets, the hotel was called "Hotel de Gink."

313 Ibid., pg. 15.

314 Ibid., pg. 16.

315 "Change of Location for Workingmen's Hotel," *True Voice*, September 8, 1916, pg. 5.

316 "In July of 1914, he moved from the Burlington Hotel to the Livesy Flats." History record of St. Patrick's Church, Omaha, Nebraska, pg. 8.

317 *Omaha World-Herald*, January 17, 1917, pg. 10.

318 *His Lamp of Fire*, pg. 19.

319 Ibid.

320 Ibid., pg. 20.

321 Ibid.

322 "Father Peter Gannon began his tenure at St. Patrick's on February 15, 1915, just thirteen days after the death of then pastor, Father Smith. Father Gannon was born in Grand Junction and grew up on a farm four miles south of there. He attended Creighton University and played on the first Creighton Football Team. He was ordained to the priesthood in 1903. He had thought of being a circuit rider priest in the Sand Hills of Nebraska but was assigned to a parish in Chadron, Nebraska instead. Six months later, he was re-assigned to Omaha as editor of the Catholic paper of that city called the *True Voice*." Parish records of St. Patrick's Church, Omaha, Nebraska, pg. 8.

323 Ibid., pgs. 21-27.

324 Ibid., pg. 22.

325 Ibid., pgs. 32-34.

326 Ibid., pg. 27.

327 Ibid., pg. 27.

328 Ibid., pg. 21.

329 Ibid., pg. 30.

Chapter 6: The First Battle for Boys

330 *His Lamp of Fire*, by the Rev. E.J. Flanagan. Unpublished manuscript, Ch. II, pgs. 32-34.

331 Oursler Notes, Ch. 14, items 7-10.

332 Willets, op. cit., Ch. 5, pgs. 24-27.

333 Ibid., pg. 30.

334 "I made friends with many waifs off the streets, boys who were forever getting into mischief because their time was not profitably employed, and I fell into the habit of trying to straighten out their tangles in juvenile court. I soon found that an

enormous number of boys under 12 years of age were being sent to the state industrial school at Kearney, simply because there was no place to send them." From a public letter of Father Flanagan about 1923, soon after moving to Overlook Farm.

335 "At the turn of the century, the status of the child in Anglo-American criminal law was no different from that of an adult. The Common Law of England, which was frequently followed in American courts, had held for centuries that seven was the age of reason... Thereafter, the child might be held responsible for criminal acts. Until the age of fourteen, however, the law presumed that the child did not understand the nature of his offense... After the age of fourteen, the accused youth was legally on the same footing as an adult. Children were also tried in the same courts as adults... The treatment of children after conviction was as harsh as the legal principles by which they were tried." *The Good Fight: The Remarkable Life and Times of Ben Lindsey*, by Charles Larsen, Quadrangle Books, Chicago, 1972. Ch. 2, pg. 27.

336 *His Lamp of Fire*, Ch. III.

337 Ibid., Ch. III, pg. 35.

338 Ibid., pg. 36.

339 *The Romance of the Homeless Boy*, by Father Edward Joseph Flanagan, 1925.

340 Willets, op. cit., Ch. 5, pg. 21.

341 "After researching with the State of Nebraska Archives in Lincoln, they referred me to the Law Library in Lincoln, Nebraska. I was told that the Judges that were on the bench in 1916 are as follows: Judge Lee S. Estelle; Judge Charles Lesley; Judge William Redick; Judge Alexander C. Troupe; Judge Arthur C. Wakely. The most well-known and the one they believed to work mostly with Juveniles was Judge George A. Day... I was also informed that there were no separate Juvenile Courts until sometime in the 70's." Communication from Cindy Vandenbroucke, Clerk of the Douglas County Court, Omaha, Nebraska. March 2, 2011.

342 *His Lamp of Fire*, Ch. II, pg. 47.

343 Ibid.

344 "I decided to spend my life in saving boys from becoming misfits and recruits to the army of crime. I had studied the program of our courts dealing with delinquents, and as far as I could see the only results were the constantly growing number of boys sent to the reform schools, and the additional expense of making reform schools larger. Then, as now, at least ninety percent of our adult criminals had started their careers as children, and I felt that there must be something radically wrong with a system which produced so many criminals. The economic and social loss to society was abhorrent.

"I felt that there must be another way – the way of love and kindness – of training and teaching – of learning to do by doing. I was certain that erring and neglected boys could be trained by a system other than bars and the cat o'nine tails, and developed into worthwhile citizens, and I set out to do it in a most humble manner. I had no financial backing, not even much sympathy, and certainly not much interest on the part of local citizens, for our soldier boys were in the trenches of France at the time, and mothers' hearts were with them." Letter from Father Edward Flanagan to Mrs. Harley J. Earl, July 15, 1939. Boys Town Archives.

345 "It did not seem right to me that these boys, just babies they seemed, should be forever branded with the stigma of having been committed to a reformatory. I felt that they were entitled to a better chance in life." Public letter of Father Flanagan about 1923, after the move to Overlook Farm.

346 Ibid., Ch. 3, pg. 49.

347 "It is not enough to see that what has been called the underprivileged child is given good food, warm clothing, and a clean bed. An army commissary can do as much. No! More than food, clothes, and shelter, what these lads have been deprived of is a mother's tenderness, and a father's wisdom, and the love of a family. We will never get anywhere in our reform schools and orphan asylums until we compensate for that great loss in such young lives.

"And what does that mean? It means you will have to develop a new class of social workers, not merely distinguished for the professional training, but, more important, consecrated to the great, the soul-lifting task of brining tenderness and solicitude and understanding and mother interest – if you please – a doting interest, if you don't mind – to the little affairs of desolate children." Quoted in *Father Flanagan of Boys Town*, by Fulton and Will Oursler, pg. 5.

[348] "One of the more important studies of juvenile delinquency was conducted by Thomas Earl Sullenger, a sociology professor at the University of Omaha, and written up in 1930 as "Social Determinants in Juvenile Delinquency: A Community Challenge." A 'careful analysis' of 1,145 cases of juveniles appearing before the courts between 1922 and 1927, Sullenger's studies echoes and supports Flanagan's emphasis on social causes of delinquency, among them family dysfunction, lack of organized recreational activities, and widespread poverty." *Making American Boys: Boyology and the Feral Tale*, by Kennedy B. Kidd, University of Minnesota Press, 2004, Note 4, pg. 210.

[349] Cf. "The Pedagogical Genius of Father Flanagan of Boys Town," by Clifford Stevens, *Homiletic and Pastoral Review*, January, 2009.

[350] Cf. *The Jane Addams Reader*, edited by Jean Beathke Elshtain, Basic Books, New York, 2002.

[351] Cf. *Thomas Maurice Mulry*, by Thomas F. Meehan, The Encyclopedia Press, Inc., New York, 1917.

[352] Cf. *The Good Fight: The Remarkable Life and Times of Ben B. Lindsey*, by Charles Larsen, Chicago Triangle Books, Chicago, 1972.

[353] Cf. *Children in Bondage*, by Edwin Markham, Ben B. Lindsey, and George Creel. Hearst's International Library Co., New York, 1914. This is certainly one of the books that Father Flanagan consulted in his study of the care of children. Passages like his would have supported his view that children were at risk in the American society of the time: "The hours these children work is well-nigh incredible. Either they toil from six in the morning until six at night, or from six at night to six in the

morning. In addition to this, the mills demand an extra half day's work on Saturday, in consequence of which the children that quit at six o'clock Saturday morning must return at noon.… It is also the truth that the dayshift is frequently asked to work two or three nights a week, so that there are days when a child works for seventeen hours at a stretch.… Amid such unremitting drudgery, such horror of monotony, how can there be talk of health, education and intelligence." Pgs. 25-26. The book is a terrifying and graphic indictment of the laxity of the law in matters of juvenile justice and brought about the passing of the Keating-Owen Act by Congress in 1916, outlawing child labor. The law, however, was overturned by the Supreme Court in *Hammer vs. Dagenhart* in 1918, over the powerful dissent of Justice Oliver Wendell Holmes, Jr.

[354] Judge Lindsey visited Father Flanagan at the German-American Home sometime between 1918 and 1921.

[355] Quoted from *The Beast* by Judge Ben B. Lindsey in *The Good Fight: The Remarkable Life and Times of Ben B. Lindsey*, pgs. 64-65. In this same quotation, Judge Lindsey blamed the greed of big business and the hopeless economic and working conditions of fathers of families for juvenile crime and the failure of legislatures to pass laws safeguarding the economic rights of workers and furthering just working conditions. Later, in his *Boys' Home Journal*, Father Flanagan would begin to explore these deeper causes of juvenile delinquency.

[356] We know the names of two of the judges, since they are mentioned in an article that appeared in the April 1919 issue of the *Boys' Home Journal*. The title of the article is "The Omaha Juvenile Court and its Functions," and the two judges named are Judge George A. Day, who presided at the Juvenile Court in Omaha from 1905 to 1918, and Judge A.C. Troup, who succeeded Judge Day in 1918. The article was written "in order that those of our readers who may never have the occasion to visit a court may gain a fair idea of its features, for it is through this court mainly that most of the boys who come to Father Flanagan's Boys' Home have been received." *Boys' Home Journal*, April, 1918, pgs. 3-4.

357 "It was out of Father Flanagan's attempt, two years ago, to save a lad from being sent by the juvenile court here to the Kearney Industrial School that the Home for Boys had its inception.

"He was a little Italian newsboy, an unusually bright youngster. Although he was only 14, he had had two years in high school. He was a natural orator and frequently acted as an interpreter for his family and friends. Even Judge Leslie, who was on the juvenile court bench at the time, was astonished at the lad's excellent command of English.

"He was charged with stealing, and admitted a long list of petty thefts. But I felt certain that there was an immense deal of good in the boy. I didn't know where or how I could keep him, but I begged the court to let me have him in my charge instead of sending him to Kearney.

"The court granted the boy to Father Flanagan who at that time conducted a downtown home for old men. The boy was turned over to Father Flanagan at the usual Saturday morning session of the juvenile court. That night the lad was housed at the home of the old men. By Monday, Father Flanagan had ten other boys who had been picked up by the police." *The Omaha Daily News Magazine*, Sunday, September 21, 1918.

358 *His Lamp of Fire*, Ch. III, pg. 53.

359 Ibid., Ch. III, pgs. 54-55.

360 Ibid., pgs. 54-55.

361 Casper, op. cit., Vol. III, *The Poles in Omaha: Sheelytown*, pgs. 182-183.

362 "It is a foreign country – Sheely station, and is a little village by itself, sustained by the not far distant packing houses. It is hemmed in by the railroad and brick yards on the eastern side, by the city at the north, and by the nothingness of the plains on the west and south. It is an aspect of peculiar poverty, yet it is not squalid. It looks distinctly un-American, but at first has difficulty in classifying its foreign aspect…. There are in fact, Germans, English, Irish, and Poles living there. Numerically considered, the Poles may not be more than half of the community, but they exercise, without doubt, a greater influence than any

of the transplanted foreigners, and form the most restless and positive force in the neighborhood….

"There are a number of grocery stores in Sheely, at which the necessaries of life may be purchased, and several saloons, at which may be obtained the luxuries of existence – as luxuries are regarded by a large part of the community at Sheely station. In the midst of these are dance halls, where, late in the morning, the sound of gay music can be heard almost every Sunday night, and where, it is hinted, the extravagances of conduct are such as to require the most aggressive work of the Parkvale Congregational Mission to counteract them….

"There are so many good and industrious and desirable citizens living at or near Sheely station that one hesitates to describe the worst features of the place, lest it should involve these, who are innocent in the contumely which it attaches to those who have made the place a by-word. But admitting the existence of these respectable men and women who are fighting poverty honestly, and raising their children safely in pleasant little homes, there is a tribe of swarthy, angry, skulking men who spend their money in saloons, who work all day and whose leisure is spent in almost any way except an innocent one. Among this tribe are certain leaders who are nothing more nor less than bandits….

"Its deserted and dismantled buildings, of which there are several, its great bleak places between the clay cuts, its odd crooked streets, its unexpected flights of stairs leading up banks over which the path runs, its little ravines and curious nooks make it a veritable paradise for the adventurous boy. And since conspiracies and plots are in the air, it is not strange that the adventurous boy has a share in the same thing.

"Yet there are good and honest little boys there, and sweet and modest girls,… as they look out of the windows of their own little homes. There are rooms which are cozy and inviting, and very dear to the occupants in those cottages, and many a loving mother in them, and a father who deprecates the necessity which forces him to live in a neighborhood where there is turbulent and treacherous elements."

Impertinences: Selected Writings of Elia Peattie, a Journalist of the Gilded Age, edited and with a biography by Suzanne George Bloomfield, University of Nebraska Press, 2005.

363 "When we got out on the street, the seven of them closed in around me. They were still in the grip of fear, and the hand of the law was not yet lifted from them. I frankly admit that I just didn't know what to do with them. I had their confidence, I knew that, for they were grouped around me looking up at me, as if waiting for directions." *His Lamp of Fire*, pg. 56.

364 "I did not doubt that there was something to be done. I must provide some wholesome activity to take them away from the street corner… I must master the situation and provide for these boys' recreation before we separated. I led the little gang to a vacant lot not so far distant and we sat down and talked about future plans. I never mentioned the past, but gave all our attention to the future. First, I wanted the boys to forget that courtroom scene, and the misfortunes of the past. We were primarily interested in the future.

"Each one entered into the plans with all the enthusiasm of boyhood. We would meet in evenings and arrange games and hikes. Since this lot was more or less centrally located, we decided to meet there regularly." Ibid., Ch. III, pgs. 56-57.

365 Ibid., Ch. III, pg. 57.

366 Ibid., pg. 58.

367 Ibid., pg. 57.

368 Ibid.

369 Ibid., pg. 59.

370 "He was, of course, a student of J.L. Gillins' 'Criminology and Penology' and the great work on the subject by F.E. Haynes. With respect and hope he followed the laboratory work of Dr. Arnold Gesell, director of the Clinic of Child Development, School of Medicine, Yale University, and his associate Dr. Frances Ilg." Oursler, op. cit., Ch. 14, pg. 116.

371 "He had studied the case histories of delinquent boys who became cashier killers and auto bandits, all as reported in the work of Healy and Bonner: 'Delinquents and Criminals, Their Making and Unmaking.' And he had studied Clifford R. Shaw's true scientific account of the career of 'The Jack Roller' and his 'The Natural History of a Delinquent Career.' He knew the theories of the new criminology expounded by Dr. Max S. Schlapp, professor of neuropathology at New York Post Graduate Medical School and Director of the New York Children's Court Clinic, and having studied his work, Father utterly rejected the glorification of chemical causation of abnormal behavior in which all crime and sorrow of the world became one vast glandular disturbance." Ibid.

372 *His Lamp of Fire*, Ch. III, pgs. 59-60.

373 "More and more youngsters were paroled to his care. In spite of parish duties – Mass, confession, pastoral duties, and all the activities of societies and sodalities of the Church – he never refused a request from the bench. What troubled him most was that it was all so haphazard. There was no equipment, no systematic way of caring for them. The park bench remained the meeting place." Oursler, op. cit., Ch. 15, pg. 139.

374 Cf. *The New York Times*, September 6, 1903, pg. 20.

375 Jeremiah Harty's dedication to his work mirrored in many ways Father Flanagan's own dedication. When he left from St. Louis for the Philippines in 1903, he was noted for his complete lack of formality and his sense of personal poverty: Under the headline "Archbishop Harty Leaves St. Louis for Manila with Limited Funds", the article read: "St. Louis, Dec. 2. – Archbishop Jeremiah J. Harty, head of the Catholic Church at Manila, Philippine Islands, and destined to become a power in the hierarchy of the Catholic Church, left St. Louis possessing only the clothes on his back.

"With only sufficient means to supply his immediate wants, he started on the long journey across the Pacific Ocean. Even the purse presented at his last public appearance in the church, Archbishop Harty turned over to the church treasury, reserving the small sum that would prove sufficient to keep body and soul together until he arrives in Manila.

"His life insurance – both regular and fraternal – his business interests, amounting to almost $14,000, were conveyed by Archbishop Harty to the Parish of St. Leo." *The New York Times*, December 3, 1903.

376 Father Flanagan wrote this about Archbishop Harty: "He was a great believer in making religion more accessible to the people. For this reason, he established many new parishes in outlying territories… born optimist, his kindliness and tenderness of heart were often repaid by ingratitude. As a result he met with much disappointment. He was a man whose great love and solicitude for the orphan and homeless knew no bounds. Once each week he would visit these poor children, and seemed most happy when he was in the midst of an informal group of youngsters who learned to love him as a father and protector. His talks to them whether in the Chapel or on the playground were masterpieces." Sermon delivered on the Golden Jubilee of the Diocese of Omaha, December 8, 1935.

377 *His Lamp of Fire*, pg. 60.

378 Willets, op. cit., Ch. 6, pg. 4.

379 *The True Voice*, December 7, 1917, pg. 5.

380 "At the request of our Archbishop, a large gathering of ladies met at the home of Mrs. Arthur Mullen over two months ago, to discuss ways and means of financing a Home for Delinquent Boys of this City, the need of which was very great, judging from the record of the Juvenile Court. The ladies were most enthusiastic over this new work, and made preliminary arrangements for the establishing of a permanent organization which would lend its untiring efforts to this noble enterprise. Mrs. Arthur Mullen was unanimously elected Chairman of the organization… the ladies present pledged most liberal donations at that first meeting and promised to secure the co-operation of many others in their work." *Father Flanagan's Boys' Home Journal*, Vol. I, No. 1, February, 1918, pg. 2.

381 Mrs. Mullen's husband was known as the "Western Democrat" and was a prominent civic leader and politician, and was the floor leader at the national Democratic Convention in 1932, which nominated Franklin D. Roosevelt for the presidency.

"She was a grand lady… much concerned about the Home and the social life of the boys, who on occasion graciously opened her spacious home to our then clandestine dances." *Boys Will be Boys: A Memoir of Boys Town*, by Msgr. Francis P. Schmitt, Part One, pg. 25.

382 "My unsatisfactory way of caring for the boys paroled to me was the best I could think of under the circumstances, but it took so much of my time going back and forth, and I saw the boys but for a short time. I felt that I could do much more for the boys if I could have them under my supervision all the time in some more satisfactory place." *His Lamp of Fire*, by the Rev. E.J. Flanagan. Unpublished manuscript, Ch. III, pg. 59.

383 Ibid., pgs. 46-47.

Chapter 7: The House on 25th and Dodge

384 Under the heading "New Boys Home Opened," *The True Voice*, the Catholic newspaper of the Diocese of Omaha, reported: "Two Sisters of the order of Nostra Domina arrived in Omaha on Tuesday from Cedar Rapids, Ia. to take charge of the domestic department of the Industrial Boys Home at 25th and Dodge Streets. The home will be opened at once with twelve boys in charge of Rev. E.J. Flanagan, who will reside at the home. His place at St. Philomena's will be taken by Rev. Father Gabriel, O.S.A." Dec. 14, 1917.

385 Willets, op. cit., Ch. 6, pg. 6. Oursler, op. cit., Ch. 16, pgs. 145-146.

386 There is some indication that he went to the U.S. National Bank for a loan, before approaching Henry Monsky. Tom Murphy, who worked at the bank, was, like the Flanagans, from Ballymoe, and came to Omaha before the Flanagans did. The families seem to have been close. Murphy claimed that Father Flanagan came asking for not only $90.00 for the rent of the building but for a larger sum to get him started with his work. Murphy claimed that he turned Father Flanagan down, since he had no collateral or salary to back up the loan. Working Notes of Gilson VanderVeer Willets for his unpublished manuscript, *Father Flanagan of Boys Town*, Ch. 16, pg. 20.

387 Cf. Address of Father Flanagan at a banquet honoring Henry Monsky at the Commodore Hotel, New York City, February 26, 1945: "A fellow worker with whom it was my privilege to engage in charitable and welfare fields." Boys Town Archives.

388 Cf. *Henry Monsky: The Man and His Work*, by Mrs. Henry Monsky and Maurice Blisger, Crown Publishers, New York, 1947. Also, "The Education of Henry Monsky," by Oliver B. Pollak, in *Crisis and Reaction: The Hero in Jewish History*, Creighton University Press, Omaha, 1995.

389 Address given by Father Flanagan at a banquet honoring Henry Monsky at the Commodore Hotel, New York City, February 26, 1945: "Unlike most of you here, I have known him as a boy, a student at the University; a young lawyer entering upon his professional career – a fellow worker with whom it was my privilege to engage in charitable and welfare fields. He is a member of the Board of Father Flanagan's Boys' Home, the legal counsel for Boys Town, and my own attorney. He is my personal friend." Boys Town Archives.

390 Although Father Flanagan adamantly refused to reveal who gave him the $90 to rent his first boys' home, he did reveal it in a conversation with S. Regensberg, who visited him at Boys Town in 1938. In the course of their conversation, Regensberg inquired about the movie *Boys Town*: "The first thing I should like to know is, how much of the motion picture is authentic and how much 'embroidered.' I am especially curious to know whether the Jewish character Dave is real or fictional. 'Dave is an actual person,' Father Flanagan replied. 'Twenty-five years ago we became acquainted and our friendship was sealed. Dave is one of the finest Jews in Omaha. When I commenced my work with the boys, my Jewish comrade loaned me the first 90 dollars to pay my first month's rent.'" *The Jewish Forward*, Dec. 13, 1938. Boys Town Archives.

391 Cf. *Two Men Shared Path to Social Justice and Interfaith Harmony*, by Leo Adam Biga, The Jewish Press, Vol. XXXVII, Nos.22 & 23, Omaha, Nebraska, Feb. 15 & 18. Also, "Father Flanagan and Henry Monsky: Men of Vision," an exhibit created by the Hall of History, Father Flanagan's Boys' Home, Boys Town, Nebraska, and the Nebraska Jewish Historical Society, Omaha, Nebraska, with an accompanying pamphlet.

392 E.W. Nash was president of the Omaha Smelting and Refining Company and later was first president of the American Smelting and Refining Company (ASARCO). He died in 1905. His wife, Catherine, was a native of Quebec and was active in the growth of the Catholic community in Omaha. She contributed to the founding of Duchesne College in 1915, and both are buried in the Nash Chapel in the Cathedral. She was early and intensely interested in the work and growth of Father Flanagan's work and in the growth of Boys Town.

393 "An auxiliary of Catholic women has been formed to promote the interests of the home, and financially back its operation. Mrs. Arthur Mullen is chairman: Mrs. C. Will Hamilton and Mrs. Lee Estelle, Vice Chairmen, and Mrs. Louis C. Nash, Secretary." *Boys' Home Journal*.

394 "The crucifix was in the Chapel at 25th and Dodge, (in the) German Home; (in the) Chapel in 1st School Building (on Overlook Farm), which is now the library; it has been placed on a base and is now in the Sisters Chapel at Boys Town." Statement of Father Flanagan to Gilson Willets, 1943.

395 Willets, op. cit., Ch. 6, pg. 12.

396 Oursler, op. cit., Ch. 1, 7, pg. 148.

397 *Omaha World-Herald*, December 7, 1917: "BYRON REED'S OLD RESIDENCE TO BE BOYS INDUSTRIAL HOME: The old Byron Reed home at Twenty-fifth and Dodge streets is to be converted into a boys' industrial home, under the supervision of the Rev. Edward J. Flanagan, founder and successful manager of the Workingmen's Hotel at 209 North Thirteenth Street."

398 This is Father Flanagan's account of the beginnings of his work for boys: "Immediately after I completed my education abroad and was ordained to the priesthood, I came to Omaha determined to make my life count for the less fortunate on earth. I saw the need for a lodging house for 'down and out' and established one at Eleventh and Mason Streets. Later, the location was changed to Thirteenth and Capitol Avenue.

In the years just preceding the war, Omaha was flooded with jobless men. In one year, I furnished beds to 27,000 'bums', only 3,000 of whom were able to pay the price of 10 cents for a night's lodging.

"It was while engaged in this work that I was struck by the enormous number of boys of tender ages without homes, without funds, and without friends, and I conceived the idea of opening and operating a home for neglected and so-called incorrigible boys.

"Naturally, I made friends with many waifs of the streets, boys who were forever getting into mischief because their time was not profitably employed, and I fell into the habit of trying to straighten their tangles with the juvenile court. I soon found out that an enormous number of boys under 12 years of age were being sent to the state industrial school at Kearney, simply because there was no other place to send them.

"It did not seem right to me that these boys, just babies they seemed, should be forever branded with the stigma of having been committed to a reformatory. I felt that they were entitled to a better chance in life.

"I was without funds. After I had borrowed the money to pay my first month's rent, I explained my plan to a number of prominent women who enthusiastically banded together into an informal organization to help me out. Mrs. E.W. Nash gave me $2,000, and several others made substantial donations.

"The first gift, other than money, ever made to the home, was a barrel of sauerkraut, which constituted our first Christmas dinner.

"With five boys, three of whom were sent to me by the juvenile court, and the other two found homeless and penniless on the streets of Omaha, I opened my home on December 8, 1917." *The Boys' Home Journal*, undated, circa 1923.

399 Five of the first boys were John Kresse, John Butsky, Sebastian Circo, James Toth, and Leo Borovac. The Boys Town records name five other boys who came within the month, all from Omaha: Paul Romana, William Sudka, Steve Sudka, Joseph Erna, and Alfio Castiglia. Alfio was the "boy with

the voice," who was a charter member of the first Boys Choristers.

Father Flanagan insisted that Kresse, Butsky, Circo, Toth, and Borovac were the first five boys, but the Boys Town Welfare Office records indicate that all five entered in January of 1918, while Romana, and the Sudka boys, Enna and Castiglio, are listed as entering in December of 1917, but later in the month than December 12th, the date on which Father Flanagan occupied the house on 25th and Dodge. It is most likely that it took a few days to put the house in order and ready for occupancy and so the first five boys may not have arrived until later in the month. If this is the case, the first five boys would have to be Paul Romana, William and Steve Sudka, Joseph Enna, and Alfio Castiglio.

Gilson Willets, while working on his manuscript on Father Flanagan and Boys Town in 1943, recorded this information about Kresse, Butsky, Circo, Toth, Borovac, and Castiglio:

John Kresse: His mother lives at 2916 11th Avenue, South Omaha. He is married. In 1944, reported as owning and operating his own farm in Brainard, Nebraska. He has been there for 8 years now. He has one child of his own and five others, his wife's by a former marriage. Admitted to the Home on January 20, 1918.

John Butksy: He was a packing house employee and also had a candy store in Omaha. Died as a result of an accident, May 18, 1930. Admitted to Home on January 19, 1918.

Sebastian Circo: Last reported as a farm worker on a farm near North Bend, Nebraska. Files show his last letters about 1941 or 1942. Admitted to the Home on January 19, 1918.

James Toth: Admitted to the Home on January 19, 1918. Left for the home of his mother in Cleveland, Ohio, on February 19, 1920. See Note 506.

Leo Borovac: Living at 1402 North Campbell Street, in Chicago, after one and a half years in the Army, with a medical discharge. He is employed by the General American Railroad Company. He is now 37 years of age and enjoying excellent health.

Married. Has or had defense job. Admitted to Home on January 19, 1918. See his letter to Father Flanagan: Note 38.

Alfio Castiglio: Born in Naples, Italy, he came to the U.S. with his mother, who died after they arrived. He had a beautiful singing voice and was a charter member of the Boys Home Choristers. Admitted to the Home on December 31, 1917. He is probably one of the first five boys. Boys Town Archives.

400 "We wish to express our sincere thanks and appreciation to Mrs. John Latenser for the beautiful Altar we received from her and made by the Bourgois Church and Manufacturing Company. We are all happy with this much needed gift, as we had nothing but a poorly constructed altar of rough boards on which the Holy Sacrifice of the Mass was being offered." *Boys' Home Journal*, Vol. 1, No. 1, February, 1918.

401 Ibid. "The domestic part of the Boys' Home is in charge of the order of Sisters known as Nostra Domina (Notre Dame), from Cedar Rapids, Iowa. These kind Sisters are most enthusiastic over the work being done at the Home, and make every sacrifice that would tend towards its success, and add to the comforts of the boys. They look after the cooking of good, wholesome and substantial food, and are firm believers in the theory that the first essential for helping those boys is to feed them well. They see to the boys' clothes and shoes and that they are in good condition, by repairing the old clothes and replacing them with new, when necessary. They supervise the sleeping quarters, so that they would be kept clean and sanitary. In a word, these kind Sisters act as devoted mothers to the boys, and this motherly care and interest taken on their behalf go a long way to winning their confidence and respect. In this way, we have a most contented and happy class of boys, who in turn manifest their appreciation by their splendid response".

402 "Two Sisters of the order Nostra Domina arrived in Omaha on Tuesday from Grand Rapids, Ia. to take charge of the domestic department in the Industrial Home of Twenty-fifth and Dodge Streets. The home will be opened at once with twelve boys in charge of Rev. E.J. Flanagan, who will reside at the home. His place at St. Philomena's will be taken temporarily by Rev. Father Gabriel, O.S.A." *The True Voice*, December 14, 1917.

403 "In Omaha the Rev. Edward J. Flanagan, at the instigation of Rt. Rev. Archbishop J. J. Harty, began to take care of neglected, homeless boys. He found a shelter for them but had no one who would take the place of a mother to these poor boys. In his difficulty, the archbishop again turned to our spiritual director, Rev. J. St. Broz, and he, by a telegram sent on November 1, 1917, asked for two Sisters for the new Boys Home. At first we definitely resisted the idea of stretching still farther the few workers we had at our disposal; there was no one to spare.

"However, when on November 17th another telegram arrived, the superior, Rev. Sister Gualberta, at the request of the spiritual director, went to Schuyler to consult with her assistant, Sister M. Symphorosa, as to what should be done. She was very enthusiastic for this meritorious task and urged that due consideration be given to the wish of the Archbishop who wanted to interest himself in our congregation.

"Shortly after that, the second assistant, Sr. M. Gustava, also gave her approval and so, with the help of God, we decided to send two Sisters to Omaha: Sr. M. Rose Slevin and Sr. M. Martha Djobek. It was an interesting pair: the first, an American, and the second, a Slovak who did not know an English word. They got along nicely because both were animated by an endeavor to help as much as possible the children whom the world despised. Because we definitely refused to teach the boys, they were sent to the nearest Catholic schools." Records of the Notre Dame Sisters, Cedar Rapids, Iowa, December 11, 1917.

404 "That spring (1918), I started a little magazine. This brought us in a little revenue, and besides gave the boys something of their own to work on. They were all excited about the magazine. We got a printer in the city to print it for us, as we had no trade equipment then. We sent the magazine to those friends who had helped us in the past, and they in turn got others interested in the work." *His Lamp of Fire*, by the Rev. E.J. Flanagan. Unpublished manuscript, Ch. III. pg. 68.

405 *Father Flanagan's Boys' Home Journal,* published from February 1918 to February 1938.

406 "I opened my first Workingmen's Hotel in a building known as the old Burlington Hotel, in November, 1913. I had to repair this old building with the aid of my men to make it livable. This building proved entirely inadequate for the demands made upon it by the guests, and so I looked around and the following spring found the Livesy Apartments were available, which consisted of about 100 apartments – about four stories and a basement. This place I renovated with the aid of my own men and some expert plumbers, and I transferred my Workingmen's Hotel in July, 1914. Here I remained until the summer of 1918, but meanwhile I opened the Boys Home on 25th and Dodge Streets on December 12, 1917, and ran both institutions for about five or six months." Notes dictated to Gilson Vanderveer Willets, August 17, 1943.

407 "While I was with the Boys Home on 25th and Dodge Streets, as there was a scarcity of priests, I assisted my friend, Monsignor Bernard Sinne, pastor of St. Mary Magdalene's Church. Monsignor Sinne was a great friend of mine, and in fact, it was through his advice and counsel that I was privileged to go to Innsbruck, as he was a former Innsbrucker himself. All during the time I was in this Boys Home, I said Mass for him on Sunday and up to the time I moved to the German Home." Notes dictated by Father Flanagan to Gilson VanderVeer Willets, August 23, 1943. Boys Town Archives.

408 *His Lamp of Fire,* pg. 62.

409 Ibid., Ch. III, pg. 63. "When one undertakes the responsibility of children, he assumes the role of parent, and must look to every part of the training and care of children. I found a great deal of difference in this work and the work at the hotel. Food and shelter were the principal problems there, while with the boys there were many additional ones. I must provide a school. I could not personally supervise fifty boys, so I must have assistants. The caliber of such assistants must be carefully investigated. These and similar responsibilities now presented themselves."

410 "The old-fashioned home with its fireside companionship, its religious devotion and its close-knit family ties, is my idea of what a home should be." From an article by Father Flanagan in *Perfect Home Magazine.*

411 *His Lamp of Fire,* pg. 63.

412 *Boys' Home Journal,* Vol. 1, No. 2, March, 1918, pg. 9. "Our boys were not slow in exhibiting their ability in selling the *Boys' Home Journal.* The lad having had the largest sale of the Journal was awarded a new suit of clothes."

413 Ibid.

414 Ibid., pg. 5.

415 "Another activity of that early time was a misguided experiment in soapmaking. This was also carried on by the boys, in a small factory set up in the yard. When the soap was finished, boys wrapped the cakes in colored tissue paper, while others, constituting their 'sales force,' peddled it in a door-to-door campaign. Results, however, were meager, and profits so slight, that Flanagan ordered that any soap made in the future would be for their own exclusive use." Oursler, op. cit., Ch. 19, pg. 167.

416 *Boys' Home Journal,* Vol. 1, No. 1, pg. 2.

417 Oursler, op. cit., pg. 7.

418 His description of the boys in the first issue of the *Boys' Home Journal* was laying the foundation for a booklet which he authored in 1925, entitled, *The Romance of the Homeless Boy.* In less than ten years, he had changed the public image of the homeless boy from a street hoodlum and youthful criminal to a loveable figure that caught the public fancy.

419 *Boys' Home Journal,* Vol. 1, No. 1, February, 1917, pg. 3.

420 Ibid., pg. 5.

421 "Among the many advantages our boys enjoy is the necessity of going to school every day. Most of them are proving that they can hold their own, and some are doing exceptionally well." *Boys' Home Journal,* May, 1918, pg. 14. He would be happily surprised, as the years went on and Father Flanagan's Boys' Home became "Boys Town," how well they did in almost every walk of life and profession. His pride in them was something he never could hide.

422 "While the home is under Catholic auspices, it will be non-sectarian in every respect. It will be open to boys from 8 to 16 years of age, regardless of their creed or nationality. No effort will be made on the part of those in charge to interfere with the religious beliefs of those not belonging to the Catholic Faith." *Omaha World-Herald*, December 7, 1917.

423 The lynching of African-American George Brown in 1919. Cf. *The Upstream Metropolis: An Urban Biography of Omaha and Council Bluffs*, by Lawrence H. Larsen, Barbara J. Cottrell, Harl A. Dalstrom, and Kay Calame Dalstrom, University of Nebraska Press, 2007, Pgs. 220-224, It may have been this incident, the most shameful in the history of Omaha, that strengthened Father Flanagan's determination to get his boys out of the city. There were African-American boys in the Home and it was hard to say when even the presence of a Black boy might incite a crowd. But although criticism of his mixed races was sharp and hostile, opposition never went beyond criticism. See Note.

424 "Carlo was stuffed – (lived 13 years) was placed at the main entrance of our Home (now the school building) inside the door – and every time the boys passed, they loved the dog so much they would fondle him and you know what happens to a stuffed dog that is fondled by 200 boys – ten or fifteen times a day – he didn't last long." Statement of Father Flanagan to Gilson Willets, 1943. Boys Town Archives

425 "A door prize of a house and a lot will be given at the dance for the benefit of the Boys' Home at the auditorium on April 11. The committee of women who were appointed by Archbishop J. J. Harty, are meeting with great success and they feel sure that the goal of $10,000 will be reached. The boys are now living at the old Byron Reed home, but when the new one is completed, they will have an opportunity to learn farming. Prominent women are sponsoring the affair." *Omaha Bee*, April, 1918.

426 The benefit for the Boys' Home was held on April 17, 1918. The idea for the benefit seems to have been Archbishop Harty's, who knew of Father Flanagan's desperate need of funds. For the first time, it brought his work for boys to the attention of the whole city. "The Charity Ball held at the city auditorium on the evening of April 11, for the benefit of Father Flanagan's Boys' Home was the greatest social success ever held in Omaha and the attendance by over 4,000 people represented every parish in the city as well as several parishes from nearby towns…. At the close of the evening, thirty of the boys from the Home, led by Mogy Bernstein, marched around the hall and called forth much cheering from everyone present." *Boys' Home Journal*, April, 1918, pg. 2.

427 *Father Flanagan of Boy Town: A Man of Vision*, by Hugh Reilly & Kevin Warneke, Boys Town Press, Boys Town, Nebraska, 2008, pg. 41.

428 "The soul of a boy is like a violin; it needs a skillful hand to play well on it. Like the violin, its harmony is perfected through time. Its mellow chords are made mellower through waiting. So long as it waits, a skillful hand is there to draw the bow and test the notes that leave its depths, and, if they jar, label them counterfeit, but when they swell like clouds across an azure sky, that skillful hand must strike again, until by quick submission to its touch the chords become one in harmony, beautiful and inspiring." *Boys' Home Journal*.

429 Cf. "From Peck's Bad Boy to Good Little Boy," *The Omaha Daily News Magazine*, Sunday, September 21, 1919.

430 Cf. *The Omaha Sunday Bee*, September 8, 1918: "Proud Folds of American Flag Smother Frederick the Great in Father Flanagan's New Home," by Ruth B. Whitney.

431 *Boys' Home Journal*, June, 1919, pg. 9. "Father Flanagan is somewhat of a linguist himself, speaking, besides English, German, Italian and French."

432 "In juvenile court recently, Probation Officer Miller made the statement that little Italian boys were their greatest problem. In solving the problem, the home is invaluable. Father Flanagan understands… the Italians. Nearly half the boys under his care are of this nationality. He speaks the language of their country." *The Omaha Sunday Bee*, September 8, 1918.

433 Cf. "The Educational Theories of Edward

Joseph Flanagan," by Clifford Stevens, *The Priest* magazine, September, 2003.

434 Cf. *International Relations in Psychiatry: Britain, German and the United States*; Ch. 11, "Alien Psychiatrists: 1930-1950," by Paul Weindling, pg. 228. "Franz Plewa, formerly Alfred Adler's assistant in Vienna, ran a clinic at Kensington in London.... In 1953 Plewa became chief of the Welfare and Counseling Services in Boys Town, Nebraska."

435 Cf. *Collected Works: Political Writings and Speeches*, by Padraic Pearse. Maunsel & Roberts, Dublin and London, 1922. "A Kieran or an Enda or a Colmcille gathered his little group of foster-children around him; they were collectively his family, his household, his clan; many sweet and endearing words were used to mark the intimacy of this relationship. It seems to me that there has been nothing nobler in the history of education than this development of the old Irish plan of fosterage under a Christian rule, when, to the pagan ideals of strength and truth, there were added the Christian ideals of love and humility. And this, remember was not the education system of an aristocracy, but the education system of a people.

"It was more democratic than any educational system in the world today. At Clonard, Kieran, the son of a carpenter, sat in the same class as Colmcille, son of a king. To Clonard or to Aran or to Clonmacnoise went every man, rich or poor, prince or peasant, who wanted to sit at Finian's or at Enda's or at Kieran's feet and to learn of his wisdom."

Chapter 8: The German-American Home

436 "On the morning of June 1, 1918, a large truck backed up against the terrace wall outside the Home on Dodge Street. Its arrival was followed by shouts of joy and intense activity as Father Flanagan and his boys helped with loading cots and mattresses, pots and dishes, food and furnishings. Then, with several bright-eyed boys who were to assist with unloading, the truck left for South Omaha. On the third trip, Carlo, and all the remaining boys scrambled onto the truck, where they cheered like wild Indians as it rattled down Dodge Street hill, through the business district, and then turned south on Thirteenth Street." Willets, op. cit., Ch. V, pg. 4.

437 "When all had gone, Father Flanagan escorted his three co-workers to a private automobile which had been loaned by a friend for this occasion. Then he returned for a last look through the building... Under a radiator (he) saw a battered old baseball, a little tobacco sack filled with marbles... in the kitchen there remained a metal drinking cup and a paring knife. He placed the ball, the sack of marbles, the drinking cup and the knife in a paper bag, and shortly afterwards left the building." Ibid., Ch. 7, pg. 5.

438 *O & CB: Streetcars of Omaha and Council Bluffs*, by Richard Orr, 1996.

439 "Carlo is a large brown and white Scottish collie. He goes to school every day and likes it better than a great many of our boys, because he starts for the schoolroom on Saturdays and Sundays and feels very much disappointed when Charley calls him back. While the school is in season, Carlo lies quietly under the table. When the small boys read over their lines, the busy squirrel runs around looking for his future meals. Carlo gets drowsy and snuggles his head under his paws and falls asleep. Sometimes he knocks his bushy tail against the table and the boys only smile while Charley remarks Carlo must be chasing a squirrel or cat. At recess, while the boys are playing, he chases squirrels. At noon he has a large dinner, for the boys give him bread and meat, but he likes candy and grapes better. Charley Daily." *Boys' Home Journal*, September, 1918, pg. 11.

440 "In the southwest room on the second floor, where the breezes of heaven have free access from three directions, are the little white beds in which the boys sleep. In the basement are the big dining room and the clean kitchen, smelling sweet and wholesome of freshly baked loaves or other substantial food." *The Omaha Sunday Bee*, September 8, 1918.

441 Oursler, op. cit., Ch. 19, pg. 164.

442 Willets, op. cit., Ch. 6, pg. 21.

443 "Are you a boy Life Saver? The Home is

trying to interest its friends in our little Boy Life Saver Society, formed some months ago to assist in carrying part of the financial burden incurred by the Home. The members pledge themselves twenty-five cents a month or three dollars a year.... join us today and help with your mite to care for these boys who we are teaching to become good citizens." *Boys' Home Journal*, May, 1919, pg. 2.

444 The name "Boys Saver" was not original with him. "The child saving movement found its roots in the Progressive Era. During this period, Americans were noted for attempting to change the injustices of the world. Anthony M. Platt, in his book, *The Child Savers*, focuses on the Chicago branch of this movement, where their impact was the greatest. Here, the child savers focused on reforming the brutality towards children as dealt by the American criminal justice system. The first juvenile court system was established by the Illinois Juvenile Court in 1899; this 'juvenile court system was part of a general movement directed toward removing adolescents from the criminal law process and creating special programs for delinquent, dependent, and neglected children.'" From *Father Flanagan: A Master Advertiser*, Mary Pat McMahon, undergraduate thesis in American Studies, Georgetown University, February 1, 1997, pg. 16.

445 In the first issue of the *Boys' Home Journal* after his arrival at the German-American Home, these items appeared: "We would be deeply grateful for some generous-minded persons of means, who would assist us toward getting a couple of cows at the Home. We have pasturage enough for them, and we need that rich, fresh milk to keep our boys' health up to the highest point.

"The ladies are all canning and preserving now, and this is but a hint that the Boys' Home has a very large empty storehouse. Send us word and we will call for your gifts in kind as well as gifts of cattle or money."

446 "I.... got into a little Model T Ford which was given to me by Dr. T.J. Dwyer." Willets, Working Notes for his unpublished manuscript, *Father Flanagan of Boys Town*, Ch. 6, pg. 42.

447 "The life in the home is not all work. There are games and a collie dog to play with, there are lessons, for which a huge schoolroom is being prepared. The dance hall will be fitted up as a gymnasium if the funds are ever forthcoming for that purpose." *The Omaha Sunday Bee*, September 8, 1918.

448 Ibid. Ch. 6, pg. 23.

449 "Some were highly talented youngsters. One, for example, had a true gift for music. He could pick up any instrument and play it, although virtually without musical education.... Father Flanagan determined that boys of such talents should be given a chance. Through volunteer aid he made sure that the lad received regular training and kept up his practice. The boy was, of course, the outstanding member of the original band which made its tour of the Middle West.... today he is one of America's most popular bandleaders." Oursler, op. cit., pg. 171. The boy musician was Salvatore Maddenti, who later changed his name to Sammy Madden. He was born in Italy in 1909 and came to the United States with an uncle when he was 13 years old in 1922 to join his family in Greenwood, Nebraska. His mother died soon after his arrival, leaving a husband and five children. The husband was not able to care for the children, so four of them were sent to orphanages and Sammy joined Father Flanagan, not at the German-American Home, but at Overlook Farm in 1923. He spoke no English when he came, but became something of a bookworm and mastered the language. His talent for music was remarkable and he became one of the favorite performers in Father Flanagan's road shows. After he graduated, he studied music at the Wisconsin Conservatory of Music and then organized his own dance band which became Sammy Madden's Polka Band and was a favorite in the Milwaukee and Chicago areas. Boys Town Archives, under the file "Road Shows."

450 "Today boys are sent to Father Flanagan's home, not only from all parts of Nebraska, but also from Iowa and even Missouri. Upon several occasions the juvenile court workers at St. Joseph, Mo., have sent boys to Father Flanagan in preference to committing the youngsters to a state institution."

The Omaha Daily News Magazine, Sunday, September, 21, 1918.

451 "Later, a group of women formed 'The Mothers' Guild' and came regularly to the Home as volunteers. Among their various contributions of time and labor was a sewing project which took care of mending bedclothes, as well as keeping pants, shirts and boyish underthings in good repair.." Willets, op. cit., Ch. 7, pg. 9.

452 "One woman provided tableware and silverware so that 'Father Flanagan could eat decently.'" Oursler, Working Notes, Ch. 21, Item 15.

453 "Another activity of that early time was a misguided experiment in soapmaking. This was carried on by the boys, in a small factory set up in the yard. When the soap was finished, the boys wrapped the cakes in colored paper, while others, constituting their 'sales force,' peddled it in a door-to-door campaign. Results, however, were so meager, and profits so slight, that Flanagan ordered that any soap made in the future would be for their own exclusive use." Oursler, op. cit., Ch. 19, pg. 167. In the 1921 Omaha City Directory, Father Flanagan was listed as president of the Sanitary Soap Products Company.

454 "Kate sold him a $5.000.00 insurance policy – 20 year endowment. Recently an insurance agent called at the office in Boys Town and handed Father a check for $6,000.00, payment in full of the policy sold him by Kate." Willets, Working Notes, Ch. 6, pg. 39, 1943.

455 Article in the *Omaha World-Herald* by Bill Billotte, from an interview with Catherine Dannehy, 1957.

456 Ibid.

457 "Young men and women who lived in the neighborhood manifested a keen personal interest in the Home and its progress. They helped out in many ways. One group came in the evenings and offered their services in any manner that Father wished to use them. Since there were no typewriters or office equipment, and considerable mail to be handled, these volunteers gladly undertook the task of writings letters in longhand and attending to other clerical duties." Willets, op. cit., Ch. 7, pg. 8.

458 "New home, new needs, new expenses and the costs of moving: all these stirred Miss Robina Kammerer to give another of her famous parties. And so on the 17th at our hall, a goodly number gathered and enjoyed themselves, while adding to the needed funds of Father Flanagan's Boys' Home. Miss Kammerer, of course, was ubiquitous and everyone… enjoyed themselves. Those who liked a progressive card game had a good long game and above on the dancing floor the light-toed danced and ate sweets to their heart's content.

"The popularity contest between the Misses Lucille Drier, Della Vanchai and Margaruite Dooley, closed at midnight, with Miss Vachal in the lead. The heat was forgotten by all who were fortunate to be present, for the joy of the event overshadowed everything else. The excellent work of Miss Kammerer cannot be too highly commended and should inspire others to follow in her footsteps." *Boys' Home Journal*, June, 1918, pg. 7.

459 "A number of prominent ladies of the city visited the Home a couple of weeks ago, under the leadership of Mrs. E.W. Nash and Mrs. C.W. Hamilton, and were pleased with the surroundings and especially the beautiful and spacious building. From remarks made by them, we feel that something is going to be done to put the Home on a more permanent and stable basis." *Boys' Home Journal*, June, 1918, pg. 7. From other sources it is known that Mrs. Nash made a gift of $10,000 to the Home and became one of Father Flanagan's most generous benefactors and a loyal friend.

460 *His Lamp of Fire*, pg. 70.

461 Ibid., pg. 71.

462 Ibid., pgs. 71-73.

463 *Boys' Home Journal*, November, 1919, pgs. 12-13. "Howard is a handsome boy, though a sad victim of infantile paralysis. He is very shy and of a quiet disposition… he laughs frequently when in the company of the boys who are not rough and who are willing to play with him in his own way."

464 "Howard, 9, is a cripple, the victim of infantile paralysis. His mother brought him to the Home a year ago. A week later

she left the city. He has heard no word from her since. Howard is the only cause for a quarrel among the other boys. They will fight with each other for the privilege of carrying him. For the little cripple cannot walk alone." *The Omaha Daily News Magazine*, Sunday, September 21, 1919.

465 "Howard Loomis may not be quite as spry as some of our boys…; but nevertheless you should have seen him get over the ground at the Catholic Daughters of America picnic at Krug Park (a photo shows Howard being carried by another boy). Reuben Ganger is the lucky 'horse' in the picture, but it is only by clever strategy that he obtained the role for there is a continual 'battle' among our older boys for the privilege of carrying little Howard." *Boys' Home Journal*, September, 1921, pg. 11.

466 *His Lamp of Fire*, pgs. 75-76.

467 Willets, op. cit., Ch. 7, pgs. 27-30.

468 "At ten o'clock in the morning, two ladies came to the German Home. They seemed to be very fine ladies, and after visiting with them a little while I knew who they were. The one was from Cedar Rapids, Nebraska, who was seeking a baby girl to adopt. The other was her sister, who helped her. I told her that this was a strange coincidence that I had a very beautiful baby, a sister of two of my boys, whom I had taken last night from an abandoned apartment, and I immediately turned this baby over to this mother." Working Notes of Willets, from a conversation with Father Flanagan, 1943.

469 "The School was honored this month by a visit of Mother Qualberta of the order of Nostra Domina, whose Sisters are the good angels in charge of our Boys. Mother Qualberta was quite pleased with the work of our Sisters (nothing else could be expected, of course), and so expressed herself." *Boys' Home Journal*, June, 1918, pg. 8.

470 "Under the care of Miss Lenore Norton our boys are being kept at their school work, two classes each morning and afternoon, while the others are at work or at the Manual Training." Ibid. June, 1918, pg. 12.

471 Lenore Norton was the daughter of Father Flanagan's older sister, Mary Jane, and came to the United States in 1906 with John and Nora Flanagan. She was educated in Ireland, New York City, and Omaha, and on graduation from St. Mary's Academy, worked for her uncle at the German-American Home as a teacher. She was the sister of Patrick Norton, who later became Father Flanagan's assistant, manager, and purchasing agent.

472 "Our School, through the kindness of Mrs. E.W. Nash, has been equipped for Manual Training, and classes under the guidance of Miss Bessie are at work each day." Ibid.

473 "A kind friend of the boys too modest to be known, sent two tickets for the Paulist Choristers entertainment, marked 'For two good boys.' Why, we had so many that we were simply compelled to draw lots and two happy boys went to bed late on Tuesday night." Ibid.

474 *Boys Town: Revolution in Child Care*, by Msgr. Robert P. Hupp: "Most notable of those who stepped forth were two professional men, close personal friends, and they were: Dr. Harry Sullivan, a medical doctor, and Dr. Henry Schultz, a dentist. They came to Father Flanagan and offered their services. A couple of years ago when visiting Dr. Schultz, I inquired of him the extent of the services they offered. He said, in his dry inimitable way: 'We took good care of all the boys. Harry cut out their tonsils and I pulled their teeth.' And this free service they continued for many years." Foreword, pg. vii.

475 Cf. "Our Elocutionary Class," *Boys' Home Journal*, January, 1920, pg. 16.

476 Cf. "Our Elocutionary Class," *Boys' Home Journal*, January, 1920, pg. 16.

477 Oursler, op. cit., Ch. 22, pg. 186.

478 *Boys' Home Journal*, August, 1918, pg. 2.

479 "Sometimes Father Flanagan does not know from whence the boys come. Recently two small youngsters were placed on a train 'somewhere in Iowa' – they didn't know the name of the town. The lads wore tags marked 'Father Flanagan's Home, Omaha,' and their fare was in their pockets." *The Omaha Daily News Magazine*, Sunday, September 21, 1918.

480 "Murphy told of the time Father addressed the Texas cattlemen… who paid him the strictest attention, and then offered him

($50,000) a year... and Father was all smiles until they qualified the donation by saying he must NOT have any n------. He rejected the cattlemen's offer which would have given him all the money he needed." Notes of Will & Fulton Oursler for their book, *Father Flanagan of Boys Town*. Boys Town Archives.

481 Oursler, op. cit., Ch. 19, pg. 169.

482 Ibid.

483 "Pastor of St. Rose's Church from January 1919 to June 1919, when I paid off the debt of $5500 and outstanding bills of from $500 to $1000, bought pews and had the altar decorated, which altar was given by Father P.A. Bought necessary church furniture (This was in the German Home)." Statement of Father Flanagan to Gilson VanderVeer Willets, Boys Town Archives, 1943.

484 Willets, op. cit., Ch. 7, pg. 6.

485 *Boys' Home Journal*, September, 1918, pg. 2.

486 *Boys' Home Journal*, October, 1918, pg. 5.

487 Ibid. "Through the attention given the boys by Dr. J.R. Dwyer, who so generously gave of his precious time each day, to visit us, the boys had splendid treatment, and through the self-sacrificing efforts on the part of our dear Sister Rose, nothing was left undone that our boys might recover."

488 "On Saturday, about noon, one of our boys, Joseph Guerin, died at the home of pneumonia. Joseph was the oldest boy at the Home, and was loved by all the boys, to whom he endeared himself by his kindness and gentleness of disposition.... The pall-bearers were six boys from the Home: Leo Beninato, Harold Goddard, Charles Dailey, Matthew Lynch, Sebastino Circo, and James Hammon." Ibid.

489 "The boys of Father Flanagan's Boys' Home are going to make everyone happy who visits New Krug Park Wednesday, June 18, on which date the Home will hold an all-day picnic. Field sports of all kinds, as well as other special features, will be given by the boys of the Home in competition, under the charge of a popular sporting promoter, and the games will be in charge of the sporting editors of the Omaha newspapers....

"The management of the park also intends to supply special entertainment features on that day, as this will be the first large and popular picnic of the season.

"Here will be a chance to study our fine company of manly boys at close range, and we guarantee to furnish agreeable surprises to people who are not familiar with the workings of the Home." *Boys' Home Journal*, June, 1919, pg. 2.

490 Ibid., July, 1919, pg. 3.

491 Ibid.

492 "One of the most pleasant events of the day took place on the stage, preceding the evening boxing contests, when Master 'Jack' O'Connor, the very popular and winsome juvenile actor, made a cute little speech to the assembled boys, outlining to them how it was possible that one of them might become president of the United States someday. Little Jack certainly made a great hit with the boys, who want to see him again soon. At the close of his speech, he sang a popular song, which was encored." *Boys' Home Journal*, July, 1919, pg. 5.

493 Ibid., pg. 5.

494 Louis Ray Bostwick was born in Mattoon, Illinois, on May 11, 1868, the son of Charles Bostwick and Cynthia Ann Patrick. He was educated at Mattoon High School, Whipple Academy in Jacksonville, Illinois, and Illinois College in Jacksonville, from which he graduated in 1890. In 1890-91, he worked at the *Evening Times* in Denver, Colorado, and from 1891-93 in the circulation department of the *Denver Republican*. From 1893-98, he worked for the *Chicago Tribune* and the *Chicago Times Herald*. From 1808-1900, he was employed by the photography department of the *New York World*. From 1900-07, he was staff photographer for the Bee Publishing company in Omaha, Nebraska. In 1907, he became the owner and operator of Louis R. Bostwick photography business in Omaha. rootsweb.ancestry.com.

495 Cf. *How the Other Half Lives*, by Jacob A. Riis, Charles Scribner's Sons, New York, 1890. Dover Publications edition, 1971.

496 In the Boys Town Archives are photos from Jacob Riis's book, with its graphic

depiction of the slums of New York City at the turn of the 20th century, just as young Eddie Flanagan had viewed them during his seminary days at Dunwoodie, enroute to the tubercular hospitals of the city. He may have remembered Riis's photographs and wanted to show Bostwick the power of images and the kind of photos that he wanted to record the life of his boys.

497 One set of photos in a local newspaper of boys with pets ran this caption: "Four-footed pets play a prominent role in a boy's life at Father Flanagan's home. Herbert, 8, the 'baby' of the Home, found the bunny a great help in becoming acclimated upon his arrival from Lincoln, Neb. this week. 'Dutchie,' whose perpetual smile has made him the sunbeam of the Home, prefers Carlo, the Scottish collie, above all other pets. Robert is an enthusiast with all his four-footed friends and spends all his spare time helping to care for them. The lamb is especially attached to him. A goat, a big sheep, pigeons, and a canary are included in the Home's 'menagerie.'" *The Omaha Daily News Magazine*, Sunday, September 21, 1919.

498 The Durham Heritage Museum in Omaha has a collection of 70,000 photos of Bostwick's work, a small portion of which is the Boys Town collection. There are others in the Boys Town Archives and Hall of History, a remarkable record of Father Flanagan's early days and his passion to change the view of the nation about the homeless boy.

499 Cf. *The Good Fight: The Life and Times of Ben B. Lindsey*, by Charles Larsen, Quadrangle Books, Chicago, 1972.

500 He was always ready to highlight the talents of his boys, whether in sports, scholastic achievement, music, etc. The picnic at Krug Park displayed the acting talents of one of the boys, who seemed to be the hit of the picnic. "One of the most pleasing events of the day took place on the stage preceding the evening boxing contests, when Master 'Jack' O'Connor, the very popular and winsome juvenile actor, made a cute little speech to the assembled boys, outlining to them how it was possible that one of them might become president of the United States someday. Little Jack certainly made a hit with the boys, who want to see him

again soon. At the close of his speech, he sang a popular song, which was encored." *Boys' Home Journal*, July, 1919, pg. 5.

501 The finest embodiment in writing of the tradition of the Seanchai is the novel, *Ireland*, by Frank Delaney (Harper/Collins, 2005). The novel shows the effect on a young boy of the "storytelling" of the Seanchai, and the rapt attention of those who listened to his stories. Delaney's novel was written many years after Father Flanagan 's time, but it is clear that the priest was deeply ingrained in this tradition.

502 Cf. "Our Elocutionary Class," *Boys' Home Journal*, January, 1920, pg. 16. "Our boys are learning daily the art of elocution and it is remarkable how well they speak... it gives him a powerful mastery over his expressions and assists him to direct his talents in a channel both artful and persuasive.... The boys enjoy this training and judging from the manner of their acting and their efforts to learn this art, we feel that they will one day show up well in their knowledge of this dramatic art."

503 A photo of the Boy Actor "Jack" O'Connor, in character, appeared on page 9 of the *Boys' Home Journal* for July, 1919.

504 *Boys' Home Journal*, April, 1919, pg. 2.

505 Ibid.

506 Ibid. In later years it was well-known that whenever Father Flanagan approached his friend, Henry Monsky, about some step he was about to take and how much it would cost, his friend would reply, "Eddie, what have you got yourself into," and then help him to raise the money.

507 *The Omaha Sunday Bee*, September 8, 1918. Also *The Omaha Daily News Magazine*, Sunday, September 21, 1919.

508 "Father Flanagan and the Sisters of the Boys' Home take this form of thanking each and all of the benefactors of the Home, in which ever manner they have shown their kindness and thoughtfulness. Donations of food are always welcome and can be readily made. Also, garments of any kind suitable for boys aged from six to fifteen. In August, Mayor Smith delighted the boys with a fine treat of watermelons. In the same month Mrs. Fred Nash sent the Home a beautiful

supply of ice cream for a feast occasion. Both the donors were lauded for their kind remembrance." *Boys' Home Journal*, September, 1919, pg. 2.

509 "Boys Will Be Boys," *Boys' Home Journal*, April, 1919, pg. 5: "The normal boy is practically the same the world over, and the old saying that 'boys will be boys' holds good in this day and age, as well as it did when was first expressed in condoning a fault.

"The prime fact in nature is to understand the boy and study his temperament; the moulding of his character thereafter becomes a simple problem…, excepting in unusual circumstances. We may take, for example, the various types of boys gathered in the Boys' Home. Some are placed there for safe keeping by either, or both parents, or by order of the juvenile court, solely because the parents cannot live together in compatible harmony, or the parents of the boy have died and left no one to take care of the child.

"The boys in most of these instances are bright, manly, and likeable little fellows, and the majority, so it is learned, are making good progress in their studies. The same may also be truthfully be said of a number of boys that have been sent to the Home, from time to time, as incorrigibles. Latent instinct is soon developed, once they come to realize that they are amongst friends and well-wishers, and the natural good qualities that are within practically every human being, come to the surface, with the result that under the kind, patient, watchful and persevering care of the Reverend Director and the good Sisters in charge of these boys, even the most fractious soon become subject to ready obedience and the discipline of the Home, which is maintained at all times.

"This Home has no semblance whatever of that of a correctional institution, but is rather like a large family school, and it is certainly a pleasure to watch the boys, either at their studies or in their classes in the schoolroom, or at play on the big grass carpeted lawn within the home grounds.

"And as they are watched at school and at play, and studied individually and collectively, the thought impresses itself, how fortunate these boys are to be provided with a home with such helpful surroundings. And again, the more one becomes acquainted with these boys, the better he likes them, and, instead of finding dross in the crucible, many of the finest little characters imaginable are discovered, who give every promise of becoming highly useful men, and they receive the proper encouragement at the Home to make the most of themselves, which has always proved the best initiative to any boy."

510 "The boys at the Home come from many nationalities, and different conditions of life, before entering this Home, but they compose a remarkably contented family, from the fact that, as a whole, there is little or no quarreling among them at any time, and they give their attendants no more concern than any similar body of healthy school boys." *Boys' Home Journal*, April, 1919, pg. 8.

511 "The first match ball game of the season between the Home team and St. Rose parish, which was played on the home grounds April 27, was won by Father Flanagan's by the score of 6-5. Kalina and Kelly were the Home battery against Anton Weine of the St. Rose team. The Home team is open for games with any club of boys 12 to 15 years of age for Saturday or Sunday afternoons." *Boys' Home Journal*, April, 1918, pg. 8.

512 Ibid. "Spring is here, and the garden of the Home, though the ground is well prepared, still needs many things to be confided into its bosom, to grow and bear fruit for the benefit and enjoyment of the boys. There goes for appeal from Father Flanagan and his helpers, to all those who are well equipped and have a great surplus left to assist the Home with seeds, young plants, utensils, or anything else, for everything is needed now, as the number of boys is continually increasing."

513 Ibid. "Our boys will celebrate Decoration Day by having a grand parade around the yard, the two boys in their soldier suits leading the whole bunch. Should anyone have some Boy Scout suits and not need them, they would be very happy to have some more."

514 "The annual Lawn Social at St. Patrick's parish was held at Rourke Park Wednesday evening, August 20. At the invitation of

lawyer William P. Lynch, a strong friend of the Home, a number of boys possessing musical and other talents, were selected to attend the social and aid in supplying entertainment to the merry-makers. Choruses, duets and solos were rendered as well as elocutionary displays by some of the boys. A highly entertaining feature of the evening was a three round boxing bout by two of the boys from the Home.

"The boys as usual conducted themselves nicely, and entered fully into the spirit of the occasion. They were the recipients of much attention from the visitors to the park and received unstinting applause on every occasion. The appearance of the boys at the festival seemed to be a popular hit and they were given extra attention by the ladies in charge who supplied them liberally with good things to eat.

"A large gift box was also made up for the boys at the Home which was taken charge of by the performers when they returned to the Home at the close of the entertainment." Ibid., September, 1919, pg. 18.

515 "The Omaha City Council has appointed Rev. E.J. Flanagan a member of the Public Welfare Board of Omaha in succession to Frank Kennedy." Ibid., June, 1919.

516 "Rev. E.J. Flanagan, Director of the Boys' Home, attended the annual convention of the National Catholic Hospital Association, which was held in Chicago, June 25th, 26th and 27th. During the convention Father Flanagan met directors and representatives of hospitals from all over the country and made many new acquaintances." Ibid., July, 1919, pg. 7.

517 Reilly & Warneke, op. cit., Ch. 4, pg. 56.

518 Boys' Home Journal, August, 1919, pg. 2.

519 Ibid.

520 Ibid.

521 Cf. Upstream Metropolis: An Urban Biography of Omaha & Council Bluffs, by Lawrence H. Larsen, Barbara J. Cottrell, Harl A. Dalstrom, and Kay Calame Dalstron, University of Nebraska Press, 2007, pg. 219.

522 Ibid., pgs. 230-236. Also, Political Bossism in Mid-America: Tom Dennison's Omaha: 1900-1933, by Orville D. Menard, pgs. 110-116.

523 Plains Crusader: C.A. Sorensen's Assault on Organized Crime and the Political Machine in Omaha, by Juliet Sorensen. Nebraska History. Volume 96, Number 3, Fall, 2015, pgs. 110-121.

524 Cf. The Gate City: A History of Omaha, by Lawrence H. Larsen and Barbara J. Cottrell, University of Nebraska Press, pgs. 181-183.

525 Boys' Home Journal, September, 1919, pg. 2.

526 George Helgesen Fitch was an author, humorist, and journalist, whose books and newspaper columns satirized urban America. From 1910, he penned a syndicated column for the George Matthew Adams news service called "Vest Pocket Essays." He died in 1915.

527 Vest Pocket Essays, by George Fitch, Barse & Hopkins, Publishers, New York, 1916, pg. 123.

528 Boys' Home Journal, September, 1919, pg. 2.

529 Lawrence Larsen, et al., op. cit., pgs. 219-222.

530 Ibid.

531 "The first farm Father Flanagan acquired was in the Florence area on the northern edge of Omaha. He bought it for fourteen thousand dollars in September, 1919, according to the warranty deed. The land, which was formerly a chicken farm, included twenty acres and was called Seven Oaks Farm. He immediately started to raise money to build up the property." Reilly & Warneke, op. cit., Ch. 4, pg. 56.

532 Ibid., October, 1919, pg. 2.

533 Ibid., December, 1919, pg. 2.

534 Omaha-World Herald, undated article, 1918, by Bill Billotte: "Mrs. Dannehy worked for Father Flanagan from 1918 to 1919, and then had to quit to take care of her household duties."

535 We know the names of two young ladies who took over the secretarial work after he lost Catherine Dannehy. One, Agnes Barta, remained with him until September of 1920, when she entered the Notre Dame Sisters as a novice. The other, Gertrude Welch, remained with him until April of 1921, and she, too, entered the Notre Dame Sisters.

536 *Omaha World-Herald.*

537 "The Commissary, Sr. M. Gualbaerta... stayed with the Sisters at Father Flanagan's Boys' Home. There by chance she learned that Father Flanagan planned to sell his ten-acre farm in Florence, in the northern part of Greater Omaha and buy a larger farm. The Superior thought much of this, and gladly accepted the invitation of Father Flanagan to go with him and the local superior to see both farms in Florence. The weather that day was very unfavorable; there were about two inches of snow on the ground and it was snowing steadily, but even at that it was possible to judge that the small 'Seven Oakes Poultry Farm' would be very suitable for a novitiate and perhaps for a future motherhouse. The high, healthy site, an abundance of ornamental and fruit trees with enough ground for the cultivation of forage and vegetables, several well-kept buildings, a nice residence equipped with city water, electricity, a furnace, not too far distant from the parish church and the street car – it seemed as if it was all created for our needs. The Sister Commissary well remembered that the deceased Rev. Mother M. Cyrilla used to say from her experience that a motherhouse is best situated on the outskirts of a large city so that there could be a sufficiency of fresh air, tranquility and home produce, and yet at the same time, enjoy the advantages of a city such as: good clergy, schools, hospitals, stores, etc. All this was concentrated in Florence. The worst was the price. Rev. Flanagan had to have the money for the small farm so that he would be able to buy the forty acres; moreover, we did not have permission for such an important act from the motherhouse. Meanwhile, we dared to take another step. We managed to scrape up the $14,000 which Father Flanagan had paid for the farm and hence asked the same from us. We loaned the money to him at 4% interest until that time when a decision would come from the motherhouse. That came on February 24, 1920; we, however, we did not take over the property until in March at Easter time." Records of the Sisters of Notre Dame, Omaha, Nebraska, 1919-1920, pgs. 38-39.

538 Willets, op. cit., Ch. 7, pgs. 33-34.

539 "(Pat) Norton took charge of the home's 40 acre farm near Forest Lawn Cemetery in Florence. He used to drive wagon loads of boys out to pick berries and vegetables." *Omaha World-Herald*, interview with Pat Norton. Date unknown.

540 "Our Home is leased until June 1st of this year, and on that day our boys must leave here, as the building has been sold for other purposes. Realizing this, we have secured an option on a forty acre farm most beautifully situated and at a very reasonable price. To collect sufficient money to buy this farm, and put up a substantial building for our boys is a stupendous work for the year 1920. According to rough estimates this program will cost about two hundred thousand dollars. With the successful completion of this program the Home will be able to care for thousands of boys annually instead of a hundred." *Boys' Home Journal*, January, 1920, pg. 2.

541 *Boys' Home Journal*, February, 1920, pg. 3.

542 By the time the mayor's letter was written, his administration was in shambles, in the wake of the public race riot that led to the murder of George Brown, an African-American who was accused of attacking a white woman. It was the most shameful event in the history of the city and the mayor's letter may have been an attempt to salvage something of decency and something of compassion for his administration. The graphic description of the hanging and mutilation of George Brown in the "Upstream Metropolis" is sick and saddening and the event occurred at the same time that Father Flanagan was arranging for the purchase of Seven Oaks Farm. An editorial note in the October issue of the *Boys' Home Journal* may have been in response to hate mail received from persons who opposed the presence of African-American boys in his Home:

"Anonymous letters find no place in our file and receive no attention from us whatsoever. Anyone having something to say in criticism of the policy of our Home, or our Journal – the organ of the Home – is at perfect liberty to do so, but please do so in a manly and honorable manner, and do not hide behind the degrading non-deplume of the anonymous." *Boys' Home Journal*, October, 1919, pg. 2.

543 "To this noble hearted woman comes the great distinction of being the first to make this great dream of ours, 'Our New Home,' a reality. Mrs. Nash... has given our Home the magnificent sum of $10,000.00 that we might find a place for the poor and neglected boys. She and she alone deserves the credit for our impetus in this most necessary movement, for without this encouragement, we should have never dreamed of this great project." Ibid., March, 1920, pg. 7.

544 "Just a few short months ago, one of Omaha's most noble ladies, visited our Home, and spent several hours with our boys.... just a few days before she died, we were summoned to her bedside and there... she handed us a check for Twenty-Thousand dollars as a nucleus for our Building Fund." Ibid., April, 1920, pg. 2.

545 Ibid., March, 1920, pg. 2.

546 "I am afraid Father Flanagan was a nuisance to the good merchants and professional men of Omaha during those lean years. I begged in the daytime, tried my best to mother the boys at night. Somehow I kept going." Remarks of Father Flanagan to the journalist Don Sharkey, about 1941. Boys Town Archives.

547 *The Gate City: A History of Omaha*, by Lawrence H. Larsen and Barbara J. Cottrell, pgs. 174-176.

548 Ibid., March, 1920, pg. 2.

549 Ibid.

550 Like this one from the President of the Lion Bonding & Surety Company, *Boys' Home Journal*, February, 1920, pg. 3: "I will subscribe $500.00, payable $100,00 each year, say on July 1st of each year, beginning with 1920 towards the Florence project. I will put you on my payment list and will send you a check of $10.00 about the first of each month for current expenses. I am not sure that I will be able to keep up this sum permanently, but I will be glad to help all I can.

"The Lion Bonding & Surety Company will carry a card in the *Home Journal*, paying $5.00 per month hereafter."

551 "In the course of a talk to our boys of the Home, some weeks ago, Mr. E.R. Gurney, President of the Lion Bonding Company here, spoke of the value of investment and the care and prudence with which prospective investors should act. Some investments are worthless, and others are most productive in dividends to the investors. The greatest investment of all is that in which unselfish and broad-minded citizens place their money in the up-building and welfare of down-trodden humanity, particularly the most helpless of these, the poor and neglected children. 'These children,' he said, 'if properly cared for are worth millions and millions of dollars to this country's welfare, by reason of their material production alone, not to speak of the unseen value they would be to society.'" *Boys' Home Journal*, April, 1920, pg. 2.

552 *Boys' Home Journal*, February, 1920, pgs. 7-8.

553 Letter from the Chamber of Commerce to the Public Welfare Board of the City of Omaha, signed by W.A. Ellis, Assistant Commissioner. *Boys' Home Journal*, March, 1920, pg. 5.

554 "One of the first boys received into his care was James Toth. James was found wandering along the river banks in Omaha, where he had been brought from St. Paul by a woman who had since neglected and abandoned him. When the attention of Father was brought to this boy, he found that James was suffering from hunger, thirst, and in rags, for the poor lad had realized that no one cared for him and had no place to go. He wanted to make something out of himself and grow up to be a real man, to take his place in the business activities of today... a few short years had developed James into a real young man, and it is with deep regret that Father sent him back to his mother on Thursday, February 19th." Ibid., March, 1920, pg. 6.

555 'Several of the boys from the Home have been placed with farmers in the country and all, so far as is known, are reported as 'making good.' Every farmer who calls at the Home remarks at the brightness of the boys." Ibid., April, 1919, pg. 8.

Later, Father Flanagan stopped the practice of boy adoptions or placing boys on farms. He found that often the boys were wanted, not for their welfare, but for some personal advantage of farm or family. Often, farm couples would come and become enchanted with a boy in spring or early summer, and then would return him to the Home when the summer was over, having worked the boy all summer.

556 "A few days ago, a certain wealthy resident gave a scholarship to an eastern college that is yet to be erected. And the happy inspiration came to us that perhaps some reader of the Journal would give a like scholarship, or even a tenth of it, for our new home, which has for its only purpose the education and training of the poor boys that never had a chance. Out of our present humble quarters, we have three boys studying at college and fitting themselves, God willing, for the future ministry of the priesthood." Ibid., March, 1920, pg. 2.

These boys, probably studying at Conception Seminary in Conception, Missouri, apparently did not continue studying for the priesthood. The first of Father Flanagan's boys to study and be ordained a priest was Henry Sutti, who arrived at the Home in 1920. After college, he joined the Jesuits, was ordained in 1939, and spent fifty years as a missionary in British Honduras.

557 "Preliminary plans are under way for the enlargement of Father Flanagan's Boys' Home, now located at 4206 South Thirteenth Street, where 100 boys, wards of the court, are educated and trained for citizenship. A forty-acre tract has been purchased north of Florence, and the home will be moved there when the present lease expires, June 1.

"Plans for a building to house 200 boys have been completed, but must now be altered, as the establishment will be erected to care for 600 boys. Widespread interest in this campaign for the salvation of unfortunate boys, is being felt throughout the state. Hence the enlarged program for this farmhouse." Undated article in an Omaha newspaper, 1921.

558 "(Tom) Murphy told of the time Father addressed the Texas cattlemen – who paid him the strictest attention, and then offered

him $50,000 a year... and Father was all smiles... until they qualified the donation by saying he must not have any n_____." Notes of Gilson VanderVeer Willets, from an interview with Tom Murphy, an Omaha banker, who arrived in Omaha before the Flanagan family and claimed to be a native of the Flanagans' home village of Ballymoe in Ireland.

559 Ibid., March, 1920, pg. 6.

560 "The future of Father Flanagan's Boys' Home looks indeed very discouraging at the present time. The lease on the Home (expires) on June 1st of this year – just a few more months and we must vacate with our poor boys at that time. To turn these poor boys loose, and have them go out in the cold, dark world again, without friends, without money, and without guidance, would be deplorable, yes, and it would be criminal." Ibid., pg. 12.

561 "Father Flanagan's Boys' Home was incorporated on February 18, 1920. The first Board of Directors consisted of Jeremiah J. Harty (Bishop of Omaha); Augustine M. Colaneri (V.G.); Dan W. Gaines; Otto H. Marmettler; Rev. E.J. Flanagan. The Name of the Corporation shall be "FATHER FLANAGAN'S BOYS' HOME." Article 1, Articles of Incorporation, Father Flanagan's Boys' Home.

562 "Articles of Incorporation, Father Flanagan's Boys' Home," Article 5.

563 "Father kept some live stock on this property, such as cows, chickens, etc.... there was a small farmhouse on it... and he would have outings, picnics, etc. there. On one occasion (he) had a group of priests including the Bishop for a dinner there." Willets, Working Notes for his unpublished manuscript.

564 "We see the entourage of the Rev. E.J. Flanagan, then 35, about to join the Ak-Sar-Ben Floral Parade, Tuesday, Sept. 20, 1921, which started south from 16th and Cuming Streets at 2 p.m. A similar picture was in the World-Herald the next morning. The 100 or so boys... and their gateway arches are headed east on Izard Street, parallel to the Holy Family Church." Omaha Sun, October 26, 1978, in an article entitled "History in Photos," with a photo of Father Flanagan and his boys on parade.

565 "Many were the admiring looks cast at the long, long trail of boys entrusted to the tender care of Rev. E.J. Flanagan, and the crowds of people practically marveled at the picturesque Puritan costumes which added greatly to the festivity of the occasion. We are proud to say that the most prominent ladies of Omaha lent their helping hand to sew the outfits, and were as enthusiastic over their work as the boys were anxious to boost Omaha on this Omaha's greatest day." *Boys' Home Journal*, October, 1920, pg. 2.

566 *Boys' Home Journal*, May 1920, p. 2. The front cover of the *Journal* had a picture of his boys, flags flying, for the American Day Parade. He was intent to keep his boys in the public eye.

567 "In the fall of 1919, Father Steiger of Earling, Iowa, called his friend, Father Flanagan, and asked that he send the boy who makes speeches on behalf of the Home to visit him for a weekend in Earling.

"On the following Sunday, Father Steiger introduced me to his congregation after each Mass and asked me to speak to them. I told them about Father's work in caring for homeless, wayward and abandoned boys. I told of current hardships and the seemingly endless struggles to keep the doors open and Father's dream alive.

"I was surprised when Father Steiger took up a collection for the Home after each speech.

"When I returned home on Monday, I handed Father Flanagan an envelope containing more than eleven hundred dollars, mostly checks. Father was amazed and overjoyed. He couldn't believe it. I explained what had happened and told Father of Father Steiger's suggestion that with a few boys who could sing and make recitations, we could travel from town to town telling our story and taking up collections.

"A few weeks later, Father Flanagan spoke to all his boys assembled in the dining room. He told them of his plan to have several of the boys who could sing or recite, travel in a group from town to town giving a free show and asking people for help in keeping the Home open.

"He asked all of those who wanted to try out for this trip to remain seated and the others were excused.

"After several weeks of intensive training and rehearsals, the boys were selected for the first trip. The others continued rehearsing with the promise of going on future trips.

"Our show was an immediate success and Father said: 'We have found a way to keep our doors open.'

"On each succeeding trip, more songs, more recitations and jokes were added. Later a twenty minute movie depicting life at the Home became the highlight of our show. It was called *Roes for Thorns*. The number of boys varied from six to twelve.

"Part of the success of our traveling show may have been due to the lack of competition. There was no radio or television.

"Most of the smaller towns had no movies. Medium-sized towns had a movie once a month and possibly a school play once a year. But even in the larger towns and cities, we were welcomed with open arms and urged to return soon. The newspaper called us the 'World's Greatest Juvenile Entertainers.'

"I was on most of these trips. I told the audiences of Father Flanagan's work for boys and his dream of a larger Home to care for hundreds of them – and to make an appeal for funds. The people responded generously.

"A band was formed and made their first trip in 1922. They traveled in beautiful circus type wagons. Their performance consisted of a minstrel show and band concert. It was a much better show than ours but because they charged only 25 cents admission and did not explain Father's work and need of help, they only made expenses.

"However it was the greatest advertising the Home ever had before the movie *Boys Town*." From an account by Charles Kenworthy, the 'Boy Orator,' on the origin of Father Flanagan's traveling roadshow. Boys Town Archives, undated.

568 A regular on these first tours was Charles Kenworthy, who became a spokesman for the Home wherever the troupe entertained.

His eloquence was remarkable and his delivery was one of the hits of the tours.

569 This ad appeared in the *Boys' Home Journal* for January, 1921, pg. 10: "Charity Ball given by the good fathers and mothers of Omaha at the Municipal Auditorium, Wednesday, January 9th, 1921," with this added note: "Father Flanagan's Boys will give a minstrel show lasting 30 minutes preceding the Ball." This is the first recorded appearance of Dan Desdunes' band.

570 "Arrangements are being made for a tour of the Knights of Columbus Councils of the state of Nebraska by a troupe of our boys who already have gained great popularity by the splendid entertainments which they have put on in many of the towns and cities of Nebraska and Iowa. This tour is made at the invitation of the Knights throughout the state, and the Committee appointed at the last Annual State Convention, to take charge of the campaign throughout the state for Father Flanagan's Boys' Home.

"The troupe consists of five of our boys accompanied by Father Flanagan himself, and the program will be made up of many interesting and entertaining features showing the great blessings that our Home has brought to so many poor and unfortunate boys. Accompanied by the entertainment will also be a moving picture of the life at the Home." *Boys' Home Journal*, July, 1920, pg. 2.

571 "Our traveling troupe of boys who have entertained various audiences over the states of Nebraska and Iowa…. are the marvel to all who have had the privilege of listening to them…. We are very proud of our boys, and we are grateful for the splendid reception accorded to them by the good people of the towns and cities so far visited. Ibid., October, 1920, pg. 2.

572 "It is with very great pleasure that we take this opportunity of extending to our very many friends a most cordial invitation to be present at a CHARITY BALL, given by the good fathers and mothers of Omaha, at the Municipal Auditorium, Wednesday, January 19, 1921." Ibid., January, 1921, pg. 10.

573 "The owners of our present rented quarters have informed us that we must vacate just as soon as it is possible, owing to the fact that the building is needed by them for another purpose. We have asked for an extension of the lease, but have been unsuccessful. We are now facing a serious situation, and the only solution to the problem is that we must build, and begin to do so immediately. Our building program will cost about Two Hundred and Fifty Thousand ($250,000.00) Dollars, and this is no easy problem to face with only Fifty Thousand ($50,000.00) on hand." Ibid., May, 1921, pg. 3.

574 "Never before has our Home been as crowded as at the present time. With the beginning of the school year, every available bed was taken and with about twenty-five on the waiting list for admittance. One of the most difficult things that we are compelled to do is to refuse the shelter of our Home to a needy boy, who has no home, no parents, no friends. Still, circumstances are such that we are forced to do this every day….

"The money thus far received would not go far in building a Home to fill our need. We need three hundred thousand dollars ($300,000) to build and equip a Home large enough to care for at least three hundred boys." Ibid., October, 1920, pg. 2.

575 Under the heading, "Frame Resolution to Protest Flanagan Home," an article appeared in the *Omaha World-Herald* in March of 1921 on the move of the Boys' Home to the former Presbyterian Seminary: "Protest against the sale of the Omaha Presbyterian Theological seminary buildings and grounds to Father Flanagan's home for boys have resulted in plans for action by a committee representing eleven churches of the community surrounding the seminary.

"The committee, composed of twenty-one men from these eleven churches, met last night to consider the matter, and framed a resolution voicing their reasons for objecting to the location of the boys' home in the seminary building. The resolution, the committee plans, will be presented to Archbishop Harty of the Catholic diocese." *Omaha World-Herald*, March, 1921.

576 *Omaha-World Herald*, March 15, 1921: "Protests of residents and churches in the

vicinity of the Presbyterian Theological seminary, proposed site for Flanagan's boys home, are due to a mistaken idea of the institution, which they claim is a reformatory, the Rev. Father Edward J. Flanagan, founder... stated yesterday."

577 "Murphy told of the time Father addressed the Texas cattlemen... who paid him the strictest attention, and then offered him $500,000 a year... and Father was all smiles... until they qualified the donation by saying he must not have any n_____. Every time I see a Negro at Boys Town, I think of this noble priest and the alacrity with which he rejected the cattlemen's offer which would have given him all the money he needed." Morris Jacobs, Oursler Notes.

578 Oursler, op. cit., pg. 188.

579 Ibid.

580 "The owners of our present rented quarters have informed us that we must vacate just as soon as it is possible, owing to the fact that the building is needed for other purposes. We have asked them for an extension of the lease, but have been unsuccessful. We are now facing a serious situation, and the only solution of the problem is that we must build, and begin to do so immediately. Our building program will cost about Two Hundred and Fifty Thousand ($250,000.00) Dollars, and this is no easy problem to face with only Fifty Thousand ($50,000.00) on hand." Boys' Home Journal, May, 1921, pg. 3.

581 This conversation with David Baum is from an interview with Father Flanagan by Gilson VanderVeer Willets for his unpublished biography of Father Flanagan in 1943, Ch. 8, pgs. 13-16.

582 "Buy Overlook Farm For Flanagan Home," Omaha World-Herald, May 19, 1921.

Chapter 9: Overlook Farm

583 His Lamp of Fire, by the Rev. E.J. Flanagan. Unpublished manuscript.

584 Al Witcofski, Oral History, Boys Town Archives, pg. 15.

585 Boys Town Archives.

586 "There was a drive to get new buildings to replace the fire traps. They were almost

praying that the old ones would burn so that they could get the insurance money." Boys Town Archives.

587 Boys Town Archives.

588 "On June 14th, our troupe, which has been playing in Colorado, called on Judge Ben B. Lindsey, famous juvenile judge, in Denver." Boys' Home Journal, July, 1921, pg. 4. A photo of Judge Lindsey and the boys appeared on the front cover of this issue of the Journal.

589 Note about Morris Jacobs.

590 "Davidson was a big Shriner, President of a big utilities company. The original drive, conducted by men with an organization that was used to raising funds... fell flat. Then Mr. Jacobs, Mr. Bozell, and Mr. Davidson ran a new campaign and raised the money. During the campaign, Davidson received many anonymous letters, threatening, scolding and abusing him. He actually read these letters at public gatherings." Boys Town Archives.

591 His Lamp of Fire, Chapter IV, pg. 77.

592 Ibid., pg. 78.

593 Ibid., pg. 78.

594 Carlo died in February, 1925, his passing noted in the Boys' Home Journal: "Every dog has its day, and so Carlo, our faithful dog, had his, and passed away after a few days' illness. We are sure that it has been a long time since such sorrow and anxiety surrounded the dying moments of a mere dog. But, dear friends, Carlo was not a 'mere' dog. He was a treasured watch-dog and was loved by every one of the boys here. Father brought him in his pocket to us when our Home opened and since then he has answered every bell with the boys. He met us at the door when we came home from school and greeted us by barking and jumping in welcome. First up in the morning, last to go into his kennel at night, he loved and was loved by everyone of us boys. Faithful guardian, Prince of Dogs, may your rest be long and peaceful and may the example of your life assist us boys in our journey through this world to be ever A FAITHFUL FRIEND." Boys' Home Journal, February, 1925, pg. 8.

595 "In the early days at Overlook, Father lived

in a pre-fabricated old garage building... cold in winter, hot in summer... it had a little potbelly stove that gave it some heat... but not enough... everything was damp... the place had a floor of just plain soil on which the building was erected... rats inhabited it with Father. He paid little attention to them... often I sat in that rickety old building and watched rats scamper across the floor. They ate his books, they made life a misery. He lived in that place almost two years." Morris Jacobs, from notes in the Boys Town Archives.

596 "A small iron stove hungrily consumed great quantities of fuel, but it failed to overcome the chill draft which swept through the place from numerous cracks and openings...." Willets, op. cit., Ch. 8, pg. 32.

597 *Boys' Home Journal*, November, 1933, pgs. 12-13.

598 Ibid., pg. 24.

599 Short bio of Dan Catlett.

600 "Playing before an audience of 300, they have given their performance before no less than 30,000 people in Minnesota." *Boys' Home Journal*, December, 1921, pg. 7.

601 "During the week prior to our drive for $300,000 for a newer building, we were honored by having as our guests at noonday luncheons, the Omaha Women's Club, the Rotary Club, The Advertising-Selling League, the Concord Club, the Kiwanis Club, and the newspaper men of Omaha, and the Campaign Women of South Omaha. Some of our boys acted as traffic directors for the parking of automobiles; others as guides through the different buildings; and still others assisted in serving the luncheons. During lunch, our guests were entertained by our band, our boy orators, and vocalists." *Boys' Home Journal*, December, 1921, pg. 7.

602 "For business conveniences we are maintaining a small office at 514 Thirteenth Street where all business matters in connection with the Home may be transacted." *Boys' Home Journal*, November, 1921, pg. 3.

603 *Boys' Home Journal*, May, 1922. "Our Two Field Agents," with photos.

604 "Mr. Kotek has received a large number of shoemaker tools... something like 100

pairs of old shoes were turned in to be half-soled last month." Ibid., March, 1923, pg. 10.

605 "February 1st our broom factory started business, with Mr. Harry Gates in charge of it. The 7th, 8th and 9th grade boys spend two days a week helping along this line." *Boys' Home Journal*, March, 1923, pg.10.

"For the year 1923 our broom factory put out 2,500 dozen brooms." Ibid. February, 1924, pg. 8.

606 *His Lamp of Fire*, pgs. 79-80.

607 "We have 13 milking cows and they sure keep the boys busy... Virgil Magers has charge of the creamery and it surely keeps him busy washing the separator... we have slaughtered three calves this month and still have two more to go... Bobby Neal has charge of Father's little home and says he likes his job... last month we churned 100 pounds of butter... talk about ice cream, we do enjoy our homemade products. *Boys' Home Journal*, August, 1922, pg. 11.

608 "Baseball! Baseball! Why can't we forget it? Even though we are tired from our daily work, we are not too tired for a game of ball... Our smaller boys seem to take great interest in baseball, and now you will find three baseball diamonds out here instead of one... Robert Prince, our little red-headed boy, believes in stopping the baseball with his nose...." *Boys' Home Journal*, August, 1922, pg. 11.

609 "These are haymaking days on our farm, and our larger boys are enjoying the privilege... Thanks be to God was the fervent prayer that rose from our hearts when the report came about striking a spring of water... Our new laundry will be ready for use before our new Home. Boys, we won't have to be careful in case we stumble in the mud... through the courtesy of the Universal Film Exchange we are furnished with six or seven reels free of charge." *Boys' Home Journal*, July, 1922, pg. 10.

610 Another minor distraction was the fact that unauthorized persons were going through the state collecting money in the name of Father Flanagan's Boys' Home. One was arrested in Madison with all the paraphernalia of the Boys' Home campaign on him. *Omaha Bee*, April 16, 1922.

611 "In most cases they will work far longer hours at harder labor than their strength justify.

"The Supreme Court decision was received with much satisfaction by mill owners.

"It says in effect that little heed can be paid in this country to the bitter cry of the children who are denied their birthright by being caught early in the wheels of industry.

"What do the American people think of a state of law which allows children, who should have a chance to grow up in health, to become cripples through long working hours, before their little bodies can stand the strain?" *Boys' Home Journal*, July, 1922, pg. 9.

These were quotations from other sources, but expressed well Father Flanagan's horror of the misuse and neglect of children in American society. It pre-dated his angry response to the misuse of children in Irish orphanages and youth detention centers in 1946. He was already familiar with the most graphic book on the subject, *The Bitter Cry of Children*, by John Spargo, and a similar work by Judge Ben Lindsey.

Chapter 10: 'The World's Greatest Juvenile Entertainers'

612 *His Lamp of Fire*, by the Rev. E.J. Flanagan. Unpublished manuscript, Ch. IV, pg. 83.

613 Ibid.

614 One of the musicians, Danny Madden, would become an orchestra leader in his own right. After leaving Overlook Farm, he entered the Wisconsin Conservatory of Music in Milwaukee and then organized his own orchestra, which became famous in the area. *Boys' Home Journal*, July, 1930, pg. 9.

615 His mind was also occupied with another first event in the home's history: High School Graduation. Ten of his boys would be leaving and provision had to be made for their futures. *Omaha-World-Herald*, April 14, 1922.

616 Ibid., pg. 84.

617 Ibid., pg. 85.

618 Ibid.

619 *Boys' Home Journal*, April, 1922, pg. 5.

620 *His Lamp of Fire*, pg. 87.

621 Ibid

622 Ibid., pgs. 88-89.

623 "Our team of horses cost more to feed than the boys. We stayed in private homes and every family treated us royally. The boys were perfect gentlemen, too, and always made us proud of them." Interview with Pat Norton, Magazine of the Midlands of the *Omaha World-Herald*, March 15, 1970, pg. 7.

624 Ibid., pg. 89

625 *Boys' Home Journal*, June, 1922, pg. 5.

626 Oscar Flakes, Oral History, Boys Town Archives, December, 1988.

627 Ibid., Boys Town Archives, pg. 10

628 Ibid.

629 *His Lamp of Fire*, pg. 91.

630 Ibid., pg. 93.

631 Oursler, p. 209. *His Lamp of Fire*, pgs. 94-95.

632 Ibid., pg. 97.

633 Ibid., pg. 96.

634 Ibid., pg. 97.

635 Ibid., pgs. 98-99.

636 "Allan, dressed in new clothes, probably for the first time in his life, pulled out of the yards with us that night. He grew up in my Home, finished high school, and is how holding a job in a city far distant from the one where he sold papers and slept in a shack near the tracks." Ibid., pg. 115.

637 Ibid., pgs.101-102.

638 The extent of the journeys of Father Flanagan's troupe during his first years at Overlook indicates the wide scale of his program to change the public's view of the homeless boy: 1922 – South Dakota, Minnesota, Iowa; March, 1923 – Nebraska, Iowa, Missouri, Illinois, South Dakota, Chicago, Milwaukee, St. Paul (MN), Wisconsin. These journeys continued through 1928. Father Flanagan Timeline: Boys Town Archives.

639 "That homeless boys will make good in life when they are given the opportunity to do so is again illustrated by the success of a

Father Flanagan boy, Sam Madden, who left the Home three years ago. Sammy's particular stronghold was music and he was started in that field through Father Flanagan's Boys' Band. When he came to the home at the age of thirteen, things looked pretty 'dark' for him, as he says in his letter. "Sammy, however, soon found new hope and ambition and worked hard. When he left the home three years ago, he was a well-trained boy, full of idealism and courage. Today he has an orchestra of his own, and he is to graduate next year from the Wisconsin Conservatory of Music." *Boys' Home Journal,* August, 1930, pg. 2.

640 "The heartfelt sympathy of all us boys go out to our founder and director in the loss of his beloved father, who died at Omaha, Nebr., on August 13, 1923, at the age of 93 years." Ibid. November, 1923, pg. 3.

641 "Father Gately is more a pal than a dean to the boys. He may be seen running across lawns, the baseball field or at the old English game of Rugby. During the winter months, Rugby teams are organized at the Home with Father Gately as captain of one side and Father Flanagan captain of the other team." Boys Town Archives.

Chapter 11: The Romance of the Homeless Boy

642 "Father Flanagan's Boys' Band, 'the world's greatest juvenile entertainers,' known far and wide for their soul stirring, heart thrilling music, their wonderful orators and unsurpassed singers, returned to Omaha on December 11, after a three thousand mile trip through Iowa, Illinois, Wisconsin and Minnesota, where they 'knocked them over,' and were greeted with enthusiastic audiences at every stop." *Boys' Home Journal,* January, 1924, pg. 8.

643 *How The Other Half Lives,* by Jacob A. Riis. Dover Publications, New York, 1971.

644 Cf. The Bostwick-Frohardt Collection in the Durham Western Heritage Museum's Photo Archive, Omaha, Nebraska.

645 Cf. "Calling a Halt to 'Profiteering in Homeless Boys,'" *Boys' Home Journal,* February, 1926, pg. 9.

Babe Ruth, who had spent his boyhood in an orphanage, joined Father Flanagan in this campaign, as well as the mayor, Senator Norris, and several prominent businessmen. He (Father Flanagan) had been keenly disappointed in the overturning of the Child Labor Law of 1916 by the Supreme Court decision in Hammer v. Dagenhart in 1918, and this was his first attempt to form a national coalition for the protection of homeless children.

646 "Five of our boys went to Conception College. Mr. Barta, Justin Hand, Merl Brehm, Charles Kenworthy and Henry Wiebelhaus." Ibid., pg. 8.

647 Homily by Father Peter Dunne, June 22, 1986, for the 60-year celebration of Father Henry Sutti., S.J., as priest. Boys Town Archives.

648 "Some are little wanderers who, until they came to Boys Town, had never slept in a bed; one helped to rob a Bank, another – that bright-faced honor pupil over there – killed his stepfather with a pitchfork." *Father Flanagan of Boys Town,* by Fulton and Will Oursler, pg. 4.

649 Canon Sheehan was a dynamo of pastoral, literary and political activity in his parish at Doneraile and brought a few minor social miracles for his parishioners, by discreelty making arrangements with English landlords for his parishioners to own their own land on the basis of the Land Purchase Act of 1903. His novels and his example encouraged others to challenge the British occupation of Ireland by careful and discreet application of existing laws. Cf. *Canon Sheehan of Doneraile,* by Herman Joseph Hauser, Longman's, Green & Co., 1917.

650 Cf. *Holmes – Sheehan Correspondence: Letters of Justice Oliver Wendall Holmes, Jr. and Canon Patrick Augustine Sheehan,* edited by David H. Burton, Fordham University Press, 1993.

651 Cf. *Boys' Home Journal,* February, 1926, pg. 6: "Character building Most Important in Education of children."

652 Cf. *Suffer the Little Children,* by Mary Raftery and Eoin O'Sullivan, New Island Books, Dublin, Ireland, 1999, Chapter 8, pgs. 189-197, and Chapter 27.

653 *The Bitter Cry of Children*, by John Spargo, Quadrangle Publications, Chicago, 1968. Originally published by the Macmillan Company, New York, 1906.

654 *Children in Bondage*, by Edwin Markham, Ben B. Lindsey, and George Creel, Hearsts International Library, New York, 1914.

655 It is possible that the new publicity ideas came from his friend, Morris Jacobs, who met Father Flanagan first in the juvenile courts as a police reporter. He became an admirer and friend and after founding the public relations firm of Bozell and Jacobs in 1921, the firm took on Father Flanagan's Boys' Home as a pro bono client.

A "Souvenir" publication on the home appeared in 1925, which was something of a supplement to the *Boys' Home Journal*, with paid ads from local businesses. But that was soon replaced in the same year with *The Romance of the Homeless Boy*, with no ads, a visual masterpiece filled with Bostwick photos and a photographic history of the Home. With this publication, public relations came alive at Boys Town.

656 "Father Flanagan brought 12-year-old Charles Kenworthy from North Platte in 1919. The child's natural speaking ability soon opened a new era of fundraising for the Home. Shortly after his arrival, Charlie accompanied Father to a luncheon where the priest described his work with homeless children. Asked to tell his own story, Charlie complied, and the impact was immediate. This small fellow's story, in his own words, made people listen and contribute. From that day on, Charlie presented a prepared speech at every opportunity." Note in Boys Town Archives.

657 "Our traveling troupe... is carrying with it a splendid film of the Home, and the everyday activities of our boys.... It is a revelation for many who knew of our work, in part, to see this splendid moving picture. It is, too, a work of art and the Chenoweth Film Company of Omaha, who made the picture, deserves to be complimented for their work." *Boys' Home Journal*, August, 1920, pg. 2.

658 Photo with caption: "These are the boys who are playing in Father Flanagan's Boys' Home Radio Band over WOAW every Monday from 5:30 to 6:00 p.m. Ibid., April, 1926, pg. 3.

659 "This month will mark the birth of a new 'city' in Nebraska, which will be governed by a mayor, a city council, and all the municipal trimmings. The name of the new city is 'Boys Town' and its area will include 160 acres, which is now known as Overlook Farm, and upon which is located Father Flanagan's Home." *Boys' Home Journal*, February, 1926, pg. 13.

660 One of the earliest experiments of self-government was the Knights of Honor, a select group of older boys who at first were responsible for keeping order when the priests or nuns were away. This developed into the first election of mayor and commissioners in February of 1926. Boys Town Archives.

661 *Boys' Home Journal*, November, 1926, pg. 12.

662 Cf. *Boys' Home Journal*, March, 1926, pg. 15. "The Knights of Honor meet in their clubroom every Sunday and hold their meetings for the purpose of discussing ways and means to aid Father Flanagan in his noble work."

663 Ibid., March, 1927, pg. 9.

664 Ibid.

665 "Father went to Omaha where he outlined to his architect tentative plans for a new dwelling... a sturdy house with solid walls of hardest brick. When the drawings were ready, Father consulted with his banker with whom satisfactory financial arrangements were completed. A few days later, ground was broken for the residence, which was built in a grove of shade trees at the head of Birch Drive. In March, 1927, Father moved into this home." Willets, op. cit. Ch. 10, pg. 18.

666 "The most prominent ladies of Omaha were very enthusiastic over the beautiful selections so exceptionally rendered by Mr. Michael Flanagan, who, having responded to the invitation of the Mothers' Guild – won the highest admiration of all." *Boys' Home Journal*, January, 1921, pg. 4.

667 "You were on the inside and became a secondary force and father to us to see that we were trained in the right way... with

love and tenderness when called for and firmness when necessary. It was a very difficult endeavor but you were up to the task." Letter of Charles Kenworthy, the Boy Orator, to Pat Norton, May 27, 1976. Boys Town Archives.

668 "Joe McCloud is our best boy violinist.... Harry Meyers and Charles Davis, our youngest violin players, seem to be making great progress with their violins. *Boys' Home Journal*, May, 1922, pg. 9.

669 "The dairy herd of Father Flanagan's Boys' Home during December produced the highest average butterfat record in Douglas County... the Home now has 500 pullets. The flock is giving the Home about 850 eggs weekly... the Home will hatch about 2,500 chicks this spring... the Home gets grapes from its vineyard and cherries from the orchard, which contains 150 apple trees and 75 cherry trees... the boys last year raised 8,376 bushels of corn... real enterprise was shown by the lads, for they rented the Blackwell farm, which adjoins the Home, and raised 6,776 bushels of corn there...." Ibid. February, 1926, pg. 3.

670 "Ted Kenny and Bill Powers are learning to become bakers... they started their lessons last June and are learning their art quickly. Soon Ted and Bill will be able to take the baker's place." Ibid., Feb. 1926, pg. 14.

671 "Joe McCloud, our expert cook, has just taken up the milk business." Ibid.

672 "Bruno Krantz is now our chief engineer. Every Monday morning about 5 o'clock he can be seen hustling towards the laundry. He starts the machines and soon has things going." Ibid.

673 "These boys are skilled musicians; others are becoming skilled printers. Some are being taught secretarial and stenographic work, and during the coming week, we are going to organize a journalist class by which we hope to train these homeless boys to become molders of public opinion, powers for good, future Pulitzers and world journalists." Ibid., January, 1926, pg. 9.

674 *Boys' Home Journal*, February, 1926, p. 15. "Nathan E. Jacobs, a graduate of the School of Journalism, is teaching the lads.... Twelve lads are enrolled."

675 "Boys Town is fast becoming a metropolitan city. During the month, two newspapers made their appearance in town. The first is called *The Snitchbaby*, and was founded by Joseph G. Leslovich, who became editor. Howard Loomis is the publisher. The other is called *Bo-Bo* and is edited and published by Francis Johnson." Boys Town Archives.

676 "Mayor James C. Dahlman and several city commissioners have already promised to help in the organization of Boys Town. Several have offered to permit the boys to spend several days in their offices in the City Hall so that they can become acquainted with their tasks." *Boys' Home Journal*, February, 1926, pg. 13.

677 "Babe Ruth Is An Example to Boys of Home." Ibid., November, 1927, pg. 6.

678 "Tom Mix visits Father Flanagan's Boys' Home." Ibid., May, 1928, pg. 9.

Chapter 12: The Anatomy of Juvenile Crime

679 Riis's chapter on "Waifs in the City's Slums" would certainly have been an echo of Father Flanagan's own experience, and its photos of homeless boys sleeping in dark alleys or rounded up like young criminals would have made him realize that he was faced with a national tragedy. It was becoming clear to him that he would have to work on a national level. His first step in that direction came in 1932, when he was visited by Governor and Mrs. Franklin Roosevelt, during Roosevelt's campaign for president in Omaha. It cemented a friendship that began to shape Father Flanagan's national image.

680 Cf. pgs. 136-137.

681 "In 1916, in what became recognized as the climax to the Progressive Movement, substantial majorities in the House and Senate enacted the Keating-Owens Child Labor Act, which utilized the Commerce Department's power to bar goods made by children from interstate commerce." *Oxford Companion to the Supreme Court of the United States*, p. 359. But in 1918, a divided court, in *Hammer v. Dagenhart*, declared the Keating-Owens Act unconstitutional.

Child labor was finally outlawed in *United States v. Darby Lumber Co.* in 1941.

682 Cf. *River City Empire: Tom Dennison's Omaha*, by Orville D. Menard, University of Nebraska Press, Lincoln, Nebraska, 2013.

683 See Note 583.

684 Jacobs accompanied Father Flanagan on some of his speaking tours and his boys' entertainment tours, and found that some priests were not happy with Father Flanagan's appearance in their towns. Ourlsers, Notes for their book, *Father Flanagan of Boys Town*.

685 Charles Dickens, Preface to the Third Edition of *Oliver Twist*, 1841.

686 *His Lamp of Fire*, by the Rev. E.J. Flanagan. Unpublished manuscript, Ch. VI, pg. 118.

687 Ibid.

688 Ibid., Ch. VI, pg. 120.

689 *Boys' Home Journal*, January, 1928, p. 3. "Father Flanagan Appeals to Governor of Missouri for Two Boys."

690 Ibid., February, 1928, pg. 3. "Father E.J. Flanagan Continues Fight for Release of 'Kid Bandits.'"

691 *Belle Ville, Illinois Advocate*, April 19, 1928.

692 Ibid., May, 1928. "Shetron Boys Paroled from Missouri Reformatory."

693 *The Good Fight: The Life and Times of Ben B. Lindsey*, by Charles Larsen, Quadrangle Books, Chicago, 1972.

694 *Boys' Home Journal*, January, 1928, pg. 3. "Father Flanagan Appeals to Governor of Missouri for Two Boys."

695 Cf. Laura Milhailoff. *Protecting Our Children: The History of the California Youth Authority and Juvenile Justice, 1938-68*, University of California Press, Berkeley, 2006.

696 Judge Lindsey's first experience with the Juvenile Justice system of Denver and Colorado was similar to that of Father Flanagan's with that of Omaha and Nebraska: "An assistant district attorney (asked) the Judge if he would mind taking a couple of minutes to dispose of a simple case of theft. Judge Lindsey agreed, and a trembling teen-ager named Tony Costello was brought before him. Tony was accused of stealing coal alongside railroad tracks on the outskirts of town. The complaining witness was a railroad detective who had caught him red-handed. The boy clearly had no defense against the charge, and was silent when asked what he had to say for himself.

"Lindsey, seeing no alternative, sent him to a term in reform school. As the Judge turned back... the air was suddenly rent by what he later described as 'the most soul-piercing scream of agony that I ever heard from a human throat.' Unknown to Lindsey, Tony's mother had been sitting in back of the courtroom. The pathetically dressed woman tore her hair and continued to shriek as a bailiff forcibly removed her to another part of the building. Lindsey, badly shaken, dismissed the court and retired to his chambers. With the memory of the mother's screams still agitating him, he phoned the district attorney and obtained his consent to suspend Tony's sentence....

"Tony's case did not end there, however. On the same night that he suspended the sentence, Lindsey decided to pay a visit to Tony's 'home.' There in a miserable hovel, he found the boy's father dying from lead poisoning contracted while working twelve hours a day in a smelter. The large family lived in two cold, filthy rooms, which Tony's stolen coal might have helped to warm. Somewhat at a loss for words, Lindsey gave Tony a gentle lecture about obeying the law and informally placed him on probation." *The Good Fight: The Remarkable Life and Times of Judge Ben Lindsey*, by Charles Larson, Quadrangle Books, Chicago, 1972, pgs. 7-9.

697 Ibid., Chapters 1, 2, and 3, pgs. 3-82.

698 *The Good Fight: The Remarkable Life and Times of Judge Ben Lindsey*, Chapter 3: "Fighting the Establishment."

699 *The Beast*, by Ben B. Lindsey and Henry J O'Higgins, Doubleday & Page Co., 1910.

700 Jane Addams: pioneer settlement worker, sociologist, leader in woman suffrage and world peace; founder of Hull House in Chicago; author of *Twenty Years Hull House*; and winner of the Nobel Peace Prize in 1931. One of the major figures in the Progressive Movement in the United States.

701 Florence Kelley: social and political

reformer; General Secretary of the National Consumers League; and close friend and associate of Jane Addams. She was also instrumental in convincing Louis Brandeis to argue *Muller v. Oregon*, which created Labor Law in the United States. She helped create the NAACP, which began to fight in the courts for the legal rights of African-Americans.

702 Julia Lathrop: social and education reformer and director of the United States Children's Bureau from 1912 to 1922; also a close friend of Jane Addams.

703 Paul Underwood Kellogg: journalist and social reformer, Chairman of the Foreign Policy Association of New York; friend and associate of Jane Adams.

704 Homer Folks: Secretary of the Children's Aid Society and the New York Charities Association; in 1901, Secretary of the National Conference of Charities and Correction.

705 Theodore Roosevelt to Ben Lindsey: "You are one of the few men who have done the most for the moral awakening of our people. When you wrote 'The Beast and the Jungle,' you rendered a service that hardly any other man would have had the courage and the knowledge to render. You attacked evil in the concrete, not merely in the abstract. Plenty of people are willing to attack it in the abstract, for no courage is necessary in such a diffuse assault. But very few are willing to face the intense bitterness of counter-attack which follows upon attacking evil in the concrete." Quoted in the Foreword of the *The Beast*, by Ben B. Lindsey, University Press of Colorado, 2009, pg. xi.

706 *His Lamp of Fire*, Ch. 6, pg. 118. "Youth in Prison Cells."

707 *Children in Bondage*, by Edwin Markham, Ben B. Lindsey, and George Creel, Hearsts International Library, New York, 1914.

708 *Belleville, Illinois Advocate*, April 19, 1928. "Father E.J. Flanagan, who directs a boys home in Omaha, Nebr., which bears his name, even went to Governor Sam A. Baker and asked that (the boys) be paroled to him."

709 "Rev. E.J. Flanagan wins long campaign for release of 'Kid Bandits.' *Boys' Home Journal*, May, 1928, pg. 3.

710 *Readers Digest*, February, 1947.

711 This is how Father Flanagan described the miraculous change in boys, whose background had almost scarred them for life: "Sometimes we receive boys who have many marks of neglect. Their character has been soiled because those in whom they have come in contact with have taken no interest in their unfortunate condition, or could not get down to the level of the poor boy's mind to understand him. Whether the boy was not given the chance needed, no matter who was to blame, it was this fact which left an impression of injustice to him. It sours him against all humanity; and because of complaints lodged against him, he begins to feel that he is good for nothing. Let a boy get into that frame of mind, and he is usually not good for anything.

"It takes a good deal of training to bring his deranged little mind back to a proper way of thinking that he can become a good for many things, and can become a useful man. Once this thought can be ushered to his mind, the change in that boy's soiled and seared mind becomes very apparent.

"Seeing these boys come back to normal is one of the great joys that we experience in our work at Overlook Farm, and once this is accomplished, the work of building up the needed structure of successful citizenship in him is not so difficult." *Boys' Home Journal*, January, 1926, pg. 2.

712 *His Lamp of Fire*, Ch. VI, pg. 118.

713 *The Beast*, by Ben B. Lindsey and Harvey J. O'Higgins, University Press of Colorado, 2009. Chapters V-VI: "The Beast and County Court" and "The Beast and Children."

714 "I took advantage of these travels to study the laws governing juvenile offenses, and found to my amazement that they were, in most cases, very similar to those affecting adult crimes. In most states, these same laws are operating." *His Lamp of Fire*, Ch. VI, pg. 118.

715 Ibid., Ch. VI, pg. 118.

716 Ibid., pg. 119.

717 Ibid., pg. 119.

718 The movie, *Men of Boys Town*, was based

partly on juvenile abuse in the Whittier School in California, covered in Chapter 23.

719 "Interview with Hubert (Hub) Monsky," July 7, 1988. Boys Town Archives.

720 The case of Donald is taken from *His Lamp of Fire*, Ch. VII, pgs. 155-175.

721 Ibid., pg. 159.

722 Ibid., pg. 162.

723 Ibid., pg. 161.

724 Ibid., pg. 162.

725 Ibid., pg. 163.

726 Ibid., pg. 164.

727 Ibid.

728 Ibid.

729 Ibid., pg. 168.

730 Ibid., pg. 169.

731 "That understanding judge and I have become the best of friends. No child under his jurisdiction would be treated other than a neglected child." Ibid., pgs. 173-174.

732 This is how this case was described in the *Boys' Home Journal* of June, 1931: It was a turning point in Father Flanagan's battle to change the laws relating to juvenile crime and lays the groundwork for his most famous case, that of Herbert Nicholls in Washington State two years later: "A few months ago, a nine-year-old, white and curly headed boy was brought to our Home with the petition that we keep him for a few weeks until his trial for murder took place.

"A nine-year-old boy charged with murder! A mere baby that should be nestling in his mother's arms, commanded to face a court of justice on that charge that he had murdered his playmate with a gun that was left behind by a trapper who happened to stay for a short time at the boy's home. Here was a mere child of 9 years facing a reformatory sentence, and being condemned by his elders to carry with him for the rest of his life the stigma of a murderer.

"Even after long years of experience with the saddest and most unbelievable of incidents, this particular case shocked me. I could not convince myself that any legal body of American law would thus charge a mere child with murder and would actually deliberate the giving of a reformatory sentence to a boy that was yet an infant.

"I immediately called a meeting of our staff to discuss this case, and a unanimous decision was made that our Home, which stood for a fair chance to every American boy, should do everything in its power to investigate this case and to stop the legal proceedings that were in action.

""We made a thorough investigation and decided that the boy must be helped and that if it were in any way possible, we must obtain custody of that lad who was plainly a victim of neglect. After consulting our attorney, I, myself, accompanied the boy to the trial and acted in his defense....

"We are proud to say that our Home not only secured custody of that boy, with the provision that we keep him until he is eighteen years of age, but we also convinced the court to change its records and thus to free the boy from the stigma of murder, which he would otherwise have had to carry throughout his life....

"This boy is today at our Home with a clear record of the past; in his contentness, and in his association with the 200 other boys at the Home, he has forgotten the tragic moments of his life; he is attending school as is every other normal American boy of his age, and he is developing himself physically, mentally and morally into a splendid type of citizen that in days to come will be a real asset to his community and to society."

733 A photo of the boy with Father Flanagan appeared in the November, 1931, issue of the *Boys' Home Journal*, pg. 9.

Chapter 13: Hard Times Again

734 "Fire has broken out four times in the five wooden buildings at our Home. These wooden shacks are fire-traps." *Boys' Home Journal*, August, 1929, pg. 8.

735 "Trades School Badly Needed at Overlook Farm." Letter from Nebraska Governor Arthur Weaver. Ibid., September, 1929. pg. 3.

736 "We have a wide variety of trades in our Home. We teach printing, carpentry, baking, farming, horticulture, dairying, poultry raising, stenography, filing, office

work, music and various other things. If a boy is serious about studying the violin as a livelihood, we give him the opportunity. If another lad wishes something similar to that, we try to give him what he wants, if it is within reason. I want to impress upon you the fact that we do not institutionalize our boys; we aim to individualize them." Ibid., July, 1929, pg. 2.

737 Ibid., July, 1929, pg. 3.

738 Ibid., August, 1929, pg. 8.

739 "The… Administration and Recreation Building will be 60 x 206 ft. with two wings, 35 x 54. This building will house the general offices, printing trades, business trades, band practice room, auditorium and gymnasium. It will give the homeless boys… a swimming pool of their own." Ibid., October, 1929, pg. 3.

740 Boys' Home Journal, January, 1930, pgs. 8-9. "Former Champions Strut Stuff Before Young Critical Eyes; Jack and Jim Tickled to Entertain Homeless Boys."

741 "Johnnie Tells Radio Audience About Babe Ruth." Boys' Home Journal, November, 1927, p. 3. "Babe Ruth was met at the entrance to the Home. The band escorted his automobile up the gravel road leading to our Home. The car was driven between two lines of boys, nearly one hundred on each side."

742 Boys' Home Journal, November, 1927, pg. 7.

743 Cf. "Letter of Archbishop Harty." Ibid., February, 1920, pg. 3.

744 Archbishop Harty was succeeded by Bishop Joseph Francis Rummel, who was installed as Bishop of Omaha on July 4, 1928.

745 Ibid., June, 1929, pg. 3.

746 In a short editorial under the heading, "Dan Desdunes," Father Flanagan paid tribute to his friend and bandleader: "There will be many who will regret his passing, but hardly more than the boys at Father Flanagan's Boys' Home where for 12 years he directed the boys band." Boys' Home Journal, June, 1929, pg. 10.

747 "Board of Directors Plan a Large Building Campaign. Wooden Buildings Must Be Replaced Because of Fire Menace." Ibid., July, 1929, pg. 3.

748 At the meeting of the Board of Directors, Bishop Rummel seems to have expressed reservations about the new swimming pool, as well as his concern that Boys Town lacked a "Catholic" character and control. Father Flanagan's letter is surprising in his frankness and in his conviction that Boys Town was eminently Catholic in its service to homeless boys and to the wider human community.

"My dear Bishop:

Since our meeting on Friday evening last, I have given considerable thought to the character of the conference on that occasion, and cannot help but feel that your attitude was, to say the least, strangely mysterious.

I was under the impression that my building program – including the swimming pool – was passed on at the last Board meeting, and since then I received written authority from the Diocesan Council on the matter. I cannot imagine, consequently, but am tempted to suspect, what caused the eleventh hour objection.

Departing from isolated incidents, frankly, Bishop, I must respectfully state here, that, recalling some experiences of our various conferences, that you do not seem to fully grasp the peculiar genius of this place.

It must never be overlooked that the general public, including, particularly, the large non-Catholic element must be considered here. From the inception of this institution, my policy has been, that all deserving boys irrespective of race, creed, or color were welcome within its portals. On that policy I have based my appeal during the years, with a the result of whatever success has been realized thus far. During these years. with the exception of a few sacerdotal friends, both within and without the Diocese, I have received nothing in the way of sympathy, encouragement or support on the part of bishops or priests; on the contrary, much amusing criticism and kindergarten opposition have been their only contributions.

After all these years of single-handed effort, with every variety of discouraging experiences, my surprise now is to witness the practically over-night interest and wonderful solicitude on the part of the Diocese. Would that this attitude were in evidence even as recently as five or six years ago, when it would mean so much to me – then struggling, and battling with the debt of two hundred thousand dollars ($200,000). During the trying experience of that period, the Diocese and the Catholic people of Omaha, with the exception of a few, manifested practically no concern either in myself or the Home's predicament. The Diocese shied clear of it. The diocesan publication has yet to give my Home the first friendly publicity. I will not say that I was not disappointed and even discouraged with the rather strange treatment by those from whom I thought I had a right to expect, at least, sympathy, even if not support. I did not, however, throw up my hands then, and appeal to the Diocese to help me out, for the simple reason that I did not consider it their obligation to accept responsibility which they had never encouragingly recognized.

One thing is certain, that not only the Diocese of Omaha but even the suffragant Metropolitan See itself, with all its Suffragants included, could never succeed in maintaining a Home of this character, if the latter were limited to financial support from these sources alone.

While following out the policy outlined above, I have always aimed at protecting the interests of this Diocese in connection with the Home, and we have done so from a conscientious sense of duty. This, however, is not the mechanical or easy task that it might seem to the average ecclesiastic, which you, no doubt, will appreciate. It continually requires the most delicate tact and diplomatic prudence that can be called into service, which I am not claiming to have always exercised, but have endeavored to. On the other hand, I am always deeply conscious of my special obligation to the Public. My reputation, veracity, and pledges to them are supremely vital here, and I do not see how in honor as a Priest or even as a man I can bluntly belie the former or cowardly betray the latter. This is my chief reason

for respectfully representing to you on more than one occasion the necessity of an external minimum in the matter of unimportant necesssories and accidental settings or our Religion here at the Home, while in reality observing and enjoying all the substantial features.

It may not be irrelevant to recall here, that Overlook Farm, with whatsoever it entails today, did not drop miraculously from the clouds, nor was it put there by the Diocese of Omaha. I trust I may not seem to be violating good taste or any proverbial canon of Hoyle when I assert that, after God, and many good friends of this great Republic, whatever measure of success has been realized here, is due to my exclusive efforts. Is it unreasonable, then, I submit, for me to presume to have some important voice in the general policy and program of this character and activities of this institution? Don't you think that by this time I ought to be fairly familiar with the various elements that promote its best interests?

The most trying experiences in my work here, as well as the hardest variety of that work, I do not fear, but in fact, enjoy. What I do not particularly relish, however, and which I think I have a right to protest against, are the continued nagging, strange criticisms and petty opposition, which seem, unfortunately, to be my portion. It is this strange and apparently dissatisfied attitude on the part of my Diocesan superiors that has evoked the foregoing, which is intended as most impersonal and essentially unselfish. I trust you will interpret and accept it in this strictly impersonal sense. Furthermore, I want to assure you, in this same connection, that I consider myself second to none among your priests in obedience and loyalty to yourself and the welfare of the Diocese.

Wishing you at this time much more than the customary Bon Voyage, I respectfully beg to remain,

Yours most sincerely,
E.J. Flanagan"

749 "The Board of Directors of Father Flanagan's Boys' Home has been increased by the addition of three more nationally

prominent citizens who have had wide experience in the social service world. The new addition brings the total of the board of trustees to seven and creates one of the strongest and most experienced board of trustees of any institution in the United States today.

"Francis P. Mathews, Henry Monsky and Mrs. Arthur Mullen are the three new members of the board. Other members are: The Rt. Rev. Joseph F. Rummel, bishop of Omaha; James E. Davidson; Very Rev. James W. Stenson and Father E.J. Flanagan." Ibid., June, 1929, pgs. 8-9.

750 "All contracts have been let and work will be started at once in the erection of three additional buildings at Father Flanagan's Boys' Home, total cost set at approximately one quarter of a million dollars…. All three of these buildings will be of complete fireproof construction. As soon as the new buildings are erected, the wooden shacks, which have housed the trade school, the band room, the recreational center and the print shop, will be wrecked and removed….

"All of the buildings will be of modern college architecture and will harmonize with the present dormitory building." Ibid., October, 1929, pg. 3.

751 "The three buildings and the new playground in the $260,000 building expansion program at our Home are fast taking shape and we hope to have them ready for occupancy by April 1st." "Father Flanagan's Page," Boys' Home Journal, December, 1929, pg. 2.

752 "I could tell you a hundred stories of the lean years, how may trips to the bank a certain policy made so Father Flanagan could meet food bills and other expenses." Catherine Dannehy, quoted in an article in the Omaha World-Herald. Undated. Boys Town Archives.

753 "Our two handball courts are now finished and we play in them every day…. Father Flanagan wants us to play this game for he says that it is good all-around exercise and that it will make us strong and healthy. You know Father himself is a wonderful player and he never loses a game regardless of with whom he plays." Boys' Home Journal, June, 1925, pg. 9.

754 "Our two handball courts are now finished and we play in them every day…. Father Flanagan wants us to play this game for he says that it is good all-around exercise and that it will make us strong and healthy. You know Father himself is a wonderful player and he never loses a game regardless of with whom he plays." Boys' Home Journal, June, 1925, pg. 9.

755 "Graduating Class Largest in History of Home." Ibid., June, 1930, pg. 2. This was not a high school graduating class, since at this time, Boys Town had only an elementary school.

756 "Former Home Boys Who Are Making Good in the World. Letters Pour into Father Flanagan Every Month Telling of the Doings of Our Lads." Ibid., February, 1929, pg. 11.

757 Ibid., March, 1929, pg. 3. "Gloom Killer Broadcasts for 25,000 Members."

758 "Will Rogers Joins Gloom Killers." Ibid., April, 1928, pg. 8.

759 "Father Flanagan's Boys Band Moulded into a Great Musical Group." Ibid., April, 1929, pgs. 8-9.

760 Cf. Morris Jacobs' description of his "garage" living quarters. Notes 602-603.

761 "Our new track field is just about completed. It is back of the new gymnasium, and it is surely a dandy. They are putting on cinders now. The track surrounds our baseball and football fields. As soon as it is finished we plan on having some field meets at our Home." Boys' Home Journal, May, 1930, pg. 12.

762 "The new Trade School is finished, too. The print shop and carpenter shop have already moved in…. Farming, shoe-making, printing, carpentry work, commercial work and music are taught. Father says that we must learn at least one trade." Ibid., May, 1930, pg. 12.

763 "It was a heavy loss that fell on Father Flanagan's Home for Boys on Sunday. Destruction of property to the tune of $50,000 to $60,000 would be felt by any institution, but to one that has been slowly built up by hard work and patient sacrifice, such a loss is a calamity indeed.

"But Father Flanagan, who has been the moving spirit of the enterprise, is a man of both courage and vision. He is already at work, making his plans to restore the workshop ruined by the fire. His boys will have a place to learn useful trades and round out their training for the responsibilities each must assume in life.

"Omaha should, and certainly does, feel a deep concern in the fortunes of this institution. Its establishment was the inspiration of a young priest, who envisioned the needs of homeless boys, waifs, who were helpless in the stream of life, and who survived only to add to the derelicts of society. It was to salvage them, to gather them into a shelter, where they could have protection and training during the time when it was most needed, that Father Flanagan set about his task. How well he has succeeded is shown by the great home he has placed on the hilltop west of the city.

"Now the home is known throughout the length and breadth of the land. Boys from all parts of the United States, from Canada and elsewhere beyond the borders have been housed there. More than housed, they there found a home, where kindly discipline unfolds their minds, trains their hands, and develops them to usefulness.

"A wonderful work, that will not be ended, or seriously halted by the calamitous visitation that has overtaken it. Out of the ashes of the workshop will arise another, perhaps better planned and equipped, and the work of Father Flanagan's home for boys will go on, for it is needed by the world." *Omaha World-Herald*, March 3, 1930, pg. 1.

764 "The boys of the eighth grade graduating class had a very happy day on May 20. It was Graduation Day and they received their diplomas. In the morning, they all attended chapel at which Father gave them all a little talk and presented each boy with his diploma…. He encouraged all to go to high school." *Boys' Home Journal*, June, 1930, pg. 12.

765 Some graduates stayed behind until private homes could be found for them for entering high school. This was actually a benefit to the Home since these were senior members whose presence and authority added to the stability and continuity of the place. Most were gone by the end of the summer. "There are still a few boys who are waiting for an opportunity to go to high school next September. We hope somebody will give them a chance." *Boys' Home Journal*, July, 1930, pg. 13.

766 "We are happy to say that eight new boys were admitted to Overlook Farm during the month of June."Ibid., July, 1930, pg. 9.

767 Ibid., July, 1930, p. 7. "It is with the deepest sorrow we announce the death of Michael J. Flanagan, second tenor of the Father Flanagan Celebrity Quartet, and brother of Father E.J. Flanagan."

768 Ibid., August, 1930, pg. 7.

769 *Omaha World-Herald*, November 6, 1932: Franklin Roosevelt "dedicated Memorial Park and visited Boys Town."

770 "Governor Roosevelt Visits Home: When Governor Roosevelt made his trip to Nebraska and to the Sumnick Farm near Omaha, he included in his itinerary Father Flanagan's Boys' Home. The boys welcomed the Governor with rousing cheers as he drove up and waved to them all. Mr. Roosevelt declared Overlook Farm the most beautiful place he had visited in his entire trip. Mrs. Roosevelt was with the Governor." *Boys' Home Journal*, November, 1932, pg. 3.

771 "We boys are always glad to see visitors around the Home. Last month more than 500 people went through our fine buildings. It is interesting to note that our recent visitors come from more than ten different states of the union." Ibid., September, 1930, pg. 8.

772 "Governor Weaver, in paying tribute to the work of Father Flanagan, expressed the conviction that the State of Nebraska and the whole nation would be better and happier because of the work done by Father Flanagan. 'We owe Father Flanagan much for his services to humanity.'" Ibid., November, 1930, pg. 6.

773 "I am one of 3,000 boys to whom Father Flanagan has given a home during the past 13 years. This is the only home that I have, and I want to thank Father Flanagan for giving it to me. If it were not for him, and

for the kindness of thousands of people who are interested in our Home, I would now probably be getting food and education in the streets." Ibid., November, 1930, pg. 6.

774 Ibid., March, 1931, pg. 4.

775 "Father Flanagan Ordered to Take Long Rest." Ibid., August, 1931, pg. 3.

776 "In accordance with our conversation on Sunday last, I am hereby extending to you a leave of absence for a period of six months, or any portion of that time which you may deem necessary to seek complete restoration of your health and strength.

I am also appointing your brother, Reverend P.A. Flanagan, administrator of the Home during your absence, leaving his parish temporarily in charge of Reverend Father O'Brien.

I regret extremely that the run-down condition of your health requires this remedy, but I am confidently hopeful that the Lord will soon restore the vigor and enthusiasm necessary to conduct your Institution and carry its many responsibilities. In the meantime you must feel with me that in your Reverend brother's hands all will go well. This should leave you absolutely without any anxieties. Enclosed you will find a celebret for your use when you find it convenient to leave.

May I assure herewith of my very profound appreciation for your very faithful services and my very fervent prayers for your speedy recovery.

Faithfully yours in Christ,
Joseph Francis Rummel
Bishop of Omaha"

777 "Broken down in health under the strain of 13 years of unselfish service to the care of homeless boys, Father Edward J. Flanagan, first citizen of Omaha, founder and director of Father Flanagan's Boys' Home, has been ordered by physicians to take a six-month leave of absence. He will leave next week for a sanitarium in the west to make a fight for recovery of his health so that he can return to his duties at the home he personally built from nothing into an institution valued at $750,000." The Omaha Bee News, August, 1931.

778 "We have requested him many times to take vacations and rests, but he has been so interested in the care of his homeless lads that he refused to leave the Home except on business trips." James E. Davidson, Chairman of the Home's first Building Campaign. Boys' Home Journal, August, 1921, pg. 3.

779 The Denver Post, August 20, 1931: "Omaha's Most Useful Citizen Is Patient At Mercy Hospital."

780 "One of the reasons for the breakdown of the health of the founder of this institution is that during the general economic depression the past year, the income of the Home has decreased more than 50 per cent. The demands of the homeless boys have been greater. Every day some homeless boy seeks admittance within our gates.... The Home cannot continue unless it is cleared of debt and enough funds are in our treasury to feed, clothe, educate and care for our homeless lads." Ibid., "Father Flanagan's Page."

781 "Boys Home May Be Forced To Close," The Denver Post, August 20, 1931.

782 Boys' Home Journal, August, 1931, pg. 2: "The first task that confronts me is the elimination of a large debt at the Home and the securing of enough funds in order to keep the doors of the Home open."

783 Ibid., pg. 1.

784 "Never in my life have I thought I would write such a letter as this. The Boys' Home for which I have worked so hard, and for so many years, must be closed, unless the necessary money is raised immediately." Ibid.

785 Boys' Home Journal, September, 1931, pg. 2.

Chapter 14: The Battle for Boys II: Herbert Niccolls

786 The Boy Who Shot the Sheriff: The Redemption of Herbert Niccolls, Jr., by Nancy Bartley, University of Washington Press, 2013.

787 Ibid., Fig. 2.

788 Ibid., pg. 7.

789 Ibid., pg. 9.

790 Ibid., pg. 17.

791 Ibid., pg. 15.

792 Ibid., pg. 39.

793 Ibid., pg. 58.

794 Ibid.

795 Ibid.

796 *His Lamp of Fire*, by the Rev. E.J. Flanagan. Unpublished manuscript, pg. 132.

797 *The Good Fight: The Remarkable Life and Times of Judge Ben Lindsey*, by Charles Larsen, Quadrangle Books, Chicago, 1972, pg. 223.

798 Ibid., pgs. 243-244.

799 Ibid.

800 *His Lamp of Fire*, pg. 32: "I told him that if no institution existed in that state which could properly care for him, I offered the protection of my home to this homeless and neglected child."

801 Bartley, op. cit., pg. 63.

802 *His Lamp of Fire*, pg. 132.

803 *Boys' Home Journal*, November, 1931, pgs. 3, 9.

804 *His Lamp of Fire*, pg. 129.

805 Bartley, op. cit., pg. 64.

806 Ibid.

807 Ibid., pg. 65.

808 Ibid., pg. 78.

809 Ibid.

810 Ibid., pg. 86.

811 Ibid.,

812 Ibid., pgs. 89-90.

813 Ibid.

814 *Boys' Home Journal*, January, 1932.

815 Bartley, op. cit., pg. 98.

816 *Boys' Home Journal*, December, 1931, pgs. 8-9.

817 Bartley, op. cit., pgs. 101-102.

818 Ibid., pg.103.

819 Ibid., pg.103.

820 *Boys' Home Journal*, January, 1932, pg. 12.

821 Bartley, op. cit., pg. 105.

822 *His Lamp of Fire*, pgs. 137-141.

823 *Boys' Home Journal*, January, 1932, pg. 9.

824 *Boys' Home Journal*, January, 1932, pg. 12.

825 Bartley, op. cit., pg. 118.

826 Ibid., pg. 119.

827 *Boys' Home Journal*, March, 1932, pgs. 8-10.

828 Ibid., September, 1932, pg. 3.

Chapter 15: Boys Town, Nebraska

829 *Boys' Home Journal*, 1933, January-June.

830 Cf. *The Forging of an American Jew: The Life and Times of Julian Mack*, by Harry Barnard, Herzl Press, New York, 1974. Ch. 10: "The Child Saver," pgs. 64-77.

831 "The Juvenile Court," by Julian Mack, Harvard Law Review, Vol. 23, 1909, pg. 120.

832 *Boys' Home Journal*, November, 1932, pg. 3.

833 "Each spring we have a full class of eighth-grade graduates who are full of ambitions and dreams. Many of them want to go to high school. The response of our friends to his plea has been edifying and may God grant that as the years go on, more and more men and women will offer their homes and their care to these boys.... Many of these boys who were placed a few years ago are now through high school and are in college." *Boys' Home Journal*, February, 1933, pg. 2.

834 Ibid., June, 1933.

835 Ibid., June, 1933, pg. 5.

836 *Boys' Home Journal*, February, 1933: "Boys Initiate Newcomers into Life at the Home," pg. 3.

837 Fulton and Will Oursler, op. cit., pg. 5.

838 Ibid., October, 1933, pgs. 4-5.

839 "Occasionally among my boys I find spark of real genius, which promises to live if the boy only can keep that spark alive. The boys take turns at the telephone switch-board and since the work does not require all of their time, they spend the intervals reading or doing something they like to do. One of the boys who has learned how to operate the board spends every minute drawing. The results are most enlightening.

I see in his work that spark of genius. He combines ability to make his characters and originality in their words and actions. His cartoons are the promise of a brilliant career." *Boys' Home Journal*, August, 1933, pg. 2.

840 *Boys' Home Journal*, February, 1933, pg. 3: "Boys Initiate Newcomers into Life at the Home."

841 Ibid., February, 1933, pg. 6: "Here Are Two Boys Who Have Found Happiness in New Homes."

842 Ibid., June, 1933, pg. 6: "Former Homeless Boy in College Now."

843 Ibid., July, 1932, pg. 7: "Kenneth Sutton Returns Home With Highest Average in His Class."

844 Ibid., December, 1933, pg. 4: "Former Boy Returns to Tell of His Success."

845 Ibid., June, 1933, pg. 4.

846 Ibid.

847 *Boys' Home Journal*, July, 1933: "Boys Issue Own Newspaper."

848 *The City of Little Men* was also the title of a public relations film that MGM released as a promotional film for the movie *Boys Town*. It was the first time the general public was given a view of Father Flanagan's work. He himself appeared in the film briefly.

849 *Boys' Home Journal*, September, 1933, pg. 2: "Can You Give a Boy a Home?"; August, 1933, pg. 7: "Wants a Home, Too,"; September, 1933, pg. 6: "These Boys Are Still Seeking Homes."

850 *Boys' Home Journal*, June, 1934, pg. 3: "Nine Boys Complete H.S. Work."

851 Ibid., September, 1934, pg. 3: "For the first time, the sophomore year has been added."

852 At one point, he seriously considered a military school, but that plan died very quickly. There is some evidence that he considered the plan of his patron, St. John Bosco, who founded a religious order to carry on his work for youth; thus, the *Boys' Home Journal* sometimes speaks of 'Brother Paul' or 'Brother Joseph.' Eventually the town concept became the most workable."

853 *His Lamp of Fire*, by the Rev. E.J. Flanagan.

Unpublished manuscript. Boys Town Archives.

854 "Father Flanagan's Page," in every issue of the *Boys' Home Journal*, is a detailed chronicle of the scope and diversity of his work, as his "Home" developed into "Boys Town," something that astonished Hollywood when it came to call and inspired the movie.

855 "A new town will spring up in Douglas County soon. It will be Boys Town and just as the name implies, its population will be made up almost entirely of boys too young to be full-fledged citizens. Father Flanagan's Boys' Home on West Dodge Street will be the new town. The Post Office department has made the home a post office and has officially designated the new point on its map as Boys Town.... The purpose of establishing a post office at the home is to handle the thousands of letters sent out from and received at the home each month." *The Omaha Bee News*. December 2, 1934.

856 *Boys' Home Journal*, December 1934, pg. 3; January, 1935, pg. 3.

857 Ibid., January, 1935, pg. 3.

858 Ibid., February, 1935, pg. 3.

859 Ibid.

860 Ibid., pg. 7.

Chapter 16: The Movie, *Boys Town*

861 "John W. Considine, Jr. was the son of a colorful former Seattle political boss who later became head of a chain of film theaters. Considine's brother Bob was a noted newspaper columnist and screenwriter, and John had been a producer at MGM since 1933." *Elvis' Favorite Director: The Amazing 52-Year Career of Norman Taurog*, by Michael A. Hoey, Bear Manor Media, 2013, pg. 116.

862 The election noted in the newspaper was that of January 1937 in which the mayor, Dan Kampan, was re-elected. Kampan had made headlines several months before during his first term by meeting with New York City mayor Fiorello LaGuardia. *Boys Town Times*, December, 1936; *Boys' Home Journal*, February, 1937, pgs. 8-9;

New York Sun, Nov. 19, 1936; *Chicago Herald and Examiner*, Nov. 20, 1936.

863 "The studios aggressively searched for source material, scouring newspapers, magazines, reading galleys of new books, catching all the Broadway shows. The story goes that MGM producer John Considine, Jr., happened upon an L.A. newspaper article about the 1936 'city' election at Boys Town. Apparently he was intrigued by an incorporated village of 200 boys who elected a mayor and six commissioners from their own ranks." Leo Adam Biga's blog, Omaha, Nebraska, May 31, 2010: "When Boys Town Became the Center of the Film World."

864 Cf. *Case History of a Movie*, by Dore Schary, Random House, 1950. A detailed account of how movies are made, from story and script to the finished picture, from a master of the craft.

865 Telegram from John Considine to Father Flanagan, June 24, 1937: "Miss Eleanor Griffin, one of our staff writers, leaves here tomorrow for Omaha where she will be joined on next Monday by my assistant O.O. Dull who is at present in New York. [stop] They will stop at the Fontenelle Hotel and get in touch with you sometime Monday." Boys Town Archives.

866 From "I Meet Myself," Father Edward Flanagan's account of his visit to the MGM studio, March, 1938.

867 Ibid.

868 "Jimmy Lang was the youngest resident at Boys Town in 1937. He inspired writer Eleanor Griffin to create the character of Pee Wee, played by Bobs Watson." Russo and Merlin, op. cit., pg. 44.

869 MGM's fears were not unfounded. Ten years later, William Rankin, who was dropped from the Boys Town team, wrote a screenplay for RKO about another priest who rescued boys from the street, Father Peter Dunne of St. Louis, in a movie with Pat O'Brien called, *The Fighting Father Dunne*.

870 *His Lamp of Fire*, by the Rev. E.J. Flanagan. Unpublished manuscript. Boys Town Archives.

871 "My new assignment at a salary of seven hundred and fifty dollars per week was to do a story for John Considine, a producer who had the idea that there was a good movie in the history of a little-known institution called Boys Town near Omaha, Nebraska." *Heyday: An Autobiography*, by Dore Schary, Little, Brown, & Co., 1979, pg. 93.

872 "The film *Boys Town* was designed for Spencer Tracy, Freddie Bartholomew, and Mickey Rooney. After reading what had been written and studying the history of Father Flanagan's unique institution, I told Considine that the error holding up the project was casting Freddie Bartholomew in an atmosphere where he clearly did not belong. My suggestion was to do away with the character completely and concentrate on the relationship between Tracy as Father Flanagan and Rooney as the rough, unmanageable new recruit into Boys Town." Ibid.

873 "On May 3… Considine sent the Reverend Flanagan a copy of Dore Schary's latest version of the screenplay, which combined early material from Eleanor Griffin with Schary's own progressive drafts…. Flanagan responded by inviting Considine, screenwriter John Meehan, and director Norman Taurog… to Omaha for a conference over the script." James Curtis, op. cit., pg. 349.

874 "Being an Orthodox Jew, Schary had never before entered a priest's home, and he wasn't sure how to behave when Flanagan came ambling down the stairs. 'I expected robes or something, but he came down in a coat and tie and said: 'How are you doing?' I said, 'Very cold.' He said: 'A little scotch will take care of that.' We had a couple of drinks and I fell in love with him. He was a darling fellow." *Spencer Tracy: A Biography*, by James Curtis and Alfred A. Knopf, 2011, pg. 344.

875 Ibid., pg. 93.

876 "The priest told his visitor that he had specifically asked Considine to send him a Jew. 'I kept saying to MGM, 'Don't send me any Catholics. Why don't you get hold of a Jewish kid? He'll know what I am talking about.'

""Now what made you say a thing like that?" asked Schary.

"How do you think I got into this business? How do you think this place was built? Because a Jewish man understood what I was doing and gave me money." Boys Town Archives.

877 Ibid.

878 Russo and Merlin, op. cit., pg. 40: "The dinner discussion inspired the writer to make Father Flanagan the main character in the screenplay."

879 "In an effort to bond with the priest, Dore agreed. Tracy was an excellent choice, and was fully certain Tracy could portray Flanagan easily because 'he had his smile and twinkle. He was going to be a cinch to catch on film.'" Boys Town Archives.

880 "Tracy apparently expressed qualms about playing the priest. To reassure Tracy, Father Flanagan wrote him: 'Your name is written in gold in the heart of every homeless boy in Boys Town.'" Leo Adam Biga's blog, pg. 10.

881 "Metro's story editor, Kate Corbaley, had been looking for another 'priest role' for Tracy since the release of San Francisco." Spencer Tracy: A Biography, by James Curtis and Alfred A. Knopf, 2011, pg. 343.

882 Russo and Merlin, op. cit., pg. 40.

883 "On June 4th, John Considine approved the final changes. John Meehan added his editorial comments and observations. His contribution to the film was to take the two diverse screen stories and join them together. First, the original Eleanor Griffin tale of the roots of the boys' home in 1917 remained as a prologue, with its own boys and conflicts. Employing montage to depict the building of the campus, the story leaped ahead fifteen years to a second storyline, this one featuring an incorrigible named Whitey Marsh." Russo and Merlin, op. cit, pg. 55.

884 "Last month, Boys Town was host to two Hollywood motion picture men. Mr. J. Walter Ruben and Mr. Dore Schary were at Boys Town to acquire actual atmosphere for a motion picture depicting life at Boys Town and the history of the township." Boys' Home Journal, March, 1938, "Father Flanagan's Page."

885 "In the end, he (Tracy) was persuaded to take the part of Father Flanagan by Eddie Mannix." Spencer Tracy: A Biography, by James Curtis and Alfred A. Knopf, 2011, pg. 344.

886 "OUR GIFT TO HOLLYWOOD," Boys' Home Journal, March, 1938, pgs. 6-7.

887 "Dear Father In view of the fact that we go into production of our picture June second believe it advisable for you to come here as soon as possible with Andy and Jimmy [stop] Taurog wants to make tests of them to find out if it will be possible for them to play parts in which we would ordinarily cast experienced youngsters [stop] In any event they can play in the picture [stop] Please wire me date and hour of your arrival so that we can meet you. Kindest Regards John Considine Jr." Telegram from John Considine to Father Flanagan, May 23, 1938. Boys Town Archives.

888 Boys' Home Journal, March, 1938: cover photo and pgs. 1, 6, 7.

889 Boys' Home Journal, April, 1938, pg. 3: "Father Flanagan is visitor to Movie Metropolis, confers with Movie executives."

890 "Will be delighted to see Mr. Jacobs and yourself whenever you can arrange to come to Los Angeles [stop] Telephone number Republic naught two one [stop] Making good progress with Boys Town script. Kindest Regards John W. Considine, Jr." Telegram from John Considine, Jr. to Father Flangana, Feb. 14, 1938. Boys Town Archives.

891 "Throughout the preproduction phase, Boys Town's founder kept up a steady correspondence with several MGM figures, particularly producer Considine, but also with Louis B. Mayer and fixer Eddie Mannix." Leo Adam Biga's blog, "When Boys Town Became the Center of the Film World," March 8, 2015, pg. 10.

892 "On February 18, he arrived in Hollywood in the company of Morris E. Jacobs, founding partner of Bozell & Jacobs.... The two men laid out an ambitious promotional plan that involved joining the reach and resources of Metro-Goldwyn-Mayer with publicity and media contacts forged by Flanagan and his organization over a span of twenty years." James Cyrtis, op. cit., pg. 345.

893 "Over lunch on that rainy Friday afternoon, Tracy met Father Flanagan for the first time. Clad in his leather flying jacket for *Test Pilot*, his face streaked with makeup, Tracy struggled to make conversation with the first living person he had ever been asked to play." *Spencer Tracy: A Biography*, by James Curtis and Alfred A. Knopf, 2011, pg. 345.

894 This is Father Flanagan's account of his first meeting with Spencer Tracy:

"I have just returned from Hollywood where I enjoyed a unique experience – that of meeting myself. It is a strange feeling to meet, face to face and for the first time, the man who is to play the part of oneself, and to match philosophies of life with this other person.

"Yes, I sat across the table from him in the lunchroom on the Metro-Goldwyn-Mayer lot at Culver City the other day and did just that.

"For a great many years, I have been building up in my own mind – as everyone does – a mental image of myself. When I comb my hair each day, looking into the mirror, I'm adding to that self-impression. So, when I was introduced to the man who will be me in a forth-coming motion picture, you can imagine my feelings.

"It was as if I had looked into my mirror and saw, not myself – not the Father Flanagan I had known these many years – but a total stranger, dressed as an aviator with grease paint streaking down his face, sporting his leather flying jacket. For my *alter ego*, my screen personality, is Spencer Tracy, who was then engaged in taking the last "shots" for *Test Pilot*. After *Test Pilot*, he was going to the hospital for a minor operation and then, for the next three months, he would be me – Father Flanagan – in the Metro-Goldwyn-Mayer production of *Boys Town*, a movie based on our incorporated township, composed of two hundred homeless boys who govern themselves. Yet, until within a month of the time the first camera would start to click, we had never met.

"'Father,' Spencer was saying, and he grinned sheepishly at the personal superstition he was about to reveal. 'I'm almost afraid of this part in *Boys Town*. They tell me I made a pretty good priest in *San Francisco*. Well out here we have a saying that 'the second time's the charm.' I wonder if I will do as well again as a priest in *Boys Town*.'

"...As he talked, I could feel his eyes upon me, studying my every little mannerism, the way I sat in the chair, the way I talked, the way I pushed the hair back from my forehead. I knew that he was studying me – the man he was going to become – as searchingly as I studied him....

"...If I am instrumental, through this picture, in giving a new opportunity, a new hope, a new life to one single child, who otherwise would not have such a chance, then I've done something. And the *Boys Town* movie will give me such an opportunity. I only hope I can do justice to the part.'" From "I Meet Myself," Father Edward Flanagan's account of his visit to the MGM studio, March, 1938.

895 James Curtis, op. cit., pg. 345.

896 "While making *Boys Town*, Mickey Rooney's status at the studio went sky high with his box office appeal. The public clamored for his next film, and the starring role in *Boys Town* was to be a top-level picture for him." Russo and Merlin, op. cit., pg. 53.

897 "Mickey Rooney exploded onto the nation's psyche with his Andy Hardy movies, but his performance in *Boys Town* solidified his drawing power. MGM decided to put a rush on the production after seeing the growing interest of their rising star." Russo and Merlin, pg. 67.

898 *Boys' Home Journal*, July, 1938, pg. 1: "Andy and Jimmy Caine Have a Screen Test; will play bit parts."

899 "Jimmy Lang was the youngest resident at Boys Town in 1937. He inspired Eleanor Griffin to create the character that later became Pee Wee, played by Bobs Watson." Russo and Merlin, pg. 44.

900 "The Day I Made Tracks to Boys Town," by the Rev. Bobs Watson, *Reminisce* magazine, July-August, 1998.

901 From "I Meet Myself," Father Edward Flanagan's account of his visit to the MGM studio, March, 1938.

902 Russo and Merlin, op. cit., pg. 42.

903 "As the script of *Boys Town* neared completion, Jack Ruben… suddenly took ill with
endocarditis… and suddenly, sadly, he was
dead. Norman Taurog… who had earned
fame as the director of *Skippy*, was assigned
to take Jack's place." Schary, op. cit., pg. 94.

904 Cf. *Elvis' Favorite Director: The Amazing 52-
Year Career of Norman Taurog*, by Michael
A. Hoey, Bear Manor Media, 2013.

905 *Boys' Home Journal*, June, 1938, pg. 1: "The
decision to make the picture at Boys Town
instead of Hollywood came after the
recent visit of John Considine, Jr.; Norman
Taurog, the newly assigned director, who
had such success with child actors in the
past and who made the prize-winning
Skippy several years ago; John Meehan,
writer assigned to polish up the script; and
John Marchant, business manager of the
producing Company, to Boys Town where
an all-day conference was held."

906 "Before he (Norman Taurog) had directed
Boys Town, he had come to know Father
Flanagan until their relationship was practically father and son. He invited the founder
of Boys Town to a dinner at his home, and
about 70 Hollywood celebs. He knew
they would be honored to meet this as yet
uncanonized saint of our time. Everyone responded beautifully. No one had a previous
engagement… or had to go out of town.

"Each one of them on being introduced to
Father Flanagan handed him a substantial
check. I knew he was desperately in need
of money… and I was touched that others
should know this, too. He never thought
anything of money, as you know too well.
He went ahead with building programs
that would have staggered even bureaucrats
raised on deficit spending. He simply knew
that God would provide.

"The next day he came to the studio and
asked if he might borrow my secretary. He
wanted to write to all those good people.
Naturally I thought he wanted to write
bread and butter letters. But when I saw
him enclosing the checks in the letters, I
became suspicious. I asked him how come?

"He explained it very simply. 'Norman,' he
said, 'I had a wonderful time meeting

all those good people at your house last
night. But I simply couldn't profane the
sanctity of your home that way.' I pleaded
with him. I told him these people did this
of their own beautiful will. There was no
pitching or prodding from me. Somebody
might have said, 'Let's surprise him,' and
they went ahead from there, but I had not
needled them into anything of the sort.

"But in his quiet, willful way, he went on
dictating those letters and returning
those checks. Of course, you know what
happened. To a man and woman they
tore up the checks, wrote out new ones for
increased amounts and mailed them to the
treasurer at Boys Town.

"From there we began confessing experiences we had enjoyed in his hallowed company.
He thought so much of home, any home,
that he once told me that a boy with his
family, no matter how poor, had advantages over the best that Boys Town could give
him." From "Scully's Scrapbook," by Frank
Scully, *Boys Town*, date unknown.

907 *Boys' Home Journal*, July, 1938, pg. 13.

908 "In March, Mr. Frank Whitbeck of M-G-M
presented to Father Flanagan his idea for
making *The City of Little Men*, a short
screen subject, wherein Father and all his
boys were to participate. It was to include
a brief history of FATHER FLANAGAN'S
BOYS' HOME, combined with the arrival
at Boys Town of a youthful hitchhiker who
is welcomed by Father Flanagan in person.
The balance of the film was to be a review
of a typical day at Boys Town showing the
boys at work and at play in every department and in all their activities."

M-G-M planned to have this miniature
feature shown in theaters as a sort of
advance publicity for the major production,
Boys Town. Unpublished manuscript of
Gilson VanderVeer Willets, Ch. 11, pg. 4.

909 "By the time this *Journal* reaches its many
readers, cameras will probably be grinding
here at Boys Town as Metro-Goldwyn-Mayer starts work on its short subject,
The City of Little Men, which it plans to release a short while before its feature picture
Boys Town is exhibited to the world. This
information is contained in a letter from
Mr. Frank Whitbeck, publicity director

of M-G-M, who is coming to Boys Town to make this short subject." *Boys' Home Journal*, June, 1938, pg. 3.

910 "Frank Whitbeck, a former Barnum & Bailey barker, was... one of the most important publicists at MGM.... He did double duty on the trip to Boys Town. He would serve as narrator to *The City of Little Men*.... (but) Whitbeck's main function was as watchdog over Tracy." *MGM Makes Boys Town*, William Russo and Jan Merlin, CreateSpace Independent Publishing Platform, 2012, pg. 47.

911 "Arrive Thursday morning. Company will arrive Saturday. Would rather you would not mention arrival, so as to keep crowds away." Telegram from Joe Cooke, MGM, to Father Flanagan, June 22, 1938. Boys Town Archives.

912 "Despite a telegram from MGM asking that a lid be kept on the cast-crew's arrival... word leaked out. Press accounts estimate some 7,000 people greeted the stars when they arrived at Omaha's Union Station." Leo Adam Biga's blog, pg. 12.

913 "Boys Town went into production June sixth Tracy and Rooney now working [stop] Next week Rooney will complete unfinished scenes in Judy Garland picture and we will continue without him until about nineteenth or twentieth when whole company including Rooney will leave for Boystown as per original plans. Best regards John W. Considine Jr." Telegram from John Considine, Jr. to Father Flanagan, June 9, 1938. Boys Town Archives.

914 "Boys Town company of fifty-eight people tonight for Omaha.... Tracy, Rooney and eight boys head players group.... Taurog, Meehan, Dull and myself and sound, camera, musical technician complete the company... believe this is largest and most important motion picture group ever sent to middle west for location work...." Telegram from John Considine, Jr. to Father Flanagan, June 23, 1938. Boys Town Archives.

915 "Of course the company... was the biggest, by far ever to hit Nebraska. When they arrived in the evening of the twenty-fifth, several thousand jammed Omaha's Union Station to get glimpses of Tracy, and par-

ticularly Mickey Rooney, who had become just about the hottest thing in pictures." James Curtis, op. cit., pg. 350.

916 "When they arrived on the late afternoon of June 26, 1938, what seemed like the entire state of Nebraska was assembled at the train station to welcome the cast and crew of the *Boys Town* film." Ibid.

917 "The first duty of the troupe was a gathering at one of the local theaters that night. It was meant as an opportunity to introduce everyone to the city of Omaha and to the village of Boys Town. Father Flanagan was also on the stage during the assembly." Ibid., pg. 59.

918 "A fleet of Omaha cabs was assigned to take cast and crew about ten miles out to Boys Town every morning with a police car escort." Ibid., pg. 61.

919 *Boys' Home Journal*, August, 1938, pgs. 6-7. Photos.

920 "A Bit of Hollywood Comes to Boys Town," *Boys' Home Journal*, August, 1938, pgs. 6-7.

921 Photo: "Mickey Rooney Greets Father Flanagan," *Boys' Home Journal*, August, 1938.

922 *Boys' Home Journal*, August, 1938.

923 "Mickey Rooney makes a hit in Boys Town. And how! Mickey is one of the grandest kids the films ever made. Off the screen he isn't so cocky, makes friends fast, and talks our lingo.

"On his arrival, Mickey or 'Mick,' as he is called by the boys, went 'around the town.' Called the gymnasium the best in the country – in L.A. anyway! He thinks the boys here are swell, because they treat him just like any other 'guy' and don't make much fuss over his being a movie star. After watching the baseball team, Mick doesn't wonder that they don't lose very often." Tony Villone, in the *Boys' Home Journal*, August, 1938, pg. 5.

924 "Kathryn Dwyer, Father Flanagan's fifteen-year-old niece, was present during the two weeks of filming and wrote of her impressions in an article she titled, 'Boys Town Looks at Hollywood.' She told her story through the eyes of a boy she had talked to each day while the movie was being made." Reilly and Warneke, op. cit., pg. 107.

925 "Filming at Boys Town was hard on everybody: 100 in the shade, of which there was very little, and then it rained for three straight days, putting the company behind schedule and forcing it to shift to night shooting to pick up the time." From *Elvis' Favorite Director: The Amazing 52-Year Career of Norman Taurog*, by Michael A. Hoey, Bear Manor Media, 2013, p. 121.

926 Leo Adam Biga's blog, pg. 13.

927 "Thomas, a tall blond kid about eighteen, took the part of the mayor in the picture. He was a nice guy, too, and he told us the story they were going to make about our town." Ibid., pg.10.

928 "Gene Reynolds is another boy star who is very active. The other day he asked Ken Corcoran, the coach, for a basketball to play in the gym. Ken obliged and Gene put on a swell exhibition, hitting the hoop from all corners. And he is only about twelve years old." Tony Villone, in the *Boys' Home Journal*, August, 1938, pg. 5.

929 "Sidney Miller, the Jewish lad in the picture, had the boys laughing when he imitated Max Schmelling's foul kidney punch. He gestured with his hands, putting one on his side, and exclaiming 'I'm parra-lized.'" Ibid.

930 "Little Bobs Watson, called 'Pee Wee' in the picture, is having more fun than anyone else. At least, so it seems. His candid cameras always active, taking shots from all angles, and dipsy-do's. He has a very active mind, knows all his lines, and the other actors' also. The other day Mickey forgot his lines, but 'Pee Wee' was there to straighten him out. A nice chap, 'Pee Wee.' Ibid.

931 *Boys' Home Journal*, August, 1938, pg. 5.

932 "By the time cast and crew arrived at Omaha, representatives of SAG had preceded the crew and apprised Father Flanagan of the rights of the boys and how much they'd be paid for appearing as extras in the film. Sizeable amounts of money were involved because the studio used over a hundred boys as extras for each day, providing Boys Town with a hefty payment." Russo and Merlin, op. cit., pg. 56.

933 "To select extras, Taurog patiently listened to many of the boys living at the town. If they played a harmonica, or could dance,

he'd sit down and intently watch for that intangible quality that the camera might love." Russo and Merlin, op. cit., pg. 74.

934 Kathryn Dwyer, op. cit.

935 Ibid.

936 *Boys' Home Journal*, August, 1938, front cover.

937 *Boys' Home Journal*, August, 1938, pg. 8: "On the Set: Backstage in filming 'Boys Town.'"

938 "Here is what you would see and hear, if you stood on a Hollywood lot and watched them film a certain sequence. The director would give an order for the 'set-up' on a certain scene. The grips arrange all the paraphernalia. Fake trees to cast leafy shadows would be put into position. The reflectors would be placed in proper alignment, and at correct angles.... 'Quiet!' calls the assistant director. 'Turn them over,' says the director to the camera crew, and the cameras start to grind. 'Quiet! They're turning,' says the sound man. When he is sure that the film is traveling past the shutter at the proper sound speed, exactly two by four exposures per second, he calls: 'Okay! Speed!; the director calls, 'Camera!' and the scene begins." *Boys' Home Journal*, August, 1938.

939 "He made me feel like we were old friends. I liked him immediately." "The Day I Made Tracks to Boys Town," by Bobs Watson.

940 "Despite Tracy's often gruff behavior, many of the child actors recalled the actor's kindness. Bobs Watson, who played Pee Wee, the Boys Town mascot in the film, was as enamored with Tracy off-camera as he was on. 'Often, after a scene, he'd reach over and hug me and take me on his lap.'" Boys Town Archives.

941 *Boys' Home Journal*, August, 1938, front cover.

942 Frankie Thomas, Russo and Merlin, pg. 78.

943 Michael A. Hoey, op. cit., pg. 122.

944 Katherine Dwyer, op. cit.

945 Russo and Merlin, op. cit., pg. 85.

946 Russo and Merlin, op. cit., pg. 131.

947 Leo Adam Biga's blog, pg. 15.

948 Gilson Vandervilt Willets, op. cit., Ch. 11, pg. 21.

949 *Spencer Tracy*, by James Curtis, pg. 350.

950 Mrs. Henry Monsky, wife of Father Flanagan's closest friend, thus describes the premiere of *Boys Town*:

"It was a festive occasion. Premieres everywhere, that attract the galaxy of stars that this one did, are wont to be exciting. But for our Midwestern city, the thrill of having with us over a period of time… Mickey Rooney, Spencer Tracy, and a host of minor celebrities, was exhilarating to most of our townspeople…." op. cit., Monsky and Bisgyer, pg. 4.

Chapter 17: Brick and Mortar and More Boys

951 *Omaha World-Herald*, January 13, 1939, article by Edward Murrow: "Boys Town Movie Has Surprise Ending: Home Donations Drop Off Instead of Rising."

952 "The shocking result of popular success for the studio and for the performers left Father Flanagan mulling the reasons he did not benefit more from the motion picture…. In analyzing the situation, Flanagan considered, most people, seeing the picture, rather took it for granted that an orphanage sufficiently famed to be the subject of a movie, was a thoroughly established institution." Russo and Merlin, op. cit., pg. 138.

953 Boys Town Archives.

954 Ibid., pg. 139: "Henry Monsky wrote L.B. Mayer, suggesting that, in view of the picture's success, the five thousand dollar fee might be hoisted a bit. Mayer replied that he'd take it up with the corporation and that he'd be glad to make a personal donation."

955 Boys Town Archives.

956 "Father Flanagan had an idea the picture might bring a shower of gold that would let him get started on his building program. He feels he must have half the money required for any project before he can start it. The rest he can borrow from Omaha banks, which have always found him a good risk." Edward Morrow, op. cit.

957 Boys Town Archives.

958 "Mayer said that a picture which his company produced, had proved an inspirational success, but that it had led many persons to believe that Father Flanagan's project did not need any more money." Boys Town Archives.

959 *Omaha World-Herald*, November 18, 1938, under the headline: "M-G-M to Aid Boys Town; May Erect New Dormitory."

960 "At a dinner in honor of Father Edward Flanagan, founder of Boys Town, near Omaha, Louis B. Mayer, Head of Metro-Goldwyn-Mayer Studios, announced last night that his company will donate a building to the Boys Town project." *Omaha World-Herald*, November, 1938.

961 *Boys Town Times*, November 11, 1938, pg. 4.

962 "Hollywood promoters expect a crowd of 40 thousand, and let everyone take his own guess at receipts. Box Seats to celebrities are selling anywhere from $60 to two hundred dollars each." Boys Town Archives.

963 As the *Kansas City Times*, December 2, 1939, put it: "Movie Stars Cheer Against Home Team in Game With Boys Town."

964 Ibid.

965 *Los Angeles Examiner*, November 23, 1938.

966 "Do you remember me, Father? I wrote two years ago, but never got no answer. I want to come there so bad I could bawl, but my father is dead and my mother does laundries, so I can't afford to come. But I sure want to come to Boys Town." *Boys Town Times*, December. 4, 1938, pg. 4.

967 "The Fraternal Order of Eagles has done more for the social welfare of human beings in the United States than any other organization…. Their latest activity, however, is the entrance into the Child Welfare Program of these United States by establishing at Boys Town a memorial building dedicated to the Fraternal Order of Eagles." December, 1939. Boys Town Archives

968 *The Aurora Eagle*, April 17, 1941.

969 *Boys Town Times*, July 28, 1939, pgs.1, 4.

970 Willets, op. cit., Ch. 11, pg. 33.

971 "Brothers Order Takes Over Teaching Duties," *Boys Town Times*, July 28, 1939, pgs. 1, 4.

972 "Father Reveals Dowd Memorial Chapel Plans," *Boys Town Times*, October 27, 1939, pgs. 1, 4.

973 "Sketch of Boys Town's New Expansion Program," *Boys Town Times*, August 11, 1939, pg. 1.

974 "M-G-M Crew Starts Production on New Boys Town Picture," *Boys Town Times*, November 8, 1940, pg. 1.

Chapter 18: The Whittier School

975 For a complete account of the history of California's Youth Correction Institutes, before and after Father Flanagan's experience with the Whittier School, see: *After the Doors Were Locked*, by Daniel E. Macallair, Rowman & Littlefield, New York, 2015, and *States of Delinquency*, by Miroslava Chavez-Garcia, University of California Press, 2012.

976 "The Death of Benny Moreno," by Daniel E. Macallair, op. cit., pgs. 129-130.

977 *States of Delinquency*, by Miroslava Chavez-Garcia, University of California Press, 2012, pg. 182.

978 Daniel E. Macallair, op. cit., Ch. 17, pgs. 131-133.

979 Ibid.

980 Ibid., pg. 183.

981 Ibid., pg. 91.

982 Letter, July 27, 1940, Hollywood Humane Society.

983 *Los Angeles Examiner*, July 30, 1940.

984 "Since the 1850s, California relied on large correctional institutions to handle its high-needs youths. These institutions were often criticized for harsh and abusive practices while offering little in the way of rehabilitation despite varied attempts at system-wide changes. Decades of criticism ultimately led the state to acknowledge the need for systematic reform." Foreword of *After the Doors Were Locked*, by Daniel E. Macallair, Rowman & Littlefield, New York, 2015.

985 Letter of Elmer R. Murphy, July 30, 1940.

986 *Boys Town Times*, August 23, 1940, pgs. 1-2.

987 *Los Angeles Times*, July 29, 1940.

988 *Los Angeles Examiner*, "Rosanoff Endorses School Terror Room."

989 "Lindsey Group Starts Whittier Report," *Los Angeles News*, October 16, 1940.

990 Cf. *Olson's New Deal For California*, by Robert E. Burke, University of California Press, 1953, pgs. 178-180.

991 Daniel E. Macallair, op. cit., pgs. 135-137.

992 Letter, January 6, 1941, with the letterhead: "The Children's Court of Conciliation."

993 "I had dinner two weeks ago at the May-flower Hotel in Washington with Mr. Edgar Hoover and I gave him a copy of the report on Whittier School." Boys Town Archives.

994 Cf. "Culbert Olson," Wikipedia Free Encyclopedia, January 18, 1941.

995 "Whittier School Youth Picked Up Here After Escape; Companion Also Taken" was a common headline.

996 *Los Angeles Examiner*, March 1941: "Why the Delay?"

997 *Los Angeles Examiner*, March 30, 1941: "Failure to Correct Evils Stirs Demand for Action."

998 The Osborne Association of New York: Founded by Thomas Mott Osborne and considered the "pioneer and prophet of prison reform. Osborne has a distinguished history of pioneering innovative and effective programs for prison reform and for those trapped in the penal system."

999 The Governor put Father Flanagan's appointment into an official state document, which reads: "I, Culbert L. Olson, Governor of the State of California, in the name and authority of the People of California, do by these presents, appoint and commission Right Reverend Monsignor Edward J. Flanagan Member of the Governor's Commission at Whittier State School and recommend a Plan of Operation for the term at the pleasure of the Governor."

1000 "Boys Town Head Is Named To Whittier," *Stockton California Record*, April 8, 1941.

1001 Sensing a new found freedom, 60 boys took off from the school. It took a few days to round them up, and most returned willingly when they realized changes were to be made. Boys Town Archives.

1002 "Flanagan Calls Whittier School Conditions Bad. Boys Town Founder Terms Situation Worse than He Ever Dreamed," *Sacramento California Bee*, April 12, 1941.

1003 "Father Flanagan and Mrs. Mellinkoff recommended that Cox be made permanent superintendent succeeding Milne." Robert Burke, op. cit., pg. 179.

1004 News Bulletin, The Osborne Association, June, 1941, pg. 1.

1005 News Bulletin, The Osborne Association, June, 1941: "William B. Cox New Head of Whittier School."

1006 Letter, April 14, 1941, from the State of California Department of Institutions.

1007 Letter from Aaron J. Rosanoff to Mr. P.J. Norton, April 14, 1941. On the letterhead of the Department of Institutions, with two names on the letterhead: that of Rosanoff and that of the Governor. It left Pat Norton and his successor, William Cox, powerless to make any changes in the policies of the Whittier School.

1008 "Cox served as superintendent of the institution… until November 1941, when he resigned after a series of squabbles with Rosanoff." Robert E. Burke, op. cit., pg. 179.

1009 William Cox's parting words to the governor expressed his indignation and keen disappointment at his inability to make the changes necessary at the Whittier School: "I am fully convinced that I was brought to California under false pretenses and that there is not and never has been an honest intention on your part or on the part of the personnel board to do ought else than practice political chicanery." Boys Town Archives.

1010 "With the assistance of the American Law Institute's Model Youth Authority Act, created in 1940, a committee of concerned legislators, judges, lawyers, social workers, psychiatrists, and others across the state, came together to propose legislation aimed at overhauling Whittier State School." Miroslava Chavez-Garcia, op. cit., pg. 209.

1011 Cf. "The Legacy of Benny Moreno and Edward Leiva," in *States of Delinquency*, by Miroslava Chavez-Garcia, pgs. 209-211.

1012 "The Birth of the California Youth Corrections Authority Act," op. cit., Daniel E. Macallair, pgs. 139-157.

1013 "Out of the sorry mess at Whittier came an important reform. A bill… setting up a *Youth Correctional Authority* passed the legislature almost unanimously and was signed by Governor Olson on July 9, 1941. The California Youth Authority has been called 'one of the most enlightened steps of recent years in the field of penology.'" Op. cit., Robert E. Burke, pg. 180.

1014 Miroslava Chavez-Garcia, op. cit., pg. 209.

1015 Karl Holton, "Youth Correction Authority in Action," ibid., pg. 210.

1016 Father Schmitt, in his memoir, thus describes how he became Director of the choir: "Fairly early, I fell heir to something besides nightly confessions… …It happened that the choirmaster and the organist both went on vacation at the same time. Would I tide things for a couple of weeks? Well, why not?

"At the first service, I managed to pull up something past an adagio. An hour or so later, I was called to the phone, and I heard Flanagan saying: 'Schmitt, that was electric!" *Boys Will Be Boys*, by Monsignor Francis P. Schmitt, Ares Publishers, Inc., Chicago, 2000, pg. 142.

Chapter 19: The War Years

1017 "Honolulu Boy Named Mayor of Boys Town," *Boys Town Times*, September 27, 1941, pg. 1.

1018 In September of 1944, the Christian Brothers left Boys Town, dismissed by Father Flanagan because one of their Brothers had hit a boy. However, the Brothers themselves were remembered fondly by one generation of Boys Town citizens who appreciated and profited by their excellent teaching. Boys Town Archives.

1019 For graduates who were uncertain about where they wanted to go to college, he told them: "Go into Omaha to Creighton University and you will see a man in a black robe walking up and down in front of the administration building. That is the President of Creighton University. Walk up to him and say: 'Father Flanagan says you are to give me four years of College.' Several of his boys went to college that way." Boys Town Archives.

1020 *History of Music at Boys Town*, by Monsignor Francis Schmitt, Sacred Music, Volume 117, Number 1, Spring, 1990.

1021 *Boys Town Times*, August 27, 1943, pgs. 1, 3.

1022 One of the first football games the Boys Town team played under Palrang was with Omaha's Creighton Prep – and Boys Town lost. Father Flanagan confronted Palrang and said: "I didn't hire you at $10,000 a year to lose." Palrang got the message. Boys Town Archives.

1023 Photo, front page, *Boys Town Times*, April 24, 1942.

1024 Service Honor Roll, front page, *Boys Town Times*, October 22, 1943. Over 400 names; 16 listed as prisoners of war.

1025 Catherine Dannehy's daughter wrote this about her mother: "She would come home at night with a pile of letters. Then she would sit at the dining room table, take out her typewriter and work until about midnight." Boys Town Archives.

1026 Willets, op. cit., Ch. 12, pgs. 29-30.

1027 *Boys Town Times*, February 8, 1946, pgs. 1, 4, photo and text.

1028 *The Battle of Bataan: America's Greatest Defeat*, by Robert Conroy, the Macmillan Company, New York, 1969.

1029 *Letters from the Front*, Terry Hyland and Hugh Reilly, Boys Town Press, Boys Town, Nebraska, 1995, op. cit., pg. 25.

1030 Hyland and Reilly, op. cit., pg. 29.

1031 Hyland and Reilly, op. cit., pg. 12.

1032 *Boys Town Times*, March 9, 1945, pg. 1.

1033 Cf. *Infamy*, by Richard Reeves, Henry Holt and Company, New York, 2015.

1034 Cf. *Children of the Camps*, documentary, PBS, 1999.

1035 "Internment of Japanese Americans." Wikipedia, the free encyclopedia., pgs. 1-29.

1036 Japanese infants were included in the evacuation and so were children adopted by Caucasian parents. And orphans, too. Federal agents visited West Coast orphanages looking for children with Japanese features. A Catholic priest in charge of an orphanage, Father Hugh Lavery of the Maryknoll Center in Los Angeles, said of Bendetsen (one of the enforcers), "He showed himself to be a Hitler. I mentioned that we had an orphanage with children of Japanese ancestry, and that some of the children were half Japanese, others one-fourth or less. I asked which children we should send. Bendetsen said: 'I am determined that if they have one drop of Japanese blood in them, they must go to camp.'" Boys Town Archives.

1037 Personal letter to the author, September 3, 2016. From Marilyn Takahashi, with a three-page detailed account of the coming of her family to Boys Town at Father Flanagan's invitation and their reception at Boys Town in 1942.

1038 "After the war in 1947, my parents wanted to return to California, so my father bought a newer truck and loaded it with bare necessities. We asked Father Flanagan to bless the truck and us before we began the 8-day drive to Los Angeles.... When the U.S. Government gave us restitution money... I received $20,000, so I decided to fly to Boys Town in 1991 and give a portion to Boys Town, because Father Flanagan had rescued us from the internment camp." Ibid., Note 1056.

1039 "One of the Franciscan Sisters was put in charge of our site school.... All grades were in one room. Father Flanagan would visit to see our school plays at Christmas and on May Day." Ibid., Note 56.

1040 Letter to Governor Thomas L. Bailey of Mississippi, December 13, 1944.

1041 "I am interested in the cases of Murice Shimnick and Joseph M. Leemon, who are both members of the Lauderdale County Jail at Meridian, Mississippi, and convicted to die on the 29th of December this year."

1042 Letter to Father John O'Brien, St. Paul's Church, Pass Christian, Mississippi, April 17, 1946.

1043 December 29, 1944. Boys Town Archives.

1044 Boys Town Archives.

Chapter 20: Suffer the Little Children

1045 *Father Flanagan of Boy Town: A Man of Vision*, by Hugh Reilly and Kevin Warneke, Boys Town Press, Boys Town, Nebraska, 2008, pg. 141.

1046 Ibid., pg. 141.

1047 Ibid., pg. 142.

1048 *Boys Town Times*, February 22, 1946, pg. 4.

1049 Reilly and Warneke, op. cit., pg. 143.

1050 *Boys Town Times*, January 25, 1946, pgs. 1, 4.

1051 Mrs. Franz (Trudy) was a concert pianist, trained in the Leschetizky school in Vienna, who taught piano at Boys Town for many years. She scheduled a piano recital every year for the Boys Town community. The author was one of her less-talented students. Cf. *Boys Town Times*, June 23, 1945.

1052 "I would like to get in touch with the Governor and have a conference with him so that when I come out there I would have his cooperation and good will when visiting the reform school at Elko." Letter to Father Thomas F. Collins, Reno, Nevada, April 4, 1946.

1053 "Their system is pretty much alike in all their institutes and I am afraid that economy plays an important part.And I may say – too much economy." Letter to Dr. William Staunton, April 4, 1946.

1054 *Criminal Youth and the Borstal System*, by William Healy, M.D., and Benedict S. Alper, The Commonwealth Fund, New York, 1941.

1055 "These children do not have sufficient play time, sufficient opportunity to develop their individuality, sufficient hobbies, sufficient cultural training in the arts, such as painting, music, sculpturing, and anything that will develop their souls as well as athletics would develop their bodies." Letter to his nephew, Dr. William Staunton: "Father Flanagan's goals for the children of Ireland," April 4, 1946.

1056 "Artane used frequent and severe corporal punishment to impose a regime of mili-taristic discipline. Corporal Punishment was systematic and pervasive. ...boys and Brothers learnt to accept a high level of physical punishment as the norm. Broth ers used a variety of weapons and devised methods of increasing suffering when inflicting punishment, and in some cases they were cruel and sadistic." CICA Investigation Committee, St. Joseph's Industrial School, Artane, Dublin, Volume 1, pg. 155, Item 7.311: Conclusions on Physical Abuse.

1057 "Christian Brothers School, Letterfrack, County Galway: 'Physical punishment was severe, excessive and pervasive, and was administered in public within earshot of other children; it was used as a means of engendering fear and ensuring control.'" Commission to Inquire into Child Abuse, known as the Ryan Commission, Chapter 8.

1058 "Christian Brothers School, Letterfrack, County Galway: 'Physical punishment was severe, excessive and pervasive, and was administered in public, within earshot of other children. It was used as a means of engendering fear and ensuring control.'" Commission to Inquire into Child Abuse, known as the Ryan Commission, Chapter 8.

1059 Letter to Frank Mascarenhas of Bombay, India, April 8, 1946.

1060 "Artane – a vast army of 800 boys worked the school's 298 acre farm of prime land and tended its herd of up to forty cows and assortment of other farm animals. It had facilities for up to one hundred pigs." "Suffer the Little Children," by Mary Rafterty, pg. 151.

1061 "Despite a solid reputation in America and around the world, his comments on the Irish and juvenile penal system earned him the wrath of many in officialdom in this country." Conor Reidy, author of *Ireland's Moral Hospital: The Irish Borstal System: 1906-1956*.

1062 Commission to Inquire into Child Abuse (CICA), May 11, 1999: "On behalf of the State, the Government wishes to make sincere and long overdue apology to the victims of childhood abuse, for our collective failure to intervene to detect pain, to come to the rescue." Statement of the Taoiseach of the Republic of Ireland, Bertie Ahern.

1063 Monsignor Flanagan managed to gravely

offend the Irish political authorities. Boys Town Archives.

1064 "I am delighted over your connection with Frank Fahy, the Speaker of Parliament. Would you mind if I write to Frank as I want him to put me in touch with the Welfare Department in Dublin so that I could get from that Welfare Department a rather comprehensive picture of the penal institutions of both adults and juveniles.... I am particularly interested in the juvenile problem." Letter of Father Flanagan to Father Thomas Collins, April 4, 1946.

1065 The CICA Report on the Industrial School Artane in Dublin, one of the juvenile schools visited by Father Flanagan, covered 235 pages, and came to 13 General Conclusions, fully justifying Father Flanagan's criticisms of the school and its treatment of children: "Artane used frequent and severe punishment to impose a regime of militaristic discipline. The policy of the school was rigid control by means of severe corporal punishment and fear of punishment. Such punishment was excessive and pervasive. The result of arbitrary and uncontrolled punishment was a climate of fear." CICA Investigation Report, Vol. 1, pg. 234, Item 7.845.

1066 The CICA Report on the Industrial School at Letterfrack in Galway, another juvenile home visited by Father Flanagan, covered 108 pages and came to 11 General Conclusions: "There was a climate of fear at Letterfrack. Corporal punishment was severe, excessive and pervasive. Violence was used to express power and status and was practically a means of communication between Brothers and boys and among the boys themselves. Punishment was inescapable and frequently capricious, unfair and inconsistent. Rules for corporal punishment were disregarded on all levels." CICA Investigation Report, pg. 394, Item 8.740.

1067 Cf. *Ireland's 'Moral Hospital,'* by Conor Reidy; "The Monsignor Flanagan Controversy," pgs. 223-227.

1068 *Irish Times*, July 8, 1946.

1069 "I hope in the winter of '47 to go to India to establish there a Boys Town example of a home for boys among the poor children of India." Letter to his nephew, Dr. William Staunton, April 4, 1946. Also, *Boys Town*

Times, February 22, 1946, pgs. 1, 4.

1070 "I intend to get in touch with Bishop Yu Pin, the Chinese bishop who spent many days here at Boys Town with his very large retinue of people." Ibid. Also, *Boys Town Times*, June 14, 1946, pg. 1, "Cardinal Tien of China Speaks on Boys Town Visit."

1071 Letter to Father Thomas Collins, April 4, 1946.

1072 Letter to Father Thomas Collins, April 4, 1946.

1073 Corrigan Park Reconstruction Committee – Program for Monsignor Flanagan.

1074 Boys Town Archives.

1075 *Boys Town Times*, August 9, 1946, pgs. 1, 4.

1076 Fifty years later, the boy, Gerald Fogarty, told his story:

"I ran away from the place that summer. I just wanted to go home and see my mother. I missed her all the time. I made it home, and they hid me for a while. I suppose I was on the run, really. But the guards caught me after a few days. They had been watching the house. They called the Brothers, who came up and brought me back.

"The next day, I was sent for by the Head Brother. I came to his office, and he roared at me to take off my clothes. As soon as I was totally naked, he took out this stick which had several leather thongs on it. He gripped me by the hand, and started laying into me with the whip. He gave me at least twenty lashes. I was crying and trying to get down on the ground, trying to curl up and get away from him, but I couldn't because of the grip he had on my hand.

"I couldn't sleep that night, and so I slipped out and ran away again. It's thirty-two miles from Glin to Limerick city, and I walked all the way, keeping to the fields. I knew they'd be searching the roads for me. I think it took me about twelve hours. By the time I got home, the bleeding on my back had stopped and the blood had dried into my shirt. I must have been a terrible sight." Boys Town Archives

1077 "Msgr. Edward J. Flanagan, director of Boys Town, said Tuesday that the treatment of juvenile delinquents in Eire is a 'disgrace.' Monsignor Flanagan arrived in New York by plane after a visit to Ireland. He said that youthful offenders are beaten with 'the cat-o-nine-tails, the rod and the fist.' Boys from 10 to 21 years old are locked in cells like hardened criminals." Boys Town Archives.

1078 Boys Town Archives.

1079 Boys Town Archives.

1080 Boys Town Archives.

1081 "Father Flanagan answers Mr. Boland." *The Standard*, Dublin, August 9, 1946.

1082 Statement to the press, July 24, 1946.

1083 Letter from the Office of the Minister of Justice, January 20, 1948. Boys Town Archives.

Chapter 21: The Far East Assignment

1084 Letter from Father Michael J. McKillop, M.M., September 3, 1946.

1085 "Secretary of War Robert Patterson and General Douglas MacArthur invited Father Flanagan to tour Japan to assist in developing public youth care facilities for war orphans and children whose parents were living but unable to care for them." "Boys Towns Around the World." Boys Town Hall of History.

1086 "I accepted the invitation and arrived in Japan on 23 April 1947 to fulfill my mission, as ordered by Secretary of War Patterson, having left San Francisco, per instructions, on 8 April 1947, making brief stops in Honolulu, Guam and Manila enroute." "Father Flanagan's Child Welfare Report," July 9, 1947, pg. 1.

1087 "Father Flanagan's Child Welfare Report." A detailed account of his work in Japan for abandoned and orphaned children.

1088 *Embracing Defeat: Japan in the Wake of World War II*, by John W. Dower, W.W. Norton & Company, New York, 1999, pgs. 45-46.

1089 *Hiroshima Diary: The Journal of a Japanese Physician, August 6-September 30, 1945*, by Michihiko Hachiya, University of North Carolina Press, Chapel Hill, NC, 1983, pg. iii.

1090 *Nagasaki: Life after Nuclear War*, by Susan Southard, Penguin Books, London, 2015.

1091 "Father Flanagan's Child Welfare Report," pgs. 1-2.

1092 Report by Byron Reed on Father Flanagan's visit to Japan, pg. 2.

1093 "Father Flanagan's Child Welfare Report," pg. 2.

1094 Cf. Letter from Mrs. Chiyo Mochida, Head of Koyoryo Boys Home, Nagasaki, Japan, to Father Flanagan, May 14, 1948. Boys Town Archives.

Chapter 22: The Mission to Europe

1095 "Left Frankfort for Vienna by private Army plane... the airport we arrived at is in the Russian zone." Diary of Patrick J. Norton.

1096 "Left Bristol hotel for USF at 9:35 AM. Met Gen. Geoffrey Keyes at 9:45 a.m. Returned to Bristol hotel for Press Conference." Patrick Norton notes.

1097 *The Lost Children: Reconstructing Europe's Families After World War II*, by Tara Zahra, Harvard University Press, Cambridge, Massachusetts, 2011.

1098 *Austria in the First Cold War, 1945-55*, by Gunter Bischof, St. Martin's Press, Inc., New York. Chapter 2: "The Anglo-Soviet Cold War Over Austria," pgs. 30-51.

1099 "Conference with socialist Youth leaders, Peter Strasser and Paul Blau, President and Secretary, respectively, who discussed their program. A sharp difference of opinion arose regarding the political indoctrination of youth at an early age as practiced by the Socialists." Boys Town Archives.

1100 Cf. Note 1127, Chapter 1: "The Quintessential Victims of War," pgs. 24-58.

1101 Cf. Note 1127, "Renationalizing Displaced Children," pgs. 118-145.

1102 *A Hitler Youth in Poland: The Nazi Program For Evacuating Children During World War II*, by Jost Hermand, Northwestern University Press, Evanston, Illinois, 1997.

1103 "The Mindset of the Hitler-Jugend," by Kyle Frabotta, Student Research Paper, June, 2004.

ABOUT THE AUTHOR

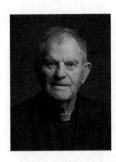 A 1944 graduate of Boys Town, Father Clifford Stevens knew Father Edward Flanagan as a caregiver, a friend, and most importantly, as a mentor who helped guide Stevens' decision to enter the priesthood.

Father Stevens was ordained in 1956, celebrating his first Mass at Boys Town's Dowd Chapel. He joined the United States Air Force in 1961, serving as a military chaplain at bases in the United States and overseas until his honorable discharge at the rank of major in 1968. A stint as the publisher of a magazine on contemporary issues facing Catholic priests and pastoral assignments at several small Nebraska churches followed. In 1984, Father Stevens fulfilled a dream he had held since his ordination when he founded the Tintern Monastery near Oakdale, Nebraska.

Father Stevens later returned to Boys Town, serving as a priest at Dowd Chapel and conducting research on Boys Town history. A widely published author, he has penned numerous books and articles, many of which focus on the work of Father Flanagan and Boys Town. Father Stevens currently resides in Omaha, Nebraska.